MAIMONIDES

MAIMONIDES

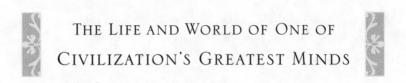

THE LIFE AND WORLD OF ONE OF
CIVILIZATION'S GREATEST MINDS

JOEL L. KRAEMER

DOUBLEDAY

New York London Toronto
Sydney Auckland

DOUBLEDAY

Copyright © 2008 by Joel L. Kraemer

All Rights Reserved

Published in the United States by Doubleday, an imprint of The Doubleday Publishing Group, a division of Random House, Inc., New York.

www.doubleday.com

DOUBLEDAY is a registered trademark and the DD colophon is a trademark of Random House, Inc.

Book design by Ralph Fowler / rlf design

Library of Congress Cataloging-in-Publication Data

Kraemer, Joel L.
Maimonides : the life and world of one of civilization's greatest minds /
Joel L. Kraemer—1st ed.
p. cm.
Includes bibliographical references and index.
1. Maimonides, Moses, 1138–1204. 2. Rabbis—Egypt—Biography. 3. Jewish philoso-
phers—Egypt—Biography. 4. Rabbis—Spain—Biography. 5. Jewish scholars—
Spain—Biography. I. Title.
BM755.M6K685 2008
296.1′81—dc22
[B]   2008032652

ISBN 978-0-385-51199-5

PRINTED IN THE UNITED STATES OF AMERICA

10 9 8 7 6 5 4 3 2 1

First Edition

This book is dedicated to my wife, Aviva Wilkov Kraemer,
who shared it all and
whose dedication made this dedication possible.

CONTENTS

PREFACE

I began to study Maimonides in 1947, when I was fourteen, at a Hebrew summer camp in Wisconsin. Some years later Professor Louis Finkelstein, chancellor of the Jewish Theological Seminary in New York, where I was then studying, established the Herbert Lehman Institute of Talmudic Ethics and offered fellowships to students. I, however, was more interested in Jewish thought. When Professor Finkelstein failed to convince me, he suggested that I speak with the eminent Talmudist Saul Lieberman.

The only way I dared take up Professor Lieberman's time was to walk home with him after he finished his day at 1:00 A.M. As we were passing Columbia University, I told him that my main interest was Maimonides' philosophy. He asked me, "For whom did Maimonides write the *Moreh nevukhim* [*Guide of the Perplexed*]?" "For the *nevukhim*," I responded. "Kraemer," he asked, "do you want to be a *navokh*?" "No, Professor." Then he said, "I don't agree with Strauss," going on to say that, contrary to the view of philosopher Leo Strauss, Maimonides' defining work was his code of law, *Mishneh Torah,* based on the Talmud, and that *The Guide of the Perplexed* was an act of benevolence for the unfortunate *nevukhim.*

The next day I went to a bookstore and bought Leo Strauss' *Persecution and the Art of Writing.* I learned how to read with meticulous care and absolute seriousness *The Guide of the Perplexed* and other texts I had been studying. As Strauss constantly cited the Arabic texts of medieval Islamic and Jewish philosophical books, as well as the Greek texts of Plato and Aristotle, I realized that I had to learn these languages. Professor Gerson D. Cohen of the seminary suggested that I go up to Yale to study Arabic with Professor Franz Rosenthal, who concentrated on Arabic, Islam, Semitic languages, and Greco-Arabic studies, namely, the transmission of the Greek philosophical heritage to the world of medieval Islam.

In the 1960s, as a graduate student at Yale, I twice visited the University of Chicago and met with Leo Strauss. I attended his class, which was an exhilarating experience. During this period I also met two other scholars who had a profound impact on me, Shelomo Dov Goitein and Shlomo Pines. Professor Goitein's specialty was the Cairo Genizah, the precious repository of manuscripts from the Ben Ezra Synagogue in Old Cairo. He was also an expert on Maimonides' life and career. I remained in touch with him over the years and went to Cambridge University every summer to pore over Genizah documents.

Professor Pines, of Hebrew University, had an incredible familiarity with languages and a command of philosophy and the history of science. He had translated *The Guide of the Perplexed* for the well-known University of Chicago Press edition of 1963. Shlomo Pines and Leo Strauss were the foremost interpreters of Maimonides in the twentieth century.

My concentrated, almost exclusive, study of Maimonides began soon after the signing of the peace treaty between President Anwar Sadat of Egypt and Prime Minister Menahem Begin of Israel on March 26, 1979. President Sadat spoke of a spirit of amity and friendship between Arabs and Jews and noted that Maimonides wrote his great works in Arabic, and that some scholars linked his writings with those of the Muslim philosopher Abu Nasr al-Farabi. President Navon observed that Arabic and Hebrew are sister languages with similar vocabularies, symbols, and concepts, and a common origin. He presented to President Sadat a copy of *The Guide of the Perplexed* in Judeo-Arabic. They agreed that Maimonides was the main cultural and intellectual bridge between the two countries.

I traveled to Egypt several times and was captivated by it. I visited Old Cairo, or Fustat, with its ancient Coptic churches and the Ben Ezra Synagogue, which housed the Genizah. I viewed the peace treaty as an opportunity to form ties with Egyptian colleagues and to help create a new cultural, social, and political reality based on cooperation and mutual understanding.

When I invited Professor Goitein to give a lecture on Maimonides' life at a conference on Maimonides in Egypt, he excused himself for health reasons, suggesting that I give the lecture instead. He had uncanny insight into what people should be doing, and his idea inspired me to write this biography.

ACKNOWLEDGMENTS

I was fortunate to be at Tel Aviv University when I began work on Maimonides. Itamar Rabinovich, former Israel ambassador to Washington and head of the Israeli negotiating team at peace talks with Syria, who was then Dean of Humanities, supported me in every way possible. Shimon Shamir, former ambassador to Egypt and Jordan, founder and director of the Israel Academic Center in Cairo, and director of Tel Aviv University's Tami Steinmetz Center of Peace Research, took my Maimonides project under his wing, introduced me to Egypt, and taught me more about the country and its people than I ever learned in books.

Moshe Gil, whose prodigious writings on Jewish cultural, economic, and social history, based mainly on Genizah documents, fill a shelf, was a guiding light at Tel Aviv University and at Cambridge. Mordechai Akiba Friedman, friend and colleague, Genizah scholar and Maimonides expert, studied manuscripts with me and read and corrected what I wrote over the years. Joseph Sadan energized me with his phenomenal knowledge of Arabic and Islamic culture and with his perpetual sense of humor. Ilai Alon was sustaining with his buoyant optimism and idealism. I first met Hagar Kahana Smilansky when she was a graduate student and over the years gained from her advice and criticism.

Stefan Reif, director of the Genizah Research Unit, and his wife, Shulie, were gracious hosts at Cambridge and imparted precious information and guidance. Geoffrey Khan answered my queries about decipherment of manuscripts. Godfrey Waller, Superintendent of the Manuscripts Reading Room, made sure that I got the manuscripts I needed. Patricia Crone was at Cambridge when I was a frequent summer visitor. I benefited from her keen mind and vast knowledge and learned not to argue with her. Elizabeth Ramsden made stays at Clare Hall memorable.

Benjamin Richler and Abraham David, of the Institute of Microfilmed Hebrew Manuscripts at the Jewish National and University Library, made my work pleasant and profitable. There, I first met Tzvi Langermann, now teaching at Bar Ilan University, from whom I learn every time I see him.

No one can approach medieval Islamic and Jewish thought and the study of Judeo-Arabic without being in touch with professors at the Hebrew University, first the fountainheads D. H. Baneth (of blessed memory) and Shlomo Pines (of blessed memory) and then following generations, including Joshua Blau, *magister* of Judaeo-Arabic. I enjoyed walks with him by the willows at Cambridge, where he turned my mind from the beautiful trees to Torah. Haggai Ben-Shammai, Sarah Stroumsa, and Warren Z. Harvey, disciples of Shlomo Pines and Joshua Blau, enhance the field with their enthusiasm and learning. Hava Lazarus-Yafeh (of blessed memory) organized a seminar at the Hebrew University Institute for Advanced Studies on the intertwined worlds of medieval Christianity, Islam, and Judaism.

I spent many precious hours walking with Bernard Lewis along the Tel Aviv promenade, seeing him often when we were both in the city. His knowledge of the cultures, histories, languages, societies, and politics of the Middle East is a unique and overflowing ocean.

Lawrence V. Berman (of blessed memory) was a beacon in the study of medieval Islamic and Jewish thought and deeply influenced my approach and understanding through conversation and his learned and eloquent studies. Likewise my friend Alfred Ivry, whom I first heard lecture more than forty years ago on the Arab philosopher al-Kindi. I have learned from Lenn E. Goodman, a philosopher with philological gifts, and Idit Dobbs-Weinstein, with knowledge from Thomas Aquinas and Christian Scholasticism to Nietzsche and modern thought. Isadore Twersky (of blessed memory) invited me to Harvard for a year, where I met Alexander Altmann (of blessed memory), Marvin Fox (of blessed memory), and Bernard Septimus. Whenever I was at Harvard during the lifetime of Harry A. Wolfson, I visited him in his study in the Widener Library and always left under the spell of a great mind.

In Paris, I got to know Gad Freudenthal, scholar and conductor of academic symphonies, the historian Maurice Kriegel, and the indefatigable Rémi Brague; and in Chicago and Munich, I had rewarding contact with Heinrich Meier, political historian and theorist and Leo Strauss authority.

Dean W. Clark Gilpin and Dean Richard A. Rosengarten, of the University of Chicago Divinity School, saw to it that I had what I needed to do my research and took an active interest in it. Clark Gilpin's incisive questions always went to the heart of the matter, helping me understand what I was trying to say. Richard Rosengarten's knowledge of religious studies and expertise on religion and literature, especially hermeneutics and literary theory, encouraged me to consider issues of interpretation and method. Wayne C. Booth (of blessed memory), whose *Rhetoric of Fiction* I have in Arabic translation thanks to him, made me think about problems of authorship and narrative as rhetoric.

I learned much from conversations with outstanding colleagues at the Divinity School and from their writings, especially those I taught with, Michael Fishbane, Bernard McGinn, and Paul Mendes-Flohr, as well as Wendy Doniger, Michael Murrin, and David Tracy. James T. Robinson made me see the genius of Samuel Ibn Tibbon, translator of the *Guide* and its first interpreter.

Ralph Lerner, friend and mentor, has done more for me than I can describe in words. He has also read everything mercilessly with his eagle eye, saving me from many a slip and embarrassment. "Reading Mr. Lerner's comments on your paper," said a student, "is like flossing your teeth with barbed wire."

I miss the warmth and wisdom of Muhsin Sayyid Mahdi (*rahimahu Allah*) and the many joyous hours with him in Paris, in the Librairie Avicenne, the Jardin du Luxembourg, and his favorite Restaurant Iranien.

I have gained much from the historian Norman Golb, a friend from youth. At the beginning of my Genizah research we studied manuscripts together when I was a guest at the Golb's home. I learned from his meticulous deciphering and mastery of paleography and from his uncompromising intellectual integrity.

Josef Stern, a fellow student of Maimonides and Jewish thought, has been a constant friend and partner in dialogue. Berel Lang is an old friend, good and true, with whom I have shared much.

Jill Kneerim was my muse and cheerleader and gave me the right advice and the right words at the right time.

My niece, Prof. Alyssa M. Gray, thrashed out some knotty legal passages with me, imparting her insights, and she read parts of an early manuscript.

My daughters, Judy, Susie, and Sarah; their husbands, Noam, Eyal, and Edo; and their children, Asaf, Itai, Alon, Ella, Inbal, Ori, Ilan, Shahar, and Ro'i, are my delight.

I honor the memory of my parents, my teachers, whose exaggerated expectations made me aim high.

MAIMONIDES

Introduction

We are the children of our landscape.

—LAWRENCE DURRELL, *JUSTINE*

MOSES MAIMONIDES, the foremost Jewish scholar of all time and one of the greatest minds in the Western world, was born circa 1138 into a distinguished family in Córdoba, Spain. As a philosopher and scientist, he wrote the illustrious *Guide of the Perplexed* and mastered mathematics, astronomy, logic, ethics, politics, and theology. As a physician, he served royalty and wrote medical works that were studied in the Middle East and Europe for centuries. As a jurist, he wrote a great compendium of Jewish law that influenced all subsequent Jewish law codes. As the Great Rav (Master) in Israel, he was the highest religious authority for Jews in Egypt and for others east and west, north and south.

Over the gallery doors in the U.S. House of Representatives Chamber of Congress are twenty-three marble relief portraits of famous lawgivers. One of them is Maimonides.

Clash of Civilizations

Even a towering genius needs favorable conditions to achieve what he does. Yet Maimonides lived in tumultuous times, in a maelstrom of earthshaking events, when the clash of civilizations between Christianity and Islam was at a point of incandescent intensity. On two fronts, Spain and the Holy Land, the rivals were locked in a colossal struggle, the Jews caught between the colliding worlds as powerless victims. Both conflicts shaped Maimonides' life. The clash in Spain and the invasion by the fundamentalist Almohads from North Africa forced him and his family to take up the wanderer's staff. Later he had a close encounter with the war between Muslims and the Crusaders in the Holy Land and Egypt.

Following itinerant years in Spain, North Africa, and the Holy Land, he arrived at a new haven in Egypt. His first years there were turbulent. Syrian and Crusader armies invaded the country. The Shi'i Fatimid dynasty (969–1171), after two hundred years of dominion, was overthrown by the Sunni Ayyubids (1171–1250), totally transforming Egypt forever.

Islamic Civilization

Maimonides lived his entire life under the aegis of Islamic civilization, first in the West—Spain and the Maghrib—and then in Egypt. In this period, the vast majority of the world's Jewish population lived in Muslim territory.

It is necessary to study Maimonides against the background of his culture and society, a demanding task requiring acquaintance with a complex civilization. We must consider his life, career, and writing as the highest expression of the intertwined worlds of Judaism and Islam. We need to know the cultural and social environment to understand our subject and to get to know his mental universe.

Islamic civilization embraced a variety of cultures and peoples, having different origins and backgrounds. It encompassed a large territory, extending from Spain and Northwest Africa to the Far East, and from Central Asia to sub-Saharan Africa. Islam was the prevalent religion, touching this civilization's political culture, worldview, lifestyle, literature, art, and architecture. We need to differentiate Islamic civilization from Islamic religion, the latter being the system of beliefs and rituals practiced by Muslims.

One reason for a prodigious Jewish achievement in the Islamic milieu was that the cultural context was Arabic, a Semitic language closely related to Hebrew. Arabic-speaking Jewish intellectuals—mainly physicians, merchants, and government bureaucrats—studied the Qur'an, grammar and lexicography, tradition (*hadith*), jurisprudence, theology, medicine, the exact sciences, philosophy, and also belles lettres and poetry. These intellectuals emulated the Muslim study of the Qur'an, grammar, and lexicography by studying the Bible and the Hebrew language, and they imitated Arabic poetry by writing Hebrew verse. In a gesture of mimetic competition, they extolled their own cultural treasures (the Bible and Hebrew) as superior to their Arab models.

The possibilities for acculturation were greater in the Islamic world than in Christendom, as so much of Islamic civilization was secular, whereas Christian culture was intimately bound to the Church and religious faith. Islamic civilization was predominantly urban and commercial, with a thriving middle class that had the desire and means to acquire knowledge. In both Islamic and Jewish societies, the social status of scholarship was high and the scholar-scribe-administrator, learned merchant, and physician were the main bearers of an elite culture.

Aside from periodic outbreaks of fanaticism, the enduring problem for non-Muslims in an Islamic state is that Islam provides a stable polity only under Islamic supremacy. The totally religious nature of the Islamic state prevents the formation of secular types of communal life and leaves no space for civil society. In Europe, civil society developed outside the church, a prospect that the unity of mosque and state precludes. The sole legitimate social order is the Islamic community, the *jama'a,* in which only free, male Muslims participate and enjoy equality. All others—slaves, women, and infidels (e.g., Jews and Christians)—are inferior. Of course, infidels can convert to Islam, and slaves can become free; however, women are consigned to permanent inferiority.[1] Religion is regarded as ethnic and national, not as confined to the spiritual aspects of life; hence, the infidel is an alien and outsider.

Islam emerged as a triumphant religious polity, with Muhammad as legislator, general, and head of state. Christianity existed without political authority for more than three hundred years before it triumphed and Constantine the Great declared it the state religion. In the course of time, state and religion could go their separate ways.

Jews, in contrast, were accustomed to being subject to alien rule and were reconciled to the absence of territorial sovereignty. After the destruction of the Second Temple in 70 C.E. and the failure of the Bar Kokhba revolt in 135 C.E., Jews lost political power and lived under Roman and then Byzantine rule, most of them dispersed throughout the Diaspora. Judaism, as we know it, came into existence under foreign sovereignty—Romans, Byzantines, and Muslims. The talmudic sages taught that "the law of the government is the law," meaning that Jews had to obey the laws of the sovereign of the land.

From the ninth to the twelfth century, Islamic culture burgeoned, as scholars translated philosophy and science from Greek into Arabic, appropriating this ancient heritage creatively and critically. Scholarship, literature, art, and architecture thrived. The Islamic world surpassed Europe in culture and learning. In Spain, especially Toledo, and in Sicily, scholars translated Arabic philosophy and science into Latin, as Islamic culture became the bridge between the intellectual heritage of antiquity and the West. The transmission of learning from Greek into Arabic and then from Arabic into Hebrew and Latin and other European languages was a momentous achievement of human civilization, and it was vital for the formation of European thought in the medieval period.

There were three great ages of cultural synthesis in Jewish history—Greek (Hellenistic), Arabic, and German. No other age compares to the Spanish experience in depth of learning, cultural sophistication, and comprehensiveness, embracing biblical and talmudic studies, linguistics, poetry, philosophy, and science.

Whereas in modern times cultural assimilation eventually led to abandonment of Judaism, the acculturation of Andalusian Jewish intellectuals within an Arab-Islamic ambience enriched their own culture and enhanced their attachment to Judaism. This was partly due to the similarity of Islam to Judaism as a religion based on a revealed law embodied in a sacred scripture, interpreted by religious scholars.

There were, however, many Jewish apostates, who found the magnet of Islamic power, the allure of Islamic culture, and the convenience of Islamic life too tempting to be turned down.

The ideal type of the Jewish intellectual in the Andalusian milieu was someone possessing *adab* (Arabic, "cultural refinement"; cf. Greek *paideia*). The cultural paragon of Andalusian Jews was the courtier-rabbi, learned in traditional scholarship and erudite in secular knowledge, who served the royal court as physician, advisor, translator, and diplomat while representing the Jewish community to the government. This model of biculturalism, versatility, and social responsibility was exemplary for Maimonides as he fashioned his career.

Unlike Christian Europe, where Jews were consigned to the margins of the economy, Jews in the Muslim world were active in the economic life of their societies. Some were merchants who managed the commercial conduits with Europe and with Muslim countries on the southern and eastern shores of the Mediterranean as well as with the Far East. Others were farmers who tended vineyards and olive groves. Still others owned shops and practiced trades and handicrafts as cloth manufacturers and dyers, manufacturers of silk clothing, goldsmiths and silversmiths, tanners, and cobblers.

Jews were not driven to moneylending in Muslim lands as they were in medieval Europe, where this societal role inflamed hatred against them. They did, however, take part in collecting taxes for the government, which inevitably aroused animosity.

A MEDITERRANEAN MAN

We are painting the portrait of a Mediterranean man. Maimonides lived his whole life near the sea in an urban environment, his scenic background always Mediterranean. Despite all of his displacements, he always resided in the same general region. He spent circa twenty-two years in Spain, then settled in Fez, Morocco, for five years before traveling eastward to Acre for one year, after which he resided in Egypt for thirty-eight years. From Egypt he corresponded with Jewish communities in the entire Mediterranean basin and beyond.

Maimonides' landscape consisted of the coasts, mountains, deserts, rivers, and cities of the Mediterranean. The sea was a barrier and a bridge connecting three continents—Europe, Asia, and Africa. It was the intersection of nations, ethnicities, languages, and cultures, traversed by ships linking North Africa, Spain, southern France, Italy, Sicily, Egypt, Syro-Palestine, and Byzantium.

The Mediterranean region is primarily an urban area, its human setting fashioned by cities and communications, with agriculture directed mainly toward towns. The great Mediterranean cities (Fez, Tunis, Alexandria, Cairo/Fustat, Tyre, Constantinople, Venice, Syracuse, Rome, Marseilles, Córdoba, and Barcelona) were adjacent to the sea or connected by accessible waterways. In the southern and eastern Mediterranean, there are also great inland cities that served as centers for roads leading through the desert.[2]

Shelomo Dov Goitein and Ferdinand Braudel made the Mediterranean the center of their historical investigations. Writing about a later era, Braudel argued for the "unity and coherence of the Mediterranean region." Braudel's colleague Lucien Febvre wrote, "The Mediterranean is the sum of its routes, land routes and sea routes, routes along the rivers and routes along the coasts, an immense network of regular and casual connections, and the life-giving bloodstream of the Mediterranean region."[3]

Goitein saw the unity of the Mediterranean world as predominant, even though it was divided into separate, sometimes warring, political units.[4] The waves lapping the northern and southern shores of the Mediterranean were no longer of a single empire, the Roman Imperium, which regarded the Mediterranean as *mare nostrum,* "our sea." Although many states, ethnic groups, and religions emerged in the Mediterranean region, political boundaries did not stifle free movement and did not interfere with the unity and autonomy of religious and ethnic groups.

BIOGRAPHICAL ISSUES

Where there are gaps in Maimonides' biography, they are often filled with legend and surmise, so that his life is surrounded by a halo of myth. Unfortunately, most biographies are derived from previous biographies and from secondary literature and fail to distinguish between fact and fiction.

We hear nothing in primary sources about Maimonides' mother, for instance. Readers like to know about mothers. There must be an explanation for this silence. So a sixteenth-century historian, writing four hundred years after the event, decided that Maimonides' mother died in childbirth.[5] This turned young Moses into an orphan brought up by a stepmother, a touching account. The story is enshrined in biographies as solid fact—in two recent biographies, for instance, written in 2001 and 2005—and I have even encountered it in serious museum exhibitions.

It is also told that Maimonides' first wife died young, and that his son, Abraham, was the offspring of a second wife. We know that he married late in life, circa 1173, when he was about thirty-five, and Abraham was born in 1186, when he was forty-eight. Biographers surmise that this could not have been with his first wife (see chapter 12).

We read in Muslim and Jewish sources that when living in Fez during a period of religious oppression, Maimonides converted to Islam. This is sensational if true. But is it true? We find in an Arabic source that when Maimonides lived in Egypt a Muslim jurist from Fez claimed that he had known him as a Muslim and that he had reverted to Judaism since then. This was an act of apostasy, according to Islam, and punishable by death. Can we give credence to this story? According to one historian, Maimonides arranged for the man's murder by having him thrown into the Nile. We shall have a look at various accounts and perspectives in chapter 7.

We often find it said that Maimonides was physician to Richard the Lionhearted. How did the story come about, and is it true?

A good narrative needs a villain, and in chapter 15 we have Zuta. The pejorative nickname Zuta means "small"; he was actually called Zuta ha-Rasha', or Zuta the Wicked. He became *ra'is al-yahud,* or head of the Jews of Egypt and its territories, by bribes and underhanded dealings with the government. When in power, he oppressed the people and pressured them for taxes. He removed judges from their posts and appointed his own candidates. Zuta informed on Jews he claimed were disloyal to the Egyptian regime, and they were imprisoned or executed. He regarded himself as the precursor of the Messiah or as the Messiah himself. Maimonides and his colleague judge Isaac ben Sason eventually got rid of Zuta and relieved Jewish

communities of their tormentor. Had Maimonides failed to defeat
Zuta, he could not have attained the leadership role over Egyptian
Jewry that he did. The problem is that no one so far has identified
Zuta. Who is Zuta? What is he that all the saints abhorred him? The
Zuta narrative is like a giant jigsaw puzzle in which the pieces don't
quite fit and some are left over on the table.

Narratives also need heroes. No one was more celebrated as a hero,
in his time and for posterity, than Salah al-Din al-Ayyubi, better known
as Saladin. He was the most famous person of the age. By chance,
Saladin and Maimonides were born in about the same year. By destiny, they became two of the outstanding figures of the second millennium. The two earned world fame in their lifetime. They were from
opposite ends of the earth and met by fortune in Egypt. Ibn Abi
Usaybi'a (1194–1270), the historian of medicine, wrote that Maimonides ministered to Saladin as one of his court physicians. Given the
historian's contact with Maimonides' son, Abraham, it stands to reason that this information is accurate.

Who was Saladin? Was he noble, generous, and pious, an idealist
who sincerely pursued jihad against the Crusaders? Or was he a prag-
matist who exploited the jihad to conquer territories in Syria and
northern Mesopotamia, to aggrandize himself and his family, pursuing
an expansionist policy in the guise of religious faith? (See chapter 11.)

THE HISTORIAN AS DETECTIVE

The above problems are examples of questions that constitute the
Sherlock Holmes component of our biography. The Yale historian
Robin Winks suggested that the historian should gather and interpret
evidence by methods like those employed by the detective, using similar
reasoning processes.[6] The detective solves a crime by reconstructing a
crime scene. We also reconstruct a scene by scrutinizing clues—names,
inscriptions, letters, legal documents, and texts. We need to authenticate, evaluate, and date them. We make inferences and construct theories on the basis of evidence that we gather slowly and painfully. We
harvest the evidence and force it to yield its secrets. We assemble a
mosaic out of pieces of varying colors, shapes, and sizes. The best evidence is often an insignificant detail, something crossed out on a page

of writing, a gesture, or a snippet of conversation. The great Greek biographer and historian Plutarch of Chaeronea (ca. 46 C.E.–120 C.E.) wrote:

> For I am writing biography, not history, and the truth is that the most brilliant exploits often tell us nothing of the virtues or vices of the men who performed them, while on the other hand a chance remark or a joke may reveal far more of a man's character than the mere feat of winning battles in which thousands fall, or of marshalling great armies, or laying siege to cities.[7]

We are fortunate to have many pages of Maimonides' writing with his deletions, additions, corrections, and afterthoughts. Philology, the handmaid of history, requires a knowledge of languages, paleography, and codicology. We have to date the texts and determine their authenticity. We need to study the author's handwriting, vocabulary, and style.

Having pertinent evidence does not mean that our analysis will be correct. We need to be aware that other interpretations are possible and that further evidence may emerge. We need to examine all facets: literary, historical, cultural, social. The biographer's writing should always be careful and never overstated. We need to distrust conventional information based on *idées reçues*. A good detective strives to unearth new evidence, even when access is difficult. At the end of the day there should be no illusion of finality to what we say.

PERSONALITY

We want to apply psychological insights into aspects of Maimonides' personality and to discover "keys to the deeper truths of his life," to its "private mythology."[8] By looking beneath the public mask of our subject, we attempt to enter his private life, to penetrate the life-myth to the mystery of a real life. Portraying a life and its private mythology gives information to readers who are curious and avid for new knowledge; it also provides insight and edification that can be helpful in the story of our own lives.

We need to portray Maimonides realistically, as a human being, a sober rationalist *and* a man of passion, a master of all that he studied but ever open to new evidence and better understanding, hence constantly revising his works.

He informs us that *The Guide of the Perplexed* contains contradictions and that they are meaningful and point to an esoteric level of truth. Maimonides' medieval commentators assumed that the *Guide* was an esoteric work, in particular Samuel Ibn Tibbon, translator of the *Guide* into Hebrew, and members of his school, such as his son Moses and his son-in-law Jacob Anatoli, as well as Shem Tov ben Joseph Ibn Falaquera, Moses Narboni, Joseph Ibn Kaspi, Isaac Albalag, and others.[9]

The *Guide* is a polyvalent text in which contradictory discourses, allusive digressions, and equivocal terms continually intersect to thwart a univocal conclusion of meaning. In his life, Maimonides had to don a mask and play the game of *taqiyya,* or prudent dissimulation, feigning Islam on the outside and being a Jew within. As a courtier in Egypt, he had to use deception to survive and remain in favor. In sum, he was used to duplicity, to living a double life for the sake of survival and for serving noble causes. His was a life of ambivalence, concealment, and inscrutable mystery.

He is often described by biographers as rejecting poetry and history. Yet all he said was that they are a waste of time compared with science and useful subjects. In fact, he wrote poetry and used rhymed prose in his letters. He began and ended *The Guide of the Perplexed* with his own verse and wrote poetic introductions to other works.

He scorned pride and extolled humility, yet he sought power and prestige. He believed that happiness is attained by solitary contemplation, yet he immersed himself in community affairs. Deploring anger, he displayed impatience and petulance in his letters and in public quarrels.

When we think about a historical figure, we try to imagine how the person looked. Many of us recognize him from the conventional portrait, but it is not an authentic likeness.[10] It first appeared in 1744, though it was said to be copied from an ancient picture (*ex antiqua tabula*).[11]

We have a few verbal descriptions of Maimonides from his own time by people who met him. A man delivering a secret message to the Great Sage visited his home and described in a letter its layout and depicted his illustrious host.[12] His letter contains many fascinating details, even the fact that his host served lemon pastilles. The messenger expected Moses ben Maimon to accept the note without receiving him in person, and his companion preferred to wait outside at the entrance. The messenger, however, was invited to come inside along with his young son, al-Jalal. He wrote in his letter that he was overcome by Moses ben Maimon's cordiality, and he proudly related how his host even discussed with him at length the contents of the message he delivered. Maimonides' son, Abraham, was present, and jestingly taught al-Jalal a term to use in addressing Rabbi Moses. When al-Jalal used it, Rabbi Moses laughed and played with him.

Although the letter describing Rabbi Moses tells us nothing earth-shaking, its simplicity, the messenger's excitement, the Master's warmth and cordiality, and his humor and playfulness speak volumes. It is in small details such as these that we discover keys to his character.

From his own description of the way a self-respecting scholar should dress and comport himself, together with descriptions by others, we may visualize a handsome figure attired in a long, flowing white robe, with sleeves to his fingertips, his turban carefully wrapped, his beard neatly trimmed. He walked slowly and deliberately, head slightly bowed. When at the royal palace, he dressed in silks and brocade.[13]

MAIMONIDES' NAMES

What's in a name? For Arabic names, the answer is everything. A name in the Arabic milieu was like a calling card. Maimonides' name, as given in its most complete form in Arabic sources, was al-Ra'is Abu 'Imran Musa ibn Maymun Ibn 'Abdallah ('Ubaydallah) al-Qurtubi al-Andalusi al-Isra'ili.

First came his title, al-Ra'is (the Head),[14] then his honorific byname (*kunya*) Abu 'Imran,[15] followed by his personal name, Musa. After his personal name came his patronymic, ibn Maymun, followed by his family's ancestral name, the name of the family's progenitor, which was 'Abdallah, or 'Ubaydallah, the Arabic equivalent of Hebrew Obadiah, hence Ibn 'Abdallah ('Ubaydallah). Thereafter came his place names (toponymics), al-Qurtubi (the Córdoban) and al-Andalusi (the Andalusian), and finally his gentilic, referring to his origin, al-Isra'ili (the Israelite). In Hebrew, he called himself Mosheh ben Maimon ha-Sefaradi (Moses son of Maimon the Sephardic [Jew]).

The name Moses does not appear among those of the talmudic sages and scholars in the early Middle Ages until Maimonides' own time. It emerged in this period, I think, because it was used so often, more than a hundred times, in the Qur'an and by Muslims, and it served well as a bilingual name. Moses ben Maimon's father praised the biblical Moses in his *Epistle of Consolation* as the best of men and noblest of apostles, citing his redemptive power, the uniqueness of his mission, and his merits, declaring his superiority to Muhammad, whom Muslims considered "the best of mankind" (*khayr al-bashar*).

Maimon claimed that Psalm 90, *A prayer for Moses, man of God*, foretells all the vicissitudes that would befall Israel from the beginning of the exile to its end. "I considered the Psalm and its secret was made clear to me, that Moses uttered it for the time of exile, and David put it in the Book of Psalms as a source of comfort and consolation."[16] Significantly, Maimon named his other son David. The name Moses and his patronymic Maimon, meaning "blessed" or "fortunate," could not but give Moses ben Maimon a sense of destiny.

Jews later called him by the acronym RaMBaM—Rabbenu (our Master) Mosheh ben Maimon. Maimonides is from the late European Middle Ages, and came about by adding a Greek patronymic suffix (*-ides*) to the Latinized name Maimon.

The epithet "Great Eagle," from the Book of Ezekiel 17:3 (*Thus said the Lord God: The great eagle with the great wings and the long pinions, with the full plumage and the brilliant colors*), was applied to Maimonides by later scholars, one of the first being Rabbi Yom Tov ben Abraham of Seville (1250–1330), a devotee of Maimonides. The title was also given to other outstanding scholars until early modern times, when it was confined to Maimonides. The idea was that the great eagle, with its enormous wings, soars in the heights of heaven and carries fledglings on its wings. The Great Eagle suddenly appeared in Spain like a star streaking across the sky, spreading its light on the horizon, then faded into the night leaving an afterglow.

In his own time and for posterity he was called ha-Moreh (the teacher/guide), or ha-Rav ha-Moreh, from *Moreh ha-nevukhim,* the

Hebrew title of his *Guide of the Perplexed,* and he was often called Moreh Sedeq (teacher of righteousness), a messianic name.[17]

The expression "Man of God" (*ish ha-elohim*) is used for the biblical Moses in Deut 33:1, Josh 14:6, and Psalm 90, and generally for men inspired or sent by God and having superhuman powers (e.g., Elijah in 1 Kings 17:24). It was a typical form of address used by people writing to and about Moses ben Maimon.

PRIMARY SOURCES

The biography is based primarily upon documents from the Cairo Genizah, the great repository of manuscripts found in the Ben Ezra Synagogue in Old Cairo and now in European, Russian, and American libraries. This treasure trove has placed at our disposal many of Moses ben Maimon's private and communal letters, some in his own handwriting, along with documents pertaining to his career and public activities. These papers are an indispensable source for knowledge of the cultural, economic, and social history of Maimonides' era.[18]

The roughly three hundred thousand manuscripts of the entire Genizah take in a broad range of subjects: the Bible, the Apocrypha, sectarian literature, the Talmud, liturgy, philosophy, medicine, personal and business letters, and commercial, legal, and communal documents. The documents were written, for the most part, in Arabic— more specifically, in Judeo-Arabic. There are also documents in classical Arabic and in Arabic script, including the Qur'an, poetry, Sufism, science, philosophy, and official chancellery records.

The Genizah contains materials pertaining to every aspect of Jewish life in the period that concerns us. It holds manuscripts vital for the reconstruction of the social history of Jews during this age. The documents give precious details about daily life, economic structure, education, and family life. We find out about material culture (housing, attire, food, furniture, etc.), court records, marriage contracts, wills and deathbed declarations, and business records. Personal letters reveal details about family relationships and friendships. Many letters from and to women in the Genizah are our only record of women's voices in this period.

As Egypt was a hub of Mediterranean trade and a mail-clearing center, the Genizah documents reflect the situation in the entire Mediterranean area. Documents come from Spain, North Africa (Morocco, Algeria, Tunisia, Libya), Sicily, Egypt, Palestine, Syria, and Byzantium.

S. D. Goitein's *A Mediterranean Society: The Jewish Communities in the Arab World as Portrayed in the Documents of the Cairo Geniza*—is based on Genizah documents, and our biography would be destitute without this remarkable resource. Goitein's working hypothesis was that the Genizah papers, while written mostly by Jews, reflect the socioeconomic situation, culture, and mentality of Mediterranean societies in general at this time. Goitein stressed that here we have records of life as it really was, especially of the middle and lower strata of society during the High Middle Ages, roughly coinciding with the Fatimid and Ayyubid periods (969–1250), which will mainly interest us.

The majority of Jews at this time enjoyed relatively normal conditions of existence. Many of the Genizah documents are business letters, which give us detailed information about the Mediterranean and Far Eastern trade. Goitein collected documents on the India trade for many years and often referred to the "India book" he was writing. However, it remained unfinished when he died, on February 6, 1985, and his student Mordechai A. Friedman has been editing and publishing it.[19]

The biography also utilizes the writings of Arab historians, geographers, and authors of travelogues and memoirs. Historians such as Ibn al-Qifti (1172–1248) and Ibn Abi Usaybi'a were contemporaries of Maimonides. The learned and reliable Ibn al-Qifti studied in Cairo until 1187 and then went first to Jerusalem and afterward to Aleppo (1201). There he befriended Maimonides' pupil Joseph ben Judah. Ibn al-Qifti's entries on him and on Maimonides are filled with precious information.

Ibn Abi Usaybi'a wrote a biographical dictionary of physicians. His father had studied with Maimonides, and Ibn Abi Usaybi'a worked with Maimonides' son, Abraham, at the Nasiri Hospital in Cairo. His biographies of Maimonides and Abraham are consequently well-informed.

The intrepid voyager Ibn Jubayr (1145–1217), an Andalusian, wrote a travelogue during this period with vivid descriptions of locales that Maimonides and his brother, David, visited around the same time.

The diaries and letters of al-Qadi al-Fadil, Saladin's chief administrator and Maimonides' patron, give a panorama of the age. Usama Ibn Munqidh (1095–1188) wrote a memoir crucial for understanding everyday life and personal aspects of the struggle between Crusaders and Muslims. Also, historians of the Fatimid and Ayyubid periods, such as Taqi al-Din al-Maqrizi (1364–1442), left valuable testimonies of events and personalities.

Only when we read Arabic sources can we have a true picture of this period, identify the actors in this drama, and have reliable knowledge of circumstances and events. Unfortunately, modern biographies of Maimonides generally neglect or fail to understand these rich Arabic mines of information.

As for Hebrew sources, there is, first and foremost, Abraham Ibn Daud, who described Andalusian Jewry in the period before Maimonides in *Sefer ha-qabbalah* (*Book of Tradition*) (1161). Benjamin of Tudela wrote a travelogue and visited Cairo in Maimonides' period. There are later writers, such as Se'adyah Ibn Danan (end of the fifteenth century), whose *Ma'amar Seder ha-dorot* (*Treatise on the Order of Generations*) is of limited historical value. The Egyptian historian Joseph ben Isaac Sambari, though late (1640–1703), is a good source for Egyptian Jewish history and has some material on Maimonides and his descendants—mostly, however, from earlier sources that we otherwise know.

It turns out that our main historical sources are written in Arabic by Muslims. This is because Jews wrote very few historical works, whereas Muslims wrote enough biographical and historical tomes to fill a good-sized library.

CONFLICT AND MISSION

The Jewish people at the time of Maimonides faced a concrete danger of physical and spiritual extinction. Opponents maligned Judaism as primitive and obsolete. Christianity and Islam viewed Judaism as superseded, the Jewish people as redundant. The Christian attitude, as articulated by authorities such as St. Augustine, justified Jewish survival only to show "how those who killed the Lord when proudly empowered have merited subjection." Jews were needed to authenticate the Old Testament, which, it was believed, predicted the coming of Jesus and the victory of Christianity.[20]

Muslims viewed their military superiority as evidence that Allah favored them. It was hard for Jews to go on believing that God had chosen them for a special mission in the world, that finally a redeemer would bring justice.

The teachings of Christianity and Islam and of philosophy and science enticed Jewish intellectuals. Peter (Petrus) Alfonsi, formerly Moses Sefaradi (1062–1110), converted to Christianity (1106) and wrote a comprehensive anti-Judaic tract, *Dialogi contra Iudaeos,* which took the form of a debate between Moses, his former self, and Peter, his new persona. He ridiculed talmudic legends that contradicted reason. The *Dialogi* became the most effective anti-Judaic tract of the Latin Middle Ages.[21]

The conversion to Islam of Samaw'al (Samuel) al-Maghribi, a mathematician and physician (ca. 1126–1175), was a celebrated case. His father was a well-known scholar and Hebrew poet. Samuel abandoned Judaism for Islam in 1163, and on the night of his conversion began to write a refutation of Judaism, *Silencing the Jews.*[22] When he was young he began reading Arabic literature, mainly stories and anecdotes, and then historical works. Muhammad's meteoric ascent from poverty to prophecy and the early conquests of Islam inspired him. Samuel went on to study mathematics, astronomy, and medicine. One of his teachers was the famous philosopher Abu 'l-Barakat al-Baghdadi, also a convert from Judaism to Islam.[23]

Samuel believed that human reason is the ultimate criterion of the truth and that it requires us to examine ancestral traditions. When we do, we discover that Judaism, Christianity, and Islam have equally valid claims.[24] All religions preach the good life, promote social well-being, and maintain political order. Islam, Samuel wrote, is superior to Judaism; for whereas Islam is the most inclusive religion, Judaism is the most exclusive. Samuel therefore decided to abandon the particularism of an obsolete faith for the greater universalism and inclusiveness of the newer and more popular religion.

He found Judaism intellectually impoverished. The Old Testament told stories discrediting the prophets and represented God as human and having human emotions. Samuel rejected the oral tradition of the Talmud, synagogue ritual, and Jewish dietary laws. Maimonides obviously knew about Samuel's conversion and was familiar with his anti-Jewish polemics and responded to them.

Christians, Muslims, and apostate Jews claimed that the Hebrew Bible predicted the advent of Jesus and Muhammad. Samuel found in the Old Testament statements announcing the prophet of Islam (Gen 17:20, Deut 18:15–18), and he used numerology to prove that Muhammad was mentioned in Gen 17:20.

Some of the strongest critiques of Judaism flowed from the eloquent pen of Ibn Hazm of Córdoba, jurist, theologian, and poet. Although he befriended Jewish intellectuals, he attacked their religion.[25]

Ibn Hazm assaulted Judaism with these arguments: (1) The transmission of the Torah was unreliable, its text corrupted and altered, beginning with Ezra's original forgery in the postexilic period. (2) The perfect revelation to the Prophet Muhammad abrogated the Torah. (3) The Jews tried to suppress biblical allusions to the Prophet Muhammad, as they had tried to remove references to Jesus. (4) Rabbinic homiletic literature contained crass anthropomorphisms that no religious intellectual could admit literally. (5) The Book of Psalms and other biblical and rabbinic writings convey materialist-atheistic views. The Torah does not mention the next world or reward after death.[26]

The rationalist critique of Judaism hit home. The Hebrew Bible indeed described God in mythopoetic language as having human features and emotions, even anger, jealousy, regret, and disappointment. God sees; he descends and ascends; he sits on a throne; he passes through the land; he dwells in Zion. In rabbinic literature, God puts on phylacteries and prays, studies the law, weeps, and mourns. Jewish mystical doctrine depicted God in the most human terms. An ancient book, *Shi'ur qomah* (*The Measure of the [Divine] Body*), portrayed God as an enormous man with quantifiable dimensions. Ibn Hazm knew this work and derided it, as did the Karaites. Maimonides wrote a responsum on *Shi'ur qomah* in which he denied its authorship by the talmudic sages and pronounced it idolatrous (see chapter 17). These myths became a laughingstock for rational critics and Karaite Jews, who rejected the Talmud and the oral tradition.

Maimonides stepped into the fray with sword and buckler to defend Judaism and to portray it as intellectually respectable. He sought to revive the ancient wisdom of the Jewish people and to assure them that God had not rejected them and that history would vindicate their case.[27] Within the Jewish community, messianic precursors and pretenders arose, who promised miracles and delivered catastrophes. Maimonides had to dampen enthusiasm for messianic movements without deepening pessimism and despair.

ABOVE ALL, Maimonides aspired to revolutionize Judaism by transforming it into a religion of reason. Maimonides wanted to change Judaism from a religion rooted in history, in great events such as the Exodus and revelation, to a religion implanted in nature and knowledge of the natural beings, God's works rather than God's words. Maimonides' main concern was science and the study of nature, the foundation of a religion of reason and enlightenment.

Maimonides teaches philosophical truths without hindering religious commitment, showing that philosophy need not disrupt social norms or destroy religious beliefs. Religion conveys the abstract truths of philosophy in the form of images and symbols. Religion, however, is not merely a mythic representation of rational verities; it also takes over where science reaches its limits. No philosophical system can give a rational account of the universe as a whole. Maimonides believed that human intelligence is limited, that there is a transcendental mystery beyond reason, and that traces of this mystery shimmer through the beauty and harmony of nature.

The Guide of the Perplexed urges human beings to become fully human by perfecting their reason and living in accordance with nature. Beyond this, Maimonides instructs us to contemplate the beauty and harmony of the universe and to experience the divine presence everywhere—in a silent room, in a storm at sea, or in the starry sky above—so that we come to a "passionate love of God." The horizon of the ordinary human world is transformed by revelatory moments ("We are like someone in a very dark night over whom lightning flashes time and time again").

Aware of how easily governments and peoples, and with them individuals, can be brought to ruin, Maimonides held aloft, amid the chaos and turmoil of his epoch, a love of order, restraint, and moderation. His ethical system is a form of therapy, a cure for excessive desires, illusions, false standards, and extreme tendencies. If people live by reason and in harmony with nature, following ethical and religious precepts and adhering to a regimen of health, they can escape the "sea of chance" as far as humanly possible.

PART ONE

ANDALUSIA

1

Córdoba

Kennst du das Land, wo die Zitronen blühen,
Im dunkeln Lau die Gold-Orangen glühn . . .

Knowst thou the land of flowering lemon trees?
In leafage dark the golden orange glows . . .[1]

—GOETHE

I F BIRTHPLACE INFLUENCES DESTINY, Moses ben Maimon
could not have chosen to be born in a city more conducive to
greatness than Córdoba.

We have knowledge of Moses ben Maimon's birth from his own
hand in the colophon to his *Commentary on the Mishnah,* completed in
Egypt in 1168. Midway in his life's journey, after years of exile and
then a newcomer to Egypt, he invoked a distinguished lineage—seven
generations of eminent scholars and magistrates.[2] He said that he
began to compose the *Commentary* when he was twenty-three and
completed it in Egypt in 1167 or 1168, when he was thirty years old.[3]
To be more accurate, then, he was born sometime in the last third of
1137 or the first two-thirds of 1138.[4] The conventional date for his
birth, 1135, which we still find in library catalogues, biographies, and

encyclopedias, is based on what Maimonides' grandson, David ben Abraham (1222–1300), wrote.[5]

According to his grandson, Maimonides' birth fell on the eve of Passover, 14 Nisan, the holiday of Redemption, a date of symbolic significance. Yellin and Abrahams, in their eulogistic biography of Maimonides, added the exact hour of his birth and created an aristocratic lineage back to Rabbi Judah ha-Nasi and King David.[6]

We do not hear about Maimonides' ancestors prior to his father, Rabbi Maimon ben Joseph. Even if they wrote legal responsa, commentaries, and treatises, nothing has survived to our knowledge.[7] Maimon (or Maymun) is an Arabic name that is common among Muslims and Maghribi Jews.[8] Aside from his father, all of Moses' ancestors and descendants had biblical names, the recurrent ones being Abraham, David, Joseph, and Obadiah.[9]

We never meet Moses' mother. Biographies of Maimonides, trying to fill in gaps, usually say that she died in childbirth, yet we have no evidence for this. If she did, then Moses' brother, David, would have been a half brother, but again there is no mention of it.

The explanation for this silence is much simpler. We hear very little, if anything, about the mothers, wives, and sisters of people we meet in this period. The historical record ignores women's lives because they were not scholarly links in a tradition of learning. Women were expected to be modest, pious, and withdrawn from public view. Unless they entered the public sphere by gaining economic power or owned important property, there was no reason for mentioning them.

THE BRIDE OF ANDALUS

Situated in a fertile plain at the foot of the Sierra Morena, overlooking the Guadalquivir River, Córdoba had been the administrative, political, military, religious, and cultural capital of Andalusia during the period of the Umayyad caliphate (976–1031).[10] The population of greater Córdoba, comprising the walled city and its outlying suburbs, was about 250,000–300,000, even greater than that of Paris.

Arab chroniclers called Córdoba "the bride of al-Andalus" and "the most beautiful jewel of al-Andalus." The Spanish historian Shihab al-Din al-Maqqari (b. ca. 1577 Tlemcen, d. 1632 Cairo) wrote that in four things Córdoba surpassed the other capitals of the world: the bridge over the Guadalquivir, its Great Mosque, the city of al-Zahra', and the sciences cultivated therein.[11]

Córdoba was made up of five connected towns, with separation ramparts, and open suburbs beyond the inner walled city, taking up a total area of about 144 square miles. The ramparts, resting on Roman foundations, had 132 towers and thirteen gates. Al-Maqqari's statistics for the city are often cited: 1,600 mosques; 900 public baths; 213,077 homes for ordinary people; 60,300 mansions for notables, officials, and military commanders; and 80,455 shops. These numbers, even if exaggerated, indicate a city of tremendous proportions.

THE CITY'S SPLENDOR

We would have to transport ourselves to Córdoba to appreciate fully the splendor of the city during Maimonides' lifetime. Córdoba basked in light, clear skies, a shimmering river, and rippling water flowing from its aqueducts. Its climate was moderate, with abundant sun and water, and its fruits were harvested all year round.[12] The Arabs had introduced exotic fruits and flowers from overseas.[13]

The Guadalquivir, Andalusia's longest river, just south of the Sierra Morena, rises in the mountains of Jaen province and takes a westward serpentine course for 408 miles, slowly meandering through Córdoba and Seville to the Gulf of Cádiz on the Atlantic Ocean. The Guadalquivir valley is the most fertile region in all Andalusia. The mountains to its north had olive groves and pine and oak trees, and were a frontier between the tropical Mediterranean and alpine Europe.

Al-Maqqari gave a poetic description of the river:

> [Córdoba's] river is one of the finest in the world, now gliding
> slowly through level lawns, or winding softly across emerald fields
> sprinkled with flowers, and serving it instead of robes; now flowing
> through thickly planted groves, where the song of birds resounds
> perpetually in the air; and now widening into a majestic stream to
> impart its waters to the numerous wheels constructed on its banks,
> or communicating to the plants and flowers of the vicinity freshness
> and vigor.[14]

The Guadalquivir was navigable in Maimonides' day from the Atlantic to Córdoba, though now only from the ocean to Seville. In his time, foreign vessels unloaded their wares at Seville and then smaller boats carried them upstream to Córdoba. He called the Guadalquivir the "Seville River," and mentioned the travel route between Seville and Alexandria.[15]

The river watered Córdoba's vineyards and olive groves. Dark-leafed orange trees, almond trees, flowering lemon trees, and wild thyme flourished along the Guadalquivir's banks. Córdoba was also a cornucopia of cherries, peaches, pomegranates, figs, apples, melons, pears, dates, bananas, quinces, and chestnuts. It was a medley of flowers and aromas—jasmine, narcissus, violets, and roses. New methods of agriculture and a sophisticated irrigation system of water mills and waterwheels, technologies imported from Syria, made food plentiful enough to sustain the city's vast population.

The city streets were paved and well lit at night, with lamps suspended on outer doors and corners of houses. Whitewashed villas, with terra-cotta tiled roofs, surrounded cool patios resplendent with flowers, pools, and fountains. The walls, verandas, latticed windows, and inner courtyards seemed to conceal deep secrets.

THE JEWISH QUARTER

Jews had been living in Córdoba from Roman times, many having emigrated to the city after the Roman conquest of Judea and destruction of the Second Temple in 70 C.E. When the Muslims conquered Córdoba in the eighth century, they garrisoned Jews there as a reward for their support against the Visigoths, expecting them to work in administration. The Mozarabs (Arabized Christians) were not allowed to reside inside the city and lived to the east of the city walls.

Moses ben Maimon and his family resided in the Jewish Quarter (*juderia*), which was in the southwest part of the city near the river and the bridge. The Great Mosque and the royal palace (*al-qasr*) were in the same vicinity. The mosque and the palace, representing Islamic sovereignty and caliphal authority, were built close to the Guadalquivir instead of in the city's center, as was more common in Islamic urban settings.[16] Situating the Jewish Quarter near the royal palace was for the Jews' protection against possible mob violence. This arrangement created a bond of mutual dependency between the Jews and the ruling establishment that contributed to popular resentment.

The Jewish Quarter was small and crowded, with narrow, labyrinthine streets and alleys, the upper stories of houses almost touching, obscuring the sky. One could easily hear voices of neighbors from across the way. This gave a feeling of intimacy, and the shade gave relief from the summer heat.

Today, the old Jewish Quarter is a charming neighborhood, with lovely white villas, gates opening onto garden patios, and geraniums cascading from flower boxes. The synagogue that we see nowadays in the Jewish Quarter, at Calle de los Judios 20, just north of Plaza Maimónides, was not the one where Maimonides prayed, although it may have been built on the site of an older synagogue that existed then.[17]

As Córdoba thrived, people poured into the city to exploit economic and cultural opportunities. The small Jewish Quarter was soon bursting at its seams, so another area for Jewish settlement was built on the northern side of the city.

As other native sons of Córdoba had crossed the ancient arched bridge—Seneca the Elder and Younger, the theologian Ibn Hazm, the poet Ibn Zaydun, and the philosopher Ibn Rushd—so too we imagine young Moses sauntering alongside the river, promenading in the evening as the sun was sinking low.[18]

In the open spaces between the mosque and the palace, one saw noblemen on their prancing mounts with proud necks and long tails, government officials, imams, preachers, scholars, and students rushing about. This was another world for young Moses. How unlike the dark warren of narrow paths, tortuous alleyways, and cul-de-sacs forming the Jewish Quarter, where pack animals and humans squeezed into sinuous lanes and could barely pass one another.[19]

THE GREAT MOSQUE

Moses ben Maimon lived a few minutes away from one of the grandest mosques in the entire Islamic world. We can picture him standing before the edifice, overwhelmed by its vastness, peering at the arcades and multiple rows of high double horseshoe arches, sensing its allure and mystery.[20]

The Qur'anic inscriptions over the mosque's entrance affirmed Islam's superiority over Judaism and Christianity, promising rewards to those who surrendered themselves to Allah and punishment to those who did not take heed. Verses assured faithful Muslims of a heavenly paradise: *You, my servants, who have believed in our revelations and surrendered yourselves, shall on that day have nothing to fear or regret. Enter paradise, you and your spouses, all in delight. You shall be served with gold dishes and golden cups. Abiding there forever, you shall find all that your souls desire and all that your eyes rejoice in* (Qur'an 43: 68–71).[21]

This mosque invited entry. The visitor walks past the courtyard with its rows of orange trees and fountains, apples of gold in settings of silver, into the cavernous interior. Eight hundred fifty jasper, marble, and porphyry columns support double arcades of horseshoe arches beneath round ones, with red and white voussoirs (the wedge-shaped stones used to build arches). The double-arched columns create a mystifying space, an extension of the orchard outside, seemingly going on forever as though reflected in mirrors. The central octagonal dome is overlaid with polychrome mosaics. In Moses ben Maimon's time, the pungent fragrance of incense and oil emanated from thousands of lamps.

At the end of a walk along the columns, one comes to the magnificent domed *mihrab,* the niche where the imam led prayers. An octagonal chamber bounded by two smaller rooms, it is adorned with Arabic inscriptions and Byzantine mosaics, which Emperor Nicephorus II Phocas sent to Caliph al-Hakam II. Abstract patterns predominate, reflecting Islamic aniconism (absence of representational art) and a sense of the geometric order that governs the universe and should preside over earth, regulating art, science, ritual, law, and society.[22]

CÓRDOBA'S SHOPS

Near the mosque were the law court and a prison. To the southeast were *suqs* (markets) and a large *qaysariyya.* A *suq* was a single gallery, while a *qaysariyya* comprised shops, workplaces, warehouses, and residences in covered galleries around an open court.[23] Close by the mosque were stalls for copyists, who also sold paper, books, reed pens, ink, and rulers. In the same area were shops of *'attarin,* druggists, who offered herbal remedies, perfume, rosewater, and spices. Names for herbs and spices were in Hispano-Romance, Arabic, Berber, and Hebrew. Nearby, locally manufactured merchandise was on sale—enameled ceramics, silk, brocade, fabrics, clothing, jewelry, and leather items. Farther out and closer to the city gates were carpenters and makers of copper and brass implements.

A variety of sounds, aromas, and bright colors stimulated the senses. A muezzin called the faithful to prayer, artisans clattered, men shouted and laughed. Close to the palace were weapons dealers and saddlers. Outside the gates, dyers worked on their fibers in a blaze of colors. Traders displayed for sale camels, donkeys, horses, mules, and sheep. By the riverside, where tanners worked on animal skins, preparing them to become shoes and bookbindings, an overwhelming odor surged from the skins and from the pigeon dung and fermented chaff used to treat goat and camel hides.[24]

Along the narrow alleys, fragrant scents arose from the bread ovens in the *suq.* Butchers hung out oxen, sheep, and birds next to the fishmongers' heaps of seafood. Pack animals and porters trudged along, the men with backs perpetually bent, and the beasts patiently accepting their fate.

Economic Prosperity

The Guadalquivir, as we have seen, brought merchandise from downstream Seville, which had one of the finest harbors in Andalusia. Seville had commercial ties with the eastern Mediterranean, with vessels sailing regularly to and from Alexandria. Córdoba exported leather products, jewelry, and textiles—woven silks and silk brocades—to the entire Mediterranean area and throughout Europe.[25]

Maimonides' incredibly detailed description of the uses of leather is a valuable source for our knowledge of the many types of leather products.[26] His powers of observation were exceptional. Córdoba was famous then, as it is now, for its fine leather goods.

During the early Umayyad period (825–925), the horizontal loom came into use along with silk thread, stimulating a thriving weaving industry. Córdoba's colorful garments were fashion favorites in Andalusia. Local industry also produced cork shoes from the cork oak trees that grew in the area along with the evergreen oak.[27]

Artisans worked in glazed and polychrome pottery. The ornamentation was rich and variegated, with bird, animal, and vegetable motifs. More than thirty forms of pottery existed—oil lamps, pots, Chinese- and Iraqian-designed bottles and bowls, imitation Persian inkwells, and Syrian-style cups.[28]

THE SPANISH UMAYYADS

The Muslims reached the peak of their conquests in the Iberian Peninsula under the Umayyad caliphs (756–1031). This was a period of cultural splendor, when the arts and sciences flourished in Córdoba as nowhere else in Europe. 'Abd al-Rahman III al-Nasir (the Victorious) (912–961) loved learning and adorned his court with scholars, poets, and scientists. Splendid libraries, mosques, madrasas, and hospitals attracted visitors from the Islamic East, who brought cultural treasures that enriched Andalusia for centuries.

The Spanish Umayyads were originally from Syria. When the 'Abbasids defeated the Syrian Umayyads in 750, 'Abd al-Rahman I (731–788), an Umayyad prince, escaped to the Maghrib, where Berber relatives of his mother protected him. He then crossed to Spain and joined the Syrian Arabs in southern Andalusia. On March 15, 756, he entered Córdoba, became amir of Andalusia, and made the city his capital.

The Umayyad caliph 'Abd al-Rahman III integrated the diverse religious communities and ethnic groups into a unified state. The Muslim majority encompassed three classes: the dominant Arab elite, the more numerous Berbers, and the *muwalladun,* indigenous Christians who converted to Islam. The caliph sought to consolidate the state's power by limiting the influence of the Arab aristocracy and producing a new elite from among the other Muslims.

Andalusia had a large population of Christians. The Hispanic Christians, called Mozarabs, were successors to the Christians of

Roman-Visigoth times.[29] There were also Near Eastern Christians, who were artisans and professionals in medicine, architecture, and translation. Attracted by economic opportunities, Christians emigrated to Andalusia from northern Spain, Europe beyond the Pyrenees, and the Maghrib.

Then there were Asturians, Catalans, Basques, Slavs, and Africans brought as slaves from the Sudan.[30] Yet the multiethnic composition of Spanish Umayyad society did not make it a multicultural utopia; instead, ethnic and religious enmity often existed among Arabs, Berbers, Slavs, Jews, and Christians. Elite Muslims, Christians, and Jews in royal courts had more in common with each other in education, wealth, and sophistication than they did with ordinary people of their own religious community.[31]

In Andalusia, most educated people were bilingual and spoke Arabic and Hispano-Romance.[32] Andalusian Jews were often trilingual, adding Hebrew to their repertoire. Arabic was the lingua franca of Moses ben Maimon's milieu. He wrote classical Arabic for a Muslim audience, as in his medical writings, and used Judeo-Arabic when writing for his coreligionists in his *Commentary on the Mishnah, Guide of the Perplexed,* and many responsa.[33] For scholars such as he, Arabic was a mother tongue and the most natural means of expression, especially for theology, philosophy, and science.[34]

The age of splendor of Spanish Jewry, from the tenth to the twelfth century, is unrivaled in its cultural achievement and is personified in Maimonides, who exemplifies the spirit of the age. Jewish intellectuals studied Greco-Arabic philosophy and were *au courant* with Arabic literature while cultivating their own classics, especially the Bible, Talmud, and Midrash.[35]

Jews exercised communal self-government, administered their own courts, collected their own taxes, and ran their own welfare and educational systems. They acquiesced to Muslim political sovereignty and did not engage in intergroup hostilities.

Al-Hakam II (r. 961–976), son of 'Abd al-Rahman III, amassed a library in the royal palace of Córdoba that allegedly held some 400,000 manuscript volumes. (The number 400,000 sounds high, but even if it were one-tenth the size, it would have been considerably larger than

any European library.) Al-Hakam's interests were broad and even extended to the religious literature of his Jewish subjects. The scholar
and poet Joseph ibn Abitur "interpreted the entire Talmud in Arabic"
for this enlightened caliph.[36]

Al-Hakam strengthened his army by increasing the number of
Berber mercenaries, and harassed the Christian kingdoms in the north
with frequent raids.[37] As a result, he received a series of emissaries
from the Christian rulers of Navarre, León, Castile, Galicia, and Barcelona, who came to Córdoba and al-Zahra' to render homage.

His death left the country under the rule of his eleven-year-old son,
Hisham II, and under the effective authority of the *hajib* (chamberlain)
Muhammad Ibn Abi 'Amir, called al-Mansur (Almanzor to the Christians), who ruled from 978 to 1002.[38] Ibn Abi 'Amir launched fifty-two
devastating expeditions against the Christians. In 997, he raided San-
tiago de Compostela, the famous pilgrimage site, and brought back
its cathedral bells to melt down and make into lamps for the Great
Mosque of Córdoba.

To prove his orthodoxy and pacify the ulema (Muslim scholars),
Ibn Abi 'Amir ended the pluralistic cultural policies of 'Abd al-
Rahman III and al-Hakam II, declaring philosophy and science heretical, destroying books, and purging al-Hakam's library of whatever
he considered offensive.[39] Those who studied philosophy had to do so
furtively; they taught cautiously and restricted their audience to fellow philosophers. They wrote discreetly in veiled language, so that
only their peers would be able to decipher their books. Maimonides
would later compose *The Guide of the Perplexed* in encoded language.

Ibn Abi 'Amir imported Berber mercenaries hostile to the Umayyad
dynasty, who eventually brought down the caliphate after a period of
civil war lasting from 1008 to 1031. Calling in the Berbers might have
been good policy for fighting the Christians, but it undermined the
Umayyad state from within.

Out of the unified state, which 'Abd al-Rahman III had created,
many small states emerged under the sovereignty of party kings (*mu-
luk al-tawa'if*; Spanish *reyes de taifas*) (1031–1091), or rulers of petty
dynasties ("the breaking of the necklace and the scattering of its
pearls," as the historian al-Maqqari put it).

THE PARTY KINGS

At the end of the eleventh century, the Muslims were losing ground to the Christians. Muslim Spain disintegrated into thirty-nine local principalities, the largest being Málaga, Seville, Granada, Córdoba, Toledo, Valencia, and Saragossa. These cities and kingdoms waged incessant war upon one another.

The local dynasties, competing for prestige, supported cultural activity. Jewish intellectuals found opportunities for service in local entourages as physicians, financial ministers, and even viziers. The polymath Samuel ibn Naghrela, or Samuel ha-Nagid (993–1056), served as vizier to the Berber Zirid rulers in Granada. He led armies on the field by day, studied the Talmud in his tent by night, and composed exquisite religious and secular poetry. Jewish communities flourished in Spain when society was multiethnic, as under the Umayyads or under local dynasties.

The ulema detested the weakness and frivolity of the local rulers, and once the Christians conquered Toledo in 1085, judges and jurists under the party kings, despising their sinful ways and indulgent lifestyle, decided to call in the Almoravids, a Berber dynasty from North Africa. The Almoravids obtained fatwas from illustrious ulema to justify their replacing the party kings.[40]

Despite the decentralization of power during the period of the *reyes de taïfas,* cultural and intellectual life flourished. The competition among local courts was beneficial, as they all vied for primacy in poetry, prose, and science, and rewarded the learned for their efforts.[41] Even under the intolerant Almoravids and Almohads, poetry, science, art, and architecture continued unabated. Still, the summit of the Arab age in Spain was the period of the Umayyad caliph 'Abd al-Rahman III in the tenth century.

THE RECONQUISTA

The Christians in the north were never reconciled to Muslim rule in Andalusia, and as the caliphate became weak, they became bold. The expeditions of Ibn Abi 'Amir into Christian territory had created bitterness and a thirst for revenge. Alfonso VI, emperor of all Spain (*imperator totius hispaniae*), spearheaded the war against the Muslims. In 1063, he defeated the Muslims at Seville. On May 25, 1085, Alfonso VI occupied Toledo, former capital of the Visigoth kingdom, a major stride in the Reconquista. In the surrender terms, he promised the Muslims possession of their mosques and extension of their privileges. Nevertheless, two generations later, in 1102, the Christians expelled the Muslims from their positions in Toledo and turned the main congregational mosque into a church.[42] The Jews of Toledo remained in their quarter in the southwestern district.

After the Christian conquest of Toledo, Jews emigrated to the city, many of them refugees from the Almohad invasion in the south.[43] They served in the Christian administration and as tax officials, despite objections by the Christian clergy and political rivals. The Pope opposed Alfonso's appointment of Jewish civil servants and ordered him not to place Jews in positions of authority over Christians.

Even so, the financier Joseph Nasi Ferruziel of Granada, known by his Hispano-Arabic name Cidellus, was physician and advisor to Alfonso and the first notable Jewish courtier in Christian Spain. His nephew Solomon Ibn Ferruziel, who also served the Castilian state, supported Judah ha-Levi (ca. 1075–1141) when the poet lived in Toledo. When Solomon Ibn Ferruziel was assassinated by Christians (May 3, 1108) while returning from a mission to Aragon, the incident distressed the poet, who wrote a bitter elegy for his fallen patron, ending with an imprecation against the "Daughter of Edom."[44] He then left Toledo. Judah ha-Levi gave vent to the anguish of being trapped between Edom (the Christians) and Ishmael (the Muslims). In 1140, he finally decided to abandon Sefarad (Hebrew for "Spain") and all its blandishments, his friends and family, and emigrated to the Land of Israel, but he perished just two months after his arrival.[45]

THE ALMORAVIDS

In 1086, a year after the Christian victory at Toledo, the Muslims summoned reinforcements from North Africa, first the Almoravids, then decades later the Almohads, who brought with them fundamentalist, militant versions of Islam.[46]

The Almoravids were Berber camel nomads of the Sanhaja group, fierce-looking with their turbans and burnooses and veils like their Tuareg descendants.[47] They had conquered most of what now we call Morocco during the 1080s. Yusuf ibn Tashufin led them into Spain in 1086, where they routed the forces of Alfonso VI at Zallaqa near Badajoz. The Almoravids did not, however, exploit their victory by retaking Toledo. Instead, Yusuf returned to the Maghrib, his home base, leaving affairs in the hands of the party kings.

The party kings could not hold off the Christians, and Yusuf ibn Tashufin had to return to Spain to fight the Christians. By 1102, the Almoravids had conquered Valencia, which Rodrigo Díaz de Vivar, called El Cid Campeador, had previously ruled as an independent territory.[48] They gained control of Andalusia, joining it to their Maghrib Empire. Soon, however, the Almohads emerged in the Maghrib. The Almoravids were now facing enemies on two fronts. Alfonso I of Aragon defeated them at Saragossa in 1118. In 1147, the Almohads deposed the last Almoravid ruler in North Africa and crossed the Strait of Gibraltar into Spain. The invasion will directly impact Maimonides' life.

THE ALMOHADS

The Almohads, a North African Berber dynasty committed to a fundamentalist version of Islam, much like Saudi Wahhabism in our own day, ended what was left of ethnic and religious coexistence in Spain.[49] The Almohad movement originated in the teaching of a messianic figure, the Mahdi Muhammad ibn Tumart (ca. 1080–1130).[50] Ibn Tumart founded the Almohad movement among the Masmuda Berbers in the High Atlas Mountains of Morocco and was recognized as their Mahdi, or messianic leader. The Mahdi was a religious revolutionary who aspired to restore the pristine faith of Islam, based on the Qur'an and the Sunna (accepted practice), and to enforce the precepts of the sacred law. He harked back to a golden age and anticipated a global rule of Islam. The Almohads were distinguished externally by their burnooses and special turbans.

The Mahdi preached a spiritual conception of the deity, free of anthropomorphism, and drew up a creed of faith for his followers.[51] Ibn Tumart was both a traditional North African holy man, saint, and

miracle worker and a Shi'i Mahdi.[52] He did not preach Shi'ism, but
was able to mobilize the Berbers, with their veneration of holy men,
by the claim that he was the Mahdi. Ibn Tumart's miracles comported
well with Andalusian Sufism and its belief in *karamat* (miraculous
signs of divine grace) by the friends of God (*awliya'*).[53] He taught a
puritanical Islam, which strictly prohibited socializing between the
sexes, drinking wine, and playing musical instruments. He intensified
the humiliation of *dhimmi*s (non-Muslim subjects of an Islamic state)
and active jihad against infidels. As Mahdi, his decisions had to be
obeyed on pain of death, and those who opposed the Almohads, such
as the Almoravids and their supporters, could be killed with impu-
nity. The same dire fate awaited any Muslims whose loyalty was in
doubt or who disobeyed the *shari'a* (Islamic law).

The pious Mahdi covered his face when he noticed ornamented
and unveiled female vendors in the streets of Tlemcen, and he sent
an Almoravid princess weeping to her brother when he caught her
unveiled.[54] In these prohibitions, he was following Islamic law to the
letter. The Almohads, in their fanaticism, puritanism, and visions of
world domination, call to mind present-day expressions of militant
Islam.

Christians and Jews were no longer an integral part of the society
and its cultural fabric. They were infidels who could be assimilated
only by conversion. The Almohads banned from their realm religions
other than Islam, and in numerous places they confronted Jews and
Christians with the alternative of conversion or death.

The first decades of the twelfth century witnessed two eschatological traditions—Islamic Mahdism and Jewish Messianism—in full
bloom. According to an Islamic tradition, God sends to the Muslims
every hundred Hijra years someone to renew, or revive, their religion.[55]
In 1102, Yusuf ibn Tashufin, the leader of the Almoravids, commanded the Jews of Lucena to convert to Islam in anticipation of the
arrival of a Renewer in the year 500 A.H. (1106/07 C.E.).[56] He claimed
that Jews had told Muhammad that by this year their Messiah would
appear and save them; and if not, they would convert to Islam.[57]

When 'Abd al-Mu'min conquered Marrakesh in 1147, he taunted
the Jews, asking where the prophet was whom they expected, presenting them with a choice between Islam and death.[58] When the Messiah

did not come, the Jews were exposed to scorn and ridicule. The question resounded in their ears—"Where is your Messiah?"

The significant years were 1106/07 C.E., the five hundredth year of Islam according to their calendar, and 1122 C.E., the five hundredth year of Islam according to the Jewish calendar. Judah ha-Levi predicted the fall of the Ishmaelites and rise of the Israelites in 1129/30, a year that may have been based on his calculation of the five hundredth year of Islam.[59]

'Abd al-Mu'min ibn 'Ali al-Kumi succeeded Ibn Tumart in 1130 and was the main leader of Almohad military expansion. Large-scale massacres of Jews occurred in various North African cities (Sijilmasa, Marrakesh, and Fez). Even during the first period of the Almohad occupation, these communities suffered from inquisitions and persecutions, as did Christians and even Muslims suspect in their belief. The Almohads destroyed synagogues, churches, and monasteries.

Many Jews feigned Islam, thereby escaping death or exile and clinging to their property. This behavior became widespread under the sultan Abu Ya'qub Yusuf (1163–1184), who enforced discriminatory practices. Many forced converts espoused their newly adopted faith and attained leading positions in the economy.

When Abu Yusuf Ya'qub al-Mansur came to power in 1184, he was dismayed to find converts praying in mosques and teaching their children the Qur'an while remaining Jews at heart. He compelled them to wear distinctive signs, and he destroyed synagogues. The mistrust of converts was based on anxiety about heresy and dread of intermingling and impurity. Even as converts, Jews remained anomalous, marginal, and menacing from the Muslim viewpoint.[60]

The Almohads united North Africa and Andalusia under the rule of a single empire. Suddenly Jews whose families had been living in Spain for more than a millennium had to prove that they belonged, and if they were unwilling to embrace Islam, they faced death. The Almohads invaded Andalusia in 1145, conquering Cádiz in 1146, Jerez in 1147, and Seville and Córdoba in 1148. Despite this religious fanaticism, intellectual life went on under the Almohads, restricted to court circles and the elite. The philosophers Ibn Tufayl and Ibn Rushd served as physicians in the Almohad court at Marrakesh. Art and architecture flourished.

JEWS IN CHRISTIAN SPAIN

The Almoravid and Almohad incursions into Andalusia changed Jewish demography and revolutionized Jewish attitudes toward Christianity and Islam. From the time of the Muslim invasion of Spain in the early eighth century until the period of the Almohads in the twelfth, Jews had tied their destiny to the lot of the Islamic state. However, when the Almoravids and the Almohads invaded Spain, most Jews from the three great Andalusian cities—Córdoba, Granada, and Seville—fled either to Christian Spain, to North Africa, or to southern France. Many went to Provence, where they brought Andalusian culture to scholars eager for learning who did not know Arabic. Among the émigrés was the family of Judah Ibn Tibbon, whose son Samuel translated Maimonides' *Guide of the Perplexed* from Arabic into Hebrew at the end of the twelfth century.[61]

The polymath Abraham Ibn Ezra—grammarian, Bible commentator, astronomer, physician, and philosopher—emigrated to Christian Europe and brought Andalusian science with him. He reached Italy, France, and even England, where his mathematical works were later translated into Latin. He found that Christian countries lacked culture, sophistication, and generosity. Pining for Andalusia, he even missed its white bread made of fine flour, which he considered superior to any other.[62]

The Christian rulers made use of Jewish expertise in finance, administration, and diplomacy, as well as crafts and commerce. The Jews' knowledge of Arabic was valuable for dealing with Arabic-speakers under Christian rule and for negotiating with authorities in Islamic Spain.

Jews living in Christian Spain began to take part in transmitting Arabic science and philosophy to Christian Europe. Toledo became the center of translation activity from Arabic into Latin in the mid-twelfth century, when Maimonides was still in Spain. The translation movement was a facet of the European cultural renaissance of the twelfth century.[63]

CONVIVENCIA AND VIOLENCE

Historians have celebrated the Spanish Umayyad period as a time of idyllic coexistence and ethnoreligious harmony. The portrayal carries a strong message relevant to the present. There is an implicit claim here that different religions and ethnic groups were able to flourish under Islamic sovereignty and that Islam is in essence open-minded and tolerant. However, no Muslim teachers of the past claimed that Islam was tolerant. In fact, even under 'Abd al-Rahman III, subjects of the realm were not permitted to hold views that conflicted with Islamic teachings. A Muslim jurist incited the caliph against the Jewish leader Hisday ibn Shaprut by accusing him of blasphemy against the Prophet Muhammad.[64] It was enough if Hisday had denied that Muhammad was a prophet, as this was tantamount to declaring him a liar (takdhib al-nabi), for Muhammad had claimed that he received revelations from Allah and was a prophet.

The Spanish historian Américo Castro used the term convivencia for the coexistence of different ethnic groups, religions, and cultures in Islamic Spain.[65] Scholars have adopted the word to depict a society of idyllic tolerance and open-mindedness. They play down periods of persecution and violence, stress harmony and collaboration, and celebrate a "golden age" of Jewish culture.[66] Actually, the convivencia was mainly an economic and cultural coexistence, accompanied by competition, mistrust, and hostility. In the economic sphere, convivencia existed as interdependence and cooperation. A Jew might provide raw silk to a Christian weaver, who in turn might sell the woven silk to a Jewish tailor, who prepared attire for a Christian gentleman.[67]

Castro believed that Spanish culture emerged as an outcome of the commingling of Muslims, Christians, and Jews—"the three castes"—from the eighth through the thirteenth century. His theory sparked a long debate with Claudio Sánchez Albornoz, who criticized Castro for having exaggerated the congenialities between Muslims and Christians, which Sánchez Albornoz regarded as discordant and unfavorable for a creative cultural interchange. He also contended that the Spanish essence, or character, arose out of Roman, Visigothic, and other elements not of Arab or Islamic origin.[68]

Historians of the Jews in Spain portray the Jewish experience either in idyllic strokes as a golden age and radiant sea of harmony or as a gloomy vale of tears. The reality was prosaically somewhere in between.[69] Having studied representations of the Jew in Arabic texts of the eleventh and twelfth centuries, the scholar of Hebrew poetry and medieval Spain Ross Brann concluded:

> The Jew remains a chimerical, slippery character as conceived in texts, a figure whose cultural and religious otherness is inconsistent, mutable, and fluctuating. He is never quite what he appears to be. Like Kristeva's "uncanny foreigner," he serves the Muslim social imagination in times of crisis as the most available and most vulnerable religious "other" upon whom the majority may project its anxiety and hostility.[70]

Jews and Christians were never really *assimilated* into Hispano-Islamic culture and could never feel truly comfortable and secure. They were, however, *integrated,* and normal daily contact among people of different ethnic and religious backgrounds provided the setting for cultural interchange. Social status made it possible for Jews and Christians to interact on equal terms with Muslims and to take part in economic activity and serve in government departments.[71]

The class stratification of Jewish society permitted affluent and cultured Jews to step out of their ethnic garb. They became courtier-rabbis, physicians, and financial advisors to sovereigns. Socioeconomic class sliced Jewish society horizontally—more or less into upper, middle, and lower strata—whereas kinship, tribe, and ethnicity divided Muslim society vertically (that is, not superimposed but contiguous). Of course, social class also defined Muslims, but it was never as decisive as kinship relations were.[72]

The study of interethnic relations in medieval Spain, as the historian of medieval Spain Thomas Glick shows, suffers from two main fallacies.[73] One is the mistaken notion that ethnoreligious conflict excludes culture contact. Historians who perceive a conflict situation either play down culture contact or seek periods of peace, supposedly required for cultural diffusion to take place. Yet culture contact happens even in periods of ethnoreligious conflict. The second fallacy is to equate acculturation with assimilation and to suppose that reducing cultural distance shrinks social distance. In fact, whereas cultural interchange was pulsating between Andalusian Muslims and Jews, boundaries of social distance were generally maintained.

ADIÓS CÓRDOBA

Moses ben Maimon's family probably abandoned Córdoba when he was ten, after the Almohad invasion (1147/48). Biographers and historians do not doubt this, but we do not know for sure, as it is undocumented. The family apparently remained in Spain for about twelve years, although we do not know where they resided. There is evidence that they lived for some time in Seville, where Moses met with Muslim astronomers.[74] They may have followed many others to the Christian north of Spain. Maimonides referred to the "country of the Franks" as something familiar in *The Guide of the Perplexed:*[75] "Now if swine were used for food [in Jewish society], market places and even houses would have been dirtier than latrines, as you see at present in the country of the Franks."[76] We find gaps in the lives of other famous men. The life of Saladin (1137–1193), sultan of Egypt and Syria, is vacant for the years 1139 to 1146, and little information exists for the years 1154 to 1164. Scholars speak of 1585 to 1592 as "the lost years" in Shakespeare's career.[77]

Fortunately, we know about Maimonides' intellectual development and writings from 1147/48 on. The life of the ten-year-old Moses was transformed by exile from his native city. Had the Almohads not invaded Andalusia and conquered Córdoba, Moses ben Maimon might well have grown into a typical rabbinic scholar like his ancestors, learned in talmudic law, a judge and communal leader. Given his intellectual curiosity, he might also have branched out into medicine and the sciences and then philosophy and perhaps theology. However, he would not have taken that mighty step into a wider world that eventually brought him to the center of the Islamic empire—Cairo—and made him one of the greatest thinkers who ever lived.

2

Andalusian
Jewish Culture

*As a result of the historic catastrophe in which Titus of Rome
destroyed Jerusalem and Israel was exiled from its land, I was
born in one of the cities of the Exile. But always I regarded
myself as one who was born in Jerusalem. In a dream, in a vision
of the night, I saw myself standing with my brother-Levites in
the Holy Temple, singing with them the songs of David, King
of Israel, melodies such as no ear has heard since the day our
city was destroyed and its people went into exile.*

—SAMUEL JOSEPH AGNON, NOBEL LECTURE 1966

MOSES BEN MAIMON was an Andalusian to the core of his
being and followed Andalusian models in law, medicine,
and philosophy. He later lived in Egypt for nearly forty years
and gained new vistas there, and he was totally immersed in the cultural life of that milieu, moving in the elite circles of Cairo. But however integrated he was into Egyptian life and manner, his speech, dress,
and demeanor surely betrayed him as a foreigner.

He was proud of his Andalusian heritage and believed, along with others, that Andalusian Jews were descendants of the Jerusalemites who went into exile when the Romans destroyed the Second Temple in 70 c.e.[1] This legacy, as well as his family heritage, gave him a sense of aristocracy and noblesse oblige. Later admirers declared that Maimonides' ancestors were the seed of David, king of Israel, portraying him as a messianic figure; however, Maimonides himself, as far as I know, did not claim to be a descendant of King David in writings available to us.

He lived in al-Andalus for about twenty-two years (ca. 1138–60) and spent another five in the Maghrib. Andalusia and the Maghrib formed a single cultural orbit. When he used the expression *'indana fi 'l-maghrib,* "by us in the Maghrib," concerning legal practice or linguistic usage, he thought of the Maghrib as including Andalusia. Likewise, when he said *'indana fi 'l-andalus,* "by us in Andalusia," he thought of al-Andalus as including the Maghrib.[2]

Maimonides placed himself squarely in a Spanish tradition of learning; he wrote in *The Epistle to Yemen,* "I am one of the least of the sages of Spain whose adornment has been stripped in *Exile*." He considered Andalusian scholars as his authorities in legal matters, above all Rabbi Isaac Alfasi and Rabbi Joseph Ibn Migash, whom he reverently called "my teacher."[3]

After the decline of learning in the Land of Israel, the dominant center of rabbinic studies had been in Iraq, where the heads of academies, called Geonim, gave instruction in the law, answered queries, and raised money for their institutions.[4] In the tenth century, the center of Jewish learning began to shift from Iraq to Andalusia and the Maghrib.

Maimonides believed that Andalusian scholars superseded the Babylonian (Iraqian) Geonim.[5] Jewish scholarship had been transplanted from Baghdad to Córdoba, and Andalusia rivaled the East in intellectual splendor, just as learning in the Islamic world had been transferred from East to West in the tenth century.

ACADEMY AT LUCENA

A new star rose as the academy at Lucena, about forty-three miles from Córdoba, became the foremost institution of higher rabbinic learning in the West. Lucena was an almost exclusively Jewish city and may have originally been founded by Jews. It was fortified and walled, and had a deep moat for defense. The Muslims lived, for the most part, outside the city walls.

Lucena's economy was based upon olive groves, vineyards, commerce, crafts, and the raising of sheep and cattle. Some Lucena residents dealt in precious stones and metals.[6] Lucenan merchants traded with Granada, Seville, Toledo, and Egypt. The independence and affluence of Lucena attracted Jews from elsewhere, especially Christian Spain. Lucena's Jewish population increased in 1013, when civil strife in Córdoba drove many people to take refuge there.

The proximity of Córdoba to Lucena enabled scholars to travel back and forth. While Lucena was renowned for its academy, Córdoba remained the meeting place for men of learning and literary taste.[7]

A rabbinic scholar, Moses ben Hanokh, is said to have settled in Córdoba at the time of Hisday ibn Shaprut (915–970), and the community appointed him rabbi and head of the academy.[8] Students flocked to Córdoba from Spain and other countries. Now Andalusian Jews could send their legal queries to local scholars in Córdoba and Lucena and be independent of Iraqian authorities. The Baghdad academy did not lose its influence elsewhere; it remained powerful in Syro-Palestine (Damascus and Jerusalem) and extended its authority into Egypt.

By the twelfth century, Andalusian culture in Arabic and Hebrew was robust, and Andalusian scholars, such as Córdoba's Abu 'l-Walid Ibn Rushd and Musa Ibn Maymun, were culturally secure and self-confident. They exhibited Andalusian pride and a drive for independence and supremacy over past authorities in the East.

TORAH AND WISDOM

Maimonides and his Jewish colleagues held aloft two torches and lived in two intellectual universes: the sacred, embodied in Torah, and the profane, embodied in wisdom and poetry.[9] They were traditional Jews, yet cosmopolitan, and they had refined taste in Arabic literature, especially poetry, a genre that enjoyed great prestige. Many participated in the indulgent life of courtiers, enjoying soirées in luxuriant gardens with wine, women, and song.

Torah and wisdom were the two pillars that sustained Maimonides throughout his life, especially at times of crisis—"And were it not for the Torah, which is my delight, and for scientific matters, which let me forget my sorrow, *I would have perished in my affliction* (Ps 119:92)."[10]

Combining study of Torah and secular subjects was the hallmark of Andalusian Jewish intellectuals. The cosmopolitan courtier-rabbi, learned in Jewish law and physician or counselor to royalty, was exemplary for Maimonides as he fashioned his career.

The secular educational ideal of enlightened Jews, as for Muslims, was the acquisition of *adab*. *Adab*, an Arabic term, had several related meanings: "courtesy," "decorum," and "urbanity," like Latin *urbanitas*—the civility and refinement of an urbane gentleman. Hence, *adab* came to mean the knowledge required to become courteous and urbane—secular culture based on rhetoric, grammar, and lexicography. It later took on the more specific meaning of belles lettres or literature, including poetry and artistic prose.[11]

THE COURTIER-RABBIS

The exemplar of Torah and wisdom, then, was the courtier-rabbi, a master of tradition and an expert in secular knowledge. He served the royal court as physician or advisor, translator or diplomat, and devoted himself to the welfare of the Jewish community. The archetypical courtier-rabbi was Hisday Ibn Shaprut, physician in Córdoba in the service of the Umayyad caliphs 'Abd al-Rahman III and al-Hakam II. 'Abd al-Rahman made Hisday head of the Jewish communities in his kingdom with the title of *nasi* (prince), and appointed him a personal advisor.

Hisday was a superb linguist who participated, along with a monk named Nicholas, in the translation of Dioscorides' *De materia medica* from Greek into Arabic. His ruler employed him for important diplomatic negotiations with a Byzantine mission to Córdoba and with a delegation of King Otto I of Germany. He carried on a correspondence with the Khazar kingdom.

Ibn Shaprut was a generous benefactor who orchestrated the Jewish cultural renaissance in Córdoba. His *majlis,* or literary salon and assembly hall, was a gathering place for poets, grammarians, Bible and

Talmud scholars, scientists, and philosophers. His day combined knowledge of logic, mathematics, and astronomy with traditional learning in the Bible, Talmud, and Midrash. He was faithful to his heritage, yet ready to adopt the cultural values of the surrounding environment.

Another courtier-rabbi was Samuel ha-Nagid (993–1055), a cultural icon in the collective memory of Andalusian Jewry, head of the Jewish communities of Andalusia with the title *nagid*. In the period of the party kings, Samuel ha-Nagid became vizier to the Zirids of Granada, led its troops, sponsored poets and men of letters, and wrote a book on talmudic law. He had an extravagant lifestyle despite his piety and learning.

Samuel was genuinely bicultural, with fine calligraphy and excellent style in both Arabic and Hebrew, and he was a sublime poet. Samuel and his son Joseph attained a rank higher than any other Andalusian Jews and were thoroughly assimilated into Arabic and Islamic culture.[12]

Eloquence in Arabic, fine calligraphy, and elevated style were rungs to success, as Judah Ibn Tibbon counseled his son Samuel: "You know that the outstanding men of our people only reached greatness and high station by means of Arabic style. You have seen what the Nagid, of blessed memory, said about the greatness he reached by it."[13]

The Nagid expressed the idea in verse:

Man's wisdom is in what he writes,
good sense at the end of his pen;
and using his pen he can climb to the height
of the scepter in the hand of his king.[14]

He served King Habbus ibn Maksan (r. 1019–38) in Granada as secretary and counselor. Granada was called "Granada of the Jews" because of its large Jewish population. He built a castle in 1052–56 to protect the area where the Jewish residents were concentrated, in the vicinity of today's Alcazaba.[15]

Samuel is comparable in his versatility with the universal man (*l'uomo universale*), celebrated by Jacob Burckhardt in *The Civilization of the Renaissance in Italy*. The education of a secretary was encyclopedic, as he had to write letters on a wide variety of topics and season them with historical anecdotes, aphorisms, and poetry. Samuel ha-Nagid was resourceful and talented, a brilliant administrator, scientist, poet, and rabbinic scholar. Like Hisday Ibn Shaprut, Samuel was a patron of the arts. His encouragement of poetry led Abraham Ibn Daud to write: "In the days of Hisday the Nasi the bards began to chirp, and in the days of Samuel the Nagid they burst into song."[16]

The Nagid wrote letters in grand style with learned allusions, arousing the admiration of Arabic-speakers. Arab historians knew him as Abu Ibrahim Isma'il Ibn Naghrela.[17] Articulate in Hispano-Romance and Berber, he studied the Qur'an, Islamic jurisprudence, tradition, and theology, and he learned Latin and read Christian Bible commentaries.[18] The Hispano-Arabic historian Abu Marwan ibn Hayyan al-Qurtubi (987/88–1076) gave a flattering portrayal of Samuel, stressing that he was eloquent in Arabic and Hebrew and cultivated knowledge of the Torah and wisdom:[19]

> This cursed fellow[20] was in his essence, though God turned him aside from his guidance, one of the most perfect men in knowledge, forbearance,[21] discerning, sharpness of wit, politeness, imperturbability, cunning, wiliness,[22] self-control, magnanimity, fame, affability to his enemy, and placating by his forbearance. [How remarkable][23] is a man who wrote with two pens and devoted himself to two sciences![24]

Al-Qurtubi added that Samuel loved the Arabic language and its literature and studied them thoroughly. He wrote in Arabic for himself and for his patron, praising Allah and his apostle (Muhammad) and noting the merits of Islam, as any Muslim administrator would do. He was expert in the mathematical sciences and in astronomy. He studied geometry and logic, and was unsurpassed in dialectic. He was reserved and reflective, a collector of books. When he died, al-Qurtubi wrote, the Jews honored his bier and wept for him openly.

In Samuel's case a dual identity was complete. Maimonides used Islamic formulae in writings intended for a general audience, such as the *Treatise on the Art of Logic,* but did not go as far as Samuel ha-Nagid in praising Allah and his apostle and lauding Islam; he was not a bureaucrat.

Samuel's mastery of the humanities and sciences, involvement in administration, and dedication to poetry did not detract from his rabbinic studies. He was "the most important link in the chain of scholars of his generation."[25] He studied with Hanokh, son of Moses ben

Hanokh, in Córdoba, and later established his own rabbinic academy in Granada. There he taught and wrote on the Talmud and produced his *Hilkhata gavrata* (*The Great Law*). It followed the Andalusian method of reducing the Talmud to its essentials in a legal compendium.

Samuel ha-Nagid groomed his son Joseph for leadership by providing him with tutors and books and guiding him in literary style. Fathers prepared their sons to become their heirs.[26] In a testament that Samuel ha-Nagid sent to Joseph from the battlefield, he advised him how to find favor with God and man.[27] When Joseph fell ill, Samuel sent him a poem from the field, saying that he was weary of war and sick of the service of kings, and lived only to see a letter from Joseph and news of his recovery.[28]

ATTACK ON GRANADA'S JEWS

After Samuel ha-Nagid died, Joseph succeeded his father as head of state.[29] He assumed the title *nagid* when he was just twenty or twenty-one, already learned and the possessor of a great library assembled by his father. Even his detractors conceded that he was cultured and competent in administration.

Joseph, like his father, participated in Granada's military campaigns, but it was with reluctance that he became entangled in the internal power struggles of the Zirid dynasty. As King Badis ibn Habbus (1038–1073) sank into a life of dissipation, Joseph had to assume more responsibility. A Muslim jurist, Abu Ishaq al-Tujibi al-Ibiri, objected to his growing influence and reviled Joseph and other Jews in an ode that incited the population against them.[30]

The poet at that time was a source of information and a propagandist who molded public opinion in a striking way. The ode ignited the embers of resentment. In 1066, a group of Sanhaja Berbers invaded Joseph's palace and massacred the Jewish vizier and other dignitaries, while others joined in and murdered hundreds of ordinary Jews, looting their property.

Andalusian Jewry suddenly awoke from illusions of comfort and security. A lesson of this bloodshed was that Jews should not risk being in positions of authority over Muslims. Only as intermediaries, diplomats, physicians, or financial advisors could they succeed, and even then only by keeping a low profile. Jews were supposed to be humble, not to wield authority. There is a certain homeostasis of the Islamic body politic, the need to return to equilibrium when threatened by a loss of control.

THE COURTIER-RABBIS AND POETRY

Not all intellectuals embraced the ideals of the courtier class. Bahya Ibn Paquda was an outspoken critic of the courtier-rabbis for their lifestyle and educational ideals.[31] They spent too much time studying language, grammar, poetry, proverbs, and astrology, he said, and did so for the practical purpose of serving royalty. These courtiers preferred general culture (*adab*) to knowledge (*'ilm*), especially religious knowledge. Bahya Ibn Paquda advocated an ascetic ideal of total devotion to God and condemned wealth and indulgence.[32] Bahya's ethical pietism influenced Maimon ben Joseph and Moses ben Maimon.[33]

The courtier-rabbis emulated Arab culture by nurturing poetry as their highest mode of expression. Poetry's ambience consisted of drinking parties, dancing girls, and pretty boys. We find it astonishing that rabbis combined wine, women, and song with learning and piety, that the same poet who wrote erotic elegies composed liturgical poems for the synagogue. After a night of revelry, Samuel ha-Nagid would arise early to pray.[34]

We find this combination of erotic poetry and devotional piety among Arab intellectuals. Ibn Hazm, a jurist and theologian, wrote a book on love, the *Ring of the Dove,* and composed erotic poetry. Recalling his youth, he wrote, "One who came from Córdoba told me . . . that he had seen our house at Balat Mughith in the western quarter. . . . I remembered my days in that house, my delights. I remembered the months of my youth there, amid full-breasted young girls who excited even the shyest man."[35] The tension between a voluptuous lifestyle and religious faith produced sober reflection as poets aged and faced the end.[36] Hence, Hebrew love poetry is often sad, filled with guilt feelings and a sense of impending doom.[37] Sorrow is not far from the floral setting, the rippling streams, the boys and girls pouring wine into crystalline cups, the furtive kisses. Throbbing ecstasy sinks into the dust. Like the "Qasida of the Rose" in the Andalusian poet Federico

García Lorca's *Tamarit Divan,* love and death intertwine as the "bitter root" of all life, the one subsiding inexplicably into the other. "To love what is fleeting is only to be reminded of death."[38]

BIBLICAL RENAISSANCE

Andalusian Jews believed that they were direct descendants of the exiles of Jerusalem—from the lily of Judea to the rose of Spain. They cited the biblical phrase *the exiles of Jerusalem that are in Sefarad* (Obad 1:20) as proof of their lineage.[39] The word *Sefarad* did not originally mean "Spain" or the Iberian peninsula, but was given that meaning by commentators.[40]

Believing in this lineage, Andalusian Jews saw themselves as a select group. They expected that their leaders, the courtier-rabbis, would bring about fulfillment of their messianic dreams and that they would be vindicated in history.[41] Andalusian scholars believed that they were bringing the ancient kingdom back to life. In their poetry, they revived the biblical epoch, when the people of Israel were free in their own land.

The poet Moses Ibn Ezra claimed that Andalusian Jews, as offspring of the nobility of Jerusalem, were linguistically gifted. They spoke Arabic and used Hebrew for poetry and much of their prose. Hebrew was a prestige language appropriate for the self-expression of a confident and unified community.[42]

As the terminology of Hebrew poetry was mainly from the Bible, poets adopted a style of embedding biblical quotations in the verse; in virtually every line of poetry there were allusions to the biblical text. The use of biblical quotations opened up countless rhetorical possibilities. The author might cite only half a verse, expecting the reader to supply the rest and be surprised how the meaning was distorted by its poetic context. He might alter meanings by creating ambiguity or by using paronomasia. Hebrew is eminently suited for wordplay. The Hebrew word *kesil,* for example, means both "the constellation Orion" and "fool." And wordplay could go back and forth between the two Semitic languages. Thus, *'ishq* in Arabic, "erotic love," is identical in its root consonants (*'-sh-q*) to *'ashaq* in Hebrew, meaning "to oppress."

Scholars revitalized biblical Hebrew and the study of Scripture, grammar, and lexicography. They saw parallels between their epoch and the biblical age and identified themselves with biblical figures. Samuel ha-Nagid was a major voice in the Andalusian biblical renaissance. The historian Ibn Daud depicted him as a replica of the biblical courtiers Joseph, Daniel, and Mordecai.[43] The Nagid identified himself with his namesake, the prophet Samuel, and saw himself as the David of his day—warrior, poet, and ruler. In his own eyes he was the Temple minister Levi, the psalmist Asaph, and the courtier Mordecai.

Maimonides shared in this biblical renaissance. He viewed his life through a scriptural lens, seeing himself in his personal myth as a Moses *redivivus*. He summoned the people of Israel to relive the biblical age, when they mastered the sciences and philosophy, which perished during the long period of exile.[44]

Arabic cultural models motivated Jewish poets and intellectuals to revisit the Bible and Hebrew and to study them in a new scientific spirit. The use of 'Arabiyya (pure, classical Arabic) and the classicizing tendency of Arabic poetry inspired Jewish poets and scholars to cultivate their own pure classical Hebrew—*sahot,* or "eloquence" (Isa 32:4). This ethnolinguistic vitality resembles the reassertion of language loyalty by other ethnic groups reacting to Arab hegemony.[45] Study of the Qur'an impelled Jewish scholars to study the Bible. Intellectuals and poets created their own cultural identity by writing Hebrew overflowing with biblical resonances.[46]

At his spiritual core the courtier was bibliocentric. If from the Greeks he took his philosophy and from the Arabs his rhetorical forms, he took from the Bible the knowledge of who he truly was. The Bible supplied the great figures, the types, the models of perfection—Joseph, Moses, Aaron, David—by which all excellence, the courtier's own emphatically included, was henceforth to be tested and proved.

The Hebrew writer, weaving biblical allusions into his poetry, letters, or prose narrative, evoked ancient echoes of his people.[47] He inlaid biblical gems into a colorful linguistic mosaic.[48] In Latin this is called *cento,* literally "patchwork," and refers to poetry borrowed from previous authors, with a clever change of meaning and a witty effect. A splendid example of this style is a garden poem by Moses Ibn Ezra, a medley of biblical themes surrounding the idea that the rose is king.[49]

Biblical Hebrew was revived in secular poetry, replacing talmudic and midrashic Hebrew of the liturgical poems, or *piyyutim*. The Spanish Hebrew poets abandoned the conflated Hebrew-Aramaic of the Talmud and the convoluted style of the liturgical poets (*payyetanim*), preferring to imitate pure Arabic with their own pure Hebrew. The Spanish linguists and poets cherished biblical Hebrew as clear, precise, and superior to all other languages. The revitalization of the language and literature of the Bible gave Jewish scholars a sense of pride and hope that God would renew their erstwhile days of glory.

This elevation of biblical Hebrew challenged the Muslim belief that the Qur'an is unsurpassed in its style. Jewish linguists and poets held that the language of the ancient Israelites surpassed in beauty the style of the Qur'an. In his book on poetics, Moses Ibn Ezra gave examples of rhetorical figures by citing Arabic and Hebrew poetry, as well as the Hebrew Bible.[50] Hebrew linguists, such as Menahem ben Saruq, Dunash ben Labrat, Judah ben David Hayyuj, and Jonah Ibn Janah, studying biblical Hebrew, used the system of Arabic grammarians and lexicographers. The new method of biblical interpretation, employing sophisticated linguistic tools and seeking the contextual and historical meaning, was consistent with the spirit of rationalism that came to life in the twelfth century.

Biblical Hebrew provided a reservoir of language and motifs for love poetry. Without the erotic lyrics of the biblical Song of Songs, Hebrew poets would not have had the inspiration or vocabulary to write about love, gardens, and wine as they did.[51] The language of the biblical Song of Songs provided inspiration and validation for erotic poetry. For erotic poetry, there was no better model than the Song of Solomon.

Arabic erotic verse could serve as an exemplar for Hebrew religious and secular poetry because it shared themes and motifs with the Song of Songs.[52] They used the same metaphors for the beloved, such as *ghazal* ("gazelle") from Arabic poetry and *ṣevi,* orthographically identical to Arabic *ṣabi* ("young man"), also meaning "gazelle," in Song of Songs.[53]

Erotic poetry on the human plane was readily transformed into sacred poetry with God as the beloved.[54] Hebrew love poetry, like the erotic poetry of the Muslim Sufi Ibn al-'Arabi of Murcia, could be interpreted as expressing either profane or sacred love, the beloved described as a handsome youth, symbolizing the divine.[55] Likewise, the Song of Songs was read as an erotic dialogue between a male lover and female beloved or as a dialogue between Israel (or the soul) and the divine.

GARDENS, WINE, AND LOVE

The Andalusian garden was the setting for wine and poetry soirées. The great Andalusian poets—Ibn Zaydun (d. 1071), al-Mu'tamid ibn 'Abbad (d. 1095), Ibn Khafaja (d. 1134), and Ibn Quzman (d. 1160)— wrote wine poems in this setting. The poet invites his companions to drink with him in a garden. Either spring has come, or the poet wishes to banish the torment caused by the beloved's absence, or he exhorts them to seize the day. The participants in wine parties lounged beneath fruit trees and strolled among vines and fresh blossoms. Everything was fragrant, as though perfumed with myrrh, with palm fronds swaying gently in the afternoon breeze, doves cooing love songs in the branches, and swallows chattering in the boughs, accompanied by the sound of water rippling in channels and pools, bordered by a colorful array of roses, lilies, and jasmine.

The Qur'an describes Paradise as a garden (*janna*), with leaping fountains, shady vales, all sorts of fruits, and pavilions for lovely maidens.[56] The Andalusian garden was fashioned as an image and anticipation of this heavenly bliss.

Gardens presented a harmony and uniformity as a counterpoint to the untamed landscape and the labyrinthine streets and alleys of towns. Culture regulated the disorder of nature. The garden displayed the essentials of Islamic art—harmony, balance, and perfection of the total composition.[57]

Poems having gardens as their theme described the fruits and the blossoms, the raindrops on the flower petals, and the shade of the trees, mingling the motifs of nature and wine. It depicted the banquet, the table where the drinkers sat, the wine cups, the sparkle of the wine, the young men—"gazelles"—and the young women, dancing, and pouring wine.[58]

Some of the loveliest Hebrew wine poems were also love lyrics about the ephebe, the young man who served the wine, or other hand-

some young men, raising the question of homoeroticism. Some scholars regard avowals of love for young boys as a poetic motif. Others
have argued that the homoerotic poems reveal a social reality.[59]

The cupbearer is a slender boy with smooth cheeks and curly hair
or a slim girl with a boyish figure and short hair, each wearing a brief
tunic.[60] The beloved is therefore an intersexual, or androgynous, figure. The young boy, or ephebe, was the *saqi,* the cupbearer, like Gany-
mede, beloved of Zeus. Girls were also addressed as gazelles, the object
of love thus being at times gender-neutral, making substitution of (intended) male for (literal) female possible.

> Before the morning raises its banners and the sun spreads its wings,
> Call a gazelle with a wine cup in his hand. When one calls for beauty,
>   it will answer.[61]

When the poet Judah al-Harizi was in Baghdad, he came across a
poet who wrote verses about his lover.

> If the son of Amram [Moses] had seen my lover's face
> blushing as he imbibed liquor,
> with his curls and glorious beauty,
> he would not have written in his Torah
> *Lie not with a male.*[62]

Muslims participated in wine parties with Jews, each side sinning
in the act. Jews may not drink wine touched by gentiles lest it had
been used for idolatrous libations. Muslims may not drink wine at all,
although the Hanafi school of law permitted date wine. In a responsum on drinking wine and listening to music, and drinking wine
pressed by gentiles, Maimonides decided that it was forbidden to
drink wine prepared by Muslims.[63] However, he added, as applied in
practice by the Geonim of the West, when a Christian or Muslim visited Jews drinking wine, the Jews quickly mixed some honey with the
wine and drank with the visitor, as the wine could not be used for an
idolatrous libation.[64] "This," Maimonides noted in his responsum, "is
what our Master Joseph ha-Levi [Ibn Migash] decided, and this is what
he did several times in practice, he and all the great men of Sefarad."
The responsum gives valuable evidence about the social life of Andalusian Jews and their conviviality with Christians and Muslims.[65]

3

Early Studies

Before I was created in the womb the Torah knew me
and before I was born, it consecrated me to its study
(cf. Jer 1:5), and made me cause its springs to gush forth
(Prov 5:16). For [the Torah] is my loving doe and the wife
of my youth, in whose love I was infatuated from my early
years (Prov 5:18–19).

—MAIMONIDES TO THE SAGES OF LUNEL

THE EARLY YEARS

In Maimonides' time, Jewish fathers began to instruct their sons in Torah as soon as they learned to speak, teaching them to repeat biblical verses. At the age of five to seven, the child was brought to an elementary-school teacher.[1] Even at that young age, studies were demanding, for society considered learning a pious act and a way of raising one's social status. The children sat in class the whole day and part of the night and had no holidays except the days before the Sabbath and festivals. Even the Sabbath, the day of rest, was spent reviewing the week's lessons, usually with the father, who also brought his son to synagogue that day for guidance in prayer and communal life.[2]

Muslim society also valued learning and encouraged children to behave maturely at an early age.[3] They memorized the Qur'an starting at age seven. Study of the Qur'an was the foundation of an Islamic education, and Islam became a great force because of it, and has remained so in our time.[4]

Traditional education in both Muslim and Jewish societies discouraged the frivolity of childhood. Al-Qadi al-Fadil (the Excellent Judge), Maimonides' patron in Egypt, instructed his son to leave childlike ways behind and praised another boy for "resembling a graybeard in his gravity." The trait of *waqar,* a kind of serious sedateness, was inculcated at an early age. Discouraged from normal juvenile behavior, outdoor play, and companionship, children were treated as young adults. This phenomenon conforms with Philippe Ariès' theory that the concept of childhood did not exist in medieval Europe, emerging only in the sixteenth and seventeenth centuries among the upper class, and among the middle and lower classes in the late nineteenth and early twentieth centuries. In medieval Muslim and Jewish societies parents naturally differentiated between gifted and promising children, who were barred from games and frivolity, and ordinary children, who were permitted the joys of youth.

THE HEBREW BIBLE

Study of the Hebrew Bible was the foundation of Jewish education. A pupil was first taught to draw Hebrew letters in preparation for reading. The Genizah preserves many examples of school exercises in which colors were used to fill in letter outlines. Lettering was taught by using biblical verses that instilled piety and virtue, such as *Blessed is he who trusts in the Lord, whose trust is the Lord alone* (Jer 17:7). The verses, implanted by repeated copying early in life, shaped the child's character as he or she learned reading and writing.

After mastering ordinary writing, a gifted child learned Hebrew and Arabic calligraphy. Along with calligraphy, pupils learned epistolary skills at a young age. Teachers used model epistles, some of which have survived in the Genizah.

Children learned the Torah along with the famous Aramaic translation (Targum) by Onqelos (ca. 35–120 C.E.). The Targum illumined the Torah and prepared the student for studying the Talmud, which is written in a mixed Aramaic-Hebrew dialect.[5] From the time of the talmudic sages the Torah was read in the synagogue in Hebrew and Aramaic, so that speakers of Aramaic, the lingua franca, would understand. However, from the tenth century on, as Arabic replaced Aramaic, reading Onqelos along with the Torah in the synagogue gradually fell by the wayside.

Boys studied the entire Bible—the Pentateuch (five books of Moses), Prophets, and Writings—not merely the Pentateuch. The many copies of Prophets and Writings in the Genizah show that the school curriculum devoted much time to them. Most quotations in Genizah letters are from Psalms, Proverbs, Job, and the Five Scrolls (Song of Songs, Ruth, Lamentations, Ecclesiastes, and Esther), and many are from the later prophets (Isaiah, Jeremiah, and Ezekiel).[6] The intensive study of the Bible on its own, apart from the Talmud and Midrash, in Moses ben Maimon's era was influenced by the emphasis Muslims placed on the Qur'an and by the special place the Karaites accorded Scripture. Bible instruction was accompanied by study of Hebrew grammar and lexicography.

The Karaites were named for the Hebrew word for Scripture (*miqra'*). As Scripturalists, they rejected the Oral law preserved in rabbinic literature and relied for religious guidance on the Written law in the Bible alone. They therefore opposed the majority of Jews who accepted the Oral law and are called Rabbanites.[7] The two groups disagreed over important issues concerning the calendar, the Sabbath, dietary laws, and personal law.

HIGHER EDUCATION

Spanish schools of higher learning abandoned the curriculum of the Babylonian (Iraqian) academy and replaced it with study of codifiers such as Isaac Alfasi.[8] Instructors encouraged secular learning, acquiring expertise in Hebrew language and poetry, and studying Arabic to enhance one's professional options. Some students studied the Bible with its Arabic translation, as this improved knowledge of the vocabulary of

Arabic books. Advanced students were instructed in Arabic and He-brew language and literary style.

Joseph ben Judah Ibn 'Aqnin and Judah ibn 'Abbas developed curricula reflecting Spanish practice.[9] The student finished the basic program in the Bible and the Talmud by the age of thirteen. Then he learned grammar and poetry and began studying the Talmud with commentaries and *halakhah* in law codes such as Alfasi's work.[10]

THE SPANISH SYLLABUS

To appreciate the uniqueness of the Spanish syllabus, it is worth contrasting it with the core curriculum of the great Ashkenazi acad-emies (*yeshivot*) of Poland, Lithuania, and Russia during the sixteenth through eighteenth centuries.[11] These *yeshivot* stressed the study of the Talmud, which a pupil started at seven or eight, to the exclusion of the Prophets, the Writings, and the Mishnah. It was possible to become a rabbi without ever studying the Bible, not to mention secular studies, which were generally ignored. The aim of instruction in the *yeshivot* of Central and Eastern Europe was to train scholars in the Talmud and its commentaries and in the law codes.

METHODS OF TEACHING

Aside from curriculum, there were also pedagogical concerns. It is more than likely that Moses ben Maimon studied privately with his father, rather than in a public school. He recorded in his code of law, *Mishneh Torah,* the talmudic principle that the number of pupils in a class should not be more than twenty-five, and that if there were as many as forty, an assistant was to be employed.[12] An overcrowded classroom was not the proper atmosphere for his nascent genius.

In Maimonides' time, boys and girls studied separately. Girls learned to read so that they could follow the prayers at synagogue. Although study was more important for boys, parents encouraged gifted girls to learn. A father, mourning his daughter's passing, recalled the precious hours he had spent teaching her. She had a quick mind, he wrote, learned Torah readily, had spoken with excellent diction, and had been kind and charitable. We sense the depth of his grief from a biblical verse he quoted—*O my dove, in the cranny of the rocks, hidden by the cliff, let me see your face, let me hear your voice; for your voice is sweet and your face is comely* (Song 2:14).[13] Fathers took pride in their children's charitable behavior and trained them early in life to be benevolent, so that compassion would be ingrained in their character.

MEMORIZING

This was a culture that treasured memory. Young boys memorized the Torah, prayer book, Mishnah, and Talmud before they understood them, following the Talmud's advice that one should first memorize the Torah and then understand.[14] Books were scarce and expensive; hence instruction was mainly by dictation and copying.

Maimonides' contemporaries believed that one could memorize without understanding, but one could not understand without memorizing. The talmudic sages sought to nurture a child's imitative faculty in speech and behavior. Consequently, traditional education fostered repetition and emulation of the character of revered teachers. They used mnemonics, or memory devices, such as *notarikon*.[15] This was a method of writing the first letter of each word of a phrase or sentence (acronym). There was also memorization by association and by enumeration. A scholar was judged by his feats of memory, and it was unthinkable that one could become an authority without having the entire Talmud at one's fingertips.

ACADEMY OF LUCENA

Moses ben Maimon was too young to attend the great Academy of Lucena before it closed, but its methods and teachings fashioned his approach to learning. His father, Maimon ben Joseph, who tutored his sons in their early years, had been a pupil of Rabbi Joseph Ibn Migash, head of the Lucena Academy. Rabbi Maimon wrote commentaries on the Bible and Talmud. His responsa and other writings indicate that he had a good command of traditional learning and some scientific knowledge. He wrote a book on the laws of prayer and festivals, another on the laws of ritual purity, and a commentary on an Arabic astronomical treatise.[16] At least five of Rabbi Maimon's responsa have survived.[17]

The son must have surpassed his father at an early age. There is a saying in the Talmud, *A man is capable of envying everyone except his son and his pupil.*[18] For the son who exceeds his father, however, the situation may be psychologically complex because it is a form of defeat for which a son may feel guilt.

The two men who had the greatest influence upon Maimonides in shaping his approach to jurisprudence—Isaac Alfasi and Joseph Ibn Migash—were both masters at Lucena.[19] Maimonides considered them his teachers, in particular Ibn Migash, whom he referred to as "my teacher," though he evidently never studied with him, as Ibn Migash died in 1141, when young Moses was three years old. We must allow for the possibility, however, as centuries later gifted Eastern European children studied the Mishnah at that tender age.

ISAAC ALFASI

The Lucena Academy reached the summit of its influence and prestige under Isaac ben Jacob Alfasi (ca. 1013–1103).[20] Alfasi emigrated from Fez in the Maghrib (hence the name al-Fasi, "the man from Fez") to Lucena in 1088 at the age of seventy-five, having been denounced to the government in Fez for some unknown offense.[21] Isaac Alfasi attracted many students, including some who were not Talmudists, such as the poet and philosopher Judah ha-Levi. People, mainly from Spain and the Maghrib, addressed legal queries to Alfasi, to which he responded mostly in Arabic.[22]

Alfasi represents the model talmudic sage whose entire life was devoted to study of the Torah without any regard for alien wisdom. His teachings, nevertheless, had a profound effect on Maimonides. Alfasi's *Book of Precepts* (*Sefer ha-Halakhot*) was a synopsis of the Talmud, Geonic writings, and earlier legal compendia. Alfasi made this intricate literature accessible to the layman, as Maimonides was to do later in his *Mishneh Torah*.[23]

TALMUD STUDY

To assess the contribution of Alfasi and his school, and his impact on Maimonides, we need to understand the problems faced by teachers of Jewish law. The Talmud was not studied as a classic detached from everyday life. It was the directive by which people lived, married, divorced, carried on business, and resolved their disputes. Hence, it was crucial to know what the law actually required; yet this knowledge was hard to derive from the Talmud.

The name Talmud means "study" and applies to two works, designated by place of origin as the Jerusalem Talmud (Talmud Yerushalmi) and the Babylonian Talmud.[24] Palestinian rabbis redacted the Jerusalem Talmud in Tiberias, Sepphoris, and Caesarea in the fourth century c.e.; "Jerusalem Talmud" is hence actually a misnomer. This work is also often called the Talmud of the West or the Talmud of the Land of Israel (the Palestinian Talmud). (From the viewpoint of Babylonia, or Iraq, the westerners were the Palestinian rabbis.) Both are commentaries on the Mishnah by scholars called Amoraim, with additions of nonlegal materials (*aggadah*) and biblical exegesis. The Babylonian Talmud, larger and more comprehensive, was redacted in Iraq at the end of the fifth century. It became the authoritative basis for determining Jewish law.

Deciding the law was a difficult task, for the Talmud is not a systematic code of law, such as the Hammurabi Code (eighth century b.c.e.), the Justinian Code (528 c.e.), or Napoleon's Civil Code (1804), where the laws are systematically set down by subject as obligations and prohibitions. The Talmud is instead a multilayered protocol of discussions, making it hard to know what the law requires. The arrangement of topics in the discussions is associative rather than logical.

The text of the Talmud is complex, as it consists of multiple sources from different generations, schools, and editors. Decisions on a single topic are dispersed throughout the entire Talmud. If you want to know about laws of divorce, you go to the tractate (treatise) on divorce (Gittin), but also to tractates on benedictions (Berakhot), the Sabbath (Shabbat), sisters-in-law (Yevamot), betrothals (Qiddushin), and vows (Nedarim). Moreover, along with strictly legal discussions, the sages included the nonlegal narratives, called Aggadah, which embraced ethical teachings, historical records, and medical and scientific matters.

The Talmud was meant not only for rabbis and scholars but also for educated nonprofessionals. Yet few students, however astute, could deduce legal rulings based on this intricate corpus. Jews needed a unified presentation that would bring order out of chaos and decide the legal precepts that guide behavior.

ALFASI'S CONTRIBUTION

This confusion and lack of decisiveness led Alfasi to clarify and arrange the law for study and practical application. His *Book of Precepts* sought to unify dispersed topics into an integrated exposition and to transform the Talmud from a disjointed conglomeration of commentary and discussion into a proper compendium of law with unambiguous instructions for actual practice.

Alfasi summarized the intricate arguments of the Talmud, explained difficult terms, integrated its diffuse treatment of topics, and decided what the law should be, providing the reasoning behind it. He postponed extended explanations and digressions to Arabic supplements at the end of his work. He incorporated talmudic legends, mainly those having legal or ethical significance. *The Book of Precepts* followed the order of the Talmud and was appropriately called the *Abridged Talmud* (*Talmud qatan*).[25] The idea was to make it easier for learners to engage in the study of the Talmud. This was a goal that Maimonides later sought throughout his writing career.

There were two kinds of codification: books of precepts (*halakhot*), corresponding to the talmudic sources, which explain the sources at the basis of the conclusions; and books of decisions (*pesaqim*), arranged topically, which omit the halakhic discussion and state only the conclusions.[26] Alfasi used the first method, seeking to unify the different customs and legal rulings that had proliferated with the dispersion of Jewish communities throughout the Diaspora.

The Book of Precepts omitted parts of the Talmud irrelevant to actual practice, such as texts dealing with the Temple sacrifice or establishing the new moon by observation. Later, in his *Mishneh Torah,* Maimonides would include all the precepts of the law, even those in

abeyance. Alfasi often cited the Jerusalem Talmud; where that diverged from the Babylonian version, Alfasi followed the Babylonian
Talmud, based on the rule that "the law follows the views of the later
authorities."[27]

JOSEPH IBN MIGASH

Alfasi died in 1103, having designated his pupil Joseph ha-Levi ben
Meir Ibn Migash to succeed him.[28] Joseph Ibn Migash (1077–1141) was
from Seville, where he had studied with Rabbi Isaac Ibn Albalia, a
friend and fellow courtier of his father in the entourage of al-Muʿtamid
ibn ʿAbbad, the poet and ruler of the local dynasty of Seville.[29] Ibn
Albalia encouraged Ibn Migash's father to provide instruction for the
boy day and night. When he was just twelve, his father sent him to
Lucena, where he studied with Alfasi until the master died at the age
of ninety.[30]

Isaac ibn Albalia praised Joseph Ibn Migash as having personal
qualities surpassing the men of the generation of the biblical Moses,
extolling him as Moses' descendant, "the most humble of men." As we
have seen, people viewed themselves and others as embodiments of
biblical figures.[31]

Maimonides wrote glowingly about Ibn Migash and made it his
business to collect notes that Ibn Migash's students (including Maimonides' own father) had written based on their teacher's talmudic interpretations.[32] He praised Ibn Migash fulsomely:

> For the mind of that man in Talmud astounds, God knows, whoever
> ponders his words and the depth of his learning, so that it can virtually
> be said of him, *There was no king like him* (2 Kings 23:25) in his way.

The great poet Judah ha-Levi, a friend of Joseph Ibn Migash from
youth, remained close to him throughout his life and wrote poems in
his honor. Judah ha-Levi described Ibn Migash as he responded to legal queries, and his students wrote down his responses as he dictated.[33]
A copy of the responsum would, of course, be sent to those who raised
the query, while the teacher's opinion was recorded by his students for
posterity. Ha-Levi wrote a letter to scholars in Provence introducing
Ibn Migash and thereby establishing contact between the sages of

Spain and the sages of Provence. Maimonides cultivated this bond later in a long correspondence with Provençal scholars, including Samuel Ibn Tibbon, translator of Maimonides' *Guide of the Perplexed*.

RELIANCE ON RESPONSA AGAINST
STUDY OF TALMUDIC SOURCES

A crucial legal opinion by Ibn Migash became a defining moment for Jewish jurisprudence.[34] Ibn Migash was asked in a legal query whether someone unfamiliar with the talmudic sources of a law could make authoritative legal decisions relying only upon legal compilations and responsa.[35] The questioners opposed this procedure, claiming that responsa may be corrupted by copyists and their authors not identifiable, and that the legal decision was sometimes retracted later. They asked Ibn Migash to clarify the issue with an ample explanation.

At first glance, we would suppose that someone who had to look up legal digests and collections of decisions without being able to consult their talmudic source would not be as reliable as someone who could also study the relevant talmudic passages concerning the law. However, this is not what Ibn Migash decided.

He instructed that whoever relies on responsa, even without understanding the Talmud, is superior to someone who relies upon himself in the belief that he knows the Talmud. Few, he argued, know the Talmud well enough to decide the law. Those who give instruction solely on the basis of the Talmud ought to be prevented from doing so. Nowadays, Ibn Migash stated, no one is qualified to make rulings without referring to the responsa of the Geonim and collections of legal decisions. A person who relies on what the Geonim have said and uses brief and clear reasoning will not err. At least he is going by the decision of a qualified court.

This view helped prepare the ground for Maimonides' great legal compendium, *Mishneh Torah*.[36] It served as a basis for legal rulings and case decisions that did not cite talmudic sources.[37]

Actual practice mirrors Ibn Migash's judgment. The Genizah contains more books on legal decisions than on the Talmud and its commentaries. Two hundred years before Maimonides' *Mishneh Torah*, these legal compendia were the main subject of study.[38]

In the academy, formal instruction focused on the Bible and the Talmud. Scientific studies were pursued outside the academy walls.[39] Talmudists and intellectuals had distinct cultural and educational aims. The Talmudists rejected Greek wisdom as either pernicious or a waste of time. The intellectuals believed that only by combining Torah with Greek wisdom could one become a gentleman and an enlightened Jew. Ironically, by writing legal digests, Talmudists, such as Alfasi, afforded intellectuals time to ponder the law without having to engage in protracted talmudic study.[40] Maimonides made it his goal to liberate students from painstaking talmudic studies, enabling them to follow an educational program combining Torah with science and philosophy.

SCIENTIFIC STUDIES

At about eighteen the student was ready to study mathematics, astronomy, logic, and physics. This was a program intended for the intellectually gifted and those who could afford to spend all their time studying, and it was the curriculum that Maimonides followed in his teens, while still living in Andalusia. Only after mastering these preliminary subjects did he go on to metaphysics, ethics, politics, theology, and medicine. How exhilarating it was for him to study mathematics and logic! He wrote with awe about the power of reason to attain scientific knowledge. Logic, he realized, was the instrument for attaining validity and mathematics was the language of the natural order. Logic, based on the writings of the Muslim philosopher al-Farabi (ca. 870–950), was studied together with medicine in Spain, following a strong Galenic tradition that the best physician must be a philosopher.[41]

Yet in Maimonides' time, the Muslim ulema and their Jewish counterparts opposed philosophy and science. For Islam, as for Judaism, the law is paramount, a comprehensive guide to life in all its aspects. Study of the Qur'an, tradition (hadith), theology (kalam), and jurisprudence (fiqh) dominated Muslim intellectual life. The ulema regarded the "ancient sciences" as foreign and useless, an insidious threat to religious faith.[42] Likewise, in Jewish societies many rabbinic authorities regarded philosophy and science as alien wisdom that eroded faith and stole time from study of Torah.

However, astronomy was useful for religion, hence tolerable. Muslims needed astronomy to determine times of prayer and the *qibla* (the direction to face when praying). Jews needed astronomy to determine the time of the new moon, to synchronize lunar and solar time, to calculate the periods of seasons, and to compute when an extra month should be added to the calendar according to the Metonic cycle of intercalated months. One could, therefore, study mathematics and astronomy without arousing suspicion of heresy.[43]

Maimonides began his scientific studies with astrology, which he may have taken seriously at first but discarded later with revulsion. He also read all the books on idolatry that he was able to lay his hands on. He needed to understand idolatry, he said, because the reason for many commandments was to distance people from its allure.

> Know, my masters, that I myself thoroughly investigated these matters. The first thing I studied was the science called astrology,[44] namely, [the science] by which a man knows what will occur in the world, or in this city, or in that kingdom, or what will occur to a certain individual during his entire life.[45] I have also studied the entire subject of idolatry. It seems to me that there does not remain in the world a composition on this topic in Arabic, which has been translated from other languages that I have not read and fully understood its contents.[46]

Scientific Reasoning

It was scientific reasoning that became Maimonides' ultimate touchstone of truth. He would write later that if Aristotle's belief in the eternity of the universe were proven, he would interpret Scripture to conform with Aristotle.[47] He did not mean that he could force Scripture to yield any meaning desired; rather, Scripture could not contradict demonstrative, or scientific, truth. If it did, then our understanding of it was deficient.

Maimonides needed to master mathematics in order to study astronomy. Mathematics conveyed the sense that the universe is orderly and rational, planned by a higher intelligence. It provided apodictic (demonstrative, certain) solutions to problems, even though some of its findings were mysterious, such as two asymptotic lines that come closer but never meet.[48] Mathematics combined pure rationality with a hint of mystery that corresponded to his conception of the universe as a place of natural laws and harmonious order along with a mystery impenetrable to the human mind.

Mathematicians in the Arab/Islamic world employed the system of Indian reckoning (*al-hisab al-hindi*), using nine figures and a zero (indicating a vacant place) as the basis for calculations in a decimal place-value system of numeration, or positional notation.[49] The place-value system and zero were as revolutionary in the Islamic world as the invention of paper, and had the same effect of making a cultural asset available to a wide cross section of the populace. The system facilitated computations in astronomy, navigation, and commerce.[50] Though the ancient Mesopotamian system was decimal, fractions were often expressed in the sexagesimal system (based on the number 60), so $\frac{1}{2}$ was 30 parts of 1 ($\frac{30}{60}$). Ptolemy used the decimal system for whole numbers and wrote fractions (hence minutes and seconds) in the sexagesimal system, which Greek astronomers had adopted from the Babylonians.

We still use the sexagesimal system for time, where a fraction of an hour is $\frac{1}{60}$, and so on, as well as for angles and degrees of a circle.[51] The numbers were written left to right (unlike Arabic and Hebrew script). The transfer of this method to Europe in the twelfth century was one of the earliest contributions of Arabic science to the West.[52]

Maimonides' knowledge of astronomy progressed over the years from general acquaintance to intimate knowledge. For instance, in his *Commentary on Rosh ha-Shanah,* which he wrote before he studied astronomy seriously, he said that the moon was visible in the east before sunrise and in the west after sunset on the same day.[53] Later, in his *Commentary on the Mishnah,* he declared that whoever believed such a thing was "nothing but an utterly ignorant man, who has no more awareness of the celestial sphere than *an ox or an ass*" (1 Sam 12:3).[54] Looking back, Maimonides deplored his juvenile folly in a self-deprecating way.[55]

Though Maimonides studied Greek philosophy and science, he could not read Attic Greek. Instead he used ninth- and tenth-century translations that had rendered Greek philosophy and science into Arabic. The translators made available the pre-Socratics (sometimes tinted by Neoplatonic ideas), Plato (mostly in paraphrases), almost all of Aristotle's writings along with works of his commentators, and Neoplatonists such as Plotinus, Porphyry, Proclus, and Iamblichus. In addition, texts by scientists such as Euclid, Archimedes, Apollonius of Perga, Ptolemy, and Galen had been rendered into Arabic and were available to him.[56] Indeed, without the Greco-Arabic translation activity in the Islamic world and the further transmission of these texts into Hebrew and Latin, medieval Jewish thought and Christian Scholasticism could not have emerged.

Maimonides justified his borrowing from the ancient Greeks by claiming that this wisdom was indigenous to Judaism.[57] The myth of a primordial Hebraic wisdom going back to Moses or Solomon was a prevalent motif in the Hellenistic period. We find the same idea perpetuated in Islamic thought.[58] The belief that Greek philosophy and science were derived from the Hebrews in ancient times made it possible to naturalize these disciplines within Islamic and Jewish culture.

4

Early Writings

Only in the mathematical sciences, as Averroes says, are things known to us identified with those known absolutely.

— WILLIAM OF BASKERVILLE[1]

TREATISE ON THE ART OF LOGIC

In typical biographies of Maimonides we read that he wrote a book on logic when he was sixteen. We don't really know how old he was when he wrote, in Arabic, his *Treatise on the Art of Logic* (*Maqala fi sina'at al-mantiq*). He probably wrote it during his Andalusian years or afterward in Fez. He would then have been in his early twenties.[2]

Logic was one of the first subjects that a budding scientist learned, and it was considered essential for the study of medicine. It was the indispensable tool of rational thought, for establishing rules of scientific method, and for distinguishing between valid and invalid reasoning. Aristotle's *Organon*—the collection of his logical works—had been translated from Greek into Arabic in its entirety, as was Porphyry's *Eisagoge,* an introduction to logic.[3]

Maimonides' *Treatise on the Art of Logic* may be said to be his only purely philosophic work with no hint of theology or anything of specifically Jewish content. Maimonides did not cite the Bible or Talmud or give any indication of his religious identity in the treatise. This makes sense, as logic is universal like mathematics and physics.[4] Maimonides also wrote purely scientific works in the fields of astronomy, mathematics, and medicine. The treatise, then, is certainly not a "Jewish book" the way *The Guide of the Perplexed* is.

It was addressed to someone said to be "an eminent man, one of those engaged in the sciences of the religious law and of those having clarity of style and eloquence in the Arabic language." Maimonides does not indicate whether this person was Jewish. The sciences of the religious law, in which he was engaged, need not involve the Jewish religious law.[5] The allusion to the recipient's clarity of style and eloquence in the Arabic language suggests that he was a non-Jew, perhaps a Muslim.[6] Maimonides used Qur'anic locutions in the treatise. He referred to Jesus, for instance, as 'Isa, the way the name appears in the Qur'an, instead of as Yeshu or Yeshua', the name used by Jewish authors.

The recipient's involvement in the legal sciences and his proficiency in rhetoric are presumably noted to explain his curiosity about logic and perhaps even to suggest a link between religious law, language, and rhetoric, on one side, and logic and philosophy, on the other. The recipient, it is said, had asked "a man who was studying the art of logic" (that is, Maimonides) to explain to him the meaning of the many terms frequently used in logic and the technical terminology used by practitioners of this art. He requested that this be done with utmost concision, as his aim was not actually to learn the art of logic but merely to understand recurrent terms as they are usually employed. The treatise, then, was not written for a philosopher, nor was it composed to clarify philosophic issues; rather, it purports to explain the terminology used by logicians.

Maimonides said that his treatise was an introductory work, not an advanced treatise on logic. It is, in fact, derivative, largely indebted to the Muslim philosopher al-Farabi, whose logical works Maimonides recommended highly. The *Treatise on the Art of Logic* consists of fourteen chapters, a significant number for Maimonides, who favored seven and its multiples.

The most important chapter of the logic treatise for our present and future purposes is chapter 8, in which Maimonides discussed four kinds of propositions that do not require proof and five types of syllogisms.

There are four kinds of propositions that are true and require no proof:

1. *Perceptions,* as our knowing that this is black, this is sweet, and this is hot.

2. *First intelligibles (axioms),* as our knowing that the whole is greater than the part, that two is an even number, and that things equal to the same thing are equal to each other.

3. *Conventions,* as our knowledge that uncovering nudity is shameful, and that repaying a benefactor with favors is noble.

4. *Traditions* are whatever is received from a single approved person or from an approved group.

Whereas perceptions and first intelligibles are the same for all human beings with sound senses and instincts, conventions differ in that they are known among one nation (*umma*) and not another. The more nations there are that accept a convention, the stronger its assent is. The same is true of traditions that may be accepted by one nation and not another.

After this preparation, Maimonides continued:

1. You must know that every syllogism whose premises are all certain, we call a demonstrative syllogism. The use of these criteria and the knowledge of their conditions we call *the art of demonstration*.

2. When the syllogism's premises or one of them is conventional, we call it a dialectical syllogism, and the use of these criteria and the knowledge of their conditions is *the art of dialectic*.

3. When the premises of the syllogism or one of them is a received opinion [tradition], we call it a rhetorical syllogism, and the use of these criteria and the knowledge of their methods is *the art of rhetoric*.

Maimonides also listed the type of syllogism used for deception and feigning, where one or both premises are the kind that a man uses to falsify in any of the syllogistic moods. These are sophistic syllogisms used in *the art of sophism*.

Lastly, there are some who praise and blame things by means of imitations. "And any syllogism whose premise is used in this way of imitation and representation is called *the art of poetry*."

Note the expression "you must know" in the first element; it is typical of Maimonides' style. When he writes for a single addressee, he naturally turns to him in the second person singular *you,* which also takes in all of his readers, including you.

Muslim philosophers (*falasifa*) correlated the types of syllogisms with the cognitive abilities of human beings. Only a few are able to comprehend scientific arguments based on demonstrative reasoning. Others are only capable of following dialectical arguments, and still others can only understand rhetorical or poetical arguments.[7] The Islamic *falasifa* and Maimonides distinguished between the few, or elite, capable of the highest form of reasoning, and the many, or the commonality, capable only of lesser types of reasoning, such as dialectical, rhetorical, and poetic.[8]

Religion uses reasoning that is dialectical (based on generally accepted premises) as well as rhetorical and poetical. Yet the person who comes to assent through these arguments is as convinced as the scientist who understands demonstrative syllogisms. Ibn Rushd identified those who could follow dialectical but not demonstrative arguments with the theologians (*mutakallimun*).

After treating logical terms and syllogisms, Maimonides proceeded to discuss the sciences. The brief survey of the sciences in chapter 14 includes "Maimonides' statement on political science."[9] The beginning reads:

> As for political science [*al-'ilm al-madani*], it is divided into four parts. First is self-governance of the individual; second is governance of the household; third is governance of the city; and fourth is governance of the great nation [*al-umma al-kabira*], or the nations [*al-umam*].[10]

The reference to "the great nation, or the nations" is intriguing, as it posits a political entity beyond the nation, a kind of united nations.[11]

The classification of human associations into city (or city-state/ *polis*), nation, and great nation or the nations, I suggest, may derive from Aristotle's remark that "as the master's rule is a sort of monarchy in the home, so absolute monarchy is domestic mastership over a city, or over a nation or several nations."[12] The idea of the great nation may have arisen from the model of the Roman Empire and from thinkers in that epoch who envisioned a world state.[13]

Maimonides distinguished the civil laws (Arabic *nawamis* = Greek *nomoi*) of the philosophers from the divine commandments in force "in these times."

> The sages of the ancient pagan nations posited governances and rules, called *nomoi,* in accordance with the perfection of the individuals among them, through which their kings governed subjects. The philosophers have written many books about these things that have been translated into Arabic, and what has not been translated may be even more extensive. But in these times, all of this has been dispensed with, I mean the regimes and the *nomoi.* For people [*al-nas*] are governed by the divine commandments [*bi'l-awamir al-ilahiyya*].[14]

There is no reason to assume that the only people governed by the divine commandments are Jews. The people who can dispense with the regimes and the *nomoi* and are governed by the divine commands "in these times" are rather monotheists, including Christians and Muslims.[15] The critical distinction is between the bygone nations that were governed by *nomoi,* on one hand, and people "in these times" who are governed by divine commands, on the other.

In this treatise Maimonides showed his leaning to numerical symbolism.[16] For instance, he observed that the treatise has fourteen chapters, in which 175 terms are considered (7 × 25). Chapter 2 treats 2 × 7 terms, and chapter 10 covers the ten Aristotelian categories. In chapter 7 he described the fourteen moods of the valid syllogism. Philosophy or science consists of seven parts. At the end of each chapter the terms studied in it are listed, except chapter 10, making the last four chapters independent of the rest. He had a preference for tetrads (multiples of 4) and heptads (multiples of 7).[17] This numerical symbolism is a mnemonic device for the reader, an aid for scribes, and a "numerical signature" of the author.[18]

REVISION OF *THE PERFECTION* (*AL-ISTIKMAL*)

An early scientific work by Maimonides was a revision of a comprehensive work on geometry and optics called *The Perfection* (*al-Istikmal*) by Yusuf ibn Ahmad I, al-Mu'tamin (r. 1081) of the Hudid dynasty, party rulers of Saragossa.[19]

The Banu Hud were patrons of learning, and many were themselves scientists and scholars.[20] The philosopher Ibn Bajja and the Jewish botanist Ibn Biklarish lived for some time in Hudid Saragossa, as did the poet and philosopher Solomon Ibn Gabirol. Al-Mu'tamin's father, Ahmad I ibn Sulayman (r. 1049–1082), was a fine mathematician. Hugo of Santalla, the Latin translator (early twelfth century), mentioned the library collection of the Hudids in his preface to a commentary on a work by Musa al-Khwarazmi (ca. 780–850), which was found "among the more secret depths of the library," a section set aside for the ancient sciences and magic.[21] Hugo stated that he was divulging secret knowledge that may not be revealed to any but worthy individuals. Note the esoteric character of philosophy and the sciences in this period.

Maimonides studied al-Mu'tamin's work because of its importance for astronomy. It incorporated several opera on geometry and optics. Separate works on related topics were often copied and transmitted together in the same manuscript. The Christian philosopher Qusta ibn Luqa of Ba'labakk (860–912), for instance, translated Euclid, Apollonius, Archimedes, and others in an anthology of ancient mathematical sources that would be studied together.

The Perfection transmits several scientific treatises on geometry and optics that had been rendered from Greek into Arabic. The treatises were eventually translated into Latin for scholars working mainly in Spain, the major bridge for the diffusion of culture from the Islamic world to Europe. The list of its contents shows that Maimonides had access to ancient scientific writings through anthologies, and it indicates the sequence in which he may have studied mathematical and astronomical writings.

Although this is not an original work by Maimonides, it demonstrates an important facet of his writing, especially in his early period. Maimonides produced books useful for instruction that organized and simplified complex material. Maimonides and his pupils, it has been said, introduced al-Mu'tamin's work into Egypt. J. P. Hogendijk found four incomplete manuscripts with discussions of number theory, plane geometry, ratio and proportion (from Euclid's *Elements,* Books V and VI), the geometry of the sphere and other solid bodies, and conic sections.[22] The fragments indicate that al-Mu'tamin had a rich library that contained many books on mathematics.

The Perfection of Ibn Hud contained the following seven works:

1. Euclid's *Elements of Geometry* and *Data*.[23]

2. Theodosius of Bithynia, a Greek astronomer and mathematician, who lived around 100 B.C.E., wrote the *Sphaerica*.[24]

3. Menelaus of Alexandria (ca. 100 C.E.) went to Rome to make astronomical observations. His *Sphaerica* has survived only in Arabic. Book II depicts the use of spherical geometry for understanding astronomical phenomena.[25]

4. The longest work of Archimedes of Syracuse (287–212 B.C.E.), *On the Sphere and the Cylinder,* in two books, was translated by Thabit ibn Qurra.[26]

5. Apollonius of Perga (ca. 260–190 B.C.E.), who lived in Alexandria, wrote a book on conic sections titled *Conics*. He was also a celebrated astronomer.[27]

6. Thabit ibn Qurra (826–901), a Sabian who lived in Harran and Baghdad and knew Greek, was a scientist and translator who wrote on amicable numbers.[28] He was also an astronomer who wrote on calculating the new moon and the relationship between physical and mathematical astronomy, a subject that greatly interested Maimonides.[29]

7. Ibn al-Haytham (ca. 965–1038), first of Basra, then Egypt, was called Alhazen by the Europeans. He wrote *The Book on Optics* (*Kitab fi 'l-manazir*), which was translated into Latin as *Opticae thesaurus Alhazeni* in 1270 and published by F. Risner in Basle (1572) as *Thesaurus opticus*. The Arabs also possessed translations of writings on optics by Euclid and Ptolemy. In the fifth chapter of his book Ibn al-Haytham solved a problem in optics that later baffled Leonardo da Vinci, who could solve it mechanically but not mathematically, as Ibn al-Haytham had done.[30] The Arab scientist improved the discipline of optics by including a theory of vision and physiology of the eye and a theory of light, including geometrical and physical optics.[31]

The historian Ibn al-Qifti mentioned Maimonides' "fine treatises on mathematics," without further specification.[32] A small mathematical work ascribed to Maimonides, titled *Notes on Some of the Propositions of the Book of Conics* (by Apollonius), was copied in Arabic letters by a Muslim scribe.[33] The purpose of the treatise was to provide the steps lacking in Apollonius of Perga's proofs. Although it was not innovative, it indicated familiarity with mathematical literature and contained a commentary on *Conics,* Book VIII, based on Ibn al-Haytham's restoration of the book.[34]

TREATISE ON THE CALENDAR

One of Maimonides' earliest works was a primer on the calendar (*Ma'amar ha-'ibbur*), written in 4918 A.M. (*anno mundi*) (= 1157/58 C.E.), when he was twenty years old.[35] The book was a reply to a request for a treatise on intercalation, the seasons, holidays, and new months to be written in an accessible style. Maimonides' aim was to provide a practical handbook rather than a theoretical treatise. He intimated that he preferred to give a more scientific account; however, this was beyond the addressee's capacity. Authors often wrote for a specific addressee, a benefactor, friend, or colleague. Then again, describing the addressee was often a literary device, a way of defining the intended audience.

Maimonides mastered the details of his subject and put them in order for ready comprehension. His command of astronomy, needed for investigating the calendar, was impressive. The great mathematician and historian of science Otto E. Neugebauer (1899–1990) commented favorably on Maimonides' mastery of astronomy.[36]

For Jews, the calendar pertained to concerns of communal cohesion and religious identity, yet it required knowledge found only in books by Greek and Arab scientists. Maimonides said that he had access to these books, whereas ancient books on these subjects that the sages of Israel, of the tribe of Issachar, composed at the time of the prophets had not reached him.[37] But as these rules have been established by sound proofs, Maimonides wrote, we need not be concerned about the ethnic or religious identity of their authors, whether they were Israelite prophets or gentile sages, for when we have demonstrative proofs, we rely on the scientist who has discovered or transmitted them.[38]

His overriding need for order expressed itself in systemization and organization of knowledge. He simplified difficult issues, making them easier to understand and memorize. A superb pedagogue, Maimonides illustrated astronomical data in tabular fashion along the lines of modern calendars, just as he later used drawings in his *Commentary on the Mishnah* and his code of law, the *Mishneh Torah*.

He wrote passionately, eager to get his points across. In his *Treatise on the Calendar,* he spoke directly to the reader as "you," as he did in the *Treatise on the Art of Logic* and in his mature writings. The second person singular was natural for an epistle, a genre he favored, and came to him easily when he was writing for a single inquirer, though he knew that his treatise would be read by many as we have seen.

As in other works, he used numerical symbolism. The calendar treatise has two sections of seven and three parts, respectively, in which he discussed lunations (*moladot*) and seasons of the year (*tequfot*).[39] Determination of lunations, or new moons, was vital for dating festivals precisely, without which communities in separate countries would celebrate at different times. Precise dating had civil legal consequences as well. Household rent, for instance, was calculated by the number of days in the month.

As the authenticity of the *Treatise on the Calendar* has been placed in doubt, it is important to survey the course of Maimonides' writings on the subject. This primer came first. Then in his *Commentary on the Mishnah,* he announced his intention to write a book on the calendar with demonstrative and irrefutable proofs.[40] The *Treatise on the Calendar* was an elementary handbook and did not fill the need for scientific information on calendar issues, which went to the heart of Judaism. We do not know when he wrote this passage in the *Commentary on the Mishnah,* which he composed in the course of seven years, from 1161 to 1168.

By 1166, he was busy writing Laws of the Sanctification of the New Moon, which was integrated into the Book of Seasons in the *Mishneh Torah*.[41] Sanctification of the New Moon was a scientific discussion of the calendar and mathematical astronomy.[42] The second part (chapters 6–10), written in 1166, was an expansion of the *Treatise on the Calendar* and appears to be the implementation of his assurance in the *Commentary on the Mishnah* that he would write a scientific book on the calendar.[43] He worked on Sanctification of the New Moon over the course of twelve years. It consists of nineteen brilliant chapters, in which he proved himself to be a master of the subject.[44]

He wrote his *Treatise on the Calendar* with tremendous enthusiasm and a profound desire to communicate the topics to the reader clearly and concisely. It was an area where religious lore and scientific procedure intersected. Only someone versed in mathematics and astronomy was capable of truly understanding the Jewish calendar. A strictly traditional approach could only transmit a body of knowledge without understanding. Here, one had to know Ptolemy and other gentile scientists and understand the nature of the universe. This belonged to the knowledge that had been available to the ancient Hebrews, Maimonides taught, but it was forgotten during the dark years of exile. Now he was reviving it and conveying it in the most comprehensible way.

Maimonides' mastery of the calendar was a component in his intellectual preeminence that eventually made him an authority figure in Egypt and in the eyes of Jewry throughout the Mediterranean and as far away as Yemen.

It is important to realize that the hours of the day for Maimonides' contemporaries had different lengths depending on the seasons. As the earth revolves around the sun, the length of the period of daylight changes. The ancients divided a day into twelve equal parts of daytime and nighttime, so the length of their hours, called seasonal hours, actually varied. In Maimonides' milieu, people counted twelve hours of nighttime and twelve hours of daytime, whatever the length of daylight. If daylight was long, each hour would be correspondingly long, and if short, the hour would be correspondingly short. An hour was one-twelfth of the length of daylight or nighttime. Instead of our sixty-minute hour, then, the ancient hour could be from forty to eighty minutes. For astronomical calculations, the hours known as equinoctial were one twenty-fourth of a day, or equal to the length of seasonal hours at equinox.[45]

The Talmud had adopted seasonal hours, following the practice of the Romans. When Maimonides referred to an hour in his writings, he naturally meant a seasonal hour.[46] He followed the talmudic sages in dividing the hour into 1,080 parts, each part (of a sixty-minute hour) equal to $3\frac{1}{3}$ seconds and each minute having eighteen parts.[47] The

Hebrew lunar day begins at sunset or the end of twilight, regulated to be at 1800 hours (6:00 P.M.).

Having seasonal hours, it was most convenient for people to tell time by using sundials. And here we have one of the amazing coincidences that occur so often in our narrative of Maimonides' intriguing life. He described a horizontal sundial in Córdoba, with the vertical gnomon in the middle of a semicircle and the hour limits marked by radii dividing the circle into twelve parts.[48]

> A piece of marble is fixed on the ground and straight lines are drawn [as radii] with the names of the hours written on them [to form] a circle. In the center of that circle there is a nail standing perpendicular [to the plane of the circle], and whenever the shadow of that nail is in the same direction as one of those lines, it is known how many hours of daylight have passed. The name of this instrument, which is used by the astronomers, is the *ballata*.

Now, a sundial found in Córdoba—bearing the name of Ahmad ibn al-Saffar, an astronomer who was active around 1000 C.E. (d. in Denia 1035)—is the oldest Islamic sundial extant.[49] The lines indicate seasonal hours of the day, proceeding from the first hour (on the right) to the sixth hour, which is at midday. A brief text ascribed to ibn al-Saffar depicted in detail a sundial that was a semicircle with the circular side pointing north and the diameter oriented east and west. The hour lines were radii at 15-degree intervals going from west to east. It was exactly like the one Maimonides described.[50]

At night, the stars marked both direction and time. People also used water clocks (clepsydras) and sand glasses, in particular aboard ships.

RABBINIC WRITINGS

Commentaries on the Babylonian Talmud

Maimonides did not neglect traditional studies during the time he was engaged in researching scientific subjects. He wrote a commentary on three of the six orders of the Babylonian Talmud, omitting four tractates that, due to lack of time, he could not finish. He also wrote a commentary on Tractate Hullin, dealing with issues of ritual purity, and glosses on difficult passages in the entire talmudic corpus. From his brief survey of these writings we gather that his scientific studies deprived him of time that he might otherwise have devoted to these works. Little of these commentaries has survived, perhaps an indication that Maimonides did not revise them to his satisfaction and did not bother to have them copied for posterity.

> I composed commentaries on three orders [of the Talmud]—Mo'ed [Festival Days], Nashim [Women], and Neziqim [Damages]—aside from four tractates which we want now to write about, but I have not yet found free time for this. I also composed something on Hullin [Profane Things] because of the great need for it.[51] This is what we were busy with along with seeking all that we did [of other knowledge].[52]

Precepts of the Jerusalem Talmud

Maimonides fashioned his *Precepts of the Jerusalem Talmud* along the lines of Isaac Alfasi's *Book of Precepts,* which had focused on the Babylonian Talmud.[53] The Jerusalem Talmud contains less nonlegal material and is more concise than its Babylonian counterpart. Rabbinic scholars used the Babylonian Talmud as the official source for legal instruction; hence the Jerusalem Talmud was relatively neglected.

Moses ben Maimon lauded the Jerusalem Talmud for explicating the reasons for normative legal decisions, whereas the Babylonian Talmud merely stated decisions without giving any rationale. His *Precepts of the Jerusalem Talmud,* therefore, supplied rationales for laws. In his *Commentary on the Mishnah* Maimonides sought reasons for the commandments. For instance, he explained why the rabbinic sages abolished the custom of reciting the Ten Commandments in the daily prayers as being due to the claim of heretics that only this part of the Torah was given to Moses at Sinai.[54]

By the time he was twenty-two, Moses ben Maimon had mastered the Bible and the Talmud, studied philosophy and science, and written religious and scientific works. Then, after more than ten itinerant years in the Iberian Peninsula, the Maimon family uprooted itself from its native soil to seek refuge in the neighboring region of Morocco.

PART TWO

FEZ TO ACRE

5

Refuge in Fez

*The mimosa tree is motionless at noon; not until night
does it start trembling, its long yellow pompom branches
brushing against the floor. The courtyard is roofless, a secret
inner world invisible from the street. Like the riad, an enclosed
garden in a house. Or the mellah [Jewish Quarter] behind
the arched gate, an intimate world turned in on itself.*

—RUTH KNAFO SETTON, *THE ROAD TO FEZ*

WHY FEZ?

By 1159/60 the twenty-one-year-old Maimonides and his family had
emigrated from Spain to Fez, Morocco.[1] Many wonder why the family
chose to move from Andalusia to Fez, where the same repressive Almohad dynasty wielded power. Most biographers say that they went to Fez
because Maimonides wished to study with the judge Judah ha-Kohen
Ibn Shoshan.[2] This explanation, however, is based on late untrustworthy
sources.[3] At this time, when he was in his early twenties, Maimonides
had no need of a teacher. Even if he did, the entire family would not
have emigrated to a dangerous place for him to pursue his studies.

Maimonides and his family may have emigrated to Fez because it was easier to live there as crypto-Jews. When Joseph ben Judah Ibn 'Aqnin (ca. 1150–1220) emigrated from Barcelona, Spain, to Fez, he expected that he would not be recognized there as a Jew.[4] Moreover, conditions for non-Muslims may have been less harsh in Fez than elsewhere, as Almohad oppression was not uniform or universal.[5]

A shift in Almohad religious policy may also explain why Maimonides and his family came to Fez. They came toward the end of the rule of 'Abd al Mu'min (r. 1130–63), founder of the Almohad state. Muslims and Jews enjoyed some respite during the second half of 'Abd al-Mu'min's reign, when he ceased conquest and expansion and turned to administration and consolidation. He needed experienced bureaucrats and found them among Jews and Christians. He made a treaty with Genoa, and in 1153 Moroccan Christians were permitted to import valuable commodities into their country. Around the same time Jews began to take an active part in the economy. These were conditions that could have made Morocco attractive for Moses ben Maimon and his family.

Jewish fortunes waned in 1163, however, when 'Abd al-Mu'min's son Abu Ya'qub Yusuf began his reign (1163–84). One reason was that in 1162 many Jews in Granada, who were forced converts, participated in a rebellion against Almohad rule. A certain Ibrahim ibn Hamushk (Hemochico in Christian sources) attacked Granada with the complicity of the Jewish and Christian (Mozarab) population.[6] The Almohads garrisoned themselves in the Alcazba (fortress), which Ibn Hamushk besieged with mangonels (Arabic *majaniq;* catapults to fling projectiles).

'Abd al-Mu'min, not far from Rabat, dispatched an army under the nominal command of his son, Abu Ya'qub Yusuf, who surprised their enemies and retrieved Granada. The Jewish rebels were killed without mercy.

The revolt contributed to a hardened attitude toward the Jews under Abu Ya'qub Yusuf. Many Jews converted in an atmosphere of fear and coercion. And so about three years after Maimonides and his family came to Fez, the situation changed for the worse. Their decision to take refuge in Fez, while reasonable at the time, eventually put them in danger.

There may have been other reasons for their coming to Fez. Many Andalusians had fled there in the wake of the Reconquista and the Almohad invasion of Spain. Hence, the migration of the Maimon family was part of a general demographic shift in the wake of ongoing hostilities. Moreover, the family may have had business ties in Fez and bonds of friendship and kinship with some of the numerous local Andalusians.

Another question is why the family, as far as we know, did not emigrate to Castile or northern Spain or across the Pyrenees to southern France. Maimonides and his family would have felt culturally alien in a Christian milieu. Yet other Andalusian Jews migrated to Christian territory even though they considered it culturally and socially inferior to Muslim Spain.

VOYAGE TO FEZ

On a clear day, you can see the coast of Morocco from Algeciras and Tarifa in southern Spain. The Strait of Gibraltar, separating Africa from Europe, is only twelve and a half miles across at its narrowest point.[7] A strong westerly wind might hinder the crossing; otherwise it was usually uneventful.

The Strait of Gibraltar was the frontier of human civilization, beyond which lay the great unknown of the Mare Tenebrosum, the Sea of Darkness, where few ventured.[8] Medieval maps showed only three continents (Asia, Europe, and Africa) enclosed by the "surrounding sea"—the Atlantic and other bodies of water that encompassed the continents. The Pillars of Hercules—Gibraltar and Mount Acha at Ceuta—marked the edge of the known world (*finis terrae*).[9]

The natural port of landing on the African coast was Ceuta (Arabic Sabta), an ancient Phoenician and then Roman site, later occupied and fortified by the Byzantines.[10] At the time, it was a major port of the Almohads, with an arsenal and a harbor for their fleet. The distance from Ceuta to Fez is about 125 miles, an overland journey of less than a week over inviting terrain of rolling hills.

When the Maimon family emigrated to Fez, Moses was in his early twenties, considered to be a mature man in those days. His father was around sixty, considered then quite elderly.[11] Moses' brother, David, a teenager, was a young adult. He had three sisters about whom little is known.

The City of Fez

Fez was at the intersection of two commercial routes, one from north to south, connecting the Mediterranean with sub-Saharan Africa, and the other from west to east, joining Morocco with the area that is today's Algeria. The city had abundant water from a subterranean table that produced springs forming the river that divides the city.[12]

The population of Fez consisted of Berbers native to the area, Arabs, Jews, and some Christians. An Andalusian influx to Fez began in the ninth century, when several hundred families came from Córdoba and Qayrawan and settled there. The city prospered under the Almoravids and remained loyal to them in their struggle against the Almohads. Eventually (in 1145) Fez was forced to succumb to 'Abd al-Mu'min, the Almohad commander. The Almohads used Fez as a base for their campaigns in Spain, while maintaining their capital at Marrakesh. The Andalusian population of Fez increased under the Almoravids and Almohads because both dynasties imported Andalusian bureaucrats for their technical expertise.[13]

The city Maimonides and his family saw showed the ravages of its resistance to the Almohad invasion. Its fortified castle and ramparts had been razed, though its large mosque, the Qarawiyyin, has survived in its elegant splendor to this day. The city walls standing today were built, for the most part, in the thirteenth century, though some segments go back to Maimonides' epoch.

The Qarawiyyin Mosque, founded in 859, a great center of learning with a magnificent library, is an enduring monument of Hispano-Muslim art.[14] It was founded by a devout woman from Qayrawan (whence its name). The mosque was brilliantly ornamented during the reign of the Almoravids. Sadly, the decoration was plastered over in 1150 in anticipation that the invading Almohads would obliterate it, as they had done elsewhere.

A university was joined to the mosque and attracted students from Andalusia, North Africa, and the Sahara. In a later period, under the Marinids (1217–1465), many madrasas were built around the Qarawiyyin Mosque that are still standing today.[15] The mosque's library is stored in an annex (built in 1349) that now houses precious manuscripts and printed books.

Fez was mystical and shadowy. The walled old city, the *medinah,* was crowded and dark, with closed markets covered by thatched roofs and a maze of narrow, winding alleyways crammed with stalls and workshops, with heavy arches over narrow passageways, and with mosques and madrasas at every turn. The tanners' quarter, with its disagreeable smells and sights, was situated close to the main mosque instead of on the outskirts of the town, as was common in Middle Eastern cities. Even nowadays, the streets in the old city are narrow and impassable except for pedestrians and pack animals. And the tanners still toil at a short distance from the Qarawiyyin Mosque, their wares sold to unwary tourists.

The description of Fez by Abraham Joshua Heschel is too apposite to omit:

> Fez was predestined for a life in hiding. The countless narrow and twisted streets intertwined into a labyrinth; the gloomy, sullen, steeply towering walls; the silence of the people, houses, and things; the Berber custom of thick veils on faces, even for men (since "it ill befits noble people to show themselves"); the Moorish architecture of sumptuous interiors but plain, barred and locked exteriors—all these circumstances favored, indeed created a fertile soil for the development of "Marrano" life, so that world history virtually had a dress rehearsal in Fez for the Spanish tragedy of the Marranos to come.[16]

THE MAGHRIB (NORTHWEST AFRICA)

The Maghrib in this era of Islamic fundamentalism was not a cultural wasteland. There was a strong doctrinal component to Almohad religious policy, which taught a pure monotheism and established fundamental principles defining the community. The religious atmosphere in the Maghrib was permeated by pietism, mysticism, and the veneration of saints.[17] The Almohads favored the ideas of the famous legal scholar, theologian, and mystic Abu 'l-Hamid al-Ghazali (1058–1111). Ibn Tumart, founder of the movement, was said to have met al-Ghazali in Baghdad, but this account is probably legendary. Nevertheless, whereas the Almoravids, who preceded the Almohads, burned al-Ghazali's books, the Almohads held him in esteem.[18]

The caliph Abu Ya'qub Yusuf (r. 1163–84) lived as a young man in Seville, where he acquired literary refinement and an interest in philosophy and poetry. He amassed a superb library and welcomed Ibn Tufayl and Ibn Rushd to his court as physicians and advisors. His son and successor, Abu Yusuf Ya'qub al-Mansur (r. 1184–99), was receptive to learning as well, although at one point he banished Ibn Rushd to Lucena and had his books torched to placate the ulema.

MEDICAL STUDIES

While in Fez Maimonides studied medicine and received clinical training. There were no formal medical schools or any prescribed system for teaching physicians at the time. Medical lore was often passed on by members of a family, and families of physicians were common. There was, for instance, the Ibn Zuhr family with five generations of physicians, including two women, who served the Almohad ruler Abu Yusuf Ya'qub al-Mansur. Maimonides' family became a medical dynasty, with each generation bequeathing medical knowledge to the next. Some physicians were self-taught, such as Ibn Sina (Avicenna) (ca. 980–1037), who studied medicine independently, while learning other subjects with teachers. Private tutoring and supervision accounted for most of the medical education and training. Some teaching took place in hospitals and some even in madrasas.

The preeminent physicians in the Islamic world were Abu Bakr al-Razi (Rhazes) (865–925) and Ibn Sina in the East and Abu 'l-Qasim al-Zahrawi (Abulcasis) (936–1013), Abu Marwan Ibn Zuhr (Avenzoar) (1091–1161), and Ibn Rushd (Averroes) in the West (Spain and Morocco). All wrote works that were translated into Latin and influenced the study of medicine in Europe for centuries.[19] Maimonides referred to his clinical training in his medical writings, where he described his contacts with physicians and shiekhs in the Maghrib, most of them Muslims.[20]

On one occasion, he tried to discover the cause of a notorious medical blunder by asking physicians who knew details of the case. Physi-

cians in Marrakesh had given the Almoravid ruler Tashufin ibn 'Ali
(r. 1142–46) an improper dose of the Great Theriac antidote for poisons, precipitating his demise.[21] Maimonides heard from a son of one
of the attending physicians that they erred by giving an excessive dosage, but later he heard from a grandson of another attending physician that the dosage was deficient. He had questioned both physicians
to learn something useful from the case, but they did not reveal sufficient details. Physicians concealed the proper dosage as a secret of an
arcane art. In addition, when the death of a sovereign was in question,
caution was imperative so as not to assign blame.

In another case, four physicians in Marrakesh had treated the crown
prince, a strapping lad in his twenties, but he failed to regain his full
health and lived on as an invalid.[22] Since he was an observant Muslim
who avoided wine, the physicians decided to give him half a dirham
of the Great Theriac, but he perished from the dosage.[23] The four
attending physicians were Abu 'l-'Ala' Ibn Zuhr (d. 1131); a certain
Sufyan; Abu 'l-Hasan Meir ibn Qamniel, the Israelite, of Saragossa;
and Abu Ayyub Ibn al-Mu'allim, the Israelite, of Seville.[24]

It is surprising to hear that Jewish physicians served the Almoravid
dynasty, which was notoriously harsh with infidels. The ruler 'Ali
ibn Yusuf, not otherwise predisposed to favor Jews, brought these
physicians from Andalusia. Jews had a reputation for their medical
skills, and so the ruler disregarded their religious identity. Nor did he
mind protecting Marrakesh with Christian mercenaries commanded
by the famous Catalan Reverter (al-Rubertayr), who was eventually
killed in a battle against the Almohads (539 A.H. = 1144/45) in eastern
Morocco.

The physician Abu 'l-Hasan Meir ibn Qamniel, mentioned in
the second case above, was a friend of the poet Judah ha-Levi. Ibn
Qamniel emigrated from Spain to Fez and served as physician to the
Almoravid rulers.[25]

Abu Ayyub Solomon ibn al-Mu'allim, who was eulogized by Judah
ha-Levi and Abraham Ibn Ezra, had a broad education in Arabic and
was a poet as well. He dedicated a poem of friendship to Judah ha-
Levi, who responded in kind.[26] Ibn al-Mu'allim gained recognition
for his poetry, his broad knowledge of Arabic, and his skill as a physician. He accompanied Ibn Qamniel on his voyage to Morocco and

ministered to the Almoravid ruler 'Ali ibn Yusuf ibn Tashufin. Both
Ibn Qamniel and Ibn al-Mu'allim were given the honorific title of
vizier.

Joseph ben Judah Ibn 'Aqnin told an anecdote about Jewish physicians in the Almoravid court, which shows the intellectual contact
physicians had with educated rulers.[27] When Ibn Qamniel once visited 'Ali ibn Yusuf ibn Tashufin, he discovered that a Jewish physician
explained the biblical Song of Songs to Ibn Tashufin in its literal sense
as an erotic poem (ghazal). This mode of erotic literalism was prohibited by the talmudic sages. Ibn Qamniel rebuked the other physician
and told Ibn Tashufin that the Jewish physician was an ignoramus
who did not understand Scripture. He then interpreted Song of Songs
for the ruler in an allegorical sense.[28]

Maimonides once referred to an experiment that he witnessed. The
best physicians in the Maghrib tested purgatives (laxatives) in his presence. He imparted the formulas and said that he received them by way
of personal instruction (talqin) from his teachers in the Maghrib and
that only scant information is found in books.[29]

We are fortunate to have the record of an actual discussion Maimonides had with a medical teacher concerning a clinical episode. He had
witnessed the case of a healthy young man with fever who was bled
and died thereafter, an incident that became notorious among physicians and the public. A learned physician under whom Maimonides
was studying explained the medical error to him, and Maimonides reported a snippet of their conversation.

His teacher asked him whether he knew what mistake the physician made by bleeding the patient.

Maimonides asked, "My master, do you also consider this to have
been a mistake?"

Laughing, his teacher replied that the patient was a man who indulged in luxury. The man was a glutton who often suffered indiges-
tion, causing a bilious humor in his stomach, in which case Galen had
forbidden bloodletting because it causes immediate fainting.[30]

These reports confirm that Maimonides trained as a medical practitioner before coming to Egypt.[31] We need to treat as dubious, however,
the statement of Leo Africanus and later historians that Maimonides

had been a medical student of Ibn Zuhr and Ibn Rushd, as this never comes up in Maimonides' writings or in contemporary sources.[32]

Maimonides admired Abu Marwan Ibn Zuhr (Avenzoar), a great experimentalist who tested special remedies, and he heard astounding things about this from Abu Marwan's son Abu Bakr, with whom he was on friendly terms. The remedies are all noted in Abu Marwan's *Easy Guide to Therapy and Dietetics* and in *Concerning Food Substances,* which Abu Marwan wrote for rulers in Andalusia. It has been suggested that Maimonides knew Abu Bakr Ibn Zuhr in Spain, as Abu Bakr resided in Seville, and we have indications that Maimonides was in touch with scientists who lived in Seville.[33]

As was customary in the Ibn Zuhr family and other medical dynasties, Abu Marwan studied medicine with his father at an early age, after having received a religious and humanistic education. He wrote his *Book of Moderation* for Ibrahim ibn Yusuf ibn Tashufin (1121). In 1140, Ibrahim's brother, 'Ali ibn Yusuf ibn Tashufin, imprisoned Abu Marwan at Marrakesh for some undisclosed reason. Abu Marwan's service to the Almoravid dynasty had made him rich and prosperous. After the Almohads replaced the Almoravids, Ibn Zuhr entered the service of the caliph 'Abd al-Mu'min and received the honorific title of vizier.

Ibn Zuhr wrote *The Book of Embellishment* on purgatives for his son Abu Bakr. In the *Book of Moderation* intended to be read before the caliph, Ibn Zuhr treated, among other things, the medicine of the body and the medicine of the soul, a topic that engaged Maimonides. Ibn Zuhr also emphasized the importance of experiment, which Maimonides valued highly. There was a difference between them, however, for whereas Ibn Zuhr believed in the efficacy of charms and prescribed them in his medical books, Maimonides denied their power to heal and permitted their use only if the patient believed that they were effective.

FORCED CONVERSION AND CRYPTO-JEWS

Maimonides launched his writing career and studied medicine and other secular subjects in Fez, yet at a certain point his life came under the shadow of Almohad oppression. Given the alternative of conversion to Islam or death, numerous Jews, wishing to save their lives, families, and property, chose conversion, many becoming pseudo-Muslims, or crypto-Jews, called *anusim* (coerced).[34] This subterfuge in twelfth-century Morocco prefigured the double life of the Marranos in fifteenth-century Christian Spain.

We need to find evidence of Almohad oppression, as there are deniers who argue that there was no Almohad policy of forced conversion, that the great loss of life in conquered territories occurred rather in battle and conquest, and that the extent of anti-Jewish measures is exaggerated.[35] In standard modern histories of North Africa, the violent and oppressive facet of Almohad domination is completely disregarded and the annihilation of its Jewish communities passed over in silence.[36]

Military violence brought bloodshed and destruction, and many Jews converted out of fear. In addition, thousands of Muslims, loyal to the Almoravids or suspect in their faith, were killed along with Jews and Christians. 'Abd al-Mu'min and his officers forcibly converted Jews to Islam, not as a specific anti-Jewish policy but as a general Almohad strategy to purge their realm of infidelity (Jews and Christians) and heresy (dissident Muslims). Physical annihilation and conversion caused entire Jewish communities to disappear.

Under 'Abd al-Mu'min's successors, daily conditions worsened for the Jews. The historian 'Abd al-Wahid al-Marrakushi (b. 1185) described the discriminatory legislation during the period of the Almohad caliph Abu Yusuf ibn Ya'qub (r. 1184–99). He wrote that Jews were compelled to live as Muslims and that their synagogues had all been destroyed. According to al-Marrakushi, Abu Yusuf ordered that the Jews in the Maghrib be distinguished by their attire and be forced to wear ridiculous clothing and headgear.[37] They had to wear dark robes with long sleeves that reached their feet. Forbidden to put on turbans, they had to wear ugly caps down to their ears. The Jewish writer Ibn 'Aqnin, a pupil of Maimonides and resident of Fez, described the discriminatory policy, adding restrictions not cited by al-Marrakushi.[38] For example, Jews could not engage in commerce, own property or slaves, or raise their own children.

The caliph Abu Yusuf ibn Ya'qub claimed that had he been sure that the Jews in his realm were sincere converts, he would have permitted them to marry and mix with Muslims. Or if he had been certain of their unbelief (*kufr*), he would have killed all their men, taken their children captive, and made their property booty for the Muslims. He acknowledged that the covenant (*dhimma*) had not been kept with the Jews and Christians from the beginning of Almohad rule, and that not a synagogue or church was left in all of the Maghrib.

The caliph said that he had to impose discriminatory rules because the Jews display Islam on the outside, pray in mosques, and have their children learn Qur'an, following Islamic tradition and custom, but no one knows what their hearts conceal."[39]

Three contemporary Jewish sources depict the disastrous events of the Almohad period and add to al-Marrakushi's description.

ABRAHAM IBN EZRA'S LAMENT

Abraham Ibn Ezra, the Spanish poet and philosopher (1092–1167), mourned the destruction of Jewish communities in a poetic elegy.[40] He was not a witness to the events he described, for he had already escaped to Christian Europe and depended upon reports.

Ibn Ezra refrained from the usual poetic ornaments of the Spanish school but used biblical intertextuality and linguistic ingenuity. He began his poem with a startling verse: "catastrophe [*ra'*] came down from heaven," meaning from God. The poet confessed in the name of the people of Israel that the calamity was brought about by their sins.[41] The exile theme combined the recent exile with exile from the Land of Israel and the Neoplatonic/Gnostic motif of the soul's exile from its permanent abode. Finally, the poet evoked the figure of Hagar, the maidservant, ancestress of the Ishmaelites, who shot arrows at her mistress until the Lord looked down from heaven.[42] The poem thereby came full circle to heaven, ultimately as benevolent and consoling.

IBN DAUD'S DESCRIPTION OF THE ALMOHAD DEVASTATION

The Spanish historian Abraham Ibn Daud (ca. 1110–1180) described the effect of the Almohad campaign on the Jewish communities in Spain

and North Africa, showing that the Almohads tried to obliterate every
vestige of Judaism. Ibn Daud bewailed the destruction of academies and
the end of learning, paying tribute to a world coming to its end.

> After the demise of Rabbi Joseph [Ibn Migash] there were years of
> war, evil decrees and persecutions that overtook the Jews, who were
> compelled to wander from their homes. *Those destined for the plague,*
> *to the plague; those destined for the sword, to the sword; those destined for*
> *the famine, to the famine; and those destined for captivity, to captivity* [Jer
> 15:2].[43] To Jeremiah's prophecy, there was now added "such as were
> [destined] to leave the faith."
>
> This happened in the wake of the sword of Ibn Tumart, which
> came into the world in [4]873,[44] when he decreed apostasy on the
> Jews, saying: *Let us wipe them out as a nation; Israel's name will be*
> *mentioned no more* [Ps 83:5].[45] *Thus, he wiped out every last name and*
> *remnant* [Isa 14:22] of them from all of his empire, from the city of
> Silves at the end of the world until the city of al-Mahdiyya.[46] Owing
> to this situation, Rabbi Joseph's sons were unable to maintain acad-
> emies and were [among] the first to flee to the city of Toledo. They
> have been making whatever effort they can to raise disciples, and the
> Holy One, blessed be he, has shown his approval of their deeds. They
> are the last of the talmudic scholars of the present age.[47]

Later, Ibn Daud described the Berber kingdom (= Almohads)
crossing the sea to Spain "after having wiped out every remnant of
Jews from Tangiers to al-Mahdiyya."[48]

SOLOMON COHEN'S DESCRIPTION OF
ALMOHAD DEVASTATION

The most concrete description of the Almohad devastation comes
from a Moroccan Jew living in Egypt, Solomon ben Abu Zikri ha-
Kohen al-Sijilmasi by name.[49] He cited eyewitness reports to the events
in a letter he wrote from Fustat (in January/February 1148) to his father, Abu Zikri Judah ben Joseph ha-Kohen al-Sijilmasi, who was returning from India and residing in Mirbat on the South Arabian coast
of Oman.[50] As the family was from Sijilmasa, Solomon and his father
were eager for news about friends and relatives still in Morocco.[51] Abu

Zikri had written to his son, complaining of hardships in business affairs and requesting news.

The family was well known. Abu Zikri Judah ben Joseph, whom his son called "Scion of the Gaons," was a leading India trader and representative of the merchants (*wakil al-tujjar*) in Cairo, where he supervised the activities of Maghribis in Egypt and the trade route to India.[52]

He presumably began as a merchant in Sijilmasa, which was on a trade route to northeast Africa, to Qayrawan (Tunisia) and the Mediterranean. Abu Zikri was well connected: he was a friend of the great trader Halfon ben Nethanel, companion of Judah ha-Levi, and he was a brother-in-law of Madmun ben Japheth ben Bundar, a famous representative of merchants in Aden.[53]

Solomon ben Judah learned about the devastation in the Maghrib from Jews and Muslims who had escaped to Egypt. He wrote an informal, typically disjointed, letter about his health, business, personal needs, and news. The *en passant* nature of his report on the Maghrib makes it more credible. The destruction of Moroccan Jewry was a calamity that sent tremors throughout Egypt and the entire region.

After the usual extended greetings, Solomon turned to his own state of affairs. He was very ill, he reported. Although his father, eighteen hundred miles away, could do nothing but worry, Solomon recounted his losses and afflictions, the point being that he needed help. After some personal remarks the writer continues:

> You certainly wish to know the news from the Maghrib, *the ears of all who hear about it will tingle* [Jer 19:3]. The travelers have arrived, among them groups of Jews who witnessed the battle [*ma'araka*]. They reported that 'Abd al-Mu'min al-Susi[54] attacked the amir Tashufin in Oran, besieged him, annihilated his army, killed him, and crucified his body.[55]
>
> Then 'Abd al-Mu'min conquered Tilimsan [Tlemçen] and killed everyone in the town, except those who apostatized.[56] When the people of Sijilmasa heard the news, they revolted against their amir, declared themselves in public as opponents of the Almoravids, drove them out of town, and sent messengers to 'Abd al-Mu'min, surrendering it to him. After ['Abd al-Mu'min] entered Sijilmasa, he assembled the Jews and

asked them to apostatize. Negotiations went on for seven months, during which they fasted and prayed.[57]

After this, a new commander arrived and demanded that they apostatize. They refused, and a hundred and fifty Jews were killed, unifying the [divine] name.[58]

. . .

The others apostatized. The first of the apostates was Joseph ben 'Imran, the judge of Sijilmasa.[59] . . . Before 'Abd al-Mu'min entered Sijilmasa, when the population rose against the Almoravids, about 200 Jews took refuge in the city's fortress [qasba]. Among them were Mar Jacob and 'Abbud, my paternal uncles, Mar Judah son of Mar Farhun, and . . . They are now in Der'a, after everything they owned was taken from them. What happened to them afterward we do not know.

Of all the countries of the Almoravids there remained in the hands of all dissenters[60] only Der'a and Miknasa [Meknes].[61] As for the congregations of the West, because of all their sins, they perished. There has not remained a single person identified as a Jew between Bijaya [Bougie] and the Gate of . . .[62] They were either killed or apostatized. And on the day I am writing this letter news has arrived that Bijaya has been taken and other matters which . . .[63]

During 'Abd al-Mu'min's conquest of Fez 100,000 persons were killed and during [the conquest] of Marrakesh 120,000.[64]

Take notice of this. This is not hearsay, but a report of people who were present at the events. Take notice.[65]

The letter continues, covering various topics. Solomon interlaced news of the catastrophe with household and business matters. He asked his father to bring him a female slave and complained of his modest circumstances, noting that his rental period was ending.

He then described the condition of refugees who settled in Egypt. One was a scholar from Sijilmasa, Mar Joseph ben Mallal, who had been ordained by Joseph Ibn Migash of Lucena.[66] Mar Joseph met with the Rav of Fustat but could not find a position because "he was crazy [majnun]." Mar Joseph sent regards to Abu Zikri and regretted not to have met him in Fustat.

Ben Qadib, a notable from Fez who had escaped with his brother, rescued a Torah scroll originally sent by Abu Zikri, which Ben Qadib had brought to Bijaya.[67] Another refugee was a *kohen* from Fez, who was a relative of Solomon's family, or "so he said." This Cohen came without means and ended up selling clothing in the bazaar of the secondhand garment dealers.[68] All these refugees sent regards to Abu Zikri (no doubt eager for his return after a successful venture).

In his letter, Solomon did not blame the apostates for converting to Islam. He conveyed the terrible news of death and destruction in a sober tone, for people considered it tactless to pour out emotion in letters. He used biblical quotations to express his sorrow and vindicated the ways of the Lord in traditional terms—"the true judge, whose judgments are just and true."

It has been claimed that Solomon Cohen's report conforms to the sequence of events given by Abu Bakr ibn 'Ali al-Sanhaji al-Baydhaq, the contemporary supporter of Ibn Tumart and 'Abd al-Mu'min, who witnessed the events and wrote a memoir about them. However, the similarity between Solomon Cohen's information and al-Baydhaq's record is in broad strokes.[69]

THE ALMOHAD CONQUEST AND ITS DEVASTATION

The sequence of the Almohad conquest followed Moroccan topography. They conquered Tlemcen early, in either 539 A.H. (1144/45) or 544 A.H. (1149/50). 'Abd al-Mu'min entered with great force, massacred many of the inhabitants and enslaved the remaining women, then remained for seven months. Harsh treatment ensued when cities resisted. The Almohad forces then headed west and conquered Fez, which refused to surrender without a protracted battle and much devastation. Meknes was next and then Marrakesh, capital of the Almoravids, where the battle lasted from June 13, 1146, to June 1, 1147, almost a full year.

After his victories over the Almoravids, 'Abd al-Mu'min instituted a second purge (*tamyiz*)—the first was at the time of Ibn Tumart in 1128/29—to separate true believers from dissidents. He distributed lists of names in various cities, forcing people to acknowledge (*i'tiraf*) the authority of the Almohads on pain of death. Al-Baydhaq, who witnessed these events, wrote that in different places 'Abd al-Mu'min killed 200, 600, and 800, and eventually a total of 2,500 people, and then went on killing more.[70] The purge had taken place in 544 A.H. (1149/1150), in the course of which 32,730 were killed. "But Allah knows best," the historian cautiously added.[71]

In Sijilmasa a list was presented, and an Almohad officer assembled people in order to put them to death. One of them, a devout Muslim, heard their protests and invoked God in their favor, after which he died.[72] Al-Baydhaq related that after the *i'tiraf*, when the country was pacified, the caliph went to Sala (Salé) on the coast near Ribat (Rabat), renewed the oath of allegiance to him, and then made his way to Bijaya (Bougie).

The Almohads killed many Jews who refused to profess Islam. However, the Jews were not the only ones who suffered. It was state policy to force everyone to recognize the Almohads as the ultimate power and their interpretation of Islam as the final truth.

6

Martyrdom or Survival

*Grievous (yaqar) in the Lord's sight
is the death of his faithful ones.*

—Ps 116:15

CRYPTO-JEWS IN MUSLIM SOCIETY

Jewish sources attest that during the Almohad period in Morocco, Jews worshiped in mosques, secretly reciting their own prayers, as Maimonides recommended in his *Epistle on Forced Conversion*. By the time the Almohad sultan Abu Ya'qub Yusuf took office in 1163, the crypto-Jews, or forced converts, were firmly entrenched in Muslim society, many having attained leading positions in the economy. The Muslim authorities were evidently satisfied with external conformity, as Maimonides maintained in his *Epistle on Forced Conversion*. But this attitude changed from time to time.

Some Jews pronounced the *shahada* (the Muslim confession of faith) with a mental reservation, to the effect that Muhammad is the apostle of Allah sent to the Arabs, instead of to all mankind, as Muslims believed.[1] This had been the practice of the Jewish 'Isawiyya sect, followers of Abu

'Isa al-Isfahani, and of the Yemenite leader Nethaniel al-Fayyumi, who described this evasion in his *Garden of the Intellects* (*Bustan al-'uqul*).

PRUDENT DISSIMULATION IN ISLAMIC SOCIETIES

Muslims living under Christian hegemony in Spain as Moriscos, or *nuevos cristianos,* in the sixteenth century, facing a similar dilemma, lived publicly as Christians and secretly as Muslims until their final expulsion from Spain (1609–14). A responsum (fatwa) by 'Ubaydallah al-Wahrani, issued in December 1504, permitted them to exercise prudent dissimulation (*taqiyya*) by pretending to be Christians. The fatwa was later translated into Spanish and Aljamia (Spanish in Arabic characters) and was widely distributed.[2]

The Moriscos' behavior was exceptional, however, and a departure from a general Islamic norm—Muslims may not convert to another religion unless their lives are in mortal danger, and then they must end their new status as quickly as possible. Islamic law leaves no room for a Muslim to live permanently under non-Islamic rule. In a world divided between the "abode of Islam" (*dar al-Islam*) and the "abode of war" (*dar al-harb*), Islamic jurists decided that Muslims had to live where they could fulfill their religious obligations and carry out Islam fully.[3]

Islam encompasses private and public duties. For instance, statutory alms, one of the five pillars of Islam, requires that there be an Islamic government to levy it. So the jurists instructed that emigration (*hijra*) was compulsory for all Muslims outside the abode of Islam. Jurists ordered Muslims to leave countries where unbelievers governed, even if they were not suffering persecution. A fourteenth-century fatwa says:

> Allah is the enemy of unbelievers, and they are enemies of [his] prophets and messengers. How is it possible for a Muslim to live as neighbor to somebody who is Allah's enemy? And enemy of His Prophet? . . . Submissiveness to the laws of unbelief is one of the most strenuously forbidden things.[4]

A Qur'anic verse exempted from the crime of apostasy those who were coerced: *Whosoever disbelieves in God after he has believed—save him who is compelled and whose heart is still content in belief—but*

For detailed information about this and other orders, please visit Your Account. You can also print invoices, change your e-mail address and payment settings, alter your communication preferences, and much more – 24 hours a day – at http://www.amazon.com/your-account.

Returns Are Easy!

Visit http://www.amazon.com/returns to return any item – including gifts – in unopened or original condition within 30 days for a full refund (other restrictions apply). Please have your order ID ready.

Thanks for shopping at Amazon.com, and please come again!

---

hipping Address:
ephen M. Gluck
2 Hillturn Ln
oslyn Heights, NY 11577–2326
nited States

Item Price	Total
$23.10	$23.10

	$23.10
	$2.86
te	−$2.86
	$1.99
	$25.09
	$25.09
	$0.00

EKG - Good

BP 130/70

CN 3/1.0

whosoever finds ease in disbelief, upon them is wrath from God and a grievous punishment (16:106). Commentators understood the verse to mean that one who is compelled to profess unbelief with his tongue to escape his enemies, while his heart still believes, is not to be blamed, because God accepts his servants according to the belief in their hearts.

In Islamic societies religious authorities pardoned deviation provided that lip service was paid to the faith and that conduct conformed with Islamic norms. The public pronouncement of heresy (not the harboring of heretical ideas) was penalized. People used concealment and wore veils. Deep inside the individual lived a private faith, which he treasured with a small circle of secret sharers.

An interaction between external and inner meaning takes place in esoteric exegesis, where the secret of a text is hidden beneath the surface. In physical phenomena, as well, we find an interface between concealing and revealing. The walled domicile and secluded privacy protect inhabitants from the encroachment of the street and public and the government.

MAIMON BEN JOSEPH'S *EPISTLE OF CONSOLATION*

Moses ben Maimon's father, Maimon ben Joseph, wrote a small treatise titled *Epistle of Consolation* (*Iggeret ha-Nehamah*) in Fez in 1471 S.E. (1159/60 C.E.), about fifteen years after the Almohad conquest of the city, prior to Moses ben Maimon's *Epistle on Forced Conversion*.[5] In his own epistle, Moses ben Maimon did not quote his father directly, but he embraced the principles of his teaching. Above all, he adopted the style and tone of consolation. Both men sought to comfort, not to cast blame or arouse feelings of guilt.

Formally addressed to a friend, as a source of consolation and delight to the soul, Rabbi Maimon's epistle was actually meant for the entire community. He consoled a people suffering the pain of exile, despondent over the remoteness of deliverance, slain for their faith. The epistle discouraged messianic movements while instilling hope in Jewish destiny, urging Jews who embraced Islam not to despair, to observe the religious law covertly and to remain faithful even after apostasy. The recognition of apostate Jews as Jews nevertheless is a principle announced in Rabbi Maimon's *Epistle of Consolation* and adhered to by his son Moses in his *Epistle on Forced Conversion*.

Islamic military and political successes crushed spirits and convinced many Jews to acquiesce and surrender to Islam. Maimon urged those who embraced Islam to observe the Jewish law as far as possible and to remain faithful. He reassured Jews who observed the commandments and prayed in secret that they would receive their reward, citing scriptural promises of salvation.[6]

A person must strive his utmost, both secretly and publicly, to perform the law and obey the commandments, to hold fast to the rope of the law. A person in exile is like someone who is drowning. The rope of God's commandments and his law are suspended from heaven, and whoever lays hold of it retains hope.[7] He who lets go of the cord has no union with God, and God allows waters to overcome him until he dies. One who clings to the rope has more hope than one who does not, and one who clings even with the tips of his fingers has more hope than one who lets go altogether.[8]

He invoked prophetic assurances of redemption. God chose Israel from among all nations and will not replace its people by another. He will not reject them or remove them from his love, as they are his sons whether he is angry or pleased with them.

He urged the people not to agonize over the power of the nations, the length of their rule, and their awesome number. They must trust in God and believe his promises, despite the sovereignty of the nations, their evil and cruelty, and the constant misfortunes day and night.

> We fear the day that darkens over us and the night when we lie down and say, "Would that we be saved from them today just as nothing awful happened to us at night." And when the night comes we say, "Who knows what new thing will come about. If only the night were like the day that passed." The prophet said, *In the morning you shall say, "If only it were evening! [and in the evening you shall say, "If it were only morning!"—because of what your heart shall dread and your eyes shall see]* [Deut 28:67].

Maimon taught that Jews who perform religious precepts in secret will receive their reward. He invoked prophetic assurances of salvation, stressing the redemptive powers of the biblical apostle Moses, the uniqueness of his mission and his merits.

Maimon's epistle is ethical and pietistic in the spirit of Bahya Ibn Paquda's *Duties of the Hearts*. It was in this atmosphere that Moses ben Maimon was raised, and it comes to expression in his writings. Rabbi Maimon described this world as a beautiful woman, her garments fine, her aroma fragrant, her demeanor seductive, her glance piercing, her speech amusing. With her legs she hunts her lover; her hand entices him so that he runs to her in his desire, while she flees from him. He runs and doesn't know what is beneath him, like a bird flying in the air. She spreads a net with seeds on it, setting a trap. In this spirit, Rabbi Maimon wrote, Solomon compared this world to a woman, saying, *A woman comes toward him. Dressed like a harlot, with set purpose* (Prov 7:10). And he said: *He is like a bird rushing into a trap* (Prov 7:23). *Beware of the temptations of the world and pursuing wealth,* wrote Rabbi Maimon, *and think of death.*

One of the strongest links between man and God is faithfulness to the obligation of prayer, reciting the eighteen benedictions thrice a day. Maimon repeated the text of the shorter version of the prayer, which, he said, one may offer in an Arabic version, the text of which he gave.[9] Nothing is more powerful than prayer when a person's intention is sincere, his heart pure, and he believes in "God and his apostle." The last phrase, like many others, is an Islamic locution. In offering Judaism as an alternative to Islam, he incorporated some of the Islamic lexicon that the *anusim* had internalized.

Rabbi Maimon mentioned the biblical Moses often, comparing him favorably to Muhammad, even assigning him Muhammad's epithets, such as "the best of mankind." Moses was an intercessor with God, pleading for the Israelites, as Muhammad was an intercessor for the Islamic community. The light of Moses' countenance was from the light of God's glory, as Muhammad was imbued with a divine light.

Commenting on Moses' prayer in Psalm 90 ("A prayer for Moses, man of God"), Rabbi Maimon found that it contains all the vicissitudes that would befall Israel from the beginning of the exile to its end. "I considered the Psalm and its secret was made clear to me, that Moses uttered it for time of exile, and David put it in the Book of

Psalms as a source of comfort and consolation."[10] "Moses prayed that God would still the waves of the seas that surround us, for the nations among whom we are dispersed encompass us about." Maimon instructed everyone to recite this psalm daily.

MAIMONIDES' *EPISTLE ON FORCED CONVERSION*

Maimonides' *Epistle on Forced Conversion* (*Iggeret ha-shemad*) was written sometime between 1160 and 1165, perhaps closer to the later date. The term *shemad* in the title means "destruction," "extermination," "uprooting religions" (Latin *extirpatio;* Greek ἐξώλεια), and it came to denote "forced conversion" and "persecution." When the rabbinic sages spoke of "the time of the *shemad*," they intended the anti-Judaic decrees of the Roman emperor Hadrian after the revolt led by Bar Kokhba in 132 C.E.[11] Hadrian's edicts imposed capital punishment for the study of Torah, circumcision, and other practices. Rabbi Aqiba and his colleagues, according to tradition, were martyred for continuing to teach Torah.

Given the forced choice of conversion to Islam or the sword, many Jews chose conversion, some becoming *anusim* (coerced).[12] As forced converts, they differed from Jews who were renegade apostates (*mumarim* or *meshummadim*) by choice and conviction.

From the report by Solomon ben Judah ha-Kohen, which we saw above, we learn that the Almohads did not always force Jews to decide immediately. In Sijilmasa, during the period of deliberation, they had time to question their sages, just as they queried the anonymous authority who gave the reply eliciting Maimonides' rejoinder. Significantly, the first recourse of the Sijilmasa Jews was to accept martyrdom.

Historians often contrast Jews in Islamic lands with European Jews. European Jews at the time of the Crusades embraced martyrdom, even sacrificing their children rather than accepting Christianity, whereas Islamic Jews supposedly preferred survival to martyrdom. But many Jews in Sijilmasa, as noted, accepted martyrdom. In Ashkenaz (Germany and France), while there were many Jews who gave their lives and even sacrificed their wives and children, still many others converted to Christianity for economic reasons or out of fear or conviction. Their religious status became a legal problem for Jewish authorities.[13] Jews in Islamic lands had a different attitude toward Islam than Jews in Christendom had toward Christianity. They did not view Islam as polytheism, as European Jews viewed Christianity. One exception in Europe was Rabbi Menahem ha-Meiri (1249–1306), a follower of Maimonides, who regarded Christianity as a monotheistic religion on a par with Judaism and Islam.[14]

Furthermore, in Christian countries, martyrdom was an ideal that Christians venerated and that Jews were likely to emulate, whereas Muslims regarded a martyr (*shahid*) to be someone who died in jihad, or warfare for the sake of Allah—an ideal that obviously bypassed the Jews. However, under duress, Islam absolved prudent dissimulation and did not insist on martyrdom. Still, both Ashkenazi and Middle Eastern Jews preferred to avert the evil decree and do whatever possible to stay alive. Both groups had their martyrs and their survivors.

By professing Islam openly and practicing Judaism secretly, Jews were (paradoxically) following the Muslim tactic of *taqiyya*. Jewish sources attest that Jews worshiped in mosques, secretly reciting the Shema‘ there, as Rabbi Maimon and Moses ben Maimon attested in their epistles.[15] The Muslim historian al-Marrakushi related, "The Jews among us only feign Islam, praying in mosques, their children reading the Qur'an, following our religion and our *sunna;* but God knows what is in their hearts or what they hold to behind closed doors in their houses."[16]

The *Epistle on Forced Conversion* was the earliest of Maimonides' communal epistles, written when he was in his early twenties and already an authority figure even in his father's lifetime. He wrote the epistle in Arabic, but it survives only in two different Hebrew translations, one consisting of just the first part.[17] The Arabic original may be lost because Jews tried to conceal it from Muslim officials and did not make many copies, preferring to convey its message by word of mouth.[18] Maimonides condoned conversion to Islam, discouraged martyrdom, and recommended migration and exile.

Maimonides did not claim—at least, according to the translations we have—that anyone asked him for his opinion; he strode into the public arena boldly. He wrote the *Epistle on Forced Conversion* in the full bloom of hot-blooded youth. Later in life, he confessed to Joseph ben Judah, when he was about fifty-three, that he had had a fiery temperament and biting tongue when he was young, referring to this period when he lived in Fez. This reminiscence suggests that Maimonides gained his reputation as a legal authority in Morocco partly through disputes with other experts as we see here.

> When I was your age and even older than you, I was more vehement than you. I would wield my tongue and pen against great and wise men when they sought to disagree with me. You surely heard what happened between me and Rabbi Judah ha-Kohen ben Mar Farhun (of blessed memory) concerning two questions about nonkosher food;[19] between me and the judge of Sijilmasa concerning the bill of divorce; and between me and Abu Joseph ben Mar Joseph (may he rest in Paradise) in the matter of the captive maiden; and many similar cases, in which I gave pleasure to my friends and tears to my enemies by my tongue and pen—by my tongue to those who were near and by my pen to those who were far.[20]

He wrote the *Epistle on Forced Conversion* in reaction to a widely circulated responsum, or judicial opinion, by an unidentified scholar. The man had been asked "whether one should profess the *shahada* to avoid being slain and having one's orphaned children become Muslims, or whether one should refuse to recite it and be slain, as the Torah requires, since uttering the *shahada* leads to abandoning all the commandments."

The first part of the question assumed that dying a martyr's death, meritorious in itself, involves loss of one's children to the Muslims, a point in favor of compromise and survival. Clearly, many Jews justified conversion by this reasoning. The second part of the question assumed that the Torah obligated them to die and not utter the *shahada*.

The respondent replied, "Whoever attests the mission of Muhammad thereby renounces the Lord God of Israel. One should rather be killed than profess the *shahada,* even if remaining alive would prevent one's children from becoming Muslims." The respondent regarded Islam as polytheism, a view held by some earlier Geonim.

Maimonides rejected the respondent's decision on legal and historical grounds. He denounced the man as a self-styled sage who had not suffered as had most Israelite communities. He deemed the responsum feeble, insipid, and superficial, packed with fallacious statements. The man's discourse, he commented, was rambling, flimsy, and muddled, unworthy even of quotation. He blathered about irrelevant things, carried away by his pen. Maimonides regarded long-windedness as a sign of foolishness. He quoted: *For dreams come with many cares, and a fool's voice with many words* (Eccl 5:2).[21]

His main point was that the anonymous respondent failed to differentiate between accepting Islam voluntarily and accepting it under compulsion. He sympathized with Jews who uttered the Muslim profession of faith under duress, and permitted doing so in the circumstances. He claimed that the Muslim sovereign merely required a verbal profession, not actions that controvert Jewish law, and he did not regard the declaration itself as an action. Those who worship idols under coercion do not deserve to be barred from the next world or to be put to death by a court of law, not even those who violate other commandments of the Torah.[22]

"Belief [*i'tiqad*]," he wrote, "is not the notion that is uttered, but the notion that is represented in the soul when it has been averred of it that it is in fact just as it has been represented."[23] The mere utterance of belief is not belief, and so the profession of Muslim faith without inner conviction is meaningless.

For some reason, discussions of this epistle overlook the Islamic position on conversion and sincerity. Most schools of Islamic law did not regard the mere utterance of belief, without sincerity and behavior, as sufficient for a valid conversion. Islamic legal scholars considered internal conviction, or belief, as essential to the act of faith. Maimonides surely knew that, according to Islam, the mere verbal affirmation of faith by pronouncing the *shahada* without internal conviction or intention was meaningless.[24]

Second, Maimonides attacked the man's claim that observing Jewish law secretly while acknowledging Islam externally is worthless, for the law must be observed openly. According to the respondent, someone who is overtly a gentile and covertly an Israelite is a gentile.

Third, Maimonides assailed the respondent's opinion that when a forced convert enters a mosque to pray to Allah and then enters his home to pray to God, he sins, for he bows both to an idol and to the Lord. The respondent, Maimonides riposted, failed to differentiate between an act done willingly and an act done under constraint.

Maimonides was furious with the man for nullifying the religious acts of converts, in particular prayer. This contradicted the advice that his father gave, that Jews should perform whatever commandments they could, especially prayer. Here the respondent hit a raw nerve. These forced converts risked their lives, yet this fellow, from his safe perch, was telling them that their courageous acts were of no avail.

A fourth issue was the respondent's statement that whoever acknowledges that Muhammad is a prophet is a wicked man, hence an invalid witness.

The final point the man made was that since Karaites and Christians preferred to die rather than acknowledge Muhammad's prophetic mission, Rabbanite Jews could do no less. Maimonides found astonishing the man's claim that Rabbanites should take Karaites and Christians as models.

Maimonides insisted that the forced converts did not rebel against God for pleasure, and did not forsake their faith in pursuit of status and temporal joys. God will not forsake them. In this forced conversion, he reiterated, Jews do not simulate idol worship but merely give lip service, and the Muslim authorities were aware that they did not believe in what they said. They were willingly deceived because all they required was a verbal utterance. Later in the epistle Maimonides spoke of the Muslim authorities in a place scrutinizing an individual, in which case the person must not dwell there at all.[25]

He used the pronoun *we* throughout the epistle in the dual sense of "we Israelites" and "we who are coerced to be Muslims." He acknowledged that he and others had sinned: *Let us lie down in our shame, let our disgrace cover us; for we have sinned against the Lord our God, we and our fathers* (Jer 3:25). *We know, O Lord, our wickedness, the transgression of our fathers, for we have sinned against you* (Jer 14:20).

Maimonides granted that martyrdom was highly meritorious and taught that even a great sinner who becomes a martyr attains immortality.

Know that whenever they (of blessed memory) said, He shall be slain and not transgress, if he is martyred he has sanctified the Name.[26] If he was among ten Israelites he sanctified the Name in public,[27] like

Hananyah, Mishael and Azariah, and Daniel[28] and the ten martyrs
killed by the government authority, and the seven sons of Hannah,
and all other Israelites martyred for the sanctification of the Name,
may the Merciful One avenge their blood soon. It is said about them:
Bring me my devotees, who made a covenant with me over sacrifice [Ps
50:5].[29] And they (of blessed memory) said:

I *adjure you, O maidens of Jerusalem* [*by gazelles or by hinds of the
field*] [Song 2:7]. *I adjure*—in generations of forced conversion. *By
gazelles*—who did what I desired so that I did what they desired. *Or
by hinds of the field*—those who shed their blood for me like the blood
of the gazelles and the hinds, about whom it is said, *It is for your sake
that we are slain all day long* [Ps 44:23].[30]

A person to whom God grants the privilege to rise to this high
rank, that is, that he be martyred for sanctification of the Name, even
if his sins be like those of Jeroboam ben Nebat and his associates,[31]
[God] causes such a person to inherit the world hereafter, and there is
none higher than he, even if he was not a disciple of the wise.[32]

Maimonides did not only cite models of self-sacrifice. He also referred to anecdotes about rabbinic sages who practiced prudent dissimulation, such as the account of Rabbi Meir, who was apprehended
in one of the periods of persecution when sages of Israel were killed.[33]
He also quoted a narrative in which Rabbi Eliezer the Great deceived
a Roman governor.[34]

Even before these sages, the people of Israel suffered forced conversion, as in the days of Nebuchadnezzar and the kingdom of the Greeks
(Antiochus IV Epiphanes), when they bowed to necessity and hence
survived. Yet the talmudic sages did not later condemn them, as they
were coerced and only pretended. When persecutors forced Jews to
perform commandments secretly, the sages did not call them "gentiles" or "wicked" but considered them perfectly righteous.

Maimonides clarified the legal aspects of martyrdom in the *Mishneh
Torah,* where he systematized what he had written in the *Epistle on
Forced Conversion.*

[1] When one is commanded to transgress rather than be slain and
is slain rather than transgress, that person is responsible for his own
death.[35]

[2] When one is commanded to be slain rather than transgress and is slain without transgressing, that person has sanctified the Name.

[2.1] If he sanctifies the Name in the presence of ten Israelites, he has done so in public, like Daniel, Hananyah, Mishael, and Azariah [Dan 1:11,19], and like Rabbi Aqiba and his colleagues.[36] This is the highest rank of martyrdom.[37]

[3] When one is commanded to be slain rather than transgress, and he transgresses rather than being slain, he has desecrated the Name.[38]

[3.1] If he does so in public, then he has desecrated the Name in public, has neglected an affirmative precept to sanctify the Name, and violated a negative precept not to desecrate the Name.

[4] But if the person transgresses under duress, he is not punished with lashes, and certainly is not put to death by a court, even if he committed murder under duress. One who transgresses under duress is exempt from punishment.[39]

The main question of the epistle pertained to the third category—how to categorize Jews who yielded to Islam and yet observed the commandments clandestinely. Were they to be considered as members of the community, though sinners, or as outsiders and apostates? Maimonides and his father considered them Jews despite their formal conversion to Islam. One must treat them as Jews during the period of involuntary conversion, and they should be welcomed back when they seek to return to the fold.

The general Jewish populace considered apostates as non-Jews, especially in matters of inheritance, and the Geonim had concurred in this.[40] However, there was a talmudic ruling that an apostate's betrothal is valid, and this provided a legal basis for considering apostates as Jews, however relapsed.[41]

Maimonides' intention was to ensure Jewish survival. If the forced apostates were condemned to exclusion, they and their children would be lost forever. One must not alienate those who desecrate the Sabbath, but encourage them to observe other commandments. Nor should the sinners be despised when they come to pray in secret.

The respondent's opinion that Islam was idolatrous and that an apostate removed himself from the Jewish faith and community was not unique or perverse. Others held the same view. He could argue that, in the long run, willingness to die for one's beliefs in critical times strengthens the faith, and that people who converted, however superficially, would eventually accept their newly adopted religion, and if not the converts themselves, then certainly their children. As the Spanish experience (1391 to 1492) later showed, many Jews who initially became *conversos* insincerely eventually became devout Christians sincerely.

The disagreement between the respondent and Maimonides had practical consequences for forced converts who wished to return to Judaism. The anonymous authority's legal opinion would rule out their return. There were consequences in everyday life. As long as the forced converts were observing commandments in private and not violating the Sabbath in public, Maimonides recognized them as Israelites and accepted their testimony in court, whereas the anonymous respondent did not, regarding profession of the Muslim faith as tantamount to swearing a false oath. Maimonides claimed that although a false oath is desecration of the divine Name, the Mishnah permitted one to make false vows to murderers, robbers, and predatory tax gatherers.[42]

THE OBLIGATION TO EMIGRATE

The result of Maimonides' diagnosis was his counsel (1) to accept Islam provisionally and avoid martyrdom, (2) to observe the commandments as far as possible, (3) and to depart to a place where one can live openly as a Jew. He exhorted Jews living under forced conversion to leave the place of oppression for a place where they could practice their faith openly without coercion.[43] The idea of leaving evil places where one cannot keep the commandments is a rabbinic admonition, which Maimonides combined with philosophic views. He stressed the duty to emigrate from a country whose customs are evil and whose inhabitants do not follow the right path.[44]

In the *Mishneh Torah,* at the end of his long discourse on martyrdom, he added,

[B]ut if he can save himself and flee from under the hand of the evil king and does not do so, he is like a dog returning to his vomit, and he is called a deliberate idol worshipper, and is removed from the world hereafter and goes to the lowest degree of Gehinnom.[45]

Addressing people suffering under similar conditions in Yemen, he advised them "to flee and run after the Lord, entering deserts and wastelands, and not mind separation from relatives or loss of property. For all this is a paltry trifle vis-à-vis God, King of kings, possessor of the universe."[46]

He wrote in the *Epistle on Forced Conversion* that a person should not be afraid to leave his house and children and all his property, "for religion takes precedence over incidental things that are contemptible to the enlightened. These things do not last, but the testament of God endures forever." One must not live in that situation but even endanger oneself to find religious freedom, especially when the eyes of the Muslims are upon him, limiting his autonomy. When someone is coerced to break one of the commandments, it is absolutely prohibited for him to remain in that place. Such an individual should abandon all he has and travel day and night until he finds a place where he can follow his faith. Maimonides rejected the excuse given by people coerced to break the commandments—that concern for household and children prevented them from leaving. We can understand this harsh advice in the light of his belief that if everyone continues to live in places of religious coercion, the Torah would come to an end and the people of Israel would perish.

His counsel was to live temporarily as a Muslim and then emigrate and settle in the Land of Israel. One should under no circumstances remain in the place of forced conversion. Whoever remains in such a place sins, desecrates the name of Heaven, and is virtually a willful sinner. The many Jews who claimed that they wanted to remain in Morocco as pseudo-Muslims and await the coming of the Messiah and then leave for Jerusalem he regarded as sinners who were deceiving themselves and leading others astray.

Hard times could be grasped as birth pangs heralding the coming of the Messiah. Maimonides discouraged this way of thinking, saying that there is no fixed time for the coming of the Messiah, just as his father, Rabbi Maimon, had written in his *Epistle of Consolation*. Maimonides insisted that the obligation to obey the commandments of the Torah does not depend on the coming of the Messiah. If people obey the Torah, and God gives them or their children the privilege of witnessing the messianic advent, this is a great boon. If not, they have not lost anything, but have gained by their observance. A person who cannot practice his religion but wants to remain until the Messiah comes and then go to the Land of Israel is wicked and destroys Judaism. This, he said, is his opinion, adding, "God knows the truth."[47]

THE PHYSICIAN AND HIS HEALING

Maimonides stated in the epistle that he diagnosed the condition of the Jews as an illness and treated them as a physician treats ailing patients, to relieve distress and ease misery. He collected pharmaceuticals and choice spices from the books of the ancients to prepare a therapeutic drug for their malady.

While praising martyrdom, Maimonides favored prudence and survival. He stressed that the divine commandments are to live by, not to die by.[48] Maimonides' interpretation of Leviticus 18:5 (*by the pursuit of which a man shall live*) diverged from the generally accepted exegesis. Accordingly, at a time of persecution a man should give his life for the lightest commandment, as is said, *You shall not profane my holy name, that I may be sanctified in the midst of the Israelite people* (Lev 22:32).[49]

The Talmud and Midrash related the obligation to sanctify the divine Name to the commandment to love God. Even in danger one does not transgress three commandments (idolatry, unchastity, and murder); as it says, *You shall love the Lord your God with all your heart and with all your soul and with all your might* (Deut 6:5). This means even if he takes your soul.[50]

Rabbi Ishmael, whose view on *and not die by them* Maimonides followed, did not interpret *with all your soul* as giving up one's soul for the love of God, but as loving God with all one's mind.

VIEWS OF EUROPEAN SCHOLARS

Maimonides' reasoning conformed with the opinion of Franco-German scholars before him.[51] In Europe, Rabbenu Gershom of Mayence, Me'or ha-Golah (Light of the Exile) (ca. 960–1028), arguing against the Geonim, permitted a priest (*kohen*) who had apostatized and repented to resume his priestly sanctity and privileges. Rabbenu Gershom argued that if he could not resume them, it would be as though, having sincerely repented, he was still being reminded of his prior misdeeds.[52] The great commentator Rashi (1040–1105) followed Rabbenu Gershom in his decision that "an Israelite who sinned remains an Israelite, especially the forced converts whose heart is turned to Heaven."[53] The principle that "an Israelite who sinned remains an Israelite" is not found in the Talmud. Rashi made it a fundamental principle in discussions of the religious status of forced converts in his day.

At a time when conversion to Christianity was widespread, during the period of the First Crusade, Rashi sought to preserve Judaism by encouraging repentance and by leaving the door open for those who hoped to return. The harsh opinion of the Geonim, that an apostate was no longer a Jew and could not return to the fold, would only further alienate relapsed Jews.[54] The decisions of Rabbenu Gershom and Rashi reveal that in Europe many Jews converted to Christianity out of fear, remaining Jews at heart, while others, though they converted out of conviction, later wanted to return to Judaism. Maimonides and his father took the same position as Rabbenu Gershom and Rashi, yet there is no evidence that they were aware of the opinions of their European predecessors.

Some European scholars were more exacting than Rabbenu Gershom and Rashi. A talmudic ruling held that if the act of coercion was not in public, meaning in the presence of ten men, a Jew is permitted, even obligated, to transgress, even to worship idols, and should not give up his life. The Tosafists, however, did not accept this. They held that in the case of idolatry one should be slain and not transgress even in the presence of one person.[55]

THE MASADA COMPLEX

Maimonides wanted to release Jews from their martyrdom obsession and esteem for sacrificial victims. The fall of Masada, a radiant chapter in the martyrdom repertoire, was an enduring national symbol. Masada is the fortress on top of a mesa-like precipice to the west of the Dead Sea, where 960 defenders defied the Romans, resisting for three years after 70 C.E. All hope gone, the men killed their wives and children, and thereafter committed suicide rather than fall into the hands of the Romans.[56] Readiness to sacrifice one's family and oneself against hopeless odds in order to preserve one's religious or national integrity or freedom has been called the "Masada complex."[57] The danger of transforming sacrificial narratives into national symbols is that a collective, like an individual, is liable to repeat past traumatic experiences obsessively (repetition compulsion). Post-traumatic stress leads to re-enactment, where individuals place themselves in the same situation repeatedly, compulsively re-creating the moment of trauma or an aspect of the traumatic scene in literal or disguised form, or returning to the scene, perhaps to alter the outcome.[58] They also tend to use projective identification onto others of roles essential for their reenactments. One may conceptualize repetition compulsion and projective identification as an attempt to integrate the traumatic scene into life in order to master it.

Authors of medieval narratives and *piyyutim* on martyrdom in the Rhineland in 1096 glorified the Masada martyrs, who killed their own wives and children and committed suicide, although killing and suicide are against Jewish law.[59]

Never did Maimonides face a greater predicament, when a legal question, whether to confess Islam and live or refuse and die, tormented individuals and communities throughout the Maghrib. He argued that the law permitted outward conversion to Islam in a situation of coercion, his aim being to uproot the martyrdom complex that was so deeply ingrained in Jewish consciousness. As physician and sage he grasped that the readiness to die was not natural or salutary for individuals or for the community as a whole. He knew that nature preserves the species, and to let oneself be killed opposes the natural instinct of self-preservation. He needed to administer a cure for a sick patient, who compulsively repeated situations of victimization and self-sacrifice. To those who would send men, women, and children to the executioner to fulfill the commandments, he replied, "*that you may live by them* and not die by them."

His solution of dissimulation, semblance, and a double life became an existential norm for Jews from the late medieval period, during the Inquisition and its aftermath, until the modern period. Indeed, in Europe it became the Jewish symptom par excellence. Many, of course, surrendered completely and apostatized. Others, willingly or not, were forced into martyrdom.

7

Did Maimonides Convert to Islam?

There is no compulsion in religion.
True guidance has been distinguished from error.
Those who reject false gods and believe in God
have grasped the firmest hand-hold
that will never break.
God is all hearing and all knowing.

—QUR'AN 2:256

JOSEPH BEN JUDAH IBN 'AQNIN

In his *Epistle on Forced Conversion*, Maimonides included himself among the forced converts who had to seek God's forgiveness. Joseph ben Judah Ibn 'Aqnin, who knew him in Fez, described the period of forced conversion, how he lived as a Muslim with guilt feelings as he secretly observed the commandments and studied Torah with Maimonides. In his *Commentary on Song of Songs,* on the verse [*At our doors are all choice fruits;] both freshly picked and long-stored have I kept, my beloved, for you* (Song 7:14), Ibn ʿAqnin commented:

> And her saying, *have I kept . . . for you* alludes to the generations of *forced conversion,* for we observe the commandments of the Torah while the edge of a sword is upon us, certainly this *forced conversion* of ours, *may God annul it,* when we nevertheless, as is known, engage in *study of the Torah.*
>
> A proof of our assertion is the appearance of *the great sage our Master Moses, son of his honor Rabbi Maimon,* in Fez, who is without equal in the extent of his knowledge. . . . If we could call upon him alone in the *forced conversion,* it would have been enough for us.[1]

Although Ibn ʿAqnin did not state that Maimonides was among the Jews who lived publicly as Muslims, his description of the circumstances and the clandestine study of Torah suggest that he observed commandments surreptitiously along with the others.

Elsewhere, Ibn ʿAqnin noted Maimonides' departure from Fez, citing lines of amorous verse that he wrote on the occasion:

> I recited these verses at the departure of the distinguished sign of the time (*ʿalamat al-zaman*), the defender of the law with the swords of proof, *Rabbi Moses, son of his honor, the sage Rabbi Maimon, son of Obadiah,*[2] *may the spirit of the Lord guide him* (Isa 63:14).
>
> When my bosom-companion sailed on wandering ships,
> my heart forgot its abode.
>
> How can it stir his love
> when my soul left with him as he departed?[3]

ABU ʾL ʿARAB IBN MUʿISHA

A man from Fez named Abu ʾl ʿArab ibn Muʿisha, visiting Cairo, came across Moses ben Maimon, whom he had known in Fez as a Muslim. His appearance as a Jew indicated that he had relinquished Islam, a crime punishable by death in Islamic law. There are various accounts of what actually happened, with most historians concurring that the event took place toward the end of Maimonides' life, around 1190 C.E. This brings us beyond the temporal scope of this chapter, but it is an integral part of the story of Maimonides' conversion to Islam, which may have taken place in Fez in the early 1160s. Another possibility is that, like his pupil Joseph Ibn 'Aqnin, Maimonides had converted to Islam in Andalusia before emigrating to Fez.

THE ACCOUNT OF IBN AL-QIFTI: AL-FADIL SAVES MAIMONIDES

The most important source for this episode is Ibn al-Qifti's *History of Sages*. The author was a contemporary of Maimonides and a close friend of his pupil Joseph ben Judah in Aleppo.[4]

This is literally what he wrote:

> When the order came into force, those with little property departed, while those with much property remained, being chary of family and wealth, professing Islam openly while harboring unbelief. Musa ibn Maymun was one of those who did this, remaining in his country [Morocco]. When, at that time, he feigned the distinguishing signs of Islam, he also adhered to its specific [rituals], including study of the Qur'an and prayer.
>
> Toward the end of his life, [Moses ibn Maimon] was harassed by a man from Andalusia, a jurist named Abu 'l-'Arab ibn Mu'isha, who came to Fustat, met [Maimonides], and accused him of having converted to Islam in Andalus, defaming him, intending to cause him harm [by having him executed]. 'Abd al-Rahim ibn 'Ali al-Fadil prevented this, claiming that when a man is forcibly converted to Islam, the conversion is not legitimate.[5]

Ibn Mu'isha al-Kinani, the main actor in this account, is a chimerical figure in Maimonides biographies, where his name is distorted and his identity undetermined. He was, nevertheless, a real person about whom we have reliable information.[6] Ibn Mu'isha was born in Ceuta and later resided in Fez, where he was active in enlarging the oratory of the Qarawiyyin Mosque. The work began under the Almoravid amir 'Ali ibn Yusuf in 1134 and was completed in 1143. Ibn Mu'isha was a jurist, theologian, poet, and chancery secretary. Familiarity with

Maimonides, then, was likely, as the two were of the religious and intellectual elite. Ibn Mu'isha may have met Maimonides in the mosque area and adjacent places of study. As Maimonides was presumably conducting himself as a Muslim at the time, there was no reason to reveal his true identity to Ibn Mu'isha.

A few Jewish writers on Maimonides' life, disturbed by the thought that he practiced Islam under any circumstances, reject Ibn al-Qifti's report as unfounded. S. Z. Havlin, the rabbinics scholar, gets rid of the notion that Maimonides and his family apostatized by claiming, on the basis of a review of Ibn al-Qifti by the French Orientalist R. Blachère, that Ibn al-Qifti is an unreliable author and that his text was epitomized and reworked.[7] Blachère wanted to show that Ibn al-Qifti borrowed many of his entries on ancient philosophy from Sa'id al-Andalusi's *Tabaqat al-umam* (*Classes of the Nations*). However, medieval Arabic authors often borrowed materials from their predecessors, sometimes very liberally. Apart from such citations, Ibn al-Qifti also preserved texts of great value that were lost in Greek and extant only in Arabic. Blachère did not impugn the reports that Ibn al-Qifti gave on his own, such as biographies of contemporaries. Havlin and others who reject Ibn al-Qifti on Maimonides' conversion to Islam nevertheless use him for data on Maimonides' marriage and writings and for the history of the era.

Joseph ben Judah Ibn Simon would naturally have been Ibn al-Qifti's informant, and neither one had a motive for fabricating the story.[8] In addition, Ibn al-Qifti would have had information about al-Qadi al-Fadil from his father or anyone else in al-Fadil's circle. Joseph ben Judah, Ibn al-Qifti's good friend, was also forced to feign Islam in Morocco, according to the historian.[9] Ibn al-Qifti could not have written a short time after these events that al-Qadi al-Fadil saved Maimonides from detractors unless it really happened. Nor was Ibn al-Qifti the only historian to report that Maimonides conducted himself as a Muslim when he was residing in Fez.

THE ACCOUNT OF IBN AL-'ADIM: DEATH ON THE NILE

The thirteenth-century Syrian historian Kamal al-Din Ibn al-'Adim (1192–1262) gives details lacking in Ibn al-Qifti's account. He related that Abu 'l-'Arab ibn Mu'isha, known as Ibn Mu'isha al-Kinani al-Sabti, was one of the veiled ones (namely, Almoravids).[10]

Taj al-Din Abu 'Abd al-Rahman Muhammad ibn Hashim, the *khatib* (preacher) of Aleppo, informed Ibn al-'Adim that Abu 'l-'Arab was one of the rarities of the time and consummate of excellence and knowledge. He also told Ibn al-'Adim that Abu 'l-'Arab escaped from the Maghrib by ship, and that prevailing winds brought him to Latakia (al-Ladhiqiya) on the Syrian coast.[11] Abu 'l-'Arab asked for the nearest town and was told it was Aleppo, so there he went. He may have left Fez because he was a follower of the Almoravids at a time when their enemies, the Almohads, had come into power.

In Aleppo, Abu 'l-'Arab dedicated a eulogistic poem to the ruler al-Zahir Ghazi.[12] Ibn al-'Adim reported in the name of Taj al-Din that Abu 'l-'Arab ibn Mu'isha traveled to Byzantium and then to Egypt in 585 A.N. (1189/90 C.E.), where he found the philosopher (*hakim*) "Abu Musa, the Jew."[13]

Ibn al-'Adim related further that in Fez Moses ben Maimon was declared as deserving death because of some wrongdoing. According to this version, Abu 'l-'Arab ibn Mu'isha gave him protection and helped him escape. Word of this reached the ruler of the Maghrib and he wanted to arrest Abu 'l-'Arab, but he also fled.

When Moses ben Maimon heard about Abu 'l-'Arab's visit to Cairo, Ibn al-'Adim tells, he gave a large sum of money to an assassin to do away with him. The assassin led Abu 'l-'Arab to a bank of the Nile and left him there. Then he circled back and, sneaking up from behind, struck him with a huge club. Abu 'l-'Arab fell into the Nile and died.

Ibn al-'Adim's account contains some plausible items of information. That Abu 'l-'Arab was a supporter of the Almoravids is confirmed by other sources. The panegyric poem became well known and was cited in other biographies of Abu 'l-'Arab. He could easily have heard about Maimonides during his visit to Aleppo.

In addition, we find here the strange report that Maimonides committed some capital crime in Fez and that Abu 'l-'Arab ibn Mu'isha helped him and consequently had to flee the country himself. The information that Abu 'l-'Arab was an Almoravid sympathizer explains why he would help someone who was being persecuted by the Almohads, the "rebels" who defeated his sect.

Nevertheless, the story that Abu 'l-'Arab helped Maimonides in Fez is odd and may be a competing narrative stressing the Jew's ingratitude to a benefactor to the point of having him killed. Ibn al-'Adim does not say explicitly that Maimonides converted to Islam, and he omits Abu 'l-'Arab's role in identifying him as a renegade. The narrative, therefore, does not make complete sense. Maimonides' arranging to have Abu 'l-'Arab killed could be justified by talmudic law if it is considered an act of self-defense, but it is unlikely that a Jew in his position would dare instigate the murder of a Muslim. This denouement is far less likely than the one Ibn al-Qifti gives.

THE ACCOUNT OF IBN ABI USAYBI'A

In his brief entry on Maimonides (whom he called Musa ibn Maymun) Ibn Abi Usaybi'a wrote: "It is said that the Ra'is Musa converted to Islam in the Maghrib, memorized the Qur'an, and studied jurisprudence. Then, when he came to Egypt and lived in Fustat, he apostatized."[14]

As Ibn Abi Usaybi'a worked with Abraham ben Moses at the Nasiri Hospital in Cairo, he could have received information about Abraham's father from him. He also knew Ibn al-Qifti's account and may have discussed it with Abraham, who would have been reluctant to verify the report. I suspect that Abraham discouraged Ibn Abi Usaybi'a enough to have him preface his remarks with "It is said." Ibn Abi Usaybi'a does not mention Abu 'l-'Arab ibn Mu'isha, but that omission is not significant, as his account is very brief.

THE ACCOUNT OF SHAMS AL-DIN AL-DHAHABI

Shams al-Din al-Dhahabi (b. 1274 Damascus, d. 1348), a famous traditionist and jurist,[15] wrote about ibn Mu'isha in his *History of Islam* (under the year 585 A.H. = 1189/90 C.E.).[16] Al-Dhahabi said that Abu 'l-'Arab went to Iraq and engaged in controversies on theological topics. He repeated Ibn al-'Adim's version of the events in the Maghrib and in Egypt and quoted Abu 'l-'Arab's panegyric to al-Zahir Ghazi.

THE ACCOUNTS OF SALAH AL-DIN AL-SAFADI

Salah al-Din al-Safadi (1297–1363), from Safad, went to Damascus when he was twenty, where he met Taqi al-Din Ibn Taymiyya (1263–1328) in 1317/18.[17] In his article on Abu 'l-'Arab ibn Mu'isha, he added nothing to al-Dhahabi's brief account. His book was basically a compendium of necrologies, and he gave Abu 'l-'Arab's year of death as 587 A.H. (= 1191/92 C.E.), not long after his visit to Cairo.

Another account from al-Safadi's biographical dictionary tells a more fabulous story.[18] Accordingly, on a sea voyage from Morocco eastward, Moses ben Maimon performed the *tarawih* prayers, recited on the nights of Ramadan, together with Muslim voyagers.[19] He arrived in Egypt and then traveled to Damascus, where he successfully treated the judge Muhyi 'l-Din Ibn al-Zaki.[20] Having been cured, Muhyi 'l-Din Ibn al-Zaki wanted to compensate Maimonides, but he refused. Afterward, Maimonides bought a house and asked Muhyi 'l-Din to predate the contract by five years. Seeing no harm in it, the judge agreed to the request.

Then, al-Safadi related, Moses ben Maimon went to Egypt and served al-Qadi al-Fadil. Thereafter, his fellow passengers revealed that "This man traveled with us from the Maghrib and prayed with us the *tarawih* prayers in such and such a year." Unruffled, Maimonides presented the contract and said, "I was in Damascus for a long time before that year and bought a house there, and here is the signature of the judge Muhyi 'l-Din Ibn al-Zaki." Al-Qadi al-Fadil recognized the signature of Ibn al-Zaki and saw that the contract had a legal authorization for the earlier date. And so the claim was rejected thanks to Moses ben Maimon's ingenuity.

We have no evidence that Moses ben Maimon reached Damascus, but it is possible that he did, for during his year in Acre he may have traveled to Tyre and other places in the area, including Damascus.[21] Abu 'l-'Arab ibn Mu'isha does not appear in this narrative. Instead, fellow passengers, who thought he was a Muslim, identified him in Cairo. The story about the Ramadan prayers is problematic, for Maimonides' voyage began on the Muslim date of 10 Jumada II 560 A.H. and ended on 3 Rajab 560, and so he was not on a ship during Ramadan. There are chronological problems as well, and the episode seems to be secondary and contrived.

This narrative may be an elaboration of the Ibn al-Qifti account with some dramatic flares, and it highlights Moses ben Maimon's cunning. Mordechai Akiba Friedman has suggested that the part about Maimonides' prescient cleverness is from a Jewish folk story about the great man.[22] Arabs ascribed cunning to Jews but in a negative sense, and in this case it involved fraud. Al-Qadi al-Fadil helped Moses ben Maimon in this version, but not by invoking Islamic law to save his life.

THE ACCOUNT OF SHIHAB AL-DIN AL-MAQQARI

Shihab al-Din al-Maqqari is a late source (b. ca. 1577 in Tlemcen, d. 1632 in Cairo). He was imam and mufti at the Qarawiyyin Mosque in Fez from 1613 to 1617 c.e., after which he traveled extensively and wrote picturesque descriptions of Spain.[23] Al-Maqqari has a brief entry on Abu 'l-'Arab ibn Mu'isha, but he repeated what we already know from Ibn al-'Adim.

SCENARIO OF MAIMONIDES' CONVERSION TO ISLAM

To summarize the evidence, the best witnesses are those closest to the events: Ibn 'Aqnin, who was with Moses ben Maimon in Fez; Ibn al-Qifti, who evidently received information from Joseph ben Judah; Ibn Abi Usaybi'a, who was familiar with the text of Ibn al-Qifti and knew Maimonides' son, Abraham; and Ibn al-'Adim, who had excellent archival resources at his disposal.

Let us build our scenario on the basis of reports that sound plausible.

Moses ben Maimon practiced Islam in Fez and eventually left and sailed to Acre. We do not know whether he was already a practicing Muslim when he came to Fez. Abu 'l-'Arab ibn Mu'isha, a jurist, theologian, and poet close to the Almoravids, knew Maimonides in Fez. Abu 'l-'Arab left Morocco and first visited Aleppo. Using his talents as an administrator and poet, he became close to the ruler of Aleppo, wrote a panegyric for him, and received rewards. He may have met

Joseph ben Judah, who served in the ruler's court. Abu 'l-'Arab did not head directly for Egypt. He first traveled to Baghdad, where he engaged in theological discussions. Then he went to Rum, meaning either Byzantium or Europe, probably the former. As he was not visiting holy sites (Mecca, Medinah, Jerusalem) or writing a travel book, his journies probably concerned business.

Abu 'l-'Arab finally got to Egypt in about 1190/91. Maimonides was then well established in Cairo, a protégé of al-Qadi al-Fadil. We get two denouements of the narrative: Ibn al-Qifti tells us that al-Fadil saved Moses ben Maimon, and Ibn al-'Adim relates that Moses ben Maimon had Abu 'l-'Arab killed. The first account is more likely.

OBJECTION OF DENIERS

Those who deny that Maimonides converted to Islam point out that his enemies never mentioned it. However, opponents such as Samuel ben Eli, Gaon of the Babylonian Academy, were not likely to endanger Maimonides' life and the lives of his descendants, for the penalty for leaving Islam was, as we have seen, death. Moreover, we don't really know what his enemies said about him beyond what has come down to us in documents, and they are limited in scope. What we need to keep in mind is that Maimonides' conversion to Islam was widely circulated, in both Muslim and Jewish sources.[24]

ADIEU FEZ

Moses ben Maimon and his family eventually left Fez. The Almohad caliph Abu Ya'qub Yusuf, who succeeded his father, 'Abd al-Mu'min, had been in power for two years. From the time of his accession to power in 1163, Abu Ya'qub Yusuf had pressured converts to adhere to their new religion.

Emigration had been the solution Maimonides recommended to the forced converts. Many others left at the same time, traveling to Egypt, Genoa, Sicily, Palestine, Tyre, Sidon, Damascus, and Aleppo. A major demographic shift took place as Jews from the Maghrib sought their fortune in other parts of the Mediterranean.[25]

8

The Beautiful Land

He it is who has set for you the stars,
that you may guide your course by them
amid the darkness of the land and sea.
We have made the signs clear
for those who have knowledge.

—Qur'an 6:97

Sea Voyage from Fez to Acre

Maimonides left Morocco on April 4, 1165, probably from Ceuta, the natural port of embarkation, and landed in Acre on May 16. His father and brother were with him, but we do not know who else accompanied him on the voyage. One sister, Miriam, wrote to him later when he was in Egypt, asking him to locate her errant son, but we do not know where she was at the time of this voyage.

Maimon ben Joseph and his two sons traveled to the Land of Israel to visit its sacred sites, an appropriate gesture for pious Jews who had been living as Muslims. Converting to Islam, even under duress, was sinful, and pilgrimage atoned for sins.

Traveling from one end of the Mediterranean to the other was not uprooting. Mediterranean people found in the region the same trees and plants, the same food, the same climate and seasons.[1] In the Mediterranean night sky, planets, stars, and constellations were faithful companions, as familiar to Maimonides as the streets of Córdoba. The stars glittered brilliantly, undimmed by city lights.

Travelers, merchants, scholars, pilgrims, refugees, slaves, and pirates crisscrossed the Mediterranean regularly. Some of the ships were huge and carried several hundred passengers. Usama Ibn Munqidh (1095–1188) mentioned a ship carrying four hundred pilgrims from the Maghrib to the eastern Mediterranean, and Ibn Jubayr described a Genoese ship bringing two hundred Maghribi pilgrims home from Egypt. A Genizah letter noted a ship traveling to Seville with thirty-six or thirty-seven Jews and nearly three hundred Muslims on board. Another document depicted a ship carrying four hundred people from Palermo to Alexandria.[2]

Sea voyages were arduous. Travelers had to carry their saddles, bedding, and equipment with them, for when they reached dry land they rode on mounts. They used their saddlebags to carry their gear—food, water, utensils, clothing, sleeping paraphernalia, books, writing supplies, and money—and slept on them to protect their valuables. The crew sold food and water to voyagers, but many passengers brought their own. Ships were congested and travelers lacked room to stretch out in ease.

Voyagers took merchandise with them to help defray the cost of the trip or to increase their capital, as ships often stopped at ports along the way. Captains kept ships near the coast, landing often for rest and supplies. Hugging the coastline, navigators evaded corsairs and kept their ships safer when gales raged.[3] When the sea was calm and the weather fair, and when ships were prey for land-based marauders, they sailed farther out. The threat of gales made sea voyages precarious all year round. Able to rely only on their sails, subject to the prevailing winds, ships were often washed ashore and onto shoals. A ship sailing east sometimes waited for days to catch a favorable west wind.

Direct long-distance itineraries without harbor visits were occasionally preferred for financial and seafaring reasons. Merchants wanted to prevent delay and extra expense caused by landing in harbors and paying customs. Moreover, breaking the coastal waves as the ships entered and left harbors was the time of greatest peril.[4]

Pilgrims regarded dangers on the way to holy places as part of their penance. Christian and Jewish itineraries and pilgrimage narratives emphasized the motif of hardship, and Muslims regarded suffering during the pilgrimage to Mecca, sometimes carried out at great peril, as enhancing their merit and reward.[5]

MAIMONIDES' DESCRIPTION OF THE SEA JOURNEY TO ACRE

Maimonides wrote a brief description of his sea journey from Morocco to Acre.[6] The text occurs at the end of his *Commentary on Rosh ha-Shanah,* as copied in Acre by Rabbi Samuel ben Abraham Siqilli, from the autograph copy of "our Master Moses, Light of the Exile, of blessed memory."[7] Samuel Siqilli said that the text was in Maimonides' handwriting.

> On Saturday night, 4 Iyyar [April 18], I set sail [from Morocco]. And on the Sabbath, 10 Iyyar [April 24], in the year 4925 A.M. [1165 C.E.], a great wave almost inundated us, the sea being very stormy. I took a vow that I would fast for these two days [every year] and observe them as a regular public fast, I and all my family and household. I shall command my descendants to do so until their last generation and to give charity according to their means. I vowed that I would remain in solitude on 10 Iyyar [every year] without seeing anyone, but rather worshiping and studying all day in privacy. Just as I found at sea that day only [the presence of] the Holy One, blessed be he, so I shall not see any person or sit with anyone [on that day] unless I am compelled to do so.
>
> On the eve of Sunday, 3 Sivan [May 16], I disembarked safely in Acre, and thus I was saved from apostasy. And so we arrived in the land of Israel. I took an oath that this day would be one of rejoicing and celebration and of giving gifts to the poor, I and my family, until the last generation.
>
> On Tuesday, 4 Marheshvan [October 12] [49]26 A.M. [1165 C.E.], we left Acre to go up to Jerusalem at a time of danger. I entered the

[ruins of] the great and holy temple and prayed there on Thursday, 6 Marheshvan [October 14]. On Sunday, 9 Marheshvan [October 17], I left Jerusalem for Hebron to kiss the tombs of my ancestors in the Cave [of Machpelah]. On that day I stayed in the cave and prayed, praise be to God, [in gratitude] for everything. I took an oath that these two days, namely, 6 and 9 Marheshvan, would each be a festive day for me, a day of prayer and rejoicing in God, [a day] for festivities and eating and drinking. May God assist me in everything, and help me realize [the verse], *I will pay my vows to the Lord* [Ps 116:18]. Amen. Just as I had the merit to pray in [Jerusalem] in its desolation, so shall I and all [the people of] Israel witness its consolation speedily. Amen.

On the eve of Thursday . . . and on Tuesday, 12 Sivan [May 14, 1166?], the Lord saw my misery, and my brother arrived safely.[8] I dedicated this day to charity and fasting.

Until here [Rabbi Samuel ben Siqilli] copied from the autograph by the finger[9] of the man of God,[10] our Master Moses, of blessed memory.

THE CITY OF ACRE

The voyage to the Holy Land lasted almost a month and a half, at the end of which Maimonides disembarked safely in Acre. At last he could live openly as a Jew. The family landed in Acre and remained there, visiting other places, such as Jerusalem and Hebron, and perhaps Tyre (Lebanon). Acre was a wise choice because of its position as an international port and an entrepôt for goods being transshipped from the Far East to Mediterranean ports. The family of Maimonides was evidently supporting itself by commercial trade at the time.

The intrepid Muslim traveler Ibn Jubayr has left us a vivid description of his entrance into Acre about the same time, giving us a richly textured account of what Maimonides must have experienced when he landed and went through customs. The customs house was a khan, a lodge where travelers would leave their mounts and merchandise on the ground floor. There were stables and stalls for horses, donkeys, mules, and camels. Outside the khan were watering places and shops where travelers bought what they needed. On the second floor, there were rooms for lodging in safety overnight for short periods of time. The khan was a place where travelers could sell merchandise they carried with them and obtain ready cash for their sojourn in the new place.[11]

Ibn Jubayr and his colleagues had no mounts, only the possessions they brought with them, for which they had to pay customs dues. The customs officers, who were Christians, sat on stone benches covered by carpets in front of the gate of the khan. They spoke and wrote Arabic and worked under the chief of customs, who was contracted by the government to collect dues from all arriving travelers except military personnel. Ibn Jubayr, whose imprecations against Christians enliven his book, admitted that the Christian agents treated travelers fairly and with respect. In contrast, he complained of the groping hands of Muslim customs officials in other places, thinking that Sultan Salah al-Din could not possibly know that this was happening and having a mind to inform him. This is Ibn Jubayr's description of his arrival at Acre:

> On the morning of Tuesday the tenth of the month, which was the eighteenth of September, we came to the city of Acre—may God destroy it. We were taken to the customs house, which is a khan prepared to accommodate the caravan. Before the door are stone benches, spread with carpets, where are the Christian clerks of the Customs with their ebony inkstands ornamented with gold. They write Arabic, which they also speak. Their chief is the Sahib al-Diwan [chief of customs], who holds the contract to farm the customs. He is known as al-Sahib [the chief], a title bestowed on him by reason of his office, and which they apply to all respected persons, save the soldiery, who hold office with them. All the dues collected go to the contractor for the customs, who pays a vast sum [to the government]. The merchants deposited their baggage there and lodged in the upper storey. The baggage of any who had no merchandise was also examined in case it contained concealed [and dutiable] merchandise, after which the owner was permitted to go his way and seek lodging where he could. All this was done with civility and respect, and without harshness and unfairness. We lodged beside the sea in a house we rented from a Christian woman, and prayed to God Most High to save us from all dangers and help us to security.[12]

Ibn Jubayr appended to his description what he called "a note on the city of Acre, may God exterminate [the Christians in] it and restore it [to the Muslims]." His negative reaction to the Europeans, or Franks, as he called them, went beyond hostility to their religion. Like many other Muslims, Ibn Jubayr found the Franks unclean and immoral. The transformation of Muslim places of worship into Christian shrines, the presence of so many churches, made Muslims feel as though their lands had been violated. Ibn Jubayr wrote:

> Acre is the capital of the Frankish cities in Syria, the unloading place of *ships reared aloft in the seas like mountains* [Qur'an 55:24], and a port of call for all ships. In its greatness it resembles Constantinople. It is the focus of ships and caravans, and the meeting-place of Muslim and Christian merchants from all regions. Its roads and streets are choked by the press of men, so that it is hard to put foot to ground. Unbelief and impiousness there burn fiercely, and pigs and crosses abound. It stinks and is filthy, being full of refuse and excrement. The Franks ravished it from Muslim hands in the first [last] decade of the sixth [fifth] century, and the eyes of Islam were swollen with weeping for it; it was one of its griefs. Mosques became churches and minarets bell towers, but God kept undefiled one part of the principal mosque, which remained in the hands of the Muslims as a small mosque where strangers could congregate to offer the obligatory prayers. Near its *mihrab* is the tomb of the prophet Salih—God bless and preserve him and all the prophets.[12] God protected this part [of the mosque] from desecration by the unbelievers for the benign influence of this holy tomb.

The Jewish traveler Benjamin of Tudela visited Acre in about 1170 and found two hundred Jewish families residing there and three rabbis, who served as leaders of the community—Sadoq, Japheth, and Jonah. He noted Acre's large harbor, which served "all the pilgrims who come to Jerusalem by ship."[13]

When the poet Judah al-Harizi visited Acre—"a city of dolts and God's wretchedest acre"— he found the righteous Sadoq, Head of Yeshivat Gaon Ya'aqov.[14] "Though Fate clanks his chains, Sadoq still reigns," he wrote.[15] Japheth ben Eli befriended Moses ben Maimon and his family and corresponded with him later.

Acre is one of the oldest (almost four thousand years) and most fascinating cities that have survived from the ancient world.[16] Many nations raised standards over it—Egyptians, Phoenicians, Greeks, Romans,

Byzantines, Crusaders, Mamluks, Ottoman Turks, British. Acre was conquered in 636 C.E. by the Arabs, sweeping out of the Arabian Peninsula and conquering adjacent territories, including the Byzantine province of Palestine.[17] The city remained in Muslim hands until it fell to King Baldwin I, Crusader king of Jerusalem, after a three-week siege, supported by the Genoese and Pisan fleet, on May 26, 1104. It then became part of the Latin Kingdom of Jerusalem. The Crusaders conquered Acre by force as they conquered Jerusalem and Haifa. The Jews of Acre fought alongside Muslim defenders.[18] The surrender terms of cities that resisted were much worse than those of cities that yielded without a fight, such as Ascalon and Tyre, which capitulated.

A Jewish merchant, on a ship off the coast, observed the Crusader siege of Acre and described it to his mother in a letter: "I arrived in Palestine before Acre was conquered and therefore witnessed the vicissitudes of the siege. We constantly faced danger of death, for we were near [the Crusaders] day and night, hearing their talk as they heard ours, and our bread was colored with blood."[19]

Acre as a strategically placed port city was vital to the Christian occupation of the Holy Land. The Crusaders fortified the city with walls and towers along the sea to the west and south, and separated Acre from the mainland on the east and north with a wall and moat. They constructed for the port an outer and an inner harbor and a new breakwater with a tower at its end. This is the Acre that Maimonides found when he landed in May 1165. Parts of the breakwater still exist in a dilapidated state.

Acre's port connected the Crusader kingdom with Christian Europe. The Crusader kings built their fortified palace in the northern section of Acre. In the vicinity of the harbor, the Italian maritime cities Venice, Pisa, and Genoa established their own quarters, each with a market having storehouses, shops, and family residences. Fine inns made temporary residents comfortable and gave merchants space for selling their wares. The military orders—Hospitallers, Templars, and others—lived in their own quarters. By the beginning of the thirteenth century, Acre was bursting with a population of about forty thousand.

The city's topography shaped its development. While most cities develop by outward expansion, Acre, resting on a peninsula, evolved in vertical layers. The Ottoman Turks built their city over Crusader structures, covering them with debris but ensuring their preservation. Excavations in the 1950s and 1960s revealed sections of Crusader buildings, and further excavations in the 1990s within and outside the city walls revealed still more of the medieval city that Maimonides knew.

Archeologists uncovered the main headquarters of the Order of the Hospitallers (the Knights of St. John), a large edifice of about 4,500 square meters with halls and rooms constructed around a spacious central courtyard, surrounded by walls and corner towers. South of the central courtyard is what is called the Crypt of St. John, a rectangular hall that functioned as a kitchen and dining area. In two corners of the hall the fleur-de-lys, symbol of the French monarchy, carved in stone, are still visible. North of the central courtyard is a row of long halls, known as the Knights' Halls, that were the barracks of the members of the Order of Hospitallers. To the east was a Hall of Pillars, which served as a hospital.

As Moses ben Maimon came from Fez, where the lanes were narrow, the streets of Acre must have impressed him as enormous. Along the streets were edifices with courtyards and rooms opening on the thoroughfare and used as shops. In the Templar quarter, a section of a main street leading to the harbor has been excavated for the length of two hundred meters, which visitors traverse nowadays.

The Crusader buildings in Acre were monumental, with high arches set on massive pillars built to last for many centuries. The Crusaders were not colonizers or temporary boarders but resident aliens who planned to stay forever.

The Crusades did not keep Muslims and Franks from engaging in local and international commerce, even socializing. During the Crusader period trade between Christians and Muslims continued unabated. Muslim merchants traveled from Damascus to Tyre, though Crusader territory, as Christians crossed Muslim lands, each imposing taxes on commodities of the enemy. The ordinary people and merchants did not get caught up in the battles of monarchs. When Ibn Jubayr was ready to sail home, he went to Acre in the Crusader kingdom to board a ship for Spain. This was at a time of active warfare, and Ibn Jubayr saw near Damascus the jubilant return of Saladin's army, loaded with spoils and leading many Christian prisoners. He nevertheless could travel to Christian Acre with a caravan of Muslim merchants.[20] 'Ali al-Harawi, a wandering ascetic and diplomat/spy, advised Saladin's son al-Zahir Ghazi, ruler of Aleppo, to support merchants who are "the providers of everything useful and the scouts of the world."[21] Surely al-Harawi, in his line of business, made ample use of commercial travelers.

Acre was in Maimonides' time a city with a very heterogeneous population, including European Christians (e.g., Italians, French, Byzantines), local Christians (e.g., Jacobites, Nestorians), Muslims, and Jews. Coming from the West, Maimonides had seen Islam as triumphant, its majestic mosques and madrasas glittering jewels in its crown. Suddenly he confronted a new world. The Muslims were defeated and demoralized, while Christians were brandishing their gaudy escutcheoned shields, bearing the cross everywhere. The khans and hostels were crowded with visitors from the Maghrib, Tunisia, Alexandria, Ethiopia, South Yemen, and India. It was a bustling, cacophonous city, conducive to trade and haggling, not to quiet study and reflection.

In the conflict between the Crusaders and the Muslims, Moses ben Maimon naturally favored the Muslims, as we see in a book dedication to al-Qadi al-Fadil. He shared the Muslim attitude to the Crusaders, which was a mixture of amusement and contempt. Usama Ibn Munqidh, a Syrian gentleman who served in the entourage of Saladin, left a book of memoirs containing precious material on everyday life with the Crusaders. He depicted the Franks and their customs with arrogant pride and sardonic humor. Usama found their trials by ordeal barbaric and their medicine primitive. He, along with other Muslims, could not grasp the idea that God has a son. He conveyed a reaction of Muslim culture shock:

> One of the Franks came to al-Amir Mu'in al-Din (may Allah's mercy rest upon his soul), when he was in the Dome of the Rock, and said to him, "Do you want to see God as a child?" Mu'in al-Din replied, "Yes." The Frank walked ahead of us until he showed us the picture of Mary with Christ (may peace be upon him) as an infant in her lap. He then said, "This is God as a child."[22]

Usama added, "But Allah is exalted far above what the infidels say about him!"

He and his friends reacted to Christian behavior toward women as modern Arab and Muslim visitors reacted when they came to Europe and the United States and were scandalized by the freedom women enjoyed.[23]

JEWISH ACRE

With its port, international trade, and multiethnic population, Acre was politically the second city in the Latin Kingdom after Jerusalem when Maimonides arrived sixty-one years after the Crusader conquest of the city almost to the day. Acre had the most important Jewish community at this time. It was still recovering from the destruction of the First Crusade at the beginning of the twelfth century (1104). A responsum of Maimonides from Egypt to a query sent from Acre shows that there was a rabbinic court in the city, which existed when he was there as well.[24] Jewish Acre came into its own after Maimonides' lifetime, in the thirteenth century.[25]

VISIT TO TYRE

While at Acre, it is likely that Maimonides visited Tyre (today in southern Lebanon), which is just twenty-five miles to the north. Later, in Egypt, he had an important correspondence with scholars of Tyre. The city had surrendered to the Crusaders in 1124, and the population had to choose whether to remain in the city or leave. The Muslim leadership and ulema left, but most of the population remained, and probably most of the Jewish populace as well. Benjamin of Tudela's description points to an active, thriving community. Along with Acre and Damascus, Tyre helped ransom Jewish captives from abroad without requiring help from Egyptian Jewry.

Benjamin of Tudela described Tyre as having a relatively large Jewish population of four hundred to five hundred households. He mentioned scholars, headed by Rabbi Ephraim al-Misri the judge, Rabbi Meir of Carcassonne, and Rabbi Abraham, the head of the community (*rosh ha-qahal*). Rabbi Ephraim may have been originally from Fustat.[26] Rabbi Meir of Carcasonne had evidently studied in France before immigrating to Tyre.

Ephraim corresponded with Maimonides, and his disciples contin-
ued the correspondence after Ephraim died. Two of Ephraim's pupils,
Rabbi Meir and Rabbi Hiyya, corresponded with Maimonides' pupil
Se'adyah ben Berakhya in 1201.[27]

PILGRIMAGE TO JERUSALEM

Maimonides and his family remained in the vicinity of Acre through
the summer of 1165. Then in October, father and sons, accompanied
by Japheth ben Eli, made a pilgrimage to Jerusalem, where they remained for three days. The Hebrew month of Tishre, falling around
September/October, was the customary time for pilgrimages to the
Holy City. It was the season of the autumn festivals—the New Year
on the first of Tishre, the Day of Atonement on the tenth, and the
Feast of Tabernacles from the fifteenth to the twenty-second. Moses
wrote that they traveled from Acre to Jerusalem "at a time of danger,"
probably alluding to the ongoing hostilities between the Crusaders
and Muslims after the second crusade. There were other dangers as
well—brigands along the way and the coercive tolls to traverse villages or encampments.

JERUSALEM AT THE TIME OF MAIMONIDES' VISIT

When Moses ben Maimon visited Jerusalem in 1165, it had been in
Crusader hands for about sixty-six years. Whereas under Muslim rule,
Jews were permitted to dwell in Jerusalem, Christian occupation
meant the end of a Jewish presence there.[28]

The Crusaders had massacred the Muslim and Jewish population
of Jerusalem when they conquered the city in 1099. Jews took refuge
in synagogues, but the Crusaders set them ablaze. Many Jews were
taken captive and sold into slavery.

In the decade after the Crusader conquest, Jews tried to return to
the cities of the Holy Land, except Jerusalem, where they were barred
from residing.[29] The Crusaders resumed a decree against Jewish settlement in Jerusalem by the Emperor Hadrian, reconfirmed by Constantine the Great. The Muslim conquest in 638 partly lifted it, and
then it was overlooked until the city returned to Christian sovereignty

at the time of the First Crusade in 1099.[30] Jerusalem became the capital of the Latin Kingdom, called also the Kingdom of Jerusalem or the Kingdom of David.

Several sources attest this ban on Jews in Jerusalem. Achard of Arrouaise, the prior of the new monastery on the Temple Mount, the Templum Domini, wrote in his *Tractatus super Templo Salomonis,* "The Lord who was born on Earth without a sin, was killed by them [the Jews] for our sins. Since then the Jewish nation was dispersed and it is absent from this place."[31] It was not until Saladin conquered Jerusalem in 1187 that Jews were again allowed to reside in the city.

The Tower of David, still standing, also called the Citadel, defended one of the main gates to the city, David's Gate (where today's Jaffa Gate is located), leading to David Street (the same nowadays), then to Temple Street (today's Street of the Chain), to a small bridge leading to the Beautiful Gate onto the Temple Mount, or al-Haram al-Sharif. Then, as today, you went past the market. In Maimonides' time, as today, you might turn one way and smell the pungent odor of poultry and lamb, or turn in another direction and inhale the fragrance of spices and herbs.

The people of Jerusalem, we learn from Benjamin of Tudela, were mainly European. There were also Near Eastern Christians—Syrians, Jacobites, and Copts, who lived in the northeastern section of the city adjacent to the church of Santa Maria Magdalena. Georgians from Caucasia lived around the Monastery of the Cross outside the city walls. The majority of Christians were of French descent, and French was the main language of communication, aside from official documents, which were written in Latin. There was a dyeing house in Jerusalem, for which the Jews paid a small rent annually to the king, on condition that no other dyers be allowed in Jerusalem. They thus gained a monopoly over a despised profession.

It was customary to view Jerusalem first from the Mount of Olives. If so, Maimonides entered the city by the Gate of Jehoshaphat, to Jehoshaphat Street, running east to west. He and his group would then have turned onto Spanish Street, past the Street of the Holy Sepulcher, to the Street of the Furriers, to Temple Street and then across the bridge to the Temple Mount. This way he would have avoided the crowded market on David Street.

The Christians had converted Jerusalem's mosques into churches, including the Dome of the Rock and the al-Aqsa Mosque. Those sanctuaries and other shrines lay within an area which Muslims call the Noble Sanctuary (al-Haram al-Sharif) and which Jews refer to as the Temple Mount (Har ha-Bayit). It is bound on the west by the Western (also called Wailing) Wall, sacred to Jews as a remnant of the Second Temple. The wall supports the western side of the plaza that King Herod constructed on the Temple Mount, which is now the Noble Sanctuary. Muslims regard the wall as the halting place of Buraq, the fabulous winged horse with a woman's face, upon which Muhammad made his heavenly ascent (see Sura 17:2).

MAIMONIDES' VISIT TO THE TEMPLE MOUNT

The Crusader ban on Jewish residence in Jerusalem meant that Jews could visit the Holy City only for business or prayer. Yet under the Crusaders Jewish pilgrimage to Jerusalem increased, even from afar, because of the improved roads connecting Christian countries with the Holy Land. Some of the pilgrims eventually settled there.

Maimonides described his visit to the Holy Land in his *Epistle to Yemen* and in a letter to Japheth ben Eli, the family's companion in Acre. In his *Epistle to Yemen,* he wrote, "When we departed from the West *to gaze upon the graciousness of the Lord, to frequent His temple . . .*" (Ps 27:4). In his letter to Japheth ben Eli, Maimonides recalled the pilgrimage to Jerusalem: "For I, he [David] and my father, my teacher (may the memory of the righteous be a blessing), and you—all four of us—walked together in God's house *in fear and trepidation.*[32] . . . I shall not forget our wandering together in wastelands and forests after the Lord."

Benjamin of Tudela had seen Jewish visitors worshiping at the Western (or Wailing) Wall, which borders the Temple Mount, and at the Golden Gate on the eastern side. It was difficult for Jews and Muslims, though not impossible, to get access to the Temple Mount.[33] Maimonides would most likely have prayed outside it at the Western Wall. At the time, the Church of St. Giles was located nearby. No matter where he looked, he would have seen one or more of the many churches established by the Crusaders in Jerusalem. Jews also prayed on the Mount of Olives, facing the Golden Gate.

The Crusader historian Joshua Prawer understood Maimonides' statement—"I entered the great and holy house and prayed in it"—to mean that he entered the Temple Mount and even the Dome of the Rock.[34] But there is no mention of the Dome of the Rock, and it is doubtful that he would have described it as "the great and holy house." Prawer finds that this raises numerous questions. For example, Maimonides ruled against Jews entering the holy precinct because of their ritual impurity. The sites that had a special importance were the Mount of Olives and the area surrounding the Temple Mount, including segments of walls and specific gates.[35] Maimonides' opinion was rejected by Rabbi Abraham ben David in his comment on the ruling, and the halakhic discussion continues to our own day.

Maimonides wrote that one must treat the ruined Sanctuary with reverence.

> Even though the Sanctuary today is in ruins because of our iniquities, we are obliged to revere it in the same manner as when it was standing. One should not enter save where it was permissible; nor should anyone sit down in the [site of] the Court or act irreverently while facing [the place where stood] the East Gate; for it is said: *You shall keep my Sabbaths, and reverence my sanctuary* [Lev 19:30]. Now just as we are obliged to keep the Sabbath for all time to come, so must we revere the Sanctuary for all time to come; for even though it is in ruins its sanctity endures.[36]

A Jewish visitor to Jerusalem would need a lively imagination to picture the Sanctuary in its glory. What Maimonides saw, aside from churches, monasteries, and the holy places of Christianity, were the mournful remnants of the Herodian wall. A Jewish visitor would experience a rush of powerful emotions—heartbreak over the ruins of Zion and confusion over the babble of foreign tongues and alien culture.

Maimonides prescribed the way a visitor to the holy places should behave:

> A person who beholds the ruined cities of Judea should say, *Your holy cities have become a wilderness* [Isa 64:9], and should rend his garment. If he beholds the ruins of Jerusalem, he should say, *Jerusalem*

a desolation [ibid.] and likewise rend his garment. If he beholds the ruins of the Temple, he should say, *Our holy Temple, our pride, where our fathers praised you, has been consumed by fire* [Isa 64:10], and again rend his garment.

At what point on the approach to Jerusalem is one obliged to rend his garment? When he is past Mount Scopus. Then, when he reaches the Temple, he must rend his garment again. If, however, one comes upon the Temple first, by approaching from the direction of the wilderness, he should rend his garment first for the Temple, and then enlarge the rent for Jerusalem.

The rending of the garments just referred to must in every case be done by hand, and while standing. Furthermore, one must rend every garment he is wearing, until his heart is laid bare. The rent may never be sewn up with regular stitching, but may be basted, hemmed, gathered, or sewn with a ladder-stitch.[37]

Considering how few Jews resided in Jerusalem, it is unlikely that Maimonides did not meet them. Benjamin of Tudela depicted one of the four Jews as belonging to the Mourners of Zion (Avele Zion).[38] This was a circle of ascetic recluses devoted to the study of the Torah, interpreting its inner meaning according to the numerical values of letters in Scripture. Accordingly, the worshiper sent his prayers to the appropriate heavenly powers governing the world so as to accelerate the descent of the Kingdom of Heaven. A Rabbi Abraham al-Constantini (from Constantine in North Africa), whom Benjamin met in Jerusalem around 1170, belonged to this circle.

HEBRON AND TOMB OF THE PATRIARCHS

After visiting Jerusalem, the small group traveled to Hebron, the site of the tombs of the Patriarchs at the Cave of Machpelah, sacred to Jews, Christians, and Muslims as the Tomb of Abraham. No Muslims or Jews were living there at the time, for shortly after conquering Jerusalem in 1099 the Crusaders occupied Hebron and drove out its inhabitants, converting the Tomb's mosque into a church, its synagogue into a monastery. The visit to the Tomb of Abraham left an indelible impression upon Maimonides, as the devotion of Christians and Muslims to Abraham matched in intensity the veneration by the Jews. Shortly after his visit in 1168, Hebron became a bishopric, and nineteen years later it was conquered by Saladin, who reconverted the church into a mosque.

The ancient Jewish community of Hebron and the Muslim population had agreed on arrangements concerning right of entry and prayer in the Herodian structure containing the tombs of the Patriarchs.[39] The Jewish community built a new prayer house there under the Fatimid vizier al-Afdal, which was represented as a regular domicile to the Muslim authorities, for Jews were not permitted to erect new prayer houses. Hebron thrived under the Crusaders as a place of pilgrimage for Jews, Christians, and Muslims.[40]

On Residing in the Land of Israel

Maimonides did not regard living in the Land of Israel to be a commandment obligating all Jews, as did Rabbi Moses ben Nahman, known as Nahmanides (1194–1270).[41] Nahmanides taught the significance of pilgrimage and the duty to settle in the Land of Israel as a precondition for the coming of the Messiah. The conflict between Islam and Christianity created the fresh enthusiasm among Jews for the Holy Land that we perceive in Nahmanides' gloss.[42] There was a resurgence of messianic hope and a rebirth of apocalyptic speculation. By not encouraging settlement in the Land of Israel as a religious obligation, Maimonides also differed from Judah ha-Levi.[43]

The description Maimonides gave of his custom on the eve of the Ninth of Av suggests "a deep sense of exile and suffering."[44] He mentioned dipping dry bread and salt in water, eating in solitude, and washing it down with a pitcher of water that one drinks "in sadness, desolation, and tears, like a person seated before his dead relative."

Leaving for Egypt

Although Maimonides did not make dwelling in the Land of Israel a religious obligation, he did regard it as preferable to living elsewhere. "A man should always live in the Land of Israel, even in a city whose population is in its majority pagan, and let him not live abroad even in a city whose majority of population is Jewish."[45]

After leaving Hebron, Moses ben Maimon, with his father and brother, returned to Acre, remaining in that vicinity until May 1166, when they departed for Egypt. Egypt was the center of Mediterranean commerce with a large Jewish population. However, a rabbinic prohibition forbade dwelling in the land of Egypt, and we wonder how the Great Sage could flout a precept that he codified later as a law.[46] Maimonides, as far as I know, did not try to justify his decision to settle in Egypt.[47] His statement of the law contains a rationale. If someone came to Egypt to do business, he was not guilty when he entered. When he settled there, he did in fact transgress, but not in a way that deserved punishment.

PART THREE

EGYPT
THE EARLY YEARS

9

Stranger in a Foreign Land

. . . for [Moses] said, "I have been a stranger (ger) in a foreign land."

—Ex. 2:22, cf. 18:3

I N 1166, Moses ben Maimon and his family arrived in Alexandria, where they resided briefly before settling permanently in Fustat (Old Cairo). He was twenty-eight. He had been moving from place to place for many years, and now he had come to stay in the country that would be his home for thirty-eight years. In Spain and Morocco he had to survive the militant Islam of the Almohad regime, and in the Holy Land he encountered the militant Christianity of the Crusaders. Egypt offered a more accommodating environment. His first years there were eventful and successful, as he achieved recognition by the ruling regime, but they were also years fraught with danger and tarnished by loss.

ALEXANDRIA

Situated on the Nile River delta, the city of Alexandria, founded by Alexander the Great in 332 B.C.E., is 129 miles northwest of Cairo.

The first sight ships had of Alexandria was the ancient lighthouse (*manar*) on Pharos Island, which could be seen from seventy miles out to sea. Built in the Ptolemaic era, the lighthouse was still standing in 1166, when Maimonides landed.[1] The thrill of sighting the lighthouse was mixed with fear of shipwreck on the breakers or attack by pirates. Safety was uncertain until one was ashore.

Once ashore, there was the ordeal of unloading belongings in a welter of confusion, the ravenous hands of customs officials groping and exploring everywhere. They levied taxes on ships, merchandise, and passengers. There were official procedures to endure. Non-Muslims had to prove that they had paid the poll tax in their previous residence. One might arrive in Alexandria in the morning and not have disembarked by evening.[2] After customs came a great crush of humanity as stevedores jostled to get hold of the baggage.

Alexandria was a brilliant metropolis with broad marble-columned thoroughfares, gleaming white residences, and sumptuous markets, although civic unrest in the middle of the twelfth century led to some looting and destruction. Benjamin of Tudela was impressed by its straight, wide boulevards. One could see for a mile down the avenue leading from the Gate of Rashid to the Gate by the Sea. Ibn Jubayr, visiting a few years later, wrote that he had never seen a city more beautiful or having broader streets or loftier buildings. The people of the city, he said, lived in comfort and affluence.[3] It was a market for all nations, with merchants coming from Europe, Africa, Arabia, and India. Alexandria imported spices, slaves, and silk and produced textiles. Indian merchants sold their wares to Christians, who shipped to Mediterranean and European ports.

The city was teeming with foreign residents, most from the Mediterranean region.[4] Alexandria had a large Maghribi population that expanded after the Fatimid conquest (969). Indeed, most of its Jewish inhabitants were Maghribi immigrants. From the eleventh century on, there was a striking migration of Maghribis, mainly Tunisians, to Egypt. This torrent increased after 1148, when the Normans of Sicily under Roger II conquered Tunisia and later when the Almohads conquered Northwest Africa.[5] The number of Jews living in Alexandria at the time may be put at about seven to eight hundred.[6]

In spite of its importance for international trade, Alexandria remained in the Fatimid period commercially subordinate to Fustat, the town that was to become Maimonides' home.[7] The urban center of Cairo/Fustat, connected to Alexandria by the Nile, was the seat of government, a great religious center, and a focal point of culture and learning. Cairo/Fustat rather than Alexandria was the hub of commerce, even though Alexandria was the port through which most commodities traveled.

FUSTAT

Passengers arriving by boat on the Nile disembarked at the quay of Fustat near the ancient Roman Fortress of Babylon, called the Quarter of the Romans (Qasr al-Rum) or Quarter of the Candle (Qasr al-Sham'). It was the earliest settlement in the region that was to become Cairo about 330 years later. The Arab-Muslim conquest of Egypt occurred more than five hundred years before Maimonides' arrival, yet Qasr al-Rum still had a considerable Christian population.

Fustat had been founded as an armed camp by the Arab-Muslim conquerors in 643 on the east bank of the Nile adjacent to Babylon. It was ideally located right below the area where the river branches into the Delta.

In its prime, Fustat was one of the most prosperous cities in the entire Muslim world. It was a principal harbor for Nile traffic to Upper Egypt and a main entrepôt along the trade routes between the Mediterranean and the Far East. It was also a thriving industrial center for ceramics, glass and glassware, steel, copper, soap, paper, sugar, and textiles.

THE MAMSUSA QUARTER, MAIMONIDES' RESIDENCE

Maimonides and his family resided in the Mamsusa Quarter of Fustat, in the Tujib district, bordering on the Roman Fortress, or Qasr al-Rum. Mamsusa had expensive and luxurious residences and a commercial area surrounded by ample open space. In 1139, a Jewish resident sold to a partner one-half of a house worth six hundred dinars, an extraordinary price for the time. Mamsusa had many Christian residents and some Muslims living alongside Jews.[8]

The population of Qasr al-Rum consisted mostly of Copts and Melkite Christians. The numerous churches and monasteries required a substantial clergy. Many men in the quarter belonged to the bureaucratic class and served in government offices. The Fortress was not a single administrative unit. Each of its communities—Coptic, Jacobite, Greek Orthodox, and Jewish—had its own independent jurisdiction, as was common in Islamic cities.

Aside from religious buildings, the quarter had regular housing and luxurious residences for the upper class and wealthy clergy.[9] The presence of this Christian enclave in a Muslim city was quite remarkable. Its walls, bastions, churches, and monasteries towered over the buildings in Fustat, a conspicuous reminder of Christian glories of the pre-Islamic past. There were about twenty churches within an area of one square mile, and a number of them have survived until today, the most impressive being the Mu'allaqa (Hanging) Church near the Coptic Museum. We usually envisage Maimonides living in a Muslim milieu, yet during the some forty years that he resided in Fustat he was also in constant contact with Christians, and they outnumbered Muslims in his neighborhood.

THE JEWISH COMMUNITY OF FUSTAT

Fustat had a Rabbanite Jewish community numbering some thirty-six hundred souls. There were also Karaite Jews, putting the total Jewish population in Cairo/Fustat at around four thousand. Eli Ashtor, a historian of Egypt and the Near East, estimated the total Jewish population of Egypt in the late twelfth century at around ten to twelve thousand persons.[10]

Three Jewish communities existed in Fustat, each with its own synagogue. The sectarian Karaites, the more affluent members of Jewish society, had their synagogue. Two Rabbanite communities were organized around their places of worship—the Synagogue of the Iraqians (Babylonians) and the Synagogue of the Palestinians.[11] The two main Rabbanite synagogues were located within the walls of Qasr al-Rum on the same street and not far from the Karaite synagogue. The synagogues were in an area crowded with churches and monasteries. It was a short walk from Maimonides' home to the Rabbanite synagogues and to the Karaite synagogue nearby.

The Synagogue of the Iraqians supported the academies in Iraq, followed their ritual, and came under the authority of their Gaonate. The Synagogue of the Palestinians adhered to the Palestinian rite and supported the Academy of the Palestinians. These two Rabbanite synagogues had different ritual customs and legal practices. The Synagogue of the Palestinians, for instance, followed a triennial cycle of Torah reading, whereas the Iraqians read the Scroll of the Five Books of Moses in one year.

Aside from being a place of worship, the synagogue was the site of the rabbinic court and the place where administrators supervised communal charities and social services.[12] The Synagogue of the Palestinians controlled matters of official authority in Egypt and was institutionally under the jurisdiction of the Jewish centers of learning of Syro-Palestine. By Maimonides' time, the Academy of the Palestinians had relocated to Cairo along with many of its scholars.

Maimonides followed the Iraqian rite and would have worshiped in their synagogue, except that they too added *piyyutim* to the blessings, to which he objected. When he achieved authority in Egypt, he sought to eliminate the special customs of the Synagogue of the Palestinians, but opposition was staunch and he failed in his efforts. Abraham ben Moses eventually accomplished this and was proud of doing so.[13]

For the most part, it appears that Maimonides did not attend either of the synagogues on a regular basis but rather attended prayer services in academies (bate midrashot) with other scholars who did not approve of certain synagogue customs.[14]

THE CAIRO GENIZAH

The Synagogue of the Palestinians, now called the Ben Ezra Synagogue, is where most of the Cairo Genizah papers were found. It still stands, refurbished and gleaming. Built in the ninth or tenth century C.E., it underwent reconstruction from 1039 to 1041. The Genizah was in a lumber loft on the upper balcony, reserved for women during prayer services.[15]

The Genizah owes its existence to the old Jewish custom of storing away worn books and manuscripts containing the divine name to prevent its desecration. Cairo/Fustat was the crossroad for much of the mail coming from the East and West and within the Mediterranean world, and letters were often copied there before being sent on their way. The Genizah therefore preserves many documents from Iraq, Syro-Palestine, Sicily, Spain, and North Africa.

The majority of documents (letters, contracts, business accounts, and court records, around ten thousand items) are from the tenth to the thirteenth centuries, during the Fatimid and Ayyubid periods, precisely the era that concerns us. Most of the documents are written in Judeo-Arabic, a Middle Arabic dialect written, for the most part, in Hebrew letters. The Genizah contains many discarded manuscripts of biblical and talmudic writings and classics from the medieval period.

The Geonic Period and early Middle Ages were the formative period of Judaism, when the talmudic and midrashic literature was edited, versions of the prayer book put in order, legal works composed, and responsa written. The Cairo Genizah is far more significant for understanding Judaism and Jewish history than the famous Dead Sea Scrolls.[16]

Consider how extraordinary it was for Maimonides' documents, letters, and works to have been preserved in a synagogue a short walk from his house. Many of his letters and responsa are in his own handwriting. They were preserved and copies were sent to addressees. Aside from letters, responsa, and legal documents, autograph manuscripts survive of parts of his major works—*Precepts of the Jerusalem Talmud, Commentary on the Mishnah, Mishneh Torah,* and *Guide of the Perplexed*. These manuscripts are precious, for his corrections and revisions reveal his thought processes.

Although Solomon Schechter is celebrated as the scholar who discovered the Genizah, he was preceded by others. Two learned book collectors, Jacob Saphir (1832–1886) and Abraham Firkovich (1787–1874), visited the synagogue in the middle of the nineteenth century. Firkovich was studying Jewish history with a special interest in the Karaites, as he was a Karaite himself. He had studied manuscripts in the Cairo Karaite synagogue in 1862 and then turned to the Ben Ezra

Synagogue and obtained documents that interested him. He sold many manuscripts to the Russian Imperial Public Library in St. Petersburg (the First Firkovich Collection). After he died, the same library purchased manuscript fragments originating in the Ben Ezra Synagogue, the Karaite Genizah, and others, and these became the Second Firkovich Collection. They remained virtually closed off to scholars during the Soviet period.

In the early 1890s, the Ben Ezra Synagogue was renovated, and manuscripts from the loft were spread out in the courtyard. It was then that they began to seep out to booksellers and eventually to libraries in Europe: the Bodleian Library at Oxford, the Cambridge University Library, the David Kaufmann Collection in the library of the Hungarian Academy of Sciences, the Archimandrite Antonin Collection in St. Petersburg, Russia, and the Elkanan Nathan Adler Collection at Jewish Theological Seminary in New York.

In 1896, two Scottish ladies, Agnes Smith Lewis and Margaret Dunlop Gibson—twin sisters, both widowed, with keen scholarly interests—traveled to Egypt and acquired from an antiquarian some fragments that came from the Genizah synagogue.[17]

On May 13, 1896, back in England, Agnes Lewis chanced upon Dr. Solomon Schechter, reader in Talmud at Cambridge, on King's Parade, and told him that she and her sister had a number of fragments at their home for his inspection.[18] He went immediately and pored over the fragments.

Dr. Schechter, a scholarly rabbi who had immigrated from Romania, was a handsome red-bearded gentleman who was attractive to women, an advantage that may have been lost on him. In any case, his imposing figure and charm helped him in achieving some of his scholarly objectives.[19]

An hour after leaving their home, Dr. Schechter sent a telegram to the sisters: "Fragment very important; come to me this afternoon." Then he wrote a letter, declaring that "the fragment I took with me represents a piece of the original Hebrew of Ecclesiasticus." He signed it, "In haste and great excitement."[20] He must have been, because he set a meeting for 11:00 P.M. the next day, intending, of course, 11:00 A.M., a more decent hour for a rabbi to visit Victorian ladies. Schechter had been working on Ecclesiasticus, or the *Book of Wisdom* of Ben Sira

(Sirach). It was translated from Hebrew into Greek in ancient times and became part of the Christian biblical canon. But the Hebrew original was considered lost, and only snippets of it were cited in the Talmud.[21]

Schechter traveled to Egypt to search for the site of the manuscript, which he found to be the Ben Ezra Synagogue. In the spring of 1896, he brought to Cambridge boxes with the contents of the Genizah room, which became the Dr. Solomon Schechter and Dr. Charles Taylor Genizah Collection, known nowadays as the Taylor-Schechter Collection (T-S).[22] The Cambridge University Library has more than 140,000 of the total 250,000 Genizah papers. It is amazing that amidst the dust of centuries, working in semidarkness, Dr. Schechter was able to identify as much as he did. For example, he had already taken note of documents pertaining to trade between Egypt and India in correspondence between a wealthy trader and his agents in Malabar.[23]

Today, the synagogue stands in renewed splendor; the storeroom is still there, though now forlorn, emptied of its treasures.

THE FATIMID DYNASTY

Maimonides continued to live amidst drama and excitement. Major events erupted around him. Soon after he arrived in Egypt a fundamental regime change occurred that altered the course of Egyptian history permanently. After two centuries of rule by the Fatimids, a Shi'i dynasty, the Ayyubids, who were Sunnis, replaced them. The twilight years of the Fatimids, which Maimonides lived through, were marred by chaos and upheaval, with regents or viziers replacing young and weak caliphs, the last two being five and nine, respectively, when they ascended the throne. Struggles for the office of vizier further undermined the tottering dynasty that became prey to outside forces—Sultan Nur al-Din of Syria and King Amalric I of the Latin Kingdom of Jerusalem—who pounced upon a supine Egypt like ravenous lions.

ORIGINS OF THE FATIMIDS

The Fatimids had emerged in North Africa, where the founder of the dynasty, 'Abdallah ('Ubaydallah) (r. 909–34) claimed to be of 'Alid descent and to be the Mahdi (Rightly Guided One), a title of messianic significance.[24]

In 969, the Fatimid caliph Mu'izz's general Jawhar, a former slave, conquered Egypt and founded Cairo.[25] It would become the political and administrative heart of the Fatimid dynasty.[26] In 970, Jawhar laid the foundation of the Mosque of Cairo, later called al-Azhar, which became Cairo's religious center for worship and instruction when it was completed two years later.[27] When Maimonides came to Cairo, al-Azhar was a place of instruction in Isma'ili doctrine and law.[28]

The Fatimids claimed 'Alid ancestry and took their name from Fatima, daughter of Muhammad and wife of the fourth caliph, 'Ali, who was Muhammad's cousin as well. The enemies of the Fatimids maintained, however, that 'Ubaydallah al-Mahdi was really a descendant of a rebel sectarian leader ('Abdallah ibn Maymun al-Qaddah) and that he fabricated his name, trumped up an 'Alid descent, and pretended to be the Mahdi when he became leader of the movement in North Africa. Some of their enemies even accused the Fatimids of being of Jewish origin. To be accused of Jewish antecedents was, however, a common form of calumny in medieval Islam.

FATIMID ISMA'ILISM

The Fatimids adhered to Isma'ilism, a Shi'i sect with a religious and philosophical teaching and a political and social agenda.[29] The Isma'ilis anticipated the advent of a Mahdi descended from Muhammad through the union of his cousin 'Ali and his daughter Fatima. The line of the Imamate went through the seventh Imam, Isma'il, after whom the Isma'iliyya were named. At that juncture they broke away from the Imami, or Twelver, Shi'is—those who carried the Imamate down to the twelfth Imam. The Shi'is in Iran and Lebanon today belong to the latter group.

Isma'ili ideology began with a Neoplatonic conception of God as beyond being, as incapable of being categorized or classified or as sharing any quality with anything else. The Isma'ilis believed that a series of prophets appeared to mankind, each founding a new religion. They called these prophets "speakers" (*nutaqa'*, sing. *natiq*).[30] Adam, Noah,

Abraham, Moses, Jesus, and Muhammad were the six speakers who
had appeared in the past. The seventh and last, the Mahdi, or Qa'im
(the One Who Arises), will bring an end to history by revealing the
deep meaning (*batin*) of Islam.[31] The Imams, successors of the prophets, taught the esoteric, philosophic interpretation (*ta'wil*) of divine
revelation. Isma'ilis considered philosophy to be the esoteric aspect of
religion, derived from a figurative interpretation (*ta'wil*) of Scripture.
Philosophy is wisdom coming from the Imam's instruction, enabling
the human intellect to attain divine knowledge.

The Fatimid idea that the inner meaning of revelation was philosophic opened the door to the study of philosophy and the sciences, and
an ethos of untrammeled inquiry and unrestricted scientific thought
lured intellectuals to the Fatimid court. The life of the intellect was accessible to all religious groups, and scientists could exercise their powers
freely and contribute to the advancement of knowledge. The Fatimid
caliphs encouraged literary activity, wrote poetry, and sponsored the
decorative arts. Under their rule Cairo became a resplendent cultural
metropolis rivaling Baghdad to the east and Córdoba to the west.

An institution called the House of Knowledge (Dar al-'Ilm) was
founded by the Fatimid caliph al-Hakim (r. 996–1021) in 1005, devoted to the ancient sciences and secular subjects.[32] Books from palace
libraries were transferred to the institute, where people could read
and copy.[33] Lectures were given not only by Qur'an readers, grammarians, and philologists but also by astronomers and physicians, logicians and mathematicians.

The Dar al-'Ilm was destroyed in riots that took place in 1068, when
disgruntled soldiers and officials plundered caliphal palaces, treasur-
ies, and libraries. The caliphal library was reassembled in a room of
the Fatimid (Western) Palace, the Qasr 'Atiq. It was a sumptuous collection that contained thousands of books on jurisprudence, grammar
and philology, traditions, history and biographies of rulers, astronomy
and alchemy, as well as Qur'an manuscripts.

ISMA'ILI MISSIONARIES

Isma'ilism was a revolutionary movement opposed to the authority
of the 'Abbasid caliphate, the central political and religious symbol of

Sunni Muslims, ruling from Baghdad (750–1258). When the Fatimid dynasty established itself in Egypt, it claimed to supersede the 'Abbasid caliphate, and dispatched missionaries to disseminate Isma'ili teachings to embrace the whole Muslim world in a single universal empire. The Isma'ilis also sent missionaries to other religious communities to convert them to Isma'ilism. Missionaries accompanying merchants brought the Isma'ili message to Yemen and India, where it has maintained a presence until today. When the Isma'ilis were a minority they concealed their true identity and practiced *taqiyya* (dissimulation), as did the Twelver/Imami Shi'is.

The Assassins were also Isma'ilis, of the Nizari branch, but their tactics of missionizing were different from the tactics of the main Isma'ili branch, and included assassination of important political figures.

FATIMID RULE

The Fatimids were relatively liberal rulers, and Moses ben Maimon benefited from the reasonably open atmosphere of Fatimid Egypt. Believing that a single truth was at the core of the different religions, the Fatimids tended to be tolerant of others. As rulers of Egypt, they encouraged their own Isma'ili rite, but they did not impose it upon the Sunni majority and even appointed Sunnis as judges. In public, however, Shi'i festivals were celebrated and Shi'i rituals were observed.

They wisely exploited the talents of Christians and Jews in administration and in science and medicine. The historian 'Ali ibn 'Uthman al-Makhzumi (1118–1189) wrote in his fiscal treatise that bureaucrats in the Ministry of War (Diwan al-Harb) were mostly Jews, while taxation officials were Christian Copts, commenting: "As Christians and Jews were unable to share rule with the Muslims, they shared with them in the general running of affairs, providing tax clerks, army clerks and doctors. I can only think that this is an affliction sent by Almighty God to test the Muslims."[34]

In the Fatimid empire, the rules for the wearing of distinctive badges by non-Muslims were evidently relaxed.[35] No public statements restricting attire appear in codes of behavior. The elites adorned themselves to their own tastes, the most fashionable color mentioned in the Genizah papers being the Fatimid color white. Evidence from Genizah documents indicates that in the Fatimid period it was hard to tell Jews, Christians, and Muslims apart in the streets.[36]

As Maimonides moved about in the streets and markets of Cairo, he came in contact with Maghribis, Berbers, Sudanese, Bedouin, Syrians, and even Europeans doing business in Egypt, in a cosmopolitan and multicultural atmosphere.

MAIMONIDES AND ISMAʻILISM

There is a striking affinity between Maimonides' philosophic theology and Ismaʻili and Neoplatonic doctrines.[37] There was, to begin with, the Ismaʻili use of prudent dissimulation and Maimonides' practice of discretion and concealment. The core of Ismaʻili teaching was the distinction between the exoteric (*zahir*) and esoteric (*batin*) aspects of sacred texts and ritual practices and generous employment of allegory, metaphor, and parable. The polarity of exoteric and esoteric was pervasive in that era, but it was so characteristic of the Ismaʻilis that they were called the Batiniyya (Esotericist) sect.[38]

The extreme formulation of an apophatic theology found in Maimonides was apparently influenced by Neoplatonic writings.[39] An apophatic theology is a negative theology, which assumes that God is unknowable and ineffable (inexpressible), meaning that God cannot be described in human language. God is unique and incomparable, and therefore cannot be categorized or classified or share a quality with any other existent being. For instance, one should not say that God exists in the usual sense of the term; all we can say is that God is not nonexistent. We should not say that God is wise, but we can say that God is not ignorant. We attempt to express knowledge of God by describing what God is not, rather than by describing what God is.

Maimonides' theological vocabulary is close in places to the terminology of the Ismaʻili missionary and philosopher Hamid al-Din al-Kirmani (d. 1091). Maimonides' statement that by a series of negations we achieve positive knowledge about something resembles al-Kirmani's "affirmation by means of negation."[40] True worship, Maimonides said, means the negation of all attributes ascribed to God, who is wholly other and transcendent—the unknowable mystery.

It is possible that a text of the Isma'ili initiatory instruction (*ta'lim*) may have been the source of an illustration Maimonides used pertaining to pedagogy. The missionary instructor (*da'i*) would say to neophytes: "For you are beginners, and a beginner is like an infant. You start by feeding him milk, and only later give him more nourishing food." The meaning was that most human beings are at an elementary level of philosophic understanding and must be brought to enlightenment gradually by first feeding them digestible accounts in the form of myth and allegory. Maimonides uses the very same example.[41]

Yet Maimonides disapproved of Isma'ili doctrine when he criticized people who interpret miracles figuratively (by *ta'wil*), as did the Islamic esotericists (*ahl al-batin*), that is, the Isma'ilis.[42] His disapproval may have been qualified, however, for he used the term *ta'wil* in the same context to describe his *own* hermeneutic system.[43] The difference was that he insisted on retaining the surface meaning of the texts as well.

Al-Farabi, a Muslim philosopher whom Maimonides esteemed, had Isma'ili leanings and influenced Isma'ili missionaries and philosophers. He may have intended his Platonic plan for the ideal state to serve Isma'ili missionaries as a model for their political objective. In describing the Imams of the state, al-Farabi used a typically Shi'i expression—"the pure Imams, who are the kings in true reality."[44] Also, similarities between Al-Farabi's prophetology and Isma'ili doctrines suggest that al-Farabi was inspired by Isma'ili ideas.[45] Al-Farabi believed there to be a common core of truth behind prophetic utterances.

Maimonides' familiarity with Neoplatonic and Isma'ili texts need not have begun with his stay in Fatimid Egypt. When the Fatimids were in Tunisia, their doctrine was disseminated throughout Andalusia and North Africa; hence he may have been acquainted with some of this literature when in Spain and North Africa. Isma'ili and Neoplatonic works, such as the *Epistles of the Sincere Brethren* and the Arabic Plotinus Corpus, were imported into Andalusia by Muhammad ibn 'Abdallah Ibn Masarra, Maslamah ibn Ahmad al-Majriti, and others.[46] Andalusia was, moreover, the abode of Jewish Neoplatonists such as Solomon Ibn Gabirol and Abraham Ibn Ezra.[47]

JEWISH ISMAʿILISM

Ismaʿilism taught the harmony of different religious doctrines and a single truth underlying all of them. It embodied Jewish and Judeo-Christian motifs, making it familiar and appealing to Jews and Christians. When proselytizing among Jews, Ismaʿili missionaries applied esoteric exegesis to the Hebrew Bible, Jewish ceremonial laws, prophecy, and messianic doctrines. Ismaʿili missionizing created a surge of Jewish converts in the second half of the tenth century, the halcyon days of the Fatimid empire. There were practical incentives for conversion. It was possible for a Jew who converted to Islam to attain a high government post in the Fatimid state, even the office of vizier.[48] Some Jews converted to Ismaʿili Islam proper, whereas others, embracing its main doctrines, espoused an Ismaʿili variation of Judaism.

Jewish Ismaʿilism was, however, a bridge to apostasy; Ismaʿili teachings regarded religious differences as negligible, leading to a type of religious relativism. Ismaʿilism was attractive to Maimonides, yet he must have viewed it as an enticement that would cause Jewish intellectuals to abandon their ancestral faith and embrace a universalistic model of Islam.

FATIMID CONTRIBUTION

The Fatimids made a lasting contribution to Islamic civilization by founding the city of Cairo, establishing the al-Azhar Mosque and the Academy of Science, and stimulating intellectual curiosity and scientific research. Even today, Ismaʿilism teaches Islam as a reflective, spiritual faith that espouses human dignity, teaches compassion and tolerance, and respects an individual's search for understanding.

Under the Fatimids, Egypt enjoyed economic prosperity despite the usual disasters of famine and urban unrest. The economy flourished with the guiding hand of an efficient state bureaucracy. When the Nile overflowed its banks, the wheat and grain harvest supplied surpluses for export. Flax was extensively cultivated and was the main agricultural export. Domestic and international trade thrived, and Jewish merchants, unhampered by discriminatory tariffs, played a vital role in commerce. From early treaties made with Italian mercantile states, Fatimid Egypt became a Mediterranean power with commercial ties throughout the Mediterranean basin, including Italy—Amalfi, Pisa, Genoa, and Venice—Sicily, North Africa, Spain, and Constantinople.

Along with Mediterranean commerce, the Fatimids restored the ancient commercial ties between Egypt and the Far East through the Red Sea.[49] Egypt was favorably located at the junction of international trade routes with access to both the Mediterranean Sea and the Indian Ocean. The Fatimids extended their control down the African and Arabian shores and established a major port at 'Aydhab on the Sudanese coast, which competed successfully with Siraf and Basra in the Persian Gulf. Fatimid agents were dispatched along the trade routes, and in Sind (today's Pakistan) and Hind (India) merchants and Isma'ili missionaries went hand in hand.

INDIA AND FAR EASTERN TRADE

The India and Far Eastern trade was the basis of international commerce in the medieval period in general and in the Islamic world in particular. The lands of Islam were a bridge between the Far East and Europe. Half of the merchandise traded in Mediterranean markets was brought from India and the Far East.[50] Europe imported spices, perfumes, pharmaceuticals, dye stuffs, and textiles and exported metals (copper, lead, tin), chemicals, and finished products. As a result of the India trade, the countries surrounding the Mediterranean (Spain and southern Europe, Sicily, North Africa, Egypt and Syria, and Anatolia) became united through commercial ties.

The India trade was the solid foundation of Egypt's prosperity during Maimonides' lifetime, with Cairo and Alexandria the main commercial conduits. International commerce created prosperous merchants and a mercantile society with a large and active middle class avid for culture and learning. This medieval globalization helped make Islamic civilization cosmopolitan and urbane. Moreover, an ethos of friendly collaboration existed among Christian, Hindu, Muslim, and Jewish traders and between the merchants and their bondservants who acted as their business agents and representatives.[51]

The Learned Merchant as Ideal Type

Arabic-speaking Jewish traders in the Mediterranean area generally carried on their business in the territory of Islam and traded with India and the Far East, as well as with Christian Europe, including the Byzantine Empire.[52] Many of these traders were highly educated. The learned merchant became an ideal type, acclaimed in Jewish communities as someone who combined religious erudition and cultural refinement with business acumen and integrity. These men were heroic in their entrepreneurship and their willingness to take enormous risks with their lives and their fortunes.

Maimonides' Life Under the Fatimids

Refusal to Serve as Physician to the Crusader King

We are fortunate to have information on Maimonides' life during his first five years in Egypt from the pen of the reliable Ibn al-Qifti.[53] Moses ben Maimon came to the attention of the ruling Fatimid dynasty shortly after he settled in Fustat, becoming a protégé of the talented administrator al-Qadi al-Fadil, who was then serving Caliph al-'Adid (r. 1160–71) and his vizier Shawar.[54] As we have seen, Maimonides had studied medicine in the West, perhaps in Spain and certainly in Fez. He was famous enough as a physician to be recommended by the Fatimids to attend to the king of the Crusaders.

Ibn al-Qifti wrote:

> They [members of the ruling dynasty] wanted to employ [Musa ibn Maymun] along with other physicians and to send him to the king of the Franks in Ascalon. For [the king] had requested that [the Egyptians] send him a physician. They chose [Musa ibn Maymun], but he adamantly refused [to perform] this service or to go along with this arrangement.[55]

As the incident occurred between 1165 and 1171, the Frankish king was probably Amalric I.[56] Why should the Fatimids send a physician to their enemies? I suggest that the event took place when the Fatimid vizier Shawar aligned forces with King Amalric. The Crusader king, then in Ascalon, apparently asked Shawar and the Egyptians to send him a physician. They turned to several, among them Musa ibn Maymun, who probably came to their attention because al-Qadi al-Fadil was then in Shawar's entourage. Maimonides prudently declined. Shawar's alliance with Amalric was built on shifting sands, and shift they did.

Moses ben Maimon's reluctance to treat the Christian monarch was wise. Had the Jewish doctor agreed to heal the Crusader king as a service to the Fatimids, who thereafter so quickly fell from power, it might have harmed his career, and the Ayyubids may have held it against him when they replaced the Fatimids in 1171.

An oft-repeated account of this same event in biographies of Maimonides relates that he was summoned to Ascalon to serve as physician to Richard I, the Lionhearted, but declined the invitation. Yellin and Abrahams, in their popular biography, say that it was because he preferred Cairo to the prospect of London. "He was well content with his position under the Vizir Alfadhel [al-Fadil], and if he was acquainted with the events which had occurred at Richard's coronation, he must have felt safer in Cairo than in London."[57]

The only data we have are from what Ibn al-Qifti wrote, and he did not name the Crusader king. That he was Richard the Lionhearted is a pure guess. However, Richard the Lionhearted was not in the Holy Land at that time. He came to Palestine in June 1191 as a leader of the Third Crusade, twenty years after the Fatimid demise.

Maimonides as Teacher of Sciences and Commercial Trader

Ibn al-Qifti also reported that during the last days of the Fatimids, Maimonides (whom he referred to as Musa ibn Maymun) taught "the [elite] people" the ancient sciences; that is, the sciences derived from the Greeks, such as mathematics, logic, and astronomy.[58] The Muslim historian recounted further that Musa ibn Maymun engaged in commerce in precious gems and the like. The family may have already traded in jewelry in Spain and Morocco, for travelers liked to deal in small articles that were valuable and portable. Precious stones were also important commodities for physicians, as they were used in medical practice.[59]

In his *Commentary on the Mishnah,* Maimonides explained how people smuggled pearls inside a stick hollowed at its end for hiding the gems from customs.[60] He explained elsewhere that if the customs officer was appointed by the sovereign, it was prohibited to smuggle because of the rule that the law of the sovereignty is the law (*dina de-malkhuta dina*).[61] However, when the customs officer is permitted to take as much as he wants or adds to what the sovereign permitted, then the situation is different.

Most precious gems were brought from India and the Far East.[62] Jewelers occasionally supplied royalty—for example, Abu Sa'd al-Tustari, a wealthy Jewish dealer in gems, who was an intimate companion of the Fatimid caliph al-Mustansir. The royal house had confidence in Abu Sa'd as a buyer of precious gemstones. Jewish dealers in valuable gems appear in the Genizah papers and in Arabic literature.

Aside from precious gems, Maimonides probably dealt in pharmaceuticals. Al-Qadi al-Fadil once asked him to procure pharmaceuticals that were not available in Egypt.[63] Jews were prominently represented in the pharmaceutical industry.

We learn from a letter he wrote in 1191 to Joseph ben Judah that he was then engaged in the India trade.[64] "When Ibn al-Mashshat [al-Amshati] comes back from India, I shall make account with him, as you have requested."

It was not unusual for physicians, such as Maimonides, to engage in commerce. Successful physicians had extensive contacts with members of the merchant class. Those who were affluent had capital to invest, and they had a professional interest in precious and semiprecious stones, gold, spices, pharmaceuticals, perfumes, paper, and books. The illustrious poet-philosopher Judah ha-Levi , also a physician, had close contacts with merchants, engaged in trade, and became very wealthy as a result.

MAIMONIDES' VIEWS ON SCHOLARS AND LIVELIHOOD

Maimonides had to earn a living because he firmly disapproved of using religious office or teaching sacred texts as a livelihood, a common practice at the time, when people were routinely compensated for religious services. Public funds from donations, charitable foundations, and contributions by community members were used to pay Heads of Academies, community leaders, judges, scholars, preachers, and cantors.

His idealistic position was unpopular and even opposed to the practice of his Andalusian colleagues. Samuel ha-Nagid had supported scholars who regarded religious study as a vocation. A full-time scholar was one who made "his Torah his profession" (*torato umanuto*). Maimonides defined someone whose Torah was his profession as a person who does no work at all.[65]

He invoked an unimpeachable precedent for his claim that study must be accompanied by labor. The talmudic sages, he said, did not seek money from people or raise funds for their academies and for their Exilarchs, judges, or teachers of Torah. They maintained themselves from ordinary employment.[66] The sages were hewers of wood and drawers of water, and some were even blind, but they devoted themselves to the study of Torah without remuneration.[67] He wrote:

> It is better to strip hides off animal carcasses than to say to other people, "I am a great sage, I am a priest, provide me therefore with maintenance." So did the Sages command us. Among the great Sages there were hewers of wood, carriers of beams, drawers of water to irrigate gardens, and workers in iron and charcoal. They did not ask for public assistance, nor did they accept it when offered to them.[68]

10

Commentary on the Mishnah

MAIMONIDES BEGAN his first major work, his *Commentary on the Mishnah,* in Fez around 1161, when he was twenty-three, and finished it in Egypt in 1168, when he was thirty. This was an overwhelming task that absorbed much of his time and energy, as he reproduced the entire text of the Mishnah with his commentary appended to it. Maimonides wrote his commentary in Judeo-Arabic, and it was later rendered into Hebrew by a number of translators, including Samuel Ibn Tibbon and Judah al-Harizi, both of whom also translated *The Guide of the Perplexed.* Only in Arabic-speaking countries did students use the original Judeo-Arabic. For the most part, the Hebrew translations have replaced it.

Why would Maimonides have written a Judeo-Arabic commentary on the Mishnah, which was in beautiful Hebrew? Perhaps it was more natural for him to write in the lingua franca of the time, the language of instruction that his fellow Jews throughout the Middle East understood. He did not yet have his sights set on "the ends of the Earth," as he did when he compiled his code of law in Hebrew in 1168–78.

THE MISHNAH

The Mishnah was the first systematic compendium of Jewish law.[1] Rabbi Judah ha-Nasi (the Prince or Patriarch) redacted the Mishnah around 200 C.E. in six orders (*sedarim*). It is then divided into sixty-three tractates (*masekhtot,* sing. *masekhet,* "fabric," cf. Latin *textus*); the tractates are divided into chapters, which are subdivided into sections, or *mishnayot* (sing. *mishnah*).

Judah ha-Nasi is said to have edited the Mishnah collections of previous sages, especially that of Rabbi Aqiba and his disciples (Rabbis Meir, Judah, Jose, and Simon). Sages in the next generation added to his edition, and the Mishnah was then concluded. Judah ha-Nasi's Mishnah came to be known as "The Mishnah" or "Our Mishnah," and all other similar texts of the Tannaim came to be called *baraita,* meaning "outside the Mishnah."[2] These *baraitot* are quoted in the Talmud and Halachic Midrashim and also appear in the compilation called the Tosefta. The Tosefta is a complementary supplement to the Mishnah edited a generation later. Whether the Mishnah was conceived of initially as a teaching manual or as a law code, it became the basis for legal discussions in the Babylonian and Jerusalem Talmuds.[3]

In the Mishnah, as in Jewish law in general, civil, personal, criminal, and constitutional law are all embraced. Aside from legal provisions, the Mishnah contains ethical norms. The tractate Avot ("Fathers") contains ethical aphorisms by sages of different periods.[4]

PROLOGUE TO THE MISHNAH COMMENTARY

Maimonides' commentary begins with a poem of six verses, three of nine words and three of ten.[5] The name Moses occurs three times, once as the biblical Moses and once as Maimonides' name—"a composition of a weak youth, Moses son of Maimon, whose cry is to God to straighten his way and make the Torah alone his desire." The third time it is ambiguous and can mean either. Maimonides constantly saw himself as a Moses *redivivus.*

In an exuberant prologue, written in florid poetry and rhymed prose, Maimonides offered up his opus. He presented it as a gift of delicious food and wine on a table set with every choice fruit, both freshly plucked and long stored, with spiced wine and pomegranate juice gliding over the lips of sleepers. He asked his companions to drink deeply of its wine from a vineyard on a fruitful hill, a vineyard of delight, a garden lovingly tended that he watched over day and night and watered every minute until its buds developed, its grapes ripened, its blossoms opened, its trees flourished, and its mandrakes yielded their fragrance.

Andalusian reminiscences are sublimated here into a lyrical overture to his first major work. The sentences are a bouquet of biblical phrases exhaling the aroma of a Spanish garden. Toward the end he compared the commentary to the majestic Tower of David and announced, "I, Moses ben Maimon the Sefaradi, erected it." He began with the "I" as someone proud of a great achievement and aware of his own worth and power. Even if this commentary had been his only work, it would have ensured his fame for perpetuity.

COMPLETION OF THE COMMENTARY ON THE MISHNAH

Maimonides completed the commentary in Egypt during the last years of the Fatimid dynasty. He was finding his way in Egyptian society, serving as a physician, giving lectures on the sciences, and engaging in commercial trade when he completed his magisterial commentary.

Hardships and wandering delayed its completion, he said, begging the reader's indulgence for its deficiencies. With the postscript there is a colophon noting the date of completion and the author's genealogy.

> I have completed this commentary as I had promised. I ask and beseech the Exalted One to save me from errors. Whoever finds herein a dubious passage, or has an interpretation of any law that is better than mine, let him draw my attention to it and give me the benefit of doubt. For what I have undertaken is not a slight thing, and to carry it out is not easy for someone honest with good judgment, especially as my heart has often been occupied with the vicissitudes of time and what God has determined for me by way of exile and

wandering in the world from one end of heaven to the other [cf. Deut 4:32]. Perhaps I have been rewarded for this, for *exile atones for sin*.[6]

The Exalted One knows that there are legal precepts whose interpretations I wrote while I was traveling along the ways, and there are matters I wrote down when I was on ships in the Mediterranean. This would be enough [to distract me], in addition to my studying other sciences. I only describe the situation to explain my apology for what may be vulnerable to an exacting critic, who is not to be blamed for his criticism. Rather he has a reward from God for this, and he is loved by me, for it is the work of the Lord. What I have explained of my situation during the time of composing this commentary[7] is what caused me to take so long.[8]

Maimonides concluded with verses from Isaiah (40:29–31):

He gives strength to the weary,
Fresh vigor to the spent.
Youths may grow faint and weary,
And young men stumble and fall;
But they who trust in the Lord shall renew their strength
As eagles grow new plumes.

SCOPE OF THE MISHNAH COMMENTARY

Maimonides explained his aims at the end of his Introduction to the commentary. He said that he elucidated the sense of the Mishnah, synthesizing, epitomizing, and simplifying what was complicated. As the text of the Mishnah could not be understood apart from its interpretation in the Gemara, Maimonides supplied what was absolutely necessary to know of the Gemara, thereby freeing the student from strenuous research and allowing him to study other subjects, such as philosophy and science. He may have made use of his unfinished commentary on the Talmud in his discussions of the Mishnah. He also clarified the legal decisions of the Mishnah to determine what actual practice should be.

Wishing to introduce a novice student to talmudic study, Maimonides gave a panoramic view of the Talmud throughout the Mishnah commentary. For the advanced student, the commentary would serve as a mnemonic, making what the student had learned accessible and organized. He tried to write briefly, he said, without sacrificing accuracy and lucidity, for he was instructing those who could understand— "I am not speaking to a stone but to an intelligent human being."

HANDWRITTEN MANUSCRIPTS

We are fortunate to have the fair copy written by Maimonides himself of nearly the entire *Commentary on the Mishnah*.[9] Though there was initially some debate whether the manuscript is an autograph copy— the script is finer than Maimonides' more common cursive handwriting—most scholars now believe that it is an autograph, making it the longest surviving manuscript written by the Master.[10] To appreciate how spectacular this survival is, consider that no handwritten manuscript of William Shakespeare, who lived four hundred years after Maimonides, has been preserved.

The survival of Maimonides' own archetype, from which other copies would be made, is due to a sequence of providential events. When Maimonides' fifth-generation descendant, Nagid David II ben Joshua (1335–1415), moved from Cairo to Aleppo, he brought with him manuscripts that were family heirlooms, including this copy of the commentary.[11] Solomon ben David I ben Abraham I, Maimonides' great-grandson, had written on the title page of the first volume, Zera'im (Seeds), a writ of ownership:

> This original copy and the rest of the original, which is in the handwriting of our Master Moses, of blessed memory, are my property. I have dedicated them to God, so that they should not be sold or bought or pledged as a security to be locked away, but should be at the discretion of the eldest of the brothers, generation after generation, until the coming of our Messiah.[12]

The manuscript remained, as a sacred relic and symbol of authority, with the family in Aleppo, until the end of the fifteenth century, when it passed into private hands. If the first miracle was the preservation of Maimonides' autograph manuscript, the second was the rediscovery of much of it by English scholars in the seventeenth century.

Edward Pococke Sr. (1604–1691) and his younger colleague Robert Huntington brought two volumes, covering three of the six parts of the commentary, from Aleppo to England.

This is an incredible story of how dedicated scholars saved manuscript treasures from oblivion. Pococke, an English Orientalist educated at Oxford, became chaplain to the merchants of the Levant Company at Aleppo in Syria, where he collected manuscript treasures.[13] After returning to England, as first incumbent of the Laudian Chair in Arabic at Oxford, he published parts of Maimonides' Mishnah commentary accompanied by a Latin translation and learned notes in a book titled *Porta Mosis* (*Gate of Moses*). *Porta Mosis* appeared in 1655 and was the first volume that Oxford University Press printed with Hebrew type. Pococke ascertained correctly that some of the texts he published in *Porta Mosis* were in Maimonides' own handwriting.[14]

Pococke urged his protégé, the Arabic scholar Robert Huntington, to apply for the chaplaincy at Aleppo in 1670. Huntington stayed there for eleven years, searching for manuscripts and filling his teacher's requests. Among the precious manuscripts he acquired were two Maimonides autographs—part of the fair copy of the Mishnah commentary and part of the *Mishneh Torah,* with Maimonides' authorization of the text.[15] Huntington eventually bequeathed his precious manuscript collection to Oxford's Bodleian Library. Pococke and Huntington have an honored place in the Elysian Fields of Orientalists.

By another providential event, two more volumes of the fair copy of the Mishnah commentary were discovered and purchased in Damascus in 1907–08 by the scholar Rabbi Jacob Moses Toledano (1880–1960).[16] These were later acquired by the Hebraist and scholarly bibliophile David Solomon Sassoon (1880–1942) and first came to his collection in Letchworth, England, some fifty miles from their companions at the Bodleian.[17] The volumes were inherited by his son, Rabbi Solomon David Sassoon (1915–85), who published the rare and exquisite facsimile edition of the Mishnah commentary.

The fair copy of the *Commentary on the Mishnah* was subjected over time to Maimonides' revisions—additions, deletions, and reformulations. In many cases Maimonides crossed out something in the text and we see what he deleted; in others, he completely expunged the original text with ink.

In addition, there are emendations by his son, Abraham, carrying out his father's intentions and oral instructions, so that after Maimonides' death his work was being improved.[18] There are also comments by his descendants, even as far down as Nagid David II ben Joshua (1335–1415). Many of the comments corrected the *Commentary on the Mishnah* in accordance with the later *Mishneh Torah,* thereby fulfilling Maimonides' own intention.[19] Then there were revisions and restorations of slips of the pen, misquotations, omitted words and passages, and even pages that had become illegible.

Aside from the fair copy, draft copies of pages from the Mishnah commentary in Maimonides' cursive handwriting have turned up in the Genizah papers.[20] The draft copies are very rough, with many corrections and deletions.

Maimonides was constantly changing his mind and correcting the commentary throughout his life in his unwavering quest for perfection. As it was copied by scribes at various times, different versions went into circulation. When Maimonides wrote the *Mishneh Torah,* he continued to revise legal formulations in the Mishnah commentary, entering the corrections in his personal copy, which served as an archetype for subsequent scribal copies.[21]

He did his utmost to ensure that his legal writings in particular did not contain contradictions, especially between earlier and later versions.[22] When a number of people complained that a passage in the *Mishneh Torah* contradicted something he had written in the earlier Mishnah commentary, Maimonides replied that the *Mishneh Torah* version was correct and that their copy of the Mishnah commentary was an early, faulty version. His son, Abraham, cited this text in a responsum, explaining that his father corrected the commentary himself and deleted a long explanation that had been there.[23] The correction appears in the margin of the *Commentary on the Mishnah* manuscript, and the next page, containing the original text, is crossed out.

In one of his letters, Maimonides commented on his corrections in the commentary.[24] He explained that he had to emend passages where he had been misguided by the Geonim, such as Rabbenu Nissim in *Megillat Setarim (The Scroll of Secrets)*[25] and Rav Hefes in the *Book of Commandments,* as well as others whom he preferred not to mention.[26] Even if he were the one who made a mistake, he said, and not the

Geonim, he had never claimed that he was perfect and never erred. Whenever he discovered something improper, he always amended it, whether in his writing or his character.

The manuscripts of the Mishnah commentary illustrate Maimonides' procedure in preparing texts.[27] First, he would make a draft copy, which he would revise. The corrections would enter a second draft, which would also be edited. When he was ready, he would have a fair copy of the entire text copied. This was done either by a scribe or by his "holy and pure hand," as later scholars described autographs. The fair copy was the exemplar from which further copies were made. Copies would be checked against the autograph original by a scribe or by Maimonides himself, who would certify that a copy had been collated with his codex.

He continued to revise the commentary throughout his life, always correcting, improving, and updating on the basis of further knowledge. Hence, the commentary was always in flux and never finished, except when time drew a curtain over it. Yet, as we have seen, his descendants continued the work, so that his writings continued to be improved without him.

INTRODUCTION TO THE *COMMENTARY ON THE MISHNAH*

Maimonides wrote three major introductions in his commentary. First he wrote a long introduction to the entire Mishnah.[28] Then he wrote an introduction to the tenth chapter of Tractate Sanhedrin, called Pereq Heleq, in which, inter alia, he set down a creed in thirteen principles. Finally, as a prelude to his comments on Tractate Avot, or Pirqe Avot (Ethics of the Fathers), he wrote eight chapters devoted to ethics. There were other introductions, such as a phenomenally detailed one to the order of Purities, but they were classifications of the material rather than theoretical discussions.[29] The introductions refer to philosophy and science, unusual denizens in a legal work. Yet he must have known his audience and that "Greek wisdom" would not be shocking. Even in the purely legal parts of the Mishnah commentary, the reader comes across science and philosophy.

In his introduction to the Mishnah, Maimonides discussed the nature of the Oral law and prophecy. Rabbanite (as opposed to Karaite)

Jews held that the Oral law was revealed to Moses along with the Written law at Mount Sinai. The Oral law, handed down by tradition and eventually embodied in the Talmud and Midrash, is the authoritative interpretation of the Written law. Elucidating the Oral law was crucial, because the Karaites denied its validity and rejected the Talmud's authority. Furthermore, Christians and Muslims emphatically rejected the Talmud. Christians believed that the true interpretation of the Old Testament was to be found in the New Testament. Muslim theologians held that the Oral law taught in the Talmud was invented by the rabbis. The true revelation was contained in the Qur'an and its proper interpretation was transmitted in traditions going back to Muhammad and his companions and expounded by the ulema throughout time.

It was imperative for Maimonides to establish an unbroken line of tradition from Moses down to the period of the Geonim and to his own time.[30] Maimonides portrayed the oral tradition not in static terms as a rigid body but rather as a basis for difference of opinion to be decided by legal reasoning and by a majority of learned authorities. The generations after the prophets differed over interpretations and used reason to reach new conclusions, thereby renewing the law. "There was never a time when there was not deliberating about the law and drawing conclusions."[31] The people of every era made the words of their predecessors a basis for judicial reasoning. When there was no difference of opinion, still the tradents (those who transmit traditions) of the law always deliberated about it and made deductions from it.

Maimonides achieved a subtle balance between preservation of tradition, on one side, and change and progress, on the other. He made jurisprudence dynamic by employing Islamic juridical instruments— e.g., the concepts of judicial divergence (*ikhtilaf*), consensus (*ijma'*), independent judgment (*ijtihad*), and legal reasoning (*qiyas*).

Jewish law therefore evolves over time, as every generation of sages derives new legislation from the Oral and Written law. Authority to interpret the law was in the hands of the sages, and prophecy no longer played a role.

In fact, Maimonides stressed that the biblical prophets were never legislators. Only Moses was a legislating prophet, and the others had to accept his authority and not add to, or detract from, the law. The

Mishnah and Talmud received their authority because the entire community of Israel concurred in accepting them.[32] As precepts are derived by logical inference (*qiyas*), disagreement occurred among the
sages because they reasoned according to their intellectual powers and
principles, not because they erred receiving traditions.

Having surveyed the judicial activity of the sages during the period
of the Talmud, Maimonides discussed its final editing, then the period
of the Geonim, and finally his own judicial philosophy. He followed
his predecessors, he said, by "seeking and by exercising independent
judgment in the law [*ijtihad*] according to my ability to acquire what
we hope will be useful before God."[33] He explained that he first wrote
commentaries on parts of the Talmud, and thereafter he decided to
compose a commentary on the entire Mishnah. He was motivated to
write a commentary that would abridge the Talmud because no one
could grasp the entire Talmud by his own reasoning.

Maimonides' discourse on the transmission of the law was not
merely theoretical. He sought to establish that the rabbinic sages in
every generation should be venerated and given a place of high honor
and that their instructions be obeyed. He stressed the necessity to
honor learned scholars and judges in his Introduction to Pereq Heleq
as well.

Maimonides' discourse on majority and minority (even individual)
views exemplifies how rabbinic democracy worked. Having established that the law follows majority opinion, or consensus, not prophetic inspiration, Maimonides noted the value of individual opinion.
The Mishnah elucidates all the precepts of the Torah, including traditions from Moses and precepts derived by reasoning (*qiyas*), about
which there may be disagreement. Judah ha-Nasi recorded both sides
of an argument, even if a single sage disagreed with the many. If Judah ha-Nasi had recorded only consensus views and suppressed individual opinions, Maimonides observed, someone later was liable to
receive the minority view from the dissenting individual, and people
would not know which opinion is valid. When all opinions are made
known from the start, this possibility is eliminated.[34] The Mishnah is
strictly speaking not so much a code of Jewish law as it is a text for
study of the law. The Mishnah explains: *Why are the opinions of the
minority included with the opinions of the majority even though the law*

does not follow them? So that a later court can examine their words and rely upon them (M Eduyot i, 3). The aim of the Mishnah was to train students in thinking about the legal issues that comprise the *halakhah*.

Judah ha-Nasi recorded the opinion of a single individual along with the majority because sometimes the law follows the single authority.

> If the reasoning is correct, even if it is the reasoning of a single individual, we listen to him, although the majority disagreed with him. This is to teach the pursuit of truth and rectitude. When these great men, who were pious and intelligent, realized that the opinion of the dissenter was superior to theirs, they acknowledged it and embraced his opinion. Even more should others, who realize that their opponent is right, yield and not be obstinate and use sophistical reasoning to defend their own opinion.[35]

Maimonides portrayed Moses and Judah ha-Nasi as the central figures in the drama of the law, the first as the lawgiver and the second as compiler of the first law book. When Moses approached death, he wrote thirteen scrolls of the Torah, giving one to each of the twelve tribes and one to the Levites, and then ascended Mount Nevo on 7 Adar.

> Moses ascended [to heaven] on midday according to what tradition has ascertained.[36] It was his death for us since we missed him, but life for him because he ascended to heaven. Thus the Sages (peace upon them) said, *Moses, our Master, did not die but ascended [to heaven] and serves on high.*[37] Discussion of this is very, very lengthy, and this is not its proper place.[38]

Rabbinic legend mentions several ascensions of Moses. The first was at the beginning of his career; the second to receive the law at Mount Sinai; the third at the time of his death.[39] The heavenly assumption of Moses at the point of his death places him in the company of Jesus, whose death was believed to be a birth into eternal life. Muhammad, according to Islamic tradition, ascended to heaven in his lifetime in the *isra'* (from Mecca to Jerusalem) and *mi'raj* (from Jerusalem to heaven).[40]

AGGADAH AND ESOTERICISM

The second part of the introduction to the Mishnah commentary considers homiletic (*aggadah* or *haggadah*) parts of rabbinic literature. Here, Maimonides introduced his hermeneutic principle of esoteric reading, commenting that certain mysterious texts of the sages should not be taught openly, a restriction pronounced by the sages themselves. The exegetical interpretation (*derash*) in the Talmud is not of minor importance or utility, but serves a high purpose and contains wondrous mysteries. When these interpretations are viewed esoterically they are seen to contain "the pure good."[41] They reveal divine truths that philosophers and scientists spent ages pondering. Only on the surface do they conflict with reason. The sages used an esoteric hermeneutic to stimulate the minds of students and to blind the ignorant, whose hearts will never be enlightened, about whom it is said, "*One does not reveal to them the secret.* For their intellect is not adequate to receive the pure truth."[42]

The sages concealed the mysteries of the Torah even from one another concerning the Account of the Beginning and the Account of the Chariot, if one did not consider others capable of learning what he knew. This can be derived from what Solomon said—*Honey and milk are under your tongue* (Song 4:11). The sages understood this to mean that the sweet things that the soul enjoys are like the pleasure of the taste of honey and milk and should not be divulged by the tongue in any way.[43] These are things that cannot be taught and one does not expound them in the sessions of wisdom, but rather intimates them in books by hidden allusions.[44] If God removes the veils from the heart of whom he wills after this person has prepared himself in the sciences, he will understand according to the power of his intellect.[45]

The common folk, including women and children, should be taught by way of parable so that when their minds are perfected they understand the meaning of these parables. For these reasons, the sages spoke of divine things by allusion. We find here *in nuce* Maimonides' view on philosophic esoteric writing, which he developed more fully in *The Guide of the Perplexed.*

INTRODUCTION TO PEREQ HELEQ:
THE THIRTEEN PRINCIPLES OF FAITH

In the introduction to Pereq Heleq, Maimonides outlined the fundamental principles, or articles of faith, of Judaism, a revolutionary undertaking, for Judaism had never been so sharply defined by a creed.[46]

Judaism had no councils to promulgate articles of faith, as did the Church, which adopted Apostolic Creeds from an early period. Christians found it necessary to establish a unity of faith, whereas Jews found it necessary to determine a unity of practice.

Islam, like Judaism, stressed performance of the law, yet Muslim scholars were used to defining faith in their canonical traditions. Collections of tradition and juridical and theological works discuss definitions of Islam, its pillars, faith and works, the essence of God, free will, and the sources of the law.[47] Ibn Tumart had spread Almohad doctrine by means of a creed ('aqida) defining Islam according to his theological understanding. Maimonides' use of the Arabic term usul for "root principles" (Heb. 'iqqarim) shows that his mission was influenced by Islamic theology.

Maimonides' starting point was the mishnah in Sanhedrin, chapter x, 1.[48]

All Israelites have a share [heleq] in the world hereafter; as it is said, And your people, all of them righteous, shall possess the land forever; they are the shoot that I planted, my handiwork in which I glory [Isa 60:21].[49]

And these are the ones who have no share in the world hereafter: he who says that there is no resurrection of the dead prescribed in the Torah;[50] he who says that the Torah is not from Heaven; and an Epicurean.

Rabbi Aqiba says: Also one who reads outside books,[51] or who utters charms over a wound and says, I will not bring upon you any of the diseases that I brought upon the Egyptians, for I the Lord am your healer [Exod 15:26].[52]

Abba Saul says: Also one who pronounces the tetragrammaton.

The world hereafter is not the messianic era or the time of the resurrection of the dead, but rather the heavenly world, where the souls
of the righteous survive eternally.[53]

When the Mishnah understands Isaiah 60:21 as referring to the
world hereafter, it is taking Isaiah's reference to the land symboli-
cally.[54] Jesus understood the verse in the same spiritual way when he
rephrased it in the Sermon on the Mount: *They shall have the earth for
their heritage* (Mat 5:4).[55]

The Mishnah does not specify what the Epicurean believes that dis-
qualifies him from having a portion in the world hereafter. Epicurus
is the only Greek philosopher mentioned in talmudic-midrashic literature, which did not ordinarily show acquaintance with Greek philosophy.[56] What the Epicurean thought, according to the rabbinic
sages, may be inferred from an aphorism of Rabbi Elazar ben 'Arakh
cited in Avot, ii, 14: *Be alert to learn Torah, and know what answer to
give to the Epicurean.*[57] Epicurean, or *apikoros*, as it was pronounced,
was an epithet for a heretic or atheist. The Epicurean contended that
the gods do not care about what happens in this world and abide in
pure tranquility.

In his comment on M San, x, 1, Maimonides explained that *Epicurean* is an Aramaic term. It means, he said, "disparaging the Torah or
its sages, and therefore whoever does not believe in the principles of
the Torah or despises either the sages or a disciple of the wise or his
own teacher." The name is actually Greek (Epikouros), of course;
however it occurs in the Talmud in Aramaic, and so Maimonides'
explanation was not entirely mistaken.[58] Elsewhere in the Mishnah
commentary, he showed that he knew what the Epicurean school represented. In his comment on Avot, ii, 14[17], Maimonides said that one
should know how to debate gentile heretics (*zanadiqa*) when they criticize Judaism, but not Jewish heretics, because the more one argues,
the more they despise, and there is no way to cure them.[59] In the *Mishneh Torah,* Maimonides distinguished three types of Epicurean: those
who deny prophecy (or knowledge coming from the Creator to the
human mind); those who deny the prophecy of Moses; and those who
say that the Creator does not know human actions.[60]

Going back to our *mishnah,* Rabbi Aqiba included those who read outside books among those who have no share in the world hereafter. Maimonides defined "outside books" this way:

> They are heretical [*minut*] books, and also the books of Ben Sira, who wrote books about the nonsense of physiognomy, lacking science and utility, rather a vacuous waste of time, such as the books found among the Arabs on chronicles, the lives of kings, Arab genealogies, books of songs and the like, in which there is neither science nor physical benefit but are merely a waste of time.

The gemara on the *mishnah* defines outside books as heretical (*minut*) books and also the book of Ben Sira, because the heretics (*minim*)—here evidently referring to Christians—included it in the biblical canon.[61] Alfasi (on B San 19b) and Maimonides found the content of Ben Sira to be vapid and useless, specifying the author's interest in physiognomy. Actually, *The Wisdom of Ben Sira* opposed dreams and divination (34:1–8) and did not mention physiognomy. They confused it with the medieval *Tales of Ben Sira*.[62]

Maimonides' comment on Arabic chronicles, the lives of kings, genealogies, and books of songs has been taken by scholars as a prohibition of history and poetry. Maimonides, however, merely said that these books are a waste of time. He may have discouraged history and poetry because apostates, such as Samuel al-Maghribi, were attracted to Islam by these genres of literature.[63] Maimonides' criterion of useful knowledge recalls a well-known *hadith* in the name of Muhammad, praising useful knowledge and condemning knowledge that is useless.[64]

The anonymous *mishnah* here bases immortality on belief, whereas Judaic sources are usually more concerned with performance.[65] Maimonides thought that it was appropriate in this place to define the Jewish faith, thereby avoiding ambiguity and confusion. The need to produce a creed appeared to him as urgent at a time when free-ranging ideas about God, creation, providence, and reward and punishment were so rampant. Maimonides wanted to wean the common folk away from superstitious beliefs, such as depicting God as having human shape and emotions.[66] He wanted the public to assent to truths of reason on the basis of authority.

In thirteen principles, he defined the true meaning of belief in a creator, prophecy, revelation, providence, reward and punishment, the messianic era, and resurrection of the dead. The principles are divided into three groups: the existence of a creator and his unity (principles 1–5), Torah from Heaven (6–9), and reward and punishment (10–13).[67] Transformed into a poetic hymn, they became part of the synagogue ritual, showing how vital they were for Jewish belief.[68]

Here is a summary of his thirteen principles:

1. *The existence of the Creator.* There is a being who is perfect in every way and is the cause of all existent beings. Everything beneath him—the intelligences of the spheres (that is, the angels), the spheres themselves, and what is beneath them—all depends upon his existence.

2. *His unity.* That this cause of everything is One, not like the unity of species or genus or anything else compound and divisible or simple and infinitely divisible.[69]

3. *Denial of God's corporeality.* This One is neither a body nor a force in a body and is not subject to the accidents of bodies, such as movement and rest, neither in substance nor in accident. When Scripture describes God physically—walking, standing, sitting, and speaking—it is by way of metaphor.

4. *Primordiality.* This One is absolutely primordial, and every other existent being is nonprimordial with reference to him. This great principle of the law of Moses our Master is that this world is created (lit. "innovated"). God formed and created it after absolute nothingness.[70]

5. *He is the one worthy of being worshiped, extolled, and obeyed.* Nothing else beneath him in existence—not the angels, the heavenly bodies, the spheres, the elements, nor what is composed of them—should be worshiped, extolled, and obeyed. This fifth principle is a prohibition of idolatry, and most of the Torah concerns this prohibition.

6. *Prophecy.* The human species includes persons possessing superior innate characteristics and great perfection. Their souls are prepared to receive the form of intelligence, then this

human intellect joins the Agent Intellect, and a noble emanation from the Agent Intellect emanates upon it. They are the
prophets, and this is prophecy and its meaning.[71]

7. *The prophecy of Moses, our Master.* We should believe that he is
father of all the prophets who preceded him and will come
after him. All of them are beneath him in rank. He is God's
chosen (*safw 'l-Allah*) from the entire human species, who
apprehended of the Exalted more than any other human apprehended or will apprehend.[72] God spoke directly to Moses.[73]

Maimonides says that to explain the power of prophecy, he needs to
speak about several relevant subjects, such as angels and their level
with respect to the Creator, the soul and its powers, symbolic forms
that prophets used for Creator and angels. He adds that *Shi'ur qomah*
(an esoteric teaching dating from the Tannaitic period) and its meaning are included here.[74]

8. *The Torah is from Heaven.* The entire Torah found in our
hands this day is the Torah that was revealed to Moses, and all
of it was from the Almighty, in what is called metaphorically
"speech" (*kalam*).[75]

9. *Abrogation.* The law of Moses will not be abrogated, and no
other law from God will come, nothing will be added to it or
detracted from it either in its text or in its interpretation.[76]

10. *The Exalted knows people's actions and will not overlook them.*

11. *The Exalted rewards whoever observes the commandments of the
Torah and he punishes those who transgress its prohibitions.* One's
great reward is in the world hereafter and one's worst punishment is excision (*karet*).[77]

12. *The days of the Messiah.* We should believe that he will come.
Even if he tarries, wait for him. One should not set a point in
time for his coming, nor interpret scriptural texts to conjecture
this time. One should believe in him and extol and love him
and pray for him. Whoever doubts him or disparages him has
denied the Torah, which promised him. The king of Israel

must be descended from David, specifically from the seed of Solomon. Whoever denies the status of this family denies God and the words of his prophets.

13. *Resurrection of the dead.*[78]

Maimonides concluded by stating that only those who believe in these articles of faith belong to the community of Israel and should be treated with love and compassion in accordance with God's commandments concerning love and brotherhood. Even if this person, overcome by desire, committed a transgression, he still merits immortality, though he is "one of the sinners of Israel." However, whoever doubts one of these articles of faith has abandoned the community and denied God (the Root), "and he is called a heretic and Epicurean and one who cuts down the shoots, and it is necessary to hate him and cause him to perish."[79] Maimonides requested that the reader rehearse the thirteen principles often and contemplate them as a spiritual exercise.

Ibn Tumart, founder of the Almohad movement, insisted on a pure monotheism and rejection of anthropomorphism.[80] Maimonides may have been influenced by Ibn Tumart's theology in his own strong stand against depicting God in human terms. The vigor of Maimonides' forceful condemnation of anthropomorphism as superstitious idolatry calls to mind the reformist zeal of Ibn Tumart.[81]

The thirteen articles of faith were intended for the entire community, not for the intellectual elite, yet they are formulated philosophically. The first principle, on God's existence, echoes Ibn Sina's concept of God as the Necessary Being. The second, on God's unity, contains a philosophic definition of oneness. The sixth, on prophecy, presents an understanding of prophecy derived from the political thought of al-Farabi, Ibn Sina, and Ibn Rushd. Maimonides stated the thirteen principles as dialectical propositions based on consensus, not on demonstrative, or scientific, proof. The underlying assumption is expressable in a hypothetical sentence: If you wish to belong to the Jewish faith community, then you need to accept these thirteen principles.

The third principle—that God is incorporeal, without image or form—is the most vital to Maimonides' educational goals. It was also the most sharply challenged by his opponents, who held that true faith was belief in a corporeal God.[82] The Hebrew Bible described God as having human characteristics and emotions, including anger, jealousy, regret, and disappointment. God sees; he descends and ascends; he sits on a throne; he passes through the land; he dwells in Zion.

The Bible and rabbinic literature affirmed that God was physical and had human attributes, and that Adam's creation in the image of God meant that God had a human appearance.[83] The Jewish mystical tradition also conceived of God in human terms. There was speculation on the form and size of God's body in the texts of the *Shi'ur qomah* (*The Measure of the Divine Stature*).[84] There was a mystical vision of God as a "figure in the form of man," which the prophet Ezekiel had seen in his vision of the heavenly throne-chariot (*merkavah*) (Ezek 1:26). Merkavah mysticism depicted the soul ascending to the divine throne and having a vision of the divine splendor in the form of a human figure.

The mystical divine body was attired in a robe of glory. Resonances of this myth appear in rabbinic narratives about God's garment of light at the time of creation.[85] In some of the extant *Shi'ur qomah* texts the anthropomorphisms are said to describe not God's essence but his "hidden glory" or the "body of the *shekhinah*" (the Divine Presence). Maimonides wrote a responsum on *Shi'ur qomah* in which he denied its authorship by the sages of the Talmud and pronounced it idolatrous.[86]

Maimonides was convinced that belief in God's corporeality is worse than idolatry, for the object of worship is not God at all. A God in human form, with human emotions, was not the Lord, God of the universe, but a fabrication of the human imagination. One who believed this did not merit a place in the world hereafter.

Not everyone can engage in speculation and arrive at knowledge of true being, but whoever refuses to accede to the authority of those who inquire into the truth and engage in investigation is not excused for his or her ignorance.[87] The unenlightened must accept on traditional authority the fundamental beliefs concerning the existence of God, his unity, incorporeality, knowledge, power, will, and eternity.[88] The purpose of teaching correct knowledge about God is to make immortality accessible to all, for without true knowledge of God immortality is unobtainable.[89]

THE EIGHT CHAPTERS ON ETHICS

Maimonides' introduction to Tractate Avot, known as the Eight Chapters, is devoted to ethics, the main subject of the tractate.[90] It is astonishing that Tractate Avot, with its ethical adages reminiscent of Hellenistic thought, found a place in the Mishnah, which otherwise mainly concerns legal topics. It gave Maimonides a welcome opportunity to import Greek ethical precepts into the *Commentary on the Mishnah*.

The first aim of Tractate Avot, he wrote, is to validate tradition that had been handed down from one generation to another.[91] He inferred from this that "it is proper to revere a learned sage and to place him in an honorable position because he transmits the tradition. He is to his generation what these earlier sages were to their generation." The point is that one should not question the judgments or enactments of judges on the ground that later judges are not the equals of their predecessors. Maimonides considered validation of tradition as the first aim of Tractate Avot because it begins by stating: *Moses received the Torah at Sinai and passed it down to Joshua, and Joshua to the elders, and the elders to the Men of the Great Assembly.*

The second aim of Tractate Avot is to elucidate the ethical teachings of the sages, so that we may learn good traits from them.[92] Judges need character training more than ordinary people do. If ordinary people do not acquire good character, they harm themselves, not the public. However, if a judge is not ethical, he harms himself and others. Therefore Tractate Avot begins with ethical teachings for judges, such as *Be deliberate in judgment* (Avot, i, 1). Judges should not jump to conclusions, nor should they delay judgment.

The general rule is that a judge should be like an expert physician, who does not resort to drugs as long as he can heal by dietary means. (Maimonides favored analogies drawn from medical practice.) However, if he sees that the illness cannot be cured by dietary means alone, he will then administer mild medications that are like food. He then progresses to strong medications. Likewise, a judge should first attempt to arbitrate a compromise between the parties. If this is unsuccessful, he should judge with kindness, humble himself, and speak gently to the litigants. If this is unsuccessful because of the truculent nature of one of the disputants, who wishes to prevail against the other, the judge should be strict with him.[93] Tractate Avot was well placed after Tractate Sanhedrin (which deals with courts), as it contains ethical teachings inducing austere behavior (*zuhd fi 'l-dunya*) in judges and respect for knowledge and scholars, as well as for righteousness and piety.[94]

ON SPEECH AND SILENCE

Tractate Avot addresses speech and silence in several aphorisms, and Maimonides makes some of his most intriguing comments on this subject.

We read in our *mishnah* (Avot, i, 16):

Simon his son said,[95] All my days have I grown up among the sages, and I have found nothing better for a person than silence. And not the expounding is the main thing but the doing. And whoever multiplies words causes sin.

Maimonides commented expansively on this saying that praises silence and condemns verbosity. He first cited books on ethics that mentioned an ascetic who kept silent and hardly spoke. Asked about his silence, the ascetic replied that only one of four categories of speech was constructive and worthy—speech about ethics and science or speech about preserving one's life.[96]

Maimonides added that "our law" divides speech into five categories:

1. *Obligatory,* such as reading and teaching Torah and devoting oneself to studying it.

2. *Prohibited,* such as bearing false witness, lying, slandering, calumniating, and vilifying, as well as obscenity and slander.

3. *Reprehensible,* which has no utility for a person and is neither obedience or disobedience to God, such as most of the conversations of the populace regarding what has happened, the conduct of a certain king in his palace, and how someone died or became rich. These the sages called "idle talk." The virtuous strive to avoid this kind of speech. It was said of Rav, the pupil of Rabbi Hiyya, that he never spoke idly in his entire lifetime.[97]

4. *Meritorious,* such as speech in praise of the intellectual and ethical virtues. It is discourse moving the soul to these virtues by speeches and poetry and restraining it from vices the same way. It is to praise virtuous persons and extol their virtues, so that their conduct will appear good to people, so that they follow their way.

5. *Permissible,* such as speech about what is specific to man, such as business, livelihood, food, drink, garments, and all he needs. One should be sincere and adjust one's deeds to one's words. And one should seek brevity, saying as much as possible in the fewest words; as they say, "One should always instruct his students by way of brevity."[98]

What Maimonides called categories of "our law" are actually from Islamic jurisprudence, which classified all human actions according to these very same five categories.[99]

Maimonides used the five qualifications of Islamic law when he expressed his view on the permissibility of songs and wine in a comment on the same text in Tractate Avot.[100] He wrote:

I have witnessed elders and pious men of our community, when they attend a drinking party or wedding and the like, disapprove when someone wishes to sing in Arabic. They do so even if the theme of the song is in praise of courage, honor, or wine.[101] These belong to the category of the recommended.[102] Yet they strongly condemn such songs and forbid listening to them.

But if the singer chants some Hebrew strophic poem, they do not condemned this or find it so bad, although what is sung may be forbidden or reprehensible.[103] This is pure folly. For speech is not *forbidden, permitted, recommended, or reprehended* or *commanded* because of its language but because of its content. For if the theme of the poem is something exalted, it would be a duty to recite it in any language; and if its theme were a vice, then it would be an obligation to exclude it in every language.

Two poems, one Hebrew and the other Arabic or some other language, both arousing and praising desire, belong to the category of reprehensible speech.[104] Listening to the Hebrew poem and reciting it would be more reprehensible because of the excellence of the language, which is suitable only for virtues, especially if a verse from the Torah or *Song of Songs* is used with this intention. At that point it is forbidden, for the Torah forbade turning the words of the prophets into songs about vices and things that are reprehensible.[105]

The sanctioned musical modes of courage and earnestness were noted by Plato in *Republic* 399, where Socrates approved for the guardians of the republic musical modes conducive to courage, firmness, and patience, or the mode conducive to peaceful voluntary action that is done intelligently, moderately, and in measure. On this basis, Averroes wrote in his *Commentary on the Republic* that the soft modes used at drinking parties and weddings are inappropriate, and that the only modes that ought to be composed for the guardians are either the kind that conduces to courage and perseverance in wars or the kind that conduces to the attainment of virtues with ease, calmness, and quietude.[106]

It is unusual to find courage and honor spoken of as virtues by a traditional Jewish thinker.[107] Maimonides found them in Plato and Aristotle, and he witnessed the courage and honor of soldiers fighting to defend the lands of Islam. He also knew the great merchants, *those who go down to the sea in ships, doing business in the mighty waters* (Ps 107: 23), and how intrepid they were, sailing in small vessels, braving storms, risking their lives on foreign shores.

The Commentary on the Mishnah was a great *tour de force,* in which Maimonides expounded the Mishnah and condensed the Babylonian and Jerusalem Talmuds, permitting students to master the essence of rabbinic Judaism without having to invest their entire lives doing so. It was a masterful display of memory, power of organization, and lucid explanation. Influenced by Aristotle and Islamic jurisprudence, Maimonides used basic principles as starting points, showing how these were exemplified in specific cases. He imported Greek philosophy into his discussion of law, the heart of Judaism. The commentary was the precursor of the *Mishneh Torah,* which followed the same agenda, yet in details contradicted the commentary and exposed some of its flaws. Maimonides spent the rest of his life revising the commentary, bequeathing the task to his descendants, for whom possession of the fair copy was a sign of learning and authority.

11

Saladin and the Ayyubids

In your light do we see light.

—Ps 36:10

For now we see in a mirror darkly,
but then we will see face to face.

—1 Cor 13:12

Allah is the Light of Heavens and Earth. The similitude of
his Light is as a niche wherein is a lamp, the lamp is in glass,
and the glass is as it were a shining star. [This lamp] is kindled
from a blessed tree. Light upon light, Allah guides to
his light whomsoever He wills.

—Qur'an 24:35

MAIMONIDES HAD BEEN LOYAL to the Fatimid dynasty, which was in power when he arrived in Egypt and for five years thereafter. He then switched allegiance to the Ayyubid dynasty, following in the footsteps of his patron, al-Qadi al-Fadil, who first served the Fatimids and then joined Saladin when he became vizier for their dynasty before overthrowing them. Al-Qadi al-Fadil became Saladin's chief administrator, and his advice and support facilitated Saladin's rise to power. Maimonides was close to the events that I shall relate here, and they set the stage for his life and career for thirty-eight years, until his death in 1204.

Syrian Army in Egypt

Saladin, founder of the Ayyubid dynasty, first came to Egypt with a Syrian army commanded by his uncle Asad al-Din Shirkuh.[1] When the Ayyubids came to power, Maimonides was about thirty-three, and they remained in power for the rest of his life and beyond. The Syrian invasion of Egypt was the beginning of foreign incursions that eventually brought about the collapse of the Fatimids and Egypt's return to the bosom of Sunni Islam under the Ayyubids.[2] Shirkuh and his brother Najm al-Din Ayyub,[3] Saladin's father, were Kurdish emirs (army officers) in the service of the Syrian ruler Nur al-Din Mahmud ibn Zangi (r. 1147–1774).[4] Shirkuh had been a friend of Nur al-Din's father and served Nur al-Din as an emir from the beginning of his reign.

Nur al-Din began a Sunni revival that Saladin consummated in full measure. The events I shall now recount show how Saladin became sultan of Egypt and, following Nur al-Din's death, ruler of Syria as well. Nur al-Din's Syrian army, under Saladin's uncle, Asad al-Din Shirkuh, invaded Egypt in 1164 to decide the outcome of a struggle between rivals for the Fatimid vizierate—Abu 'l-Ashbal Dirgham and Abu Shuja' Shawar. Shawar, overcome by Dirgham, went to Damascus, where he begged Nur al-Din for assistance, promising in return a third of Egypt's revenues and other payments and hoping to command the armies fighting for him. In response, Nur al-Din, seeing an opportunity for getting a foothold in Egypt, sent a Syrian force under Shirkuh to reinstate Shawar. They departed on April 15, 1164, the twenty-six-year-old Saladin with them, according to the historian Ibn Shaddad.[5] Saladin's role is obscure, however, and we are not even sure that he participated in this expedition.

While Shirkuh helped militarily at the beginning of hostilities, Shawar eventually took the initiative and conquered Fustat on his own. The Fatimid caliph al-'Adid reinstated Shawar as vizier, hardly mentioning Shirkuh's role. Shawar then did a volte-face, ordering Shirkuh to leave Egypt without fulfilling his promises of payment. Shawar wrote to the Crusader king Amalric, asking for his support to drive out the Syrians, promising allowances and a grant for the Hospitaller knights, and warning Amalric that Syrian control of Egypt would be detrimental to the Frankish kingdom. Many Egyptians, including al-Qadi al-Fadil, then serving Shawar, approved of this move to achieve Egypt's independence from Syria even at the price of joining the Crusaders. Shawar engaged in a dangerous game, playing the Syrians and Franks against each other. The Crusaders and Shawar besieged Shirkuh at the town of Bilbays, beginning in August 1164. Shirkuh and his troops subsequently departed for Syria.

Shirkuh led another Syrian expedition into Egypt in 1167.[6] This time he definitely brought along his nephew Saladin, whom he left in Alexandria, where there were many Sunnis ready to support the Syrians. King Amalric, having his own plans, invaded Egypt in the autumn of 1168, conquered Bilbays in October, and besieged Fustat/Cairo in November, as result of which a great conflagration destroyed much of Fustat.

The fire is usually ascribed to a Fatimid scorched earth tactic to prevent the Crusaders from using Fustat as a staging area for attacking Cairo. However, rioting sailors from the Fatimid fleet and Sudanese troops were responsible for much of the destruction.[7] The damage was extensive, and many people fled their homes. The areas around the Mosque of 'Amr and Qasr al-Sham' (al-Rum) were left more or less intact, though, and were restored and repopulated later by Saladin.[8] The Fatimid caliph informed Nur al-Din of the perilous situation. Maimonides was, of course, in Egypt at this time, and was certainly influenced by the chaos, but the area where he lived was evidently not harmed by the fire.

In 1169, Shirkuh brought his Syrian troops into Cairo for a third time, and the Crusader army threatened to abandon Shawar unless he paid them more money. Al-Qadi al-Fadil was in Shawar's service then, and recounted a policy discussion in a tent with Shawar, Shawar's son al-Kamil, and his brother Najm.[9] They concurred that it was impossible to defend Egypt without the help of the Franks.

Once the Franks had departed this time, Shirkuh decided to throw in his lot with Egypt, and he began to act independently of his chief, Nur al-Din. Shirkuh realized that to gain control he needed first to remove Shawar, which Syrian soldiers, including Saladin, did on January 18, 1169. Shirkuh then became vizier. Unfortunately, he died two months later (March 23), his death, it is said, brought on by a hot bath after a heavy dinner.[10]

MAIMONIDES' ROLE

Maimonides was already associated with al-Qadi al-Fadil, and we have every reason to believe that he supported him and the Fatimid policy as decided by Shawar. For Maimonides and al-Fadl the situation was bizarre. Al-Fadil was, after all, a Sunni Muslim in the entourage of Fatimid Isma'ilis, making common cause with Christians to protect Egypt's independence from Sunni Turks ruling in Syria. Maimonides was a Jew in the entourage of Fatimid Isma'ilis, supporting his Sunni Muslim patron's policy of alignment with the Christians.

The constant fighting in Egypt had a devastating effect on the Jewish populace, as many were taken captive in the conflicts, especially by the invading Crusaders. They were ordinary citizens, not soldiers who could pay or bargain their way out of captivity. It was the Jewish community that had to raise money to ransom them. Maimonides' earliest communal activity in Egypt was raising funds for redeeming captives, especially those taken prisoner by King Almaric's forces at Bilbays in October 1168.

SALADIN AS FATIMID VIZIER

Nur al-Din made Saladin commander of the Syrian army, and Caliph al-'Adid made him vizier, presenting him with a robe of honor, turban, and insignias of the office, with the title al-Malik al-Nasir (the Victorious King). As his name was Joseph (Yusuf), and as he came to Egypt from Syria and became vizier, he was compared to Joseph of the Bible and Qur'an (Surah 12). The diploma of investiture was drafted by al-Qadi al-Fadil, who at this point was in Saladin's camp as his chief administrator; he remained in Saladin's inner circle until the sultan's death.[11] After the demise of the vizier Shawar, there was every reason for al-Qadi al-Fadil to transfer his allegiance to Saladin and the Ayyubids.

First Saladin had to pacify Cairo and eliminate any signs of Fatimid resistance. After he became vizier, thousands—the number given is fifty thousand—of Sudanese slave-soldiers, faithful to the Fatimid caliph and motivated by racial solidarity (*jinsiyya*), revolted in Cairo on two sweltering days in August 1169, supported by Armenian troops of the Fatimids.[12] Saladin ordered his soldiers to burn their homes in the Mansuriyya Quarter. The Ayyubid force then drove the Sudanese soldiers—thirsty, dusty, and exhausted—against a closed gate.[13] Demoralized, the Sudanese troops surrendered in exchange for a guarantee of safe conduct to Gizeh, across the Nile. But when they got to Gizeh, Saladin's brother Turan Shah slaughtered them mercilessly.

AYYUBIDS REPLACE FATIMIDS

As vizier over Egypt, Saladin was not about to remain subordinate to Nur al-Din or to the Fatimid caliph for that matter. On 10 Dhu 'l-Hijja 565 (August 24, 1170), he suppressed the Shi'i call to prayer and had the four Rashidun caliphs mentioned in the Friday sermon (*khutba*).[14] Then on the first Friday of the new year, 7 Muharram 567 (September 10, 1171), Saladin had the *khutba* said in Fustat in the name of the 'Abbasid caliph. That having passed without incident, on the second Friday of Muharram 567 (September 17, 1171), Saladin went further and had the 'Abbasid *khutba* declared in Fustat and Cairo.[15] Saladin took the title Muhyi Dawlat Amir al-Mu'minin (Reviver of the Empire of the Commander of the Faithful), one that appears often on his inscriptions. The Commander of the Faithful (*amir al-mu'minin*) referred to the 'Abbasid caliph.

In September 1171, the month when Saladin became caliph and the Ayyubids replaced the Fatimids, Maimonides became Ra'is al-Yahud, or Head of the Jews. He was not avid for the office, which was demanding and meant being responsible for *dhimmi* taxes and enforcing *dhimmi* restrictions. Nonetheless, with a new dynasty in power he felt the need to assist the transition and secure for the Jewish communities a favorable position with the Ayyubids. Many Jews had served in

Fatimid chanceries and had residual loyalties to their erstwhile masters. Maimonides remained in office, by my estimation, for only two years or so (1171–73), enough to accomplish his purpose.

The Fatimid caliph al-'Adid died on the night of the Shi'i holiday of 10 Muharram (September 12) or early in the morning of September 13, 1171).[16] The cause of al-'Adid's death is related from various perspectives. It was reported, for instance, that, being ill, he asked Saladin to visit him, and requested that Saladin take care of his children, who were young. The more accepted story is that Saladin suspected treachery and refused to visit al-'Adid but regretted it later. Before this time, Saladin had befriended al-'Adid and spent many hours with the Fatimid ruler in his palace.

Al-Qadi al-Fadil issued an official proclamation, stating that al-'Adid died of natural causes and received a dignified burial. This is essentially the version that has been accepted by Western historians.[17] It is a stretch, however, to believe that the Fatimid caliph died from an illness so well timed to the week between the two sermons that deposed him. Al-'Adid had ruled for eleven and a half years. He died at the age of twenty, ten days short of his twenty-first birthday.

It was Saladin's good fortune that the vizier Shawar, his uncle Shirkuh, and Caliph al-'Adid died so conveniently, paving the way for him to take over Egypt.

FATIMID INSURGENCY AND SUPPORT OF NIZARI ISMA'ILIS

The Ayyubids obliterated vestiges of Fatimid rule and destroyed or transformed remnants of their physical presence. As Isma'ili diehards struggled to restore the Fatimid regime, the Ayyubids put down opposition and removed people suspected of Fatimid sympathies. In 569 (1174), a pro-Fatimid conspiracy in Egypt, led by the Yemenite poet 'Umara al-Yamani and others, and including Christians and Jews, blacks, the palace guard and Egyptian emirs, plotted to overthrow the Ayyubids and restore Fatimid rule. 'Umara and his coconspirators made common cause with the Crusaders and with the Normans of Sicily. The Franks sent a messenger to Saladin, assuring him of their friendly intentions. The messenger, however surreptitiously met with the conspirators. The plotters wrote to Rashid al-Din Sinan, leader of the Nizari Isma'ilis (the Assassins), imploring him to join them, as they had a common mission.[18]

The conspiracy failed, according to one version, because a certain Zayn al-Din 'Ali was approached by the conspirators. He got in touch with al-Qadi al-Fadil, told him about the plot, and agreed to be a double agent.[19] Al-Qadi al-Fadil revealed the plot to Saladin and drafted a letter to Nur al-Din in the name of Saladin, describing the conspiracy and its ultimate failure.[20] Another version has al-Qadi al-Fadil sending Zayn al-Din to investigate why a secretary of 'Umara al-Yamani avoided al-Fadil. Zayn al-Din discovered that 'Umara and others were engaged in a plot against the sultan. Al-Qadi al-Fadil rushed to Saladin, who was at Friday prayers, and revealed the details of the plot.[21] A fatwa of the ulema declared 'Umara al-Yamani an infidel, bringing about his crucifixion under Saladin's authority. When Saladin wavered in his resolve, al-Qadi al-Fadil urged him to execute the man al-Fadil knew so well and whose company he enjoyed in scholarly sessions.

Saladin's eradication of the Fatimid caliphate made him an enemy of the Isma'ili cause. The repression of Isma'ilism in Egypt and the restoration of the *khutba* in the name of the Abbasids demonstrated that Saladin wanted to establish the supremacy of the Sunni caliph over the entire Islamic world. All this was a casus belli for the Nizari Isma'ilis, otherwise known as the Assassins.[22] The Nizaris set up a new Isma'ili mission outside Egypt, occupying the mountain fortress Alamut in northwest Persia. From there they made guerilla attacks on the Sunni Seljuq state. Under their new leader, Rashid al-Din Sinan (d. 1192), one of their agents succeeded in assassinating the famous vizier Nizam al-Mulk (in 1092), founder of the first Sunni madrasa, the Nizamiyya, in Baghdad. The event shocked Sunnis throughout the region. The Nizari Isma'ilis made use of the dagger, which meant that they had to get close to their victims, sacrificing their own lives as *fida'in* (those who sacrifice themselves). They terrorized Sunnis, who called them Hashishiyyun (or Hashshashun), "users of hashish," believing that the Nizaris were stimulated by hallucinatory drugs. The word *assassin* passed from the designation of an Isma'ili sect to the sense of murderer, and as such entered the literary lexicon when it was used by Dante.[23]

The Assassins gained strongholds in Syria from which they struck awe in the hearts of the Crusaders, who called Rashid al-Din Sinan the "Old Man of the Mountain."[24] The Nizaris attempted to kill Saladin several times.[25] The first attempt was in December 1174 or January 1175; the second was on May 22, 1176. Sinan, then at his fortress at Masyaf, sent a suicide team disguised as Ayyubid soldiers. The Nizaris entered Saladin's camp, mingled with his soldiers, and succeeded in enrolling his bodyguard in the conspiracy. When they attacked Saladin in his tent, a cap of mail protected him from severe injury.[26] Saladin invaded Nizari territory and besieged their stronghold at Masyaf on July 30, 1176. He eventually made a truce with Rashid al-Din Sinan and withdrew his army.[27]

WARFARE AGAINST THE CRUSADERS

Saladin's main concerns were not inside Egypt but rather in expanding Ayyubid territory to include Syria and in pursuing jihad against the Crusaders.

In October 1187, Saladin's troops conquered Jerusalem, restoring the Holy City to Islam. Posterity would come to regard this as Saladin's greatest victory. The sultan quoted a *hadith* at the al-Aqsa Mosque before battle: "My God! my earthly means have been devoted to the aid of your religion. There is nothing left but to trust in you, hold fast to your rope [cf. Qur'an 3:103] and rely on your goodness. You are my sufficiency and what an excellent trustee!"[28]

Saladin's task after securing Jerusalem was to reinstate the Dome of the Rock and the al-Aqsa Mosque as Islamic sacred shrines. Seeking to give Jerusalem an Islamic character, Saladin built madrasas, including one named for him, al-Salahiyyah, and established a hospital and lodges for scholars and mystics. One of his earliest acts after conquering Jerusalem was to permit Jews to resume residence there.

The loss of the capital of the Latin Kingdom of Jerusalem shocked Christian Europe and unleashed the Third Crusade (1189–92), bringing Richard the Lionhearted into the fray.

Saladin maintained that he had to unify Muslim territories by controlling Syria and Upper Mesopotamia to wage war successfully against the Crusaders. Syria and Egypt were the foci of Saladin's career, the two centers of the Ayyubid empire.[29] Most of his energies were spent expanding the Ayyubid realm in Syria and Northern Mesopotamia. After Nur ad-Din died in 1174, Saladin occupied Damascus and solidified his legitimacy as ruler there by marrying Nur al-Din's widow, 'Ismat al-Din Khatun, in 1176.[30] Her son by Nur al-Din, al-Salih Isma'il, in a Hamlet-like role, still ruled Aleppo, and led Zangid resistance to Saladin's takeover.

Egypt was the breadbasket that supplied Saladin's armies and made his victories possible—and whose assets he depleted. He never disguised his preference for Syria and his ultimate ambition to control it. After Saladin departed Egypt to conquer Syria and northern Mesopotamia, conditions in Egypt deteriorated, a situation that distressed al-Qadi al-Fadil. He wrote alarmed letters to Saladin, but the sultan could only chant the praises of Damascus and compare the Egyptian phase of his career to being with a prostitute: "Egypt was a whore who had tried in vain to part me from my faithful wife." Al-Fadil reacted strongly, rebuking Saladin for maligning the chaste woman (Egypt) by calling her a prostitute (*mumis*).[31] The exchange put a great strain on their relationship, alienating al-Qadi al-Fadil from his leader. But it was Syria that was Saladin's power base, where he had many relatives, Kurds and Turkomans, and it was Syria that he loved.

After suffering a number of defeats by Richard I and the Crusaders, the sultan died March 4, 1193, in Damascus after a two-week illness. Two people were present—al-Qadi al-Fadil and an imam. Saladin is buried in a tomb in a small garden on the north side of the Umayyad Mosque in Damascus.

AYYUBID EGYPT

With the Ayyubid accession to power, Moses ben Maimon witnessed Cairo's transformation from an Isma'ili center of rule and missionary activity to a Sunni capital loyal to the 'Abbasid caliphate.[32] As a Sunni restoration after two centuries of Shi'i-Isma'ili domination, Saladin's coup d'état was a spectacular turning point in Egyptian history. The Shafi'i and Maliki legal schools replaced the Isma'ili rite, with the chief judge being appointed from the ranks of the Shafi'is.[33] The 'Abbasid ceremonial color black replaced the white of the Fatimids.[34]

The Ayyubids founded many new madrasas to replace Isma'ili centers of instruction.[35] From 1170 until the advent of the Mamluks (1250), they erected more than thirty new religious colleges. Saladin himself sponsored four madrasas in Cairo. These were primarily for study of the religious sciences, but language was also studied as ancillary to them, including *adab* (belles lettres), one of his appointees being a famous Andalusian teacher of *adab* named al-Ru'ayni (d. 1194). The al-Azhar college continued to flourish, but no longer as a center of Isma'ili teaching. The Ayyubids transformed Shi'i institutions to serve the ideology of Sunni Islam. They also established lodges (*zawiya*s) for Sufis. Saladin changed a Fatimid pious foundation named Sa'id al-Su'ada' into a Sufi lodge, serving Sufi mendicants (*fuqara'*) and functioning as a center of popular piety.

Ayyubid Administration

The Ayyubids retained the Fatimid bureaucracy, including its administrative officials and physicians, who made the transition from Fatimid to Ayyubid rule with ease, as did the majority of the population. In the social structure of Ayyubid society, the Muslim elite (aside from the ruling entourage) belonged either to the class of high military officers (emirs) or to "men of the turban" (*muta'ammimun*)—scholars and administration officials, many with a madrasa education. Maimonides had close contacts with both groups, the military officers and government officials. In his medical practice, he treated army officers, and as a religious authority, he had to deal with state officials and judges.

The civil administration was not a rational bureaucracy; it was more a pyramid-like patron-client hierarchy, in which lower echelons paid higher echelons to get appointments and were then repaid out of profits. In this period, the cement that held societies together, whether the Muslims and the ruling dynasty or the Christians and Jews, was "a network of personal relationships."[36] The institutional structures supporting the Ayyubid regime and even the Jewish communities of Egypt were diffuse. Power was transmitted along many lines, all connected by family and personal ties.

AL-QADI AL-FADIL

At noted previously, Maimonides was a protégé of the most famous person of the time after Saladin, his counselor, al-Qadi al-Fadil (1135–1200), administrator, statesman, poet, litterateur, model stylist, and avaricious bibliophile.[37] Al-Qadi al-Fadil's letters are a major source for Saladin's life and career and give an aperçu into the landscape of the age.[38] He was the most influential person of the era after Saladin and surely the most important person in Egypt for Maimonides.

Al-Fadil's family was from Ascalon, where his father had been a judge and, according to one account, sent his son to Egypt for training in administration.[39] Judges did not only preside over court cases; they supervised coinage, taxes, and tariffs, and they were concerned with social welfare and raising forces for jihad. In al-Fadil's case, the title al-Qadi was honorific and referred to his function as administrator. Along with the epithet al-Fadil, meaning "the Excellent," it was conferred upon him by the Fatimid vizier Shawar.

Ascending the rungs of Egypt's political and social hierarchy required the protection of a powerful patron, and Maimonides' career followed the meteoric rise of his benefactor. The elite class was ranked hierarchically, with patronage and friendship (*mahabba*) from above extending to clients below in return for their service (*khidma*).[40] A patron mediated between his clients and higher sponsors, such as the royal entourage. Administrators tried to compensate for the shakiness of their position by constructing a network of personal ties in the administrative system. The wider these ties were, the better were his chances of survival. The employment of members of the same family in administration, such as father and sons or several brothers, was scandalously common.

Al-Qadi al-Fadil studied the secretarial art in Cairo/Fustat and then moved to Alexandria, where he was a government administrator (*katib*).[41] The vizier Ruzzik ibn Tala'i' (r. 1161–62) brought him from Alexandria to Cairo/Fustat and made him head of the Ministry of the Army.[42]

After his coup d'état, Saladin made al-Qadi al-Fadil his counselor and chief administrator, as we have seen.[43] The author of a medieval biography wrote: "No scribe is known to have reached a position with regard to his master comparable to that achieved by al-Fadil with Saladin."[44] Al-Qadi al-Fadil assisted Saladin in deposing the Fatimid caliphate and in launching the Ayyubid regime in Egypt.[45] He made internal reforms, including tax restructuring, reorganized the Egyptian armed forces and intelligence system, and planned the logistics of Saladin's military campaigns. Saladin acknowledged the role of al-Qadi al-Fadil and is quoted as having said, "I have not conquered the countries with the sword, I conquered them with the pen of al-Qadi al-Fadil."[46]

With the Ayyubid accession to power, al-Fadil, together with Saladin's brother al-'Adil, ran Egyptian affairs during Saladin's long absences from Cairo on military campaigns in Syria. Al-Fadil managed domestic and foreign affairs, brought information to Saladin, and wrote letters in his name.[47]

He identified himself as a Muslim by birth and an Egyptian by adoption.[48] Unlike his leader, Saladin, he had a special love for his adopted homeland. Once when crossing the Euphrates into northern Iraq he recited:

> Bear me a message to the Nile,
> Tell it that I could not quench my thirst
> with the waters of the Euphrates,
> And inquire from my heart, for it is my witness,
> If my eye has been a miser in shedding tears.[49]

He loved even the pyramids, which he compared to "the breasts of a woman, symbolizing beauty, prominence, and vitality."[50]

Looking out for the welfare of Egypt and for reducing its tax burden, al-Qadi al-Fadil was distressed when Saladin's wars exhausted Egypt's treasury. In general, he opposed Saladin's warfare against Muslims in Syria and northern Iraq. Whereas al-Fadil wanted to make Cairo the capital of the Ayyubid dynasty, Saladin preferred Damascus.

Al-Qadi al-Fadil was physically unimpressive. He had a large head and a hunched back. The philosopher Abd al-Latif al-Baghdadi described meeting him during the Crusader siege of Acre in 1191: "We came into the presence of al-Fadil and saw a frail old man [he was then fifty-six] all head and heart. He was writing and dictating to two people, with all kinds of contortions of the face and lips caused by his eagerness to get his words out. It was as though he was writing with his whole body." Al-Fadil went on talking to 'Abd al-Latif al-Baghdadi while dictating.

Al-Qadi al-Fadil was a wealthy merchant, invested in Mediterranean and Indian trade and having a high annual salary. He owned a huge tract of land in the area of al-Luq in Cairo, where he planted a large garden that produced vegetables and fruits, including grapes and dates, for Fustat residents.[51] It had spring wells, a large pavilion, and several houses. The garden partly overlooked the Nile. On the garden's edge he constructed a mosque and surrounding buildings. Bab al-Luq, which exists today and gives the area its name, was built in the mid-thirteenth century.

The Excellent Judge was ascetic in his demeanor. "An ascetic life amid wealth," he observed, "is superior to an ascetic life of poverty." He had a basic knowledge of medicine and law.[52] A magnanimous man, al-Qadi al-Fadil founded a religious college, called al-Madrasa al-Fadiliyya, in 580 (1184/85), and a school for orphans nearby. He endowed the madrasa for two legal schools, the Shafi'i and Maliki. His residence was in this complex of buildings, which also contained his enormous library and a hall for readers. His library comprised a hundred thousand bound volumes, originating in the great Fatimid library, which had been auctioned over a period of years. Maimonides presumably availed himself of the riches of this collection and the facilities of the madrasa.[53]

Al-Qadi al-Fadil's *majlis,* or literary salon, was studded with the most brilliant luminaries in Egypt's intellectual firmament.[54] We have every reason to believe that Maimonides was in touch with some of these figures. 'Umara al-Yamani (d. 1174), born in Yemen, emigrated to Egypt and was a member of the Fatimid court and confidant of the vizier Shawar. His memoirs describe court life and intrigue. His history of Yemen, written in 1167/68, under the sponsorship of al-Qadi al-Fadil, is an important source for our knowledge of that country. He was unique in the Qadi's circle for his steadfast loyalty to the Fatimids after the Ayyubids overthrew them, and paid the price for his loyalty, an event described above.

Al-Qadi al-Fadil had good reasons for sponsoring Maimonides and bringing him into the royal entourage. He was an influential force in the Jewish community. He was a physician and scientist used to communicating with men of the world. From al-Qadi al-Fadil's viewpoint, Maimonides could be an ally and secure the Jewish community's support for the new dynasty and its policies. The Ayyubids needed to stabilize the regime and eradicate residual Fatimid loyalty. And there were the state coffers, to which the Jewish community could contribute, as Saladin's munificence and expansionist policy came at a price. From Maimonides' viewpoint, al-Qadi al-Fadil could promote the interests of the Jewish community in the corridors of power. Furthermore, al-Qadi al-Fadil and Maimonides had mutual commercial interests. The Qadi had accumulated great wealth in the India and Maghrib trade. Their friendship was based upon mutual benefit, respect, and shared intellectual interests.

Moses ben Maimon dedicated to al-Qadi al-Fadil his book *On Poisons and Antidotes,* which came to be known as *al-Risala al-Fadiliyya (The Fadilite Treatise).*[55] Al-Fadil had requested advice on first aid for poisonous bites or stings when medical help was unavailable, and he wanted information about precautions against poisons. This was a practical guide for a high official who needed to know how to help friends and harm enemies.

In a lovely dedicatory encomium in this book, which was flattering but truthful, Maimonides lauded al-Fadil's devotion to helping people and saving them from harm by means of his wealth, station, intellect, and eloquence. He satisfied the needs of the poor, nurtured orphans, redeemed prisoners, and built places of learning, increasing the number of scholars. He saved individuals, communities, and towns through his eloquence. He rescued people's property from booty-seeking Crusaders and from despoiling rulers.[56] He made peace among believers and waged war against polytheists (Christians), seeking to open their minds to recognize the oneness of God and to disseminate monotheism in all their countries. He did this with his tongue and his pen. He guided rulers in ways of justice and truth. His counsel and guidance made the people of Cairo more prosperous than people of all other cities known.

A strange story regarding Maimonides and al-Qadi al-Fadil is told by the thirteenth-century author al-Ghazi ibn al-Wasiti, a civil administrator, who held government positions in Cairo, Aleppo, and Damascus.[57]

> I have been told by the most trustworthy witnesses that when the physician Moses fell ill, al-Qadi al-Fadil went to visit him. Now, this Jew was a learned and decent fellow.[58] So he said to al-Fadil, "I owe you a favor for your coming to visit me. I advise you not to employ a Jew as a physician.[59] With us whoever desecrates the Sabbath has forfeited his life." So al-Qadi al-Fadil forbade employing Jews as physicians.

The story is odd for several reasons. First, Maimonides himself was a physician to al-Qadi al-Fadil. Furthermore, he would not have wanted to deprive Jewish physicians of a livelihood. Moreover, they did not need to desecrate the Sabbath any more than he did.

The writer was evidently trying to discourage Muslims from hiring Jews (and Christians) as physicians and civil service officials, as their skill and cleverness made them tough competition for Muslims. He was not impressed by *dhimmi* conversions to Islam, which he viewed as opportunistic.

Although al-Ghazi ibn al-Wasiti's anecdote is apparently spurious, the possibility has been raised that it contains the proverbial grain of truth.[60] Perhaps Maimonides in a moment of irritation made a derisive remark about Jewish physicians who sometimes lacked knowledge and experience and thereby harmed their patients. His criticism may have been conveyed to al-Qadi al-Fadil, and this became distorted by al-Ghazi or his source into advice to refrain from employing Jewish physicians altogether.

Al-Qadi al-Fadil died on January 25, 1200, and was buried at the foot of the Muqattam Hills in Cairo.

AYYUBID COMMERCE

The Ayyubids under Saladin resumed trade, which had flourished under the Fatimids, developing the main routes from Egypt to Africa, the Indian Ocean, and the Far East.[61] The Crusaders had interrupted trade with European merchants. Saladin, therefore, signed commercial treaties with Italian cities and permitted Italian merchants to settle in Alexandria. After first collecting a double tariff from *dhimmi*s, he authorized Christian and Jewish merchants to pay the same tariff as Muslims. The Karimi merchants, from the Fatimid period, dominated international trade between the Indian Ocean and Egypt.[62] They were an association of partners who owned ships and had a collective legal position. The Ayyubids gave them protection and set up storehouses and port services for them.

AYYUBID RELIGION AND THEOLOGY

The Shafi'i and Maliki schools replaced the Isma'ili rite, with the chief judge (*qadi 'l-qudat*) being appointed from the ranks of the Shafi'is.[63] As a judicial authority, Maimonides had close ties to the Muslim chief judge, and he refers about ten times to Muslim judges in his responsa. Saladin employed scholars and bureaucrats with local knowledge and reputation and established charitable foundations to provide for Sunni ulema.[64]

The Ayyubids favored the Ash'ari school of *kalam* (theology).[65] The Ash'aris did not shun anthropomorphic references to God and ascribed to him real eternal attributes. According to the Ash'aris, Qur'anic references to God's hand and face or to descending and sitting must not be reinterpreted abstractly but are real attributes of God, whose true meaning is unfathomable. We need to accept them without asking how (*bi-la kayfa*).[66] The Ash'aris rejected Mu'tazili *tanzih* (demythologizing) as emptying the notion of God of meaning and being tantamount to atheism (*ta'til*). (In due course, however, even Ash'ari theologians relaxed their hermeneutic fundamentalism and interpreted Qur'anic anthropomorphisms metaphorically.)

The Ash'ari theologians embraced an atomistic theory of the physical world, but unlike Greek atomists they did not believe that chance rules the cosmos. Where ancient atomists, such as Leucippus, Democritus, Epicurus, and Lucretius, detected chance, denying the purposive theories of the Peripatetics, Stoics, and Platonists, the Ash'aris perceived God, who creates, combines, and annihilates individual atoms, maintaining his omnipotence. God's sovereign will is the immediate cause of all occurrences. There are no laws of nature, no permanent world order, or cause and effect; only God creates events anew every moment. Laws of nature are customary recurrences of isolated events, as the Scottish philosopher David Hume (1711–1776) was to maintain.

The Ash'ari school refused to impose rational criteria upon God's actions. His will is inscrutable, and whatever he determines is thereby good and just. The Ash'aris opposed Mu'tazili rationalism, which posited that what God requires of human beings is just and rational. The Ash'aris claimed that good and evil are determined by divine revelation, not by reason, by which God is not bound or limited. A rhymed epitome of the Ash'ari theology dedicated to Saladin became a textbook in schools.[67]

Maimonides' harsh strictures against Ash'ari *kalam* (theology) in *The Guide of the Perplexed* (I, 71 and 73) sharply contradicted the prevailing doctrine of the Ayyubid religious establishment. He claimed that the Ash'ari denial of cause and effect undermines the possibility of science.[68] In his philosophic outlook, Maimonides was closer to the deposed Fatimids than to the reigning Ayyubids.

The Sunni orientation of the Ayyubids had an adverse effect on the *dhimmi*s. To begin with, Shirkuh in his brief time as vizier enforced the sumptuary (pertaining to dress) laws on non-Muslims.[69] Then at the beginning of Ayyubid rule the government prohibited hiring Christians to serve in the fiscal administration. Christian historical sources blame al-Qadi al-Fadil for this policy. Emirs, or army commanders, however, continued to employ *dhimmi*s on their estates and in general had excellent relations with them. The Ayyubid emirs were "a foreign body grafted onto Egyptian society," having come from Syria, and they tended to be sympathetic to *dhimmi*s, who were also viewed as alien.[70] The Ayyubids enforced the provisions of the Pact of 'Umar, which regulated *dhimmi* behavior, and a number of Christian administrators and physicians converted to Islam.

The Ayyubids zealously stamped out dissent and heresy. The most significant act of oppression was the execution of the mystic martyr Shihab al-Din Yahya al-Suhrawardi (b. 1154) in 1191 by al-Zahir Ghazi, Saladin's son and ruler of Aleppo. We may assume that Maimonides knew about the incident. Saladin himself gave the execution order, and the letter to al-Zahir Ghazi conveying the order was written by al-Qadi al-Fadil. Maimonides' pupil Joseph ben Judah Ibn

Simon was in Aleppo at the time. In the year of the execution, Maimonides wrote his *Treatise on Resurrection,* affirming his belief in its literal sense in a prudent exhibition of traditional faith.

Al-Suhrawardi, founder of the Illuminationist, or Ishraqi, school of philosophy, based on a synthesis of ancient Zoroastrian, pre-Socratic, Platonic, Aristotelian, Hermetic, and Pythagoreanizing Neoplatonist doctrines, along with Islamic/Sufi teachings, such as the "science of lights," had substantial influence in his own time and down to the present. *Ishraq* was inner illumination, related to the Qur'anic concept of *sakina* (Heb. *shekhinah*), to which Maimonides referred in *The Guide of the Perplexed* (see below, ch. 19). Al-Suhrawardi arrived in Aleppo around 1183 and eventually became a confidant of the prince al-Zahir Ghazi.[71] He taught that only the truly wise and enlightened recipients of illuminationist wisdom have the right to rule. He conceived of the ruler as a philosopher-king, according to the model of Plato and al-Farabi, adding that the ruler had to be a recipient of divine light, meaning special knowledge, and be able to perform extraordinary acts and predict the future. Potential rulers, he taught, should study "the science of lights" and acquire both intuitive and discursive wisdom.

After al-Suhrawardi gained prominence in Aleppo, he was accused of declaring the religious law abrogated. He was thought to possess magic powers and divine secrets, and was believed by some to be a prophetic messenger of God, placing his authority above that of the Islamic law. He was denounced as an infidel and sorcerer who wanted to contaminate the faith and corrupt the young prince al-Zahir Ghazi, and he was charged with denying positive divine attributes and following ancient wisdom and philosophy.[72] Suhrawardi was suspected of being involved in a conspiracy to announce al-Zahir Ghazi as ruler of the age, as divinely supported, and guided by the divine philosopher al-Suhrawardi himself.

This episode was a *cause célèbre.* Baha' al-Din Ibn Shaddad, Saladin's biographer, qadi of the army and Jerusalem, described Saladin as believing literally in resurrection of the dead and despising philosophers and deniers of the divine attributes. He gave the execution of al-Suhrawardi as a shining example of the sultan's adherence to these beliefs. Maimonides was on unsteady ground with his vehement rejection of Ash'arism. We can understand Maimonides' discretion in these matters—his reluctance, for example, to have *The Guide of the Perplexed* written in Arabic characters and his affirmation of resurrection in its literal, physical sense.

Saladin was familiar with philosopher-kings—the early Fatimid caliphs and the leader of the Isma'ili Assassins—and was naturally wary of the type. Al-Suhrawardi's plans could have brought about the defection of Aleppo or abandoning the jihad against the Crusaders. He therefore ordered al-Suhrawardi's execution, and al-Zahir Ghazi reluctantly carried out his father's wishes. The Mausoleum of Shihab al-Din Ahmad al-Suhrawardi is located in Aleppo.

AYYUBID CULTURE

When we speak of the Ayyubid era, we must realize that Egypt and Syria, including northern Mesopotamia (al-Jazira), formed a single culture sphere. Politically, Egypt and Syria were connected by means of the alliance—uneasy as it was at times—between Nur al-Din of Syria and Saladin of Egypt until Nur al-Din died in 1174 and Saladin became supreme commander of the Egyptian and Syrian armies and brought Syria and Northern Iraq under Ayyubid control. Intellectuals moved about freely from one area to the other, as did Joseph ben Judah when he moved from Cairo to Aleppo.

Prominent among the intellectuals and culture bearers during the Ayyubid age were the *kuttab*—the clerks, bureaucrats, and officers of the administration. Individuals such as al-Qadi al-Fadil, 'Imad al-Din al-Katib, and Baha' al-Din Ibn Shaddad were religious scholars, as well as historians, litterateurs, and poets. The *kuttab* were expected to have a broad humanistic education and encyclopedic knowledge in grammar, rhetoric, mathematics, natural science, foreign languages, Qur'an, hadith, dialectics, law, genealogy, history, poetry, and *adab*.[73] They laced their letters with rhymed prose having clever tropes and tantalizing allusions.

We see a similar *jeu d'esprit* in Maimonides' correspondence, especially in his exchanges with Rabbi Anatoli, the sages of Lunel, and Joseph ben Judah.[74] Jewish intellectuals exchanged letters in rhymed prose, embroidered with subtly irreverent biblical allusions in a dazzling display of ingenuity spiced with humor.

Unlike their Fatimid predecessors, the Ayyubids did not establish regular institutions for the study of the secular sciences. When the philosopher-physician 'Abd al-Latif al-Baghdadi visited Cairo in 1191, he found two philosophers there, one being Musa ibn Maymun, whom he was eager to meet (see below).

The absence of philosophers in Cairo is not surprising in view of the sultan's suspicion of their religious sincerity and his partiality to Ash'ari theology. This does not mean that Maimonides lived in a cultural wilderness. His close acquaintances among the Cairo elite were men of refinement and sophistication, though not philosophers and scientists as were Muslim colleagues in the West.

IBN SANA' AL-MULK

Maimonides had personal ties of friendship with the poet Ibn Sana' al-Mulk, who was like him a protégé of al-Qadi al-Fadil. The Qadi was a friend of Ibn Sana' al-Mulk's family, and he took the poet under his tutelage and improved his literary style.[75] Ibn Sana' al-Mulk had a busy correspondence with his mentor when al-Fadil accompanied Saladin on his campaigns in Syria. He joined his patron there in 571 (1175/76) and met 'Imad al-Din al-Isfahani, secretary to Saladin, who was impressed by Ibn Sana' al-Mulk's intelligence and literary talent. In 572 (1176/77), he became a *katib* in the government chancery (*diwan al-insha'*) with the support of al-Qadi al-Fadil.

Ibn Sana' al-Mulk was first and foremost a poet, an anthologist of poetry, and a poetry critic. He wrote a famous book on strophic poetry, titled *Dar al-tiraz fi 'amal al-muwashshahat* (*The Embroidery Factory for Creating Strophic Poetry*), and made this Andalusian genre known in Egypt, where it gained popularity in literary circles.[76] He wrote enthusiastically about strophic poetry, enchanted by the novelty and diversity of the genre. He also provided conventions for composing strophic poetry and cited examples, adding specimens of his own along with an analysis of the genre's poetics. His book is a valuable source for our knowledge of this Andalusian genre. He also wrote a *diwan* with strophic poetry, as did his companion 'Umara al-Yamani. Maimonides was naturally familiar with the strophic form and discussed the permissibility of singing songs of this genre at weddings.[77]

Ibn Sana' wrote verses about Maimonides, combining adulation and wit.

Were [Moses ben Maimon] to treat the [present] time with his
  knowledge,
He would cure it from the disease of ignorance.
Were the full moon to ask him for treatment,
It would obtain the perfection it claims.
On the day of the full moon, he would give it medicine against its
  brownish freckles,
And cure it of disease on the last day of the month.[78]

Maimonides participated in Ibn Sana' al-Mulk's circle of companions. Al-Fadil mentioned some brilliant remarks by the poet that were eagerly welcomed in his circle, described as "lovers who love discourse, in particular that dealing with theology ['ilm al-kalam]."[79]

Ibn Sana' al-Mulk explained: "The theology to which [al-Fadil] referred is a section in a letter I wrote to him in which I mentioned a disputation (munazara) that had taken place between me, Sharif Abu 'l-Qasim al-Halabi, and al-Ra'is Abu 'Imran Musa al-Yahudi. It is a long session and there is no room for discussing it in this book."[80] The conversation took place in Ibn Sana' al-Mulk's literary salon (majlis) sometime before 582 (1186/87), the date of Sharif Abu 'l-Qasim's death. Thus, as Franz Rosenthal observed, we find an Egyptian Sunni, a Shi'i scholar from Aleppo, and the Andalusian Jew Maimonides convening in Cairo, in a circle of "lovers who love discourse" to discuss theology. Maimonides accordingly participated in disputations with contemporary mutakallimun, although his attitude toward kalam in The Guide of the Perplexed was, as we know, disapproving.[81]

Maimonides is mentioned along with Ibn Sana' al-Mulk in a deathbed declaration of a certain Abu 'l-Faraj Ibn al-Kallam on March 24, 1182.[82] They were creditors of the man, as were Shaykh al-Muwaffaq (perhaps the physician Ibn Jumay') and a Muslim jurist by the name of Ibn Sawla. Abu 'l-Faraj stated that he owed money to "our teacher and master Moses" (2.5 Egyptian dinars) and to the illustrious Qadi Ibn Sana' al-Mulk (1 dinar and 12 dirhams).[83]

As Goitein observes, we have here two distinguished Jews and two outstanding Muslims belonging to a circle of intimate friends who were brought together by shared cultural and intellectual interests. Abu 'l-Faraj was admitted to their circle, as merchants sought the company of intellectuals, offering them services and receiving help when needed.[84] The document reflects the intellectual vitality of the early Ayyubid period, which facilitated contacts among members of different religious groups. One may add that the moribund Abu 'l-Faraj was evidently a Jew and that the debts may have been incurred from business rather than from friendly interchange. If so, this text attests that Maimonides was engaged in investment banking along with sedentary trading. We do not, however, have enough evidence to say this with certainty.

JAMAL AL-DIN IBN AL-QIFTI

A contemporary of Maimonides who may have known him in Cairo was the historian Jamal al-Din Ibn al-Qifti. He is our main source for information on Maimonides' life.[85] Ibn al-Qifti lived in Cairo until 1187, and then went to Jerusalem, where his father served as a deputy to al-Qadi al-Fadil, more reason for supposing that Maimonides knew him. In 1201, he settled in Aleppo, where he became a close friend of Joseph ben Judah. Ibn al-Qifti related that when the Christians and Jews of Morocco were forced to convert to Islam or be expatriated (during the Almohad persecutions), Joseph concealed his true religion and practiced Islam in public. Then when he could, he left for Egypt. This is, of course, similar to the account Ibn al-Qifti gave concerning Maimonides in his entry on Joseph, from whom he heard it.

'ABD AL-LATIF AL-BAGHDADI

'Abd al-Latif al-Baghdadi was a philosopher and physician who hailed from Iraq.[86] His career is fascinating and deserves attention as illustrative of the intellectual currents of the era. Moreover, he actually met Maimonides, and is the only one to have done so and to have left us his impression of the Great Eagle.

In an extended travelogue, or autobiographical essay, 'Abd al-Latif told of his journey from Baghdad to Jerusalem, and then his visit to Saladin's camp outside Acre in 587 (1190). He was introduced to al-

Qadi al-Fadil, who gave him a small note addressed to Ibn Sana' al-Mulk, his representative (*wakil*) in Cairo. In Cairo, Ibn Sana' al-Mulk provided 'Abd al-Latif with a house and a salary, and presented him to the chiefs of the administration (*arbab al-dawla*) as a guest of al-Qadi al-Fadil.

'Abd al-Latif said that he came to Cairo to see three people: Yasin al-Simiya'i (the Magician), al-Ra'is Musa ibn Maymun al-Yahudi (as he called Maimonides), and Abu 'l-Qasim al-Sha'iri. The first turned out to be a deceitful liar and trickster. As for Musa ibn Maymun, al-Baghdadi wrote, "Musa came to see me."[87] "He was of superior merit," he went on, "but he was overcome by love of authority [*riyasa*] and serving the high and mighty." As the testimony of the only person who met the Great Eagle and left word about him, it is intriguing, as Maimonides commended humility so strongly. 'Abd al-Latif then commented on *The Guide of the Perplexed*: "He wrote a book for the Jews and called it *Kitab al-dalala* (*The Book of the Guide*) and cursed whoever would write it in a non-Hebrew script.[88] I read it and found it to be a bad book which destroys the foundations of laws and beliefs, whereas he thought that he was restoring them." This remark is fascinating, as it is made by a Muslim close to the time of composition. Notice that 'Abd al-Latif regarded the *Guide* as a book written for Jews.[89] He found that it is damaging not only to the Jewish religion but also to religious laws and beliefs in general. He did not, however, elaborate. If he read *The Guide of the Perplexed*, as he said he did, it would have been a version transcribed into Arabic letters, unless someone read it to him.

'Abd al-Latif's next meeting is important for us as revealing the intellectual orientation of a philosopher living then in Cairo. It was in a mosque that 'Abd al-Latif met Abu 'l-Qasim al-Sha'iri, who took his guest to his home, where they dined and discussed philosophy. Al-Sha'iri introduced him to the books of Abu Nasr al-Farabi, Alexander of Aphrodisias, and Themistius. Al-Sha'iri's philosophic orientation was close to that of Maimonides, who respected these thinkers and used them in his writings.

In a different version of his autobiography, 'Abd al-Latif related that he found two scholars studying the ancients in Cairo, one a Maghribi Jew, called Musa ibn Maymun, "who has extensive knowledge and great intellectual gifts, but was too much concerned with worldly success and frequenting the great."[90]

When Saladin signed a peace treaty with the Crusaders in 588 (1192), 'Abd al-Latif went to meet him in Jerusalem, bringing as many of the writings of the ancients as possible. At the beginning of the evening he attended Saladin's court. He found the assembly hall filled with learned men discussing different sciences. Saladin, he wrote, enjoyed these assemblies.[91] Saladin arranged a pension for 'Abd al-Latif in Damascus, and after the sultan died in 1193, 'Abd al-Latif remained in Damascus, where he studied the ancients.

'Abd al-Latif returned to Egypt in 1197 with al-Malik al-'Aziz 'Uthman, Saladin's son. He taught in the al-Azhar Mosque. Then at midday he gave instruction in medicine and other subjects, probably the ancient sciences. This he must have done in private because he said that afterward he would return to al-Azhar.[92]

He was in Cairo during the great famine in 1199–1202, which he described in gruesome detail. The famine followed a drought caused by the Nile's failure to rise, leading also to plague and contagion and resulting in flight and depopulation of cities and towns. 'Abd al-Latif vividly described horrific acts of cannibalism.[93] Maimonides referred to the famine in his Responsa.[94] I mention this dreadful episode because it gives us a sense of the tenor of life at the time, the constant threat of catastrophe, and the total breakdown of civilized behavior when calamities struck. To understand the *mentalité* of the age we must reckon with the unbearable insecurity and precariousness of life.

When al-Malik al-'Aziz died (595/1198), 'Abd al-Latif went to Jerusalem and taught at the al-Aqsa Mosque. He traveled to Damascus in 1207, where he wrote and delivered lectures on medicine and the sciences, including a book on diabetes.[95] He then moved on to Aleppo, where he remained from 1216 to 1220, and thereafter went to Byzantium. In Aleppo, he got to know Joseph ben Judah, whom he described as a Maghribi shaykh who had converted to Islam but reverted outwardly to Judaism, though Jews do not believe this.[96] Joseph had been poor, 'Abd al-Latif wrote, wandered around in the service of merchants, and became a physician later in life. 'Abd al Latif accused him of killing his patients, specifically blaming him for the demise in Aleppo in 613 (1216) of al-Zahir Ghazi, who had been treated unsuccessfully by Joseph and others.

Abd al-Latif al-Baghdadi's philosophical interests can be gauged from several of his works.[97] His sources and general outlook are close to Maimonides.

The material in the second version of his autobiography complements the narrative in that of Ibn Abi Usaybi'a. He gave an epitome of al-Farabi's account of Plato's philosophy, compressing the text and quoted passages from Plato's *Republic, Timaeus,* and *Laws*.[98] He also made use of al-Farabi's summary of Aristotle's philosophy, believing that Plato and Aristotle taught the same philosophy and that it cannot be improved.[99]

'Abd al-Latif complained that people use logical terms without understanding their meaning. (It was such a situation that had caused Maimonides to write his *Treatise on the Art of Logic*.) He observed that philosophers warned against teaching logic and philosophy to all people indiscriminately, citing the religious laws as advocating restraint, a sentiment shared by Maimonides. It is imperative, he wrote, to observe the religious law before philosophizing. He expressed his opposition to alchemy and to frauds and dupes. The father of this false science, he observed, was Jabir ibn Hayyan, who led astray scholars of later generations such as Abu Bakr al-Razi, who in his work on physics and in his *Doubts Concerning Galen* exhibited weakness in the theoretical part of philosophy and medicine. Maimonides had a low opinion of al-Razi, criticizing him for affirming that there is more evil in the universe than good. In his letter to Samuel ibn Tibbon, he wrote that al-Razi was merely a physician.[100]

Al-Sha'iri, Musa ibn Maymun, and 'Abd al-Latif had similar philosophical bearings.[101] They made ample use of Plato, especially his political philosophy. They knew Ibn Sina but were not impressed by him, and they shied away from alchemy and the "pseudosciences." They studied Aristotle thoroughly with his commentaries, in particular Alexander of Aphrodisias and Themistius. They also used Neoplatonic texts, especially those that were believed to have emanated from Aristotle.

Ayyubid Hospitals and Medical Care

Saladin emulated Nur al-Din by sponsoring religious colleges (madrasas) and hospitals. Devoted to improving public health, Sultan Saladin established the Nasiri Hospital, a large institution in his name (al-Malik al-Nasir). Saladin's models were the Nuri hospitals that Sultan Nur al-Din built in Damascus and Aleppo. If the level of medical care and hospitals is a measure of a society's civilization, then Ayyubid Cairo receives high commendation. The hospitals in Syria and Egypt in the twelfth and thirteenth centuries were administered on rigorous standards, with careful treatment of patients, meticulous records, frequent clinical visits, and lectures.

After a visit to the Nasiri Hospital in 1182, the intrepid traveler Ibn Jubayr gave an enthusiastic description, praising its administration and staff.[102] He was impressed that the sultan, when he was in town, supervised everything, examining and questioning, and demanding that the greatest care and attention be given to everything in the hospital.

The Nurid and Ayyubid hospitals were founded and financed on the basis of pious endowments called *awqaf* (sing. *waqf*), donated by rulers, the elite, and the wealthy. The profit-yielding property of hospitals was extensive, including caravanserais, mills, and shops, even entire villages. The hospitals had fountains with clean water for drinking and baths and separate areas for women, prevalent diseases, surgical cases, and the mentally ill. Appointed physicians made the rounds, checking patients and prescribing medicine, with the help of orderlies and male and female attendants. Maimonides' son, Abraham, as we have seen, had an official appointment at the Nasiri Hospital, although Maimonides himself is not said to have had a hospital appointment.[103]

Saladin's Christian and Jewish Physicians

Ibn Abi Usaybi'a mentioned twenty-one physicians in Saladin's service—eight Muslims, eight Jews, and five Christians.[104] I mention these physicians who administered to Saladin because they formed a network of medical experts, most of them brought into government service by al-Qadi al-Fadil, and they were colleagues of Maimonides. Great as Maimonides was as a physician, in his own day he was eclipsed

by the most illustrious physician in the early Ayyubid era—Hibatallah
Ibn Jumay' (or Jami', d. 594 [1198]), called al-Muwaffaq (the Successful), chief physician at the court of Saladin. If you had lived in Cairo/
Fustat at the time and needed the services of a physician, your Cairene
friends would most likely send you to Ibn Jumay'.

IBN JUMAY'

The Jewish physician Abu 'l-Makarim Hibatallah Ibn Jumay' al-Isra'ili
(d. 1198) was born in Fustat.[105] He studied medicine with the famous
physician Abu Nasr al-'Aynzarbi.[106] Maimonides was in close contact
with him and on one occasion—there must have been more—he recommended a medical student to him.[107] Ibn Jumay' gained renown by
reviving a man believed dead after a cataleptic fit. As the dead man
was being carried on a bier for burial past the clinic of Ibn Jumay' in
Suq al-Qanadil, Ibn Jumay' noticed that his feet, protruding from under the hearse cloth, were erect and not flat as they should be if he were
in fact dead. The populace believed that he had revived the man.

Ibn Jumay' dedicated to Sultan Saladin his *al-Risala al-Salahiyya fi
ihya' al-'ulum al-sihhiyya* (*The Salahid Treatise on Reviving the Medical
Sciences*), dealing with ethical and social issues in the medical art.[108]
The book was the outcome of a conversation with Saladin about the
decline of medicine.[109] He described the deficiency of medicine in his
time, the ineptitude of physicians, and lack of suitable medical training. We shall see later (ch. 22) that Maimonides too had a generally low
opinion of medical practice in his time. In the final chapter on medical
education, Ibn Jumay' wrote that it is not enough for a medical student to study the Greek physicians Hippocrates and Galen. A student
needs to have clinical training, preferably in hospitals, where he can
make rounds with physicians as they treat patients. Clinical training is
something we take for granted, but in those days a medical student
could avoid it, a practice that the sultan and Ibn Jumay' deplored.

Ibn Jumay' dedicated a short treatise on the entire science of medicine, *al-Irshad fi masalih al-anfus wa-'l-asjad* (*Guide to the Welfare of
Souls and Bodies*), to al-Qadi al-Fadil. He also wrote a brief treatise on
Alexandria and another on administering first aid when a physician is
not available.

He knew Arabic literature and wrote his *al-Risala al-Salahiyya* in an elevated style. Ibn Abi Usaybi'a said that Ibn Jumay' always consulted al-Jawhari's *Sihah,* a dictionary of classical Arabic. In their medical writings, Jewish physicians sought a high style of classical Arabic (*fusha*). They wrote in Arabic characters and tried to avoid solecisms and dialectical features of Judeo-Arabic.

AL-MUWAFFAQ IBN SHU'A

Another famous Jewish physician at the time was al-Muwaffaq Ibn Shu'a (or Shaw'a) (d. 1183/84), who served as personal physician to Saladin. He practiced medicine, surgery, and ophthalmology. Along with his learning, he was a free-spirited poet and musician. His instrument was the *qitara*.[110] An anecdote about Ibn Shu'a enlightens us about the ambiguous status of *dhimmi* physicians. They were respected for their medical skills, yet they remained *dhimmi*s with restricted rights. Ibn Shu'a liked horseback riding, which was forbidden by the Pact of 'Umar governing *dhimmi* conduct. An austere and devout Shafi'i jurist, Najm al-Din (Star of the Faith) al-Khabushani, criticized the royal palace for not enforcing the *dhimmi* regulations.[111] Whenever Najm al-Din saw a *dhimmi* riding a horse, he would assault the person. When he saw Ibn Shu'a riding, he threw a stone that put out one of the physician's eyes. Ibn Shu'a wrote a sardonic poem about the occasion:

> Do not wonder that the sun's rays dim the eyes,
> for this is not unusual.
> Rather wonder how I was blinded
> by an obscure and tiny star [*najm*].[112]

The Karaites were among the wealthier and more intellectual members of the Jewish community, and many were physicians, some in the royal court. Although Maimonides, as a Rabbanite Jew, regarded the Karaites as heretics (*minim*) for their deviation from rabbinic Judaism, he treated them with respect socially, and presumably befriended Karaite physicians in the sultan's entourage.[113]

The medical staff of the Ayyubid palace included prominent Christian physicians as well. The Syrian Christian Asad ibn Ilyas Ibn al-Matran (d. 1191) studied grammar and lexicography and then immersed himself in Christian theology in Byzantium, thereafter studying medicine in Baghdad.[114] He became physician to Saladin, whom he accompanied on his campaigns, and for whom he wrote a treatise on the regimen of health. Saladin persuaded Ibn Matran to convert to Islam. His *Bustan al-atibba' wa-rawdat al-alibba'* (*The Garden of Physicians and the Meadows of the Wise*) is a rich resource of excerpts and quotations on the ancient sciences. He amassed great wealth and, employing three copyists, built an enormous library of ten thousand volumes.[115]

MAIMONIDES, PHYSICIAN TO SALADIN

According to Ibn Abi Usaybi'a, Moses ben Maimon served as physician to Saladin.[116] As Saladin did not return to Egypt from wars in Syria after 1182, Maimonides' entrance to his service was presumably prior to this year. This makes sense, of course, seeing that Maimonides was Head of the Jews from 1171 to 1173. It was natural to be simultaneously Head of the Jews and court physician to the sultan. Maimonides was, of course, the protégé of Saladin's chief administrator, al-Qadi al-Fadil, who brought many physicians to serve Saladin and the royal entourage.[117] Ibn Abi Usaybi'a, colleague of Abraham Maimonides, was in an excellent position to know whether Maimonides served as physician to Saladin. I see no reason to doubt Ibn Abi Usaybi'a's report, especially as al-Qadi al-Fadil was the one who introduced physicians to Saladin.

Some historians maintain, though, that Ibn Abi Usaybi'a's statement about Maimonides' service to Saladin is unsupported and untrue.[118] It is argued that Maimonides' assertion in a letter to Joseph ben Judah, in 1190, that he had "attained great fame in medicine among the eminent" means that he had no success as a practitioner prior to about 1190. Also, Maimonides did not dedicate any medical writings to Saladin, as he did to Saladin's son al-Afdal, whom he served later.[119] Furthermore, it is strange that Ibn al-Qifti did not mention Maimonides' service to Saladin. We must recall, however, that we have only an abridged version of his book.

12

The Great Rav in Israel

You know, my honored son, that these great things and high offices
that Jews attain in our time are not in my eyes happiness and
perfection worth striving for, and are not—by the life of God
(the exalted)—a minor evil but an appalling vexation and burden.

—Letter to Joseph ben Judah Ibn Simon

THERE HAS BEEN so much discussion about the office of Ra'is al-Yahud that it is worth clarifying what it was, not only because Maimonides was Ra'is at a crucial time but also because, in my view, he took over many functions of the Ra'is when he was not in office, mainly by supervising personal law, synagogues, pious foundations, and social services.

The office of Nagid or Ra'is al-Yahud was not based upon law or tradition, as were the ranks of Gaon, Nasi, and Exilarch.[1] It was created in eleventh-century Egypt to give the government a spokesman responsible for the Jewish community. The Head of the Jews, though, was not a supreme leader who organized all of Egyptian Jewry. The political/social reality was more complex and power much more diffused, dynamic, and shifting. For one thing, there were always challenges to the Head's authority from different sources.[2] In addition, he could not govern on his own; he needed a broad consensus of the elders and the educated and wealthy and consent of the common people.

The regime of the Jewish community was an oligarchy, or rule by the few, with support of the many, who were capable of disruption. Local judges and *muqaddams* (community leaders) also wielded power, as did Geonim and Nesi'im.[3] Instability of the Islamic state impacted the Head's position, as we have seen with Nagid Samuel ben Hananyah.

The Jewish community referred to the Ra'is by the biblical title Nagid.[4] However, after Nagid Samuel ben Hananyah's tenure of office the title fell into abeyance until Maimonides' son, Abraham, used it. The historian Joseph Sambari concluded, incorrectly, that from the time of Samuel ben Hananyah to Abraham ben Moses there were no Nagids.[5] Maimonides did not have the title Nagid, although he was addressed as Nagid in some letters and documents. However, five generations of his descendants were called Nagid, spanning more than two hundred years down to the fifteenth century.[6]

The government appointed the Head of the Jews after leading members of the local communities, the territorial community, and the ecumenical authorities had agreed on a candidate.[7] He was thereby elected from below and confirmed from above, the double selection signifying his position as mediator between the community and the government.[8] The candidate either reached high office on his own, as did Maimonides, or succeeded his father or other family member in office.

Muslim sources depicted the Ra'is as equivalent to the Christian Patriarch.[9] Administrative handbooks and letters of appointment state that the Jews were divided into three sects (Rabbanites, Karaites, and Samaritans), that the Head of the Jews was to be selected from the majority Rabbanite faction, and that he had authority over all three denominations.[10] He was required to avoid partiality toward his fellow Rabbanites, "a tendency which his own baser instincts [*nafs ammara*] might lead him into," and he must have the Karaites' complete confidence.[11] During the Fatimid and Ayyubid periods, the authority of the Head of the Jews extended to Jewish communities in Syro-Palestine.[12]

The Ra'is was not supposed to seek office ambitiously but should accept it when it was thrust upon him. "He should be a man of immoveable principle, not to be deflected from the right course by disappointment or embarrassment; and he should be outspoken and not keep silent in the face of what he knows is really wrong."[13]

The appointee had to be a person who gave good counsel in private

and public.[14] One letter of appointment noted the candidate's outstanding skill in medicine: "Being the authority in the field of medicine, on
which good health depends and endures. By his skill the symptoms of
illness and disease are removed." In matters of health, he submits to the
laws of religion, doing "what is permitted in earthly life."[15]

Administrative handbooks stressed that the offices of Patriarch and
Head of the Jews made possible fulfillment of the Pact of 'Umar, the
famous covenant between Muslims and *dhimmi*s, granting them permission to reside in Islamic lands and protection of their lives and their
well-being in exchange for submission to the Islamic state and payment
of the poll tax. The appointment of a Ra'is provides for the Jews, according to an administration handbook, "the best possible choice and
respect for their dignity and honor. It allows them the free exercise of
all their religious affairs in accordance with the original covenant to
which they have subscribed, and grants to them all the rights permitted
by virtue of their agreement with the Muslim authorities."[16]

The document of appointment stressed the Jews' obligation to pay
the poll tax "cheerfully and willingly."[17] The Ra'is had to make sure
that the restrictions placed upon the *ahl al-dhimma* were not neglected.
He had to see to it that the dress codes were observed, and those of the
community who proudly refuse to wear the yellow badge on their garment or the badge on their turbans had to be compelled to conform.
The Ra'is had to make sure that no new synagogues were built.

When Muslim authorities wanted to enforce *dhimmi* regulations,
they would summon the Patriarch and the Head of the Jews to renew
the Pact of 'Umar. Muslim theologians debated with them and reproached them for not compelling their communities to observe the
rules of discrimination. Sometimes the Ra'is appeared before government representatives with notables from his community.[18] The government summoned the Head of the Jews when the financial situation
was bad, and demanded large sums. The Ra'is defended his coreligionists, exerting his influence on government officials, or the police
and the army, and at times on representatives of foreign nations.[19]

The Head of the Jews was the highest judicial authority in the Jewish community, with broad communal responsibilities. As a rule, he
did not give judgment in person, but instructed his chief judges or the
local courts how they should deal with cases that he referred to them.[20]

The Ra'is was responsible for justice and law and order and for up-holding the precepts of the Torah. However, he generally did not have power of constraint, because he had no police or prisons to enforce his decisions.[21] This kind of power was in the hands of government au-thorities. He had only his status and respect (*hayba*), which instilled fear and a willingness to obey, and he could use fines, lashings, and excom-munication against recalcitrants.[22] *Hayba* is much more than is connoted by the English word *respect;* it is an aura of invincible authority that in-timidates and arouses awe, dread, reverence, and veneration.

He had to serve the Jewish communities as legal authority in confor-mity with their law. "The duty laid upon him is to join his community together and to prevent their separation by means of their obedience to him, and by his pronouncing judgment for them according to the laws of their religious body and the customs of their community when it is evident to him in matters relating to his rule."[23] He supervised marriage and divorce, inheritance, circumcision, alms and dues, pronouncing of excommunication, and synagogues. He had to raise money to redeem Jewish captives taken by war or by pirates at sea. He was responsible for public property, social services, and charities. The Head of the Jews ap-pointed and supervised the local leaders (*muqaddams*) of the sect.[24] He appointed the judges, and they appointed community officials with his consent, or they were appointed by him directly. He selected ritual slaughterers and cantors. Those appointed by the Head, working under his supervision, set aside fixed percentages for his coffers—for example, the revenue from meat markets and from writing legal documents.[25]

In matters of justice, the Ra'is resembled the Muslim ruler. He had to give equal treatment to the elite and the common people and ad-minister justice to the strong and the weak. He was "the judge of wid-ows and father of orphans" and "the hope of the poor and the shield of the oppressed."[26] Like Muslim rulers, he was concerned with everyday matters and minute details. Moses ben Maimon and his son, Abra-ham, wrote receipts for tiny sums of just a few dirhams.[27]

The Ra'is and his associates acted as a supreme court, dealing with its own cases and with cases of lower courts. People protesting the decision of a lower court appealed to the Head of the Jews, who in-structed the court or the local community on how to deal with the complaint. This kind of judicial remedy existed in Islamic societies and was called "commanding right and forbidding wrong" (*al-amr bi'l-ma'ruf wa-'l-nahy 'an al-munkar*).[28] An aggrieved person could appeal to the Head of state or local ruler (caliph, vizier, governor, etc.) for a redress of grievances.

I have spent time delineating the office and functions of the Head of the Jews because often in biographies of Maimonides this is not defined in precise detail. In addition, this portrayal is needed to support my thesis that Maimonides fulfilled many of the functions of Ra'is without occupying the office.

THE HA-LEVI FAMILY

When Maimonides arrived in Egypt, the Head of the Jews (Ra'is al-Yahud) was Nethanel (Arabic Hibatallah), son of Abu Sa'd Moses ha-Levi, of the family of the Sixth, Gaon of the Palestinian Academy.[29]

The ha-Levis were a well-established Egyptian family, representing the old leadership of the Palestinian Gaonate and having a prominent role in communal affairs during the lifetime of Moses Maimonides and his son Abraham, competing with them for leadership and influence, constantly thwarting their plans for synagogue and institutional reform. Members of this family served as physicians in the courts of Egyptian rulers and in governmental hospitals, enjoying close connections with Muslim government officials.

Moses ha-Levi ben Nethanel, the first prominent member of the family, was President of the Court (*av bet din*) of the Academy of the Palestinians in Egypt and served in a government hospital in Cairo. Moses ha-Levi attempted to replace Nagid Samuel ben Hananyah as head of the Jews by bribing a chamberlain, who was Moses's patron, claiming that he had documents to prove that he was worthy of the office.[30] He intended to convene community leaders, expecting their support. Samuel ha-Nagid, however, appealed to the Fatimid ruler, who appreciated his service and confirmed his friendship in exchange for it. (Later, in ch. 14, we shall meet a certain Zuta the Wicked, who may have been a name tag for Moses ha-Levi and two of his descendants. Zuta was said to have replaced Samuel ben Hananyah for a brief period of time.) Two key terms for patronage appear in the text: friendship (*mawadda*) from the patron—in this case, the caliph—and service (*khidma*) from the client, Samuel ben Hananyah. The informal bond between caliph and Nagid was hence one of patron-client.

NETHANEL BEN MOSES

The Geonim Nethanel and Sar Shalom ha-Levi, sons of Abu Sa'd Moses, likewise held the office of Gaon of the Academy of the Palestinians.[31] Nethanel was Head of the Jews for several years between 1160 and 1169. He grew up among "the *jeunesse dorée* of the Egyptian capital," cavorting with some unsavory cronies nicknamed "Devil" and "Bird of the Jinnies."[32] His father paid him the huge sum of twenty-five dinars to stay home and study medicine, grammar and lexicography, Talmud, and theology. Nethanel objected to staying indoors and would invite a friend ("brother") to visit in the morning, when his father was busy in the hospital. Nethanel matured to become Gaon and a prominent physician as well.

When Nethanel's position was challenged, he secured a document in September–October 1161 from the Exilarch in Baghdad, Daniel ben Hisday,[33] confirming his right to the office and crowning him with the titles Head of the Academy of the Diaspora and Presiding Head, the Great Gaon. The Exilarch declared that Nethanel was "the great judge in all the cities of Egypt. He shall give legal opinions and adjudicate and establish judges in every province. All of the sages and officials and the rest of the holy people shall obey him and listen to his words."[34]

The Exilarch's letter was read in Baghdad in the presence of civil officials and notables, with the crowd answering, "Amen."[35] He mentioned in his letter to Nethanel that he expected to get fixed payments (*ha-huqqim ha-haquqim*) from Nethanel in return for his support.[36] Claiming poverty, the Exilarch also alluded to dissension between him and Gaon Samuel ben Eli of Baghdad, a circumstance of great interest to us, as Maimonides and Joseph ben Judah were eventually caught up in this controversy.

Benjamin of Tudela described Nethanel as the chief government official (*sar ha-sarim*), Head of the Academy, and the Head of all the communities of Egypt.[37] Ibn Abi Usaybi'a included him in his *Classes of Physicians,* calling him by his title and Arabic name, al-Ra'is Hiba-tallah, stating that he was an excellent and famous physician, court physician to the last Fatimids, from whom he received a generous stipend and incessant gifts, so that after their dynasty collapsed he was able to support himself until he died in about 580 A.H. (1184/85).[38]

SAR SHALOM HA-LEVI

In Adar (February-March) 1170, documents were issued under the authority (*reshut*) of Sar Shalom ben Moses ha-Levi Gaon.[39] Sar Shalom was head of the Academy of the Palestinians with the titles Crown of the Geonim (*keter ha-Geonim*) and Gaon, Head of the Academy (*ha-ga'on rosh ha-yeshivah*).[40]

THE *RESHUT* CLAUSE

People recognized the authority of the Ra'is al-Yahud by invoking his authority (*reshut*) in the synagogue, at meals, at circumcisions, at engagement and wedding celebrations, and on documents that stated under whose authority they were signed.[41] This recognition generated income for the holder of authority, who received payments from clerks who wrote documents, slaughterers (*shohatim*), circumcisors (*mohalim*), and other functionaries. Given this situation, a candidate for high office sometimes offered payment for the appointment.[42]

This practice of invoking a leader's authority or jurisdiction was similar to the Islamic procedure of giving permission or authority (*taswigh*) in documents. The state bureaucracy adopted this system for contracts and other official papers.

Sometimes documents were signed under the authority of more than one person in the same period, either because there were two claimants or a Gaon or Nasi was recognized along with the Head of the Jews.[43] Maimonides mentioned in a responsum on the *reshut* that authority was invoked for individuals who were not Heads of the Jews, such as Exilarchs, Heads of Academies, Nesi'im, and Geonim.

MAIMONIDES AS HEAD OF THE JEWS

Maimonides became Head of the Jews (Ra'is al-Yahud) in August-September 1171, precisely when Saladin and the Ayyubid dynasty replaced the Fatimids.[44] At this time, al-Qadi al-Fadil extended his patronage and gave him a stipend for service to the dynasty.[45] As Saladin's chief administrator, al-Fadil was instrumental in the Ayyubid accession to power, and he was therefore an ideal patron to have.

There is no reason to doubt that Maimonides was head of the Jews at this time.[46] Ibn al-Qifti and Ibn Abi Usaybi'a reported that he was, and they had impeccable sources and no motive for being untruthful.[47]

Maimonides was the right person at this moment to represent the Jews in the corridors of power. It was a critical time, for the Ayyubids not only instituted a new regime but introduced a new era. There were pressing issues to resolve—autonomy of the Jewish legal system, the *dhimmi* pact, taxes and tariffs, and the question of material and moral support of the new government.

DOCUMENTS 1171–72

Documents were written under the authority of Moses ben Maimon in the years 1171–72. He was, in my view, Head of the Jews for that one brief but critical period of time.[48] The official protocol read, "Under the authority of our lord Moses, the Great Master [Rav] in Israel."[49] *Rav* means "jurisconsult" (Arabic *mufti*), one who decides legal questions and issues responsa or legal opinions (*teshuvot*/Arabic *fatawa,* pl. of *fatwa*). Although Maimonides was Head of the Jews for a brief period, his title, the Great Rav in Israel, lasted forever. Previously, he was called simply Master (Rav).[50] The longer title is found at least nineteen times in his surviving responsa, spanning his entire career. Other scholars had been known as the Rav or the Great Rav, but only Maimonides was known as the Great Rav in Israel. We know the word *rav* in the form *rabbi,* meaning "my master." (The accent is on the *i*, pronounced like the i in *marine*.)

At least six documents survive of the many that were signed under Maimonides' jurisdiction during the years 1171–72.[51] The earliest was a dissolution of an industrial partnership between two smelters, dated in the Hebrew month Elul, beginning August 4, 1171.[52] Another document, dated during the first ten days of Tishre (September 2–11), concerned a widow who wished to remarry. Having agreed to take an oath that her deceased husband left her nothing, she was spared the need to take it when her eldest son confirmed her testimony.[53] The third document signed under Maimonides' jurisdiction was an acknowledgement of the receipt of a dowry dated October 1171.[54] The fourth is a marriage contract (*ketubbah*) written under his authority and dated 1171/72 C.E.[55] The fifth document was dated in the first ten days of the Hebrew month that began on January 29, 1172.[56] Another document drawn up under his jurisdiction was an inventory of a legacy left by a physician named Abu 'l-Rida ha-Levi, dated April 13, 1172, during the intermediate days of Passover.[57] The text reads:

> Inventory of what was left by the shaykh Abu 'l-Rida al-Tabib [the Physician] ha-Levi, kept as a deposit for his orphan 'Imran, by order [*amr*] of his Excellency, our lord Moses, the Great Rav, may his name last forever, Thursday, 17 Nisan 1483.

The date follows the civil (Seleucid-era) calendar, probably because legacies were submitted to the civil administration (diwan al-mawarith) to assess taxation. Maimonides may have been involved because of the profession of the deceased and concern for a young orphan.

DOCUMENTS PERTAINING TO APPOINTMENT AS HEAD OF THE JEWS

Two surviving documents pertain to Maimonides' appointment as Head of the Jews. Goitein describes the first as the cover of a proclamation.[58] Although the term *riyasa* (Headship) occurs, there is no indication that this was a proclamation declaring Moses ben Maimon Head of the Jews. However, the document does mention the seat of his office and his Headship over Egyptian Jewry and evidently relates to his being Ra'is al-Yahud.

A letter that a student wrote, commending Maimonides on his appointment, clearly indicates that Maimonides was Head of the Jews. The writer began with a string of honorific titles.[59]

> To his honor, greatness and holiness, his eminent dignity, diadem of glory, our teacher and master, our [lord][60] and holiness, pride [*ge'on*] of our sanctuary, splendor of our sun, diadem of our head, delight of our

soul, *our chariots and horsemen*,[61] *the breath of our life*,[62] light of our eyes, our leader and chief,[63] our teacher and master, our lord Moses, Head of Heads,[64] chief of the holy ones, delight of souls,[65] who gives wisdom to elders [cf. Job 12:12], *skilled artisan and expert enchanter* [Isa 3:3], *right column* [1 Kings 7:21], upon which the house of Israel is established [cf. Judge 16:26, 29], the distinguished Rav . . .[66]

The main part of the letter, in Arabic, began with the writer's expression of desire and love for his teacher and his regret that he was far from his court (*majlis*), presence, and teaching. He then mentioned Maimonides' appointment as Ra'is.

> When I heard of the happiness which God (the exalted) restored to the nation [*umma*] and elevation of the headship [*al-riyasa*] by the promotion of his honor, our lord, the Great Rav (may his glory be raised and his honor exalted), my joy and happiness abounded, and I said, *For the Lord will not forsake his people; he will not abandon his very own* [Ps 94:14].
>
> I thanked God (the exalted) and said, *Blessed be the Lord, who has not withheld a redeemer for his people Israel* [Ruth 4:14]. I congratulate the community [*milla*] and the high office for the honor which God has bestowed through his Excellency's Headship.

The writer's enthusiasm for the appointment was diminished by his concern that occupation with community affairs would deflect the Master from scholarship and writing. He also mentioned "the harm of whoever seeks to injure him," leaving us in the dark as to what the harm was and who these seekers were.[67] The writer then welcomed his teacher's "sublime command," but the rest is lacking and we do not know what the command was.

Maimonides could not have been eager to undertake the demands of administration, nor did he crave service as courtier and court physician, an adjunct to the office that was literally dangerous. After a brief tenure as Head of the Jews, he returned to his first love, study and writing. Having presided over the transition to a new dynasty, Maimonides was ready to lay down the burdens of responsibility. He expressed his attitude toward high office and the risk of government service in a letter to Joseph ben Judah:

You know, my honored son, that these great things and high offices that Jews attain in our time are not in my eyes happiness[68] and perfect goodness worth striving for, and are not—by the life of God (the exalted)—a minor evil but an appalling vexation and burden.[69] For the perfect man who attains ultimate happiness is the one who attends to the refinement of his religious life, carrying out his obligations and avoiding the evil of all men, their base ways and depraved moral qualities. For the one who holds high office there is much agony and grief. The gentiles may disgrace and humiliate him, and he may fall into the hands of the authorities, and they then torture him and break his bones. And if he attends to people's affairs and strives to be acceptable to them, he violates the Torah of the Lord (the exalted) and behaves with flattery and partiality. The Torah explicitly warned us not to honor transgressors. In this matter the prophet of the Lord, the man of God, said to Eli the Priest, *You have honored your sons above me* [1 Sam 2:29].[70]

Being Ra'is brought honor and status accompanied by responsibility and risk. Representing the Jewish community before the government imposed unpleasant tasks. Saladin needed vast funds for his projects and wars, and the Head of the Jews had to meet the sultan's demands by pressing his community. Nor would the ceremony and pageant have enticed him. The question we need to ask is not what titles Maimonides held but what his function was. His communal leadership was not dependent upon his being Ra'is. As the great Rav in Israel, he had power as a religious authority of the first order, not only in Egypt, but in other lands as well.

Sar Shalom as Ra'is al-Yahud in 1173

Maimonides was succeeded as Head of the Jews by Sar Shalom ha-Levi, the man whom he had replaced. Sar Shalom was out of office, then, only these two years, and again we find documents signed under his jurisdiction in 1173.[71] A court record under Sar Shalom's authority in Iyyar (April–May) 1173 is written by Mevorakh ben Nathan. Also, a letter congratulates Sar Shalom ha-Levi on reinstatement of his family to the Headship over Egyptian Jews.[72]

Sar Shalom was in office, all told, for more than twenty-five years.

His tenure was followed again by Moses ben Maimon in the 1190s. There are documents indicating, though not conclusively, that Maimonides was Ra'is in circa 1198–1199.[73] At this stage of his life he was in poor health, hardly equipped for the demands of high office and administration. Although I do not believe that he was striving against the ha-Levi family to be Head of the Jews, his relations with them were strained because he did not regard them as worthy of office, and they blocked his efforts at religious reform.

CRITICISM OF GEONIM AND THEIR TITLES

In his criticism of the Geonim of the Land of Israel, Maimonides alluded to Nethanel and Sar Shalom ha-Levi and other scholars who did not deserve the titles they held aloft.[74]

Maimonides explained that the reader should not be confused by

> the well known names in Syro-Palestine [al-Sham] and Iraq,[75] where people are called *Head of the Academy* and others *President of the Court* and where they distinguish between the *Head of the Academy of the Pride of Jacob* and *Head of the Academy of the Diaspora*.[76] [....] *These things are merely embellishments*, such as nicknames [*alqab*] and titles [*nu'ut*].[77]
>
> I have seen in *the Land of Israel* people called *fellows* [*haverim*] and in other places someone called *Head of an Academy* yet *who is not even a tyro*.[78] We are not discussing titles, but rather substantive things [*ma'ani*], and I have explained to you that one appointed is tested by substantive things and given *authorization* (*reshut*) according to his knowledge [*ma'rifa*].

Maimonides did not disparage fancy titles in this passage. The thrust of his criticism was that the candidates were not deserving of them. After all, he permitted himself to be addressed in queries with very exalted titles. The titles Nagid and Ra'is al-Yahud were not fancy, and he did not disdain them per se.

RAV AND NOT DAYYAN

After serving as Ra'is, Maimonides remained the Great Rav in Israel, the highest authority in Jewish law, and people continued to call him

Ra'is as the presiding authority on law.[79] The mainstay of Maimonides' authority was his extraordinary learning, which made his legal opinions decisive.[80] Even a Muslim judge was unwilling to decide a case involving Jews that came before him without having a written opinion from Maimonides, whom he addressed as Ra'is.[81]

A jurisconsult (*mufti, rav*) wrote legal opinions without being a judge himself.[82] In the Islamic judicial system, the judge (*qadi*) and jurisconsult (*mufti*) differed in that the judge adjudicated legal procedures, consisting of adversarial litigation, proceedings of evidence, binding decisions, and state enforcement; whereas the jurisconsult gave non-binding opinions (*fatawa;* sing. *fatwa*) in response to legal queries.[83]

Aside from the Geonim, spiritual leaders of academies, there were independent religious authorities called ha-Rav (ha-Gadol), as his contemporaries addressed Maimonides, a title corresponding to Grand Mufti. Maimonides was not formally a judge, but rather a jurisconsult, a respondent, or decisor.[84]

A Rav was a leading scholar or jurisconsult, the ranking scholar authorized to give legal opinions and instruct lower courts. As such, a Rav was more exalted than a Dayyan (judge), who had litigants appear before him daily, listened to witnesses and weighed evidence, and turned to the Rav for instruction in the law if necessary.[85] Maimonides' colleague Isaac ben Sason was the judge of Cairo/Fustat, not Maimonides. Isaac ben Sason called Maimonides the Presiding Rav (*ha-rav ha-muvhaq*), as Isaac was called the Presiding Judge (*ha-dayyan ha-muvhaq*).[86] Maimonides achieved his international stature as Rav.[87] He was addressed as "our lord, Mufti of the religious community."[88]

Giving instruction in the law was based on knowledge and judgment, not authority and power. Maimonides and his son Abraham, were approached as legal authorities, not as heads of the community. The Ra'is did not have unlimited authority in the definition and application of the law.[89] Having reproached certain persons for mishandling a case, Abraham wrote in a responsum: "If, however, anyone, and were he the youngest of students, should prove that my decision is wrong, I shall accept the correct ruling." He acknowledged that his authority was based on learning and that he was willing to be corrected. The decisor's authority derived also from the chain of transmission leading to him. He personified a tradition of learning inherited from great teachers and prominent relatives, such as Maimon ben Joseph. Maimonides' own descendants maintained the tradition of their ancestor and used his private books as sources of knowledge and authoritative instruction.

Maimonides presided over his own *moshav* (Arabic *majlis*), that is, council, or *moshav bet din*, court—a place of instruction in the law, where legal decisions were made in consultation with colleagues.[90] A *majlis* is a session or assembly, or the place where a session was held—an assembly room or court.[91] Maimonides, as Head of his council, was often called Gaon, as were Heads of Academies in Iraq and Palestine.

Maimonides' *majlis* consisted of judges, elders (Hebrew *zeqenim*, Arabic *shuyukh*), and scholars (*talmide hakhamim*).[92] He and his *majlis* carried out many of the prerogatives of the Ra'is al-Yahud and his entourage. Aside from replying to legal queries, they supervised pious foundations and synagogues, looked after the poor, organized the release of captives, and supervised marriage and divorce.[93]

As supreme religious authority in Egypt and abroad, as the Great Master (Rav) in Israel, Maimonides' fame spread throughout the Jewish world, from France in the north to Yemen in the south and from Morocco in the west to Iraq in the east.

His authority as jurisconsult and communal leader was based on his superior knowledge of the law, his judicious application of the law to real-life situations, his ability to attract superb colleagues and students to his *majlis,* his command of medicine and the sciences, his contacts with elite members of Ayyubid society, and his personal stature and integrity.

Judges turned to Moses ben Maimon for legal opinions and instruction on how to proceed in thorny cases.[94] Courts in Egypt and elsewhere issued rulings in accordance with the court of Maimonides. The legal opinions were read aloud in the synagogue on the Sabbath when it was necessary to publicize them.[95]

Maimonides responded to many queries addressed to him in person,[96] although when complicated cases came before him, when the ruling of a lower court had to be reversed, or when he issued legal enactments (Hebrew *taqqanot,* sing. *taqqanah*), distinguished colleagues, such as Isaac ben Sason and Samuel ben Se'adyah, cosigned.[97] This was not a token of weakness or proof that he was not Head of the

Jews or that he lacked authority.[98] In Baghdad, colleagues normally cosigned decisions of the Gaon, such that the responsa conveyed the consensus of the academy. The fact that Maimonides had elders in his council shows that he had to act in concert with others.

We may picture how he filled his role as the Great Rav in Israel from his guidelines for communal leaders and judges.[99] The leader of the community must not be domineering and arrogant. He must wield authority in humility and reverence. He should not instill great fear in its members for anything but a religious aim. He should never treat people with disrespect, though they be ignorant, and he must never force his way through them to get to his place. He should be patient with them, as was Moses, *as a nurse carries a child.*[100]

MARRIAGE AND FAMILY

As far as we know, Maimonides had not been married before he came to Egypt, and when his father and brother died, he was still single. He evidently married when he was in his early thirties.[101] A newcomer to Egypt, Maimonides needed social acceptance and economic security to gain status within the Jewish community. Marrying into a prominent family was a natural way of gaining entrance.[102] It was vital that members of his wife's family be learned and pious as well. To get anywhere in that society, one needed a powerful patron and influential friends. In addition, one needed strong family ties and a network of dependable relatives to succeed in business, social life, and politics.

Maimonides' bride was the daughter of al-Shaykh al-Thiqa (the Reliable Shaykh) Abu 'l-Mahasin Mishael ben Isaiah ha-Levi, a government official and physician, whose ancestors were active in communal affairs for many generations.[103] His paternal lineage included scholars, physicians, and public figures, and his maternal lineage went back to the House of Dosa, a prestigious family originally from Jerusalem.[104]

The bride's brother, Abu 'l-Ma'ali 'Uzziel, married Moses' sister, becoming Maimonides' brother-in-law twice over, thereby reinforcing family solidarity.[105] Abu 'l-Ma'ali was a government official, secretary to the mother of Saladin's eldest son, Nur al-Din al-Afdal.[106]

This sister of Maimonides gave birth to several children, among them Abu 'l-Rida, who became a physician. Ibn al-Qifti described him as a quiet and intelligent doctor who served the Seljuq ruler Qilij Arslan in Anatolia. At the end of a letter to Joseph ben Judah in 1191, Maimonides sent regards from Abu 'l-Ma'ali and his brothers and from Abu 'l-Ma'ali's son Joseph Abu 'l-Rida.[107] Hence, it has been suggested that Maimonides sister's family and her brothers-in-law with their families were all members of his household.[108] Extended families often lived under one roof or in close proximity to one another.

A letter of congratulations, written to Moses ben Maimon on the occasion of his wedding,[109] describes the bride, whose name is not given, as being from a good family (*bat tovim*).[110]

Her father, Mishael ben Isaiah, is called in the letter *haver* (member of the academy) rather than *hasid* (pious), the honorific usually appended to his name and other names of the family.[111] After his name is a phrase—*may the memory of the righteous be a blessing* (Prov 10:7)—indicating that he was no longer living. This may explain why Ibn al-Qifti began his description of the marriage by mentioning the bride's brother Abu 'l-Ma'ali, as he was at the time her legal guardian.[112]

As the document is not dated, we do not know for sure when the wedding took place.[113] It was evidently after Maimonides was thirty-three, as he is called "the Great Rav," a title he held at least from around 1171 on.[114] He was described as "son of the rabbi, his honor, greatness, and holiness, our teacher and master, our lord Maimon, the Great Rav (may the memory of the holy be a blessing)."[115] He was called "ark of our covenant,[116] "unique in our generation," "our teacher, Moses," "the Great Rav," "the Nagid of a people not bereft,"[117] and "unique in his generation and time."[118]

We can also estimate Maimonides' age when he married from a letter to Joseph ben Judah (October 1191), in which he sent greetings from "our young man Abu 'l-Rida."[119] Abu 'l-Rida, son of Moses' sister, was a member of his household and studied medicine with him. He was then a mature man, and Maimonides' sister had to have been married some twenty years before. Maimonides married, then, a few years after he arrived in Egypt, say in around 1173, when he was in his early thirties, apparently close to thirty-five.[120] If so, he married almost twenty years after the time set down by custom. Some of his descendants also married late in life. Maimonides' son, Abraham, was thirty-six when his only child, David, was born in 1222. David was fifty-five when his youngest son, Jacob, was born, and David's son Abraham married when he returned to Egypt from Acre at the age of forty-four.

Moses ben Maimon was forty-eight when Abraham was born in 1186, ten to fifteen years after his marriage. Some scholars assume that Maimonides was unmarried until shortly before his son was born. It is, however, possible that during the fifteen years he had a daughter or daughters who are not mentioned, at least in documents that have come to light. In a letter to Joseph ben Judah, he mentioned the death of a little girl or young daughter (*ha-bat ha-qetanah*), which some scholars take to be a reference to his own daughter.

As Maimonides had notified Joseph of the little girl's death from Fustat, it is unlikely that he was referring to a daughter of Joseph, who would have been in Aleppo with her father. Moreover, telling Joseph not to mourn or be sad would be indecorous if Joseph's daughter had died. Yet if she were Maimonides' own daughter, he should not be consoling Joseph as he did in this letter. However, she may have been a daughter of Maimonides to whom Joseph had become attached, in which case Maimonides' condolence was appropriate. This is the second letter concerning the young girl's death that Maimonides wrote to Joseph ("I have already informed you . . ."). In the first, which we do not have, he had announced the misfortune, and there he may have been more emotional, as we expect of a bereaved father. His saying "May God make her death an atonement" is appropriate if the little girl was his own daughter. Perhaps someday a new document will shed more light on this question.

13

Epistle to Yemen

Strengthen the hands that are slack; make firm the tottering knees!

—Isa 35:3

IN 1172, Maimonides—then in Egypt for six years and Head of the Jews for one—wrote an epistle to the Jews of Yemen, who were suffering the torment of forced conversion, as had the Jews in Spain and North Africa. The *Epistle to Yemen* is one of his best-known writings, and it endeared him to Yemenite Jews forever.

THE ADDRESSEE OF THE EPISTLE

The formal addressee of the *Epistle to Yemen* was Jacob ben Nethanel Fayyumi, who had sent a letter to Egypt describing the plight of the Yemenite Jews. Maimonides' preamble, in superb rhymed prose, extolled the hospitality that the dwellers of Yemen extend to merchants. (The port of Aden was an important stop on the India trade route.) Merchants and all traders, he wrote, had found among the people of Yemen a lovely and pleasant plantation with faithful shepherds, a goodly pasture where everyone who was lean would become fat. Their hand was extended to every traveler and their home was open wide. Along with their hospitality, they studied the Torah of Moses, pursued justice, preserved God's commandments, and held fast to his covenant.

Jacob ben Nethanel said that he had heard a number of Maimonides' brethren eulogize him as being comparable to the mighty Geonim. Moses deflected the compliment: "I am one of the least of the sages of Sefarad, whose adornment has been stripped in exile. Ever vigilant in my studies, I have not attained the learning of my ancestors." Maimonides made "Sefarad" rhyme with *hurad* (stripped), echoing Abraham Ibn Ezra's lament (*Sefarad . . . yarad*) (see ch. 5).

Although he wrote to Jacob ben Nethanel, Maimonides' epistle was addressed to all "our brothers, our scholars, all the disciples of the communities in Yemen." He wanted the epistle to be read by the general public, and hence wrote in Arabic, asking the recipients to instill his message in the youth, children, and women, to reinforce their weakened and unsettled faith.

The Anguish of the Yemenites

Maimonides first cited the shocking news of the forced conversion imposed by the Qa'im, 'Abd al-Nabi ibn al-Mahdi.[1] The Mahdi made Jews abandon their faith just as the Almohads had done in the Maghrib. Maimonides placed their anguish within a divine plan, assuring them that their trials would end. As in his *Epistle on Forced Conversion,* Maimonides wrote as a physician, a healer, who sends a pharmacopoeia, a medicine of the soul, a restorative, relieving pain and distress.

The main body of the epistle reacted to three emergencies: (1) the appearance of a Mahdi in Yemen, who compelled Jews in all the places he had conquered to convert to Islam; (2) the emergence of a Jewish apostate, who was persuading Jews that Muhammad was prefigured in Scripture; and (3) a Jewish messianic pretender, who attracted many followers among the Jews.

The Historical Background

Yemen was then part of the 'Abbasid empire, which had its capital in Baghdad. It was a distant province and rebels were constantly arising against its authority. Many of them accepted the Fatimid ideology of the Isma'ili sect in opposition to the 'Abbasid caliphate. In 545 A.H. (1150/51 C.E.), 'Ali ibn al-Mahdi, a charismatic preacher, who advocated an ascetic way of life, rebelled openly.[2] Summoning people to repentance and religious revival, he attracted supporters. In 554 (1159), shortly before he died, he conquered the fortified city of Zabid. The Mahdist movement continued with 'Ali's son 'Abd al-Nabi ibn 'Ali ibn al-Mahdi assuming leadership. He is the Qa'im mentioned in the *Epistle to Yemen*.[3]

'Abd al-Nabi held the view that sin is tantamount to infidelity to Islam and the sinner subject to the death penalty, a position usually associated with the Khariji movement.[4] He also enforced the death penalty on those who opposed his doctrines, drank wine, listened to music, missed Friday prayer or his sermons, or had illicit intercourse. Believers had to surrender all their property to him.

His strict puritanism among coreligionists was accompanied by fanaticism against outside religions such as Judaism. 'Abd al-Nabi continued his father's policy of marauding, pillaging, and conquering territories in Yemen. The ascetic and fanatic fervor of his edicts expressed his Mahdist (messianic) claims. According to the *Epistle to Yemen*, 'Abd al-Nabi's triumphs aroused messianic fervor among Jews.

Saladin dispatched an Ayyubid force commanded by his brother Turan Shah in 569 (1173) to put an end to the Mahdist insurgency.[5] Turan Shah invaded Tihama, subdued the town of Zabid, and captured and executed 'Abd al-Nabi in 571 (1176). The Ayyubids subsequently ruled Yemen until 1250, when the Mamluks replaced them as rulers of Egypt and its territories.

One of Saladin's aims in sending an armed force to subdue the distant province of Yemen was to assert Egyptian control over the Red Sea.[6] Turan Shah had pacified Upper Egypt, and he used its revenue to impose Egyptian hegemony over the Hijaz and Yemen. Sovereignty over the holy cities of Mecca and Medinah bolstered Ayyubid assertions of legitimacy. Al-Qadi al-Fadil obviously favored the Ayyubid intervention, far away as it was. Maimonides wrote his epistle one year before the campaign, and must have viewed the Ayyubid conquest of Yemen with relief and satisfaction.

PHILOSOPHY OF HISTORY AND MESSIANISM

In both the Maghrib and Yemen, Maimonides wrote in his epistle, Jews were being coerced to convert to Islam. The ubiquity of this forced conversion "at the two ends of the world, East and West," was painful. He offered a philosophy of history to cope with the calamity, quoting biblical verses, mainly from the Book of Daniel, anticipating all the vicissitudes that came to pass. If the ordeals were the unfolding of a grand design, they were easier to comprehend and endure. There were divine promises of ultimate triumph, yet these promises were not an adequate explanation of the suffering. Maimonides sought meaning in the suffering itself. The torment, he explained, was intended to test and purify, so that only the saints and the pious, the pure and chaste seed, would hold fast to Judaism and survive.

PANGS OF THE MESSIAH

Maimonides perceived catastrophe, wars, upheavals, and revolutions as presaging the footsteps of the Messiah. He said that many of his contemporaries, confidence shaken, depressed by the infirmity of the Jewish people and by the exultation of its adversaries, went astray, abandoning the faith, while others never strayed into doubt or betrayed their belief.

Maimonides viewed the Crusades as the ultimate dramatic showdown between the two great world powers and as a prelude to the final Redemption of Israel. He saw these events as messianic travails, "the pangs of the Messiah," harbingers of the restoration of prophecy and the Messiah's arrival in the near future.

In patent disregard of the rabbinic prohibition against calculating the End of Days, Maimonides claimed to possess an extraordinary family tradition going back to "the beginning of our exile from Jerusalem," according to which the statement of Balaam in Numbers 23:23—*Jacob is told at once, yea Israel, what God has planned*—alludes to the future restoration of prophecy in the year 4976 of creation (= 1215/16 C.E.).[7] The calculation is based upon a temporal symmetry and a doubling of the time from Balaam's utterance in 2485 A.M., which was thought to be the midpoint of world history. Accordingly, a perfect symmetry exists from creation to Sinai, the midpoint, and from Sinai to Redemption. The restoration of prophecy to Israel is preliminary to the messianic advent. Maimonides ended with a qualifying proviso—"God is the best knower of the truth"—leaving room for error and arousing the suspicion that the prediction was a balm in his pharmacopoeia.[8] Yet how could he make such a daring prediction, sure to be tested, unless he meant it?

Anticipation of eschatological denouements drove Maimonides' historical outlook. He perceived himself as a leader who would help bring about the restoration of prophecy. His references to the biblical Moses intimate that he saw himself as Moses *redivivus,* a redeemer and savior of his people. A mainspring of his personality was identification with the first Moses. Maimonides composed the *Mishneh Torah* and *Guide of the Perplexed* to reconstitute the Jewish people as strong, wise, and discerning, to prepare them for a new age. This was an active messianism built on natural preparation, not a passive messianism based on visions of divine interventions. His messianic expectation was not extraordinary in that age.[9]

CHRISTIANITY AND ISLAM

Confronting oppression and persecution in the Muslim West and East, with pervasive hatred of Jews in Christian Europe, Maimonides raised a question: Why this intense hatred for the Jewish people?

Maimonides' theory was that the root of hatred for Jews is envy. God distinguished the Israelites from all of mankind. *Yet it was to your fathers that the Lord was drawn in his love for them, so that he chose you, their lineal descendants, from among all the peoples* (see Deut 10:15).[10] This was not by their merit but by grace, on account of their ancestors having known God and obeyed him.[11] Their preeminence was evident in God's rules and regulations: *What great nation has laws and rules as perfect?* (Deut 4:8).[12]

Therefore, the nations have fought against the Jews out of envy, and kings have pursued them unjustly and aggressively. Every king, tyrant, or conqueror has tried to destroy their law by violence, such as Amalek, Sisera, Sennacherib, Nebuchadnezzar, Titus, Hadrian, and others.[13]

The second class of opponents comprises the most learned among the nations, such as the Syrians, Persians, and Greeks, who wish to abrogate the law by disputation. They attempt to destroy by their words, as the conquerors did by their swords.

Then a new faction arose combining conquest with controversy, striving to remove the last vestige of the Jewish community.[14] This faction claimed prophecy and produced a new law, claiming that it came from God and was his true word. Thus doubt and perplexity would result, as both laws are ascribed to one God. This paves the way for the destruction of both.

The first to undertake this was Jesus the Nazarene.[15] He was a Jew because he was the son of a Jewess. Even if his father was a gentile, he is a Jew, since the law states that *the offspring of a union between a gentile or slave with an Israelite woman is legitimate*.[16] We only call him illegitimate by way of hyperbole.[17] He claimed deceivingly that "he was sent by God to explain difficulties in the Torah, and that he was the Messiah promised by every prophet. He interpreted the Torah in a way that leads to the complete nullification of the law, to suspending all its commandments, and to transgressing all its prohibitions in accordance with his intention and aim. The sages (may their memory be a blessing), aware of his aim before his fame became firmly established among the [Jewish] community, treated him as he deserved."[18] Daniel warned us of this, saying that an impudent and rebellious Jew would claim prophecy and presume blasphemous things by saying that he is the Messiah. Daniel said that God would cause Jesus to stumble as he did, to wit: *"and the lawless sons of your people will assert themselves to confirm the vision, but they shall fail"* [Dan 11:14].[19]

A long time after Jesus a religion ascribed to him became prevalent among the descendants of Esau [the Christians], although this was not his aim.[20] Jesus did not harm the people of Israel, nor did anyone of them have any doubt about him. For they foresaw his ruin and his falling into our hands and meeting his end.[21]

After Jesus there arose Muhammad, who followed the path Jesus had opened for him.[22] He added a new dimension. He sought sovereignty and obedience to himself and innovated what we know.[23]

All of these opponents attempted to imitate the religion of God. There cannot, however, be any resemblance between the divine and the human artifact. The difference between our religion and the others compared to it is like the difference between a "living, rational human being and a statue resembling a human being."[24] When someone ignorant of divine wisdom sees a statue that superficially resembles a man, he supposes that it is exactly like a man because he is oblivious to the interior [*batin*] of each. The wise person, however, who knows the interior of both, is aware that the statue's interior is not skillfully made, whereas a man's interior contains true wonders indicating the Creator's wisdom.[25]

Maimonides' discourse on Christianity and Islam in the *Epistle to Yemen* is his most extended discussion of these religions.[26] Jesus' interpretation of the Torah, Maimonides believed, leads to the total abrogation of the law and suspension of all its commandments. The synoptic Gospels, in contrast, represent Jesus rather as not opposing the law and as carrying out all the commandments. Jesus, he understood, was the first to give an allegorical interpretation of the Torah, which abolishes its legislation. What Maimonides had to say elsewhere about the Batiniyya (Esotericists)—Isma'ilis who practiced *ta'wil* (allegorical and metaphorical interpretation)—applied as well to Christians. Both, in his view, used a spiritual interpretation of Scripture in an antinomian way.[27]

In Maimonides' version of Christian history, Jesus never intended that a new religion should emerge from his teaching. Pauline Christianity was an outcome that Jesus had not envisioned.[28]

Christians and Muslims employed the prefiguration motif to show that the Hebrew Bible predicted the coming of Jesus and of Muhammad as savior and prophet.

Daniel gave prior warning of Muhammad, saying that someone would arise who would initiate a religion similar to the divine religion, claim inspiration and prophecy, speak profusely, and claim to abrogate the Jewish law. Prolixity in Maimonides' vocabulary indicates foolishness, whereas concise speech is subtle and suggestive, containing more than meets the eye. The Muslim assertion that Islam abrogated the law brings Islam into direct confrontation with Judaism.

Maimonides viewed Christianity and Islam as imitations of Judaism. Jesus and Muhammad aspired to replicate Judaism, but the resemblance is merely superficial. The wisdom of the true divine law resides in its inner meaning. The rituals, laws, and customs of the three religions are outwardly similar and cannot be distinguished by an outside observer. The internal sense of the Torah, however, its true essence, sets it apart from the other religions.

Adumbrating an idea developed later in *The Guide of the Perplexed* (III, 27), Maimonides wrote that the Israelite community, which he called a "divine community," becomes preeminent (*fadil*), attaining two perfections, those of the moral and the rational virtues.[29] Maimonides' formulization of the idea that the Israelite nation is divine and preeminent, paradoxically reprises themes from the Muslim philosopher Abu Nasr al-Farabi (d. 950).[30] Responding to the humiliation and sad condition of the Jews, Maimonides stressed the essential and primordial preeminence of their polity and offered assurances that it will be revived.

He also drew his understanding of the history of religion and the relation between Judaism and its daughter religions from al-Farabi.[31] Accordingly, religion conveys to the common people the theoretical truths of philosophy by imaginative symbols. Al-Farabi even envisioned the possibility that a religion may be transferred by imitation from one nation to another, an idea that Maimonides employed here in the *Epistle to Yemen*.[32] If Christianity and Islam were imitations of Judaism, as Maimonides claimed, they were in al-Farabian terms twice removed from the truth.

Maimonides wrote at the end of the *Mishneh Torah* that Jesus of Nazareth and the Ishmaelite (Muhammad) have paved the way for the advent of the Messiah.[33] As imitations of Judaism, Christianity and Islam have brought its message to the ends of the earth. In the *Epistle to Yemen* he predicted that the Messiah will appear when the kingdoms of the Christians and Muslims spread to the entire world. He assigned a vital eschatological role to Jesus and Muhammad, or to Christianity and Islam.

Life Under Ishmael

Notwithstanding his rather favorable view of Islam elsewhere, Maimonides gave a most disparaging portrayal of life under Ishmael in this epistle. He explained to his Yemenite brethren that because of the Jews' dreadful sins God has cast them among the nation of Ishmael, adding these somber words: "Never has a people arisen against Israel more hurtful than it, nor one that went so far to debase and humiliate us and to instill hatred toward us as they have."[34] Maimonides alluded here to Qur'an 2:61, where it is said: *Debasement and humiliation were stamped upon them [the Jews] and they were visited with wrath from Allah.*[35] Maimonides' alluding to the Qur'an suggests that debasement of the Jews is not the arbitrary policy of some Islamic dynasty, but rather built into Islam from its foundation.

The acerbity of Maimonides' condemnation is startling, and historians have been puzzled by its bitterness. We have seen him living among Muslims, within the embrace of Islamic civilization, assimilating its cultural legacy. We need to understand how he came to this dismal assessment of life under Ishmael.

Let us observe that just six years prior to the appalling events in Yemen Maimonides arrived at a safe haven in Egypt. He could look back on the Almohads and the destruction of Jewish communities in Andalusia and the Maghrib as a horrific episode circumscribed in place and time. But here it was happening again, this time in Yemen. One could easily conclude that oppression was unending. The historian and Genizah scholar Mark R. Cohen perceives here a feeling that the *dhimmi* bargain had come to an end, that this was a time of transition.[36]

In speaking here of the harmful legislation of Islam, Maimonides used an Arabic word, *nikaya,* which means "spiteful harm," intimating that the hatred sprang from malicious envy.[37] It is harm inflicted out of resentment and spite, and it satisfies the perpetrator because his opponent has suffered loss.

In the face of overwhelming power Maimonides recommended passive resistance.[38]

And we have borne their humiliations and their falsehoods and their absurdities that are beyond human ability to bear, and have become as in the words of the prophet, *But I am like a deaf man hearing, like a dumb man who cannot speak up* [Ps 38:14]. And the sages (may their memory be blessed) have instructed us that we bear the falsehood of Ishmael and his absurdity and obey in submission and silence, seeing an allusion to this in his sons' names: Mishma, Dumah, and Massa [Gen 25:14]—*Obey, be silent, and bear.*[39] We have trained ourselves, young and old, to sustain their humiliation, as Isaiah decreed, *I offered my back to the floggers, and my cheeks to those who tore out my hair* [Isa 50:6]. Despite all this, we do not escape their terrible harm, their constant outbursts and all that we bear. We prefer peace with them, yet they prefer strife and wars with us, as David said, *I am all peace; but when I speak, they are for war* [Ps 120:7].[40] How much more would we throw ourselves to perdition were we to stir up trouble and claim sovereignty over them by nonsense and absurdity?

Maimonides' advice, then, was to remain passive in the face of extreme provocation, as the prophets and sages counseled. The prophets warned that when the coming of the true Messiah approaches, pretenders and deceivers will increase, but their missions will fail; they will die, and many with them. Solomon explained by the holy spirit that this community in exile will rouse itself at the wrong time and suffer calamities. He warned of this and adjured the community figuratively: I *adjure you, O maidens of Jerusalem, [by gazelles or by hinds of the field: do not wake or rouse love until it please]*.[41] Maimonides cautions them, "Now, you our brethren, our friends, abide by his oath, *and do not rouse love until it please.*" The messianic claimant in Yemen was just the kind of charismatic leader who could stampede the community to perdition.

14

Moses and David

Some lost their way in the wilderness,
in the wasteland;
they found no settled place.
Hungry and thirsty, their spirit failed.
In their adversity they cried to the Lord,
and he rescued them from their troubles.
He showed them a direct way to reach a settled place . . .

Others go down to the sea in ships,
ply their trade in the mighty waters;
they have seen the works of the Lord
and his wonders in the deep . . .

Let them praise the Lord for his steadfast love,
his wondrous deeds for mankind.

—Ps 107: 4–8, 23–24, 31

EGYPT IS THE GIFT OF THE RIVER," said Herodotus. Medieval Egyptians knew this to be true. The narrow strip that supplied Egypt with food could be cultivated only because of the annual flooding of the Nile. Everything depended on the inundation—

food, prices, the economy, and therefore the country in general. The absolute dependence of the country on the Nile was expressed not only in administrative structure but also in the long history of Nile religious cults. But the Nile was not an unequivocal blessing, and the river could be impetuous: too little water, and famine ensued; too much, and there was mass destruction.

Early in Maimonides' sojourn in Egypt, in the 1170s, his younger brother, David, went on a business trip, first to Qus on the Nile, then to the Red Sea port of 'Aydhab in what is today the Sudan, and finally to India. David set sail from the port of Fustat. This was near the famous mosque of 'Amr, to the north of Musasa, where the Maimonides family lived. The mosque was surrounded by markets filled with local fruits and vegetables and foreign commodities. The port was crowded with Egyptian and foreign ships and merchants and travelers from Christian and Muslim countries. The docks were loaded with exports, mainly pottery and glass, metalwork, leather, and paper. Moses surely accompanied his brother to see him off, and both would have made their way through the commotion to the Nile boat on which David booked passage. He had to bring with him supplies for the journey and some wares for trading when he got to markets along the way and at his destination. He had to provide his own food supply, utensils, and bedding as well, as we have seen. In addition to money, one carried letters of credit, which served as checks, and safe-conduct passes if possible, and it would be foolish to start without a prayer.

Many types of vessel, mostly oar-driven galleys, sailed on the Nile.[1] Sea travel was hazardous; yet even the Nile had its particular dangers. Navigating the Nile was risky because of abrupt squalls and shifts in the riverbed. When vessels ran aground, boatmen got into the water and pushed with their shoulders and used long poles to dislodge the ship from the mud.

Boats were usually overcrowded and overloaded; passengers were vulnerable to piracy, and feared theft by fellow travelers. Nor could they trust the ship's crew, and we hear of murder on the Nile by boatmen.[2]

As a craft made its way up the Nile, passengers saw the lofty houses and palaces of the city, the walls, forts, domes, and minarets, brilliant in the sun, receding.

The riverside scenery, opulent in tropical splendor, the eternal current of the beautiful river, the perpetual silence of the desert ridges beyond, awoke in the onlooker a sense of tranquil power, repose, and permanence. Rising out of the mist in East Africa, the Nile flowed south to north. The river valley offered stark contrasts, strips of alluvial earth cultivated by irrigation surrounded by vast stretches of arid land, the Eastern Desert on one side and the Libyan Desert to the west.

As the boat made its way, travelers gazed at the thicket along the Nile, the huts and the fellahin. A wooden-beamed water hoist was outlined against the horizon; it had turned patiently for centuries, driven by men moving gracefully and singing. The boat moved past date palm plantations, huge dovecotes, and women doing laundry on the banks of the river. The domes and minarets of villages seemed to rise out of the trees. Along the riverbanks crocodiles basked, opening lazy eyes, patient and seemingly indifferent to the human spectacle gliding by. Glimpsing crocodiles in the water, with their bulky reptilian bodies submerged, their eyes protruding, the onlooker felt the gaze of ultimate peril. Passengers watched as the docile water buffalo swam across the river, awkwardly regaining land on the other side. Oxen on the riverbank pulled wooden plows, as did their ancestors portrayed in ancient tombs. Donkeys grazed unfettered along the shores, oblivious to the scenery around them.

Nile boats tied up along embankments for rest and supplies. Passengers roamed the edge, some hunting, others watching birds bedecking trees and sky. Mooring was dangerous, as bandits attacked boats casting anchor for overnight rest.[3]

About forty miles from Fustat was the Fayyum district, a fruitful and lush region famous for its flax industry. It was also the center of Coptic Christianity and boasted numerous monasteries.[4] Jews called it by its biblical name, Pithom (Exod 1:11).[5] For David Maimonides and his companions, the entire Egyptian countryside evoked biblical associations. Near Fayyum a famous canal flowed from the Nile, believed to have been dug by the biblical Joseph.[6]

Further up the river, boats stopped at Akhmim, where travelers had to pay customs.[7] The predatory officials at the tollhouse fleeced travelers.[8] It was not unheard of for customs officials to detain a Nile boat at Akhmim for five days.[9] Akhmim was a main anchorage on the east bank before the river turned sharply right, coming closer to the Red Sea. Akhmim was a town surrounded by lavish cultivation, with date palms and sugar cane. There was a substantial Jewish community and a great number of Christians as well, with their many churches.

Akhmim was the site of an ancient pagan temple, associated with Hermes Trismegistus, the Thrice-Great Hermes. Ibn Jubayr, describing its grandeur, wrote that it was one of the wonders of the world, beyond description or defining, although he could intimate something of it.[10] (The shrine was destroyed in the fourth century, its ruins used for a madrasa.) Hermes Trismegistus was a hero to the Sabians, whom Maimonides described in *The Guide of the Perplexed* as pagan opponents of the biblical Abraham and enemies of monotheism still posing a threat.

Akhmim was the first of the towns in Upper Egypt dominated by colossal temples of ancient gods. The mysteries of the sacred places and the secrets in the caves and cliffs of the Nile valley were alluring. The half-covered shrines of Amun at Karnak, Luxor, and other holy sites marked in late antiquity the stages of one's passage along the Nile valley toward Upper Egypt. Egypt, marked by these sacred sites, was described in Hermetic texts as an image of heaven, temple of the whole world, and focus of celestial emanations.[11]

Forty-five miles further upstream, boats passed the site of Naj' Hammadi, in the silent cliffs of the east bank, where a priceless treasure lay buried, a clay jar concealing papyri of Christian Gnostic, Jewish Gnostic, and Hermetic writings.[12]

From Qus to 'Aydhab

David arrived in the caravan town of Qus, about 350 miles from home, just before the Passover holiday, probably in early April.[13] Galleys arriving at Qus sometimes returned to Cairo after a day or two.[14]

David left his Nile journey at this point and rested for a few days. The Jewish community of Qus was large and prosperous and hospitable to visitors.[15] A traveler reaching the place after a hard Nile voyage writes that he was welcomed with warmth beyond measure.[16]

Qus was just eighteen miles north of the ruins of Luxor. It was the administrative capital of Upper Egypt, its population mostly Christian. Linking the Red Sea ports with Cairo, it was an entrepôt on the trade route to East Africa, India, and the Far East. Merchants came there from Alexandria and Cairo in the north, and from Aden, Yemen, Ethiopia, Zanzibar, and India in the south. Goods brought by caravan from Red Sea ports were transferred there onto Nile boats, mainly heading north for Cairo and Alexandria. It was a place of rest for pilgrims to Mecca from the Maghrib, Cairo, Alexandria, and adjacent lands. From Qus they crossed the desert to the Red Sea, and they returned on their way back from the pilgrimage the same way.[17]

After Passover, David and his travel companion (rafiq) hired a caravan heading for ‘Aydhab.[18] They proceeded first to Bir al-Bayda near Luxor—the site of ancient Thebes, Homer's "city of a hundred gates," royal capital of ancient Egypt, with its tombs and monuments. At Bir al-Bayda, travelers hired camels and drivers, weighed and loaded their baggage, and supplied themselves with food and water.

David's companion, Ma‘ani, persuaded him that they should go off on their own, separating themselves from the main group. Either they did not trust the caravan leader and the guides or they feared that a large group would be a more tempting target for marauders. Whatever their calculation, as they trekked along through the desert, they realized that they had made a dreadful mistake. It was a disastrous move, David wrote, done out of sheer ignorance, but God saved them: *The Lord preserves the simple* (Ps 116:6).

The route from Luxor to ‘Aydhab was three hundred miles over the Eastern Desert, covering rugged terrain, split by wadis and fringed by rough mountains in the southeast, some reaching more than six thousand feet above sea level. A person could not survive more than three days without fresh water, though camels could make it up to seven. Travelers would arrive at oases only to find that the water had dried up, at times drained by parched camels. Along the trails, they would see the white bones of travelers who had succumbed to the cruelty of the desert.[19]

Most travelers rode camels, sitting astride their baggage, exposed to the heat of the sun. The wealthy could afford more comfortable transportation. Tying two litters across the camel with a canopy shielding them from the sun allowed them to read and even play chess for diversion.

The Beja tribesmen, who served as camel drivers and guides, were wild and frightening, and they squeezed the most out of travelers needing their help. There was also protection money to pay other tribesmen along the way.

David and Ma'ani trudged on, regretting with every step the choice they had made and calling upon the Lord to lead them out safely. Finally, after almost three weeks of the blazing sun by day and the cold sand and windy desert by night, they reached 'Aydhab safely with all of their baggage. None of their former companions was there, as the main caravan had not yet arrived. While they were unloading their belongings at the town gate, the main caravan appeared. Marauders had robbed and wounded the travelers, and some had died of thirst. David and Ma'ani had suffered unspeakable ordeals, but the main group experienced worse. The son of an acquaintance, 'Atallah Ibn al-Rashidi, was among those who had been robbed. David was frantic imagining Moses' anguish—"When I imagine all day how you will hear the news that 'Atallah Ibn al-Rashidi was robbed, knowing that I was with him, I lose my senses."

The town of 'Aydhab, with its fine deep harbor, was an important terminal for traffic coming from South Arabia, East Africa, India, Ceylon, Burma, and China.[20] Ships from the Orient deposited on its wharfs silks and celadon, cinnamon, cloves, ginger, pepper, and other spices for shipment to Cairo, the Nile Delta, Alexandria, and Mediterranean ports in North Africa, Sicily, and Europe. They loaded for export to the east glassware, dates, cotton, sugar, pearls, tortoiseshell, shark fins, and mother-of-pearl.[21]

There was little about the town that was remarkable aside from the harbor. It was a small village of a hundred or two hundred primitive enclosures, its houses mere booths of reed, with a few solid buildings, the mosque and houses of officials, and a cluster of simple huts and tents on its outskirts. It had no vegetation and was entirely dependent on imported food. Its natives, mainly Beja tribesmen, exploited the transit trade and the pilgrim traffic as well.[22]

'Aydhab was unbearably hot and exposed to severe summer sand-storms. People told legends of its abominations, recalling the story that King Solomon took it as a prison for the *ifrit* demons (Qur'an 27:39).[23] The great India trader Abraham Ben Yiju, forced to lodge in 'Aydhab, called the place 'Adhab, meaning "agony," "pain," "torture."[24] Debtors took refuge there on account of its remoteness from civilization.[25]

The town was across the Red Sea opposite the holy cities of the Hijaz, Mecca and Medinah. 'Aydhab gained importance during this period be-cause Muslim pilgrims could not take the overland route through Trans-jordan to the Hijaz, as it was blocked by Crusader strongholds at Karak, Montréal, and Aylah. The pilgrimage route had to be diverted to the Nile, going by way of Qus and the Eastern Desert to 'Aydhab, then crossing the Red Sea to Jedda, the port of Mecca.

DAVID'S LETTER

We know about David's journey and his thoughts from a letter he wrote to his brother Moses when he arrived in 'Aydhab. The letter's survival is a sheer wonder. First, it had to make its way from 'Aydhab to Fustat and arrive safely in the hands of Moses. It must then have been placed in his archive and eventually was deposited in the Genizah at the Synagogue of the Palestinians (now the Ben Ezra Synagogue), where it survived until it was brought to Cambridge, England.

There it was placed in a crate that was almost discarded but for the astuteness of S. D. Goitein. Before a trip to Cambridge in 1954, Goitein gave a lecture on his *India Book* to the American Academy of Jewish Research in 1954. I listened carefully as Goitein, a small, lithe, sprightly figure, spoke in a pleasant foreign accent and with great excitement about his Genizah discoveries on the India trade.

Saul Lieberman, the great Talmudist, commented in the question-and-answer period that it would be a fine thing if the Genizah could furnish us with a letter from David to his brother Moses ben Maimon. Goitein answered that he could write a story about David but would not dare to fabricate a letter. Shortly thereafter, Goitein traveled to Cambridge. He asked the librarian if he could inspect Genizah papers acquired before Solomon Schechter's visit to Egypt in 1897, which had remained unclassified. The very first document Goitein selected was the letter from David to Moses.[26] It was as though an invisible hand guided Goitein. There was something uncanny about him. He was ingenious at reassembling Genizah fragments, sometimes from as many as three different libraries. He was able to re-create the story behind them. He was skillful in recognizing handwriting and identifying the writer. Goitein realized that it was David's letter when he saw the Sudanese port of 'Aydhab mentioned.

When I first set eyes on the letter at Cambridge in the manuscript reading room, I read the letter emotionally word by word, line by line, imagining how Moses felt as his eyes went down the same page.

When this letter was written, Moses was thirty-one years old and his brother was in his early twenties. Moses felt an unbounded love for David. During the time that his family was uprooted and suffered years of exile and religious persecution, Moses was caring and protective of his little brother. In their society, as life expectancy was brief and fathers became ill or weak and died young, an older brother helped raise and educate younger siblings. A younger brother kissed the hands of his older brother.

Writing from 'Aydhab, David first assured Moses that he was well but distraught thinking how anxious he must be.[27] He wandered about the marketplace aimlessly, without knowing where he was going or even why he went out, imagining how his brother was worrying.

David mentioned God often in his letter, as was customary in this religious age, when pious idioms permeated everyday language. People such as David felt a particular grace when they survived adversity, and as son of Maimon, a name meaning (in Arabic) "blessed" or "fortunate," he may have felt especially protected.

David then wrote that when he got to 'Aydhab, no imports had arrived recently; he found only indigo to purchase. So, he told his brother, he had decided to go on to India by sea.[28] Recalling the frightful ordeals in the desert, he thought a sea voyage would be easy. This time he would take a different traveling companion, a man named Mansur. He did not want Ma'ani, he wrote, for it was because of Ma'ani that he endured all the trials in the desert; *you know the man and his discourse* (2 Kings 9:11).[29] David promised that when he returned home he would relate in detail all that occurred on the journey from Fustat to 'Aydhab.

At the end of the letter, David named those who would be his other companions on the upcoming India voyage, people obviously known to Moses. They were Ibn Abraham; Salim, the son of the female broker;[30] Salim's nephew, Makarim al-Hariri (the Silk Merchant) and his brother; and the brother of Sitt Ghazal (Lady Gazelle).[31] David's former companion, Ma'ani, boarded another ship along with a man named Ibn al-Kuwayyis.

David reported in the letter that some voyagers who had sailed earlier had run into trouble soon after embarking. The ship of a certain Bu 'l-'Ala' foundered near Dahlak, though he survived without losing any of his baggage.[32] Ibn 'Atiyya was in another *jalba* boat along with Ibn al-Maqdisi and they were shipwrecked, losing everything except their money.[33] David carefully reported these incidents so that Moses could inform relatives of the men that they were safe and sound. So far, lives had been lost only in the desert, not at sea.

Despite these ominous mishaps, David told Moses not to worry about his impending voyage. "He who saved me from the desert and its terrors will save me from the sea." He implored his brother to calm the heart of David's wife ("the little one") and her sister, not to alarm them or make them despair. And he implored Moses not to pray, for *if a man cries out [to God] over what is past, his prayer is in vain.*[34]

David informed Moses that he was undertaking the voyage because of his constant efforts on Moses' behalf, even though his brother had not imposed any of this upon him. "Be steadfast," he urged, "and God will compensate you and rejoin me with you." Then, falling back on the fatalistic leitmotif of the letter, David cited a brief Arabic proverb, current even today—*wa-ma fat fat,* "what is done is gone." David said that by the time his letter reached Moses he would have traveled a good part of the way to India, *but it is the Lord's plan that is accomplished* (Prov 19:21). Along with his sense of salvation, David was resigned to his destiny, believing it to be in God's hands. The journey would probably begin, he wrote, in the middle of Ramadan. He gave the Muslim month because the ship owner or captain would have set the time of sailing.

David said that he was writing the letter on 22 Iyyar, as the express caravan was about to depart and he was rushing to send it off in time.[35] As he did not give the year, we need to ascertain when 22 Iyyar was

close to Ramadan.[36] That date was close to the beginning of Ramadan
in the years 1169–1171,[37] giving us a time frame for the letter. [38]

We associate the India trade with Portuguese commerce in the sixteenth century. In fact, the Portuguese *revived* contact between the
Mediterranean and India. When Vasco de Gama sailed around the
Cape of Good Hope to India in 1498, he was restoring a connection
between Europe and the Far East that had existed for centuries, beginning in Ptolemaic and Roman times. In the Fatimid and Ayyubid
period, the era of Maimonides, trade with India thrived.[39]

Shipbuilders constructed vessels bound for the Indian Ocean by sew-
ing planks together rather than nailing them.[40] The builders fastened
stitches of coir, palm fibers, and rushes through holes in the wood, a
technique in use from antiquity.[41] The ships were more flexible and able
to maneuver in unsafe harbors, and repair was easier, yet such ships
required substantial maintenance and were leaky and fragile. [42] Faced
with the perils of storms, reefs, and shallows, ships usually traveled in
convoys (sing. *sanjarah*, Persian *zinjir*) or pairs for greater safety.

There were sites of great threat to navigation. Ships often sank in
Bab al-Mandab, or at Abyan east of Aden, outside the Yemeni port of
Ghulayfiqa, or near the Indian Shore.[43] The waters of the Indian
Ocean were shark-infested. When a boat was in danger of sinking,
sailors would cast baggage overboard, to lighten the ship, so merchants
divided the load among different boats to distribute risk, just as they
would send several copies of the same letter. As there was no insur-
ance, losses could be staggering. It was customary to divide the cost of
lost baggage among all the passengers, a practice based on both Islamic and Jewish law.

Announcing loss of life, people would write that there was no recourse from what God had determined. When property was lost, they
comforted themselves that everything had a substitute save life itself.
These were people who lived by proverbial wisdom, which helped
them cope with everyday loss and tragedy.

DAVID SAILS TO INDIA

As David's ship made its way toward Aden, a journey of 875 miles, the
Red Sea grew more treacherous, demanding expert navigation, sail-

ing close to shore, and anchorage at night. The occasional ship traveled to the seaport of Ghulayfiqa in southern Yemen without halting at Aden, and from there sailed directly to India.

At the mouth of the Red Sea, Aden, with its fine harbor, lay half the distance between Cairo and India, making it a center point of the Indian Ocean trade.[44] As Cairo was the port of transit between the Far East and the European West, so Aden was the major emporium for transport between the Far East and Red Sea ports. The commercial importance of Aden was partly due to its location at the entrance to the Red Sea. Ships could come to Aden and sell their commodities without having to risk the unsafe journey to Jedda or Suez.[45]

From Aden, many ships made their way to the coast of East Africa and down to Mogadishu, Zanzibar, Kilwa, and Mozambique. During the summer months, enjoying the favorable monsoons, they sailed eastward to the Arabian Sea and the Persian Gulf for the ports of Hurmuz and Siraf in Persia, or Abbadan, Ubulla, and Basra in Iraq. Some sailed straight across the Arabian Sea to the Malabar Coast of India; others went further on to Ceylon (Sri Lanka), the Bay of Bengal, China, Burma (Myanmar), Malaya, Sumatra, and Borneo. From Aden to the Malabar coast of India was a journey on the open sea of 2,100 miles. All told, a journey from Fustat to India, via 'Aydhab and Aden, was 3,615 miles, a journey the same distance as a flight between New York and Paris.

Before departing, travelers would recite:

When you pass through water,
I shall be with you;
Through streams,
They shall not overwhelm you. (Isa 43:2)

And upon returning, they would recite:

Let them praise the Lord for his steadfast love,
his wondrous deeds for mankind. (Ps 107:31)

Though we have no record of the shipwreck that sealed David's fate, the descriptions we have in Genizah papers and elsewhere suggest horror and despair over other wrecks at sea during the same time. Skies turn black. Winds and rain rage. The waves surge onto the decks and sweep into the cabins. The ship rocks and creaks as if to break. Like drunken men, the seamen stagger, their skills of no avail. Fearing death, the passengers cry out, each in his own language to his God. Yet the waves are not stilled. The prayers become hysterical, the voices mount to screams. Through the storm the terrified passengers grow resigned to death. Family and friends pass before their eyes as they bid them farewell. The feeble vessel shatters to splinters, disgorging its contents. Soon all are dead, the storm a whisper.

Moses Writes to Japheth

The loss of his younger brother was a core experience that transformed Maimonides' life and left an indelible mark on his thinking. By another piece of good fortune, a letter is preserved in which Moses described his reaction to David's drowning. He wrote to Japheth ben Elijah in Acre, whom he and his father and brother had befriended during their stay in that city.[46] The letter was preserved in literary form and transmitted in collections of Maimonides' letters. In it Maimonides described his extreme reaction to David's drowning.

The letter is written in Hebrew with a salutation in fine rhymed prose. Japheth's letter must also have been in Hebrew, as Maimonides always replied in kind. Moses' letter is a vivid mosaic of biblical resonances, as though his deepest emotions could be expressed only in the voice of Scripture.

Moses addressed Japheth with conventional deference as "our esteemed, great and revered teacher and master, Japheth, the wise and astute sage[47] and discerning judge (may his Rock preserve him), son of the esteemed, great and revered teacher and master, Elijah, the pious judge (may the memory of the righteous be a blessing)." Maimonides referred to himself as "the one who loves him, who yearns for him in his absence and prays for the increase of his honor." The gracious sentiments are a disarming preamble to the strident message that follows.

Japheth's letter, we infer from the reply, was a stunning affront to Moses. Japheth had complained that Moses had not taken the initiative and written to inquire about Japheth from the day Moses and his family had left the Holy Land. Japheth must have assumed that etiquette required Moses, as Japheth's guest who had departed, to write first.

The reprimand from Japheth infuriated Moses, who listed his own grievances in his letter to Japheth. A few months after his family had left the Holy Land, his father died. Letters of condolence arrived from distant places, yet Japheth had not written.

Moses therefore did not write to Japheth. Further setbacks still elicited no word from Japheth. Then for years there was silence. Suddenly Japheth sent a request for help, but before stating what he wanted he unburdened his heart with complaints. Maimonides replied, admonishing Japheth and explaining how difficult his life had been, and stressing the loss of his brother David.

> Moreover, a few months after we departed [from the Land of Israel], my father and master [*abba mari*] died (*may the memory of the righteous be a blessing*). Letters of condolence arrived from the furthest west and from the land of Edom, a distance of several months, yet you disregarded this.
>
> Furthermore, I suffered many well-known calamities in Egypt,[48] including sicknesses, financial loss and the attempt by informers to have me killed.[49]
>
> The worst disaster that struck me of late, worse than anything[50] I had ever experienced from the time I was born until this day, was the demise of that upright man (*may the memory of the righteous be a blessing*), who drowned in the Indian Ocean while in possession of much money belonging to me, to him and to others, leaving a young daughter and his widow in my care.
>
> For about a year from the day the evil tidings reached me, I remained prostrate in bed with a severe inflammation, fever and mental confusion, and well nigh perished.[51]
>
> From then until this day, that is, about eight years, I have been in a state of disconsolate mourning. How can I be consoled? For he was my son; he grew up upon my knees; he was my brother, my pupil. It was he who did business in the market place, earning a livelihood, while I dwelled in security.
>
> He had a ready grasp of Talmud and a superb mastery of grammar. My only joy was to see him. *The sun has set on all joy* [Isa 24:11]. For he has gone on to eternal life, leaving me dismayed in a foreign land.[52] Whenever I see his handwriting or one of his books, my heart

is churned inside me and my sorrow is rekindled.[53] *In short, I will go down mourning to my son in Sheol* [Gen 37:35].[54] And were it not for the Torah, which is my delight, and for scientific matters, which let me forget my sorrow, *I would have perished in my affliction* [Ps 119:92].

In spite of this, while I complain not of any sage, disciple, friend, or acquaintance, I should complain about you above all others. For I, he and my father, my teacher (may the memory of the righteous be a blessing), and you—all four of us—walked together in God's house in fear and trepidation. But you did not seek or inquire. I would be justified in not answering your letter that has now arrived pertaining to power of attorney.[55] But my affection is drawn up in full and secured.[56] I shall not forget our wandering together in wastelands and forests after the Lord, and therefore I do not ascribe to you sin and transgression. *Love covers up all faults* [Prov 10:12].

God knows how much I am distressed by the hard times you mention. The whole matter grieved me deeply unto death.[57] If you were here with me, I would care for you properly, and I would honor and please you according to my ability.[58]

I rejoice greatly over this son whom God has given you—Rabbi Elijah, the astute pupil. I heard that he studies Torah and that he is a clever fellow,[59] and treads the right path. *Your sons will succeed your ancestors; you will appoint them princes throughout the land* [Ps 45:17].[60] May this be God's will.

Shevat 1496 s.e. (January 1185)

With all the polite phrases, kind assurances, fond memories, and gentle thoughts that Maimonides conveyed here, his letter to Japheth was brusque and betrays barely repressed anger. The letter reveals the sage's agitated state of mind as he recalled his sojourn in the Holy Land and the loss of his father and brother. Epistolary etiquette considered the emotional display of personal misfortune a breach of decorum.[61] Japheth's letter reminded Moses of the pain he suffered as a newcomer to Egypt, and he relived it as he wrote. The anger he displayed in the letter released a torrent of feelings—fury and also tender sentiments of love and nostalgia and a sense of deprivation.

The allusion to the biblical Moses as a stranger in a foreign land is a clue to an aspect of Moses ben Maimon's character and self-image, namely, his strong identification with Moses son of Amram. Like the biblical Moses, the son of Maimon was also a stranger in Egypt. Moses is an idealized figure for Maimonides. He is not simply the one who led the people of Israel out of Egypt and received the Torah at Sinai; he has achieved the highest degree of wisdom attainable by a human being. He was "the master of those who know," superior to "the chief of the philosophers" (Aristotle).[62]

MOURNING AND MELANCHOLY

Maimonides' anguish at his brother's death left him overwhelmed with grief and a sense of irretrievable loss, as though his own life had ended. His paralyzing illness and protracted sorrow, which lasted for years, point unmistakably to a serious depression. This may occur when a person sensitized by stressful life events, especially traumatic separation, suffers the loss of a loved one.[63]

David's death was a financial blow to the family of Maimonides. We are surprised at his mentioning loss of life and loss of money in the same breath in his letter to Japheth—"the demise of that upright man . . . who drowned in the Indian Ocean while in possession of much money belonging to me, to him and to others, leaving a young daughter and his widow in my care."

We sense disapproval and resentment that David's improvident venture harmed his own family and all who had invested in his enterprise. The financial catastrophe drastically affected Moses' life and sense of security.[64]

Moses' extreme reaction to his brother's death was conditioned by the sensibilities of his age, when the precariousness of life made people nervous, overreactive, and high-strung. Goitein notes the "nervousness in the Genizah period, the epidemics, disruption of life, horrors and panics and losses."[65] Living on the edge of disaster causes hypersensitivity and emotivism.[66] Maimonides was hyperattuned to survival in a time when famine, plague, and illness were constant threats. Such was the insecure tenor of life in this age.

A Life Transformed

The loss of money and sudden burden of having to support David's widow and daughter disturbed Maimonides' sense of well-being. Biographers have written that David's death caused Maimonides to relinquish the life of a scholar and take up medicine as a profession. However, there is no sign of such an abrupt transition.[67] Maimonides had studied medicine in North Africa and attained prominence as a physician in his early days in Fatimid Egypt, before David's demise. When he says in his letter to Japheth that David went abroad on business, permitting him to dwell in security, this does not mean that he was unoccupied. He was already a practicing physician, he taught the sciences and philosophy, and—as we see—he engaged in commerce as a sedentary trader.

Still, there was a momentous transformation in Maimonides' life after David's death. Religious study and scientific research had restored his spirits in his most dejected phase. Maimonides came to realize that we cannot avoid "the sea of chance"—sudden death and loss—by prayer and good works; rather, we must live a life of reason in accordance with nature, avoiding risks that may bring enrichment but expose us to the chance of poverty and loss as well.

PART FOUR

EGYPT
THE MIDDLE YEARS

15

Zuta the Wicked

There are evils ... that men inflict upon one another, such as
tyrannical domination of some of them over others.

— THE GUIDE OF THE PERPLEXED, III, 2

A MAN CALLED ZUTA THE WICKED became Ra'is over Jewish communities in Egypt several times during Maimonides' career. Zuta paid, or bribed, rulers for the privilege of office and the right to collect taxes, which he did with high-handed and oppressive measures. Zuta was, in fact, a derogatory nickname conferred by his enemies. His parents called him Yahya, his full name being Yahya Abu Zikri (John, father of Zachariah). He called himself Sar Shalom, meaning "Prince of Peace" (Isa 9:5b), a name we have met with Sar Shalom ha-Levi. He was said to have regarded himself as the precursor of the Messiah or as the Messiah himself.[1]

In Alexandria, Zuta led lower-class people in an uprising against the elders of the Jewish community. By his actions and messianic claims he inevitably aroused the attention of the high-ranking Muslim authorities. Maimonides was deeply involved in the Zuta affair. He and his colleague Isaac ben Sason eventually overcame Zuta and relieved Jewish communities of their tormentor. Had Maimonides failed to crush Zuta, it is unlikely that he would have become leader over Egyptian Jewry.

SCROLL OF ZUTA THE WICKED

Zuta and his nefarious deeds were depicted in the *Scroll of Zuta the Wicked,* written by Abraham ben Hillel, a supporter of Maimonides and the anti-Zuta camp. We should not, therefore, expect complete objectivity from the author. The Zuta scroll is written as a parody of the biblical Book of Esther, inlaid with biblical allusions and quotations.[2] Its layering of rhymed prose and poetry is typical of the *maqama,* which features a charming rogue as the main character. Here, the main character is more rogue than charming. The scroll is hyperbolic and elusive, making re-creation of events difficult. Abraham ben Hillel claimed that his father told him about some events, while others he observed himself, indicating action over a long period of time.

INTERPRETATION OF THE SCROLL

We can only tentatively identify the characters and historical situations to which the *Scroll of Zuta* alludes.[3] Zuta's attempts to seize the Nagidut began in the 1140s and were renewed on different occasions in the 1170s and even later.

He first attempted to supplant Samuel ben Hananyah, who was Nagid (r. 1140–59) and court physician to the Fatimid Caliph al-Hafiz (r. 1131–49) and Caliph al-Zafir (r. 1149–54). The avaricious ruler was presumably one of these caliphs or one of their viziers, as viziers wielded effective power at this stage of Fatimid rule and were even called "king" (*malik*) and "sultan." The vizier Najm al-Din ibn Masal was in office for about sixty days in 1149, and this period may have corresponded with Zuta's sixty-six-day tenure of office, but this is only a surmise.

When Zuta informed the authorities that ten thousand dinars had been concealed beneath Samuel's head when he was buried, the sovereign discovered that this was false. He may have been Caliph al-Fa'iz (r. 1154–60) or his vizier, al-Malik al-Salih Tala'i' Ibn Ruzzik (r. 1154–60).[4]

A new sovereign rose over Egypt, from whom Zuta purchased high office for two hundred dinars a year, remaining in power for four years, probably between 1166 and 1169. The caliph was then al-'Adid, with four viziers serving him: Dirgham ibn Suwar (1162), Shawar ibn Mujir (1162–68), Shirkuh (1168), and finally Saladin (1168–71).

Then Moses ben Maimon, who had come to Egypt in 1166, overcame Zuta, "restored the law to its former state, removed the image from the temple" and brought "the beginning of salvation."[5] The *Scroll of Zuta* does not say how Maimonides created this dawn of deliverance; however, it is intimated later that he went to the sultan. The scroll mentions communal bans against Zuta and son, and Maimonides was a principal on one of these occasions.[6]

Zuta and his son thereafter encountered a sultan who was righteous and would not accept a bribe. Having no other recourse, they told the sultan and his officials that some Jews were traitors to the regime and should be investigated. The sultan's suspicions were confirmed and he kept the Jews under scrutiny. Zuta held power for two years, keeping his eye on his fellow Jews in service to the dynasty. Scholars identify the righteous sovereign with Saladin, pointing out that supporters of the Fatimids, including some Jews, plotted against his new regime.[7]

At the end of two years, a government official, who helped Zuta, went to Syro-Palestine, and the people were hopeful that they would be saved from Zuta. We do not know who the official was or when he went to Syro-Palestine. As Saladin went there in October 1174, accompanied by army commanders and government officials, including al-Qadi al-Fadil, the official who supported Zuta may well have gone along with the royal entourage at this time.

Zuta informed the royal chamberlain that three insurgents entered Egypt from outside the country and were being hidden by local Jews. They were apprehended and died in prison.[8] The Jews then placed Zuta and son under a ban and a curse, and declared their excision (*karet*) from the world hereafter.

After this Rav Isaac ben Sason, with full backing of the community, went to speak with the sultan and saved his people from oppression. The sultan promised to remove Zuta and his son. The people banned them a second time, "and they fell, never to rise again."

As Abraham ben Hillel finished the scroll in 1197, celebrating Zuta's final downfall in the Hebrew month of Adar, it is usually assumed that his activities extended to this period. If so, when Isaac ben Sason went to speak with the sultan, Saladin was no longer living (d. 1193). He was followed by al-Malik al-'Aziz I 'Uthman (r. 1193–1198).

If 1197 is the date of this copy of the Zuta scroll and not of the original composition, then the final stage of the conflict could have been in the early 1180s. We shall see below that by about 1185, according to Maimonides, Zuta was a toothless lion.

Abraham ben Hillel depicted Zuta as an ignoramus who acceded to office by bribes and then went on to wield authority tyrannically. Paying for office was a common practice at the time. The government farmed out the collecting of taxes to private individuals or groups, who paid a sum to the treasury and received in return a percentage of the taxes.[9] People paid taxes under duress, sought ways of evasion, and were vulnerable to extortion and torture.

It was natural for a Ra'is to farm taxes, as he was responsible for the collective poll tax (*jizya*) and raised taxes for his own treasury. Zuta, however, was excessively cruel and attempted to replace popular local leaders with agents loyal to him. Perhaps Isaac ben Sason succeeded in getting the sultan to depose Zuta by promising to have the Jewish community pay a greater amount of taxes to the state treasury.

A LETTER DESCRIBING ZUTA

Zuta is depicted as a rabble-rouser and messianic figure in a letter narrating events in Alexandria during a communal crisis in about 1180—a power struggle between the incumbent judge Elazar ha-Kohen and a newcomer, judge Ephraim, said by his opponents to be a follower of Zuta.[10] Judges were leaders of the Alexandrian Jewish community, representing them to the government, supervising taxes, adjudicating legal issues, raising funds for social services and release of captives, and presiding over synagogue services. The power struggle divided the Jewish community and came to the attention of the Muslim authorities in Alexandria and Cairo/Fustat.

The rivals eventually reached a compromise by agreeing to a power-sharing partnership. Ephraim and his colleagues wrote to Maimonides asking for his opinion. Unfortunately, the document is unclear at this point, and we do not know whether Maimonides approved of the compromise.

A letter written by Judge Ephraim, the newcomer to Alexandria, to an important person in Cairo/Fustat portrayed his controversy with the incumbent Judge Elazar and the popular rebellion led by Zuta.[11] Ephraim recounted efforts to delegitimize him by supporters of Elazar and by Muslim government authorities who were brought into the fray by Elazar's camp. He claimed that he was conciliatory and mentioned the division of authority with Elazar ha-Kohen, which they reached by compromise.

Ephraim's opponents, supporters of Elazar, revealed to Muslim officials Ephraim's sin: "He incited people—dyers, oyster gatherers, and rabble of the helpers (al-ansar)—and put them in authority over the elders."[12]

A session (majlis) of Muslim worthies was convened, including the jurist Ibn 'Awf,[13] the Qadi, Shaykh Abu 'l-Qasim,[14] and a group of jurists, to establish that Gaon al-Iqtidar, who called himself by the name al-Masih (Messiah),[15] and all who shared his view deserved to be burned.[16] That a charismatic, pietistic leader, as Ephraim was, should be drawn into the orbit of the messianic claimant Zuta is certainly believable. Accordingly, we have on one side Judge Elazar, a man of the law, loyal to the communal elders, confronting two outsiders, Ephraim and Zuta, who enchant the crowd and challenge authority.

Afterward, Ephraim's opponents began to slander him to every passerby in the city and inclined the hearts of the people against him, persuading the Qadi and the jurists that Ephraim worshiped idolatry—a reference to his alleged association with Zuta. Again, as with the idol in the temple, we are not told why Ephraim was accused of worshipping idolatry.

A certain Rabbi Manasseh and a small delegation went to Cairo/Fustat and appeared before al-Qadi al-Fadil.[17] "God knows what they said about me," Ephraim commented. Al-Qadi al-Fadil wrote a letter to the Qadi, to Abu 'l-Qasim, to the jurist Ibn 'Awf, to the jurist al-Za'farani, and to a certain Ben Elisha.[18] We do not hear about the content of the letter, yet as the delegation comprised enemies of Ephraim, and as al-Qadi al-Fadil wrote to Muslim dignitaries who were concerned about the Zuta movement, we may infer that he intended to warn the dignitaries about the threat and to urge them not to support Ephraim.

Ephraim, the newcomer, and his colleagues decided to inform "our Master," presumably Maimonides, concerning the partnership agreement between him and Elazar ha-Kohen, the incumbent judge. The reason for turning to Maimonides was to seek a judicial opinion on the legal force of the partnership agreement, for matters had apparently come to a standstill. Maimonides was evidently not Ra'is al-Yahud at the time, yet he was the authority to whom Ephraim turned for resolution of the issue.

Ephraim's letter describing the controversy is of great value, for it shows that at the time, around 1180, Zuta was in Alexandria fomenting a rebellion of the lower classes against the traditional leadership, claiming to be a messianic figure and instituting new ways of worship that were considered idolatrous and troubled both the Jewish and Muslim authorities.

MAIMONIDES' LETTER TO RABBI PHINEAS

Maimonides gave a brief description of Zuta, called Abu Zikri, in reply to a query by Phineas ben Meshullam, a French rabbi who emigrated to Egypt around 1185. He was appointed, perhaps by Maimonides, as a judge in Alexandria.[19] His letter to Maimonides may have been written close to the time of his arrival in Egypt.[20]

Judge Phineas asked Maimonides about "the business of Abu Zikri, who took over authority in wickedness and cruelty." The judge's inquiry was a matter of personal concern, as Zuta evidently remained in Alexandria. Maimonides reassured Phineas by diminishing the seriousness of Abu Zikri's threat:

> [Abu Zikri] fears the most insignificant member of the community and has no one to support him. Do not mind him, and let not the words of transgressors alarm you. He turned over ninety dinars futilely without receiving any writ [of appointment] from the ruler, but only permission as follows: "If the Jews want him, let them [have him]." He [then] came and said to the elders, "If you expel me I shall leave,"

and he wept at night in their presence until they let him be. This is
the truth of the matter. May your peace increase.

WHO WAS ZUTA?

Our problem is that Yahya Abu Zikri, the man called Zuta, who called
himself Sar Shalom, was on different occasions Ra'is of the Jews, yet
we cannot identify him with a known figure. Some scholars have argued that he was the Gaon and Ra'is Sar Shalom ha-Levi.[21] The pro-
ponents of this view cite as their main proof a statement by Abraham
Maimonides that his father tried to unify synagogue practices in the
two main synagogues of Fustat, the Iraqian synagogue, which had the
same customs as all the exiles, and the Palestinian synagogue, which
had its own customs.[22] However, Abraham said, the "supremely evil
one" (*sharr al-ashrar*) and others forced Maimonides to be silent. *Sharr
al-ashrar* appears to be a satirical allusion to *sar ha-sarim* (chief official),
a title of the Head of the Jews, which Sar Shalom ha-Levi used.[23]

However, others were also addressed as *sar ha-sarim* and *sar shalom*.
The Alexandrian judge Anatoli ben Joseph, in a letter to Maimonides,
called him *sar ha-sarim*.[24] The Lunel scholars, in their query on astrology, applied to Maimonides the appellations in Isa 9:5b: *Wonderful Counselor, Mighty God, Everlasting Father, Prince of Peace (sar
shalom) is his name.*[25] Moreover, even if Abraham ben Moses alluded
to Sar Shalom ha-Levi, this does not mean that he was identical with
Zuta.

Furthermore, the description of Zuta as a despotic ignoramus
hardly tallies with what we know about Sar Shalom ha-Levi, who was
from an aristocratic family of Geonim, descendants of Moses the Sixth.
His brother Nethanel, as we have seen, was a physician and courtier
and Head of the Jews. Sar Shalom succeeded Nethanel by a normal
process, and we have no evidence that he was regarded as oppressive
and wicked. Some argue that Abraham ben Hillel, author of the Zuta
scroll, was biased and made Sar Shalom ha-Levi, who was in fact
Zuta, sound more ignorant and wicked than he actually was. Yet other
reports about Zuta depict him in lurid shades as well, and Abraham
ben Hillel could not have exaggerated very much.

Menachem Ben-Sasson and Mordechai A. Friedman believe that Zuta was not simply Sar Shalom; rather (because of the long time line), he was a composite of members of the ha-Levi family—Moses ha-Levi ben Nethanel and his sons Nethanel and Sar Shalom. This is a daring hypothesis, and it remains to be seen if it can be sustained.

16

Communal Affairs

*The ransoming of captives has precedence over the feeding and clothing
of the poor. Indeed there is no religious duty more meritorious.*

MISHNEH TORAH, GIFTS TO THE POOR, XIII, 10

AMONG MAIMONIDES' FIRST ACTS IN EGYPT was ransoming captives taken prisoner in warfare with the Crusaders. All three religious communities had to deal with releasing prisoners captured in war, seized by pirates, or taken hostage as travelers. The usual ransom for a single captive, whether Muslim, Christian, or Jew, was 33⅓ dinars, or 100 dinars for three people (= $620.78 in 2007 terms). This sum varied, as important individuals were held for higher ransom. When Christian and Muslim combatants or civilians were taken prisoner in warfare, their representatives negotiated prisoner exchanges with their captors. Jewish communities, however, did not have armies to negotiate prisoner exchanges, and their only recourse was to pay ransom money.

Muslim leaders had Muslim prisoners released as swiftly as possible to safeguard their faith, and Islamic law regarded ransoming prisoners as an act of piety.[1] The traveler Ibn Jubayr admired Syrian efforts to ransom Maghribi prisoners captured by the Crusaders, who merited special consideration as foreigners far from home.[2] The Syrian ruler Nur al-Din sent twelve thousand dinars to ransom these Maghribi foreigners only to discover that some were actually from Hamah in

Syria. He ordered that the Syrians be returned to captivity and had more Maghribis released on the assumption that the Syrians could be ransomed by their friends and relatives nearby.

Christians also considered captives as objects of charity, like the poor, and regarded ransom money as alms.[3] Some religious orders, such as the Mercedarians in thirteenth-century Spain, devoted themselves to ransoming captives. In general, however, the Crusaders regarded payment for redemption of captives as shameful, preferring to liberate them by force.

Aside from the many Jews taken prisoner in warfare, pirates were constantly bringing captured Jewish merchants and travelers to shore for ransoming. In the beginning of the eleventh century, piracy in the Mediterranean increased as Byzantine and Fatimid navies fought for control. Muslim pirates brought Jews to Alexandria, and local Jews ransomed them and cared for them until they returned home. The cost was so burdensome that they had to ask other communities for help, often turning to the Jews of Fustat.[4] Combined fund-raising appeals by Karaites and Rabbanites were normal, as captives belonged to both denominations.

Communities had to mobilize the energies of the entire population to raise ransom money. The released captive needed clothing and support until he or she returned home, and costs of the journey, poll taxes, and port duties had to be paid to the Muslim authorities.

Queries about ransoming captives were sent to Maimonides, who ruled on them in his responsa. He decided, for example, that the ransomed captive is not obligated to repay those who did the ransoming because it was done as a religious obligation, not as a loan.[5]

Maimonides viewed ransoming captives as equivalent to saving lives:[6]

The ransoming of captives has precedence over the feeding and clothing of the poor. Indeed there is no religious duty more meritorious than the ransoming of captives, for not only is the captive included in the generality of the hungry, the thirsty, and the naked, but also his very life is in jeopardy.[7] He who turns his eyes away from ransoming him, transgresses the commandments, *You shall not harden your heart, nor shut your hand* [Deut 15:7], *Neither shall you stand idly by the blood of your neighbor* [Lev 19:16], and *He shall not rule ruthlessly over him in your sight* [Lev 25:53]. Moreover, he nullifies the commandments *You shall surely open your hand unto him* [Deut 15:18], *Let him live by your side as your kinsman* [Lev 25:36], *You shall love your neighbor as yourself* [Lev 19:18], *If you refrained from rescuing those taken off to death* [Prov 24:11], and many other admonitions such as these. To sum up, there is no religious duty greater than ransoming captives.[8]

In giving priority to ransoming captives and stressing its merit, Maimonides followed rabbinic precedent, yet the passage contains a special urgency and personal emphasis.

FUND-RAISING CIRCULARS

We find in the Cairo Genizah four fund-raising circulars sent out by Maimonides and a receipt that he signed for nine dinars.[9] Three of the documents and the receipt are dated, which helps ascertain their circumstances.[10] Two of the circulars may pertain to captives taken prisoner by the Crusaders when they conquered Bilbays.[11] The captives were frequently held in Palestine, many having been taken prisoner in Egypt and then transported to Crusader territory.

Maimonides' campaigns to raise money for release of captives may have begun before he was Head of the Jews and continued after he left office in 1173. The circulars were issued by his council, or court, the scribe being the court clerk and judge Mevorakh ben Nathan, a gifted stylist whose letters were written in eloquent rhymed prose—a perfect medium for circulars, which had to appeal to the heart.[12]

Maimonides adopted a strict policy of central command, controlling details and eliminating chance and risk. He requested that funds, donor lists, and sums pledged should all be sent to him. He designated officials to make the rounds and read aloud the fund-raising letters, and he appointed representatives to be in contact with the captives, supervise their ransoming, and appoint negotiators to work out details of their release, entrusting the ransom money to these representatives.

Circular to the Countryside

Maimonides sent a circular to communities in the countryside of Egypt to raise money for the ransom of captives, apparently taken prisoner at Bilbays, which the Crusaders, commanded by King Amalric, conquered on November 4, 1168, burning its dwellings, killing civilians, and taking many captives as prisoners of war.[13]

The circular addressed elders, scholars. and *muqaddam*s, indeed entire communities, who were urged to ransom captives as the law prescribed and support one another generously as other communities had done.

Whatever was collected should be sent to Maimonides, and it would be combined with contributions from the people of Cairo/Fustat,[14] who showed pity, undeterred by the stressful times, acting out of their generosity.

The judges in Syro-Palestine (al-Sham), Hiyya and Ephraim, were instructed to be in contact with the captives and supervise the release of these abandoned people (*munqati'in*).[15] The agent should receive the sum of money from Maimonides against their signatures.[16] A certain Aaron ha-Levi volunteered to make the rounds among the communities and read out the letter; despite his own poverty and need, he desired to merit this reward.[17] The circular ended with Maimonides' justification of his strong tone and the hope that his addressees would be blessed and spared adversity and suffering.

Ransoming Captives Letter
Signed by Moses ben Maimon

This important letter on ransoming captives was first published by S. M. Margulies in 1900, thus being one of the earliest Genizah documents to be published.[18] S. D. Goitein later edited it using available facsimiles of poor quality.[19] Subsequently, Professor Menahem H. Schmelzer, librarian of the Jewish Theological Seminary collection, informed Goitein that the original manuscript was in the Marshall Case of the library.[20] Although the beginning is lacking, Moses ben Maimon's signature and the date are preserved at the end. Unfortunately, the date is hard to decipher. It appears to be 1484 s.e., which began June 14, 1173 c.e.[21] Goitein believed that this document, like the previous one, relates to captives taken prisoner by the Crusaders at Bilbays in 1168. However, if the document is from a later period, then the occasion may not have been Bilbays, although fund-raising campaigns did sometimes last for years.

As in the first document, Maimonides asked the addressees to consider the generosity of others and strive to emulate them.[22] He informed them that he was sending a letter with Aaron ha-Levi, who would read it out in public. A welfare official (*firnas*) belonging to Maimonides' entourage accompanied him.[23] Maimonides urged them to pay attention to the letter and seize the opportunity.[24]

They should do what Maimonides and his colleagues—judges, elders, and scholars—had done. "We all go about night and day and encourage people in synagogues and bazaars and at gates of residences, to obtain funds for this momentous task only after we ourselves have contributed according to our means. So must you act for [the captives] according to your noble status, and your well-known kindness and your eagerness to earn merit [*zekhut*]."

Whatever sum they obtained for ransoming the captives they should transfer to Maimonides. He urged them to strive to collect the money quickly and to dispatch it to him with Aaron ha-Levi. At the end, he wished that God not let them fall upon hard times, and blessed them: "May he protect and guard you in His great mercy. And may your welfare increase forever."

RELATIONS WITH KARAITES

The calendar was the main cause of disagreement between Karaites and Rabbanites. Rabbanite Jewish communities followed a calendar regulated by astronomical calculations.[25] The Karaites, however, retained the ancient method of determining the new month by witnesses' observation of the new moon's appearance, which was less accurate and tended to vary from place to place. Karaites and Rabbanites consequently celebrated holidays on different days, leading to disorders when, for instance, one group was observing the Day of

Atonement solemnly and the other was opening stores, or when one group was observing Passover by eating matzot and the other was not observing and eating bread.

Moreover, the Karaites observed the Sabbath strictly, prohibiting lights in the house, heating, warm food, and sexual relations. The Karaites prohibited entry into Rabbanite synagogues illuminated by lamps on the Sabbath.

They also expanded the definition of incestuous marriages beyond the scriptural forbidden degrees, making it difficult to find marriage partners within their own community and necessitating mixed marriages with Rabbanites on all social levels.

Despite differences, Rabbanites and Karaites considered themselves a single religious community and were so recognized by the Muslim authorities. The Ra'is al-Yahud was responsible for both groups, as we have seen (ch. 12). When Karaites and Rabbanites intermarried, the partners adhered to their own denominations while respecting the customs of the other, although in some cases one member of the married couple would adopt the traditions of the other.

In his *Commentary on the Mishnah* and *Mishneh Torah,* Maimonides declared the Karaites heretics (*minim*). In his responsa, however, he tended to be more flexible and to view the Karaites as fellow Jews. When asked by an esteemed scholar how the Rabbanites should conduct themselves toward Karaites with respect to circumcising their sons, greeting them, visiting their homes, and drinking their wine, he responded:[26]

> These Karaites, who live here in Alexandria, Cairo, Damascus, and other places of the Land of Ishmael [Islam] and outside, should be treated with respect and approached with honesty. One should conduct oneself with them with modesty and in the way of truth and peace, as long as they conduct themselves with us with integrity, avoiding crooked speech and devious talk [cf. Prv 4:24] and preaching disloyalty [cf. Isa 32:6] toward the Rabbanite Sages of the generation; all the more that they avoid mocking the words of our holy Sages (peace upon them), the Tannaim, the Sages of the Mishnah and the Talmud, whose words and customs we follow, which they established for us from Moses and the Almighty. Therefore, we should honor them and

greet them, even in their houses, and circumcise their sons, even on the Sabbath, bury their dead, and comfort their mourners.[27]

OVERSEEING SYNAGOGUES AND PIOUS FOUNDATIONS

As Head of the Jews and as the Great Rav in Israel, Maimonides had broad communal responsibilities, and despite his onerous schedule, he supervised minute details of communal activity. A major task of his was overseeing synagogues and pious foundations.

Moses and his son, Abraham, as well as Abraham's father-in-law, Hananel ben Samuel, directed the upkeep of the sanctuary of Dammuh, which was a pious foundation.[28] The Synagogue of Moses (Kanisat Musa) at Dammuh was a highly venerated site.[29] It was located across the Nile from Fustat, on the western bank, outside the city, near the pyramids of Gizeh, surrounded by monasteries. Like the Christian cult of the saints and Islamic veneration of holy tombs, Dammuh was an object of pilgrimage for all segments of the population—elites and commoners, young and old, men and women, possibly even apostates and non-Jews. The phenomenon by which believers of one religious community venerate the holy sites of another is a feature of the cult of saints in the Mediterranean region.

The pilgrimages to the Synagogue of Moses at Dammuh took place on Shavuot (Pentecost), a holiday commemorating the revelation of the law to Moses on Sinai, and on 7 Adar (which falls in February-March), the day when Moses was believed to have been born and died. The seventh of Adar was a fast day and was followed by a feast on the eighth. The Muslim historian Taqi al-Din al-Maqrizi wrote that the Jews went with their families to Dammuh on Pentecost as a substitute for making the pilgrimage to Jerusalem.[30] The most detailed account of the pilgrimage is given by the Egyptian Jewish historian Joseph Sambari (1640–1703), who notes that the eighth of Adar was a day of festivity and joy when "men, women and children and the heads of the thousands of Israel would assemble."[31]

We know about religious festivals at Dammuh from a community enactment prohibiting certain customs.[32] The purpose of the enactment was to repress the bacchanal atmosphere that prevailed during

pilgrimages to the Dammuh sanctuary, to restore boundaries that had
been breached, especially between the sexes, the area of most potent
danger to the strict social hierarchy and the most threatening to communal (male) anxieties. Women's travel was restricted in general, but
they were permitted to go on the pilgrimage to Jerusalem and to visit
synagogues. Nevertheless, behavior at holy sites was under firm control, and men and women were strictly separated.[33] An important provision of the Dammuh enactment stipulated that a woman could not
attend the synagogue unaccompanied by a male relative unless she was
very old. Another requirement stressed the strict segregation of the
sexes in the synagogue. The statute also prohibited homosexuality in
the sanctuary precincts. One ruling apparently (the text is unclear) forbade the pilgrim to bring with him a gentile or apostate. The enactment banned frivolity and jesting and the kind of entertainments and
amusements known to take place on similar occasions at Christian and
Muslim religious festivals, such as marionette shows and gambling;
here chess and other games are mentioned. Singing and dancing with
rhythmic banging and clapping were forbidden. The statute evidently
applied not only to festivals but to sanctuary visits in general.

Maimonides alluded to coarse behavior at festivities in a passage of
his law code in which he condemned revelry and drinking in celebration of holidays lest the carnival mood lead to sexual immorality.[34]

He raised funds for operating the Dammuh sanctuary after a period
of neglect.[35] Several documents pertaining to the sanctuary are from
the time of Maimonides and his son, Abraham. S. D. Goitein suggests
that the religious revival of Egyptian Jewry inspired by Maimonides'
teaching and reforms and by his son's pietism may have rekindled veneration for this ancient holy sanctuary.[36] Abraham's father-in-law, the
judge Hananel ben Samuel, was also engaged in maintenance of the
Dammuh sanctuary. He received a letter from an acquaintance in Alexandria in which the writer wistfully recalled the days spent with him
at the sanctuary, sending fifty dirhams for its repair.[37]

The main instrument controlling the activities of a pious foundation was the court, which even in antiquity had a crucial role in the
administrative system. The legal maxim *The court is the hand of the
poor* is invoked by a Geonic responsum and later by Maimonides as
the rule for management of dedicated communal property.[38] The

court was not represented by a single presiding judge. It was connected with the *majlis* (council) and the leading scholars, who were its members. The historian Moshe Gil explains why a distinguished person such as Maimonides dealt with minuscule details of synagogue administration. One reason was the sacred character of the pious foundation, which required attention to every item of expenditure. Another was the influence of the Islamic state's centralism. The caliph attended to minor administrative details required of him as a dispenser of justice.

ISAIAH HA-LEVI'S APPOINTMENT

Isaiah ha-Levi ben Mishael was the father of Moses ben Maimon's father-in-law, and thereby the grandfather of Maimonides' wife. A letter of appointment issued in Adar 1461 s.e. (February 1150), under the authority (*reshut*) of Nagid Samuel ben Hananya and his court, made Isaiah ha-Levi supervisor over affairs of the Jews in Fustat, communal property (*qodesh*), synagogues in the city, and the Dammuh sanctuary with its gardens, the scrolls of the Torah, the vessels for oil, books, and all other things.

The privileges given to Isaiah ha-Levi were extensive, yet the court's supervision over him was limited. There was to be no power or opinion over his. Anything he deemed right and any expenditures he approved were to be carried out independently of higher authority. He was allowed to appoint his own deputies, since his righteousness and upright conduct were acknowledged by all. The rest of the document stressed his prerogatives and immunity from any interference by the court. How he managed to obtain such flagrant privileges we do not know. A judge who made arrangements with him attested: "Rabbi Isaiah was appointed over the pious foundation because he excelled in piety and faith in what he supervised for the people of Israel. I have testimony to this from the presiding judges of the time, with the signatures of our teacher Hiyya ben Isaac and our teacher Jacob ben Joseph ha-Kohen and their associates." Isaiah's letter of appointment was presented a century later, in Nisan (March–April) 1252, to Nagid David ben Abraham (Moses Maimonides' grandson), as it had become the legal basis for all claims of pious foundations under supervision of

the community. David ben Abraham was the great-great-grandson of
Isaiah ha-Levi.

A COMPLAINT AGAINST ISAIAH HA-LEVI

A letter of complaint to Moses ben Maimon from Meir ben Hillel ben
Rabbi Sadoq Av concerned Isaiah ha-Levi's management. The beginning and end of the letter are lacking, and there are no clear signs of
writer or addressee, yet the handwriting and content indicate who
they were.[39]

Meir ben Hillel was a professional judge who began his career
in the town of al-Mahalla, then became deputy judge in Fustat, and
thereafter chief judge in Alexandria, where he may have written this
letter. His grandfather, Rabbi Sadoq Av, was Av Bet Din (chief of the
court) of the Palestinian Academy, then located in Egypt. Meir ben
Hillel related in a letter that our lord (*sayyiduna*) the Head of the Jews
offered him the judgeship in Alexandria in return for an annual payment of twelve dinars.[40]

Meir ben Hillel complained to Maimonides that Isaiah ha-Levi had
revoked provisions that Isaiah had originally put in place, allowing
Meir to rebuild a ruined plot of the pious foundation and live there,
offsetting the cost of upkeep by the rent he received from leasing the
property. Meir argued that similar provisions affecting others should
likewise be rescinded, claiming betrayal of trust and discrimination.

A representative brought the letter to Maimonides' court and presented the case. The letter is a curious blend of polite esteem and pa-
tronizing impropriety. Meir ben Hillel switched from the respectful
third person to the more familiar second, pressing for expeditious
handling of his case and claiming that delay would make Maimonides
an accessory to injustice. I suspect that this was not Meir's first appeal
on the subject.

Meir proposed that if Moses ben Maimon were to decide in his favor,
he would pay for a copy of the *Commentary on the Mishnah*. Meir also
wanted him to reply to previous queries about astronomy according to
talmudic sources and some texts in the *Book of Commandments*. Instead
of acceding to Meir's request, with its offer of a bribe, Maimonides an-

nulled the arrangement that had been made by his wife's grandfather as inappropriate for the regulation of communal property.

LETTER TO A COMMUNITY OFFICIAL

The letter is on the verso side of a petition sent to Moses ben Maimon.[41] Both the recto (which is unrelated) and verso sides of the document show us Moses ben Maimon dealing with minute details of community administration. The letter is written in Maimonides' handwriting to Abraham ibn Yahya al-Najib, called al-Shaykh al-Watiq.[42] A piece of *waqf* land was leased to him in Dammuh, near the synagogue located there.[43] The land had been donated by Moses ben Maimon's brother-in-law, Isaiah ha-Levi ben Mishael, who had been made its administrator.[44]

In the letter, Maimonides asked al-Shaykh al-Watiq to attend to clearance of earth (*turab*) and repairs of the synagogue, not to continue to hire out the cow, and not to depart from the advice of al-Hajj 'Ali al-Sharawi [a Muslim] or let any other lessee enter the place.[45] Nothing should be done in the garden until another agreement was made with the lessee, which Maimonides said he would take care of himself. Moses ben Maimon also gave the addressee dietary advice. It was not unusual for him to combine medical advice with other matters, as in his letter to an anonymous inquirer. Similarly, the wife of a Jewish devotee to Sufism sought medical advice from Nagid David II Maimonides.[46]

DECISION IN MAIMONIDES' *MAJLIS*

In a decision of Maimonides' *majlis,* judges and elders in attendance agreed to pay 1²/₃ dinars as the poll tax (*jizya*) for the supervisor of the Dammuh sanctuary, al-Najib Abraham ibn Yahya.[47] The sum came from the income of the pious foundation and was for overlooking repairs in its caravanserai.[48] The document stressed the need to save al-Shaykh al-Najib from harm if he failed to pay the tax.[49] The decision was agreed upon in the *majlis* of "our teacher Moses, the Great Rav, in the presence of the judges and the elders in attendance."

The document shows how Maimonides presided by consensus of the judges and elders who were members of his council. That he did not administer justice independently does not indicate that he was weak or lacking authority. In this case, although the sum was small, it had to be transferred from the revenue of the pious foundation to defray the poll tax of a single individual, and this required authorization. It was normally the Head of the Jews who was responsible for problems concerning the poll tax. Yet here and elsewhere Maimonides assumed this burden, indicating that he discharged the responsibilities of the Head of the Jews without occupying that office for much of his career.

CORRESPONDENCE WITH
JUDGE PHINEAS BEN MESHULLAM

Among Maimonides' communal responsibilities was administration of justice by appointing judges and supervising the judicial system. Phineas ben Meshullam, who emigrated to Egypt from France, served as a judge in Alexandria, evidently as an appointee of Maimonides, and the two corresponded about communal and legal affairs. Phineas sent queries to Maimonides when he needed guidance.[50] The judge had written a letter to Maimonides in Hebrew and Maimonides responded, as usual, in the same language. Phineas may not have known Arabic at the time. The letter shows a breakdown of confidence between the two.

At the beginning of his letter Maimonides excused his delay in responding. It was because he was ill, not because of the slander he had heard reported about himself in an earlier letter from Phineas (see below), as he was not a person who paid heed to slander and he realized that gossip distorts the truth. "Even if I heard with my own ears and knew for certain that some person glorified himself at my expense, or rejected my words, or even vilified me, I do not—thank God—become emotional and lose my temper but relent and forgive." We shall see later how in his ethical writings Maimonides condemned anger and pride. As previously noted, however, he admitted later in life that when he was young he had trouble controlling his anger.

Phineas had made Maimonides swear that he would not forsake him [surely by removing him from office] and wanted assurance that this promise was in effect. Maimonides responded, "God forbid that I should uproot what I have planted or demolish what I have built up. Let it never occur to you, neither you nor any disciple, all the more a sage, that I should cause you harm or sorrow, if only by vexing with words." Maimonides acknowledged that when the pious judge Isaac ben Sason had told Phineas that Maimonides was angry because of an earlier letter Phineas had sent, he spoke the truth. Maimonides said that a letter had come to him from Phineas "full of drivel, while I was sick and on the verge of death. How could I avoid being angry?"

What was the incident that infuriated the Great Eagle?

Phineas had reported that the entire Jewish community in Alexandria had come to him, claiming that it was an ancestral tradition for an Israelite not to pray if he had had a seminal emission until he bathed in a bathhouse or in the sea and purified himself. Phineas had permitted such a person to pray, to enter the synagogue, and to recite from the Torah without bathing and purification. Maimonides responded:

> Now consider whether your words would anger even Hillel the Elder or not. You said that the entire people, old and young, rose up. It is well known, however, that it was not all of them but only a few of the idiotic ignoramuses. Also, you reinforced their statements and construed them to be like the words of great sages, men of tradition who received [tradition] from their ancestors.

After the complaint by people from the community, Phineas gave a judicial opinion (*teshuvah*) that after a seminal emission one may not enter the synagogue and recite the Torah without bathing. Maimonides objected that bathing after a seminal emission was customary only in Iraq and the Maghrib, whereas people in all the cities of Byzantium and France and all the people of Provence never observed this custom. Whenever great sages and teachers came from southern France to Spain and saw Spanish Jews bathe after a seminal emission, they would laugh and say, "You learned from the hygiene of the Muslims."

Maimonides criticized Phineas for not rebuking the people and for not teaching them the law properly without mincing words— "informing them that the law of Moses, our Master, is that the Torah does not receive impurity, and that one who has had a seminal emission may enter the synagogue and recite from the Torah scroll." As for praying, the issue depended upon custom. Jews in Islamic countries followed the custom of washing, whereas those who lived among the Christians did not. One should not change the custom of one's ancestors. This, Maimonides insisted, was what Phineas should have said.

Maimonides had to deal with a personal attack that Phineas mentioned to him in his letter:

> This wretched fellow who said that I do not bathe after a seminal emission spoke falsely. May heaven and earth testify on my behalf that I never failed to bathe unless I was ill. How can I change my own and my ancestors' custom for no reason? How did he know in his naiveté whether I was observed washing or not? His words are nothing but hazy dreams. It is certainly pointless to go on about this trivial matter; however, I wished to inform you why I was angry.

The question whether impurity from a seminal emission required bathing before Torah study and prayer was debated from the Tannaitic period on. In the Land of Israel, bathing was customary even among the common people, and when they considered discontinuing the custom, rabbinic authorities urged them to continue. In the Geonic period it was one of the legal differences between the Land of Israel and Iraq.

Maimonides' observation that in Islamic countries Jews bathed after having a seminal emission is proven by the practice of the Babylonian (Iraqian) Geonim, who sought to sanctify the Name of God before gentiles by conducting themselves as the Muslims would approve. The practice of bathing was not generally observed in Christian Europe, however.

Maimonides commented that the Jews of Christendom were incapable of giving opinions on the law because the Christians did not permit them to adjudicate as the Muslims did. The Jews living in Muslim countries had communal autonomy allowing them to adjudicate in civil and even some criminal cases, whereas the Jews of Christendom did not. Jews and other *dhimmi*s could administer their own courts, collect their own taxes, and manage their own welfare and educational system. Each minority community governed itself by its own leaders and judges. The Jewish community's courts had jurisdiction over civil and personal law (marriage, divorce, and inheritance) and some criminal cases.[51]

We see here the power of ancestral and local custom in the legal thinking of Maimonides.[52] This entailed recognition of different legal practices and the application of sociology of law. His leniency regarding ablutions after seminal emissions, especially compared with Islam's strictness, is significant. He insisted on a point in Jewish law, that the Torah does not receive impurity, and was not deterred by anxieties about purity and public opinion.

ANATOLI BEN JOSEPH

Maimonides corresponded with Anatoli (in French, Anatole) ben Joseph, of Marseilles, a judge in Alexandria who wrote beautiful liturgical and secular poetry.[53] Many judges who were in Egypt in the twelfth century came from overseas, and Anatoli was one of several judges from the land of the Franks. These French scholars did not know Arabic and needed interpreters for their work. They had little prior experience with practical application of civil law, as Maimonides observed in the letter to Phineas ben Meshullam just cited. After the death of Anatoli (ca. 1229), a dissident group brought forth an old statute that French or Byzantine Jews could not serve as judges in Alexandria because they were not conversant with Arabic. A French rabbi who knew Arabic became Anatoli's successor.

As Anatoli's letter to Maimonides alluded to *The Guide of the Perplexed*, it was written after 1190 or so. Anatoli sent legal queries along with a long, florid introduction in rhymed prose. Like Phineas ben Meshullam, he evidently had been appointed as a judge by Maimonides, who respected the learning of these French immigrants and overlooked their linguistic handicap.

Maimonides sent a responsum to Anatoli and another in reply to a question sent to him from Syracuse that Anatoli forwarded to him. Some scholars have suggested that Anatoli resided in Syracuse before coming to Egypt.

COMMUNAL ENACTMENTS

The Jewish community (*qehillah*) was a social unit with considerable autonomy and authority to control secular and religious aspects of its members' activities.[54] One of the ways communities reformed current practices was to pass enactments, called *taqannot,* that were binding and enforceable on all members. The enactment was a measure developed by Jewish law in the Hellenistic-Roman period, passed by the scholars or the majority of the community, to effect reforms and to adapt the law to new circumstances.[55] The most famous *taqannah* in the medieval period was by the German Rabbenu Gershom ben Judah, "Light of the Exile," forbidding polygyny, which was permitted in talmudic law and continued to be permitted by Jewish communities in the Islamic world where it is still practiced.[56]

In the early phases of communal legislation, the terms of communal enactments were not clearly defined.[57] For instance, there was a question whether an enactment had to be approved by all the members of the community and in their presence, or whether selected representatives could pass an enactment in their name without their approval. If all the members voted, could a majority impose its will on a minority, or did an enactment obligate only members who accepted it?

Eventually, communal enactments were adopted by the majority of members, obligating the minority. Isaac Alfasi stated in a responsum: "The basic requirement for [effective] legislation is that the majority of the community, with the advice of its elders, enact whatever they wish, and they [all] abide by it; this is [effective] legislation."[58]

These enactments had to be accepted by a scholar, if one was present in the town, or by a distinguished person selected to be a communal leader.[59] Joseph Ibn Migash required that the person be a distinguished communal leader versed in knowledge of Torah.

Egypt was not a bastion of Jewish learning, and Maimonides found serious violations in legal practice that he believed had to be resolved by strong measures.[60] Under his leadership, with the cooperation of members of his court and judges in other towns with whom he cooperated, he succeeded in reforming some Jewish practices.[61] The principle enactments in which he participated were:

1. A ban on recognizing the authority (*reshut*) of a Gaon or Exilarch

2. Remedying the situation of Rabbanite women who were following the postmenstrual customs of Karaite women by

having water poured over them by another female instead of using the ritual bath (*miqweh*)

3. Making marriage and divorce uniform and official under the proper supervision of rabbis learned in the law

4. Requiring proof of single status of men who immigrated to Egypt

5. Rejecting the appointment of a mayor in a town by a Ra'is who wanted to farm taxes through him

6. Arrangements for the Synagogue of the Palestinians

Ban on Taking Permission

The responsum concerning the ban was issued around 1170, not long after Maimonides arrived in Egypt and before he became Ra'is in 1171.[62] The issue resulted from the transition from the Fatimid to the Ayyubid dynasty and the disorder that roiled the Jewish community. People objected to invoking the authority of the Exilarch and the Head of an Academy (Gaon). During the last days of the Fatimid empire, Nethanel ha-Levi was the Head of the Jews (see above, ch. 12). The Exilarch in Egypt at the time may have been Judah ben Josiah.[63] As we have seen, people recognized an official by invoking his authority in the synagogue, at meals, circumcisions, engagement and wedding celebrations, and on documents, which stated under whose authority they were signed.

In this situation and in others, when a ban was issued by a majority of the community, who took an oath, and was opposed by a minority, who did not take an oath, a question arose whether the majority could coerce the minority to be bound by the oath and sustain the ban. In other words, how does majority rule work in these circumstances? Maimonides' solution was compound. The majority cannot impose its will on the minority, yet the minority must not recognize the authority of any official because such an overt act would create factions and divide the community.

The author of the query asked Maimonides about the ban that some people placed on recognizing authority. They said that they would not obey anyone, not the Exilarch and not the Head of an Academy. The question they asked was who was bound by oath to uphold the ban.

Maimonides responded that whoever was present in the synagogue at the time of the ban and responded "amen" was bound by the oath. Conversely, whoever did not respond "amen" was exempt; this certainly applied to someone who was not in the synagogue at all. Maimonides declared that the majority cannot impose its will on a minority—those who were present but did not bind themselves by an oath to the ban, or others who were not present at all.

If the minority wished to recognize the authority of an official, however, it was forbidden from a different aspect, namely, "Do not make yourselves into factions."[64] "Rather the entire house of Israel, called by the name of Jacob, who adhere to the religion of Moses our teacher (of blessed memory) are obliged to be—every assembly ['eda] and community [kahal]—one faction, and there should not be among them a controversy in anything at all." Maimonides' paramount concern was to avoid factions and to create accord in the community.

Enactment on Female Ritual Baths

An enactment on female purity was issued by Maimonides' court, which rejected the Karaite custom of having menstruant women bathe in drawn water (sukub) instead of immersing in a ritual bath in accordance with talmudic legislation. Maimonides drafted the enactment in Fustat, and ten leading Rabbanite scholars signed it and had it read publicly in synagogues.[65] It is dated May/June 1167, only a year or so after Maimonides arrived in Egypt. Many of the authorities who supported him and his council were from the Maghrib. There was a significant demographic shift from the Far West to Egypt during this period, as has been mentioned before. Maghribi Jews, coming from a milieu of Maliki law and Almohad rule, tended to be more strictly observant than Egyptian Jews.

The historian Avraham Grossman calls this "the Miqweh [ritual bath] Rebellion in Egypt," in which many women, for their comfort and convenience, flaunted rabbinic authority until Maimonides and his colleagues, taking extreme measures, got them under control.[66]

The enactment was ascribed to "scholars living in the Land of Egypt" who were gathered there from distant lands and far-off regions and whose viewpoint agreed with that of the local Rabbanite scholars they found in the country. Each scholar separately and thereafter all of them in unison examined communal matters to restore to the fold those who strayed from the right path.

The date of the document and the active participation of scholars from the Maghrib imply that they formed a power base that influenced the religious life of Egyptian Jewry and reinforced Maimonides' authority.

These newcomers to Egypt discovered that Jews throughout the entire country followed the custom of the Karaites of bathing in drawn water, claiming that this brings about purity, permitting the menstruant woman to resume sexual relations with her husband. In most cases, the menstruant woman took a nonmenstruant woman to pour clean water upon her. The menstruant woman believed that if she poured the water on herself, she would not be purified or permitted to her husband. Some of them waited until twilight, following the custom of the Karaites.

The authors of the enactment decided to have it read publicly in synagogues as a warning and to inform every woman that she may marry only on the conditions of the enactment. If not, she would give up the right to her divorce settlement.

The authors of the enactment concurred that every court in Egypt would adjudicate according to the enactment starting with Sivan 4927 A.M. (May/June 1167). They agreed that whoever knowingly had intercourse with his wife after she committed one of these transgressions and was silent about it should be excommunicated, banished, degraded, removed from the community, and lose his property as far as the power of the court reaches. The ten signatories were Moses ben Maimon; Samuel ben Se'adyah ha-Levi; Isaac ben Sason, the judge; Mevorakh ben Nathan, the *haver*; Samuel ben Joseph; Elazar ben Michael; Daniel ben Joseph ha-Melammed (the Teacher); Elazar ha-Levi ben Japheth; Judah ha-Kohen ben Tobias; and Abraham, the *haver*, son of ————.[67] The only one called "judge" was Isaac ben Sason. The men who joined Maimonides in this enactment from his earliest phase in Egypt also supported later enactments and were, it appears, the core members of his *majlis* at this time.

Enactment on Marriage and Divorce

The rabbis of Egypt issued an enactment imposing a ban on anyone who performed a marriage or carried out a divorce except the local *muqaddam*s in the towns of Damanhur, Bilbays, and al-Mahalla.[68] These were Rabbi Halfon, the judge of Damanhur; Rabbi Judah ha-Kohen, the judge of Bilbays; and Rabbi Perahya, the judge of al-Mahalla. They passed the enactment in the last third of the month of Tevet in the year 1498 s.e. (January 1187) in Fustat, about twenty years after the enactment on female purity. It was signed by Moses ben Maimon, Isaac ben Sason, Samuel ben Se'adyah, and Menasse ben Joseph.

The Alexandrian Jews later sent a query to Abraham Maimonides with a copy of a statute from 1235 declaring a ban against anyone who performed a marriage in the city aside from the local *muqaddam*s. The 1235 statute referred to the enactment of Maimonides and his court. Abraham Maimonides cited the earlier enactment in his responsa.[69]

On Foreigners Marrying in Egypt

This enactment is called in its prologue one of the new enactments that Moses ben Maimon passed for the benefit of young women in Israel.[70] It does not carry a date. This was another effort Maimonides made to improve the status of personal law in Egyptian Jewish communities. Jewish women in Egypt would marry men from other countries whose marital status was obscure. While polygyny was permitted, the problem was that if a Jewish woman in Egypt married a foreign man, say from Syria, who was already married without knowing of her husband's existing marriage, children from the same father but a different mother might marry, unaware of their relationship. Maimonides and his colleagues wanted to end this.

The enactment stated:

> We shall not marry a woman to a foreigner in all the land of Egypt unless he brings proof that he is unmarried or swears on a Pentateuch

to this effect.[71] If he has a wife, he should divorce her, and then we shall marry him here. If a foreigner marries a woman in Egypt and wishes to travel to another country, we do not permit him to go, even if his wife agrees to it, until he writes a bill of divorce and delivers it to her for whatever interval of time they agree to—one, two, or three years, not more.[72]

Signed by Moses

Maimonides appears to follow Rabbi Eliezer ben Jacob's dictum in the Talmud: *One should not marry a woman in this city [or country] and go and take another wife in another city, lest a match is made between the children, and a brother marry his sister.*[73] The heading "for the benefit of the daughters of Israel" means, however, that Maimonides was mainly concerned not with incest but with women being deserted by their husbands or separated from them for long periods of time.[74] From Maimonides' point of view, the intent of this stipulation was to prevent the woman from becoming a deserted wife (*'agunah*) should the husband not return.[75] This was a highly mobile society, and men were often on the road. Merchants engaged in foreign trade could be absent for ten or twenty years. The custom of giving conditional bills of divorce before leaving the country had been in practice for some time.[76] Maimonides strengthened this measure and shortened the period to three years at which point the woman could consider herself as divorced and remarry. The signatories of the enactment also concurred that if there was a dispute, the litigants should not go to the courts of gentiles.[77]

This ban was signed by Moses bar Maimon, Isaac ben Sason, Samuel ben Se'adyah and Menasse bar Joseph, all with the title Dayyan. The enactment was not directed against polygyny per se, for in his legal writings Maimonides taught that a man was permitted to marry as many wives as he could maintain.[78]

Before he came, Egyptian Jews followed the Palestinian ruling that a wife could restrain her husband from a second marriage.[79] This was done by inserting a condition in the marital contract stipulating that the husband could take a second wife or hire a female slave only if his first wife approved (not very likely). Maimonides reversed this custom and permitted a local Jew to take a second wife whether his first wife consented or not.[80]

Following Spanish authorities, Maimonides insisted on levirate marriage (in which a man would marry his brother's widow if there was no offspring from the marriage), whereas other authorities in Egypt preferred that levirate marriage be avoided by having the act of release (*halisah*) performed by the widow.[81]

The al-Mahalla Enactment

Maimonides was queried about an enactment passed by a community—its elders, prominent men, and the rest of the people—pertaining to Rabbi Perahya ben Joseph, the *muqaddam* and judge of al-Mahalla.[82] Perahya ben Joseph was a nephew of the great India trader Abraham Ben Yiju and migrated from Sicily to Fustat to marry Sitt al-Dar, Ben Yiju's daughter. The marriage took place in August 1156.[83] Ben Yiju had died by then, but not before showing his displeasure with his son-in-law, for Perahya was not the shrewd man of affairs Ben Yiju was seeking.

Abu Zikri, who was Ra'is at this time, and who has been identified as Zuta, pressured the *muqaddam* Perahya ben Joseph to pay for his appointment over al-Mahalla or else be removed from office. The notables in al-Mahalla did not lend their hand to this because of Perahya's "piety, old age, abstemiousness, and learning, the testimony of the learned in his favor, and his superiority over his peers in the entire countryside."

They refused to accept the authority (*reshut*) of any other *muqaddam* who came to al-Mahalla in the name of this Head. They would not participate with him in a quorum, for worship, give him public taxes, or obey his orders. They obligated themselves to Perahya the judge as long as he remained alive and stayed in the country, not requesting to leave it for the Land of Israel. All of them "agreed to this wholeheartedly and with a perfect mind,[84] and have entered into God's covenant and its sanctions.[85] Not one of us will infringe upon anything we have mentioned. Whoever transgresses this and violates it without necessity shall not be one of them and be isolated from the community of Israel." The elders and notables of the community and many people signed this.

They queried Maimonides whether it was permissible for anyone of the community to transgress the enactment and abandon its provisions by accepting the authority of a new *muqaddam* who came under the auspices of Ra'is Abu Zikri.[86] We have the impression that after the elders and notables pledged themselves to the enactment in support of Perahya, Abu Zikri attempted to force a new *muqaddam* upon them. His pressure and threats, perhaps with government support, made some of those who took an oath in favor of the enactment try to get out of their commitment. The enactment was copied word for word, signed by two witnesses, and sent to Moses Maimonides.

Maimonides replied in his own handwriting. He instructed that every provision of the enactment obligated everyone who signed it, or before whom it was read, or who heard it and accepted its provisions. Whoever broke its provisions intentionally "has broken his oath and sworn falsely, and he is incompetent to testify and will not be exculpated from the judgment of hell as is the rule of all those who transgress an express oath wantonly."[87] If someone transgressed before witnesses after having been forewarned, he would be flogged, as he accepted an oath with the divine name and sanction. The responsum was signed by Maimonides and cosigned by his colleagues Isaac ben Sason, Samuel ha-Levi ben Se'adyah, and Manasseh ben Joseph.[88]

Goitein and some others who identify Abu Zikri as Zuta believe that this is Maimonides' defeat of Zuta that is celebrated in the *Scroll of Zuta the Wicked*.[89]

The Two Synagogues

Moses ben Maimon appeared as a signatory to a well-known enactment concerning the arrangements for the Synagogue of the Palestinians.[90] Its members adhered obstinately to its own rituals. He did not mention these rituals in the *Mishneh Torah,* noting only the custom of finishing the Torah readings in a cycle of three years. He wrote: "Some complete the reading of the Pentateuch in three years, but this is not a prevalent custom."[91]

Maimonides attempted to unify the prayer customs of the two synagogues by means of a legal decision.[92] However, his efforts to abolish the distinctive customs of the Synagogue of the Palestinians, which he found legally objectionable, were unsuccessful. On the contrary, at the time of his son, Abraham, the specific customs of the Synagogue of the Palestinians of Old Cairo were reconfirmed by a solemn pact.

Enactments Summary

Soon after Maimonides arrived in Egypt he became involved in community affairs. His *majlis* issued enactments that were intended to raise standards of conduct within the Jewish community. The first enactments are dated in 1167 and 1170, before he became Head of the Jews, showing that he had considerable power already under the Fatimids. His court was the instrument for exercise of authority. (Likewise, he believed that optimal medical treatment comes from a consilium of physicians after they have reached a consensus [see ch. 22].) The numerous Maghribi Jews, who had emigrated to Egypt, served as a power base. He guided affairs by consensus, his ultimate aim being the harmony and unity of the Jewish community.

17

Responsa

RABBINIC RESPONSA

Rabbinic responsa, or, more precisely, queries (*she'elot*) and responses (*teshuvot*), appeared in the talmudic era and became prevalent during the period of the Geonim, when thousands were written, many of them still unpublished.[1] During the period of the Geonim, scholars turned to the Baghdad academies for guidance. People sent queries from Spain, North Africa, France, Syro-Palestine, and Yemen, often accompanied by a financial donation. Many of these documents found their way into the Cairo Genizah. Let us recall that Egypt was a central postal junction where notable documents were often copied before being forwarded.

Legal responsa resemble the Roman *jus respondendi,* and the scholars giving legal counsel are like the Roman *prudentes*. From the time of the emperor Augustus Caesar (63 B.C.E.–19 C.E.), certain jurisconsults were authorized to answer legal questions in the name of the emperor. It was later determined that when the opinions of official jurisconsults were unanimous, they should have the legal force to compel judges; when they were not unanimous, the judge might accept the opinion that he considered most equitable. Some Roman jurists, then, had the "right of responding on the authority of the ruler" (*ius respondendi ex auctoritate principis*).[2] Muslim and Jewish jurisconsults had no power of coercion and were not backed by the authority of a ruler. Their authority was derived from learning and reputation.

Rabbinic responsa had the effect of case law, based on the legal opinions and precedents of judges and legal scholars. The responsa were copied by assistants and filed for further study and reference as precedents. They were usually bound in small collections, and these were further bound until they formed a book.[3] Most of Maimonides' responsa were preserved this way and were consulted by later scholars for making their own legal opinions. The decision of the respondent was often recorded from his dictation. On certain occasions, learned colleagues cosigned, expressing the consensus of the academy. Consensus (*ijma'*) among jurisprudents was an important principle of Islamic law as well.

When lower courts could not resolve problems, they appealed to recognized respondents, who constituted an informal supreme tribunal.[4] In the Geonic period, there were supreme courts in Palestine and Iraq. The Head of the Palestinian Academy claimed to have jurisdiction over world Jewry and authority over all judges, while the Iraqian Geonim saw themselves as heirs of the ancient High Court (Sanhedrin) in Jerusalem. As these centers declined, individual jurisconsults acted as supreme tribunals.

Maimonides' responsa demonstrate how he applied a theoretical legal system to actual life situations. He received queries on all aspects of law. More than five hundred of his responsa survive, ample evidence of how his mind worked as a decisor. His responsa provide a record of his opinions on a wide range of subjects—synagogue decorum, business partnerships, marriage, divorce, inheritance, orphans and widows, ownership and rental of property, trusteeship, debts, conversion to Judaism and apostasy, circumcision, menstruation, charity, court procedure, legal documents, and so on.

Community leaders, judges, and scholars turned to him, asking about points of law and ritual as well as questions of faith, seeking explanations of his legal writings, questioning decisions by lower courts, and asking for advice on communal issues.

He replied to legal queries according to the level of the addressee.

To the learned he explained the law in detail with proofs from Scripture and Talmud, whereas to the untrained he was brief, using just a few words, even one.[5]

The queries and responses disclose socioeconomic conditions, material culture, interpersonal relations—especially within the family—and business practices. Whereas historical works focus on the political and social elite and on political events and wars, responsa mirror the lives of ordinary people—workers, communal servants, women, villagers and urbanites, people about whom we hear little in historical sources.

Draft copies of responsa in Maimonides' handwriting have survived. These original copies were preserved for reference, deposited in a family archive, and eventually placed in the Genizah in the loft of the Ben Ezra synagogue.[6] These drafts show that Maimonides often wrote on the paper containing the query, on the blank bottom part of the page and continuing, if necessary, on the reverse side. He sometimes wrote his replies at the end of the day when he was tired, lying down and writing while leaning on his side. A professional scribe would then make a fair copy to send to the questioners. Like other decisors, he dictated important responsa to students and colleagues. At times, when he thought it was necessary, he discussed the case with them and asked colleagues to cosign.

The first of Maimonides' extant responsa date from 1167, a year after he came to Egypt, and they continue to the last year of his life, 1204.[7] Writing responsa was therefore an activity he engaged in during every phase of his career. He had an affinity for the responsum style. Many of his main writings were in their form responses to questions, including the *Epistle on Forced Conversion*, *Epistle to Yemen*, *Epistle on Astrology*, and *Treatise on Resurrection*. *The Guide of the Perplexed* is a long epistle written to his pupil Joseph ben Judah. Some of his medical writings as well were replies to queries.

QUERIES FROM A DISTANT LAND

Some queries sent to Maimonides traveled far, as we learn from a Genizah letter that portrays how a query reached him from Europe.[8]

A physician, Abraham ben Elazar of Alexandria, wrote to Moses ha-Kohen, the representative of the merchants (*peqid ha-soharim*) at the warehouse (*dar wakala*) in Cairo/Fustat, which was used as a postal address. Abraham ben Elazar reported that a ship in a convoy arrived from Marseilles. The trip from the port of Marseilles to Egypt was direct and took about twenty-five days.[9] On board was a certain Rabbi Ephraim, who had been in Alexandria the previous year, apparently on a similar mission. Rabbi Ephraim brought queries (*she'elot*) from a distant country for "our Master Moses ben Maimon."[10] Abraham informed Moses ha-Kohen that he hired a special messenger to carry the queries from Alexandria to the Egyptian capital.

The reverse of the letter has greetings for Maimonides from scholars in Alexandria, such as Rabbenu Anatoli ben Joseph, and there was news about Rabbi Phineas ben Meshullam.

FAMILY ISSUES

Many of the responsa concern personal law, in particular marriage, divorce, and inheritance, an area where Jewish law remained in force and was applied largely without interference by government authorities.

A Man Regrets Divorcing His Wife

A query sent to Maimonides concerned a man who divorced his wife, with two witnesses signing the bill of divorce and delivering it to her.[11] She completed her period of waiting and married another man, with whom she had children.[12] Seeing this, her first husband regretted divorcing her.

He wrote a document in the presence of two competent witnesses to the effect that the witnesses to the bill of divorce were disreputable sinners, rendering their testimony null and void. These sinners had admitted to having intercourse with menstruating women in a spirit of defiance, fully aware that the law forbids this.

The man presented this document to the court to invalidate his divorce from his former wife and nullify her marriage to the new husband, rendering children from him illegitimate. The question was

whether the testimony of the witnesses to the divorce had legal force
or not.

Maimonides responded that whoever permitted witnesses of this
type to testify made a gross error. The testimony of a sinner should not
be accepted either in civil or criminal law.[13]

Anyone who had sinned in the presence of others who had forewarned him that his behavior would be a sin would be an ineligible
witness. Hence any bill of divorce for which he served as witness would
be invalid, and the children of the woman's second marriage would be
illegitimate.[14] However, if competent individuals testify that they saw
the witness commit a sin but failed to warn him, the first husband
would be obligated to write his ex-wife another bill of divorce in the
presence of eligible witnesses, and she may remain with her second
husband and need not be divorced by him.[15]

Maimonides' solution left the wife with her second husband, because the chance that the immoral witnesses to the divorce were forewarned was presumed slight, as they were infamous transgressors.

Jewish and Islamic law approach the question of remarriage after
divorce differently, although having the same intent. According to
Jewish law, a divorced woman who remarries may *not* return to her
first husband (after divorce or the death of her second husband).[16] In
Islamic law, however, a man may take his wife back *only on condition*
that she has married another and the marriage is consummated.[17] In
both cases, in the developed system of the law, the aim was to discourage men from divorcing their wives frivolously. In the Jewish system,
the divorcing husband risked seeing his wife remarry and thereby become forbidden to him; in the Islamic system, she was obligated to
remarry before she could return to him, which reduced the chance
that she ever would.

A Widow Remarries and Her Second Husband Dies

Another query involved a woman who married twice and was widowed twice. She was therefore considered a "killer wife" (*qatlanit*)
who could not marry a third time, according to talmudic law.

The purveyors of the question explained that a woman had married and lived with her husband for a long time.[18] He then died, leaving behind a male child, who also later died.[19]

The woman then married another man, and he lived with her for a number of years; however, she derived no pleasure from him and they often quarreled. She confirmed before witnesses her intention to release (lit. "redeem") herself from the marriage by renouncing the settlement of her marriage contract and her delayed payment (mu'akhkhar). Seeing that she had redeemed herself from the marriage and was demanding its dissolution, the husband left that very day without telling her. After he arrived in the countryside, he fell ill and died.

The dead husband had owned land that was mortgaged to a number of Jews, and the creditors now demanded payment of the debt from the land. The creditors then discovered that the deceased's wife had already released herself from the marriage by renouncing the settlement of her marriage contract and the delayed payment. The court ruled at the time that the land the deceased had mortgaged must be sold and the debt paid from the proceeds. The court's argument was that by renouncing her rights the wife was not in a position to put in a claim for the land or for any other part of the husband's estate.

The woman declared to the court: "As my husband did not write for me a bill of divorce [get], grant me my delayed payment and the settlement of my marriage contract, which my husband's estate owes me, for I released myself from the marriage only on condition that he write a final bill of divorce for me." The woman contended that as her husband died before giving her a bill of divorce, her renunciation never went into effect since she renounced only on condition that she would be divorced.

The court responded: "You may not receive anything that you would otherwise be entitled to, for you renounced all that is in your marriage contract." The case remained suspended. The land that had belonged to the deceased was sold, the creditors collected the debt due them, and his family took the rest. The widow, however, was left with nothing.

After this, someone came along who wanted to marry the widow. She went to a court to consult about this. The court restrained her from marrying, saying to her: "You are a killer wife [qatlanit], as two husbands of yours have died." The woman was thus left in dire straits during a difficult time of famine (*qilla*).[20] She could neither get sustenance from the land her second husband had left nor marry someone to provide her with a morsel of bread.

The questioners wished to know whether this woman might marry, as she had renounced the delayed payment and the dowry in her marriage contract, intending to be released from her second husband, who then died. This, they stressed, "is a serious matter that may eventually lead to the laws of the gentiles."[21] The questioners concluded:

> Necessity[22] requires that this matter be brought before your sublime council [*majlis*] (*may it be exalted*), so that you may consider what is of best interest [*maslaha*] and rule according to your preference.[23] Further, instruct us thoroughly whether the woman's redeeming herself is valid or not, and whether she can go back to the creditors and recover from them her due, *as you have been shown by Heaven, and may your reward be twofold.*

Maimonides' response was as follows:

> If someone betrothed her before *two* [witnesses], *the betrothal* is valid.[24] He should then write a *marriage contract* for her *in the court, and she should be married there.* One ought to be lenient in these matters, and *the judge* should feign inadvertence, for punctiliousness on this minor point leads to very serious consequences.

> Signed by Moses

In fact, Maimonides did not accept the talmudic belief that the woman was the cause of her husbands' deaths. We can begin to understand Maimonides' legal activism when we consider the parallel system in Islam and the constructive, proactive role of the jurisprudent, or mufti.

As the Muslim mufti could exercise independent judgment (*ijtihad*) and actually modify the law, so Maimonides' rejection of the talmudic concept of "killer wife" revised the law.[25] The talmudic law was based on an unscientific view that made the woman responsible for the deaths of her husbands.

Maimonides, whose life ambition was to reformulate Judaism as a rational religion, a religion of reason, viewed the notion of the "killer wife" and the prohibition of her marrying a third time, enshrined in the Talmud, as a superstition harmful to women.[26] The woman had to bear the loneliness of widowhood and the burden of guilt as the agent of her husbands' deaths although she was not an agent at all.

Maimonides was willing to oppose the authority of the talmudic sages when he deemed their thinking to be based on superstition, his authority being scientific reasoning. Husbands died for may reasons, some as a result of violence, and Maimonides could not accept the talmudic view that wives were responsible. He insisted that this woman's third marriage be performed in a rabbinic court, even though it was against the law, so as to elevate her status in society and remove irrational fear of her.

Dealing with the "killer wife" problem in another responsum, Maimonides made it clear that he regarded the belief as superstitious. Some authorities compared the "killer wife" situation to the custom of not circumcising the third male child of a woman whose two previous infant sons had perished from the operation. Maimonides rejected the analogy because in the case of circumcision there was a medical reason for not performing the operation on a third son.[27]

Maimonides noted that in Spain sages had devised a way to permit a "killer wife" to remarry, lest such a woman seek satisfaction without the benefit of marriage. He noted that the court of our Master Isaac the Rav (Alfasi) and the court of our Master Joseph ha-Levi (Ibn Migash), his disciple, did likewise. "And so we have instructed and done in the land of Egypt ever since we came there."[28]

In questions of this sort, Maimonides was also concerned with communal survival. Maimonides' ruling was a beacon to later centuries, especially during the Black Plague and the persecutions of 1391 in Spain, when countless Jewish men lost their lives. Rabbis, with misgivings but appealing to Maimonides' authority, permitted "killer wives" to remarry.

The *Zohar*, however, the classic work of the Kabbalah, opposed remarriage of widows even after one marriage, and certainly if two husbands had died. This instilled in men fear of marrying a widow, as they believed that the deceased husband was in Paradise awaiting his wife.[29] At the end of the medieval period, this Kabbalistic view was disseminated throughout Spain and among Spanish exiles, countering the rational-scientific concept of Maimonides and his followers.

The questioners had also asked Maimonides to instruct them whether the woman's redeeming herself from the marriage was valid or not. In Jewish and Islamic law divorce is generally a unilateral right of the husband. But Islamic law has a provision (called *khul'* or *iftida'*) that permits the wife to buy her freedom through payment of compensation to the husband, usually the *mahr* (bridal price) or a part thereof (see Qur'an 2:229). In our query, the woman similarly renounced her marriage contract settlement and the delayed payment to free herself from the marriage.[30]

When Maimonides said "for punctiliousness on this minor point leads to very serious consequences," he alluded to the possibility that the validity of the wife's self-ransom might be brought to a Muslim court, which Maimonides wanted to avoid. He implied that the ransom-divorce was invalid, as he regarded the woman as being married when her second husband died. Though she was therefore a "killer wife," he did not wish to prevent her from remarrying, for then she was liable to appeal to a Muslim court to confirm the legality of her divorce from her previous husband.

A Woman's Right to Marry the Man of Her Choice

The case concerned a man who objected when his married daughter decided to give part of her dowry to her husband, although she was a mature woman no longer under her father's jurisdiction and free to dispose of her dowry as she wished.[31]

The case was brought before a Muslim judge. A Jewish judge in attendance at the hearing assured his Muslim counterpart that the woman was under the jurisdiction of her father, empowering him to object. This might not have appeared irregular to the Qadi, but it was not a precise statement of Jewish law. I surmise that the woman's father preferred to bring the case to a Muslim court in anticipation that the Muslim judge would be more understanding of his position than a Jewish judge would have been. The presence of a Jewish judge, who gave information in the father's favor, was presumably not accidental.

Another Jew present in the Muslim court contradicted the Jewish judge, pointing out that the father had no jurisdiction over a mature female. Having heard conflicting views, the Qadi decided to wait for the decision of the Ra'is. Our document is a fine example of the cooperation of Muslim legal authorities with Maimonides.

Islamic law provides that a legal guardian can marry off his minor ward against her will, but she may rescind once she is of age; some Muslim authorities hold that a minor bride may not rescind if her father or grandfather gave her in marriage.[32] A mature, fully responsible Muslim woman can give herself in marriage; however, her legal guardian can object if the groom is not of equal socioeconomic status.

Maimonides was irritated with the Jewish judge for exhibiting ignorance of the law, as even a married female minor is no longer under her father's jurisdiction, and certainly a mature woman would not be. He suspected that the Jewish judge was testifying under pressure of the Muslim court and decided that the case should be clarified before witnesses who could substantiate what occurred in the Qadi's court.

A Christian Concubine

Maimonides was questioned about a female Christian captive who became the concubine of a Jewish bachelor after he purchased her from her captors.[33] It was an intricate case, and the summary here omits some of the subtler legal issues.

The captive woman stayed with the bachelor in a family residence, including his father's wife and her three small daughters.[34] The man's brother quarreled with him and summoned him to court, complaining that he had acquired a Christian slave girl, had converted her to Judaism, and was having sexual relations with her.

Now, it was illegal for the man to cohabit with the woman while she was a slave. Jewish and Christian legal systems prohibited sexual relations with slaves, something that was permitted by Islamic law. Nor could he free her and then marry her, for having lived with a woman illicitly, he was not permitted to marry her thereafter. Maimonides replied, however, with great latitude, that the man should free the captive woman and then marry her.

He explained that he had issued similar decisions previously so as to give men a chance to mend their lives, relying on the verse *It is a time to act for the Lord, for they have violated your teaching* (Ps 119:126), which was interpreted to mean that one might pay regard to God by disregarding his law.[35] The court should help the man marry her and set a time for the marriage or else remove her. He concluded by saying, "May God (the exalted) correct our wrongdoing as he has promised, saying, *I shall remove your dross*" (Isa 1:25). Maimonides accepted in practice a widespread custom that was theoretically against the law.

Maimonides' legal opinion had bearing on the marital status of the great Indian trader Abraham Ben Yiju, for he also had lived with a female slave in India and then emancipated her, converted her to Judaism, and married her. While in Aden, on his way back to Egypt, Ben Yiju wrote a legal opinion justifying his conduct, but it did not convince local scholars there, and his reputation remained tarnished.

SYNAGOGUE DECORUM

Maimonides received many queries on worship and synagogue etiquette. The synagogue was the center of Jewish communal life. Two things disturbed him: the ritual differences between the Palestinian and Iraqian synagogues and the general lack of synagogue decorum.

Elder Offends Preacher

Maimonides was once asked what should be done about an elder who offended a preacher in the synagogue by shouting out in the middle of a sermon, "How long will you go on with this senseless jabber [*hadhayan*]?[36] All that you are saying is utter nonsense that should not be seen or heard!"[37] The authors of the query, unsympathetic to the elder, commented:

He thus described *the words of God* as nonsense.[38] Those present, scandalized by these remarks, exclaimed, "We have never seen or heard anyone do something as horrible. While speaking in public, he nevertheless depicted the sublime law in such a way!"

They asked Maimonides whether the elder deserved punishment or banishment and what his responsibility was to the *muqaddam* whom he offended in public. Having examined the words of the sermon, Maimonides responded that the elder had indeed committed a grave sin by embarrassing his fellow in public.[39] Yet he observed, with a touch of humor, that "the comments are such as preachers usually make," adding that if the offending elder were not a sage, one would simply rebuke him and add some penalty. But as the elder was renowned for his piety and learning, it would be improper to criticize him until his side was heard, "for the sacred law requires that we honor scholars, give them the benefit of the doubt, and overlook their slips and lapses, if the plaintiff wishes.[40] Or the plaintiff may go to court with him to hear his response if he prefers."

Maimonides did not want the community to issue a ban against the elder and did not even answer the question about it (assuming we have his complete response). As it involved insubordination to the *muqaddam*, the disturbance was serious, and it became a public scandal. By shifting the solution onto the *muqaddam* and his supporters, Maimonides was evidently hoping that the incident would evaporate.[41] Acknowledging that the elder had transgressed, Maimonides yet respected him as a pious scholar, and empathized with his impatience while listening to a tedious sermon.

Intoxicated Prayer Leaders

It may come as a surprise to you that prayer leaders in synagogues were frequently intoxicated during services and behaved inappropriately.[42] Cantors, as virtuoso performers, were often on the road and appeared in different towns, and they were rewarded for their creative efforts. They sang at weddings and were generously remunerated by appreciative audiences. They traveled to display their talents and to make public announcements, act as envoys, and even to engage in commerce, conveying goods from place to place. Cantors in Fustat were brought from various countries, including Spain, France, and Iran. They were like opera singers, and, as Goitein observes, "[n]ot few of them manifested a certain predilection for the bottle."[43]

The query concerned a prayer leader (*shaliah sibbur*) who drank to the point of intoxication and behaved improperly. When he entered the synagogue late and found another prayer leader in his place, he would object that his replacement intervened between God and the congregation.

Inebriated, he carried a Torah scroll on one of the holidays and threw it down, breaking its pomegranate.[44] When the congregation asked him what he had done, he replied, in his inebriated state, "What is a Torah scroll [anyway]?"

Since the man had done this not once or twice but many times, the congregation asked Maimonides whether it was permissible for the man to be a prayer leader, to carry a Torah scroll, or perform any of these services. They asked what, in Maimonides' judgment, should be done and whether the man should be punished.

Maimonides responded:

> It is in no way permissible to allow someone of this sort to be a *prayer leader* or to carry a *Torah scroll*. And whoever prays behind him, certainly whoever supports him or does not seek to depose him, demeans the law and is included among those *who despise and desecrate the Torah*, who is guaranteed to *be himself dishonored by mankind*.[45]

Signed by Moses

ON THE PERMISSIBILITY OF MUSIC

Maimonides wrote a long response to a brief query from Aleppo on the permissibility of listening to vocal renditions of strophic poems and *al-zamr,* or "reed pipe music."[46]

A *mizmar* is "an instrument of piping," generally in the woodwind family.[47] Al-Farabi, musical theorist and artist, described the reed pipe as having eight holes for fingering. One type of reed pipe was the *buq,* similar to a saxophone. Here, however, Maimonides used the term "reed-pipe music" as a generic expression for instrumental music.

Maimonides replied to the questioners by saying that the rabbinic prohibition of instrumental music was well known and that there was no difference between instrumental music and singing. Anything producing delight and excitement is forbidden, for the sensual faculty must be suppressed—a reason not present in Scripture or Talmud. The Talmud passage he cited discussed the prohibition of music as something needed at "this time," meaning after the destruction of the Temple. Maimonides deftly turned a traditional reason for a ban on music into a teaching of philosophic ethics.

Maimonides explained that music is prohibited to most people, as legal rulings are posited for the majority, not for the rare exceptions. There are people for whom music is permissible, as they use it for religious devotion and intellectual stimulation. He was presumably thinking of (Jewish) Sufis, who engaged in *sama'*, the Sufi technique of listening to music that transported them to states of grace (*ahwal*) and ecstasy (*wajd*).[48] *Sama'* was often accompanied by *dhikr,* the rhythmic chanting of Allah's name or some other mantra. Maimonides permitted music for the enlightened for its calming influence and as an aid to concentration and meditation. He also recommended music as a cure for depression.

He gathered from the question that the people of Aleppo had a specific problem with Arabic poetry; hence he stressed, as he did in his *Commentary on the Mishnah*, that there is no difference between Arabic and Hebrew, that something is prohibited or permitted according to its meaning, not the language in which it is expressed. Even prose is prohibited if it is senseless.

It was impossible to discuss music without considering its social context. Music in his milieu was associated with poetry, wine, erotic dancing, and young boy and girl entertainers—graceful gazelles with lustrous eyes. Maimonides listed five prohibitions against singing and playing music. One prohibited a woman singing, because her voice is always arousing, especially when she sings.

The intention of the prohibitions against music, Maimonides taught, is that the Jews be a holy nation, and that they not abandon themselves to amusement and play. He did not say here that Jews should not rejoice because of the destruction of the Temple, as the Talmud stated.

In fact, there were objections to music before the destruction of the Temple. The biblical verses that may be cited (Amos 6:5, Hos 9:1, and Isa 5:12 and 23:15–16) as well as Jesus ben Sirah (Ecclesiasticus 9:4) already denounce, "wine, women, and song."[49] After the destruction of the Temple, mourning became the main motivation for avoiding music with rejoicing, and it was then that the comment was made—*The ear that listens to the reed-pipe shall be cut off*—that Maimonides quoted approvingly.

The legal scholars of Islam also decried music, and the four Sunni schools strictly forbade listening to it. But as with the Islamic prohibition against wine, reality was stronger than legislation, and music and dance were the center of court life in Islamic societies. There were reactions among the Muslims, such as Ibn Abi 'l-Dunya (823–894), who wrote a work condemning musical instruments (*Dhamm al-malahi*). Sufi authors wrote books defending their *sama'* recitations.

Music was studied by philosophers and scientists as part of the scientific curriculum.[50] (Jews excelled in the Middle Ages as skilled musicians despite the prohibition.) Maimonides' learned predecessors praised music and wrote about it—Plato and Aristotle, al-Farabi, who wrote a large book on music, Ibn Sina, al-Ghazali, and Ibn Bajja. Al-Farabi and Ibn Bajja were virtuoso performers. There were Muslims who held a moderate position on listening to music, such as al-Ghazali, in his *Revivication of the Religious Sciences*. Interestingly, he gave five instances when listening to music and singing was forbidden, the first being that the player or singer is a woman.

Maimonides compartmentalized his functions. When he was asked about the law, he replied in terms of the law. And when he was asked about medicine, he replied in terms of medicine. Here, he was approached as a legist, and he gave the reply of a legal scholar. In the Eight Chapters, he wrote as a physician of the soul about the benefits of listening to the music of stringed instruments and reed pipes, looking at beautiful human forms, strolling in lovely gardens, and wearing fine raiment.

BUSINESS AFFAIRS

Partnership in Business with Muslims

A query touching everyday life and ordinary relations between Muslims and Jews concerned Jewish and Muslim partners in a single craft of goldsmithing and glassmaking.[51] They agreed on their own to split the profits for Friday and Saturday, so that the Jews would benefit from work that Muslims did on the Sabbath, when work is strictly forbidden for Jews. The existence of the responsum and records of the Geonim suggest that this was a common arrangement. Here is an excellent example of responsa providing historical information. Muslim and Jewish artisans formed a partnership and were able to keep their business running seven days a week by each working on the other's weekly holy day. Maimonides permitted it, saying that the profit of the Sabbath should go to the Muslim, the profit of Friday or of any other day should go to the Israelite, and they should share the profit of the rest of the days. It would not be wrong even though tools belonging to the Jews were being used on the Sabbath.[52]

Appointment of an Attorney

Many great merchants of the India trade were scholars who mastered Bible and Talmud, read Hebrew and Aramaic, and even wrote legal opinions.[53] There were occasions when they had to appear in court, yet use of an attorney to appear on their behalf—what the Romans did as a matter of course—was rare. Only if a party was unable to attend court was power of attorney turned over to another person. The fear was that an attorney would not represent the best interests of his client. He might take the case because he enjoys litigation, and then he may be more uncompromising than the client would be if he were to appear on his own.

Maimonides disapproved of power of attorney except under extenuating circumstances. Nevertheless, he personally affirmed a power of attorney as a judge in the case of a legacy, which must have been one of those special circumstances.[54] The inquirer in this case wished to know if an attorney might be appointed to argue a case for a client.[55]

The query mentioned two healthy Israelites, living in different towns, one of them owing the other a sum of money. The creditor asked whether the law permitted an attorney to be appointed for him to retrieve what the debtor owed him. And if both creditor and debtor resided in the same town, the questioner asked, was the creditor permitted to have an attorney appointed for him to litigate and retrieve what was owed to him or not?

Maimonides responded that power of attorney is objectionable, citing the sages, who said, *And he did what is not good [among his people]* [Ezek 18:18]; *this refers to one who comes with power of attorney.*[56] A person is not permitted to plead for his colleague,[57] he wrote, as is well known from the fact that the sages avoided the office of judge.[58] In accordance with these premises, it is not permissible, in Maimonides' opinion, to appoint an attorney except in case of *force majeure,* either because the creditor and debtor are in different towns or because the creditor is indisposed or has a similar excuse. But if there are no excuses, there is no place for power of attorney. Rather, the two litigants should appear in court, as there is nothing restraining either of them.

TEACHERS

Rumors About a Teacher

A man who was a teacher of young children, the Torah being his profession, was accused by an elderly widow of jesting about having sexual relations with her.[59] Those who sent the query, obviously on the teacher's side, said that he was never known to have had an amorous disposition and that he was a man of integrity. They also noted that there were no witnesses or evidence for her claim and that, in their view, she intended to harm the teacher by humiliating him publicly. They asked whether what she said was credible and whether, in order to clear his name, he could impose a public ban on anyone who accused him of doing such a thing or who lied about him and suspected him unfairly.

Given the lack of evidence, Maimonides viewed the woman's accusation as unacceptable, and he recognized every person's right to have banned whoever gives him a bad name.[60] He added, however, that the correct way was to cease all discussion, not to impose a ban, and not to pursue a public debate.

This sounds like the kind of case that would come before a judge, but it was sent to Maimonides as a decisor, indicating that there may have been judicial efforts to resolve the conflict that did not satisfy the teacher and his supporters. As in the case of the pious elder who disturbed the sermon, Maimonides sought to quiet things down, to head off a public scandal and preserve the reputation of the people involved. The elderly widow deserved compassion, and the teacher (who appears not to have been married), against whom there was no incriminating evidence, depended on a blameless reputation for his livelihood.

Man Swears Oath Not to Teach Girls

This responsum is about a blind teacher of young girls who had words with someone, evidently a father of one or more of the girls, and took an oath that he would not continue teaching the girls.[61] Oath taking was a serious business in those days, as it entailed invoking the name of God, and the oath taker had to be formally released if (s)he regretted. The teacher, in fact, later regretted his oath. The girls would not study with any other man, and having a woman take his place was unrealistic, because they tended to read incorrectly, according to the writers of the query. I am giving a literal translation of the text to show how lavishly Maimonides was addressed in queries. The questioners presumably thought that the more profuse the praise, the more expeditious and thorough the response would be. The query and response are in Judeo-Arabic. I have italicized the words that are in Hebrew.

> *What says his eminent dignity, diadem of glory, his honor, greatness and*
> *holiness, our teacher and master, our Lord (adon) and Pride (gaon),*
> *Moses, the Great Rav, the mighty hammer, may his name be eternal, who*
> *has exercised authority in truth and justice, removes the hedge, reinforces*
> *the repairs, applies the measuring line to judgment, causes the kingdom of*
> *idolatry to vanish,*[62] *raises the banner of the Mosaic religion, expounds the*
> *Talmud of Rav Ashe, composes and arranges, and magnifies and glorifies*
> *the Torah,*[63] concerning a teacher of young girls, who had words with
> someone.
>
> [The teacher] swore an oath that he would not teach the daughters
> of so-and-so, being irritated by the words. Afterward he regretted this.

The young girls did not remove their veils before anyone else, and no one could replace him as their teacher. He thought about his gain from [the girls] and their fathers. There is no benefit in having women teach, for they teach *incorrectly*. The teacher *is blind* and no one takes *his place*. He suffers a loss, for he supported himself from [teaching].

May our lord and pride instruct us whether he is permitted to teach them, *and may his reward from Heaven be twofold*.

He explains the prayers to them in Arabic, *as if the early rain had covered it with a blessing.*[64]

Maimonides' response was as follows:

If he regrets [his oath], let him pronounce his regret before three *Israelite men and they will release him.*[65] Thereafter he may teach [the girls] as usual, and there is no sin upon him.

Signed by Moses

Obadiah the Proselyte

This is the third of three responsa Maimonides wrote to Obadiah the Proselyte.[66] Obadiah is identified as a Muslim who had converted to Judaism and lived in Jerusalem.[67] The contents of the responsum confirm this. He should not be confused with Obadiah the Norman, a Christian convert to Judaism, formerly the Italian priest Johannes of Oppido, who converted in 1102.[68]

We have Obadiah's query only as rephrased by Maimonides. From it we learn that Obadiah had believed that Muslims are not idolaters, whereas his Jewish teacher insisted that they were, comparing Islamic practices to idolatrous customs mentioned in the Talmud. His teacher shamed Obadiah and called him a fool. Now the teacher was obviously rude, but his view that Islam was idolatrous was not idiosyncratic. Se'adyah Gaon and others believed that Muslims kept idols in the Ka'ba.[69]

Maimonides replied that there is no idolatry in Islam, that Muslims believe in a pure monotheism. He tried to reverse the ill effects of Obadiah's teacher by reassuring the convert that his ancestors were pure monotheists and that he was a true son of Abraham who would be rewarded in this world and in the next.

The language of the responsum is Hebrew, probably because Maimonides did not want it to be read by Arabic-speakers. A renegade from Islam is subject to the death penalty. When Judah ha-Levi was in Egypt, he tried to help a Muslim convert to Judaism, but he landed in serious trouble for his efforts. Had Maimonides been caught encouraging a Muslim to join the Jewish people, both he and the man would have been sought out and killed. Whereas we find many examples of Jews converting to Islam, few Muslims converted to Judaism.

Concerning these Muslims whom you said are not idolaters, whereupon your teacher informed you that they are, and that the stones they cast during their [hajj] festival are intended for Mercurius,[70] thereby answering you improperly so that you were grieved and humiliated, and he proclaimed, *Answer a fool according to his folly* [Prov 26:5].

These Muslims are not idolaters at all. Idolatry has been removed from their tongues and hearts, and they ascribe a unity[71] to God (may he be exalted) in which there is no defect.[72] Because they misrepresent us, falsely alleging that we say that God (may he be exalted) has a son, we should not likewise falsely allege that they are idolaters.[73] The Torah testifies concerning them, *whose mouths speak lies, and whose right hands are false* [Ps 144:8, 11]. It testifies concerning us, *The remnant of Israel shall do no wrong and speak no falsehood; a deceitful tongue shall not be in their mouths* [Zeph 3:13].[74]

He ended his response:

Should someone [like you] who has attained this station be called a fool? Far be it for you! The Lord has called you not fool [kesil] but rather wise [maskil], discerning and righteous, the disciple of Abraham our father, who abandoned his ancestors and birthplace and inclined after the Lord.[75] And he who has blessed Abraham, your Master, and rewarded him in this and the next world will bless you and reward you as you deserve in this and the next world, and lengthen your days until you teach the statutes of the Lord to his entire congregation. And he will grant you the privilege of witnessing all the consolations prepared for Israel. And the benefit that the Lord shall bestow upon us we shall bestow upon you. For the Lord has ordained benefit for Israel.

Moses, son of Maimon (may the memory
of the righteous be a blessing)

SHI'UR QOMAH

Maimonides' pupil Se'adyah ben Berakhot sent a group of queries to him in 4961 A.M. (1200–1 C.E.), said to be a disastrous year. It was, as we have seen above (e.g., ch. 11), a time of famine and plague.

One of the queries pertained to *Shi'ur qomah,* literally "the measure of God's stature [or body]," the name of texts on this theme.[76] The query on *Shi'ur qomah* appears to have been raised by people in the Maghrib.[77] Maimonides said in his responsum that he regarded the *Shi'ur qomah* texts as a fabrication of European preachers.[78] He considered *Shi'ur qomah* as idolatrous and felt the need to refute what he judged to be vituperous assaults on rabbinic irrationality.[79]

> *May his honor instruct us* also how one should reply to someone who raises a question concerning *Shi'ur qomah.*[80] Should one follow the view that it is a composition of one of the Karaites, as has been transmitted in your honor's name, or is it one of the secrets of the *Sages (of blessed memory),* which contains great matters in physics or metaphysics, as Rabbenu Hayya (*of blessed memory*) said in one of the quires concerning questions relating to [the talmudic tractate] *Hagigah. May your reward from Heaven be twofold.*

Maimonides answered:

> I never ascribed [*Shi'ur qomah*] to the *sages (of blessed memory)* in any way, and God forbid that it should be by them. It is rather a composition of one of *the European preachers [darshanin al-rum]* and nothing else. In sum, to eradicate this book and obliterate every vestige of its contents is a *very meritorious deed. Make no mention of the name of other gods,* etc. [Exod 23:13]. For one who has *stature is* undoubtedly *other gods.*

Signed by Moses

Maimonides had a more positive attitude to *Shi'ur qomah* texts when he wrote his *Commentary on the Mishnah*.[81] He must then have interpreted these texts as having an esoteric philosophic meaning. He wrote about *Shi'ur qomah* in the commentary and later deleted it with ink.[82] He had declared in his discussion of the seventh of his thirteen principles of faith that Moses spoke with God immediately, without the intermediacy of angels. He then explained that he could not elaborate on this idea because it required too many premises, proofs, and explanations about the angels and the soul and its faculties. This would include, he said, *Shi'ur qomah* and its meaning. A hundred pages, he added, would not suffice for this subject alone, even if it were covered with the utmost brevity. Therefore, he left it for its proper context either in the *Book of Interpretation of Homilies* (*Kitab ta'wil al-derashot*), which he planned to compose, or in the *Book of Prophecy* (*Kitab al-nubuwwa*), which he was then writing, or a book that he would produce interpreting these fundamental principles.[83]

ASTRONOMY AND THE LOVE OF GOD

Following the questions of Se'adyah ben Berakhot in the printed edition of the responsa, there is a group of queries from the sages of Tyre, pupils of Ephraim, called the pious judge.[84] The sages of Tyre asked Maimonides about the meaning of a rabbinic dictum concerning someone who knows astronomy but does not make use of his knowledge. In his response, Maimonides made a moving comment on contemplating nature.[85]

> Concerning the saying [of the sages],[86] "*He who knows how to calculate seasons and celestial bodies and does not,*" etc.[87] How is this *calculation* done, and what comes of it, and is this a *legal ruling* or *not*?
>
> Maimonides responded:
>
> The calculation of seasons and celestial bodies is the science of astronomy in general. And the saying [*of the sages*], *All those who know and do not calculate,* that is, whoever has the ability to understand it and has a good mind and has studied the premises of this science but does not deal with it.

As for your question, "What does this mean?"—Rabbi Meir has explained in the *baraita*, *Contemplate God's works, for thus you recognize him who spoke and the world came into being.*[88] At the beginning of our great composition these principles will be explained.

MAIMONIDES' METHOD AS DECISOR

Maimonides' responsa give us access to his thought process as he applied the law to actual situations. We have looked at a small selection of responsa, yet we can grasp what his tendencies were.

1. He stated what the talmudic law was, whether he thought it had to be applied in the specific case or not.

2. He did not adhere to the law when it conflicted with science and reason.

3. He did not recommend that the law be applied when conditions required flexibility.

4. He was willing to give leeway when the law was honored in the breach.

5. He attached great importance to local custom even though it undermined the unity of legal practice.

6. He acted with compassion and did not press the full extent of the law.

7. His rulings often elevated the status of women.

18

Mishneh Torah

A tree by Wisdom's waters blooms—
no further seek for shade or fruit.
Many the books our Sages wrote,
but they be branches; this is the root.

—The Book of Tahkemoni,
trans. D. Segal

IN THE YEARS 1168–77, Maimonides, then in his thirties, compiled his monumental compendium of Jewish law, the *Mishneh Torah* (*Repetition of the Torah*), in fourteen books, the numerical value of the Hebrew word for hand (*yad*, y = 10, d = 4) and therefore called *ha-Yad ha-hazaqah* (*The Mighty Hand*) (see Deut 6:21).

BOOK OF COMMANDMENTS

First, Maimonides wrote the *Book of Commandments* as a prelude to the *Mishneh Torah,* listing the 613 commandments, positing fourteen guiding principles for identifying and enumerating them, and dividing them into positive and negative.[1] He did this because he perceived a lack of clarity in the enumeration of the commandments done by liturgical poets and others.

He wrote the *Book of Commandments,* it appears, between 1168 and 1170.[2] It was translated during his lifetime from Judeo-Arabic into Hebrew by three scholars: Abraham ibn Hisday, Solomon ibn Job, and Moses Ibn Tibbon, the first using Maimonides' first version and the second two using the second.[3] Maimonides wanted to systematize the classification of the laws, distinguishing between Scriptural and rabbinic commandments, negative and positive commandments, and commandments between man and man and those between man and God.[4] The *Book of Commandments* provided a guideline for the *Mishneh Torah,* ensuring its completeness and preventing slips and omissions.

MISHNEH TORAH

The *Mishneh Torah* established Maimonides' reputation worldwide and for all time as the authority par excellence on Jewish law, the backbone of Judaism. Whereas at the end of the *Commentary on the Mishnah* Maimonides appeared as diffident and apprehensive of criticism, he was now confident, knowing that this great work on jurisprudence was unprecedented in intention and scope. The *Mishneh Torah* was also unsurpassed and transformed the whole realm of rabbinic literature.

This great composition became the benchmark for all subsequent writing on Jewish jurisprudence. No serious work on the subject could be written without reference to the *Mishneh Torah.* His authority was so great that even Joseph Caro (1488–1575), author of the *Shulhan 'arukh (The Set Table)*—a code of law that is authoritative for Orthodox Jews—took the *Mishneh Torah* as a foundation for formulations and normative decisions.

LANGUAGE AND STYLE OF THE MISHNEH TORAH

Maimonides preferred not to write the *Mishneh Torah* in biblical language, as he thought it inadequate for expressing the intricacy of the law in its later development. "I deemed it advisable not to compose this book in the language of the Prophetic Books, since that sacred language is too limited for us today."[5] Aramaic, the language of the Talmud, was also out of the question, as only a few understood it, and even those who did were befuddled by its occasionally foreign (Greek and Latin) vocabulary. Maimonides decided to write the *Mishneh Torah* in the language of the Mishnah, to make it linguistically accessible to most people. This was a brilliant choice, for the Hebrew of the Mishnah is concise and lucid.[6] Maimonides went beyond the Mishnah's language and created a style of elegant Hebrew that serves even today for legal writing and was an inspiration for the Hebrew author Samuel Joseph Agnon, who won a Nobel Prize for literature in 1966.

While the *Mishneh Torah* emulates the style of the Mishnah, it has many more citations of Scripture. The Book of Knowledge, for instance, having 455 sections, gives 400 biblical citations.[7]

Maimonides employed rhetorical questions throughout the law code as a pedagogical device to capture the reader's attention. He must have used the same method in teaching. He embraced a moving lyrical style at the end of books, treatises, and chapters, or when he wrote on sublime topics, such as love of God. His legal language had a poetic tenor.[8] Every word is in place as though chiseled in granite, yet his draft copies we have were thoroughly reworked by deletions, additions, and alterations.

His organization of laws was designed to make it easy for the student to learn by memory. His compositional technique, as in his medical works, was to divide the text to be remembered into short pieces (called *halakhot*) that are easy to memorize and in a logical sequence. He lived in a memory culture, in which knowing meant knowing by heart.[9] He explained composition and memory in the *Mishneh Torah*.[10] "I have seen fit to divide this compilation by laws according to topic; and I shall divide the laws into chapters according to that topic; and each and every chapter I shall divide into smaller laws so that they might be committed to memory."

Composing his writings for memorization shaped his style.[11] He relied on enumerations to make the text easier to recall. Above all, Maimonides wanted to facilitate and simplify the law, to make it comprehensible and intelligible. The governing passion of his mind was a quest for order and harmony, clarity and simplicity, having everything in its proper place as in a perfect cosmos.

The *Mishneh Torah* exemplifies this drive for simplicity and system by topically arranging the dispersed and scattered statements in the Talmud into books, each containing from three to ten treatises. Although he imitated the Mishnah's language, he did not follow its division of orders and tractates. He reorganized the material under different rubrics and in his own sequence. He combed all of rabbinic literature, the Talmuds and Midrashim, for references to specific topics, relying mostly on his memory, something we can do nowadays only with concordances, databases, and electronic texts. He was understandably proud of this feat of memory and organization.

The fourteen books of the *Mishneh Torah* were subdivided into eighty-three treatises. If we count the introduction, we have eighty-four, the product of two significant numbers [= 7×12]. These were further divided into 982 chapters according to subject matter, and the chapters into smaller sections (*halakhot*). Maimonides wanted the text to serve as a basis for repetition and contemplation that would deepen the reader's devotion to the way of life described in the law code. Memorization was a spiritual exercise; it internalized teachings and deepened their effect, transforming the reader's consciousness.[12]

OMISSION OF SOURCES

Maimonides did not name the talmudic authorities he used and the rabbinic sources—the Mishnah, Tosefta, Babylonian Talmud, Jerusalem Talmud, Midrashim, and writings of the Geonim—he relied upon. Every previous legal work specified the names of authorities and transmitters of traditions. Maimonides believed that quoting all opinions and referring to talmudic sources and names of authorities might confuse the reader and limit the usefulness of his law code.

Although he did not give references to rabbinic sources from which laws were derived, he was able to recall each specific source. His own memory was phenomenal, a gift nurtured by steady training and use of memorizing techniques. On one occasion, however, when it took him some time to recall a source from memory, he was disconcerted by his temporary lapse.[13] He regretted then that he had not given references to his sources and planned to remedy the situation in a separate book, but this never happened.

Whereas the Mishnah dealt mainly with case law, Maimonides wanted to combine case law with legal principles, just as Islamic jurisprudence balanced positive laws ("the branches") with principles of the law ("the roots"). Maimonides incorporated this distinction into Jewish jurisprudence.

Motivations for Compiling the Mishneh Torah

Intellectual Decline and Cultural Pessimism

Maimonides elucidated the motivations and aims of the *Mishneh Torah* in the *Book of Commandments,* in the introduction to the *Mishneh Torah* itself, in *The Guide of the Perplexed,* and in letters to colleagues.

A strong motivation for compiling a totally new legal compendium was his sense of intellectual decline resulting from difficult and stressful times, making the two Talmuds and Midrashim difficult to understand, certainly the interpretations, responsa, and legal precepts of the Geonim.[14] "Excessive troubles and distressful times press upon all now, and *the wisdom of our wise men has perished, and the discerning of our prudent men is hidden* [Isa 29:14]."

This motivation, based on cultural pessimism, resembles Maimonides' account of Judah ha-Nasi's motives for transforming the Oral law into writing by compiling the Mishnah.[15] Judah ha-Nasi realized that the number of disciples was diminishing, with fresh calamities overwhelming them, the evil (Roman) empire expanding and growing more powerful, and the people of Israel taking flight to the ends of the earth. Maimonides wanted to justify in both cases—the Mishnah and the *Mishneh Torah*—the necessity for writing down oral traditions. The accepted rule was that the oral tradition should not be written down; however, Maimonides believed that Judah ha-Nasi and he were compelled to infringe the rule.

He gave a gloomy description of Torah study in his age in a letter to the rabbis of Lunel.[16] He informed them that there were no men at the time to raise the banner of Moses and to study carefully the words of Ravina and Rav Ashe[17] except for the sages of Lunel and all the towns about them.[18] They constantly establish houses of study and are men of discernment and wisdom.[19] "But in all other places the Torah has vanished from the prudent."[20] In all of Syria there is only Aleppo that has a few sages studying Torah, but they are not killing themselves in its tent.[21] In all Iraq *there are two berries or three* [Isa 17:6]."

> In all the towns of Yemen and in all the towns of Arabia there are a few who study Talmud, but they know only how *to interpret and receive a reward.*[22] .... The Jews in India do not know the Written law, and do nothing but observe the Sabbath and circumcision.[23] And in the towns of the non-Arab[24] Muslims there are those who study the Written law according to its literal meaning. What has been decreed for the towns of the Maghrib, on account of our sins, is well known.[25]

Maimonides preferred, as did Socrates in Plato's *Phaedrus,* that teaching be oral, with the written word serving merely as an aide-mémoire. But he saw that the community lacked a true legal compendium with correct, precisely formulated opinions. The vicissitudes of the times and the general loss of knowledge made such a compendium a pressing necessity.

Letter on Motivations and Aims of the Mishneh Torah

There is no better statement of the motivations and aims of the *Mishneh Torah* than we find in a letter by Maimonides to Joseph ben Judah.[26] When the disciple wrote to him that he was aware of people who did not welcome the *Mishneh Torah,* Maimonides replied by stating four points about his motivations and expectations:

1. He did not compose this compendium to gain authority or to achieve fame. He composed it in the first place for himself, to be released from study and searching in his old age.

2. He knew when he composed the *Mishneh Torah* that it would fall into the hands of some evil and envious person who would denigrate it and act as if it were dispensable or faulty, and some foolish ignoramuses who would consider it useless. It would reach some raving, befuddled novice who would struggle and fail to grasp precisely what he had formulated precisely. It would also reach some rigid, dull religionist who would attack the foundations of belief it contains. These would be the

majority. Yet it would certainly reach *the survivors whom the Lord calls* (Joel 3:5), fair people with good sense, who would appreciate the value of what he has achieved, Joseph being the first among them.[27]

Only in this time people will not receive it well. "But in the time to come, when envy and ambition disappear, all Israelites will be satisfied with it alone, everything else lying fallow, except for those who seek something to busy themselves with throughout their lives without attaining any objective."[28]

3. The *Mishneh Torah* is not comparable to the Torah, which is the true guidance for mankind, or to the words of the prophets. Yet only some people have followed those. If Maimonides were to yield to anger or be miserable because of everyone ignorant of some truth who resists something certain or stubbornly follows some caprice, then *all his days his thoughts are grief and heartache* (Eccl 2:23).

4. There were people in Maimonides' city without fame, status, or competence. Yet they were so arrogant and envious that they would not study this great composition and had never even seen it, to avoid it being said that they must learn from it and were therefore beneath Maimonides in knowledge. They merely lent support to the common people in this, and were always *as the blind grope in darkness* (Deut 28:29).

Not seeking authority and power, he composed the *Mishneh Torah* for the sake of the Lord, to serve as a guide to enlighten those who misunderstood the teachings of earlier scholars, and to escort people to the true significance of religious principles. Maimonides realized that it would be wrong to try to explain the branches of religion, the positive law, and to neglect its roots, or principles. He attempted to deal with confusion about God's incorporeality and the view of sages from other countries who believed that God is a physical body and who regarded deniers of this false belief to be unbelievers and heretics.

As Maimonides was addressing both intellectuals and the uneducated, he propounded religious principles in the *Mishneh Torah* and his other legal compositions by way of tradition, not by adducing proof, which required proficiency in many sciences about which the jurists knew little or nothing. In the absence of intellectual leadership he had to take on the mantle of a *spiritus rector* to cope with primitive beliefs about the nature of the deity.

COMPREHENSIVENESS OF THE *MISHNEH TORAH*

Maimonides' treatment of the law in the *Mishneh Torah* was comprehensive. It included laws tied to the Land of Israel and to a recovered national sovereignty, such as ordinances concerning agricultural tithes and ritual sacrifice that were irrelevant in his own time. It has been suggested that this sweeping range indicates that he drafted his law code to be the constitution of a revived Jewish sovereignty.[29] In the messianic age "all the ancient laws will be instituted . . . sacrifices will again be offered; the Sabbatical and Jubilee years will again be observed in accordance with the commandments set forth in the law."[30] He described the Mishneh Torah's comprehensiveness in the introduction, stressing that it contains the entire Oral law and that it frees everyone from needing any other legal compilation.[31] Surprising as it may sound, he included the Talmud and Midrash in the category of books that no longer need to be studied.

> Rather, this compilation will gather together the entire Oral law including the ordinances, customs, and decrees made from the days of Moses our Master until the compilation of the Talmud. . . . Accordingly, I have titled this compilation *"Mishneh Torah"* [i.e., repetition of the Torah], because a man who first reads the Written law and after that reads this will know from it the entire Oral law and will have no need to read any other book besides them.

The code of law is a compendium of the entire Hebrew law in topical order. *Mishneh Torah* is "repetition of the Torah" and should not be confused with Mishnah, which means "teaching [of the *halakhah*]." The Talmud is a record of rabbinic discussions of legal and nonlegal issues, with topics dispersed over many tractates, without any systematic exposition of the law and without ascertaining the actual law that is to be put into practice. The *Mishneh Torah* is a systematic codification of the law, a classification of legal topics according to subject matter. It is a comprehensive legal compendium that determines the law in every detail, freeing the individual from having to study Talmud.

Maimonides instructed Joseph ben Judah to get to know the entire *Mishneh Torah* and teach it everywhere, for the intended objective of the Talmud had been lost. This is because scholars spend time on talmudic discussions as though the objective were training in dialectic (*jadal*) and nothing else. Discussion and dialectic argumentation are only accidental to it.[32] However, the primary intention is none other than recognizing what a person is obligated to do and what he should avoid. Therefore Maimonides abstracted the primary intention so that it would be easy to remember, for it has become lost in all the words of dialectic.

The *Mishneh Torah* effectively replaced the Talmud, Maimonides boldly substituting his own authority for that of the talmudic sages. He decided not to record differences of opinion of these sages but to expound only the established normative law. He explained in the Introduction that he wrote plainly and concisely, so that the entire Oral law may become known systematically without citing different views of the sages. Instead, he mentioned all the talmudic sages collectively. "[All this while] leaving aside argument and counterargument, or that one says this and the other says that, but rather [limiting the exposition to] clear, plausible, juridically correct things, as is made clear from all those compilations and interpretations that have existed from the days of Our Holy Teacher [Judah ha-Nasi] down to now."[33]

CRITICISM OF THE *MISHNEH TORAH*

Maimonides' undertaking was so audacious—introducing philosophy and omitting rabbinic sources and names of sages—that even in his lifetime the *Mishneh Torah* came under a barrage of criticism. Rabbi Phineas ben Meshullam, whom we met above, reported scholarly criticism to Maimonides. For instance, it was said that omitting the names of the Tannaim and Amoraim would cause them to be totally forgotten, and people would cease studying the Talmud, as the *Mishneh To-*

rah would replace it. This may have been Maimonides' intent, but it was not shared by many others.

In contrast, it was claimed, Rabbi Judah ha-Nasi had assigned statements in the Mishnah to their authors to preserve the continuity of legal transmission, since omission of scholars' names would have broken the chain of transmission from one scholar to another. Maimonides accomplished this—or so he believed—by listing the names of all the scholars collectively in the introduction to the *Mishneh Torah,* seeking to riposte the Karaite claim that the Rabbanites rely on the opinions of individual scholars. He therefore wrote down the chain of transmission in his introduction "in order to teach that the tradition consists of many on the authority of many, not a single individual from a single individual."[34]

Maimonides told Phineas that he continued to teach the Talmud and the *Precepts* of Alfasi and did not restrict his teaching to his own *Mishneh Torah*. Even after he had composed it, most of his students wanted to study Alfasi's work. However, only two wanted to study the Talmud.[35]

Critics were disturbed by Maimonides's effort to impose system upon the traditional multilayered and dynamic fluidity of talmudic discourse. One hears this criticism even nowadays. Some claim that Maimonides imposed a congealed legal framework onto a dynamic tradition and enforced a homogeneous talmudic hegemony upon a pluralistic Judaism. In reality, Maimonides created his code of law to remove the Talmud from its hegemonic position and give people time to study other things, especially the sciences.

The *Mishneh Torah* was criticized by Abraham ben David of Posquières (ca. 1125–1198), whose strictures were printed on the margins of editions of the *Mishneh Torah,* eloquent testimony to the pluralism of Jewish legal thought.[36]

His critics regarded the philosophic foundations of the law, which Maimonides considered its necessary basis, as alien wisdom imported into the sacred precincts of tradition. Despite the criticisms, the *Mishneh Torah* gained an international following even in Maimonides's own lifetime.

Teachings of the *Mishneh Torah*

Book of Knowledge

Foundations of the Law

In the Book of Knowledge, Maimonides discussed philosophic and ethical subjects, a total novelty in Jewish legal codification.[37] The Book of Knowledge was divided into five treatises: Foundations of the law, Ethical Qualities, Torah Study, Idolatry, and Repentance.

The Foundations of the law proceeds along two intersecting lines. Ten religious commandments intertwine with a philosophic theology. For instance, defining the commandment to love and fear God, Maimonides wrote that when one contemplates God's wondrous works and perceives his infinite wisdom, one comes to love God and senses one's own lowliness.[38] Knowing the nature of the universe is a way to attain love of God, which is realized only through apprehension of the whole of being and the contemplation of God's wisdom manifested in it. This contemplation consists of correct opinions concerning the whole of being, which correspond to the various theoretical sciences by which these opinions are validated.[39] This philosophic interpretation of the love of God is closer to Spinoza's intellectual love of God (*amor dei intellectualis*) than to any description of love of the divine in the Talmud and Midrash. Maimonides clarified at the start that his main concern was science and the study of nature, the foundation of his restoring Judaism as a religion of reason and enlightenment.

The Necessary Being. Maimonides began Foundations of the law by alluding to a proof for the existence of a deity, following Aristotle's cosmology as formulated by al-Farabi and Ibn Sina. He did not begin, as we expect in a Jewish theology, with the Exodus from Egypt or the revelation at Mount Sinai. It is hard to find words to describe how innovative and radical his beginning is. It transforms Judaism from a religion rooted in history, in great events, to a religion implanted in nature and knowledge of the existent beings, God's works rather than God's words.[40]

The fundamental principle and the pillar of the sciences is to know that there is[41] a first existent who causes to exist all existing things.[42] All existing things, from heaven and earth and what is between them exist only through the reality of his existence.

If it be supposed that he does not exist, nothing else would be able to exist. And if it be supposed that no other beings aside from him existed, he alone would exist, their absence would not entail his absence. For all existent beings need him and he, blessed be he, does not need them or any one of them. Therefore, his reality is unlike the reality of any of them.

This is what the prophet says: *But the Lord is truly God* [Jer 10:10]. He alone is true and none other has a truth like his reality. It is what the Torah says: [*The Lord alone is God*] [Deut 4:35], that is, there is no true existent being beside him that is like him.

This existent being is God of the universe, the Lord of the whole earth. He it is who guides the sphere with a limitless power that is never interrupted.[43] For the sphere revolves forever, and it cannot revolve without something that makes it revolve. He, may he be blessed, causes it to revolve without hand or body.

Maimonides began with a demonstrative proof for the existence of God based upon the premise of the eternity of the universe. He explained later in *The Guide of the Perplexed* that he wanted to prove the existence of God by an indisputable method, based on the eternity of the universe, that would appeal to philosophers and scientists.[44] Moreover, the eternity of the universe is the foundation for the ensuing proofs of the oneness, eternity, and incorporeality of God.[45]

The declaration that the Necessary Being is identical with the "God of the universe, the Lord of the whole earth" sets up an equivalence between the Necessary Being and the God of creation, the God of Abraham, Isaac, and Jacob.[46]

However, the God of Abraham, Isaac, and Jacob is not the God of philosophers. Judah ha-Levi's *haver,* his spokesman for Judaism, had clarified in the *Kuzari* that he placed his faith in the "God of Abraham, Isaac, and Israel, who brought the Israelites out of Egypt."[47] Similarly, the French mathematician and philosopher Blaise Pascal

(1623–1662) later declared, "God of Abraham, God of Isaac, God of Jacob, not of philosophers and scholars."[48]

Maimonides projected the proof from the eternal motion of the sphere onto Abraham, who is depicted as having employed independent reasoning, inferring from the necessity for a mover of the sphere the existence of a single deity who guides (*manhig*) it and created the universe.[50] Maimonides combined a rabbinic *midrash*[51] with an Aristotelian argument, and as a result the God of Abraham is identified with Aristotle's first mover.[52] By transforming Abraham and then Moses into philosophers, Maimonides succeeded in naturalizing philosophy and the sciences within Judaism.

Maimonides made the same equation between the first mover of the universe and the biblical God in *The Guide of the Perplexed*. There cannot, however, be an equivalence between the first mover and the biblical God. An equivalence can exist only in different realms of discourse, on a vertical axis, where the higher level is of philosophic concepts and the lower level is of religious images.

God of philosophers ≠ God of Abraham

God of philosophers

$\updownarrow$

God of Abraham

At this point, we are wondering how Foundations of the Law relates to the famous thirteen principles of faith that Maimonides had set down in his *Commentary on the Mishnah*. There, he began with (1) the existence of the Creator and continued with (2) God's unity and (3) his incorporeality. Then came (4) God's primordiality and the world's being innovated. In the *Mishneh Torah* the thirteen principles appear later summarily along with other beliefs by way of portraying the twenty-four classes of those who do not have a portion in the world hereafter.[53]

Maimonides astonishingly omitted creation in Foundations of the Law, despite the fact that he taught elsewhere that creation is undoubtedly a foundation (*qa'ida*) of the law of Moses our Master and second to the foundation of the unity of God.[54] Belief in eternity, as Aristotle viewed it, Maimonides claimed, destroys the law in its principle and negates miracles.[55] Nevertheless, he preferred to proceed in the *Mishneh Torah* on the premise of the eternity of the universe and the proof of a first mover because it was a solid proof and a foundation for the principles of God's oneness and incorporeality.

Command to Love and Fear God. Having established the existence, oneness, and incorporeality of God, Maimonides elucidated the commands to love and to fear him. He explained that we come to love and fear God by pondering his works in nature and realizing his infinite wisdom. When we do, we fear and tremble, aware that we are small and lowly compared to the vast universe.[56]

And what is the way to loving him and fearing him? When a man reflects upon his wondrous great works and creatures and perceives from them his inestimable and infinite wisdom, he at once loves, praises, glorifies, and yearns greatly to know the Great Name—as David said: *My soul thirsts for God, the living God* [Ps 42:3].

And when he meditates on these things themselves, he at once recoils in a start, and will fear and tremble and know that he is a small, lowly, dark creature standing with slight, insignificant understanding before [him who is] perfect in understanding, just as David said: *When I behold your heavens, [the work of your fingers, the moon and stars that you set in place,] what is man that you have been mindful of him, [moral man that you have taken note of him,]* and so on [Ps 8:4–5].

And in accord with these sayings, I shall explain important principles concerning the work of the Lord of the Worlds[57] so that they might be an entry for one who understands to love the Name [= God]. As the sages said concerning love: *Thereby you come to acknowledge him who spoke, and the world came to be.*[58]

Maimonides referred to this passage in *The Guide of the Perplexed:*

We have already explained in the *Mishneh Torah* that this *love* is realized only through the apprehension of the whole of being as it is and through the consideration of his wisdom as it is manifested in it. We have also mentioned there the fact that the *Sages* (*may their memory be blessed*) call attention to this notion.[59]

The biblical Song of Songs, an originally earthy love poem, was understood by Maimonides in a traditional mode as an erotic dialogue between God and the human soul. He took the words *for I am sick with love* (Song 2:5) parabolically as the soul's love for God. It "shall be knit up with the love of God, and one should be continually enraptured by it, like a love-sick individual, whose mind is at no time free from his passion for a special woman, the thought of her filling his heart at all times . . . Even more intense should be the love of God in the hearts of those who love him."

God's Knowledge and Human Knowledge. The Muslim theologian and mystic Abu Hamid al-Ghazali (1058–1111) claimed that the philosophers did not believe in God's knowledge of particulars, such as individual human beings and their acts. Ibn Rushd defended the position of the philosophers by asserting that God's knowledge and human knowledge are radically different. Maimonides discussed the issue of God's knowledge in Foundations of the Law and later in *The Guide of the Perplexed*.[60] In both texts he emphasized a dictum of the philosophers, that "God is the intellect, the intellectually cognizing subject and the intellectually cognized object."

> All existent entities exist by the power of God's reality.[61] God's knowledge of the world is totally different from human knowledge. He knows himself, and knowing himself, he knows the whole universe, and nothing escapes him. He knows his reality as it is, not by a knowledge external to himself the way we know. For we and our knowledge are not one, whereas the Creator and his knowledge and life are one in every respect. "He is the knower, he is the known, and he is the knowledge itself, all of it being one."

In *The Guide of the Perplexed,* Maimonides said that he cited in the *Mishneh Torah* the dictum of the philosophers that God is the intellect, the intellectually cognizing subject, and the intellectually cognized object, and that these three form in him a single notion.[62] He repeated the philosophers' dictum three times in the same chapter of *The Guide of the Perplexed.*[63]

The statement that God is the intellect, the intellectually cognizing subject, and the intellectually cognized object has far-reaching implications, for if God knows the system of forms, or natural laws, existing in the universe, we must consider him as identical with these forms and laws, which constitute the scientific world system. If so, Maimonides' God is like Spinoza's divine attribute of intellect.[64]

ETHICAL QUALITIES

Maimonides had written about ethics in his *Commentary on the Mishnah,* especially in his introduction to Avot, called the Eight Chapters. In the *Mishneh Torah*, the treatise of the Book of Knowledge called Ethical Qualities (*de'ot*) is devoted to ethics, etiquette, and rules of health. The term "ethical qualities" corresponds to Arabic *akhlaq* (sing. *khulq* or *kuluq*), meaning "nature," "temperament," "disposition," "character," and "morals."[65] The term *de'ot* is already used in this sense in rabbinic literature.[66]

The more common Hebrew term in rabbinic and medieval Hebrew texts for moral qualities is *middot,* one that Maimonides may have avoided because it is also (in the sense of "measurements") the title of a tractate of the Mishnah and thus would have been confusing. The popular translation of *de'ot* as "opinions" rather than "ethical qualities" gives a dictionary meaning that disregards content.

Ethical Qualities and the Mean. Maimonides first determined that people have different moral dispositions by birth and are habituated in different ways. He explained that the intermediate ways are best, and he explained how to achieve them.[67]

The famous Greek physician Galen of Pergamon (b. 129 C.E.), followed by Islamic philosophers and physicians, accepted the theory of innate temperament, based upon a mixture of the four humors. This did not imply that environment had no influence on disposition, only that people could be classified as being by nature choleric, sanguine, phlegmatic, or melancholic.

Most psychologists nowadays try to avoid using the idea of innate characteristics because of its social and political implications. Some psychologists, nevertheless, hold that the ancient Greeks were right in believing that human beings have an innate personality or temperament, thereby challenging the regnant theory of developmental psychology, which says that environment determines human growth.[68] The ideal temperament, in Galenic psychology, is a moderate and balanced mixture of the four cardinal humors.[69] Each of the other four temperaments was an excess of one of the bodily humors. Galen's theory was not radically different from ideas nowadays that schizophrenics have a surfeit of dopamine and depressives lack norepinephrine.[70]

Maimonides believed that human beings have some moral dispositions innately and that other moral dispositions are learned from others, or from experience, and become ingrained in one's behavior. He and his contemporaries did not, of course, have a concept of "personality," which became current only in the eighteenth century, but they did have a notion of character alongside individual disposition.

Different Ethical Qualities. Human beings, Maimonides said, have many different moral dispositions.[71] One person is irascible and another is even-tempered and never angry, or only slightly and rarely. One person is excessively proud, and another is extremely meek. One is an insatiable sensualist and another does not desire the minimum the body needs. People differ in other moral dispositions, such as hilarious and melancholy, miserly and generous, cruel and merciful, cowardly and courageous.

Between the extremes are intermediate dispositions, equidistant from the extremes. Some dispositions one has from the beginning of one's existence and depend on one's physical nature.[72] Then there are dispositions that one learns from others, or come from oneself, or are learned and ingrained in one's behavior.

The right way is the mean in every disposition.[73] One should not be irascible and easily angered, nor should one be like a corpse without feeling, but rather one should be in the middle. One should get angry only over a serious matter, so that it will not occur again.

Similarly, one should desire only what the body needs to survive. Nor should one be miserly or wasteful with one's money; rather, one should give charity according to what one can spare, and lend as fitting to the needy.

One should not be frivolous and jesting, nor should one be sorrowful and miserable, but one should rejoice all one's days, calmly, with a joyful demeanor. This, Maimonides says, is the way of the wise.

The Sick of Soul. Maimonides considered immoral people as lacking taste and good judgment; their desires resemble the needs of sick people.

> Those whose bodies are sick taste the bitter as sweet and the sweet as bitter. Some of the sick desire and long for foods that are unfit to eat, such as soil and charcoal, and they hate good foods, such as bread and meat. It all depends upon the extent of the illness. Likewise, people with sick souls crave and love the bad character traits and hate the good way. They are careless about following it, and it is very difficult for them depending upon the extent of their illness.[74]

They may be cured if they consult the sages, the physicians of the soul, who restore them to the right path.[75] This passage corresponds to an earlier discussion in the Eight Chapters, and both are virtually identical to a text in al-Farabi's *Selected Aphorisms*. Those who are conscious of their illness yet do not attend to the advice of a physician, of them Solomon says, *fools despise wisdom and instruction* [Prov 1:7]."

The physician analogy appears in al-Farabi's *Virtuous City* and his *Political Regimes*.[76] Al-Farabi compared the infirm who think they are healthy and do not heed the advice of a physician to the psychologically afflicted who think they are virtuous and psychologically sound and do not heed the words of a guide, a teacher, or a reformer.[77] A person's practical reason discriminates between good and evil. These are not scientific judgments and cannot be proven, and therefore are not true or false. Rather, they depend upon the consensus of most human beings or the wise among them.[78]

Evil qualities should be cured by moving to the opposite extreme in order to return to the mean.[79] Al-Farabi, using the medical analogy, observed that the physician ought to know that extremes need to be opposed by extremes in order to effect a cure.[80]

Pride and Anger. While a person of an intermediate disposition is called wise, one who is scrupulous and moves from the middle way to either extreme is called pious.[81]

Maimonides stressed in all his ethical writings the need to subdue one's anger and contain one's pride.[82] It is better to be offended than to offend. He advocated passivity and silence in crises of persecution. At all times he counseled compassion and self-restraint, forgiveness and moderation. Yet he also praised the virtue of courage, which is rarely esteemed by Jewish ethicists. In classical rabbinic sources courage is equated with self-control.[83]

In some cases, one is forbidden to adhere to the mean; rather, one should remove oneself to a far extreme, as in the case of pride.[84] A person should not be simply modest, but meek and of lowly spirit to the utmost. Moses our Master was very humble, not just humble (Num 12:3). The sages commanded, *Be very, very lowly of spirit.*[85]

Anger is a very defective moral disposition (*de'ah ra'ah*), and one should go to its opposite extreme. One should train oneself not to get angry even when anger is justified. If one wants to instill fear in one's children and members of the household, or in the community if one is a welfare official, in order that they return to good ways, then one should *feign* anger to correct them, but one should remain composed.[86]

Maimonides condemned anger so resolutely because, among other things, it was a loss of control, as were pride and the inclination to offend others. He coped with anger and pride in his personal life and, as we have seen, admitted to his pupil Joseph ben Judah that he was irascible as a young man.

Asceticism. Maimonides recommended deviating from the mean toward an extreme as a therapeutic move in behavior modification and as an antidote to anger and pride. Otherwise, he did not recommend extreme or ascetic behavior, which he associated with the life of Christian monks.[87] He did not mention Sufis or philosophers, although many of them led ascetic lives as well.

He disapproved of pietistic extremes and refraining from meat, wine, and marriage, a path he considered sinful. One may think, he wrote, that since envy, lust, and honor lead to ruin, one should abandon them for the opposite extreme.[88] A person then does not eat meat, drink wine, marry, live in an attractive house, or dress in fine clothes, but dons only sackcloth and coarse wool like Christian monks.[89] This is a wrong path and one who follows it transgresses.[90] The Torah regards the Nazirite as a sinner: *He shall make atonement for him because he sinned against his soul* (Num 6:11).[91] The sages said, *If a Nazirite, who only abstained from wine, needs atonement, then how much more anyone who abstains from all things?* Therefore, the sages commanded that one should not abstain from anything other than things the Torah has forbidden. About these and similar things Solomon said, *Do not be too righteous, nor make yourself too wise; why should you destroy yourself?* (Eccl 7:16).[92]

TORAH STUDY

Maimonides began the treatise of Torah Study by observing that women, slaves, and minors are exempt from the study of Torah. There was general consensus that a woman was not *obligated* to study the Torah, but there was disagreement over the question whether she was *permitted* to do so. Ben 'Azzai said that a man ought to impart to his daughter knowledge of the law, whereas Rabbi Eliezer ben Hyrcanus said that if a man imparts to his daughter knowledge of the law it is as though he taught her frivolousness.[93] The view prohibiting women's study became a legal precept, as a result of which few women in this period were learned.[94] We hear of the daughter of Samuel ben Eli, Head of the Baghdad Academy (1161–93), who was learned in the Bible and Talmud and taught male pupils through a latticed window so that they could not see her.[95] We also know of female scribes, though copying was basically a mechanical task.[96] It was natural for young women who assisted their fathers in the scribal profession to enter the same vocation. Women's literacy was relatively high, as they had to learn to read to follow prayers in the synagogue.

Although Maimonides ruled that women are exempt from studying Torah, he did not prohibit it, as did others.[97] He said that a woman who studies Torah has a reward, although it is not equal to a man's reward, as she is not obligated to study, and his discharging an obligation makes his act superior.[98] He cited Rabbi Eliezer as saying that women transform the words of Torah into nonsense (*divre havay*),[99] taking the statement to refer to the Oral Law, but he decided that even the Written Law should not be taught. However—and this is the important point—if a woman's father *did* teach her, it is not as though he taught her nonsense.

These legal strictures presupposed that women lacked the capacity to learn or to take studies seriously. The pessimistic opinion of women's cognitive abilities was certainly influenced by the low estimation of women current in late Hellenistic antiquity, which carried over to the medieval period. A vicious cycle was created, as low expectations and neglect of female education created a female population lacking cultural ambitions.

Yet, as we have seen, Maimonides believed that women were capable of being instructed in Talmud and even that women can be prophetesses, as was Miriam, sister of Moses. In the modern period, the greatest Talmudist since the Gaon of Vilna, the Gaon Rabbi Saul (GeRaSH) Lieberman, an admirer of Maimonides, encouraged women to study Talmud and admitted them into his Talmud classes.[100]

Book of Adoration

The Book of Adoration, following the Book of Knowledge, is concerned with the love of God through divine service. There are five prerequisites for proper recital of the synagogue service: cleansing the hands, covering the body, purifying the place of prayer, removing distractions, and concentration of the mind. For the morning service, the face, hands, and feet were washed before the prayers were recited, as we see Muslims preparing for worship nowadays. The requirement of concentration gives prayer its inward, spiritual aspect.

> How does one achieve correct intention? One must free the mind of all thoughts and see oneself as standing before the divine Presence. Therefore, one should sit awhile before prayer in order to direct the mind, and then pray gently and beseechingly. One must not pray as if it were a burden to be cast aside before one continues on the way. Thus, one should sit awhile after prayer and only then leave. The early pietists would wait an hour before prayer, an hour after prayer, and spend an hour praying.[101]

Maimonides gave a description of synagogues, based on traditional custom and contemporary practice.[102] Wherever ten Jews live, they must build a synagogue, and it should be at the highest place in the city.[103] Its doors should open toward the east. The holy ark (*hekhal*), in which the Torah scrolls are placed, is built in the direction toward which the people pray. In the center a reader's platform (Greek-Hebrew *bema*) is erected for the congregation to hear the Torah and sermons. The reading desk with the Torah scroll is set up in the middle, its back to the shrine and its front to the congregation.

The elders (*zeqenim*) sit facing the congregation, and the people sit in rows, so that they all face the shrine, the elders, and the holy ark. The prayer leader stands in front of the ark, facing the shrine like the rest of the congregation.

Speaking of synagogue decorum, Maimonides observed a difference between Jews of Christendom and Jews of Islamdom:[104]

> Synagogues and study halls are to be treated with respect. They are swept, and water is to be sprinkled on their floors. It is customary for all the Jews of Spain, the Maghrib, Iraq, and the Holy Land to light lamps in the synagogue and sit on mats spread on the floor. In the Christian cities they sit on chairs.[105]

Book of Women

MARRIAGE

Rabbinic tradition presented marriage as a state of joy and contentment.[106] Jewish law made marriage obligatory for the man. The purpose of marriage in Jewish tradition was both procreation (*Be fruitful and multiply,* Gen 1:28) and companionship (*It is not good that the man should be alone,* Gen 2:18).

In his discourse on marriage, Maimonides combined rabbinic precepts with his own personal accents and nuances.[107]

> The sensible course is for a man first to choose an occupation that will give him a livelihood, then buy himself a home; and after that, take a wife; as it is said: *Is there anyone who has planted a vineyard but has never harvested it? . . . Is there anyone who has built a new house but has not dedicated it? . . . Is there anyone who has paid the bride-price*

for a wife, but who has not yet married her? . . . [Deut 20:5–7].[108] But
the foolish first marry; then if one of this sort can afford it, he pur-
chases a house; and, last of all, toward the end of his life, he sets about
seeking a trade or lives on charity. Thus it is said in the imprecations,
If you pay the bride-price for a wife, [another man shall enjoy her]. If
you build a house[, you shall not live in it]. If you plant a vineyard[,
you shall not harvest it] [Deut 28:30]. That is, all your activities shall
be in the reverse order of what they should be, so that you will not
prosper in your ways.[109] And a blessing is conveyed in the scriptural
text: *David was successful in all his undertakings, for the Lord was with
him* [1 Sam 18:14].[110]

A man should always first study Torah and then marry; for if he
takes a wife first, his mind will not be free for study. But if his physical
desires are so overpowering as to preoccupy his mind, he should marry
and then study Torah.[111]

The obligation to be fruitful and multiply is incumbent upon the
man and not the woman.[112] A man must assume this obligation from
the age of seventeen upward. If he passes twenty without marrying, he
is transgressing and nullifying a positive commandment. If, however,
he is engaged in the study of Torah and is anxious about taking a wife,
for earning a livelihood might prevent him from studying Torah, he is
permitted to delay his marriage.[113] This is because someone performing one religious duty is released from another, certainly when it concerns the study of Torah. A man who desires to study Torah constantly,
like Ben ʿAzzai, and cleaves to it all his life, without taking a wife,
does not sin in this as long as his passion does not regularly overpower
him.[114] If, however, his passion frequently overcomes him, he is obligated to marry, even if he already has children, so as not to fall victim
to unchaste thoughts.

In the Genizah period, the first stage of marriage was engagement
(*shiddukhin*), when the financial terms and other conditions and obligations were negotiated; then came betrothal, when the partners were
consecrated in marriage (*qiddushin*) without intimate relations being
permitted; and lastly there were nuptials (*nisu'in*), or consummation
by wedding, when the marriage contract was written. In actual practice, the first two stages, engagement and betrothal, were merged. Af-

ter the Genizah period, it was more common to combine the second two, betrothal and nuptials.[115]

From ancient times, Jewish marriage was a private transaction between bride and groom.[116] The community's involvement was minimal and was simply to ensure that the contractual obligations between the two parties were truly kept.[117] In fact, the presence of an official was unnecessary and became only customary for someone to supervise the proceedings. The *ketubbah*, or "written instrument," establishes the terms of marriage. In Islamic law also marriage is basically a contract (*'aqd*) between the bridegroom and the guardian (*wali*) of the bride. A Jewish wedding takes place in the presence of a minyan (ten worshipers) to make it public and solemn, but neither a minyan nor the presence of a rabbi is formally required by Jewish law.

Maimonides' *Mishneh Torah* influenced the development of jurisprudence in seventeenth-century England and Holland. John Selden (1584–1654), the great English lawyer and jurist, had an abiding interest in Maimonides' *Mishneh Torah,* and the great Dutch juridical scholar Hugo Grotius, who was in contact with Selden, made ample use of Maimonides' *Mishneh Torah* in his writings as well. Christian Hebraists regarded the *Mishneh Torah* as the classical text on Jewish law and appreciated its lucid style.[118]

John Selden sought to demonstrate that biblical law, interpreted in the Talmud and in Maimonides' *Mishneh Torah,* contains the heart of the natural law common to all humankind.[119] His *Law of Nature and the Nations According to the Hebrews* (*De jure naturali et gentium juxta disciplinam Ebraeorum,* 1640) deals with the seven Noahide laws, which Selden regarded as an articulation of natural law and the basic text for the law of nations. The Noahides are the immediate descendants of Noah, the progenitors of humankind, to whom God gave seven basic laws, according to Jewish lore.

John Selden's *Uxor hebraica* (*The Hebrew Wife,* 1646) presented sex not as a way to avoid sin but as a blessing. Instead of the New Testament's attitude toward marriage as a concession to human nature, *better to marry than burn* (1 Cor 7:9), Selden's book celebrated marriage. *Uxor hebraica* was a major source for John Milton's attitude on marriage and divorce.[120] Selden provided material for Milton in his attempt to eliminate church and state from interference in the marriage institution. Jewish marriage is not a sacrament and does not require the presence of a rabbi, and it is made binding by consummation. Milton found in *Uxor hebraica* Selden's reference to Maimonides' formulation of Jewish marriage law, that it is leading into the chamber (*chuppah*), or consummation between husband and wife, that constitutes marriage. Intercourse need not actually take place, but it must be assumed or permissible. This chapter establishes that neither the state nor the clergy have any authority over the marriage institution, a position that Milton embraced wholeheartedly.

BIRTH CONTROL

Although Maimonides believed that the purpose of marriage is procreation, he also understood that relief of sexual tension was conducive to good health.[121]

Birth control was not an insuperable problem in Judaism. First of all, only the man was commanded to procreate, and since the command did not obligate the woman, she was permitted to use a preventive device, as a talmudic precedent permitted a woman to use a compress (*mokh*) during intercourse.[122] A passage in the Talmud explicitly permitted certain women under specific conditions to use a compress. The passage speaks of three categories of women who must (or may) use a *mokh* when having marital intercourse—a minor, a pregnant woman, and a nursing mother.[123] Maimonides did not cite this passage.[124] There was a tendency to interpret the permission expansively and to permit other women having health risks to use the compress. Maimonides (like Alfasi before him), it appears, did not object even to a precoital compress for women in general.

As the talmudic sages and codes of law permitted women to use contraceptive compresses, it was possible in modern times by extension to regard birth control pills as an approved method of contraception.[125]

A WIFE'S MODESTY

After itemizing the garments and cosmetics that a husband is obligated to supply his wife,[126] Maimonides stated that where it was customary for a woman to go out into the street wearing a veil covering her entire body like a cloak, the husband is obligated to include in the garments he gives her such a veil of the least expensive kind.[127] If he is wealthy, however, he must give her a more expensive veil. In any case, she needs a veil when she goes out to visit.

Maimonides ruled that a woman is entitled to visit her father's house, a house of mourning, or a wedding feast,[128] in kindness to friends and relatives, so that they visit her on similar occasions, "for she is not in a prison where she cannot come and go."[129] Yet he was stern in restricting women to the household. He had come from an austere religious culture in the Maghrib to Egypt, a country he thought lax in its sexual mores.

[I]t is unseemly for a woman to be constantly going out abroad and into the streets, and the husband should prevent his wife from going out except once or twice a month as the need may arise. Rather, it is proper for a woman to sit in the corner of her house, for it is written, *The honor of the King's daughter is within* [Ps 45:14].[130]

The daughters of Israel, Maimonides said, observe the custom of modesty.[131] The following were infringements of this custom: going out into the street or into an open alley with head uncovered and without the veil, even if her hair was covered with a kerchief; spinning in the street, with a rose or a similar ornament in front of her face, on her forehead, or on her cheeks, in the manner of brazen gentile women, with her arms exposed to the public; frolicking with young men; and demanding intimacy with her husband in a voice so loud that her neighbors could hear her.

POLYGYNY

Polygamy [Greek *gamos,* "marriage"], or more correctly polygyny [Greek *gynē,* "woman"], means that a husband can have multiple wives concurrently. The Hebrew Bible, the Talmud, and Islamic law permit it. The chance of being replaced by a younger and more attractive bride was a constant source of female anxiety. One way for a wife to avert this threat was by adding a condition in her marriage contract that her husband could not take another wife or hire a female servant without her permission.[132]

European Jews prohibited polygyny by an enactment of Rabbenu Gershom, the Light of the Exile, and his synod. He also passed an enactment imposing a ban on someone who divorced his wife without her consent. These arrangements established a more balanced symmetry between husband and wife.[133] The prohibition of polygyny, however, did not affect Jewish communities in Muslim countries.

Maimonides did not prohibit polygyny or even declare it reprehensible or suggest that the standard of piety required monogamy. Although Jewish marriage in Andalusia was basically monogamous, polygyny did exist, and a second wife was an arrangement that the first wife could not veto. One of the reasons for its persistence was that Andalusian men were away from home for long intervals.[134] This remained the case in Egypt, where merchants, most of them Maghribis, were far from home for extended periods of time.

> A man may marry several women, even a hundred of them, either at the same time or one after another, and his wife may not hinder him therein, provided that he is able to supply each one of them with the food, raiment, and conjugal rights due her. He may not, however, compel them to reside in the same residence, but must let each one reside by herself.[135]

The condition that the husband should be fair to his multiple wives is stated in the Qur'an and is used in some modern Islamic states to outlaw polygyny, on the assumption that a man cannot treat all of his wives equally.[136]

With a plurality of wives there was a problem of conjugal rights.[137] "It depends on their number," said Maimonides. A laborer with two wives schedules each once a week. If the laborer has four wives, then each has a turn once every two weeks. If a sailor has four wives, then each has a turn in two years. Hence the sages prescribed that a man should not take more than four wives, even if he is wealthy, so that each wife's turn is at least once a month.

Some scholars understand Maimonides' strictures against prostitution as also banning concubinage.[138] Prohibiting secondary wives, or concubines, was an innovation, as they were permitted in Scripture and the Talmud. A number of later legal scholars criticized Maimonides for this, including Rabbi Abraham ben David of Posquières.[139]

MUTUAL RESPECT IN MARRIAGE

A man should caution his wife against infidelity, yet he should not be jealous beyond reason or have sexual relations with her against her will, but only with her consent amidst pleasant banter and enjoyment.[140] The wife should act with discretion in her house and not indulge in jesting and levity in her husband's presence, nor demand to have intercourse. She should not withhold herself from her husband in order to torment him or to increase his love. She should submit to her husband when he desires.[141]

> The sages have likewise ordained that a man should honor his wife more than his own self, and love her as himself; that if he has money, he should increase his generosity to her according to his wealth; that he should not cast undue fear upon her; and that his discourse with her should be gentle—he should be prone neither to melancholy nor to anger.
>
> They have likewise ordained that the wife should honor her husband exceedingly and hold him in awe, that she should arrange all her affairs according to his instructions, and that he should be in her eyes as if he were a prince or a king, while she behaves according to his heart's desire, and keeps away from anything that is hateful to him. This is the way of the daughters and the sons of Israel who are holy and pure in their mating, and in these ways will their life together be seemly and praiseworthy.[142]

When Maimonides said that the husband should not be unreasonably jealous or coerce his wife to have sexual relations, he alluded to an issue that surfaces nowadays under the heading of marital rape. He strongly disapproved of a man coercing his wife to have intimate relations with him but he did not make it a crime.

Though he prescribed that a man should honor his wife even more than himself, there was no penalty for failing to do so.

PHYSICAL PUNISHMENT OF A WIFE

In medieval societies—Jewish, Christian, or Muslim—the wife was subjugated to the husband and lived under his authority and control. These societies had hierarchical structures of dominance and inferiority.[143]

Physical abuse of women by husbands cannot have been rare in Maimonides' time.[144] Husbands were permitted to use force to prevent their wives from going out. Violence against women was an extension of the husband's custodial role. A Geonic ruling permitted wife beating: "Even if he beats her, she should be silent as modest women are."[145] The Geonim had various views; however, many concurred that if the wife refused to perform household chores, the husband or the courts had the right to compel her. Women were expected to mill, bake, launder, cook, nurse children, make beds, and weave wool.[146]

Maimonides posited: "A wife who refuses to perform any kind of work that she is obligated to do may be compelled to perform it, even by lashing her with a rod."[147] This judgment sounds extremely harsh and unfair, indeed appalling. It is a statement that has been widely misunderstood, even by scholars who write on Maimonides.

Rabbi Isaac Klein, translator of the Book of Women, in which this text appears, observes in his introduction, "Coming from Maimonides, whose ethical standards were uncommonly high, such a rule is, to say the least, surprising."[148] He then explains that Maimonides "found it advisable to yield to the prevailing mores of the Muslim society in the midst of which he lived." But why, we may ask, did he find it advisable to yield to these standards? His European contemporaries, Klein observes, represented Jewish tradition more authentically in this instance. Abraham ben David of Posquières commented, "I have never heard of women being scourged with a rod," advising that the husband should rather reduce support of her needs and her food supply until she relents. Scholars have followed Rabbi Klein's lead, taking Maimonides to be permitting the husband to beat his wife and blaming it on his Islamic milieu.

The historian Avraham Grossman suggests that Maimonides' ruling should be contextualized within the Islamic environment. Physical violence against women is sanctioned in the Qur'an: *As those you fear may be rebellious admonish; banish them to their couches, and beat them* (4:34). Grossman thought that both the Geonic ruling and Islamic influence account for Maimonides' decision.[149] This strict measure, however, may have been due to Maimonides' own stern Maghribi attitudes and dismay at the loose morals of Egypt.[150]

In any event, there is no evidence that wife beating was more rampant in the Islamic environment than in Europe.[151] European rabbinic authorities may have been more strict in prohibiting it.

Daniel Boyarin gave a highly speculative sociological explanation: "Maimonides permitted (recommended) scourging a wife with a rod if she refused to perform her duties (Nashim 21:10)."[152] Boyarin explained this precept as influenced by different sociopolitical conditions from those of Europe. Maimonides, says Boyarin, belonged to a socially dominant class and was close to ruling circles. Even if this were true, however, it does not explain why he would permit Jewish women to be treated so intemperately. Moreover, his explanation does not apply to the rulings of the Geonim that were a precedent. Aristocrats and the ruling elite had slaves, and their wives did not do the palace housework.

The main point is that Maimonides did *not* decide that a husband could force his wife even with a whip. He distinctly referred the case to *the court*. He wrote *"they* compel her" (*ḳofin otah*), which is plural, and in other places where he used the words "they compel," he meant the court. The rest of the paragraph affirms this. It speaks of "what the judge may consider feasible" evidence. The husband brings his wife to court, where both present their sides and witnesses are summoned. The court then decides. The talmudic sages never permitted a husband to beat his wife, and neither did Maimonides. It contradicts everything he said about a husband having to honor his wife even more than himself. Wife beating was, in his view, the custom of uncivilized gentiles.[153]

Similarly, Maimonides legislated that a man who refused to divorce his wife when he was obligated to do so should be flogged until he consents. "They compel him" (*ḳofin oto*), "they" being the court.[154] And he ruled: "He who refuses to give alms, or gives less than is proper for him, must be compelled by the court [*bet din ḳofin oto*] to comply, and must be flogged for disobedience until he gives as much as the court estimates he should give."[155]

Flogging was not a punishment but a disciplinary measure to force compliance.[156] The community had recourse to excommunication, bans, and floggings to coerce members to live up to their obligations.

There were no other sanctions, such as incarceration, which was used by the Islamic government to enforce compliance.

DIVORCE

In Jewish law the husband has the right to divorce his wife, but she does not have the right to divorce him. According to biblical law, if he finds something unseemly about her, he writes her a bill of divorce, hands it to her, and sends her away from his house (Deut 24:1–4). The sages interpreted *something unseemly* in different ways.[157] The School of Shammai maintained that *something unseemly* meant unchastity; the School of Hillel said it was whatever brought about incompatibility, even if she spoiled his food, while Rabbi Aqiba extended the source of incompatibility to the husband's finding another, fairer woman.

Maimonides emphasized that the husband must divorce of his own free will, and if it is against his will, she is not divorced. "The woman, however, may be divorced with or without her consent."[158] Rules of divorce in Islamic law were similar in that the husband did the divorcing. He did not need a reason and could divorce her on a whim, but she could not divorce him. This glaring asymmetry created a problem for women and for the entire system of personal law in Judaism and Islam. In the Genizah period, Islamic law was innovative in creating ways for women to get out of their marriages. Jewish legists imported Islamic practice into their own legal system. Often a kernel of the Islamic solution already existed in Jewish law, making reception much easier.

Book of Agriculture

THE LADDER OF CHARITY

In Maimonides' time poverty was ubiquitous. Although the social services of the community tried to help, and the poor could appeal to the community in the synagogue and even petition worshipers during a service, still the poor were seen begging and making the rounds of homes and stores. Maimonides included a treatise of gifts to the poor within the Book of Agriculture because in Scripture so many commandments pertaining to the poor had to do with an agricultural economy—to leave a corner crop (Lev 19:9–10), gleanings (Lev 19:9), defective vineyard clusters (Lev 19:10), grape gleanings (Lev 19:10), the forgotten sheaf (Deut 24:19), and a tithe for the poor (Deut 14:28). To these Maimonides added two general commandments on poverty: to give charity to the poor in accordance with one's means (*You shall surely open your hand unto your poor and needy brothers,* Deut 15:11) and not to harden one's heart against the poor (*If, however, there is a needy person among you . . . do not harden your heart and shut your hand against your needy kinsman,* Deut 15:7).

He wrote, without having a talmudic source for it: "He who, seeing a poor man begging, turns his eyes away from him and fails to give him alms transgresses a negative commandment."[159] And he advised, "One must feed and clothe the heathen poor together with the Israelite poor, for the sake of the ways of peace." When a poor man goes from door to door, one is obligated to give him at least a small gift. It is forbidden to let him depart empty-handed: *Let not the downtrodden be put to shame* (Ps 74:21).[160]

Maimonides liked to embellish his code of law with lyrical passages, and he poeticized his praise of charity to make it inspiring and memorable for the reader:

> We must be more careful in charity than in any other positive commandment, for charity is the mark of the righteous man who is of the seed of our father Abraham. . . . The throne of Israel cannot be established, nor true faith made to stand up, except through charity, nor will Israel be redeemed, except through the practice of charity. . . . He who has compassion upon others, others will have compassion upon him.[161]

Maimonides described eight rungs in the ladder of charity.[162] The highest rung is helping the impoverished get employment. Then come three rungs concerning the identity of the giver and receiver. In the highest of this group, neither knows the identity of the other. Then there are four rungs on the manner of giving. As he has established that one must support the poor among gentiles as one supports the poor among Israelites, the ladder may be taken as universal.

1. The highest degree is supporting an Israelite who is impoverished by giving him a gift or a loan, or entering a partnership with him, or finding him work.

2. Below this is giving charity to the poor without knowing to whom, nor does the recipient know who the donor is. This is by contributing to a charitable fund.[163]

3. Below this is giving to a known poor person, whereas the recipient does not know who the donor is.

4. Below this the poor person knows the identity of the donor, to whom he is unknown.

5. Below this is giving charity to the poor person before being asked.

6. Below this is giving charity to the poor person after being asked.

7. Below this is giving the poor person less than what is proper, but with a friendly face.

8. Below this is giving charity with a frowning face.

Maimonides taught that charity begins at home.[164] We should support our grown sons and daughters, whom we are not obligated to support, so that sons may study Torah and daughters learn to follow the right path and not expose themselves to contempt.[165] Providing for one's father and mother is accounted as performing an act of charity.[166] Indeed, it is an outstanding act of charity, since one's relatives have precedence over other people.[167] He listed them in order of priority as (1) relatives, (2) household, (3) city, and (4) other cities. The household is defined as everyone living under one's roof, including male and female servants, apprentices, and students.

Book of Torts

ABORTION

Abortion did not come up as a question of early termination of pregnancy or as an issue of pro-choice or pro-life as we know it. It presented itself as a question when at the time of birth a preference had to be made between the life of the mother and the life of the child when both were in extremis. The issue of when the soul enters an embryo ("quickening") was not decided in Jewish law and does not enter the decisions about abortion.[168] The fetus was not considered a person, from a legal viewpoint, until it was born. Abortion was discussed in the Mishnah in regard to when an embryotomy was required to save the mother's life. We read:

> [1] If a woman has [life-threatening] difficulty in childbirth, one dismembers the embryo within her, limb by limb, because her life takes precedence over its life.
>
> [2] Once its head has emerged, it may not be touched, for we do not set aside one life for another.[169]

The second part of this *mishnah* was discussed elsewhere in the Talmud. In other cases, if a young child threatens a person's life, the child may be killed without due process to save the person whose life is in danger. Why, it is asked, should the life of the child of a woman in life-threatening labor not be set aside in the same way? The reply given is that the infant being born is innocent and that this is an "act of God." Another reason given is that we cannot determine who is the aggressor in the case of an infant in the process of being born.[170]

The discussion of these cases went on for many centuries as result of Maimonides' reformulation of the issue in the *Mishneh Torah*.[171]

> [1] This is, moreover, a negative commandment, that we have no pity on the life of the pursuer [*rodef*].[172] Consequently, the Sages have ruled that if a woman with child is having difficulty giving birth, the child inside her may be taken out, either by drugs or by surgery, because it is regarded as though it were pursuing her and trying to kill her.[173]
>
> [2] But once its head has appeared, it must not be touched, for we may not set aside one human life to save another human life, and what is happening is the course of nature.[174]

Maimonides altered the first part of the *mishnah* by applying the aggressor condition to the situation before birth and omitted the reason given that the mother's life takes precedence.[175] That reason was based on the principle that the fetus is not a person until born.[176] Maimonides' aggressor argument suggests that only when the child is an aggressor is abortion permitted, but not for anything less serious. This position differs from the opinion of the Talmud.[177]

His provision in the second part of the *mishnah,* that once the child is being born its life cannot be set aside, implies that it has become a person. Yet his regarding the fetus as an aggressor in the first part of the *mishnah*, when it is not yet a person, while not considering the newborn an aggressor in the second part is illogical.[178] Indeed, by declaring the fetus an aggressor, he implies that it is a person.[179] In any case, his position was understood as saying that the fetus was a person, which clashed with the view of Rashi (Rabbi Shlomo Yishaqi) that the fetus was not a person.

We need to find out Maimonides' reasoning, because he was dealing with an issue of life and death that demanded clear thinking. The statement in the first part of the *mishnah* that the mother's life has preference over the life of the fetus is not explained, and it may be that he wanted to give the reasoning behind that judgment.[180]

The authors of the Tosafot (twelfth to fourteenth centuries), in their comments on the Talmud, prohibited abortion on the basis of the precept that it was a capital crime for the Noahides, a view that Maimonides codified.[181] The Tosafists combined this with the principle that nothing is permitted to a Jew that is prohibited to a non-Jew.[182]

Later scholars discussed whether Maimonides' position should be taken in the strict sense, that only when the fetus is threatening the mother's life (as in the first part of the *mishnah*) can abortion occur. Some scholars took this to imply that, in general, only life-threatening situations justify abortion. Most authorities take Maimonides' use of the aggressor argument at the time of birth to imply that abortion at an earlier stage is not to be taken into consideration.[183]

Abortion, although prohibited, does not constitute murder in Jewish law. If someone assaults a woman, even unintentionally, and the child is born prematurely and does not survive, the offender is obligated to compensate the woman and her husband for loss of the child and for injury and pain, but he is not guilty of involuntary homicide because the fetus is not a person.[184] A Noahide, however, who kills a fetus has committed a capital crime.[185]

In modern times, rabbinic authorities have expanded the concept of "life-threatening" to include lesser threats, such as hazards to a woman's health and sanity. The principle that a fetus is not a person has contributed toward implementation of this less restrictive trend. Nevertheless, for Maimonides abortion had to be therapeutic, and it was not condoned by him or by later codes and responsa, medieval or modern, for convenience, practicality, or choice.[186]

EUTHANASIA

The preservation of human life takes precedence over all other considerations, and one may violate the Sabbath to save someone who is precariously ill. This implies that one must not do anything to accelerate the death of a dying person. The highest concern was life itself, not the quality of life.

Maimonides followed the rabbinic rule that a dying person is regarded as living in every respect.[187] The main concern was to avoid doing anything to the dying person that would hasten or delay death or cause additional suffering. The people surrounding a dying person must not speak as though he is going to die and may not make any preparations for his death.

One may not bind his jaws, stop the organs of the lower extremities,[188] place metallic or cooling utensils upon his navel to prevent swelling, rub or wash him, or place sand or salt upon him until he dies.[189] Whoever touches the dying person is guilty of shedding blood. "To what may he be compared? To a flickering flame, which is extinguished as soon as one touches it. Whoever closes the eyes of the dying while the soul is about to depart is shedding blood. One should wait a while; perhaps he is only in a faint."[190]

Later authorities held that one may not delay the death of a dying person by medical treatment, and one may remove causes hindering the departure of the soul, such as nearby noise. Still, no halakhic authority permitted hastening death by active euthanasia, which is considered murder.[191] Yet some permit using narcotics or powerful analgesics to alleviate pain and distress, even though this may depress respiration and accelerate death.[192] Indeed, this is a merciful way of giving the patient final peace and tranquility and an easier death. Scripture says, *Love your neighbor as yourself* (Lev 19:18). *Choose a beautiful death for him.*[193]

Book of Judges

THE SEVEN COMMANDMENTS OF THE NOAHIDES

The Noahide laws are the elementary moral standards of civilized behavior for all of mankind. Six go back to Adam, and are thus ultimately Adamic or universal human laws, and one was added at the time of Noah. They are the prohibition of idolatry, blasphemy, murder, incest, robbery, and eating a limb from a living animal, and the obligation to have courts of law. Maimonides wrote:

> A gentile who accepts the seven commandments and observes them scrupulously is a "righteous gentile," and will have a portion in the world hereafter, provided that he accepts them and performs them because the Holy One, blessed be he, commanded them in the law and made known through Moses, our teacher, that the observance thereof had been enjoined upon the descendants of Noah even before the law was given. But if his observance thereof is based upon a reasoned conclusion he is not deemed a resident alien, or one of the pious of the gentiles, rather one of their wise men.[194]

The Noahides include Jews, but Jews have the obligation to fulfill 613 commandments. Yet in some respects the law is more strict with a Noahide. If a Noahide kills a person, even an embryo in its mother's womb, or if he performs a mercy killing for the terminally ill, he is to be put to death.[195]

Maimonides stressed that the gentile who observes the seven Noahide laws must accept them because God commanded them even before the Mosaic law was given. If his observance is based upon a reasoned conclusion only (and not divine revelation), he is not one of the pious gentiles, rather one of their wise men.[196]

This statement has received wide attention, with much discussion focusing on the last phrase, which in printed editions has the reading *we-lo' me-hakhmehem* ("and *not* of their wise men"), meaning that he is neither one of their pious nor one of their wise men. But the reading *ella me-hakhmehem* ("rather one of their wise men") is commended by the textual evidence of many later citations and contextual sense.[197] I believe that the original reading, "rather one of their wise men," was altered (one letter was deleted) so as to make the statement more restrictive.

This passage has become the focus of attention because Spinoza relied on it to deny Judaism's universalism. Thereafter, Moses Mendelssohn and Hermann Cohen took issue with Spinoza. He used a printed edition of the *Mishneh Torah* that had the reading "and not of their wise men," meaning that a righteous gentile was considered neither pious nor wise and did not merit immortality. Even according to the more favorable reading ("rather one of their wise men"), however, these gentiles are excluded from the world hereafter. Moses Mendelssohn found this exclusion from immortality objectionable.[198]

The seven Noahide laws, when reached by reasoned determination, are rational laws. As the barest minimum laws necessary for the order of society, they pertain to a natural right in the sense that natural right pertains to a just order.[199]

JESUS AND MUHAMMAD

The true and only test of the Messiah, Maimonides believed, was success or failure. A purported Messiah who failed was not the Messiah. It is not necessary, he explained, that the Messiah perform signs and wonders, innovate things, or revive the dead and the like.[200] Yet if the Messiah does not succeed fully, or is slain, he is not the Messiah promised in the Torah.

The section in which he wrote about the Messiah and Jesus and Muhammad, at the end of the *Mishneh Torah,* was suppressed by Christian censors, yet preserved in early editions, and cited in works based on uncensored printed editions and manuscripts.

> But if he does not meet with full success, or is slain, it is obvious that he is not the Messiah promised in the Torah. He is to be regarded like all the other wholehearted and worthy kings of the House of David who died and whom the Holy One, blessed be he, raised up to test the common people, as it is written *Some of the wise shall fall, so that they may be refined, purified, and cleansed, until the time of the end, for there is still an interval until the time appointed* [Dan 11:35]
>
> Even of Jesus of Nazareth, who imagined that he was the Messiah, but was put to death by the court, Daniel had prophesied, as it is

written, *The lawless sons of your own people shall lift themselves up in order to fulfill the vision, but they shall fail* [Dan 11:14]. For has there ever been a greater stumbling than this? All the prophets affirmed that the Messiah would redeem Israel, save them, gather their dispersed members, and confirm the commandments. But he caused Israel to be destroyed by the sword, their remnant to be dispersed and humiliated. He was instrumental in changing the Torah and causing the world to err and serve another beside God.

But it is beyond the human mind to fathom the designs of the Creator; for our ways are not his ways, neither are our thoughts his thoughts. All these matters relating to Jesus of Nazareth and the Ishmaelite [Muhammad] who came after him, only served to clear the way for King Messiah, to prepare the whole world to worship God with one accord, as it is written, *At that time I will change the speech of the peoples to a pure speech, that all of them may call on the name of the Lord and serve him with one accord* [Zeph 3:9]. Thus the messianic hope, the Torah, and the commandments have become familiar topics—topics of conversation [among the inhabitants] of the far isles and many peoples, uncircumcised of heart and flesh. They are discussing these matters and the commandments of the Torah. Some say, "Those commandments were true, but have lost their validity and are no longer binding;" others declare that they had an esoteric meaning and were not intended to be taken literally; that the Messiah has already come and revealed their occult significance. But when the true King Messiah will appear and succeed, be exalted and lifted up, they will forthwith recant and realize that they have inherited naught but lies from their fathers, that their prophets and forebears led them astray.[201]

THE DAYS OF THE MESSIAH

The days of the Messiah are yearned for not for any material rewards they might bring but for the tranquility that permits untrammeled pursuit of wisdom leading to perfection and immortality. Just as the material blessings promised in the Torah, Maimonides said, strengthen one's ability to fulfill the law, and thereby to attain immortality, and are not an end in themselves,[202] all Israelites, their prophets and their sages longed for the days of king Messiah so they might have relief from the wicked kingdom which does not let them occupy themselves properly with the Torah and the commandments and find tranquility and devote themselves to wisdom so that they are worthy of the world hereafter. . . .[203] The ultimate and perfect reward, the final bliss which will suffer neither interruption nor diminution, is the life of the world hereafter. The days of the Messiah are this world, and the world goes it customary way, except that sovereignty will be restored to Israel.[204] The ancient sages have said, *There is no difference between this world and the messianic age except [the end of] subjection to [alien] powers.*[205]

The Messiah brings prosperity and peace. Maimonides did not envisage, however, a social upheaval: there will be rich and poor, strong and weak, even in the days of the Messiah. Yet livelihood will be considerably easier for people and a small effort will produce plenty.[206]

The absence of hunger is a condition for the attainment of peace, as though the struggle for survival were the chief cause of envy, competition, and warfare. In the *Treatise on Resurrection,* Maimonides envisioned the aggressiveness of animals diminishing, and their becoming amiable with one another when cultivation is prolific and the country prospers.[207] He cited Aristotle as having observed that if there were no lack of food, animals wild by nature would be tame and familiar with man and with one another, as is shown by the peaceable conduct of fierce animals in Egypt. They are constantly supplied with food and tamed by kindness, a phenomenon that occurs also elsewhere.[208]

He later expounded another view, that the evils human beings inflict upon one another all stem from ignorance.[209] He wrote that by knowledge of the truth, envy and hatred are removed and mutual harm abolished, citing Isa 11:9: *For the land shall be filled with devotion to the Lord as water covers the sea.* The reason for abolition of these enmities, discords, and tyrannies will be men's knowledge of the true reality of the deity.

Likewise, Maimonides said elsewhere that following desires, as the ignorant do, increases mutual envy, hatred, and strife.[210] Just as the reestablishment of national sovereignty restores a previous condition—the Davidic monarchy—so the fruitfulness of the earth, harmony, and knowledge of God restore Paradise (Garden of Eden). A symmetry in world history is established, and the messianic era recapitulates a primordial period of paradisiacal peace and tranquility.

This noble vision, I think, reflects a description of the *eschaton* in a letter ascribed to Aristotle, known to medieval Jewish scholars living in Spain, in which the Greek philosopher envisioned a splendid future for mankind consisting of peace, tranquility, and the pursuit of wisdom.

> I know that if mankind in general is destined to reach true felicity within the duration of this world, there will come about that concord and order which I shall describe. Happy is he who sees the resplendence of that day when men will agree to constitute one rule and one kingdom. They will cease from wars and strife, and devote themselves to that which promotes their welfare and the welfare of their cities and countries. They will enjoy safety and quiet, dividing their days into parts, part for rest and welfare of the body, part for education and attention to that noble pursuit, philosophy—studying what has been achieved and seeking what has not yet been attained. I would love to remain alive and see that age—if not all, at least part of it. I wish that my friends and brethren may see it; if they, too, will not obtain this privilege, then those who are like them and follow their ways.[211]

Maimonides ended the *Mishneh Torah* on this note:[212]

> The sages and prophets did not long for the days of the Messiah that Israel might exercise dominion over the world, or rule over the gentiles, or be exalted by the nations, or that it might eat and drink and rejoice. Their aspiration was that Israel be free to devote itself to the law and its wisdom, with no one to oppress or disturb it, and thus be worthy of life in the world hereafter.[213]
>
> In that era there will be neither famine nor war, neither jealousy nor strife. Blessings will be abundant, comforts within the reach of all. The one preoccupation of the whole world will be to know the Lord. Hence Israelites will be very wise, they will know the things that are now concealed and will attain an understanding of their Creator to the utmost capacity of the human mind, as it is written: *For the earth shall be full of the knowledge of the Lord as the waters cover the sea* [Isa 11: 9].[214]

PART FIVE

EGYPT
THE LATE YEARS

19

The Guide of the Perplexed

In Jorge Luis Borges' "The Garden of the Forking Paths"
Ts'ui Pen, the narrator's father, isolated himself in the Pavilion
of Limpid Solitude, in the center of a garden, most intricately
laid out, like a labyrinth, to write a book that was confused
and indistinguishable from that labyrinth. The book-labyrinth
is infinite, as it is cyclical and its last page is identical with the
first. Ts'ui Pen's book contained contradictory chapters and in
the mire of its perplexities left several possible forking paths.

THE ADDRESSEE: JOSEPH BEN JUDAH IBN SIMON

Maimonides began his celebrated masterpiece, *The Guide of the Perplexed*, around 1185, when he was about forty-seven, and completed it around 1191, when he was about fifty-three. This is the third of his trilogy of masterworks, beginning with the *Commentary on the Mishnah* and the *Mishneh Torah*. He wrote *The Guide of the Perplexed* in Judeo-Arabic, and it was translated in his lifetime into Hebrew by Samuel Ibn Tibbon and by Judah al-Harizi, and thereafter into Latin and other European languages.

When his pupil Joseph ben Judah departed for Aleppo (ca. 1184–85), Maimonides could no longer teach him face-to-face, so he continued to instruct Joseph by sending chapters of *The Guide of the Perplexed* as an extended epistle. He wrote the treatise for Joseph and "for those like him however few they may be."[1] Maimonides addressed the reader as "you," meaning in the first instance Joseph, but in effect every reader of the treatise. By making Joseph the formal addressee, Maimonides signaled who his target audience was—intellectuals learned in the law and initiated into the arcana of philosophy and science who were perplexed by Scripture's contradictions of reason.

Joseph ben Judah had emigrated from Morocco to Alexandria (ca. 1182–84) and sent letters and *maqama*s from there to Maimonides, who appreciated his intense desire for study and great longing for theoretical matters.[2]

A *maqama* was an extended literary creation combining ornate rhymed and rhythmic prose (*saj'*) interlaced with verse.[3] It usually depicted two fictional characters, a narrator and a protagonist or hero, whose escapades the narrator portrayed. The narrator was a naive, bourgeois type of fellow, whereas the protagonist was usually a bohemian roguish vagabond and adventurer. Ahmad Badi' al-Zaman al-Hamdhani (968–1008) created the genre of *maqamat*, or *séances*. Abu Muhammad al-Hariri (1054–1122) imitated the *maqamat* of al-Hamadhani. The genre found a home in Andalusia, where the Hebrew *maqama* (*mahberet*) imitated its Arabic model.[4]

Maimonides at first suspected that perhaps Joseph's craving for learning exceeded his ability. However, when he studied the science of astronomy and the mathematical sciences with him, his joy increased as he encountered Joseph's fine mind and quick grasp. He saw that Joseph craved mathematical sciences and let him study on his own.

Later, when Joseph studied the art of logic with him, he realized that Joseph was worthy of having the secrets of the prophetic books revealed to him, that he might comprehend what the perfect should understand.[5] Maimonides taught by hints and allusions. Joseph requested that he explain metaphysical topics and tell him about the intentions of the *mutakallimun* and whether their methods were demonstrative.[6]

Maimonides could not help noticing that Joseph had already picked up a smattering of metaphysics and theology with some other teacher. As a result, Joseph was perplexed, his noble soul demanding of him "to discover useful sayings" (Eccl 12:10).[7] But Maimonides discouraged him from plunging into metaphysics and theology, directing him to study systematically, so that he might attain the truth by a proper method, not by serendipity. While he remained with the Master, whenever a biblical verse or text of the sages came up that signaled some wonderful matter, Maimonides explained it to him.[8] This was Maimonides' method in *The Guide of the Perplexed*, where he explained verses as intimating philosophic truths. During this period of study, Joseph appears to have been living in Maimonides' household, as close pupils did.

The direct encounter of teacher and pupil was interrupted by a physical separation. Joseph left for Aleppo, something Maimonides says God decreed.[9] Since this is the first mention of God in *The Guide of the Perplexed*, the assertion should not be dismissed as a mere *façon de parler*.[10] His meetings with Joseph, Maimonides said, aroused in him an earlier resolution to write on these subjects. Now Joseph's absence was a further incentive.

He told Joseph that the chapters would reach him gradually wherever he was.[11] Maimonides first wrote the book in a draft copy but did not publicize any part of it until he finished and corrected at least that part after rereading. Some pages of early drafts have been found in the Genizah.

We get an inkling of the way the *Guide* was sent from a letter that Maimonides wrote to Joseph.[12]

> I have sent you six quires of *The Guide of the Perplexed*, which I have taken from someone else, that are the end of the First Part.[13] I am uncertain whether I sent you the Introduction [*sadr*], which I am appending to them, hence I am sending it to you now.[14] The ones who copied them were none other than the *pious judge* and Abu 'l-Mahasin.[15] Be chary with them and do not lose them lest I come to harm at the hands of the *gentiles*.[16] *For the wicked among Israel are many.*[17]

In a subsequent letter, Moses mentioned chapters of *The Guide of the Perplexed* concerning divine providence that will reach Joseph. "Perhaps when the chapters of *The Guide of the Perplexed* that consider this matter reach you this principle will become clear to you, with the help of God (the exalted)."[18]

Along with this letter in Judeo-Arabic (Epistle Dedicatory), which is printed in editions of *The Guide of the Perplexed*, Maimonides sent a Hebrew letter to Joseph, beginning, "Concerning the son who was given to us[19] when there is none to restore the soul."[20] The letters were written at the same time and both said that *The Guide of the Perplexed* was composed for Joseph and for those like him. The preamble states that Maimonides sent the letter to Joseph along with *The Guide of the Perplexed*.

The Hebrew letter is a splendid mosaic of verses woven into rhymed prose, written in the florid style of the period. Moses wrote that he was sending a gift of his wondrous love to Joseph on the wings of morning stars and gazelles. He then compared Joseph to a pleasant sapling, an apple tree, and a noble vine. Joseph was like a son at a time when he had no one to restore his soul. When the light of Israel was extinguished in the West, Joseph gave light from Aleppo. Maimonides reaffirmed his love for Joseph and said that he thought of him always. He wrote, "I am Moses, and your lovely mouth attracts me, and has aroused me to love you."

Maimonides praised the linguistic beauty and contents of Joseph's prior letter, which aroused the admiration of his colleagues in Egypt, who considered it "words of a vision." He mentioned Joseph's study of logic, mathematics, and astronomy, with detailed references to astronomy, and we gather that it was a major preoccupation of both.

The Master advised his pupil to imitate the ways of the sages and saints of the time.[21] Intuitive knowledge, which is like prophecy, is the ultimate goal after obeying the law. Maimonides encouraged Joseph to pursue secular and religious studies, but to dedicate his best time to the law of Moses.

In the verse superscription to the Introduction, Maimonides hinted that the *Guide* was directed to the elite and the common people.[22] For in the verse *Unto you, O men, I call, and my voice is to the sons of men* (Prov. 8:4), the word *men* refers to the elite and the words *sons of men* refer to the common people.[23] Maimonides said that the treatise's purpose was not to make its *totality* understandable to the unlettered, beginners in speculation, or those engaged solely in the law.[24] He wrote, "I know that, among men generally, every beginner will derive benefit from some of the chapters of this Treatise, though he lacks even an inkling of what is involved in speculation." He addressed both the elite and the general public by employing multiple levels of meaning.[25]

The lexicographic chapters in Part I appear especially suited for the common folk. He promised instruction to all concerning the words of the wise, hinting that he would add to their words, that he intended to revise traditional wisdom.

Joseph had studied the propaideutic sciences, especially astronomy and logic, but he was not initiated into the study of physics or metaphysics. His rank was that of those who, having studied mathematics and logic, are among those walking around the palace searching for its gate.[26]

Maimonides viewed the addressee of *The Guide of the Perplexed* as a potential philosopher, a young man who desired to know, who had the capacity to develop if brought gradually and systematically along the way of enlightenment.[27]

IBN AL-QIFTI AND JOSEPH BEN JUDAH

Who was Maimonides' beloved disciple Joseph ben Judah Ibn Simon?[28] Our best source is the Muslim historian, the reliable Ibn al-Qifti, who was his friend in Aleppo.[29] Ibn al-Qifti gave a biographical entry to the man he called Yusuf ibn Yahya ibn Ishaq al-Sabti al-Maghribi Abu 'l-Hajjaj, resident of Aleppo.[30] According to Ibn al-Qifti, Joseph was known in his hometown of Ceuta, Morocco, as Ibn Sam'un (Simon), Sam'un being his ancestor, who had been a physician at Fez. Joseph's father traded in the marketplace, whereas Joseph, according to his friend, excelled in philosophy and the mathematical sciences. He suffered during the Almohad period and, like Maimonides, had to live a double life. Ibn al-Qifti wrote:

> During the Almohad period, [Joseph] concealed his faith and tried to emigrate to Egypt, which he did. There, he joined Musa ibn Maymun the Córdoban, the Head of the Jews [Ra'is al-Yahud] in Egypt. Joseph studied with him and resided with him for some time.[31] He asked Maimonides to revise the astronomy of Ibn Aflah al-Andalusi, which

he had brought with him from Ceuta. He and Moses revised and edited it.

Joseph then left Egypt for Syria and settled in Aleppo, where he resided for some time. He married the daughter of an Aleppan Jew named Abu 'l-'Ala'. He traveled as a merchant from Aleppo to Iraq and visited India, returning in good health.[32] Having become wealthy, he gave up traveling, took up local commerce, and purchased property.

People came to study with him, and he taught a group of Aleppo residents and visitors. He served among the select physicians for the Zahirid dynasty in Aleppo.[33]

Ibn al-Qifti added that Joseph and he had a long-standing friendship, about which he told some lively anecdotes.

IBN ABI USAYBI'A ON JOSEPH BEN JUDAH

Ibn Abi Usaybi'a, the historian of physicians, added some details to Ibn al-Qifti's account in his entry for Abu 'l Hajjaj Yusuf al-Isra'ili.[34] He said that Joseph excelled in the art of medicine, geometry, and astronomy and that he studied medicine in Egypt with al-Ra'is Musa ibn Maymun al-Qurtubi.[35] Aside from King al-Zahir Ghazi, who depended upon Joseph ben Judah in medicine, he also served Amir Faris al-Din Maymun al-Qasri.[36] Ibn Abi Usaybi'a ascribed two books to Joseph, one on diet and the second a commentary on the Aphorisms of Hippocrates.

JUDAH BEN SOLOMON AL-HARIZI

Aside from Ibn al-Qifti and Ibn Abi Usaybi'a, our best source of information on Joseph ben Judah was Judah ben Solomon al-Harizi (1165–1225), a poet and translator who was born in Spain, traveled extensively in southern France, Egypt, Palestine, Syria, and Mesopotamia, and disseminated Andalusian-Hebrew culture.[37] Both he and Joseph ben Judah came from the Maghrib and both were followers of Maimonides, though we have no record of al-Harizi studying with the Master or knowing him personally.

Permit me an extra word on al-Harizi, as he was vital in the transmission of the Master's works. He translated Maimonides' *The Guide of the Perplexed* into biblical Hebrew. His translation, however, was not as reliable as the earlier version by Samuel Ibn Tibbon.[38] Still, it was by means of it that Maimonides reached the Christian world. An anonymous Latin translation of *The Guide of the Perplexed*, published in Paris by Agostino Giustiniani in 1520, was based on Al-Harizi's translation, as was Pedro de Toledo's Spanish rendition. Al-Harizi also translated into Hebrew Maimonides' Introduction to the Mishnah and his commentary on the first five tractates of the Mishnah order Zera'im. He translated the *Treatise on Resurrection*,[39] accompanying it with a poem in praise of Maimonides, which he sent to Jonathan of Lunel.[40]

Al-Harizi met Joseph ben Judah in Aleppo, where he found him "in all his glory." He described Joseph as a great poet, a famous physician, a sage and communal leader, and a generous patron. He praised Joseph's vast wisdom, intellect, and eloquence, and called him a prophet. Al-Harizi assessed that among poets in the Maghrib only "the great sage" Joseph ben Judah was outstanding, singling out for special praise his *Speech of Toviyah ben Zidkiyya*, the *maqama* that Joseph ben Judah first sent to Maimonides.[41]

ALLEGORICAL LETTERS BETWEEN MAIMONIDES AND JOSEPH

Maimonides and Joseph ben Judah remained in touch by correspondence, in the course of which they had a sharp disagreement about Joseph's privileged status as addressee and recipient of *The Guide of the Perplexed*.

Joseph complained in an allegorical letter to Maimonides from Aleppo that he had legally married Maimonides' daughter Pleiades[42] but that his bride was faithless even in the bridal chamber.[43] "All of this was before two firm witness friends, Ibn 'Ubaydallah and Ibn Rushd. While still in the bridal chamber she was unfaithful to me and turned to other lovers,"[44] without her father protesting, and perhaps with his encouragement. Joseph demanded that his wife be returned to him, "for he [Joseph] is a prophet or will become one."

Moses replied with his own allegorical letter in rhymed prose, denying the allegation with witty biblical allusions, ridiculing Joseph and his claim to prophecy. Maimonides said that the allegation was false and based on envy. He called Joseph *kesil*, meaning both "Orion" and "fool."[45] As for Ibn Rushd, Joseph wrote "contrary to the law,[46] summoning a mixed kind of witness."[47] Maimonides' wit was caustic: "She [*The Guide of the Perplexed*] was reared to be steady / in the [heavenly] sphere[48] / *and he took her for a harlot, / for she had covered her face*" (Gen 38:15).[49]

Salomon Munk suggested that the bride in the allegory represented Maimonides' teaching.[50] However, D. H. Baneth gave a more persuasive interpretation, identifying the daughter as *The Guide of the Perplexed* itself.[51] Maimonides had copies of it made but delayed sending them to Joseph, who portrayed this as the daughter's betrayal in the bridal chamber. Others enjoyed her before he did. Ibn 'Ubaydallah (= Maimonides) in Joseph's letter evidently symbolized Torah, and Ibn Rushd represented philosophy, the two facets of *The Guide of the Perplexed*. Maimonides' reference to her covering her face is an allusion to the outer exoteric veil of the text masking an inner esoteric meaning. You may be shocked by Maimonides' crude metaphor and desacrilizing use of the Hebrew Bible, but this was an era when sexual repartee and piety coexisted in perfect harmony.

AIM OF *THE GUIDE OF THE PERPLEXED*

The first purpose of *The Guide of the Perplexed*, Maimonides explained, is to instruct a religious person, who believes in the law and has studied philosophy and is perplexed by the contradictions between the two.[52] He is in a dilemma whether he should follow his reason and renounce the literal sense of the biblical text, thereby abandoning the law, in his view, or take biblical terms literally and discard his reason. If so, he harms himself and his religious faith, for he remains with imaginary beliefs that cause his fear and difficulty and he would go on suffering heartache and great perplexity.

For these people and others, Maimonides wanted to make the law respectable to philosophy and make philosophy compatible with the law. This dual endeavor required showing the true meaning of the law and the true nature of philosophy.

The second purpose of *The Guide of the Perplexed* (related to the first) is to explain obscure parables that occur in biblical books. An ignorant or superficial reader thinks that they have only an external meaning. Even an educated person, who interprets them according to their literal meaning, is overwhelmed by perplexity. Only if these parables are explained to him can he take the right road and avoid this perplexity.

The aim of *The Guide of the Perplexed* is to enlighten a religious individual who believes in the truth of the law, who fulfils his or her moral and religious duties, and succeeds in philosophic studies. Human reason has attracted the individual to abide within its realm, and he or she finds it difficult to accept the literal interpretation of the law. It is for this reason, Maimonides said, that he called his treatise *The Guide of the Perplexed*. As in the *Mishneh Torah*, Maimonides presented himself in the first person as the man of destiny to carry out the task.

> To sum up: I am the man who when the concern pressed him and his way was straitened and he could find no other device by which to teach a demonstrated truth other than by giving satisfaction to a single virtuous man while displeasing ten thousand ignoramuses— I am he who prefers to address that single man by himself, and I do not heed the blame of those many creatures. For I claim to liberate that virtuous one from that into which he has sunk, and I shall guide him in his perplexity until he becomes perfect and finds rest.[53]

An aim of *The Guide of the Perplexed* is to give peace and tranquility to body and soul through enlightenment. "And when these gates are opened and these places are entered, the souls will find rest therein, the eyes will be delighted, and the bodies will be eased of their toil and of their labor."[54] Note the often-overlooked reference to *bodies* being eased of their toil and labor.

Maimonides wanted to move the individual away from imaginary beliefs that cause fear and toward a rational awareness that brings equanimity. The reward is not merely intellectual relief but an existential transformation and inner spiritual conversion. He sought to move the individual to a deeper appreciation of religion that was in harmony with reason and brings equanimity.

The Guide of the Perplexed begins with a poem by the author:

> *My knowledge goes forth to point out the way,*
> *to pave straight its road.*
> *Lo, everyone who goes astray in the field of Torah,*
> *Come and follow its path.*
> *The unclean and the fool shall not pass over it;*
> *It shall be called the Sacred Way.*[55]

The poem is about paving a straight road, following pathmarks, and passing over the Sacred Way.[56] Pierre Hadot, the French historian of philosophy, showed that in late antiquity philosophy was viewed as a way of life, a life focused on the pursuit of wisdom, and the philosopher as a wise man engaged in dialogue with students and colleagues. This kind of philosophy, which is not merely intellectual but transformative of life, leading to a life of wisdom, is rooted in the writings of Plato, Aristotle, and the Stoics.

The life Maimonides is exhorting the reader to follow is not merely a way of life, it is the *Sacred* Way.

The poem has twenty-six words, 26 being the *gematria*[57] of the tetragrammaton, the ineffable name of God (YHWH), as Y = 10, H = 5, W = 6, H = 5, and hence 10 + 5 + 6 + 5 = 26.[58]

The *Guide* also ends with a poem by the author.[59]

> *God is very near to everyone who calls,*
> *If he calls truly and has no distractions;*
> *He is found by every seeker who searches for him,*
> *If he marches toward him and goes not astray.*

The very last word of the poem, and hence of *The Guide of the Perplexed,* is *yit'eh* ("go astray"), which occurred in the first poem, "everyone who goes astray" and echoes the end of the Isaiah verse on the straight way: *No traveler, not even fools, shall go astray* (Isa 35:8).

The *Guide* is a *dalala*, a pointing, guidance, indication, pathmarker for the *ha'irun*, those who are disconcerted, perplexed, confused, straying, and astray.[60] It shows the path, the Sacred Way, to those who search for God if they march toward him and do not go astray.[61]

The words *ḥayra* and *taḥayyur* often render Greek *aporia* (*aporein*).[62] An *aporia* is an impasse, literally meaning that "no passage" (*poros*) has been found to the solution of a puzzle.[63] The word *ḥayra* has to do with being dazzled and unable to see one's way, to lose one's course, go astray, wander about lost in the desert, confused and dismayed. The implied reader, then, is a person who has come to an impasse and needs to be shown the way. The impasse is cognitive and existential, affecting mind and body.

Maimonides defined perplexity when he described the primary purpose of his treatise.[64] He depicted the main dilemma between philosophy and the law and mentioned the possibility that the person may remain with "imaginary beliefs that cause his *fear and trouble* and continues *suffering heartache* and *great perplexity*."

The *Guide* carries forward the psychagogical (the art of leading souls) character of Socrates' speeches, aimed at the spiritual edification of interlocutors, the fundamental question being "How should we live?" The philosopher is a compassionate physician, whose skill heals human suffering and whose foremost concern is "care of the soul" (Apology, 29d–30b). Socrates announced to the Athenians that their eagerness to have wealth, reputation, and honors must never be preferred over wisdom, truth, and care of the soul.[65]

Philosophy as therapy treats not only cognitive questions but also irrational fears and anxieties. The wise are "physicians of the soul," and care of self in the widest sense includes diet, physical exercise, training in the virtues, and rational enlightenment.

Maimonides followed Plato's *Phaedrus* in privileging the oral over the written word, the purpose being "to produce a certain psychological effect in the reader or listener."[66] Ancient philosophy sought "to form more than to inform," "to form people and to transform souls." Philosophers taught orally, because only "the living word, in dialogues" can accomplish this.

As Socrates taught that knowledge was not a set of propositions, but a way of being, conveyed through dialogue, so the *Guide* leads the reader along the Sacred Way, transforming every aspect of a reader's being—intellect, imagination, emotion, and will. It offers the counsel of Rilke's poem "Archaic Torso of Apollo": "You must change your life."[67] The *Guide* is not merely an exposition of ideas, a theological discourse; it is a spiritual journey through an intricate labyrinth to a clearing in the forest, pierced by the sun's dappled rays.

STYLE OF *THE GUIDE OF THE PERPLEXED*

We need to examine the *Guide*'s form of discourse and the parameters of genre and audience that influenced its creation. Maimonides did not call it a book (*kitab*) or an epistolary essay (*risala*), but a *maqala*, which means "statement" or "utterance," having the root sense of speech.[68] *The Guide of the Perplexed* is recorded speech, the style intimate and conversational.

The second purpose of *The Guide of the Perplexed,* Maimonides said, is to explain obscure parables in Scripture and point out that they are parables, thereby delivering the educated reader from perplexity.[69] However, Maimonides could not explain the meaning of the parables exhaustively, not even when he taught orally, and certainly not in writing that is public and would be a target for the uninformed, who, supposing they have knowledge, would only denigrate it.

Maimonides encapsulated his truth in two of the great mysteries of *The Guide of the Perplexed*—Ma'aseh Bereshit (Account of the Beginning) and Ma'aseh Merkavah (Account of the Chariot). He explained that the Account of the Beginning is natural science and the Account of the Chariot is divine science, or metaphysics.[70]

The Mishnah relates the Account of the Chariot with speculations concerning the Throne of Glory and the chariot bearing it (Ezekiel, 1).[71] The term *merkavah* is from 1 Chron 28:18 and has this sense in Ben Sira 49:8: *Ezekiel saw a vision, and described the different orders of the chariot.*

In the Talmud and Midrash, Merkavah mysticism was a sacred and potentially dangerous esoteric tradition that could not be taught in public. The famous Tannaim Rabbis Johanan ben Zakkai, Aqiba, and Ishmael engaged in this type of speculation.[72] The sages said that Merkavah mysticism was a great subject in comparison with legal casuistry, which was a small subject, a view that Maimonides espoused.[73]

Mystical speculation on the divine chariot and throne is found in the Dead Sea Scrolls and related texts, such as the Book of Enoch, as well as in early Gnostic writings. The Hekhalot literature belongs to this genre, and the *Shi'ur qomah* (Measurement of God's Body) was related to it in an early period.[74] Jewish converts brought Merkavah mysticism to Christian Gnostics—Ophites and Valentinus, and some Coptic texts discovered at Nag Hammadi, among others.

The Cairo Genizah contains some early Merkavah and Hekhalot treatises. These texts sought to preserve a mystical reminiscence of the temple by means of heavenly shrines. Ezekiel's vision of the Chariot converted the terrestrial temple into a celestial shrine, transforming terrestrial cultic motifs into celestial visions.[75]

Merkavah mysticism developed a doctrine of seven heavens and angelic hosts. This motif enabled Maimonides to identify Merkavah speculation with an Aristotelian-Ptolemaic cosmology having heavenly spheres and sphere movers (intelligences = angels).[76] He interpreted rabbinic myths, speculations, and visions of the Chariot in a philosophic mode, consistently giving a philosophic interpretation of mythology. For instance, he replaced a mystical interpretation of the myth of God's garment of light with a philosophic understanding.

In his Introduction to *The Guide of the Perplexed*, Part III, Maimonides said that he was going to write down his interpretation of the Chariot to save knowledge from perishing. He was, he stated, following his own conjecture and supposition, and he had received no divine revelation, nor did he learn what he believed in these matters from a teacher. He had no tradition and was, in his estimation, the first. Transforming rabbinic myth into secular science was revolutionary.

The Account of the Beginning should not be taught even to one man unless he is wise and able to understand on his own, and then he is taught only chapter headings.[77] Yet whoever elucidates these matters in a book instructs thousands of men. Scripture veiled these subjects in parables and the sages wrapped them in riddles and parables, for natural science (the Account of the Beginning) is close to metaphysics (the Account of the Chariot).

Hence the recipient of the *Guide* should not expect anything beyond chapter headings, and these are imparted in a disjointed way among other subjects.[78] The message of the *Guide* is dispersed throughout its chapters, so that the reader must pick up hints and join them to form a coherent meaning, as one strings pearls together to create a necklace. The *Guide* imitates the perfection of nature, where superficial chaos hides harmony and order. Maimonides gave keys for unlocking its secrets throughout the text, signaling when a fragment was to be found in the subtext. The writer claims authorial control and writes by "the law of logographic necessity"—nothing in the text occurs by chance.[79]

These great secrets are not fully known to any human being. Maimonides used the image of lightning to depict the different stages of access to the truth.[80] Sometimes the truth flashes as bright as day; then our matter and habit obscure it as though it were night. We are like someone in a very dark night over whom lightning flashes time and again. (1) There is one for whom lightning flashes time after time so that he is in perpetual light, such as Moses. (2) There are some to whom the lightning flashes once in their entire night, as those who prophesied one time (Num 11:25). (3) There are others whose lightning flashes are at greater or shorter time intervals. (4) Some do not attain illumination by any lightning flash; their darkness is illumined by a polished body or the like, which lights the night's darkness in flashes and then is hidden. The degrees of those who seek perfection vary in accordance with these states. (5) Then there are persons who never see a light and grope about in darkness.

The teacher who understands these secrets makes the topics appear in flashes and then be concealed. Hence the metaphysician who knows the truth uses parables and riddles.[81] Every metaphysician who desired to teach without using parables and riddles had to make his exposition obscure and brief so that obscurity and brevity replaced parables and riddles. He alluded here, I propose, to a text that describes an exchange between Plato and Aristotle, in which Plato accused Aristotle of revealing philosophic secrets, and Aristotle replied that he substituted obscurity and brevity for Plato's parables and riddles.[82]

Al-Farabi demonstrated, following a late Hellenistic motif, that the different literary styles of Plato and Aristotle perform the same rhetorical function of concealment. Plato refrained from inscribing the sciences in books, favoring pure hearts and congenial minds. When he was old and afraid of forgetting, he wrote things down, but used symbols (*rumuz*) and enigmas (*alghaz*), so that only the deserving would understand.[83] Aristotle, however, communicated in writing by elucidation and exhaustive discussion, thereby making philosophy accessible. When Plato objected, it was explained that Aristotle's style was nevertheless abstruse, obscure, and complicated regardless of the superficial clarity.

Maimonides combined the method of Plato with the method of Aristotle. He used allegories, as did Plato, and he wrote in an abstruse style, as did Aristotle. By dispersing his message throughout the *Guide*'s chapters and repeating certain things with minor changes, as Scripture did, he could shade meanings and invite subtle interpretation.

The Guide of the Perplexed, as we have seen, was addressed to someone who had already studied philosophy and the sciences and believed in the law but was perplexed about its meaning because of obscure terms and parables.[84] The key to Scripture unlocks the meaning of figurative language and parables. As only philosophers can discern the deeper meaning, they are the privileged interpreters of Scripture. Maimonides made reason the criterion of exegesis and the philosopher the supreme exegete. The enlightened intellectuals, not the rabbinic sages, become the chief arbiters of the meaning of Scripture.[85]

Scripture has two levels of meaning, a deep meaning and a surface meaning. A saying that conveys two meanings is like an apple of gold overlaid with silver filigree, with tiny holes through which the gold is visible. Biblical parables have an external meaning useful for human welfare and an internal meaning pertaining to the truth. Here Maimonides employed a vivid parable to explain parables.[86]

SEMANTIC EQUIVALENCE

Maimonides used a technique of semantic equivalence to convey esoteric messages.[87] For instance, once he has made the equation "the divine actions, I mean to say the natural actions," we may anticipate that when he calls something "divine" it may be natural.[88] Natural things are called "the work of God," as in the verse *They have seen the work of God* (Ps 107:24), so the expression *the tablets were the work of God* (Exod 32:16) signifies that they were natural and not artificial. When Maimonides refers to nature in this way, he means nature as an active, creative force, not nature as the natural world we perceive. Spinoza expressed the difference as between *natura naturans* and *natura* naturata,[89] defining "the universal laws of nature" as "nothing but God's decrees."[90] Elsewhere, when Spinoza mentioned God's decrees, he assumed that the reader would understand that God's decrees/laws/precepts are the same as the eternal laws of nature. Although Spinoza disagreed with Maimonides' biblical exegesis, he evidently learned the technique of metaphorical equivalence from Maimonides.

We need to be attentive to the equivalences Maimonides used, some quite covertly:

Religion	Philosophy
account of chariot	metaphysics
account of creation	physics
God	first mover
divine will	divine wisdom
acts of God and angels	acts of nature
divine determination	natural/contingent events
created light/glory/*shekhinah*	divine presence
angels	intelligences of spheres
angel, holy spirit	Agent Intellect
divine inspiration	uniting with Agent Intellect
good rewarded evil punished	guidance by intellect
prophet (Moses)	philosopher-king
creation from nothing	eternal emanation

There are other ways of conveying esoteric messages; for example, use of contradictions (between a conventional, traditional belief and a philosophic version of that belief). Whenever we find a contradiction between a traditional belief, often framed in the name of "we," as opposed to a philosophic account, which is based on demonstrative arguments, we ought to infer that the philosophic account is the doctrine and the traditional account the public teaching.

The *Guide* is an encoded text, containing hints and deliberate contradictions, drawing the reader into an amazing labyrinth, a dark forest. But there are paths marked out and clearings. On a deep level the reader enters into a dialogue with the author, and the author is a partner lending a hand to the reader and leading him or her along the way.[91]

This exoteric-esoteric binarity was not simply a hermeneutic mode for interpreting Scripture but a way of writing and a total *mentalité,* a way of observing the world and of constructing it.[92] Sufis visualized the entire cosmos as an array of symbols, similar to the verbal symbols of revelation, requiring hermeneutic exposition. Some people can comprehend the deep meaning of these cosmic symbols by unveiling mysteries (*kashf, mukashafa*), while others sense only superficial meaning. The cosmos cascades with signs and meanings, with numerical and verbal symbols and divine names. Everything in the world is a figure and a sign of an inner reality, a speculum of God.

Maimonides was trying to hide philosophic truths not merely from his religious community but from the eyes of the entire public, including Christians and Muslims. Many of his views were too sensitive to insert into the public domain, and therefore he did not wish his treatise to be transcribed from Hebrew into Arabic characters.[93] The most sensitive topics were creation, prophecy, and providence.

He was apprehensive about writing these things in a public treatise. "They are concealed things that have never been written in a book in the Jewish community in these times of Exile."[94] He relied on two rabbinic sayings: *It is time to act for the Lord, [for they have violated Your teaching]*[95] and *Let all thy acts be for the sake of heaven.*[96]

CONTENTS OF *THE GUIDE OF THE PERPLEXED*

These are the thematic topics of *The Guide of the Perplexed*:

- Biblical language and hermeneutics

- Divine attributes

- Creation versus eternity

- Prophecy

- Providence

- Commandments

- Human perfection

Biblical Language and Hermeneutics

The first purpose of *The Guide of the Perplexed* is to explain the meanings of multivalent terms in prophetic books, which are understood by the uninformed in only one of their possible senses. The first purpose is therefore exegetical and lexicographic.[97]

Scripture uses human terms in speaking of God and depicts him as seeing, descending and ascending, sitting, rising, standing, approaching, filling, passing, coming and going, dwelling, and being sorrowful or angry. The prephilosophical folk take these terms literally, but those who follow reason find these expressions perplexing.

The Guide of the Perplexed is, to a great extent, a commentary on biblical terminology. The chapters in Part I, with few exceptions, treat biblical terms. This concern goes on in the rest of the treatise, as Part II has two chapters (6 and 7) on the term for "angel" and *Guide*, II, 41 discusses "vision."[98] The treatise culminates with two lexicographic chapters on the meaning of "loving-kindness," "judgment," "righteousness" (III, 53), and "wisdom" (III, 54).

After Part I, Maimonides discusses creation, prophecy, and providence, never averting his eye from biblical exegesis. He gives extended interpretations of Gen 1–4 (*Guide*, II, 30), Exod 23:20 (II, 34), Ezek 1 (III, 1–7), the book of Job (III, 22–23), and Abraham's trial in Genesis 22 (III, 24). Although Maimonides' explanations of lexemes follows Andalusian lexicography and Aramaic translations of Scripture, the method of linguistic analysis is strongly Aristotelian. He classifies biblical expressions as (1) equivocal (homonyms), (2) metaphorical, and (3) sometimes equivocal and sometimes univocal, or amphibolous.[99]

Part I, 1–45 concern lexicographic questions, specifically equivocal terms that occur in Scripture, with digressions on related matters. We need to attend to every word of the discussion, even if it does not belong to the main subject of the chapter. When we go through these chapters, we discern certain interwoven motifs that constitute a coherent subtext.

The method of Onqelos for demythologizing gave Maimonides a rabbinic precedent and legitimacy for his project. In Maimonides' campaign against literal readings of Scripture and belief in God's corporeality, Onqelos was a powerful ally. His fondness for Onqelos must have begun in childhood, when he first studied him and thought about biblical language. He praised Onqelos for his knowledge of Hebrew and Aramaic and his rational theology.[100] Maimonides regarded Onqelos as an authority on the law and scriptural interpretation.[101] He cited Onqelos twenty-four times in *The Guide of the Perplexed*, more than any other author except Aristotle.[102] He considered Onqelos a talmudic sage, as he studied with Rabbi Eliezer ben Hyrqanos and Rabbi Joshua ben Hananyah, "who are the Sages of Israel par excellence."[103]

When necessary, instead of the name of God, Onqelos substituted epithets, such as *memra* (Word), *shekhinta* (Indwelling), and *yeqara* (Glory).[104] A good example is his translation of the verse *And the Lord passed before [Moses'] face* (Exod 34:6) as *The Lord caused his Indwelling [shekhinta] to pass before [Moses'] face.*[105] *Shekhinah* (Heb) is from biblical texts that depict God as dwelling (*shakhan*) among the Israelites in the Tabernacle,[106] in Jerusalem,[107] or Mount Zion and the Temple, the bush[108] or Mount Sinai, where God's Glory dwelled.[109]

The terms "Word," "Indwelling," and "Glory," which Onqelos used to signify the divine presence, were essential to Maimonides' understanding of prophecy and providence. He described them as "created light" and as intermediary between God and the world.[110] The "created light" had been used by Se'adyah Gaon, and it merged with illuminationist mysticism that was current in Maimonides' era, especially in the works of Shihab al-Din al-Suhrawardi.[111]

MEANING OF IMAGE OF GOD

The discussion of image (*selem*) and likeness (*demut*) clarifies the meaning of *Let us make man in our image, after our likeness* (Gen 1:26).[112] Maimonides began by citing what people have thought—*selem* in Hebrew is something with shape and configuration, hence God has human form and corporeality (*tajsim*).

People believe that God is the same as they, only greater and more splendid and not of flesh and blood. The term in Hebrew for shape and configuration, well known to the common people, is *to'ar*, as *beautiful of form* (*to'ar*) in Gen 39:6. But image (*selem*) denotes *the natural form,* what comprises the essence and true reality of the thing. In man, his natural form is what gives him intellectual apprehension. Maimonides concluded that it was owing to the divine intellect in human beings that they are said to be created *in the image of God and in his likeness,* not that God is corporeal and has a shape. Human beings are the only creatures in the cosmos who share a quality with God, namely, reason. Humanity is like God in this most important sense.

BE LIKE ELOHIM

Chapter 2 is concerned with *Elohim* as an equivocal term, meaning "the deity, the angels, and the rulers governing cities." Onqelos the Proselyte explained that the verse *And you shall be as Elohim, knowing good and evil* (Gen 3:5) means the rulers of cities.[113] An objection had been raised by "a learned man"[114] that when Adam disobeyed and ate the fruit, he was not punished as God had promised but *rewarded* by a capacity to distinguish between good and evil. Maimonides replied that the intellect that God gave man, his ultimate perfection, because of which it was said that he was created in the image of God, is the intellect that distinguishes between true and false.

Adam in the Garden of Eden was unable to consider conventional opinions, so he did not regard uncovering the genitals as immoral. Only after his disobedience, when he yielded to desires of the imagination and gratification of his senses—as is said, *The tree was good for food and it was a delight to the eyes* (Gen 3:6)—was he punished by the loss of intellectual apprehension.

Human law and morality, apart from revelation, in Maimonides' view, are based upon convention. Maimonides maintained in *Guide,* I, 2, that moral judgments of noble and base belong to things generally accepted (*mashhurat = endoxa*).[115] He subsumed generally accepted things, as uncovering the genitals is base (*qabih*) and compensating a benefactor is good (*jamil*), under the kinds of propositions that are self-evident and require no proof (*dalil*) for their validity.[116]

Likewise, Spinoza claimed that "if men were born free, that is, guided only by reason, they would form no conception of good and evil."[117] Maimonides and Spinoza held that the knowledge of good and evil is conventional, that it depends on the consensus of society, whereas knowledge of true and false is understanding of what is necessary. Maimonides maintained that "with regard to what is of necessity, there is no good or evil at all, but only the false and the true."[118]

Spinoza said that, "It is not in the nature of reason to regard things as contingent, but as necessary."[119]

Although Spinoza objected to Maimonides's philosophic interpretations of Scripture, he accepted this distinction between awareness of good and evil and knowledge of true and false.[120]

GOD'S INDWELLING

Several times in the lexicographic chapters (*Guide*, I, 1–70) Maimonides used the term *shekhinah* (Indwelling)[121] and the Arabic equivalent, *sakina*.[122] In the lexicographical chapters, he was only concerned with biblical vocabulary, yet *shekhinah* does not occur in Scripture, which rather uses *kavod* as the "glory" of God in the Ark (Exod 40: 34–35).

Shekhinah, being grammatically feminine, was often (yet not always) pictured in Midrash as the feminine manifestation of God. She is exiled from the Sanctuary and weeps for God and yearns for him. In Proverbs and elsewhere, wisdom, or *hokhmah*, *sophia* in Greek, is God's consort. The idea is then taken up in the Kabbalah, where the Shekhinah is the feminine aspect of the divine. For the coming down of the Indwelling, Maimonides had recourse to an Arabic theological term, *nazala*, used in the Qur'an for coming down by revelation. Se'adyah used *nazala* and other forms of the word in the same sense in his Arabic *tafsir* (translation) of Scripture.[123] Maimonides understood biblical "to pass" (*'avor*) as used figuratively for descent of the light and the Indwelling (*sakina*) seen by the prophets in their visions of prophecy.[124]

Maimonides used God's Indwelling as semantically equivalent to his providence (in I, 25, p. 55). "The verb *shakhon* is applied figuratively to the permanence of the deity's Indwelling or his providence in whatever place it subsists or toward whatever matter providence is permanently guided." As *The Guide of the Perplexed* progresses, providence replaces *shekhinah* and governance then replaces providence.[125]

We need to be alert when Maimonides substitutes one term for another. God's Indwelling is his "created light."[126] The created light, God's Indwelling or Presence, and providence are semantically equivalent.[127] Maimonides permitted an individual of insufficient capacity, who does not try to reach a high intellectual rank, to consider the words as indicating sensual perception of created lights, whether angels or something else.

Divine Wrath

The lexicographical chapters weave back and forth on the theme of divine presence and absence. Discussing the verb "going out" (*al-yesi'ah*) with respect to God, Maimonides went on to the term "returning" (*shivah*), meaning the terminating of an act willfully, as *I will go and return to my place* (Hosea 5:15).[128] This signifies that the Indwelling that has been in our midst departed from us, followed by a privation of divine providence, as Scripture says, threateningly, *I will hide my face from them, and they shall be devoured* (Deut 31:17). Maimonides understood "God's face" to mean providence, just as "eye" means providence.[129] A privation of providence leaves one a target to all that may happen, and one's fortune and misfortune then depend on chance. This is a terrible threat, referred to in the verse just cited, *I will go and return to my place* (Hos 5:15).

Maimonides' concern was to minimize chance occurrences in life and to increase moments in the divine Presence, when we are in harmony with the Mind of the universe.

The verse *And the anger of the Lord was kindled against them, and he went away* (Num 12:9) combines two meanings—withdrawal of divine providence, expressed by going away, and the anger that went forth and reached them, so that Miriam became *leprous, white as snow* (Num 12:10).[130]

Divine distance, we see, is expressed mythically as divine wrath.[131] He stressed that in Scripture we find the expressions "wrath," "anger," and "jealousy" applied to God only in connection with idolatry, and that only the idolater is called "enemy, adversary, or hater of the Lord."

One ought therefore recall that by believing in God's corporeality or that any physical state pertains to God, one provokes his wrath.[132] Maimonides addressed the one who holds wrong views about the nature of God:

> Know accordingly, you who are that man, that when you believe in
> the doctrine of the corporeality of God or believe that one of the states

of the body belongs to him, you *provoke his jealousy and anger, kindle the fire of his wrath*, and are *a hater, an enemy, and an adversary* of God, much more so than *an idolater*.

The apostrophe is filled with irony. Maimonides warned the person who believes that God can be angry that God will be angry with him. Since that person believes that God gets angry, the threat is real, especially as he or she fails to understand that divine anger is a figure of speech signifying God's distance from us.

Divine Attributes

The critique of biblical language is the foreground to a systemic deconstruction of biblical anthropomorphism. Maimonides held that belief in a God with human attributes is tantamount to idolatry, which is a denial of the entire Torah. If God is at all to be depicted in human terms, it is because he and mankind share in reason.

Human beings can know God only through the natural world, Maimonides asserted, since his essence is unknowable. We can only apprehend God's existence (Ar *anniyya,* Grk *to einai*) by contemplating the existent beings (Ar *mawjudat,* Grk *ta onta*). Moses conveyed a true notion of the existence of God in the words "I will be what I will be" (Exod 3:14).[133]

Here Maimonides brilliantly merged biblical and philosophic themes. The meaning of the phrase *ehyeh asher ehyeh* is obscure. It has been translated "I am who I am" or "I will be whatever I will be." It is presumably related to the tetragrammaton which occurs in the next verse.[134] The sense of "I will be what I will be," Maimonides says, is "My nature will become evident from my actions."[135]

The meaning is that God is the being that always exists, or the Necessary Being. It can be proven that there is a Necessary Being that is never nonexistent. Existence is an accident pertaining to all things, hence an element superadded to essence.[136] Only God has no cause for his existence.

His existence does not depend on any other being; nothing brought it into being, and nothing will cause it to cease being.[137] We can imagine other existent beings as not existing, but we cannot imagine God as not existing.[138] We are only able to apprehend the fact *that* he is, and we cannot apprehend *what* he is.[139]

When essential attributes are ascribed to God, they must be thought of as ascribed in a negative sense.[140] When we say that God exists, we mean that his nonexistence is impossible. To say that he is living means that he is not nonexistent. This approach is the *via negativa,* the "negative way," which denies that God can be described by positive attributes, such as "alive" and "knowing," but only by saying what he is not, as in "God is not ignorant." Nothing about God can be expressed in language; he is ineffable. The most appropriate phrase is the saying in Psalms: *Silence is praise to you* (Ps 65:2).[141]

Creation and Eternity

ANTINOMIES OF REASON

In the dilemma of creation versus eternity, Maimonides declared unproven both the Aristotelian eternal world order and the biblical creation by the divine word. Aristotle, Maimonides contended, did not claim that his proof of the world's eternity was demonstrative. In these difficult matters, Maimonides said, his theories were merely tentative. He represented Aristotle as a seeker of truth, offering more or less plausible theories. Maimonides stressed the limitations of human knowledge, a theme that recurred in the first part of *The Guide of the Perplexed.*[142]

While eternity and creation are vulnerable positions, the theory of eternity, Maimonides believed, is more so. Hence, one should prefer over Aristotle's agreement with pagans the consensus of the believers in the revealed laws—the Jews, Christians and Muslims—that the world was created. Moreover, creation makes possible belief in prophecy and miracles.

The Muslim philosopher al-Farabi understood Aristotle's assertion that the question whether the universe is eternal or not is too vast for us to solve with convincing arguments to mean that the issue rests on dialectical arguments, that no solution based upon demonstrative, or scientifically true, syllogisms exists.[143] The physician Galen, al-Farabi observed, could not demonstrate the eternity of the universe, as all proofs, he discovered, are of equal validity.[144]

Ibn Tufayl, in his philosophic novel *Hayy ibn Yaqzan,* presented arguments for creation and eternity as equivalent truth claims. The implications of both arguments, he argued, are the same, for a created universe must have an agent, and an eternal world having eternal motion implies the existence of a first mover.[145] One can accept reason over revelation only on the basis of a decision of the will, for reason is not self-validating.

Averroes, a devout Aristotelian, affirmed the existence of an eternal world order and was convinced that *creatio ex nihilo* weakens causation and hence precludes natural science. Yet he used the language of creation, or innovation. The world is coeternal with God as eternally moved by God (a nontemporal prior cause) in a process of eternal innovation. Existent beings are innovated by being brought from potentiality to actuality. Averroes could describe this eternal process in the language of creation because God is the cause of the continuous motion of the heavenly spheres and thus the cause of the existence of all other beings. God is an intelligent, creative agent that eternally brings the world from the nonbeing of potentiality to the being of actual existence.[146] This realization of being Averroes called "creation" by the communicative strategy of rhetorical accommodation.[147]

FROM DISORDER TO ORDER

Maimonides gave a Platonic interpretation to a mystical passage on creation in Pirqe de Rabbi Eliezer, an eighth-century midrashic pseudograph, ascribed to the second-century Tanna Rabbi Eliezer the Great, son of Hyrcanus. (Maimonides evidently accepted the ascription of the Midrash to Rabbi Eliezer the Great as authentic.) This, in my view, is one of the key chapters in *The Guide of the Perplexed.*[148] Maimonides quoted Rabbi Eliezer as saying:[149]

Wherefrom were the heavens created? From the light of his garment.[150]
He took some of it, stretched it like a cloth, and thus they were extending
continually, as it is said: [Bless the Lord, O my soul; O lord my God,
you are very great; you are clothed with glory and majesty,] wrapped in

the light of your garment, you stretch the heavens like a tent [Ps 104:1–2].
Wherefrom was the earth created? From the snow under the throne
of his glory. He took some of it and threw it,[151] as it is said, *For to the
snow he says, fall on the earth* [Job 37:6].

Maimonides commented that it is the most extraordinary statement
he has seen made by someone who follows the law of Moses our Master.[152] He wondered whether Rabbi Eliezer believed that it was impossible for something to come into being out of nothing and that there
must be matter for generation to occur. Rabbi Eliezer's statement
would be reprehensible, Maimonides claimed, if he wanted to signify
by *the light of [God's] garment* and *the throne of [God's] glory* uncreated
entities, because this admits the eternity of the universe, if only according to Plato's opinion.[153] Maimonides' declaration that Rabbi
Eliezer's statement would be objectionable if he meant that the light
of the garment and the throne of glory are uncreated entities is probably disingenuous, for this is apparently what he secretly believed.

The most wondrous thing of all, Maimonides observed, is Rabbi
Eliezer's saying *the light of [God's] garment.*[154] This reference is confusing
even for the learned, for it has no accepted figurative interpretation.
Despite the difficulties, Maimonides observed, Rabbi Eliezer has effectively clarified that the kinds of matter in heaven and earth differ, the
matter of heaven being from *the light of God's garment* and terrestrial
matter from *the snow under the throne of his glory.* That the universe has
two different kinds of matter, Maimonides commented, is a great mystery: "For it is one of the mysteries of being and a *mystery among the
mysteries of the* Torah."[155] Similar *midrashim* about light emanating from
God's splendor existed that Maimonides did not cite here.[156]

Let me suggest tentatively that Maimonides hinted in this chapter
that creation was out of a primary matter. The biblical text does not
actually teach creation out of nothing (*ex nihilo*), but rather creation
out of primeval chaos: *When God began to create heaven and earth —
the earth being unformed and void, with darkness over the surface of the
deep and a wind from God sweeping over the water — God said, "Let there
be light'; and there was light"* (Gen 1:1–3). A temporal clause, *When
God began to create the heaven and the earth* (Gen 1:1), leads to a circum-

stantial clause about the earth (1:2) and then two main clauses (1:3) telling how God created cosmic order out of primeval chaos. This is the way the commentator Rashi understood Genesis 1:1, and it is an interpretation that would not have eluded Maimonides.

The traditional doctrine of creation out of nothing is present only if we translate it as "In the beginning God created the heaven and the earth," and take it as a reference to a creative act on the first day.[157] If we search through biblical cosmogonies, such as Psalm 104, which may be earlier than the Genesis account, we find that creation is bringing order out of chaos rather than creating something out of nothing.[158] Maimonides devoted an entire chapter to Pirqe de Rabbi Eliezer because it was already an important text in the mystical tradition. It later became one of the main sources for the mythopoesis of the Zohar.[159] Maimonides substituted a philosophic Platonic interpretation for the mystical explanation of the garment of light. Maimonides alluded elsewhere to Plato's *Timaeus,* quoting the sages as having said, *The Holy One, blessed be he, as it were, does nothing without contemplating the host above.*[160] He marveled at the term *contemplating,* for Plato used the same expression when he said that "God contemplates the world of the intellects" and what comes into existence then emanates from it.[161] In other places, the rabbinic sages said that God *does nothing without consulting the host above.*[162] Maimonides quoted these rabbinic dicta to convey the idea that God works through angels. He then equated angels with natural forces. The meaning of the saying, Maimonides asserts, is that God acts through natural forces, or secondary causes, not directly; hence we must study causality and nature. The idea of natural forces and secondary causes separates Maimonides from a traditional Jewish and Islamic understanding of God's actions in the world, according to which everything that happens is a direct result of divine activity. Later, in his *Epistle on Astrology*, Maimonides returned to the Platonic theory.[163]

Maimonides cited other philosophic theories in rabbinic texts that posited some existence before creation. Several sages held that time existed before the creation of the universe, which Maimonides identified as the opinion of Aristotle, for whom time had no beginning.[164] The rabbinic text reads:

And there was evening [and there was morning, a first day] [Gen 1:5].
Rabbi Judah son of Rabbi Simon said: *Let there be evening* is not
written here, rather *And there was evening*, hence we know that a
temporal order *[seder zemanim]* existed before this.[165]

Rabbi Abbahu said: This proves that the Holy One, blessed be he,
went on creating worlds and destroying them until he created this
one and declared, "This one pleases me; those did not please me."

Rabbi Phineas said: This is Rabbi Abbahu's reason: *And God saw
all that he had made, and found it very good* [Gen 1:31]: this pleases me,
but those did not please me.[166]

As often happens, Maimonides did not cite the rabbinic text as we
have it.[167] In any event, his version is more crisp and logical. Accordingly, Rabbi Judah son of Rabbi Simon said that since Scripture mentioned "one day" and "a second day" (Gen 1:5, 8) before the heavenly
bodies were created (that mark time), the days had to be measured by
a temporal order existing prior to their creation. Rabbi Abbahu, in
Maimonides' version, derived his view that God used to create worlds
and destroy them from the same interpretation.

Maimonides commented that if Rabbi Judah and Rabbi Abbahu
believed that an order of time existed eternally *a parte ante,* then all
those who adhere to the law of Moses ought to reject it. It calls to
mind, he observed, the passage in which Rabbi Eliezer says, *Wherefrom were the heavens created?*[168] Notice, however, that the ground for
rejection is a consensus of the religious community, not a flaw in reasoning, and Maimonides intimates that it is valid.

Islamic philosophers intended by the word "nothing" in "creation
out of nothing" the One beyond being and attributes; for God is called
"nothing" or "no thing" because of his incomprehensibility and inef-
fability.[169] The world is created from the essence of God (*creatio ex es-
sentiai dei*). This had been the view of the Christian philosophers
Dionysius the Areopagite and John Scotus Eriugena.

By "nothing" (*al-'adam*) the Islamic philosophers sometimes meant
matter, following Plotinus and others, who regarded matter as nonbeing (Greek *mē ōn*), and hence the sense of creation out of nothing was
that the world was created out of matter.

The public teaching of creation required the language of creation out of nothing, whereas the private teaching was the Platonic concept that creation was bringing the world from chaos into order.[170]

Averroes, we have seen, used the language of creation, or innovation, in the sense that existent beings are innovated by being moved from potentiality to actuality. He could use the language of creation because God is the cause of the continuous motion of the heavenly spheres and thereby the cause of the existence of all other beings. God is an intelligent, creative agent and eternally brings the world from the nonbeing of potentiality to the being of actual existence that called "creation."

Prophecy

QUALITIES OF THE PROPHET

Maimonides affirmed that God causes human beings—not only Israelites— to prophesy.[171] In biblical religion, a prophet is a charismatic figure endowed with the ability to receive and communicate the divine message. He does not choose to prophesy and does not become a prophet by means of an innate or acquired faculty, nor does he need ethical or intellectual preparation. God elects him, sometimes against his will, to communicate the divine word.

In a departure from the biblical image of the prophet as an ordinary man visited by miraculous divine inspiration, Maimonides stressed intellectual and leadership qualities. Prophecy, he said, rests only upon a sage great in wisdom, heroic in character, whose reason overcomes his passion, and who has a broad and sound mind.[172] The talmudic sages set down requirements for prophecy, yet he did not invoke these in his discussion.[173]

Maimonides' formulation brings to mind al-Farabi's qualifications for the philosopher-prophet. These qualifications comprise physical, ethical, and intellectual traits.[174]

PROPHETS AS PHILOSOPHERS

In keeping with al-Farabi and his intellectual heirs, Maimonides described the prophets as philosophers who apprehend theoretical concepts and transform them into images. The Agent Intellect causes an

emanation to overflow upon the prophet's rational faculty and then
upon his imaginative faculty.[175] The prophet receives theoretical truths
from the emanation of the Agent Intellect upon his rational faculty.
This emanation actuates his faculty of imagination, thus giving rise to
symbolic representations of the truth on a level the common folk can
understand.[176] The prophet communicates these symbols to the public
by way of myth and ritual. Religion is an imitation of philosophy, and
whereas philosophy is appropriate for the few, religion serves the many.

PROPHECY AS A NATURAL PROCESS

Maimonides saw the prophet as a statesman and lawgiver, who brings a
law to his people and cautions them to comply with it. The prophet-
statesman is like the philosopher-king of Plato's *Republic,* who founds
and governs the virtuous, perfect, or excellent, state (*al-madina al-fadila*).

Maimonides modified the philosophical-naturalistic concept of
prophecy by bringing in a moment of divine election. A person may be
prepared for prophecy, having perfected his ethical and rational qualities, and yet God may withhold prophecy. In natural terms, the meaning is that there may be impediments preventing a person from
realizing his potential. The potential prophet is intellectually gifted,
healthy, wise, and restrained, yet some circumstance prevents him
from attaining the rank of prophet.

Providence

The section on providence builds up from Part III, chapters 8–24, on
divine providence, to Part III, chapter 51, on human perfection and
divine providence. It contains the parable of the palace, which depicts
ascending levels of proximity to the king.[177] The finale of *The Guide of
the Perplexed* is in the last three chapters (III, 52–54) on God's governance of the universe. Maimonides does not offer us consolation and
solace, yet he does provide a view of human experience that is realistic
and ultimately more supportive than comfort level theologies.

EVIL IN THE UNIVERSE

Maimonides described Epicurus and his sect (*shi'a*) as those who believed that things are due to chance and that there is "no one who

governs and orders being." Epicurus did not believe in the existence of a deity or in prophecy. Regarding providence, Epicurus taught that all things happen by chance and that there is no agent who orders, governs, or is concerned about anything, only atoms that interact by chance.[178] The first two times Maimonides mentioned Epicureans, he said that there was no point in citing their views; however, the third time he gave their view on providence, where the main clash with Epicureanism occurs. Maimonides grasped the great divide between monotheists, who believe that an intelligence guides the universe, and Epicureans, who believe that everything happens by chance. The argument continues nowadays between intelligent adherents of intelligent design and Darwinian atheists who believe in chance mutation. If someone were to ask, "What is the most important idea taught by Maimonides in his scientific and philosophic writings?" A good answer would be that it is the idea of an orderly universe governed by laws of a cosmic intelligence.

Human beings suffer afflictions, Maimonides said, because they have a physical nature that makes them vulnerable to pain and loss. There are three kinds of evil in the world.[179]

1. *Natural evils* occur because we are made of matter, of flesh and bones, and we are subject to generation and corruption. We thereby make room for others of our species. As we are physical beings, illness and paralytic afflictions befall some individuals. Evil comes about because of changes in the elements, through bad air, thunderstorms, landslides, floods, and fires. It is absurd to think that an individual can come into being and not be subject to change and passing away.[180]

   Maimonides quoted Galen as having said: "Do not set your mind on the vain thought that it is possible that out of menstrual blood and sperm there should be generated a living being that does not die, is not subject to pain, is in perpetual motion, or is as brilliant as the sun."[181]

2. *Human beings inflict evil upon one another* by tyrannical domination and wars. These evils are more numerous than natural evils. The reasons are known and come from us, yet the one who is wronged and who suffers cannot avoid them. On a

broad scale this kind of evil is not predominant in the world,
and it is rare that someone murders and robs his neighbor at
night. This kind of evil afflicts many people in major wars,
but they are not the majority of events if we consider the world
as a whole.

3. *Individuals inflict evil upon themselves* by eating, drinking, and
indulging in sexual relations to excess. A bad regimen produces
diseases of the body. And there are also diseases of the soul due
to a poor regimen of the body. The soul is a corporeal faculty,
and its ethical qualities are affected by the body's temperament.
The soul becomes habituated in superfluous things and has
infinite desire for things unnecessary for preservation of the
individual or the species. If you desire silver plate, then you
think it would be better to have gold, and some have crystal
plate, or emeralds and rubies. Individuals are despondent
because they cannot attain the luxury others have. They endanger themselves by going on sea voyages and serving kings,
aiming to attain these luxuries.[182] And when misfortune strikes,
the person complains about God's decree and blames fate for not
helping him to attain wealth to buy wine and be drunk and have
many concubines bedecked in gold ornaments and precious
stones, and to indulge in sex more than he is able to experience
real pleasure, as though the aim were simply pleasure.

Yet people who are virtuous and wise comprehend God's
wisdom manifested in the universe. They seek the aim for
which humanity was created, which is knowledge and understanding. They seek what is necessary for the body, *bread to eat
and clothing to wear* (Gen 28:20), without luxury. Whatever is
necessary for living—air, water, and food—is more accessible
and less expensive than luxuries. No sane person would say
that humans have a strong need for musk, amber, rubies, and
emeralds, unless for medical treatment, and these can be
replaced by herbs.

Natural evils are infrequent, and hence most of the evil in
the world, which is caused by human beings—as in tyranny,
wars, and self-destructive health regimens—can be remedied.

If we consider the entire universe, we realize that it is not for the sake of a single individual or even for the entire human species. We must judge the world from a universal perspective, not from a limited human viewpoint. We must be aware that no being is alone, that we are all parts of a whole, all humanity and the totality of the universe. Then we feel serene, aware that the only evil is moral evil, and this depends upon us.

Maimonides' explanation of evils in the universe is superior in my eyes to modern post-Holocaust theologies, such as the claim that God was absent, in hiding, limited in power, etc., as though he were a weak or wayward parent and not Lord of the universe. Human beings have been inflicting evil upon one another in wars and tyrannical domination from the beginning of history. This is not a justification of God's ways, or a theodicy, as it is called, but an exclusion of God from responsibility for human actions, whether they harm others or themselves.

PROVIDENCE AND INTELLECT

Divine providence, Maimonides wrote, is consequent upon the divine overflow.[183] The human species, with which the intellectual overflow unites, is endowed with intellect, and is thereby accompanied by divine providence.[184] Our intellects protect us from danger by foreseeing the consequences of our actions.[185] We are suspended between our intelligence on one side and chance, nature, and fortune on the other. As long as we use our reason and do not divert it by misconduct, we succeed in understanding and avoid misfortune. In this way the righteous are truly rewarded. This is not by a calculus of divine reward and punishment for good and evil deeds, for in truth God is beyond good and evil. It pertains to the nature of the universe designed by the divine mind.

Providence is commensurate with intellect and can only come from a perfectly intelligent and supreme being.[186] People will come under providential care to the extent that they develop their intellect. The idea that only the person who participates in the divine intellect is the object of divine care is consistent with both philosophy and the law according to Maimonides.

He cited Abu Nasr al-Farabi as being among the philosophers who refer to this idea.[187] In the Introduction to his *Commentary on Aristotle's*

Ethics, known from quotations, al-Farabi stated that those who can make their soul pass from one moral quality to another are those of whom Plato has said that God's providence watches over them to a higher degree. The commentator Shem Tov ben Joseph ben Shem Tov (fifteenth century) wondered why Maimonides did not cite Aristotle's view on providence in his *Ethics*.[188] He saw the Aristotelian view in Maimonides' notion that providence is proportionate to intellect.[189]

Shem Tov criticized Maimonides' version of Aristotle's opinion as holding that providence ends with the sphere of the moon, for Aristotle believed that the wise man comes under divine care.[190] Aristotle's view, as stated by Maimonides (who relied on Alexander of Aphrodisias), was that providence extends only to terrestrial species and not to individuals.

Shem Tov may have hit the mark when he implied that Maimonides deliberately suppressed the true source of his doctrine of providence as proportionate to intellect, for he had assigned to Aristotle the view that everything in this world happens by chance.[191]

For instance, according to Aristotle (as Maimonides understood him), if a hurricane or strong wind blows, it will cause leaves to fall, break branches, topple stones, raise dust, and agitate great waves, making a ship founder and people on board drown. For Aristotle, there is no difference between a falling leaf or stone or the drowning of excellent people on board a sinking ship. And there is no difference between an ox that defecates upon a host of ants, killing them, or a building that collapses on people who are praying, so they die. There is no difference between a cat devouring a mouse, a spider devouring a fly, and a ravenous lion devouring a prophet. This view, Maimonides said, arises from Aristotle's opinion on the eternity of the universe and the impossibility of what exists being different from what it is.

Shipwrecks are mentioned in conventional arguments against astrology as being the kind of disaster that proves that many people born under various astral configurations were all destined to perish together at the same time and place. Maimonides does not use this example in his argument against astrology.

It is, then, by the overflow of the intellect from God to us that we have cognition and right guidance.[192] Our minds understand the rational order and causal system of the world because they are activated by the Agent Intellect.

Maimonides declared that *In your light do we see light* (Ps 36:10) means that intellect is the bond between human beings and God.[193] As humans apprehend the deity by means of the light that he made over-flow toward us, so does he scrutinize us by this very light and is present with us. This constant presence of the deity in our lives induces humility, reverence, and temperate behavior in ways that pertain to reality and not imagination.

Why, then, do righteous individuals suffer evils and premature death?[194] Speaking of an extraordinary insight[195] that occurred to him, eliminating doubts and disclosing divine secrets, Maimonides said that if providence shelters someone whose mind is taken up with God, then when that individual is not thinking of God, providence with-draws or decreases because the person's intellect is not active. Evils befall prophets or righteous people at this time of mental distraction, and the calamity is proportionate to the extent of the disruption and the baseness of what occupies them. This, Maimonides claimed, an-swers the question raised by philosophers about the misfortunes of good people.

When someone is with God and God is with him or her, that person cannot be afflicted by any evil, for the intellectual overflow brings divine protection and deliverance from "the sea of chance."[196] Our intellect protects us by revealing the causation and order in the cosmos. Knowledge of nature saves us from accidents and miscalculations. We must live intelligently and not rely upon superstition and fantasy in coping with contingency.

Maimonides insisted that providence extends in this world only to humans, never to other species, including animals, as in his view they are not endowed with the kind of intelligence that humans have, and cannot raise themselves above the sea of chance.[197]

In contrast, the fourteenth-century astronomer and philosopher Levi ben Gerson, known as Gersonides (1288–1344), later maintained that animals come under providential care by instincts that act as a life-preserving protectors. During the tsunami in December 2005, for instance, flamingos that breed on India's southern coast sought refuge in forests before the tsunami struck.[198] Large animals, such as elephants, leopards, tigers, wild boar, deer, water buffalo, and monkeys, as well as smaller mammals and reptiles, escaped unharmed. Animals behave strangely before natural catastrophes hit, and are keenly sensitive to environmental stimuli, especially to vibrations, sounds, and changes in temperature and magnetic fields. They became anxious and seek higher and safer ground. This is Gersonides' providence.

MAIMONIDES' INTERPRETATION OF THE BOOK OF JOB

Maimonides understood the Job narrative as expressing philosophic views of providence. After losses and great suffering, Maimonides said, Job came to the conclusion that the world is ruled by chance, as Aristotle thought. Then in the prophetic revelation that came to him (Job, chs. 38–42), Job realized that God's providence and governance are mysterious.[199] He heard in God's speech a description of Leviathan, a primordial creature that is God's plaything. The implication is that divine providence and governance are totally alien to us. A sea monster that terrifies human beings is God's plaything. Job repented for having believed that the world is guided by chance: *Wherefore I abhor myself and repent of dust and ashes* (42:6).[200] The sages said, *Those who do out of love are joyful in sufferings.*[201]

Maimonides made a startling distinction between the traditional view of providence and his own opinion.[202] He then portrayed the message of Job as the true view on providence. The most primitive views on providence surfaced at the time of the early revelation in the Five Books of Moses, when people needed tangible rewards, such as rain and fertility. The Book of Job was deeper and more sophisticated.

If Maimonides' view differed from the traditional view and the true view emerged in Job, then Maimonides agreed with the message of Job. His thinking developed from his earliest position—that people get their just deserts, though we do not understand God's ways—to a new awareness manifested in his ideas on intellect and providence. Yet, as often is the case, Maimonides leaves embedded in his text the traditional view along with his philosophic insight. "As for us," he wrote, "we believe that all the human circumstances are according to the deserts, that he is exalted above injustice, and that among us only those deserving punishment are punished."[203] It is love of God by contemplating his works that makes us joyful. If we are aware that God's governance is ultimately mysterious, we will bear every misfortune lightly, and misfortune will not add to our doubts concerning God and providence. God's speech to Job shifts the ground from human suffering to the nature of the universe. It is only when we contemplate the entire universe that we begin to understand human suffering.

When we view the universe from a human perspective, we see it as evil and threatening and as governed by chance. Human beings are not the purpose of creation, however. We realize this when we consider the immensity of the cosmos in contrast with our insignificance. The earth is an infinitesimally minute part of the universe, so what is the proportion of a human being to all of creation?[204] How, then, can we imagine that all existing things are because of us and for our benefit? Human love and fear of God arise from contemplating his wondrous works and infinite wisdom. We are frightened when we realize that we are tiny, lowly, obscure creatures having slight intelligence.[205]

This is the opposite of the Sophists' principle "Of all things the measure is man, of the things that are, that [or "how"] they are, and of things that are not, that they are not."[206]

Knowing the nature of existence is to be aware of the universe and the place of human beings in it. Wisdom is the capacity to see the cosmos as it is in the light of reason and the manner of being compatible with this vision. This is the meaning of the chapters on Job in *The Guide of the Perplexed*.

The final message of Job is that after all is said and done, we really do not understand very much, and the most appropriate response to this world is one of humility. Job's friends thought that they had all the answers, but the finale is the God speech that says, *Where were you when I laid the earth's foundations?* And further on, *Who is wise enough to give an account of the heavens?* (38:37). It may not give us all the answers, but it helps us to reconcile ourselves to our limitations, to get a sense of the very miraculousness of any existence at all, the grandeur of existence, and to get on with making the most of our lives.

When the Lord replied to Job out of the tempest, Job realized his error and understood that we cannot get beyond knowing natural things, the elements, the natures of various species of animals and meteorological phenomena, but little else.[207] Our suffering comes from our finitude and vulnerability to the afflictions of nature.[208]

Human beings should live according to nature, in harmony with the world order. When we do that, we place the right value on things. We seek the things that are truly good, such as wisdom and virtue, and not the things presumed to be good, such as money and property.

We achieve a proper disposition by contemplating the truths of things and knowing the nature of existence. We then realize that the goods and evils in this world are paltry compared to death. Being mindful of death gives us the right perspective and the proper attitude toward happiness and suffering.

Job gains wisdom in the end. He understands the nature of the cosmos and realizes what is truly good and that death is not an evil. We consider our own death as an evil, since death is nonbeing, as are illness, poverty, and ignorance.[209] God acts only for the good, for good is being. If Maimonides viewed creation as the formation of a preexistent matter, then his statements that only good, or being, comes from God takes on new meaning. This was later the view of Gersonides.[210]

DEATH OF A YOUNG GIRL

In one of his letters, Maimonides consoled his pupil Joseph ben Judah for the death of a young girl, urging him not to mourn or be despondent, for the good circumstances of the human species, in the opinion of everyone who has understanding, is only by the continuation of the coming-into-being of its individuals.[211] Maimonides did not consider it an absolute good but the most apposite and the one holding forth a minimum of sorrow. There is a general providence that may affect individuals and groups in ways that are not optimal, but this does not mean that all of existence is not good. "With regard to this world, which has a wondrously ordered structure, and which is very good, as the wisdom of its Creator has determined, we must assume that everything that is created in it is for the good, even death.[212] Therefore, a man should contemplate in the best way the existence of the species, not the good of individuals."[213]

Maimonides mentioned this *midrash* in the *Guide* in a section on providence that Joseph had not yet received. He ended the chapter with a further quotation from Genesis Rabbah: *Nothing that is evil descends from above.*[214]

The Great Sage did not proffer immortality as compensation for human suffering in this world. The consolation for death is that it is good for the species, and the consolation for evil is the harmony of the universe, which our minds comprehend imperfectly because our perspective is limited.

Maimonides' philosophical theology is not constricted by the picture of the universe that he and his contemporaries had. He was aware of its grandeur and how minute we and our planet are in the vast scheme. Cosmologists estimate the universe to be about 15 billion light-years in extent, making us even more infinitesimal than he thought.

Commandments

The last part of *The Guide* (III, 25–54) pertains to human actions. The first section of this (25–50) is on actions commanded by God.[215]

SACRIFICES

Maimonides discussed sacrifices in two chapters of the section pertaining to reasons for the commandments.[216] He began his discussion with a survey of ancient forms of worship, a kind of anthropological history of religion, focused on Sabian forms of worship. For instance, the Sabians used to consume the blood of animals or ate the flesh of a slaughtered animal close by the blood, believing that they achieved brotherhood among themselves and with the *jinn,* eating at the same table at the same gathering.[217] Therefore, the law prohibited consuming blood in the same language that it forbade idolatry (Lev 17:10 and 20:4–6) and offering sacrifices to the goat-demons (*se'irim*) (Lev 17:5, 7).[218] These sacrifices were usually made in the open desert, as Maimonides was aware. Townsmen went from the city to isolated places in the desert to converse with the *jinn*. Could he perhaps have used the term *jinn* to satirize the Qur'an, as though it preserved an ancient Sabian notion?[219]

Maimonides admitted that he was perplexed by the offering of wine in the holy sanctuary, since the idolaters offered it and he could see no reason why God commanded that it be offered. He could only give someone else's forced interpretation.

The great attention that Maimonides gave to the sacrificial cult has puzzled scholars, since Maimonides taught that human beings had gone beyond that primitive level of worship and reached a more spiritualized way of serving God. Human nature, Maimonides expounded, is incapable of abandoning customs and habits abruptly, and so God, by a gracious ruse, gradually weaned them away from sacrifices toward prayer and meditation. Maimonides used his own historical anthropology to explain how people were moved away from Sabian types of worship. In his discussion of reasons for the commandments he shifted from the natural sphere of God's actions to the sphere of history and the question of a rationale for the commandments. Nahmanides criticized Maimonides' anthropological approach to sacrifices, which rendered them obsolete. He rather viewed them positively as theurgic actions and supreme symbols.

In the chapter that begins by considering the divine or natural actions, Maimonides spoke of God's wisdom and wily graciousness (*talattuf*) in natural phenomena, as for instance, the human body.[220] He showed how limbs and organs and nerves are perfectly adapted to their function. Maimonides used the term "wily graciousness" six times in the chapter along with the related word *lutf*, meaning "graciousness." Samuel Ibn Tibbon translated *talattuf* by the Hebrew '*or-mah*, meaning "cunning." Pines observes that this wily graciousness or cunning calls to mind Hegel's cunning, or ruse, of reason (*List der Vernunft*). Reason channels the passions of world-historical individuals to its own purposes unknown to them.[221] Nature, having the continuation of the species in mind, has made individuals sexually attractive, so they are aroused to have intercourse and reproduce.

Since human beings are incapable of sudden transitions to the opposite of custom and habit, God leads them gradually to the desired end, which is the primary intention. When service of the divine was universally by sacrifices in temples with images, his gracious ruse was to permit these sacrifices to survive and be transferred to his name. He commanded the Israelites to build a temple, bring sacrifices, and burn incense before him. People were moved to belief in God without feeling repulsion toward the forms of worship to which they were accustomed.

Human Perfection

The final chapters of *The Guide* (III, 51–54) concern the ideal of human perfection. Although the matrix is Jewish, the significance is human and universal.[222]

THE PARABLE OF THE PALACE

Chapter III, 51, is the bright summit of *The Guide of the Perplexed*. It is about the supreme form of worship, the ultimate attainment of the truth, and the highest knowledge and love of God. Maimonides moved from the supreme intellectual attainment of an Aristotelian rationalist, which is knowing the truth about the nature of reality, to the higher mystical attainment of a true worshiper, knowing and loving God. He insisted that the chapter does not include anything added to what is in the other chapters of *The Guide of the Perplexed*.

Yet this is a chapter in which Maimonides stated that he had a most extraordinary insight into the nature of divine providence. Moreover, he gave spiritual exercises for attaining the intellectual worship of God and then to reaching a passionate love of God, stations that can only be described as mystical. It was from this chapter in particular that the ecstatic Kabbalah of Abraham Abulafia drew its inspiration.

Maimonides began the chapter with a parable (*mathal*) about a king in his palace and people who are at a distance from the palace or approaching it.[223] It is a lengthy and difficult journey from the walls of the city to the center of the palace, but the reward is great when one reaches the inner sanctum of the king's palace (*dar al-sultan*).

The ruler (*sultan*) is in his palace (*qasr*) and his subjects are within the city and outside the city. There are seven levels:

1. Outside the city are those who are irrational, who have no doctrinal belief by speculation or tradition and are barely human.[224]

2. Some of those who are within the city have turned their backs to the ruler's residence (*dar*). They have opinions and speculate but hold incorrect opinions because of great error in theorizing or because they follow incorrect traditional authority. The more they proceed, the farther away they are from the ruler's residence.[225]

3. Those who seek to reach the ruler's residence and enter it and present themselves before him but have not seen the wall of the residence are the multitude of the adherents of the law, the ignorant who observe the commandments.

4. Those who have gone up to the residence and search for its gate are the jurists who have true opinions based on traditional authority and do not speculate about the foundations of religion.

5. Those who have entered the gate and walk around in the antechambers (Arabic *dahaliz*) have begun speculation about the fundamentals of religion.

6. Those who entered the inner court of the residence and have come to be with the king (*malik*) in the same place in the ruler's residence (*dar al-sultan*), in the inner part of the residence, have attained demonstrative knowledge and have resolved metaphysical questions as far as possible for humankind. This does not mean that they see the ruler or speak with him.

7. Once the aspirant is inside the residence, he or she must make another effort and then he or she will be in the presence of the ruler (*sultan*) and see him from a distance or from nearby, or hear the ruler's speech or speak with him.[226]

The parable of the palace is reminiscent of Gnostic myths of ascent, in which the aspirant travels through the heavens to reach a palace. After relating the parable of the palace, Maimonides addressed Joseph ben Judah ("Know, my son . . ."). As long as Joseph remains on the level of mathematics and logic, he is walking around the palace searching for its gate; as the sages said in a parable, *Ben Zoma is still outside.*[227] Whereas this had a mystical sense in rabbinic sources, Maimonides gave it a philosophic interpretation, taking outside to mean not yet engaged in physics and metaphysics. One who understands physics has entered the residence and is in the antechambers. Understanding metaphysics means that you have entered the inner court. This is the rank of scientists (*'ulama'*) according to their different ranks of perfection. Some after mastering metaphysics turn toward God, renounce all else, and direct their intellect to investigating all existent things to draw from them a proof (*istidlal*) concerning him, to know his governance of them in whatever way possible. They are present in the ruler's council (*majlis*), and this is the rank of the prophets. Some because of their understanding and renouncing all that is not God have it said of them, *And he was there with the Lord* (Exod 34:28).[228] Because of his great joy, he did not eat or drink and the various kinds of the sense of touch ceased their function. The prophet, Moses above all, was also a philosopher, who attained the highest degree of knowledge and the greatest proximity to God. The roles of prophet and philosopher converge on this level.

The Torah has clarified that the highest worship is only possible after one acquires knowledge of God.[229] It says, *Loving the Lord your God and serving him with all your heart and soul* (Deut 11:13). One's love (*mahabba*) of God is proportionate to knowledge of him. Love precedes the worship that the sages called *service of the heart.*[230] One concentrates all of one's thoughts on the first intelligible and devotes oneself (*infirad*) to this as far as possible. David therefore exhorted Solomon to acquire a true knowledge of God and to worship him after this knowledge has been acquired (1 Chron 28:9).

In a "call to attention" (*tanbih*) Maimonides said that he has explained that our intellect is the bond (*wusla*) between us and God.[231] You can strengthen it or else weaken it gradually until it breaks. You strengthen it by love (*mahabba*) of God. Even if you are advanced in metaphysics, you break that bond when you turn away in order to eat and carry out necessary business, for then you are not with God and he is not with you. The virtuous resent having to turn away from God to other occupations, following the warning of the sages, *Do not let God be absent from your thought.*[232]

Maimonides gave the reader guidance in the spiritual exercises that bring one close to God and loving him.

1. You begin by performing the commandments and reciting prayers with intense concentration, not being distracted by worldly things. Then afterward you may occupy your mind with worldly things, as you eat, drink, or bathe, or talk with your wife and small children, or with common humanity. You have plenty of time for tending to property, your household, and care of your health.

2. When you are alone, awake on your sofa,[233] you should be careful to meditate during these precious moments on the intellectual worship of God, which is being near to God and in his presence.[234] There may be a person who knows the truth and has joy in this knowledge. His mind is always in God's presence, while outwardly he is with others, tending to physical necessities.[235] This was expressed in poetic parables: *I was asleep, but my heart was awake. Listen, my beloved is knocking,* etc. (Song 5:2).[236]

   This is not the rank of all the prophets, but it is of Moses our Master, who was with the Lord in his presence, and it was the rank of the Patriarchs. For the Patriarchs and Moses our Master, union with God (*al-ittihad bi'llah*), which is knowing and loving him, was apparent in the texts of Scripture, and God's providence protected them as they prospered, although they were busy governing people, increasing wealth, and trying to acquire property.

3. God's providence over these four—the Patriarchs (Abraham, Isaac, Jacob) and Moses our Master—and over their posterity was great. While occupied with governing, increasing their wealth, and acquiring property, their minds were constantly in God's presence, and his providence attended them even when they were increasing their fortunes by tending their sheep, farming, and running their household. Their purpose was to come near to God, "and how near!" Their aim was to guide people to love God. Their actions were the ultimate pure worship of God. As described here, the mystic's ultimate experience of oneness with God is not achieved in solitude by

abandoning the world, but rather while occupied in this world with one's mind meditating on a higher world.

Here, Maimonides inserted a personal note: "This rank is not one to which someone like me can give guidance."[237] We hear an echo of Maimonides' own religious life, as he strived to perform his public duties and engage in economic activities while seeking moments of solitude when he could achieve a blissful state of union with God.

He confessed that he could not be in God's presence while tending to ordinary affairs. He needed moments of quiet and contemplation away from the crowd. This kind of personal self-reference is rare in the *Guide* or in his other writings. The two competing forces in his life were, on one side, the drive to help people and be of service to them and, on the other, the craving for solitude and contemplation. We know him well enough to say that his essential need was for solitude and study, whereas the rest he did out of a sense of responsibility. People distracted him, and he could not emulate the Patriarchs and Moses, who could dwell in this world with their minds in another.

One may aspire to the rank previous to this one through the spiritual exercises that Maimonides described. We must implore God to remove the veils that separate us from him, most of which come from us. *Your iniquities have been a barrier between you and your God* (Isa 59:2).

The chapter moves from the intellectual love of God to providence and the close relationship between them. The reason providence protects the individual who is close to God is that he has known and loved God. *Because he loves [hashaq] me, I will deliver him; I will keep him safe because he knows my name* (Ps 91:14).[238] It is as though the Psalmist said that this individual is sheltered because he has known God and then passionately loved him. "You know the difference," Maimonides went on, "between the terms one who loves [Hebrew *ohev*] and one who loves passionately [*hosheq*]; an excess of love [*mahabbah*], so that no thought remains that is directed toward a thing other than the beloved, is passionate love [*'ishq*]."[239]

Maimonides apprehended the order and harmony of the universe and intuited a supreme intellect evident in nature. Nature is a wondrous structure that we can understand only imperfectly, and that must imbue us with a feeling of humility. To know that what is mysterious for us really exists and manifests itself as the highest wisdom and the most radiant beauty is the essence of true religious feeling. This is the *amor dei intellectualis* that he speaks of as a rapturous obsession.[240]

After gaining knowledge of God, one should seek total devotion and employ one's thought in constantly loving him. The vocabulary of passion and bliss indicates that this is a mystical state, a philosophic mysticism. This chapter is the ultimate statement Maimonides made on religious experience.

The passions of youth impede us from attaining the kind of perfection that leads to passionate love of God. As the fire of the desires is extinguished, the light of the mind becomes purer and it rejoices in what it knows. When a perfect human being is stricken with years and is near death, his knowledge increases, his joy in the knowledge is stronger, and his love for the object of his knowledge more intense, and it is in this great delight that the soul is separated from the body.[241] This state is bliss and passionate love. The sages referred to the deaths of Moses, Aaron, and Miriam as being death by a kiss.[242]

The sages indicated that these three died in the pleasure of their knowledge of God due to the intensity of their passionate love. They accepted the poetical convention of calling knowledge of God combined with passionate love for him a kiss, following the saying, *Let him kiss me with the kisses of his mouth* (Song 1:2).

FOUR PERFECTIONS

The climax of the *Guide* is a description of four perfections in mounting order of excellence.[243] The four perfections are:[244]

1. The perfection of possessions—such as money, land, a house, and clothing—pertains to things that are not really connected with what a person is. Being a great king belongs to this kind of perfection. Most pleasure from these things is purely imaginary and they have no permanence. Even if they remain forever, a person cannot achieve through them perfection of self.

2. The perfection of the body's constitution and shape, its harmonious temperament and well-proportioned and strong limbs, is

more closely linked to the person's self. Yet this perfection, being corporeal, pertains to man not as man but as animal, and it does not touch the soul.

3. The perfection of the ethical virtues exists to a great extent in the individual's self. One's moral habits reach their ultimate excellence. Most of the commandments have as their aim this kind of perfection. But it is not an end in itself. The disposition to be useful to people is always for someone else. One cannot be virtuous on one's own.

4. The "true human perfection" resides in the rational virtues and belongs to the person alone. It is permanent and through it a person is human. You ought to strive to attain this perfection that remains permanently with you, "and do not weary and trouble yourself for the sake of others, O you who neglect your own soul so that its whiteness has turned into blackness through corporeal faculties having gained domination over it."[245]

Maimonides explained that the ethical virtues that we exercise by being useful to people and troubling oneself for others involve submission to the physical and neglect of the soul.

The prophets have explained these things to us, just as the philosophers have understood them. Both philosophy and the law construe ultimate human perfection in the same way. The perfection one can take pride in and desire is knowledge of God, which is the true science. The prophet Jeremiah said concerning these four perfections:

> Thus said the Lord: Let not the wise man glory in his wisdom; let not the strong man glory in his strength; let not the wealthy man glory in his wealth. But only in this should one glory: in his earnest devotion to me. For I the Lord act with kindness [hesed], justice [mishpat], and righteousness [sedaqa] in the world; for in these I delight, says the Lord (Jer 9:22–23).

The prophet mentioned them in an order befitting the opinion of the common people, for whom the greatest perfection is wealth, then might, and then wisdom, by which he meant the moral virtues.

Jeremiah made clear in this verse (Jer 9:23) that the actions that we should know and imitate are kindness, justice, and righteousness. The ultimate perfection is knowledge of God and of his providence extending to his creatures by bringing them into being and governing them. The way of life of this individual, who has attained this knowledge, will have in view kindness, justice, and righteousness "through assimilation to his actions (may he be exalted)."

The ultimate vision vouchsafed man is contemplation of God's governance in the world, study of the rational structure of the universe.[246] The supreme vision is apprehension of God's attributes, of God's actions in the world.

Maimonides' perfect man is ideally a philosopher-statesman or prophet, exemplified in the supremely perfect man, Moses. These individuals, in varying degrees, are to the body politic what God is to the universe. The happiness and perfection that they achieve overflows to others through their benevolent governance.[247]

Only one who has attained supreme knowledge of the nature of the universe and of God's providence in it is capable of exercising the political virtues. These virtues should be distinguished from the ethical virtues that are a preparation for the life of reason, for they flow from the activity of contemplation and assimilation to God.

Maimonides drew the *Guide* to a close with a prayer:

> This is the extent of what I thought fit that I should set down in this treatise. It is a part of what I consider very useful to those like you. I hope for you that through sufficient reflection you will grasp all the intentions I have included therein, with the help of God (may he be exalted); and that he will grant us *and all*
>
> > *[the people of] Israel, being fellows,* that which
> > he has promised us: *Then the eyes of the blind*
> > *shall be opened, and the ears of the deaf*
> > *unstopped* [Isa 35:5]. *The people*
> > *who walked in darkness have*
> > *seen a great light; those*
> > *who lived in a land*
> > *of deep darkness,*
> > *on them light*
> > *has shined* [Isa 9:1].

20

The Treatise on Resurrection

Many of those that sleep in the dust of the earth will awake,
some to eternal life, others to reproaches, to everlasting
abhorrence. And the knowledgeable will be radiant like the
bright expanse of sky, and those who lead the many to
righteousness will be like the stars forever and ever.

—DANIEL 12:2–3

Now if Christ is proclaimed as raised from the death,
how can some of you say there is no resurrection of the dead?
If there is no resurrection of the dead, then Christ has not been
raised; and if Christ has not been raised, then our
proclamation has been in vain and your faith is in vain.

—1 COR 15:12–14

Then he will make you die; then he will make you live;
then you will return to him.

—QUR'AN 2: 28

BELIEF in resurrection is shared by the three Western mono-theistic religions.[1] resurrection is the conviction that the dead will arise in their own bodies and live again. Belief in resurrection is one of Maimonides' thirteen principles of faith. It is mentioned in the main prayer of the liturgy, the 'Amidah. Yet important as it is for Judaism, resurrection is even more important for Christianity and Islam. The resurrection of Jesus Christ is at the heart of Christian faith, and the day of resurrection (*al-qiyama*) comes up no less than seventy times in the Qur'an.

JUDAISM ON RESURRECTION

The prophet Ezekiel had a vision of a valley full of dry bones that took on flesh and breath and came to life again, symbolizing the restoration of the people of Israel to its land (37:1–14). Ezekiel was speaking figuratively, alluding to a collective, not to individuals, but once belief in resurrection took hold in postbiblical Judaism, Ezekiel's vision was taken literally as referring to the revival of the dead before judgment day.

Later tradition saw an allusion to resurrection in Isaiah 26:19–21: *Your dead shall live, their corpses shall rise. You who dwell in the dust, awake and sing for joy! For your dew is a radiant dew, and the earth will give birth to those long dead.*

The first unambiguous scriptural reference to resurrection is in the book of Daniel (Dan 12:2–3).[2] In contrast to the visions of Isaiah and Ezekiel, these verses refer to individual resurrection, after which a judgment will take place, some of the deceased awaking to eternal life and others to everlasting shame.

In 2 Macc 7:14, 23, the seven martyred brothers were promised that they would get back breath and life and be raised again to a new existence. Some of the apocryphal writings speak of all humankind rising from the dead for judgment. Others declare that only the just will rise to life and the wicked will not experience a renewal of life.

In the Second Temple period, especially in apocryphal literature, the soul's immortality prevailed over resurrection. Immortality means that the individual soul survives with consciousness of a personal identity and memory of a past life. The philosopher Philo believed that immortality of the soul was the true reward, and resurrection was merely a figurative way of speaking about it.[3]

The doctrine of resurrection became a fundamental principle for rabbinic eschatology and distinguished the Pharisees from their Sadducean adversaries. The Talmud determined that numerous biblical passages alluded to resurrection.[4] Though the idea of resurrection appears only once or twice in the Hebrew Bible, the Mishnah goes so far as to state that *whoever says there is no resurrection of the dead [prescribed in the Torah]* has *no share in the world hereafter.*[5]

CHRISTIAN VIEWS

Jesus taught the doctrine of resurrection and argued against its denial by the Sadducees, who knew not the power of God and Scripture.[6] St. Paul preached the belief that *Christ died for our sins* and was resurrected on the third day and appeared to the believers (1 Cor 15:3–9).

Paul expounded the Christian doctrine of resurrection before skeptical Jews and philosophers in Athens.[7] First, in the synagogue he debated Jews and God-fearers, and in the marketplace he debated Epicurean and Stoic philosophers, who ridiculed his preaching about Jesus and the resurrection. He then addressed the Athenians in front of the Areopagus, and when they heard about the resurrection of the dead, some scoffed and others wanted to hear about it again.

The creeds of the church defined resurrection of the body as an article of faith. The earliest ecumenical creeds, the Apostles' Creed (second century) and the Nicene Creed (325 C.E.), adopted by the Council of Chalcedon in 451 C.E., taught: "[Jesus] descended into hell. The third day he rose again from the dead; he ascended into heaven, and sits at the right hand of God the Father Almighty. From there he shall come to judge the quick and the dead." "No doctrine of the Christian faith," said St. Augustine, "is so vehemently and so obstinately opposed as the doctrine of the resurrection of the flesh."[8]

ISLAMIC VIEWS

Resurrection is a fundamental article of faith for Muslims. In the Qur'an it comes after the annihilation of all human beings and before the day of judgment (*yawm al-din*).[9] The eschatological unfolding begins with prophetic signs followed by the world's final annihilation, leaving God in his solitude, *as all shall perish save his face. His is the judgment, and unto him you shall return* (Qur'an 28:88). Denying the teaching of resurrection is disbelief (*kufr*) (6:29–30).[10]

The great theologian al-Ghazali taught belief in resurrection in the literal sense and accounted it as one of the heresies of the philosophers that they did not believe and tried to conceal their disbelief.[11] He considered the philosophers infidels who should be put to death for three of their beliefs: (1) the pre-eternity of the universe, (2) the assertion that God's knowledge does not take in particular things, and (3) the denial of the resurrection of bodies and their gathering on the day of judgment. Al-Ghazali had studied philosophy and knew enough to strip the philosophers in public by showing that their professed belief in creation, divine knowledge of particulars, and resurrection was a facade.

The beliefs of the philosophers, al-Ghazali maintained, contradict Islam. They imply that the prophets spoke falsehoods and merely aimed for social utility, conveying salutary ideas in figurative language. Al-Ghazali's influence was enormous, and his branding the philosophers as infidels deserving the death penalty placed them in a very tenuous position.

PHILOSOPHERS

Philosophers saw no point in having body and soul reunited after death. Rather, they envisioned the soul's ascent to the Agent Intellect and an ultimate blissful union with God in the afterlife. Philosophers viewed immortality as the survival of the rational part of a human being and reason as the link between the human and divine.[12]

Aristotle had suggested a kinship between the human and the divine by saying that during intellection the subject becomes one with its object, intellect becoming its intelligible, like the first mover, which is self-intelligized intelligence.[13] The philosophers regarded the religious vision of personal immortality and the belief in physical resurrection as socially beneficial myths as al-Ghazali claimed.

Al-Ghazali's strictures against the philosophers were aimed mainly at al-Farabi and Ibn Sina. In works addressed to novice philosophers, Ibn Sina confirmed the doctrine of resurrection according to Qur'anic teachings. "The law affirms and reason does not deny that the body also will enjoy pleasures or partake of misery and suffering."[14] Ibn Sina defended the philosophers against the accusation that they believed resurrection to pertain to the soul alone and showed that resurrection should be understood as a symbol that encourages the common people to pursue virtuous conduct.[15] In actuality, "it is known that the true well-being of man is opposed by the very existence of the soul in his body, and that physical pleasures are other than true pleasures, and that the fact of the soul returning to the body would be punishment for the soul."[16]

Reading this, we can understand how traditional thinkers could accuse philosophers of not embracing the teaching of the Qur'an concerning resurrection.

Averroes' theological works, such as *The Decisive Treatise* and *The Incoherence of the Incoherence*, were an effort to refute al-Ghazali and make room for philosophy in Islamic societies.

He insisted that Muslims reached a consensus that it is not obligatory for all the utterances of the law to be taken in their literal sense, but some may be interpreted in a metaphorical or allegorical way. There is only disagreement over *what* should be interpreted. Al-Ghazali himself, Averroes emphasized, was among leading thinkers who said that infidelity cannot be ascribed to someone for going against consensus for interpreting these things.[17] He was eager to reserve for the intellectual elite the right to understand the Qur'an and *hadith* on the basis of their own interpretation. He wished to overcome al-Ghazali's view that philosophers should be put to death as infidels. Also, he had to refute the assertion that philosophers believed resurrection to be a socially useful myth. Yet he made a forthright statement of the philosopher's position in his *Incoherence of the Incoherence*. I know of no passage quite like it by one of the Islamic philosophers that defines so clearly the attitude of Islamic philosophers to religion.[18]

SAMUEL BEN ELI AND THE BAGHDAD ACADEMY

When Joseph ben Judah traveled to Baghdad, he encountered critics
of Maimonides and found himself defending his teacher in public.
The Gaon Samuel ben Eli, Head of the Academy in Baghdad, was the
most influential and outspoken detractor of Maimonides. His cohorts
included the Head of the Court, Rabbi Zechariah ben Berachel, his
son-in-law.[19]

Samuel ben Eli was Maimonides' formidable opponent in a struggle that was both personal and political, fought on the battlefield of
the law. Leadership of the Jewish communities of the Middle East—
Egypt, Syro-Palestine, Yemen, and Iraq—was at stake. Samuel assessed
that Maimonides' belief in resurrection was halfhearted, detecting a
vulnerability that could be exploited to undermine him. The doctrine
of a literal resurrection was problematic for Maimonides, but he could
not afford to let that be known.

The authority of Gaon Samuel ben Eli extended to Syria and even
to Egypt. In the past, Andalusian scholars had gained independence
from Baghdad by superior scholarship and teaching. Now Maimonides, the leading religious authority of Egyptian Jews, was in a ri-
valry with the Baghdad Academy and its claims to hegemony over a
wide territory.

Samuel's first dated document is a responsum concerning blessings
after a meal, dated October–November 1164 (query) and April 1166
(response). The last preserved document is from May 1197. He was
Head of the Academy for about forty years, from around 1160 to
around 1200, overlapping Maimonides' career in Egypt (1166–1204).

Samuel ben Eli claimed a genealogy going back to the biblical Samuel.[20] He had sixty slaves, armed with whips to force the people into
obedience. Whoever did not carry out orders was flogged. Samuel resided in a large house covered with tapestry and wore colorful garments adorned with gold like a king. Every Jew in Iraq paid a gold
dinar annually to his treasury.

Genizah documents provide evidence indicating that Samuel ben
Eli was forceful in demanding financial support. In one letter the
Gaon threatened that he would send a representative to communities
that did not contribute to the Academy. They must show respect to

the agent and send generous fixed payments for the Academy. He threatened strong measures against those who refused.

Maimonides criticized this method of raising money from individuals and communities. He opposed the hierarchical leadership of the Iraqian Geonim. His concept of leadership was far less authoritarian. As we have seen, decisions were made in his council by judges and elders together with him. His critique of the socioeconomic foundations of the Iraqian Geonate was combined with contempt for their trappings of office and rejection of their curriculum, which left no room for anything other than Talmud studies.

A battleground in the struggle between Maimonides and the Iraqian Geonim was the *Mishneh Torah,* which, as we have seen, replaced the Talmud with a systematic compendium of law. But Talmud study was the core of the Baghdad curriculum, and the growing influence of the *Mishneh Torah* threatened the Gaon's authority.

Samuel ben Eli attacked Maimonides, and Joseph ben Judah reported the attack to his mentor. Upset over the anti-Maimonidean propaganda coming from the circles of Samuel ben Eli, Joseph sent a copy of the Baghdad Gaon's polemical work, to which Maimonides later responded in his *Treatise on Resurrection.*

Joseph himself came under fire, and complained of it in a letter to his teacher. He wondered, in view of their conduct and speech, how these Iraqian Jews could be considered pious. Joseph also asked Maimonides to write to the Exilarch concerning a controversy between the Exilarch and Samuel ben Eli.

Joseph eventually returned to Aleppo, which, as part of Syria, was under the influence of Samuel ben Eli. In Aleppo, he began to teach and disseminate the *Mishneh Torah* and Maimonides' teachings, thereby acting with disrespect toward the Gaon. In addition, he intervened in the appointment of a new Exilarch, and got Maimonides to back his candidate. This was unacceptable to Samuel ben Eli, who opposed the appointment and, in fact, the institution of the Exilarchate. From his viewpoint, only the guidance of the Geonim was needed.

Gaon Samuel and Rabbi Zechariah were dismissive of the Exilarch and derisive toward Joseph ben Judah and even Maimonides. They wrote to Maimonides with finesse in order to elicit polite replies from him that they could exploit in their debates with Joseph. Joseph was incensed by their insults to his teacher and their demeaning the *Mishneh Torah,* and he fought back with vitriolic expressions. Nevertheless, the Baghdad scholars went on assailing him.

Maimonides instructed his pupil to calm down and act with prudence and circumspection and avoid intemperate language. His words to Joseph expressed his personal ethic, which he wrote about and communicated in speech to those who encountered him in daily circumstances.[21]

In a brief letter written around this time, Maimonides discussed the issue of anger with Joseph and replied to Joseph's question why he teacher carried on a correspondence with a Baghdadian named Joseph Abu 'l-Khayr Ibn Jabir, who was unlearned.[22] Maimonides began his reply with the verse *I am ever mindful of the Lord's presence* (Ps 16:8), which he had placed at the head of his letter to Jabir.[23] He addressed Joseph with great respect, calling him "my dear son and precious pupil, the esteemed, great and revered, our teacher and master Joseph, Rosh ha-Seder."[24] He knew, he assured the younger man, that Joseph's love for him was genuine—"and if you imagine that someone doubts this, you well deserve reproach." Somehow, Joseph had gotten the impression that Maimonides doubted Joseph's love for him.

As for the dispute with the Gaon and his academy, Maimonides explained to Joseph that he strived to be modest always even if that hurt him in the eyes of the public. He forgave those who wished to show their superiority by demeaning him, even if that person was among the least of scholars. Those who showed the way to eternal happiness (the sages) said: *If a friend requires unloading, and an enemy loading, the enemy has priority in order to subdue one's evil inclination.*[25]

Maimonides reminded Joseph that when they had spoken face-to-face, he had told him that if in "this time of ours" one tried to requite in word or deed each person according to his actions, by way of following Scripture, *and with the crooked you show yourself perverse* (2 Sam 22:27), he would accustom himself to committing all sorts of evil, for most people he sees are crooked. Therefore, if a man wishes to be human, he should consider how to perfect his moral qualities and develop his intellectual virtues and not occupy his thoughts with vanities.

Joseph's grief and intense anger at deceivers and liars Maimonides ascribed to his youth. When he had been Joseph's age and even older, he was even more irascible than Joseph.

We constantly find Maimonides repressing anger and advising that others do the same. His comments are similar to Seneca's book *On Anger*, in which anger is seen as a loss of reason and control that is bad for the angry person and counterproductive in conflicts. However, know that turning anger inward has its price as well, for it creates bitterness, melancholy, and resentment.

LETTER TO JOSEPH IBN JABIR

In Maimonides' correspondence with Joseph Ibn Jabir, which we have just mentioned, the issue of the Baghdadians' criticism of the *Mishneh Torah* was central.[26]

Ibn Jabir had studied the *Commentary on the Mishnah*, written in Arabic, his native language, but struggled with the *Mishneh Torah*'s Hebrew. He had heard scurrilous critiques of Maimonides from the Baghdadians, and requested replies to their strictures and guidance in his own studies, all this in Maimonides' handwriting.

Maimonides referred to the love (*ahavah*) between them, although no previous meeting is mentioned. In fact, toward the end of the letter, Maimonides said that the friendship was based on "what you saw of my discussion of the law."

The date of the letter can be inferred from the reference to Maimonides' responsum concerning travel on large rivers on the Sabbath, written in June–July 1191, and to the *Treatise on Resurrection*, which was also written in 1191. The letter to Joseph ibn Jabir was hence written sometime after 1191.[27]

In the salutation, impressed by the man's sincere scholarly efforts and personal devotion, the Sage of Fustat reassured him that his rudimentary level of knowledge was no barrier to further study and that he should strive to achieve perfection. "The first thing you should know (may God perpetuate your glory and increase your success) is that you are not an ignoramus but our pupil and dear friend. Whoever cleaves to study, even if he understands but a single verse or precept, whether he understands that concept in the holy tongue [Hebrew],

Aramaic or Arabic—the intention is to understand concepts in whatever the language is."[28] Ibn Jabir should study enough Hebrew to understand the *Mishneh Torah*.

In the main body of the letter Maimonides responded to the criticisms by Baghdadians that Ibn Jabir had forwarded. The first concerned resurrection. The Baghdad scholars, Ibn Jabir reported, had
maintained that Maimonides rejected resurrection, an allegation that
Maimonides vigorously denied, referring to his *Treatise on Resurrection,* which Ibn Jabir would receive. "As for mentioning that you
heard [the Baghdad scholars] state that I denied the resurrection of the
dead—I mean, the restoration of the soul to the body—this is a grave
slander against me.[29] The one who says this about me is either a cunning knave, who accuses me of saying what I have not said, or an ignoramus who has difficulty understanding my discourse [*kalam*]
concerning the world hereafter and supposes it is the resurrection of
the dead."[30] As Ibn Jabir was untutored, he belonged to the target audience of the resurrection treatise, which Maimonides explicitly said
was written for the common people.

Ibn Jabir had also asked Maimonides to explain immortality of the
soul and the world hereafter. This was his own query, not raised in the
name of critics, though related to the question of resurrection. Maimonides advised Ibn Jabir to avoid profound matters and stick to what
his mind could grasp. His religious faith would not be impaired if he
believes that the denizens of the hereafter are corporeal and even eat,
drink, and copulate. Nevertheless, Maimonides invoked the authority
of the Talmud to deny corporeal existence in the world hereafter. We
may conjecture why Maimonides was so permissive on this issue. It
may be because Islam offered believers comfort in visions of a rapturous future life, where they would enjoy beautiful virgins, flowing
springs, and gardens.[31]

Maimonides ended his letter by alluding to the love "for the sake of
heaven" that existed between him and Ibn Jabir. This would have
been a fitting conclusion. But he then took up rumors concerning the
attempt on the part of some Baghdadians to denigrate him for their
self-aggrandizement. They had distorted the meaning of the *Mishneh
Torah*. Maimonides had heard that Ibn Jabir had protested this cal-

umny. He forgave them and dissuaded Ibn Jabir from taking up arms on his behalf.

THE EXILARCH

The conflict between Maimonides and Gaon Samuel ben Eli was intertwined with a quarrel between the Exilarch Daniel ben Hisday (d. 1174/75 C.E.) and the Gaon. As a result of the tension, the Exilarch opened an academy in Baghdad independent of the Gaon's academy. This was not unusual. Other Exilarchs opened academies and compensated for their academic deficiencies, if necessary, by selecting a scholar to be the actual head.[32]

Gaon Samuel ben Eli's aim was to weaken the Exilarchate and to promote the interests of the Heads of Academies at its expense.

Maimonides wrote to Joseph that if it were not for him, "the Exilarch would have been in his [Samuel's] hands like a chick in the talons of a hawk, and he would have denounced him for the matter of the bill of divorce and other things, and would have torn him to shreds."[33]

A letter from the Exilarch in Baghdad to Maimonides arrived, which he had read aloud to an assembled crowd in his house.[34] "All the people of Fustat" were in the house to celebrate a circumcision that took place there on the festival of Tabernacles. The double celebration made the crowd unusually large. Rabbi Samuel ben Se'adyah[35] read out the letter, while all the elders of the community took their places on a dais (*dikka*) to his right and left.[36] A house with a very large courtyard, with an ample reception room off the courtyard and open areas about the domicile, would be spacious enough for hundreds of people.

THE TREATISE ON RESURRECTION

Audience and Style

Maimonides requested that no student of the sciences criticize him, for he composed this treatise for the common people, who struggle to understand what is crystal clear in what he said, and for all those who criticized his brevity on resurrection. For those perfect in knowledge a hint suffices. They do not require explication and repetition, but only chapter headings, as he has done with all these obscure things in *The Guide of the Perplexed*. The reader understands that speaking with the perfect in knowledge does not require elaboration: *Instruct a wise man, and he will grow wiser* (Prov 9:9). But the common people need both, *precept after precept, precept after precept, line upon line, line upon line* (Isa 28:10, 13). And despite this, they understand a little, *here a little, there a little*. Therefore, each group should be addressed according to its capacity.

His treatise, Maimonides insisted, did not contain anything beyond what he had written in the *Commentary on the Mishnah* or the *Mishneh Torah*. It was simply a reiteration of themes and a popular embellishment that the common people would understand.[37] Maimonides' rhetoric was multitiered, as he addressed more than one audience. Here, he indicated distinctly that the treatise was intended mainly for the uneducated. As always, he conveyed a beneficial message to the enlightened as well. The treatise is a masterful piece of rhetorical accommodation.

The treatise has four parts. (1) Maimonides first elucidated his previous statements, insisting that he always regarded resurrection as a fundamental belief. (2) He then discussed reactions to the *Mishneh Torah,* the main target of his critics. He found that some of his followers misunderstood his intentions and other people were confused. (3) He added comments on two new questions: (i) Why did some verses in the Prophets and Writings deny resurrection? (ii) Why was resurrection not mentioned in the Pentateuch? (4) In conclusion, he explained that his intended audience was the general public, not the intellectual elite.

He reiterated throughout the treatise that its arguments were not scientific or demonstrative but rhetorical and persuasive, geared to the popular imagination. At the same time, he stressed his belief in the literal sense of resurrection. Maimonides emulated God's accommodation to the spiritual level of his audience and the wily graciousness with which he shows the way to higher levels.

Maimonides had to treat resurrection cautiously for several reasons. One was because it was a fundamental belief in Islam. Baha' al-Din Ibn Shaddad, in his laudatory biography of Saladin, gave his order to execute Suhrawardi as an example of his piety.[38] Saladin believed in resurrection and despised philosophers and those who denied positive divine attributes. We can readily understand Maimonides' discretion in writing about these subjects.

Distortions of Maimonides' View

Maimonides stated that if he did not mention resurrection in his writings frequently enough, as his critics claimed, this did not imply that he denied its importance.[39] It is not unusual, he wrote, for someone to explain the meaning of an issue clearly and precisely only to have people who are sick of soul misinterpret what he says. This happened when Moses tried to teach that God is one by announcing, *Hear, O Israel! The Lord is our God, the Lord is one* (Deut 6:4). Yet the Christians inferred that God is the third person of the Trinity.[40] They interpreted the words *the Lord, our God,* and *the Lord,* followed by *one,* as proof that God is three and the three are one (*may He be exalted* above what the ignorant suppose).[41] "If this occurred with the discourse of God, then it is even more likely to occur with the discourse of mankind, as in the case of some simpletons[42] in interpreting my discourse concerning one of the foundations of the law."

Maimonides had asserted in Introduction to Sanhedrin, x (Pereq Heleq), that resurrection of the dead is a foundation of the law accepted by consensus within the religious community, which must be believed by all who adhere to it.[43] Yet the true end of human life is immortality of the soul in the world hereafter. Maimonides taught that after resurrection people would die (again) and only their intellects would survive.

TEACHING FUNDAMENTAL BELIEFS

The discipline concerned with religious principles was *kalam,* or theology.[44] Maimonides' formulation of the thirteen principles of faith was therefore a theological endeavor. The principles were based upon tradition and communal consensus, defining who belongs to the community and who does not.

Maimonides sought to teach members of the community the meaning of immortality and to avert their minds from crude physical no-tions. He explained the true essence of immortality, without bothering with resurrection, in the Introduction to Sanhedrin, x (Pereq Heleq). He focused on immortality, he said, because people deliberated about resurrection and whether people shall arise naked or clothed and such absurd questions, yet they ignored immortality of the soul.[45] He explained that while resurrection is one of the foundations of the law, it is not the ultimate goal, which is life of the world hereafter.[46] For "this is the reward beyond which there is no reward and the good beyond which there is no good."[47] He stressed this because it was widely held that the Pentateuch offers reward and punishment only in this life, and that reward and punishment in the afterlife are not mentioned there at all.[48]

Existence in the Afterlife

Maimonides discussed these themes in the *Mishneh Torah*.[49] There, he catalogued those who do not have a portion in the afterlife, among them someone who denies resurrection. He explained that the afterlife is the final goal, the ultimate reward, and the ultimate good.[50] The world hereafter does not admit the existence of bodies, as the sages said: *It consists of neither eating or drinking or intercourse.* He used the term "intercourse" (*tashmish* [*ha-mittah*]), whereas the talmudic source, as we have it, spoke of procreation (*periyah u-reviyah*).[51] Maimonides evidently thought that procreation was a euphemism and that the real intention is that there is no sexual intercourse in the world hereafter. He wanted to stress this, I think, in order to contrast Jewish with Islamic belief. The Qur'an portrays sexual relations in Paradise with virgins—the black-eyed houris, "spotless virgins, amorous, like of age," "with swelling breasts," untouched and modest, "enclosed in pavilions" (56:22–23, 56:34–39, 78:33, 55:56, 58, 72, 74).[52] Jews of simple faith could easily be enticed by such attractions, especially when the Jewish vision of immortality promised only that *the righteous will be seated, with crowns on their heads, and will bask in the splendor of the divine presence [Shekhinah].*[53]

The common people imagine that eternal life is corporeal, as they believe that only body has real existence.[54] Hence, most of them think that God is a body. If not, in their view, he does not exist. But true men of science know that what is separate from matter has a more real existence than what is embedded in matter, for it is not affected by change. All separate created beings, such as the angels and the intellect, are permanent and more real than any body. By angels Maimonides meant the intelligences that move the celestial spheres, and by intellect he meant the Agent Intellect. The angels are incorporeal, and the denizens of the world hereafter are separate souls, or intellects. He reminded the reader that he had adduced proofs for this on the basis of the law in *The Guide of the Perplexed*.[55]

Resurrection as a Parable

In the *Treatise on Resurrection,* Maimonides recapitulated the events that led to composing the work. Maimonides' brief and vague remarks on resurrection in his Mishnah commentary and code of law suggested to some of his readers that his discourse was not to be taken literally and that resurrection is nothing but a myth.[56]

This interpretation was not confined to his opponents but was shared by his own followers.[57] After the *Mishneh Torah* had been widely disseminated, Maimonides heard that one of his followers in Damascus taught that there is no resurrection and that the soul does not return to the body after their separation, citing Maimonides' view in the *Mishneh Torah* that the final goal is an incorporeal existence in the afterlife.[58] The man's critics appealed to the general opinion among the religious community and to many texts of the sages. The fellow replied, "They are all a parable." When Maimonides was told about it, he said that he took no notice, commenting, "This is inconsequential, for no one could be ignorant of this or have any problem understanding what I said."

Yet in 1188/89, Maimonides received a query from Yemen telling him that some people there had decided that the body disintegrates, the soul does not return to the body after separation, and reward and punishment pertain only to the soul—there is no bodily resurrection—citing Maimonides' views on the afterlife. When clear texts of the prophets and sages concerning resurrection were quoted to them, they replied that resurrection is a parable and should be interpreted figuratively. The questioners informed Maimonides that this opinion had spread among the Yemenite Jews and requested instruction in a responsum.

He replied that resurrection is a foundation of the law, that it should not be interpreted figuratively, and that the afterlife follows resurrection.[59] He had explained this in the Introduction to Sanhedrin, x (Pereq Heleq) and thought that this amount of explanation would suffice.[60] Maimonides' statement there is very brief. He said that resurrection is a foundation (qa'ida) of the law of Moses, and whoever does not believe it has no connection with the Jewish community. He stressed that it is for the righteous, for there were other views, for instance, of Islam, that the righteous and wicked are all resurrected, followed by the judgment that separates the righteous from the sinful. Further on, he said that the ultimate aim is spiritual immortality.

Maimonides observed that resurrection was a common opinion about which all Jewish sects, including the Karaites, concurred.[61] It is often mentioned in prayers, sermons, and invocations composed by the prophets and the great sages of the Talmud and Midrash. The community is unanimous in believing it without resorting to figurative interpretation, and one must believe in it to be a member of the community.

The general recourse of intellectuals confronted by the doctrine of resurrection was to interpret it figuratively, and this was an obvious option for Maimonides. He did not avail himself of it because the reference to resurrection in the book of Daniel (Dan 12:2, 13) was decisive and left no room for symbolic interpretation.

Maimonides forcefully denied the accusation that he considered resurrection a parable. This was, he claimed, an outright lie and pure calumny. Maimonides' writings have become public, and so this can be verified. He regarded the vision of dry bones in Ezekiel (Ezek 37:1–14) a parable, but this is what the sages of Israel, or some, had already said.[62] Maimonides established a clear criterion for assessing the force of Aggadah in the Talmud. As long as a difference of opinion did not entail changing behavior, there was no reason for preferring one view over another.[63] "I have mentioned this in the *Commentary on the Mishnah* several times."[64] In any case, the individuals whose souls return to their bodies eat, drink, have sex, give birth and die after very long lives like the lives of those who exist in the days of the Messiah."[65]

What really mattered to Maimonides was not belief in the long physical lives of the resurrected but the spiritual afterlife.

The Miraculous

What he denied and that for which he was innocent of before God was the judgment that the soul never returns to the body.[66] This denial leads to the denial of all miracles, just as the denial of creation leads to a denial of all miracles. The denial of the miraculous is a denial of the root principle and renunciation of the law.[67]

THE WOLF SHALL DWELL WITH THE LAMB

Maimonides' purpose in the treatise was to remove any doubt that he interpreted resurrection figuratively. He had to deal with criticism of his parabolic interpretation of Isaiah's statement, *The wolf shall dwell with the lamb, the leopard lie down with the kid,* etc. (Isa 11:6).[68] Maimonides said that competent exegetes proposed this interpretation before him.

Maimonides believed that Isaiah's vision of a transformation in animal behavior in the messianic era is parabolical because of his conviction that in the messianic era no change in the nature of things will occur.[69] The world will follow its regular course. Maimonides recognized a natural order, except for some rare phenomena that are miraculous.

These promises in Isaiah and others like them, which Maimonides said are a parable, may not be, for no divine inspiration had come to him instructing him that they are so.[70] He never found a tradition of the sages on the authority of the prophets declaring that these things are a parable.[71] His desire and the desire of intellectuals differed from the desire of the common people. The common people love to set the law and reason at variance, to detach everything from reason and to claim that what happens is miraculous. The common people steer clear of anything being according to nature, whether in the past, the present, or the future. Maimonides wanted to unite the law with reason, and he regarded all things as following a natural order, except what is distinctly miraculous and cannot be given a figurative interpretation. Only then would he recognize something as miraculous.

Yet the Isaiah prophecy may not be a parable. It is possible to explain the transformation of animal temperament in a natural way. When the inhabited world develops and lands become fertile, the hostility of animals will diminish and they will become sociable with one another. Aristotle mentioned this in the *Book of Animals* when giving the reason for the lack of dissension among animals in Egypt, even though this is exaggerated. Maimonides explained in the *Guide* that many parables appear in the words of prophets. He did his utmost to explain this so that no arrogant ignoramuses could deny it.[72] For this reason, he and the excellent exegetes who preceded him say that these are parables, as he interpreted them.

Following a literal interpretation of Isaiah's prophecy, it will be a miracle that will appear specifically on the Temple Mount, as it says, *in all of my sacred mount* (Isa 11:9). It will be like the sages' saying, *And never did serpent or scorpion do harm in Jerusalem.*[73] "In sum, all these things are not foundations of the law, and one should not make an issue over how they are believed," Maimonides wrote.

These matters cannot be determined until they appear and it becomes clear whether they are a parable or a miracle. In the final analysis, Maimonides wished to avoid having to acknowledge a change in the order of creation. "It is known that I strongly reject a *change in the order of creation*."[74] We must distinguish between miracles, which occur on account of necessity or to validate a prophecy, and the constant natural things that are the custom of the world, about which the sages say, *The world follows its course,*[75] and *We do not summon proof from miracles.*[76] Solomon said that *whatever God does will be forever and cannot be added to or diminished* (Eccl 3:14). The natural things remain constant according to their custom.

Necessary Beliefs

Some scholars have claimed that the vehement tone and the outlandish literalism are not typical of Maimonides and force the conclusion that he was not the author of this treatise, that it was a later forgery.[77]

We can dismiss these doubts, as we now have the writings of Samuel ben Eli and Joseph ben Judah that were part of the ongoing debate that provoked Maimonides' *Treatise on Resurrection*. Moreover, Maimonides emphasized throughout the treatise that the unsophisticated belief in resurrection of the body was intended for the general public, not for intellectuals. And we have noted the force majeure that compelled him to embrace resurrection in the literal sense.

Resurrection of the body is one of the beliefs that are necessary in a society. Maimonides noted two kinds of belief.[78] (1) First are correct opinions by which one attains ultimate perfection, which the law invites us to believe in a summary way, such as the existence of the deity, his unity, and incorporeality. (2) The second class includes beliefs that are necessary for the sake of the welfare of political affairs, such as the belief that God is violently angry with those who are disobedient, so that one should fear him and avoid disobeying him.[79] The common people adhere to the law only when they are promised rewards or threatened with punishment, and the necessary beliefs give this incentive. They are superfluous for philosophers, who obey the law without regard to reward and punishment. The concept of "necessary beliefs," which are untrue, such as Plato's "noble lie" (*Republic* 414c), is found in al-Farabi's discussion of political governance in his summary of Aristotle's *Topics*.[80] He listed ways in which dialectical arguments were useful, though not scientifically true.

Aristotle often said regarding his exoteric philosophy that he wanted to teach the masses the generally accepted opinions. The philosopher shares these with them. He is then protected, and his project is not rejected, for the common people tend to reject what is alien to them. A philosopher, said al-Farabi, may intend to teach the public opinions that are true, certain, and demonstrative. But as the proofs of these statements are remote and alien for them, he will prefer to teach them these opinions by way of dialectic or rhetoric, thereby disseminating among them necessary opinions (*ara' daruriyya*) that are beneficial to them.[81] He does this by means of political governance (*al-tadbir al-madani*).[82]

21

Epistle on Astrology and Lunel Correspondence

Nonsense is nonsense, but the history of nonsense is a very important science. In certain respects it is more revealing than the history of sciences based on reason.

—SAUL LIEBERMAN[1]

MAIMONIDES' *Epistle on Astrology* was written in response to a question that the rabbis of southern France sent to him. The writers of the query were not students of astrology but heard much about it and read some astrological books. The questioners were members of a group surrounding Rabbi Jonathan ha-Kohen and they requested that Maimonides send his reply to Jonathan in Montpellier. The query may have first been posed by Jonathan himself, and when the Master's reply was delayed, Jonathan's colleagues wrote again, as occurred later with questions on the *Mishneh Torah*.[2] The Provençal scholars had studied the *Mishneh Torah* and in the course of their correspondence with Maimonides raised questions about it. One of them, the well-known Rabbi Abraham ben David of

Posquières (RaBaD), wrote critical comments on the *Mishneh Torah*, as we have seen.

The Epistle on Astrology was the first in a series of letters exchanged between Maimonides and the rabbis of southern France. Their learning in law was impressive, but they admittedly lacked training in philosophy and the sciences, hence his replies on scientific questions were elementary.

Jonathan ben David ha-Kohen (ca. 1135–1210), the main spokesman, was a Talmudist who may have studied with Meir Ibn Migash in Spain and was a pupil and colleague of Abraham ben David of Posquières.[3] Jonathan became interested in Maimonides when he found a copy of the *Epistle to Yemen*. It may have been the section condemning astrology that generated the query on astrology that the Lunel scholars sent to Maimonides. The validity of astrology was a current issue, one reason being that it was sometimes tied in with medicine. Rabbi Jonathan, the leader of the group, was still in Montpellier in 1194, when Maimonides replied to the query on astrology.[4] Soon after, Jonathan relocated to Lunel.

Maimonides' correspondence with Jonathan and the sages of Lunel is marked by stylistic grace and learning, and is a classic of Hebrew letters. Both sides were deferential. Thus, toward the end of his life (he was about sixty), he found a group of serious scholars who appreciated what he had done and defended him against detractors. He was optimistic about the blossoming of a new center of Jewish learning in southern France.

The Provençal sages wrote to Maimonides that they received a letter relating that men from a distant land told Maimonides that a prophet arose in Israel[5] who announced the advent of the redeemer, and that Maimonides informed the people of Fez about it in a letter. Maimonides explained to them in his *Epistle on Astrology* that the letter to Fez was probably a copy of the message he had sent in the *Epistle to Yemen*. The Yemenite Jews had made copies of Maimonides' letter and sent them to other communities. Fez was a natural address because its people had suffered a fate similar to the fate of the Yemenites.

Maimonides restated the circumstances of the Yemen episode in the astrology epistle. Accordingly, an individual appeared in Yemen claiming to be a messenger preparing the way for a Messiah who was to appear in the land of Yemen. Actually, in the *Epistle to Yemen* the man was described as claiming to be the Messiah himself, but this is a common ambiguity.[6] Maimonides also related in the *Epistle on Astrology* that Arabs were among the people who rallied to the messianic claimant, something he did not mention in the Yemen letter. He said that he feared for the Jews in Yemen and wrote to inform them about the true signs of the Messiah, warning them to caution this claimant lest he and the communities perish. In the *Epistle to Yemen,* as we have it, he told them to apprehend the man.

According to the *Epistle on Astrology*, the man was apprehended after a year, and all who had joined him fled. The Arab ruler who had imprisoned him asked him for a verifying sign: "What is your miracle?" The fellow replied, "Chop off my head and I shall recover." The ruler thereupon accommodated him by chopping off his head on the spot. The man's prediction did not come true. Until now, said Maimonides, ignoramuses in Yemen expect him to come back to life and resume his career.[7]

The inconsistencies between the two epistles may be due to some imprecision in the astrology letter, as Maimonides wrote it in great haste.[8] Another possibility is that by the time he wrote the astrology letter he knew more details about the Messiah of Yemen.

QUERY BY RABBIS OF SOUTHERN FRANCE

The rabbis of Provence were concerned with astrology as it influenced genethlialogy, hemerology, and menology. Genethlialogy is the technique of compiling a horoscope from the position of the stars at the time of birth. Hemerology and menology have to do with choices of auspicious and inauspicious times for undertaking a project. One of the main functions of the astrologer, especially in royal courts, was to predict when enterprises could be embarked upon successfully. In addition, there was a political or universal astrology, calculated by periods and cycles according to the location of the planets in the signs when the earth was fashioned. Maimonides had discussed this kind of astrology in the *Epistle to Yemen.*

The authors of the query lamented that formerly in Israel some-one setting out on a journey could consult a seer, but those days had passed because of troubled times.[9] Wisdom was bereft and exiled. *There is no one to guide her* (Isa 51:18) until God sends a savior (cf. Isa 19:20), making known the paths of righteousness (cf. Isa 26:7). We realize here that Maimonides' cultural pessimism was an attitude shared by others.

Referring to Maimonides, they wrote:

Then wisdom went out, and wore royal robes and embroidery.[10] Wisdom then conceived and bore a precious son: *Mighty God, Everlasting Father, Prince of Peace is his name.*[11] *Authority rests on his shoulders.*[12] *Justice shall be the belt around his waist, and faithfulness the belt around his hips.*[13] He opened the chambers of the Torah[14] to illumine eyes and made it accessible.[15] He erected her siege towers[16] and raised her citadels.[17] *There the weary are at ease* [Job 3:17] and find a resting place [cf. Lam 1:3] at *that good hill country and the Lebanon* [Deut 3:25],[18] where the tree of knowledge is [cf. Gen 2:9, 17]. *Its branches grew long* [Ezek 31:5]; *it was beautiful in its prominence, in the length of its branches* [Ezek 31:7]. *The waters nourished it, the deep made it grow tall* [Ezek 31:4]. There will lie down the poor sheep, the driven away and the lame [cf. Micah 4:6]. For this is the [place of] repose.[19]

Some members of the Provençal fellowship (*havurah*)[20] wished to ask Maimonides about a saying of the sages: "Israel has no patron star" (*mazzal*).[21] They noted that the Geonim Rabbi Sherira and Rabbi Hayya (his son) had classified astrologers in a response to a query.[22] (1) Some astrologers ascribe all events to a patron star, even a person's movements and emotions, but they do not acknowledge God and hence are of no concern. (2) Some of them say that a person may influence astrological determination. (i) Some of these say that the human soul and spirit can alter the influence of the heavenly bodies. (ii) Some of them ascribe this power to the Lord of the worlds, saying that he created in a person the capacity to influence his star.[23] When a planet causes a fever to come in the person's appointed time, that person can drink something cold and cool off, alleviating suffering. However, precaution does not affect someone destined to die on a specific day according to his horoscope.

The rabbis of southern France objected to astrology because it entailed that astral and planetary decrees (*gezerot*) are fixed in the world from creation. But this discourages those devoted to Torah and inhibits prayer. For everyone will consider how the order of creation affects him and how to elude astrological predictions. The sages said, *Behold, this is a vain prayer.*[24]

If astrology were valid, if everything were foreordained, a person would not do righteous deeds and pray for the dying to recover. But life, wealth, and joy are to be sought from the Creator. Sherira Gaon and Hayya Gaon relied in their responsum upon the view that *Israel has no patron star.*

The rabbis of southern France wondered how the science of astrology differed from other sciences; the medical sciences are very useful, but this science of astrology contains much vexation. They wanted Maimonides to tell them the truth about the misfortunes astrologers predict: whether they know for every occasion, and if it is possible to take precautions by consulting a wise man.

The writers chronicled some of the predictions of astrologers. The list is arresting, for it indicates the recurring catastrophes that triggered anxiety: The person will die by unusual diseases. He will die at the hands of brigands. He will languish in prison. He will die an unusual death along with many people. He will suffer a permanent defect. His property will be confiscated. Circumstances will cause him to kill himself. He will be captured while on a journey and brought into captivity. Misfortune will come upon him in midlife. His end will not be good. Many tribulations will come over him. He will be forever poor. He will spend all his days in desolation, anxiety, and fear of death. A chronic illness will overtake one of his brothers. All his brothers will die during his lifetime. Most of his children will die. There are other accidents, including the sword, fire, water, or wild beasts; collapse of a building, wall, or roof; and falling from a high place.

They wanted to know whether a wise man can have prior knowledge of an affliction in all these future contingencies and whether there was an advantage in trying to save a man from his dreadful fate in every astrological decree. Can the astrologers discern whether they come about by human means or by divine agency? And as for troubles, poverty, desolation, anxiety, and fear of death mentioned before, they asked Maimonides if there is a remedy for these things.

A Muslim philosopher who was in their country, they heard, stated that no astrologer has the power to determine clearly that such-and-such will come about. For the supernal sphere emits forces upon creatures that change every moment, just as stars and planets do. No person can withstand them. At times the forces of the supernal sphere reverse the force of the stars. No wise person can calculate this. Therefore no one can make a correct astrological prediction. Nothing is hidden from Maimonides, they said, and he knows if there is substance to what the Muslim philosopher claimed.

The Provençal sages asked the Master to remove their doubts and quiet their dismay by general and particular rules clearly and explicitly presented without omitting anything. They extended to Maimonides an invitation to visit them: "It would be well if you were to visit our country and rest in our land."[25] They asked him to reply in a single letter in his hand concerning this matter that should be communicated only to people who have discretion.

They ended with instructions to the Master on how to address his letter if he considered it right to reply in this way. He should send his letter by way of a trusted messenger to another trusted messenger, until he came to a place named Montpellier near the cities of Narbonne and Marseille. It should be written and sealed as a sign of good faith[26] in the name of Rabbi Jonathan, one of the teachers and pious men of their land.

In a manuscript preserving the Provençal scholars' query we find their return address, "May the letter be delivered to the mighty council [*moshav ha-etanim*],[27] the foundations of the earth,[28] the sages of the land of France, may God preserve them, who dwell in Montpellier, at their head, the Rav, the sage Rabbi Jonathan ha-Kohen, the worthy scholar. May God preserve him."

MAIMONIDES' RESPONSE

The exchange of letters with the rabbis of southern France began in around 1194 with the query on astrology. Maimonides' reply was dated September 27, 1194. This was followed in 1195/96 by a letter from Jonathan, as leader of the group, with a flattering letter in rhymed prose and an attachment with questions on the *Mishneh Torah*. Maimonides was ill often during these years and delayed his replies for a long time. His letter to Samuel Ibn Tibbon, whom they agreed should translate *The Guide of the Perplexed*, was dated September 30, 1199. He sent another letter after that one and the French scholars sent two more.

It was uplifting for him to receive letters from scholars who appreciated what he had done and asked friendly and constructive questions, although Abraham ben David of Posquières, who wrote animadversions on the *Mishneh Torah,* belonged to this circle.

Maimonides' contact with the rabbis of southern France began about four years after his quarrel with Gaon Samuel ben Eli, which was crushing and disappointing. After Maimonides had worked for ten years on the *Mishneh Torah*, learned colleagues found it wanting, accused him of self-aggrandizement, and tried to destroy his reputation.

Now in southern France he found scholars who valued his work, who were sincerely puzzled by some passages, and addressed him with veneration. The Spanish origin of many Provençal scholars surely pleased him. His hopes for a continuation of learning were centered on southern France. It was in this environment that Samuel Ibn Tibbon, translator of *The Guide of the Perplexed*, emerged. Samuel was from one of the prominent families of Andalusian scholars that settled in southern France. The sun set on Andalusia and rose in Provence, the next great center of Torah and the sciences.[29] Aside from that single ray of light the rest of the Exile was bleak.

Maimonides addressed the scholars of southern France as *our companions and familiar friends* (cf. Ps 55:14), the keen sages *who know law and custom* (Esth 1:13), who dwell in the city of Montpellier.[30] Maimonides praised the learning of the Provençal sages. Aside from them there was no one to raise the banner of Moses and to ponder the Talmud.[31] They had established houses of study and were men of discernment and wisdom.[32] But in all other places the Torah had vanished from the prudent (cf. Jer 49:7). He urged them:

And so no help remains for us except you, our brethren and redeemers. *Let us be strong and resolute for the sake of our people and for the cities of our God* [2 Sam 10:12; 1 Chron 19:13]. Strive to be valiant men, for the issue depends upon you. You are obligated by the command of levirate marriage, whether to refuse or to marry.[33] Do not depend upon my waging war. *I today can no longe sally forth and come in* [Deut 31:2].[34] I have become old and gray, not from the many years but from the nature of my body, which is *familiar with illness* [Isa 53:3].[35] And may the Creator (blessed be he) help you and make you renowned and famous upon the earth.[36]

Maimonides had rejected astrology in the *Mishneh Torah* and thought that they had received the work, but their query indicated that either they had not or they did not pay sufficient attention to what he had said.[37] "It is obvious that my compendium on the laws of the Torah, which I named *Mishneh Torah,* has not reached you." I do not believe that Maimonides was being sarcastic. We know from Judah al-Harizi that not all of the Book of Knowledge, which includes the Treatise on Idolatry and the section on astrology, had arrived in France but only parts of it.[38]

Their question whether astrology was a science induced him to formulate criteria for assenting to truth claims.

It is only proper for a person to believe one of three things: (1) something for which there is a demonstrative proof based upon reasoning, such as arithmetic, geometry, and astronomy; (2) something that a person perceives through one of the five senses; or (3) something that a person receives from the prophets or from the righteous.[39]

The vast majority of people err, Maimonides observed, in thinking that what is written in books, especially ancient ones, is true.[40] Since many people study and discuss those books, the rash person immediately concludes that its words are wise.

Maimonides blamed astrology for the destruction of the second commonwealth and the holy temple in Jerusalem. Jewish tradition, embodied in rabbinic sources and in the daily prayer book, says that the catastrophe was "because of our sins." Maimonides, in contrast, gave a natural explanation.[41]

What annihilated our kingdom and destroyed our temple and brought us to this pass is that our forefathers sinned and perished because they found many books about these matters of the stargazers, these things being the root of idolatry, as we explained in Laws Concerning Idolatry.[42] They erred and were drawn to them, imagining them to be illustrious sciences having great utility. They did not study the art of war or the conquest of lands, but imagined that those things would assist them. The prophets therefore called them foolish and stupid [cf. Jer. 4:22]. And surely they were foolish, for they followed worthless things that cannot profit [cf. 1 Sam 12:21 and Jer 2:8].

Astrology, Maimonides argued, is in no way scientific but mere foolishness, as can be demonstrated.[43] The Greek sages, who were really sages, never studied this subject or wrote about it.[44] Only the Chasdeans, Chaldeans, Egyptians, and Canaanites made the error of calling it a science.[45] The Persian sages also realized that all the sciences that the Chasdeans, Chaldeans, Egyptians, and Canaanites produced are falsehoods and lies.[46]

The philosophers, who affirm that everything is ultimately caused by the spheres and the astral bodies, say that whatever occurs to human beings is accidental and has no cause from above, and neither one's nativity nor one's nature will help.[47] They ascribe everything to accident or chance occurrence.[48] The adherents of the true religion assign what strikes people not to chance but rather to judgment: *For all his ways are judgment* (Deut 32:4).[49] The sages said, *There is no death without sin and no afflictions without transgression.*[50]

This was written after completion of *The Guide of the Perplexed,* yet Maimonides appealed to a traditional notion of divine providence, omitting his more sophisticated opinion that providence is consequent upon intellect.

One of the principles of the religion of Moses, acknowledged by all the philosophers, is that all human actions are in their control, nothing coerces them, and no nature or nativity compels them.[51]

Whatever occurs, he contended, does so by *judgment and justice* (Job 36:17), and we cannot fathom God's wisdom to realize by what *judgment and justice* he decreed one thing to be this way and another to be a different way: *For my ways are not your ways, nor are my plans your plans* (Isa 55:8).[52] One should not think that many people behaved righteously without being successful. Either they had committed a sin that caused their failure or were suffering afflictions to attain something better.[53] Our minds cannot comprehend divine judgments in this world and in the afterlife.

Every scientific investigator considers all the talk of stargazers as false.[54] We may find statements by individual sages in the Talmud and Midrash that appear to say that the stars determine the future of every newly born child. One ought not discount rational proofs and accept the words of an individual sage, who may have overlooked something, alluded to something, or spoke for the occasion and the specific case before him.

Maimonides asked his correspondents not to blame him for the brevity of his comments, for he wrote them to fulfill a momentary need. He was very occupied by gentile affairs, meaning service in the court. The excuse he offered was obviously real, yet he also conveyed the idea that the epistle should not be examined too carefully for logic and consistency. He wrote at the end:

> Written under great pressure on 11 Tishre 1506 S.E. = 4944 A.M. (September 27, 1194)[55] in the land of Egypt, may salvation be nigh [yesha' yiqrav]. Let my masters not blame me for brevity, for the letter shows that I wrote it for the present time, and I am very busy with gentile affairs. God knows that were it not for Rabbi Phineas [ben Meshullam] (may God protect him), who sent an envoy and entreated me to the point of embarrassment, and did not leave me until I wrote it, I would not answer now, for I have no time. For this, judge me leniently. May your peace, my brethren, friends, and teachers increase.

SAMUEL IBN TIBBON

The Hebrew translation of *The Guide of the Perplexed, Moreh ha-nevukhim,* by Samuel Ibn Tibbon (b. ca. 1160 in Lunel; d. ca. 1230 in Marseilles) has throughout the centuries been the version used by the vast majority of readers rather than the original Arabic (*Dalalat al-ha'irin*). Samuel was not merely a translator. He turned out to be an important philosopher whose works have recently attracted considerable scholarly attention.[56]

His father, Judah Ibn Tibbon (ca. 1120–90), called "Father of Translators" had created a vocabulary and laid the foundations for translation technique. Judah translated Se'adyah Gaon's *Beliefs and Opinions,* Bahya ibn Paqudah's *Duties of the Heart,* Judah ha-Levi's *Kuzari,* Solomon Ibn Gabirol's *Improvement of the Moral Qualities,* and works by the grammarian Jonah Ibn Janah.[57]

As often, there was a patron, Meshullam ben Jacob of Lunel (d. ca. 1170). He and his five sons were wealthy, learned in Torah and the secular sciences, and pious. They established a *bet midrash* (college) and aided students who came there. Meshullam supported Judah Ibn Tibbon. Judah amassed a great library that later served his son well and would naturally be passed on to his descendants. He and his descendants were instrumental in transmitting the Arabic sciences and philosophy to southern France in their new Hebrew garb.[58]

Judah Ibn Tibbon left Spain in approximately 1150, around the time when Maimonides' family left Córdoba and for the same reason, the Almohad invasion. Along with many other Spanish Jews, Judah crossed the Pyrenees to towns in Provence and Languedoc and settled in Lunel. Benjamin of Tudela met him there in 1160 and described him as a prominent physician.

Judah Ibn Tibbon's *Ethical Will* (1190), to his son Samuel, is a touching human document.[59] He taught Samuel the love and care of books and the importance of calligraphy and style, which he noted had helped Samuel ha-Nagid reach a high station. Judah was from Granada, where the Nagid had resided, and regarded him as a model to be emulated. He expressed annoyance with his son, who as a youth was lazy and neglected his studies. He reminded Samuel that he paid liberally for tutors in the secular sciences and Hebrew and wanted to see a return on his investment.

Lunel Sages Request a Translation of *The Guide of the Perplexed*

The Lunel rabbis asked Maimonides to translate *The Guide of the Perplexed* for them, along with other of his Arabic works.[60] This he said he could not do and instead recommended Samuel Ibn Tibbon, then in his thirties, out of respect for his father's work. Jonathan ben David and his colleagues turned to Samuel, at the time residing in Lunel.[61]

Ibn Tibbon's Hebrew version of *The Guide of the Perplexed* is a masterly work.[62]

Samuel had learned Arabic in a Christian environment and was diffident about his knowledge. Maimonides was surprised that someone who grew up in the lands of Edom (Christendom) could be so proficient. In the Preface to his translation Judah was very modest about his abilities:

> And it was I, Samuel son of Rabbi Judah Ibn Tibbon (may his memory be a blessing), whom they summoned, and to me they turned; for they recognized me as someone who knew a bit of the Arabic language. And as there was no one in their country who understood this language, they entreated with me to translate it for them according to my ability. Although I told them about my limitations in translation for the reasons I have mentioned, they said to me: "In any case, we shall have some benefit from it. And even if the translation be weak and of limited benefit in the sublime matters contained in this book, it is still considerable in our eyes." I could not refuse them, and I made myself into a fool who rushes in confidently. And so I translated it despite my lack of understanding.

Samuel assured his readers that he would check every doubtful word against the books that "the father of translators, my father and teacher (of blessed memory) translated" and in Arabic grammars and Arabic books that he owned. If any doubt remained, he would ask the Great Rav for elucidation. He had already asked him many questions about doubtful places in the text, some of them errors or lacunae, for the book sent to him was uncorrected. Indeed, in many places where Maimonides objected to Samuel's translation, the problem was with the faulty text that Samuel had received. The sages of Lunel were eager to have the translation, so he did it from the inferior manuscript he had. He indicated doubtful places in the marginalia of copies he gave to people, promising to provide corrections in due course.

The poet Judah al-Harizi, as we have seen (ch. 19), translated *The Guide of the Perplexed* shortly after Ibn Tibbon. He said that he was invited to do a new translation by some Provençal scholars. Al-Harizi's translation was written in a loftier style, but it was less accurate and consistent. Ibn Tibbon's translation was occasionally inelegant, but it was faithful to the source. Ironically, Ibn Tibbon succeeded precisely because he rejected Maimonides' advice not to translate literally but to render concepts in the idiom of the target language. Al-Harizi followed Maimonides' method, using many words to translate one and rearranging sentences. The Arabist D. H. Baneth praised Ibn Tibbon's translation and the contribution it made to the study of the most important book in Jewish thought. He called for a modern translation that would combine the virtues of terminological fidelity and elegance of style for the modern reader.[63]

Maimonides' Letter to Ibn Tibbon on Translating The Guide of the Perplexed

Maimonides wrote a long letter to Samuel Ibn Tibbon, answering his questions, giving him general guidance on translation and specific pointers on sentences and terms, and recommending a reading list of philosophers. His letter was dated 8 Tishre 4960 (September 30, 1199), around the time when he wrote to Jonathan ben David after a long delay.

Abraham ben Moses mentioned that "at the end of his father's life he received letters of Rabbi Samuel Ibn Tibbon, who translated *The Guide of the Perplexed* into Hebrew, and he replied to his letters and questions, for Samuel was an esteemed and discerning sage."[64] This is the version in the three manuscripts that the editor used. In the printed edition there is more: "My father and teacher (may the memory of the righteous be blessed) attested that [Samuel] went deeply into the secret matters of *The Guide of the Perplexed* and his other compositions and understood his intention." The longer version actually reflects what Maimonides wrote to Ibn Tibbon (see immediately below). Samuel's query on Maimonides' theory of providence proves that he understood *The Guide of the Perplexed* well.

Maimonides' letter to Samuel is bilingual. The opening, which is a polite prelude, is in Hebrew, and the main part, which concerns the translation, is in Arabic. The letter is lengthy and heterogeneous, but it is an integral letter and not several letters strung together. There are six sections.

1. Opening greetings; friendship

2. Instructions on how to translate

3. Answers to questions on text and translation in first two parts

4. Answers to questions on content in second part

5. Response to request to come to Egypt, his daily schedule

6. Instruction in studying philosophy

Maimonides' translation technique was to reformulate the content of the source language as befits the natural idioms of the target language.[65] He suggested improved translations to Ibn Tibbon but advised the younger man not to depend on his translations alone, which he had written quickly, if he found more appropriate language. The fact is that Maimonides' proposed translations are not better than Ibn Tibbon's initial attempts, and Ibn Tibbon did not use them. Adhering to his theory, Maimonides sometimes translated one word in the source language by six words in the target language. He was a great literary stylist, and his philosophic language in the *Mishneh Torah* is superb, but his translations leave something to be desired. Ibn Tibbon rather followed his father's method, trying to keep to the order of words and using the same translation for the same word throughout.[66]

Maimonides was satisfied with Ibn Tibbon's translation and understanding of the *Guide*. He wrote at the beginning of his letter:

You are certainly qualified to translate from one language to another, for God has given you a perceptive mind for understanding proverb and epigram [*the words of the wise and their riddles*] [Prov 1:6]. I discern from your words that your mind has penetrated to the depths of the matter and has revealed hidden secrets.

I rejoiced to find a wise son, and I was amazed how the nature of a son born among non-Arabic-speakers could be such that he pursues the sciences and is skilled [*mahir*] in the Arabic language, which is undoubtedly a slightly distorted dialect of the Hebrew language, and further how he understands linguistic subtilités and profound matters. This is certainly *like a tree trunk out of arid ground* [Isa 53:2].

May the Lord illumine your eyes with the light of his Torah so that you be of his friends *as the sun rising in its might* (Judg 5:31).

In the fifth section of the letter, Maimonides mentioned his physical weakness and explained that he could not accept a visit from Samuel.

The Creator of the world knows how I wrote to you this amount and that I flee from mankind and seek seclusion in a place they are unaware of, sometimes leaning against a wall, sometimes writing while lying because of the great weakness of my body, for its powers have failed and I am old.

As far as what you mention about coming to visit me, come blessed of visitors. I rejoice at the prospect, wish, yearn, and desire, and shall be happier to see your face than you will be to see mine, although your risking the danger of a sea voyage would distress me. Indeed, I advise you not to risk your life, for by coming you will only gain by seeing my face and what you obtain of my hospitality according to my ability. But do not hope to study any science or be alone with me for even a single hour, day or night, for my affairs are as I shall relate to you.

Maimonides then described his daily schedule.

I dwell in Fustat while the king resides in Cairo, and between the two places there are two Sabbath limits [4,000 cubits = slightly more than one mile]. I have a very difficult assignment with the king. I must see him daily at the beginning of the day. When he is weak, or when one of his sons or concubines is ill, I do not leave Cairo, and most of my day I spend in the king's palace. And I must attend to the king's officers every day. One or two officials is invariably ill, and I must administer their medical treatment.

In sum, every day I go up to Cairo early in the morning, and if there is no mishap or incident, I return to Fustat after midday in any case. As soon as I arrive, in a state of hunger, I find all the vestibules [of my home] filled with gentiles, noble and common, judges and magistrates, a mixed multitude, who know the time of my return. I dismount from my riding animal, wash my hands, and go out to them to persuade them to wait for me while I have a light repast, which I do from time to time. I then go out to heal them and write [prescriptions] for them. They come in and out sometimes until night, and at times, by faith in the Torah, until the end of two hours into the night [around 8:00 P.M.]. I speak with them while lying down because of great fatigue. When night falls I am so utterly exhausted that I cannot speak.

The result is that no Israelite can speak with me or meet with me except on the Sabbath. Then they all come after the [morning] prayer, and I direct the community concerning what they should do all week. They study light things until noon, and then go on their way. Some of them return and study again until the evening prayer.

This is my daily schedule, and I have only told some of what you would see, with the help of God (may he be exalted).[67]

In an earlier letter to Jonathan of Lunel, depicting an illness, he had written:

Most of the day I lie in bed, and the yoke of the gentiles is on my neck regarding medical matters, which have sapped my strength, and have not left me one hour, neither day or night. But what can I do now that my reputation has reached most countries?[68]

A LETTER OF EXPLANATION FROM MAIMONIDES TO SAMUEL

It appears that Samuel asked for a reason for Maimonides' unwillingness to meet him, and in an autograph letter published by Mordechai A. Friedman, we find Maimonides addressing the problem. As often happens, one document is more valuable than a hundred theories.

It is a letter of apology in Hebrew which Maimonides wrote to a Samuel the sage, whom Friedman tentatively identifies as Samuel Ibn Tibbon.[69] He suggests that the apology relates to Maimonides' inability to meet with Samuel.[70] As in other letters, Maimonides complained of time pressures and ill health. The absence of signature and address may mean that the document is a draft or a copy of the letter that was sent. Another possibility is that Maimonides intended to send the letter and then changed his mind. He requested of Rabbi Samuel the sage,[71] the pious, to give him the benefit of doubt in everything. He is surely aware of Maimonides' esteem. But Maimonides said that his capacity was limited and time pressing, "nor can a man reveal all the circumstances for various reasons. In any case, *the Merciful One desires the heart*."[72] At this time, he was probably Head of the Jews.

Maimonides' explanation is persuasive. He was ill and weak, with the end in sight and so much to do, when even pleasant visits of friends were demanding and enervating, certainly a fervid admirer who would come with great expectations. His refusal to meet with Samuel was not an expression of disesteem. Sadly, after Maimonides' death, Samuel came to visit Egypt, but it appears that he stayed in Alexandria and never visited Fustat.

In the fifth section of the first letter to Samuel Maimonides gave him instructions for studying philosophy:

> Be careful not to study the works of Aristotle without the commentaries on them, the commentary of Alexander or the commentary of Themistius, or the commentary of Ibn Rushd. However, the books you mentioned to me that you have with you, including the *Book of the Apple* and the *Book of the House of Gold,* are all drivel, inane and vapid. These two books belong to the spurious works ascribed to Aristotle.
>
> The book of *Divine Wisdom,* which al-Razi wrote, is authentic, but it is useless, for al-Razi was merely a physician.[73] The same is true of the *Book of Definitions* and the *Book of Elements,* which Isaac Israeli composed. They too are drivel, esoteric and vapid, for Isaac Israeli was also merely a physician.[74]
>
> But the book *Microcosm,* which Rabbi Joseph ha-Saddiq composed, I have not seen, however, *I knew the man and his discourse* (2 Kings 9:11), and I recognized his eminence and the value of his book, for he undoubtedly followed the system of the Sincere Brethren.[75]
>
> In general, I say to you: Do not concern yourself with books on logic except for what the philosopher Abu Nasr al-Farabi composed; for all that he wrote in general, and in particular his *Principles of the Existent Beings,* is wheat without chaff, and one should pay attention to his words and understand what he says, for he was exceedingly wise.[76] Likewise, Abu Bakr Ibn al-Sa'igh [Ibn Bajja] is a great philosopher, and his words and compositions—*all are straightforward to the intelligent man, and right to those who have attained knowledge* [Prov 8:9].

The books of Aristotle are the sources and foundations for these compositions on the sciences. They are not understandable, as we have mentioned, except with the commentaries on them, [namely,] the commentary of Alexander or Themistius or the commentary of Ibn Rushd.

But as for other compositions, such as the books of Empedocles, the books of Pythagoras, the books of Hermes, and the books of Porphyry—all these are ancient philosophers on which it is not worth wasting one's time.

The discourse of Plato, the teacher of Aristotle, in his books and compositions, contains enigmas and parables and are also superfluous for an intelligent man; for the books of his pupil Aristotle cover all that was composed previously. His opinion—I mean to say, the opinion of Aristotle—is the ultimate of human opinion, save for those who received the divine overflow, so that they attained the rank of prophecy, which is the highest rank.

The books of Abu 'Ali Ibn Sina, although they are accurate and contain subtle speculation, are not comparable to the books of Abu Nasr al-Farabi. His books are nevertheless useful. He too is a man whose discourse you should study and whose compositions you should scrutinize. I have guided and instructed you concerning what you should study and wherein you should occupy your precious soul.

May your peace, my friend, son and pupil, increase and may salvation be at hand for a poor and miserable people.

> Signed by Moses, son of Rabbi Maimon the Sefaradi
> (may the memory of the righteous be a blessing),
> on 8 Tishre 1511 s.e. [September 30, 1199 c.e.] Peace.

22

The Physician

Life is short, and Art long; the crisis fleeting; experience
perilous, and decision difficult. The physician must not only be
prepared to do what is right himself, but also to make the
patient, the attendants, and externals cooperate.

—HIPPOCRATES, *Aphorisms*, TRANS. FRANCIS ADAMS

FAME AND ITS PRICE

Maimonides moved in the highest circles in Cairo thanks to his skill as a physician. He informed his pupil Joseph ben Judah (1191) that he had acquired a reputation in the practice of medicine:

> Know that I have attained great fame in medicine among the eminent, such as the chief judge,[1] the emirs, the house of [al-Qadi] al-Fadil, and other heads of state, without recompense.[2] As for the common people, I am above them and inaccessible to them.[3]
>
> This has necessitated my always spending the day in Cairo attending the sick. When I return to Fustat, I am able at most during the remainder of the day and night to peruse what I need in medical books. You

know the length and difficulty of this art for one who is conscientious and exacting and wishes to avoid saying anything without knowing a proof for it, its source, and the manner of reasoning in that subject.

Because of this, I do not find an hour for studying anything of the law, and I only study Scripture on the day of the Sabbath. As for the rest of the sciences, I do not find time to study any of them. I am deeply aggrieved by this.

It was around the same time that 'Abd al-Latif al-Baghdadi visited Cairo (see above, ch. 11), where he met Maimonides and described his "love of authority and serving the high and mighty."[4]

Serving in the Ayyubid court conferred prestige, but it was not an undiluted blessing. Maimonides complained on several occasions that attending the royal entourage was an irksome and onerous burden. We hear his fatigue and frustration, yet we also sense that his fame was a source of satisfaction to him.

COURT PHYSICIAN

Outstanding physicians, such as Abu Bakr al-Razi, Abu 'Ali Ibn Sina, Abu Marwan Ibn Zuhr, and Ibn Rushd, served in royal courts. Jewish court physicians were ideally suited to represent their community as Head of the Jews as did Maimonides, his predecessors and his descendants down to Nagid David ben Joshua (1335–1415). The rank of court physician demanded a range of talents—scientific knowledge, linguistic aptitude, and diplomatic skill. Royal courts were arenas of dissemblance, deceit, intrigue, and betrayal, where one might easily forfeit one's life by displeasing the sovereign or hasten his demise by some inadvertent blunder.

Maimonides studied medicine in the West, perhaps first in Spain, and then he had clinical training in Fez.[5]

When the Ayyubids came to power in Egypt, al-Qadi al-Fadil extended his patronage to Maimonides, giving him an annual stipend. Maimonides cooperated with other court physicians and did not work independently because, said Ibn al-Qifti, he lacked experience in the practice of medicine, nor was he qualified for management of health. Ibn al-Qifti may have meant administration at one of the hospitals.

Maimonides, Physician to
al-Malik al-Afdal

Saladin had divided the administration of his empire among his sons and close relatives. When he died in 589 (1193), the territories were partitioned among them as appanages. They ruled the three principal provinces: al-Afdal 'Ali ruled in Damascus, al-Zahir Ghazi in Aleppo, and al-'Aziz 'Uthman in Cairo. Al-Afdal held power in Egypt itself briefly (January 1199 to December 1200). It must have been at this time that Maimonides ministered to him and served his second tenure as Head of the Jews. Maimonides' brother-in-law, Abu 'l-Ma'ali, as we have seen (ch. 12), served as secretary for al-Afdal's mother.[6]

Maimonides, then, served as physician to the sultan's eldest son, al-Afdal Nur al-Din 'Ali (1169–1225).[7] The resourceful Qadi al-Fadil administered as al-Afdal's vizier and apparently introduced Maimonides to the ruler. Al-Afdal encouraged and subsidized scholars and litterateurs. It is pointless to ask exactly when al-Afdal was in Cairo, because Maimonides said at the beginning of *The Regimen of Health* that he received al-Afdal's command via a messenger who explained his master's symptoms to him. In 1200, when he was himself ill and confined to his home, Maimonides composed *On the Cause of Symptoms* (*Maqala fi bayan al-a'rad*) for al-Afdal. He explained that his own infirmities and weak constitution prevented him from visiting the prince in person. He wrote his opinions, answered questions, and evaluated counsel given by other physicians.

Saladin's Nephew Taqi al-Din

Saladin's nephew, Taqi al-Din al-Malik al-Muzzafar, beset by a bevy of young maidens, desired to have his ardor enhanced, his overexertion having drained him to the point of febrile emaciation.[8] Maimonides wrote a medical work for the prince, *On Sexual Intercourse* (*Fi 'l-jima'*), prescribing aphrodisiac concoctions yet counseling temperance in erotic pursuits.[9] These, he claimed, debilitate, enfeeble, and attenuate the body. We know how intensely Maimonides denounced "concupiscence for eating, drinking, and copulation."[10] Here we find the Sage of Fustat, the Great Eagle, applying his vast medical knowledge to the awesome task of resuscitating the waning vigor of an impotent potentate.

The Maghribi satirist Ibn Muhriz al-Wahrani had different advice for Taqi al-Din:

> You should resign from this service, settle in the orchards of Damascus, turn away from repentance, and collect together the sinners of Damascus, the prostitutes of Mosul, the panders of Aleppo, and the singing girls of Iraq, delighting the five senses . . . and relying on the forgiveness of the Forgiving and Merciful God.[11]

Although Maimonides stressed that sexual intercourse weakens the body, he did give positive advice about aphrodisiacs and other stimulants. He applied a model that he used in other works: the psyche controls emotional processes, and the emotions influence intercourse. Some emotions are beneficial, such as happiness, laughter, and rest, and some are detrimental, such as anxiety and sorrow, as well as aversion. The woman should be attractive, not too young and not too old.

Among the aphrodisiacs he prescribed was black pepper, the most popular commodity imported from India (but not only for this purpose). Hot spices are often used as aphrodisiacs, because they increase the heart rate and cause perspiring, which are like physical responses that occur during intimacy. He also recommended honey water and wine. 'Umar Khayyam (1048–1122) had it right: "A jug of wine, a loaf of bread, and thou." Alcohol lowers resistance; it is, however, a depressant. "It provokes the desire, but it takes away the performance."[12]

Maimonides recommended "a wondrous secret" never before described. (This was in the middle of quotations from Ibn Zuhr and Ibn Sina, as if to say, "Now listen to me.") He advised the prince to mix some oils with saffron-colored ants and use the blend to massage the penis for two or three hours before sexual intimacy. The erection, he said, remains even after the act.

He also prescribed a potion that he mentioned often in his medical books—a cocktail of a plant called oxtongue with wine (or with honey for someone who is forbidden to drink wine). Maimonides may have used this himself as a mood drug, since he mentions it so often as an antidepressant. He also advised the prince to inhale the aromatics myrrh, amber, and nutmeg.[13]

Maimonides ended his brief treatise with a blessing: "And may the Lord lengthen his days with pleasures, and may those delights be attached to eternal delights for the sake of God's kindness and goodness." He seems to be hinting, seeing that he was advising a Muslim prince, that his eternal delights would be an extension of the hedonistic delights in this world.

The reader may be surprised at Maimonides' expertise in aphrodisiacs, but as a physician serving royalty, emirs, judges, and other eminent men, he had to keep files with this kind of information.

THE MEDICAL PROFESSION

Doctors were among the main culture bearers in this society. Medical training entailed mastery of logic, mathematics, astronomy, physics, and the biological sciences. The libraries of some Jewish physicians, known from their bequests found in the Genizah, show that they were men with broad intellectual horizons. S. D. Goitein describes the medieval physicians of the Mediterranean area as masters of secular erudition and expounders of philosophy and the sciences.[14] Physicians served in the courts of caliphs, sultans, or viziers partly because the ruling elite wanted to have experts in ancient texts in the vicinity. Their reverence for venerable religious books was transferred to ancient books in general. The general stance of a highly scholastic age with its respect for science solidified the position of the medical practitioner in this society.

The Genizah has preserved lists of physicians' libraries, from which we can gauge their intellectual pursuits. The library of a physician, Abu Sa'd, sold in November 1190, contained works on all branches of medicine, pharmaceuticals, philosophy, theology, logic, ethics, politics, physics, and the history of medicine; six volumes of an anthology of Arabic verse (*Kitab al-aghani*); and books on physiognomy and geomancy.[15]

The library of Abraham he-Hasid, a pietist and colleague of Abraham Maimonides, sold in the spring of 1223, contained medical books, biblical books and commentaries, prayer books, *The Guide of the Per-*

plexed, one tractate of the Talmud, and a large collection of books on language.[16]

Many of these physicians were intellectuals who used medicine as a livelihood, not a profession. The linguist Ibn Janah and the poet Judah ha-Levi exemplify this type. S. D. Goitein observed:

> The medieval doctors of the Mediterranean area were the torchbearers of secular erudition, the professional expounders of philosophy and the sciences. While the lawyers studied and applied the sacred laws of their religions and denominations, and therefore were limited in outlook by their very profession, the physicians were the disciples of the Greeks, and as heirs to a universal tradition formed a spiritual brotherhood that transcended the barriers of religion, languages, and countries.[17]

MEDICAL CARE

Maimonides advocated personalization of medical treatment and involvement of family and friends in health care. The physician should give the family detailed instructions about diet and all other external factors that have to be weighed for the individual patient. This is an early example of family-centered patient care.[18] Family caregiving is prevalent in our own societies and is supported by organizations such as the American Red Cross, which has a Family Caregiving Program and a family caregiving reference guide. This benefits the increasing senior population.

Every patient, Maimonides taught, requires *individual* consideration. The doctor should not say, "This disease is similar to that other case"; rather, he should treat each patient independently according to the patient's natural constitution, individual psychology, and specific circumstances. The physician should try to cure not a disease but a diseased person.[19] Maimonides cited Galen as saying that in deciding on a treatment the physician needs to observe seven things: "the nature of the sickness, the nature of the patient, his age, his habits, the nature of the town, the season of the year, and the constitution of the surrounding air."[20]

Maimonides counseled physicians to treat patients humanely. At the beginning of his *Commentary on Hippocrates' Aphorisms,* he wrote a long gloss on the Hippocratic aphorism "Life is short, the art [of medicine] is long," in which he discussed the physician's responsibility.[21] The physician must concern himself with external matters affecting the patient. If the patient is poor, the physician must supply him with food, medicine, and whatever is needed to restore his health. Maimonides' "medical humanism" conformed with the ancient idea that medical care was an act of *philanthropia* (love of mankind) and *humanitas* (humanity). The Hippocratic *Precepts* calls for a physician to give his services free when necessary, but not food and medications, as Maimonides prescribed. Nothing of the sort, it has been said, appears in Galen's comment on this aphorism or in the many commentaries on it in Greek, Latin, Arabic, and Hebrew.[22]

The Genizah has documents showing that Maimonides and his descendant, Nagid David II gave medical advice to poor persons who turned to them as heads of the Jewish community.[23] And a Genizah letter tells of a Christian army surgeon who gave medical treatment to a Jewish woman, injured in an accident, without taking a fee.[24]

Muslim physicians were obligated to treat the poor and sick without compensation.[25] Care of the poor took place in hospitals, which were basically secular institutions open to all people, whether male or female, military or civilian, adult or child, rich or poor, Muslim or non-Muslim.

MEDICAL WRITINGS

Maimonides wrote most of his medical works in the decade of the 1190s and slightly before, when he was in his fifties.[26] After finishing *The Guide of the Perplexed* (ca. 1191), he did not write philosophic or legal works (aside from responsa). He devoted his time to theoretical and clinical aspects of medicine. Despite frailty and declining health, it was during this decade, in the latter part, that he ministered as physician to the royal entourage.

Medicine in the Arab-Islamic world was based mainly on the Greek Hippocratic corpus and the works of the Roman physician Galen.[27] As we have seen above (ch. 18), Arabic medicine presupposes Galenic humoral pathology, according to which physical and mental illness arise from disruptions in the equilibrium of the four basic humors (blood, phlegm, yellow bile, black bile). We are familiar with these humors from terms for human temperaments, such as melancholic, sanguine, choleric, and phlegmatic. The dispositions come about, according to Galenic medicine, from imbalances of the humors. Maimonides worked with a theory of human nature that presupposed a natural disposition or temperament as the basis of personality.[28]

This balance (Greek *eukrasia, symmetria;* Arabic *i'tidal* or *mijaz*) produces well-being. The terminology also had an ethical connotation and relates to the idea of *mesotes,* the mean between two extremes. Excess or deficiency of a humor upsets the balance, and causes illness. The term "melancholia" denotes an excess of black bile, a physiological imbalance affecting the mind.

The classical medical library, including virtually all of Galen's works, was translated into Arabic in the tenth century and became accessible to Muslim physicians, who added their own experience and wisdom. Many of their works were translated into Latin and studied in European universities until the sixteenth century.

In medicine, as in other fields, Maimonides sought to reduce complexity to system and order. He chafed under Galen's prolixity and reduced the Roman physician's massive literary output to a single book, *Extracts from Galen (The Art of Cure)*, which a physician could carry around in his pocket.[29] He also wrote a work called *Medical Aphorisms,* containing about 1,500 passages culled mainly from Galen, with critical comments, providing the physician with a handy desk manual and reducing Galen's 129 books to one.

Maimonides composed ten medical works: *On Hemorrhoids, On Cohabitation, On Asthma, On Poisons and Their Antidotes, Regimen of Health, On the Cause of Symptoms*, and (prepared for fellow physicians) *Extracts from Galen (The Art of Cure), Medical Aphorisms, Commentary on Hippocrates' Aphorisms,* and *Glossary of Drug Names*.

RATIONALISM AND EMPIRICISM

As a medical theorist, Maimonides advocated individual research, a critical attitude toward authority, and attention to both theory and practice. The two main schools of classical medicine—empiricism and rationalism—differed over the relative importance of experience and reason in medicine. Empiricists believed that medical knowledge is acquired by experience, practice, and reliance on observable data. Rationalists emphasized reason and advocated the study of nature and the investigation of causes. Empirical knowledge could not provide causes for what happens in treatment. Yet a proper explanation, according to Aristotle, requires that there be causes if there is to be scientific proof. Maimonides, following Galen, combined rationalism and empiricism, relying on experiment and observation and also using reasoned hypotheses and logical demonstration as much as possible. He favored theory on the assumption that experience without theory was merely probable and that theory offered cogent explanation.

A physician cannot achieve competence by mere practice, Maimonides wrote, without having gained knowledge of theory. As medical experience is recorded in books for many generations, one can learn medicine without practical experience by studying this literature. The greatest mistake is the belief that experience in medicine is of the individual physician in his own time. Medical experience is rather the accumulation of experience over the course of past generations, from before Galen, in what has been written in medical books. Some of the drugs and compound remedies were tested for hundreds of years and only thereafter were written about in books.[30] Experience is often claimed by pseudo-physicians, who make people believe in something unproven to conceal their lack of experience.[31]

To be competent without any theoretical knowledge is impossible, he said, for medicine is not like carpentry or weaving, which are acquired by habit.[32] Abandoning reason means becoming vulnerable to chance.

In his comment on the first aphorism of Hippocrates, which is long and detailed, Maimonides cited al-Farabi, who divided theoretical and practical medicine into seven parts.[33] They are (1) the science of anatomy, (2) the types of health for the body and for each organ, (3) the types of diseases and their causes, (4) interpretation of symptoms, (5) rules for the regimen of health, (6) general rules for restoring health, and (7) foods, medications, binding, bathing, bandaging, physiotherapy, and surgical instruments.

Maimonides said that even if someone knew all seven parts by heart, which would take many years, that person would not yet be an accomplished physician. He needs to observe healthy and sick individuals, learn symptoms and how patients describe them, and know how to determine patients' general and particular constitutions. The physician needs to examine many different patients to be able to adjust the proper treatment to each one of them.

Maimonides described his respect for the theoretical study of medicine in the letter to Joseph ben Judah cited at the beginning of this chapter.[34]

MEDICINE AND NATURE

Medical practitioners must let nature heal. If a physician errs and prescribes a therapy that is contrary to the course of nature, he may impede the cure or aggravate the illness. Al-Farabi asserted that medicine, sailing, and physical labor are similar in that their activity does not necessarily lead to a positive result. This is like a farmer who does everything required, yet the seed does not produce when nature does not cooperate. Or the seaman may navigate his ship in the best possible way, build it well, and sail the sea at the usual time, yet the ship may come to grief.[35] The reason for all these failures is that the goal is achieved only through the action of two agents, one doing all that is necessary, while the other falls short.[36]

The good physician knows when to leave nature alone, whereas the incompetent physician goes by chance. Sometimes it is better to let nature run its course.[37] "And sometimes a man will find a change in his digestion or he will experience some heaviness in his head, or some pain in one part of his body; in such cases be very careful and do refrain from treating these symptoms and from hurrying to use medicines."[38] Maimonides adopted a conservative approach that would prevent drug reactions and fatalities. Rashness, according to ancient medicine, reveals incapacity and ignorance.[39]

Even if a person is scrupulous about health, there is no way to avoid minor illnesses.[40] The digestive system may be irregular, or one may have a headache or pain somewhere or any other minor ailment. One should not be hasty to take medications. The greatest physicians have advised against it, because one's nature is adequate. One should rather follow a healthy regimen, Maimonides advised. If you medicate minor ailments, you either go contrary to your nature or accustom it to being passive and in need of external assistance. It is best to refrain from interfering with nature when life is not in danger, as medications lower the body's resistance.[41] "For this reason," Maimonides wrote, "I have warned you and advised you and urged you to rely on nature, because it is quite adequate in most cases if left alone and undisturbed."[42] Maimonides depended on Hippocrates' aphorism: "Nature cures diseases."[43] Hippocrates said that nature finds and evaluates the ways to cure by itself and nature does what is necessary because it is well trained and educated.[44] Hippocrates thought that people should imitate the actions of nature because nature is wise.[45]

We find an intriguing equation of divine providence and nature's wisdom in Maimonides' statement that the intestines are cared for by providence when yellow bile secretes into them and cleanses and purifies them, yet not even a tiny amount of the bile secretes to the stomach, as this would cause great harm.[46]

MEDICINE AND RELIGION

Maimonides' medical writings contain little reference to talmudic medicine, nor is there any hint of magic, superstition, or astrology, common then in medical practice.[47] When religion and science clashed, he viewed religion from the perspective of a scientist.[48] In one vital respect, however, medicine and religion were related: "By keeping the body in health and vigor, one walks in the ways of God."[49]

In his *Medical Aphorisms,* he cited magic medicaments that he had learned from Abu Marwan Ibn Zuhr, whom he admired, but he disapproved of their use. In his commentary on the first Hippocratic aphorism and in part 22, Maimonides referred to magical concoctions of Ibn Zuhr.[50] He was flexible, however, when it was clear that the power of suggestion assisted the patient, as when women in childbirth used amulets or when people whispered spells over scorpion or snake wounds.[51]

Separating medicine from religion, he recommended wine and music for al-Afdal's melancholy, both strictly forbidden to Muslims:

Let not our Master [al-Afdal] censure his minor Servant [Musa] for what he has stated in this treatise of his about the use of wine and

songs, both of which the [Islamic] law [*shari'a*] abhors. For this
Servant has not commanded that he do this. He has merely noted
what his art [medicine] calls for. The legislators have known, as have
the physicians, that wine is beneficial to mankind. The physician, qua
physician, must give counsel on the conduct of a beneficial regimen,
be it lawful or permissible. The sick then have the option to act or not
[on this advice].

If the physician refrains from prescribing all that is of benefit,
whether it be prohibited or permissible [by the *shari'a*], he misleads
by not giving sincere counsel. It is known that the law [*shari'a*]
commands what is beneficial and prohibits what is harmful in the
next world, whereas the physician gives counsel about what benefits
the body and warns against what harms it in this world.[52]

It is hard to know for sure what Maimonides' intention was. He was
convinced of the curative powers of wine. He wrote: "It is known among
all physicians, that the best of all nutriments is that which was prohibited in Islam."[53] It was said in the Talmud, *At the head of all medicine am
I, wine; only where there is no wine are drugs required.*[54]

Ibn Ridwan, a Muslim physician, recommended matured wine and
raisin liquor as suitable drinks.[55] In his *Aphorisms* Maimonides was
more guarded.[56] He approved of Galen's advice that wine should be
taken in moderation, and that it is very good for the elderly.[57]

Recommending wine to a Muslim, Maimonides may have been
considering the independence of the patient and his freedom of choice.
He was certainly protecting himself against possible criticism by traditional Muslims. Or he may have anticipated that the sultan would
welcome the advice to drink wine.

The majority of Muslim, Christian, and Jewish physicians in the
Islamic world relied on the heritage of ancient Greek and Roman
medicine. Muslim physicians did not refer to the Qur'an, nor did
Christians cite New Testament doctrines when they treated medical
problems.[58] Folk medicine was very popular, and books on the medicine of the Prophet, still current in the Islamic world, offered much
utilizable lore.

PHARMACEUTICALS

Maimonides' book on drugs continued the work of the Spanish school
by using Sulayman Ibn Juljul, 'Abd al-Rahman Ibn Wafid, Muhammad Marwan al-Ghafiqi, and Marwan Ibn Janah. Maimonides' work
gave names of drugs in Greek, Arabic, Hispano-Romance, Berber,
and colloquial Egyptian, but not in Hebrew.[59] This is puzzling, as he
knew Hebrew terms for drugs from the Bible and Mishnah and used
them in his *Commentary on the Mishnah* and *Mishneh Torah*. Moreover,
even the Arab author Abu 'Abdallah al-Idrisi (ca. 1100–1165) and the
Jewish physician Abu 'l-Muna' al-Kohen al-'Attar gave Hebrew synonyms.[60] The explanation may be that Abu Muhammad Ibn al-Baytar,
the Spanish Muslim pharmacologist who later lived in Egypt, edited
Maimonides' text and could have omitted Hebrew terms.[61] Without
further evidence, however, we cannot know for sure.

LIMITS OF MEDICAL KNOWLEDGE

Maimonides was aware of the limits of medical knowledge and the
high risk of failure. He stressed the ancient rule that physicians must
take care not to harm the patient. Hippocrates is quoted as having
said, "One [who is a physician] should devote himself to two things:
one is to benefit the patient, and the other is not to harm him," or in its
well-known Latin form, *primum non nocere*.[62]

In the *Regimen of Health* and *On Asthma,* Maimonides stressed the
hazards of medical treatment:

> The dangers are obvious to the wise while the fools do not find
> anything difficult. How easy is healing in the eyes of the practitioners
> [lit. "sons"] of our art, and how long and deep it had been in the eyes
> of Hippocrates. Behold: inasmuch as a man be perfect in this wis-
> dom, new doubts arise in him which lead to additional reflection. But
> inasmuch as he is bare of knowledge, each difficulty is easy in his
> eyes, he exceeds in follies and in the rashness of answering to what he
> does not understand.[63]

Maimonides believed that one can dispense with a physician unless
the healer is exceptional and knows how to assist nature without di-

verting it from its way.[64] Rash physicians make serious errors, yet even then the sick recover.[65] This, however, does not mean that physicians' errors do little harm. The physician may overlook something that he and the patient consider minor yet which causes the patient's death.

Galen agreed with Hippocrates that medicine is difficult and time-consuming.[66] This is not unique to medicine, Galen observed, but is true of other sciences as well. The more proficient a person is in a science, the more precisely he investigates. He raises doubts and difficult questions, deliberates, and is hesitant in replying. Galen once thought that this was something minor, not worthy of mention by Hippocrates.[67] He supposed that nobody doubts that the physician should want to benefit his patients or at least not harm them. But later Galen saw that numerous famous physicians harmed many patients, and he said that he would not do anything unless it was clear that if he was not able to cure the patient, he would not harm him.[68] Maimonides concluded the discussion with these words: "And [since] most physicians are incompetent, the result is as Aristotle has said, namely, that most people die as a result of medical treatment."[69]

We need to recall that medicine in the classical period and in Maimonides' age was archaic and crude, and that significant advances were not made until modern times. Even in the early nineteenth century, Benjamin Rush saw all disease as an overstimulation of nerves and blood, the cure being bleeding, purging, and vomiting to readjust the natural balance. Surgery was painful and often fatal. Only in the middle and end of the nineteenth century do we find the development of antiseptic surgery (Joseph Lister) and the beginnings of bacteriology. In the late 1880s, Dr. William Mayo began using antiseptic surgery in his clinics.[70]

Maimonides was not just a critic of others; he was aware of his own limitations.

> Having heard my words, do not assume that I am the one into whose hands you should deliver your soul and body for treatment.[71] May God be my witness that I know for certain about myself that I, too, am among those who are deficient in this art, [who] stand in awe of it, and who find it difficult to achieve its goal. There is no doubt that I know myself better than anyone else does and that I can criticize my own knowledge or the knowledge of others better than someone

with less scientific insight. Again, may God be my witness that I do not state this out of modesty, nor in the customary manner of the erudite [al-fudala'],[72] who say about themselves that their knowledge is deficient even when it is perfect and that their deeds fall short even when they are very diligent. But I state the truth of the matter as it is. I have adduced this chapter strictly for fear that, when you look into it, you would suspect me of that of which I am innocent and would therefore find it difficult to accept my advice, since you would think that it is partly motivated by self-interest. Consequently, you would act according to my advice only rarely and would thus frustrate my intention.

At the end of *On Asthma,* Maimonides referred to quarreling among physicians, and advised the recipient to dismiss all of them and rely upon nature alone.[73] He then described three causes for dissension, which he derived from Alexander of Aphrodisias' *On the Principles of the All (Universe).* These are: (1) the drive for power and domination, preventing one from seeing the truth as it is; (2) the subtlety and obscurity of the subject; and (3) the ignorance of the one who apprehends. A fourth cause Alexander did not mention because it did not exist in his time as a way of life, and that is upbringing and habit and rejection of opposite opinions even when they are closer to the truth. Pines commented on the fourth cause:

> In other words, Maimonides contrasts his own times, which he seems to have held to be dominated by superstition, to use Spinoza's term and that of the philosophers of the Enlightenment, with Greek antiquity, in which the philosophers who aspired to know the true nature of things did not have to struggle against the dead hand of traditional belief. Maimonides was indubitably aware that the Greek philosophers lived in a pagan society, i.e., a society with religious beliefs and observances of its own, but apparently he chose not to mention this fact.

Need for Concilia

Because physicians so often err and no one remembers everything, Maimonides recommended the system of the consilium, the joint consultation among several physicians. But when physicians in a consilium compete to prove their own superiority, then they bring harm and honesty is impaired.

The optimal medical treatment is that which is recommended by a consilium of physicians after they have reached consensus.[74] Maimonides said that it is best when a group of physicians gather, as in the instance of kings and rulers, and debate until they reach a decision about procedure. Together they can attain the goal and perfection they seek.

Folk Medicine

Medical treatment, as we have seen, depends on experience and reasoning on the basis of experience, Maimonides intended the accumulated knowledge of former generations recorded in medical books.[75] Pseudo-physicians have neither experience nor reasoning, and hence perpetrate errors. In cases of harsh treatments, such as draining superfluities by bleeding, purgatives, vomiting, and enemas, the patient should by no means consult a folk doctor.[76] Theriacs and all other strong medicines should only be taken on the advice of a professional physician.[77]

People in Maimonides' time tended to consult folk doctors and believed in amulets and charms, magic bowls, and special potions. Maimonides loathed superstition in all shapes and forms, though he appreciated the power of suggestion and permitted use of amulets by women in childbirth, as we have seen above. We gather from Maimonides' references to the beliefs of people he lived among that they tended to consult folk doctors for their *experience,* which is what they deemed counts.

One who goes to doctors who have practical experience but who do not know how to reason or think scientifically and who have not studied medical books is like someone who trusts a sea captain who sails by experience, relying on the winds, without knowing navigation. This is an analogy that Maimonides used more than once.

After describing the expert physician, whom people should consult, Maimonides protested, "However, people do not do so, and they seek medical help from anyone whom they may meet by chance and from everything which seems new."[78] Going on in a more humorous tone, he described how people sought second, third, and fourth opinions: "I saw things practiced in the land of Egypt by the noble as well as by the populace, for seldom is a physician called to treat a patient from the beginning of his illness till its end; rather they wander from one physician to another. . . . This practice has disadvantages to which I shall call your attention. First, the perplexity of the patient himself who does not know with whom the truth lies."

> [Medicine] is an art that requires experience and reasoning. What we know through experience is greater than what we know through reason. Since people know this, they rely so much on experience that the multitude has a well-known saying: 'Ask the experienced [practitioner] but not the [theoretical] physician." So people perish as they are deluded by old women and common folk and rely on anyone claiming to have [medical] experience. Any deceiving and impudent person can gain access [to medicine] by saying, "I have remedies that I have tested." And most of the elite prefer physicians either because they consider them experienced or because they are advanced in age. Often they say: "So and so is not a learned [physician]; but he has experience, practical training, and skill." All these are errors which cause those eventualities against which we have warned.[79]

SOME DIETARY ADVICE

Maimonides advocated a moderate diet, daily exercise, and emotional tranquility to fend off the onset of illness. In his medical, ethical, and legal writings, Maimonides emphasizes that we should eat foods that are easily digestible in moderate amounts.[80] He observed in his *Regimen of Health* that if we conducted ourselves as we care for the animals on which we ride, we would be saved from many illnesses.[81] Overeating is a deadly threat to any physical constitution and the main cause of all diseases. We should avoid consuming a large variety of foods during a single meal.[82] Maimonides quoted Galen as recommending that light foods be taken before heavy ones. One should eat only when hungry and drink only when thirsty, and not eat to satiety.

In his treatise *On Asthma* he talked about his personal experience. Sometimes in winter one ate once a day or in summer one ate earlier and lighter than usual. When he spent the night on an empty stomach, it became filled with bad humors. He discovered that the best recourse was to have light tasty foods that are easy to digest.[83] Sometimes he drank soup made from young roosters and then went to sleep. Sometimes he boiled five or six eggs and ate the yolks with cinnamon and salt. Sometimes he ate pistachio nuts and seedless raisins, or raisins with almonds [cf. Yiddish Rozhinkes mit Mandlen] and drank a beverage of sugar or honey. In the winter, when it was cold, he took a glass of wine. Instead of wine he advised his patient, obviously a Muslim, to take refined hydromel, honey mixed with water.

When an asthma attack occurs, Maimonides recommended to his patient, among other cures, chicken soup.

Chapter 7 of *On Asthma* is concerned with beverages. There he said that small quantities of wine, such as three or four glasses, when food is being digested are beneficial for one's health by improving digestion and expelling superfluities in perspiration and urine.

Drinking water with meals keeps food from being properly digested. The best drinking water is "sweet, pure, light, free from any change in odor, drawn on the same day from running water. One should boil the water in a new polished pot a few times, let it cool off, and then drink it." The precautions Maimonides recommended were justified by local conditions. The Nile was a breeding place of leprosy, bilharziasis, fever, and dysentery.

Maimonides advised that sleeping right after a meal is harmful for everyone, as it fills the brain with vapors, and one should wait three or four hours. Going to the bathhouse is harmful for asthmatics, and they should be careful to avoid cold drafts when leaving the bathhouse, and then sleep for an hour. Galen had recommended sleep immediately after a bath. Maimonides said: "Since I have come to know about this, I have not bathed except at the time of sunset, and I go directly from the bathhouse to the deep and beneficial sleep of the night. I was very happy with its effect [on me]." Massage in the morning upon waking and in the evening at bedtime is a good regimen for all healthy people.

Excessive indulgence in sexual intercourse is injurious to all people, as even the general public knows. A man should decrease his sexual activity as he grows older for the benefit of the body and the purity of the soul and ethical qualities of "tranquility, modesty, and temperance." Sexual intercourse is especially harmful for the brain because of the depletion of humors. When someone with a weak brain indulges, he will suffer from different mental disturbances. Sexual intercourse, Maimonides thought, was especially risky for someone recovering from acute fever. Maimonides and others observed that some lost their strength on the same day, fell into unconsciousness at the end of the day, and died that night.

PHYSICIANS OF THE SOUL

Galen emphasized the influence of mind on body and was aware that extreme emotional states, such as anger and excessive elation, may even cause death. Maimonides made the interdependence of body and soul a primary rule of therapeutics. The *Regimen of Health* gave a complete psychotherapy to calm the emotions and achieve equanimity.

The physician, said Maimonides, should keep the patient's emotions in equilibrium at all times, free of passions that cause anxiety. Cheerfulness alleviates sickness, especially sickness of soul, and the physician should give greatest care to the emotions of people overcome by grief, obsessive thoughts, inappropriate aversions, and diminished pleasure.[84]

The physician in ancient medicine was a counselor who cared for the human being as a whole, for body and soul, holistically, as we say nowadays. They are physicians who are also philosophers—physicians of the soul.[85]

Just as the physician, who cures the body, must have a perfect knowledge of the body, so the practitioner who treats the soul, improving its moral qualities, must know the soul, what makes it sick and what preserves its health.[86]

Maimonides contended that a physician should not expect his art to impart knowledge of how to eliminate these passions.[87] One acquires this knowledge from practical philosophy and from the exhortations and aphorisms of the religious law.[88] The wise are either philosophers or teachers of the law. The philosophers wrote many books on improving moral qualities and disciplining the soul to acquire the moral virtues, so that it generates only good actions. They warned against moral imperfections and taught the way to remove them, so that the

character trait leading to evil actions vanishes. Likewise, the aphorisms of the law, and the exhortations and maxims of the prophets or
their followers, and knowledge of their virtuous lives, improve the
moral qualities of the soul, so that it acquires virtuous dispositions and
only good actions flow from it.

One finds, therefore, that these passions have great influence only
on those individuals lacking knowledge of philosophic ethics or exhortations and aphorisms of the law. These people become anxious
and despair because their souls are very vulnerable. If harm comes to
them and some calamity of this world befalls them, their anxiety increases and they cry out and weep, slap their cheeks, and beat their
breasts. Sometimes the misfortunes become so great that one of them
dies suddenly or after some time from the grief and worry that overwhelm him.

Similarly, when these people acquire one of the goods of this world,
their joy is magnified. Some suppose, for lack of discipline of the soul,
that they have acquired a very great good, and their delight and excitement exaggerate what they have acquired. They are greatly affected by this, and their laughter and giddiness increase, so some of
them die from excessive joy.[89] The cause of all this is the soul's vulnerability and its ignorance of the truth of things. We must reverse our
way of looking at things and move from our human view of reality to
the perspective of universal nature.[90]

Like the philosophical schools in late antiquity, Maimonides taught
that a main cause of disorder and suffering were the passions, unregu-
lated desires and exaggerated fears. Philosophy or the law is a therapeutic of the passions, a transformation of the person's mode of seeing
and being.

The training that Maimonides prescribed, like Stoic training, required exercising the soul to be unmoved by passions. The goal is a life
of virtue, equanimity, and imperturbability. In living this kind of life,
we are not subservient to the play of chance that affects us when we
seek physical pleasure or material things, for wisdom and virtue depend upon ourselves alone.

Whereas in his Eight Chapters and *Regimen of Health* Maimonides
used psychotherapy to treat the emotions, in *On the Causes of Symptoms*
he prescribed drugs. Nowadays the two main treatments for psycho-

logical disorders are psychotherapy and drug therapy. Psychotherapy treats psychological conflicts that may be causing the illness and provides emotional support to the patient. Drugs affect the brain's chemistry and remedy the chemical imbalance causing the symptoms. For al-Malik al-Afdal's melancholy, Maimonides advised an extract of the plant known as oxtongue, to be taken along with wine, which increases the delight of the spirit and was hence called "the drink that exhilarates."[91] Maimonides believed that the plant exerted a psychotropic effect.[92] In ancient medicine the plant was called euphrosynum, because it was believed to induce a good mood. Aside from the exhilarating effect, Maimonides recommended oxtongue as an aid for sleep, digestion, and removing "vapors" from the blood. The use of oxtongue in a concoction with other pharmaceuticals is also prescribed in the *Regimen of Health* to dilate the soul and invigorate the heart.[93]

Maimonides said that he already treated other royalty suffering from melancholy, a disorder tending toward mania. In these cases he added to the recipe powdered jacinth (ruby), which was greatly beneficial. The description he gives is that of a manic-depressive illness, or bipolar depression, which was not properly defined until the nineteenth century.[94]

PHILOSOPHIC ETHICS

People trained in philosophic ethics or in the aphorisms and exhortations of the law acquire a truly courageous spirit.[95] Their souls are only affected slightly by events. The more a person is disciplined, the less that person is affected by prosperity or adversity. So when acquiring one of the great goods of this world, which the philosophers call presumed goods, he is not affected by them, and he does not exaggerate those goods. Likewise, when one of the great evils of this world befalls him, which the philosophers call presumed evils, he does not become anxious or despair, but endures it patiently.

The physician should not insist that his art is the only remedy for removing these passions. This remedy, as we have seen, is by "practical philosophy and the admonitions and rules of the law." Those who are trained in philosophic ethics or the admonitions and rules of the law have a balanced disposition and display composure and fortitude in all circumstances.

The proper disposition of soul comes from consideration of the truths of things and knowledge of "the nature of existence." For even if one possessed the highest worldly good for an entire lifetime, it is a paltry and perishable thing, since a person dies like other animals. Similarly, the greatest evils of this world are inferior when we consider death, which is inevitable. Remembering death induces the appropriate worldview and produces the right attitude to happiness and suffering.

We must eliminate distressing thoughts by not brooding over the past or being anxious about the future. Rational observation teaches us that brooding over the past is futile and comes from a lack of true understanding. We must not be anxious about the future and what it portends. Everything that one expects is within the realm of possibility, so it may or may not occur. Hence, just as we are distressed by anticipated disaster, so ought we hope for the opposite, for both outcomes are possible.

This psychotherapy recalls Socratic and Stoic ideas and anticipates modern forms of psychotherapy. Maimonides' assertion that knowing the nature of existence means understanding the world and man's place in it and viewing reality from a universal perspective is akin to Stoic teachings. Stoic ethics commended a life according to reason and living according to nature in harmony with the world order. When we follow nature and reason, we place the right value on things and seek what is truly good, wisdom and virtue, not what is presumed to be good, such as money and property. Poverty, pain, and death are not evils; money, health, and pleasure are not goods. Irrational passions must be eradicated. The training Maimonides prescribed, like the Stoic *askesis,* requires exercising the soul to be unmoved by passions. The goal is a life of virtue, a life of equanimity and imperturbability. In living this kind of life, we are not subservient to the play of chance that affects us when we seek physical pleasure or material things, for wisdom and virtue depend upon ourselves alone.

MELANCHOLY

In his Eight Chapters on ethics Maimonides prescribed a psychotherapy for melancholia, permitting the patient pleasures that he prohibited in the law.[96] "If melancholia comes over [an individual], he should expel it by listening to songs and various kinds of instrumental melodies, by strolling through gardens and beautiful buildings, by sitting with beautiful forms,[97] and the like, which gladden the soul and banish the disturbance of melancholia from it."[98] A person should aim at making his or her body healthy. The purpose of a healthy body is for the soul to pursue the sciences and the ethical and rational virtues, and ultimately the knowledge of God. From this aspect, the art of medicine is vital for attaining the virtues and true happiness.

He contended in his medical works that a depressed person cannot engage in creative intellectual activity and achieve the aim of human life, which is the intellectual love of God. This view of melancholy and its impairment of creativity contrasts with another assessment that sees melancholy as related to greatness and genius. The Aristotelian *Problemata physica* (XXX, 1) posited that whoever becomes eminent in philosophy, politics, poetry, or the arts is melancholic, giving as examples Empedocles, Plato, and Socrates.[99] Melancholy is associated with exaltation and ecstasy. This view occurs in medieval Scholastic thought (Albertus Magnus and William of Auvergne) and appears in Kant, who endowed melancholy with traits of the sublime.[100]

Maimonides raised his theory of the inverse proportion of creativity and depression to a group level. Prophecy cannot come to any but a cheerful spirit. Thus the cessation of prophecy in ancient Israel was the result of poor socioeconomic conditions.[101] Exile produced a loss of wisdom and creativity.[102] Israel's subjection to the nations of the world caused its native wisdom to vanish. Maimonides used a current pun based on a biblical verse—*but mingled [wa-yit'arvu] with the nations [goyim] and learned their ways* (Ps 106:35)—to indicate that assimilation to Arab/Muslim culture and adopting their opinions, morals, and actions led to a loss of native wisdom.[103] He twice said that the opinions were of the ignorant (*jahiliyya*), a word that Muslim sources applied to the Arabs of the Period of Ignorance before Islam. Because of this mode of assimilation the philosophic views appeared foreign to "our law," as they are in the view of the ignorant. "However, matters are not like this," he added. Maimonides evidently had in mind the antagonism to philosophy on the part of the Muslim ulema.

Maimonides permitted the therapeutic use of pleasure to dispel the despondency that might attend the solitary contemplative life. He was aware that pursuit of the ultimate goal, knowledge of God, restricts one's actions and social interaction with other people. One who pursues this goal will not bother to decorate walls with gold or affix a gold-embroidered border on a garment. He will do this only to gladden his soul for the sake of its health and to drive sickness from it, so that it will be polished and ready to apprehend the sciences. The sages have said: *An attractive dwelling, an attractive wife, attractive utensils, and a bed prepared for the disciples of the wise give delight to the mind of a man.*[104] He appreciated that the soul becomes weary and the mind dull by continuous reflection upon abstruse matters, just as the body becomes exhausted from undertaking toilsome labors until it relaxes and rests and then returns to its equilibrium. Similarly, the soul needs to rest and to give relief to the senses, looking at beautiful decorations and objects, so that weariness be removed from it.[105]

If doctors, mathematicians, or astronomers ponder, brood, memorize, and investigate too much, they can fall prey to melancholy.[106] The soul becomes ill and is affected by disorders of the understanding and the memory due to fatigue and overexertion, as Hippocrates said in Book VI of the *Epidemics:* "Fatigue of the soul comes from the soul's thinking." Just as bodily overexertion leads to severe illnesses, of which fatigue is the least, so does mental overexertion lead to severe illnesses, the worst being melancholy.[107]

Maimonides' diagnosis and treatment of melancholy appear to be beset by contradictions and tensions. He cured his own melancholy by intense study and philosophic contemplation, and prescribed this for others as well. Yet he and other physicians found that intense scientific activity can also produce melancholy. Furthermore, he noted that melancholy is a malady afflicting royalty in particular, but he also made the point that grief and obsessive thoughts distress the philosophically ignorant, who are weak and irresolute.

While it is paradoxical that study should be both cause and cure of melancholy, this was evidently what people experienced. Intense and prolonged thinking about scientific problems could release melancholic symptoms. Yet contemplation of the nature of being, leading to greater understanding of the whole, removed beliefs that brought on grief and a sense of loss.

Maimonides' psychotherapy sounds like methods of therapy prevalent today that resemble the insights and techniques of ancient philosophy. His advice to give up negative ways of thinking that distort reality and cause distress resembles the teachings of cognitive therapy. These dysfunctional ideas arise, as Maimonides noticed, because we overestimate threats and concentrate on negative outcomes. The distorted cognition stirs emotional and physiological responses, such as anger and anxiety, and these emotions affect cognition, creating further dysfunctional thoughts. Maimonides' opinion that harmful emotions and dysfunctional behavior are the product of irrational thinking links up with the teachings of existential psychotherapy, which sees emotional disturbances as caused by our failure to act authentically by pursuing our own objectives rather than those of others.

BANISHING GRIEF

Maimonides made use of a genre of writing concerned with banishing grief, which concerned despondency and various ways of dispelling it. It has much in common with consolation literature.[108]

The Arab philosopher al-Kindi, in a treatise on banishing grief, stressed living in accordance with nature. Sadness is psychic pain caused by loss of loved ones or the vanishing of things desired. No one can be free of these things because it is impossible that one can obtain all his desires or be safe from losing things he loves, for permanence is absent in this world. Loss of loved ones and property is natural in this world. Calamities are due to universal generation and corruption. If we grieve over loss, we shall be grieving all the time. We should not be sorrowful when our loved ones and things we cherish vanish. A great many people have perished, and many reconciled themselves to the loss. Some lost children; others lost property. We must not harm our souls by being sad, for sadness is pain of the soul and makes us irrational. We banish physical ailments with medicines. Curing the soul of pain is more important, as the soul is superior to the body. Care for restoring it to equilibrium is more important than caring for what perishes.

Philosophical psychotherapy, or philosophical counseling, inspired by Socrates' maxim that "the unexamined life is not worth living," assumes that many personal difficulties are philosophic in nature. Philosophical counseling deals with healthy people and helps them understand the structure of their world and possibilities for life in the world. It helps people examine their lives and predicaments, deepen their understanding of themselves and their world, and transform their narrow, personal perspective into a global view and wisdom.[109]

ENVIRONMENT

Maimonides expressed concern for a healthy environment in *On Asthma,* which treats the affliction in the context of health in general.[110] Concern for clean air, Maimonides wrote, is the foremost rule in preserving the health of one's body and soul. He discouraged living in an urban environment. In the city, the air becomes stagnant, turbid, thick, misty, and foggy because of high buildings, narrow streets, and what its inhabitants produce—their waste, their dead, the carcasses of their animals, and the corruption of their decaying food. The body alters accordingly, perhaps imperceptibly to the person. If you have no choice in this, as you may be accustomed to city life or cannot emigrate, you should at least live in a city that is spacious, high in the hills or on treeless mountains where there is clear air. Try to live in its outskirts. Live in a tall building with a wide court, traversed by the north wind and accessible to the sunlight. Try to place the toilet as far as possible from the dwelling place. Purify the air and dry it with fine aromatics, vapors, fumigation, and drying agents, according to atmospheric conditions.

CONCLUSION

Maimonides was in all his activities the Great Healer. He acted as a physician of the soul in his communal epistles, in which he compared his words to medications, signifying that his aim was to heal and pacify. The *Guide* is a therapeutic treatise in a deeper sense. The epistles treated specific emergencies, whereas the *Guide* cured a chronic existential condition of numbing perplexity.

Epilogue

*When I consider the condition of this world, I find consolation
only in two things: in contemplating and studying and in my
son Abraham, for God (the exalted) has given him grace and
blessing from the blessing of his namesake, who believed in God
and in his promise. May God give him long life, for he is most
modest and has fine moral qualities, and he has a subtle mind
and fine nature. With the help of God he shall no doubt have a
name among the great. I entreat God (the exalted) to protect
him and to shower upon him his mercy to the utmost.*

—LETTER TO JOSEPH BEN JUDAH IBN SIMON

MAIMONIDES' DEMISE

The writer of a letter to Maimonides, whose name is not mentioned,
said that he had acquired a rudimentary knowledge of philosophy but
needed an instructor to make further progress.[1] He added that he had
studied part of *The Guide of the Perplexed*, yet did not fully understand
what he read. He therefore wished to meet Maimonides in person or
else someone recommended by him who could help him. In addition,
he desired advice on dietary matters to enhance his ability to pursue
knowledge. The inquirer thanked the Lord for bringing him into the
world at the time of the great Master.

Moses ben Maimon declined the man's request for a meeting.
He rejected similar appeals by people who wished to meet with him
around 1199, when he was old and infirm. He invoked illness and fatigue as a reason for not answering letters on time even when he was
younger. His frail health and his depression following the death of his

brother David, which he revealed in his letter to Japheth ben Eli, indicates perhaps a tendency to malaise, but Moses ben Maimon also used
his fragility to fend off invasions of privacy.

Along with his poor health, Maimonides explained to the man that
he had little time for study and teaching, and he had to lie down most
of the time. He explained that he could only meet the man on the Sabbath, when he attended the study hall, and expressed his hope that he
would find time later to deal with his questions.[2] He recommended
for the man's diet raisins and almonds and occasional date honey.

Maimonides often referred in his letters to his fragile health. His
complaints became more frequent during the last decade of the twelfth
century, when he was occupied with service to the court and communal matters.

We see it in his writing as he becomes old and more ill; his hand
naturally trembles. In a letter to Jonathan of Lunel, he said: "I was seriously ill for one year and now out of danger but my hand trembles."[3]

The writer of a letter preserved in the Genizah described an illness
of the sage, calling for an emergency visit of a physician. He had received on 21 Tammuz "disturbing and alarming news about our lord,
our Master Moses, may he live forever." He requested that a physician
come as quickly as possible. Now, 21 Tammuz fell on a Wednesday
in 1196 and 1197, so the date was either June 19, 1196, or July 9, 1197.
Maimonides was ill again in 1199 when he wrote letters to people
complaining of an extended indisposition. And when he wrote his
medical work, *On the Cause of Symptoms*, in 1200, he was too ill to visit
Sultan al-Afdal in person. A severe famine and epidemic struck Cairo
in the years 1201–2, one that he mentioned several times in his responsa. His frail health could have been undermined even more during this period of crisis.

According to his grandson David, Moses ben Maimon died on
December 13, 1204. Given his age and feeble condition, this date may
well be correct. His nephew Abu 'l-Rida copied a medical work of his
in 1205 and said that his illustrious uncle was already dead.

We have further confirmation from a poem of al-Harizi that Maimonides died in 1204.[4] He wrote that there was a year of lamentation
(*nehi* = 65 in *gematria,* the year being [49]65 A.M. = 1204/5). The poet
says, "We heard that there was *shever* in Egypt" (alluding to Gen 42:1),

where *shever* means "grain," but its homonym means "breaking, collapse, disaster, calamity." The poet went on: "Moses ascended to heaven," alluding to the verse *And Moses went up to God* (Exod 19:3) and to legends on the ascension of Moses.

According to Ibn al-Qifti, Moses ben Maimon requested that his descendants have him buried in Tiberias, and this was done. A tombstone marks the gravesite where he is believed to be interred. But like the biblical Moses, *no one knows his burial place to this day* (Deut 34:6).

ABBREVIATIONS

Biblical translations are from the NJPS and NRSV with necessary adjustments to make the text compatible with Maimonides' understanding of it. Talmud translations are from the Soncino edition, and the *Mishneh Torah* translations are from the Yale Judaica Series volumes. Qur'an renditions are based mainly on the translations of A.J. Arberry and M. Pickthall. All other translations from Arabic and Hebrew texts are by the author unless otherwise indicated.

HEBREW BIBLE

Amos	Amos	Hos	Hosea
Mic	Micah	1 Chron	First Chronicles
Isa	Isaiah	Nah	Nahum
2 Chron	Second Chronicles	Jer	Jeremiah
Neh	Nehemiah	Dan	Daniel
Job	Job	Num	Numbers
Deut	Deuteronomy	Joel	Joel
Obad	Obadiah	Eccl	Ecclesiastes
Jonah	Jonah	Prov	Proverbs
Esth	Esther	Josh	Joshua
Ps	Psalms	Exod	Exodus
Ezek	Ezekiel	Judg	Judges
Ruth	Ruth	Ezra	Ezra
1 Kings	First Kings	1 Sam	First Samuel
Gen	Genesis	2 Kings	Second Kings
2 Sam	Second Samuel	Hab	Habakkuk
Lam	Lamentations	Song	Song of Songs
Hag	Haggai	Lev	Leviticus
Zech	Zechariah	Mal	Malachi
Zeph	Zephaniah		

NEW TESTAMENT

Mt	Matthew	Eph	Ephesians
Heb	Hebrews	Mk	Mark
Phil	Philippians	Jas	James
Lk	Luke	Col	Colossians
1 Pet	1 Peter	Jn	John

1 Thess	1 Thessalonians	2 Pet	2 Peter
Acts	Acts of the Apostles	2 Thess	2 Thessalonians
1 Jn	1 John	Rom	Romans
1 Tim	1 Timothy	2 Jn	2 John
1 Cor	1 Corinthians	2 Tim	2 Timothy
3 Jn	3 John	2 Cor	2 Corinthians
Titus	Titus	Jude	Jude
Gal	Galatians	Philem	Philemon
Rev	Revelation		

Ar	Arabic
Aram	Aramaic
b.	born
d.	died
DSB	Dictionary of Scientific Biography
Enc. Tal.	Talmudic Encyclopedia [Heb]
Fr	French
Grk	Greek
Heb	Hebrew
JSB	Jewish Study Bible
KJV	King James Version
Lat	Latin
Med. Soc.	*A Mediterranean Society*
NJB	New Jerusalem Bible
NJPS	New Jewish Publication Society
NRSV	New Revised Standard Version
OED	Oxford English Dictionary
OF	Old French
Port	Portugese
r.	reigned
Span	Spanish

A.H.	Anno Hegirae (Hijra year) (began July 16, 622 C.E.)
A.M.	Anno Mundi (Year of Creation, Hebrew Calendar) (began 3761 B.C.E.)
B.C.E.	Before the Common Era (= B.C.)
C.E.	The Common Era (= A.D.)
S.E.	Seleucid Era (began 311 B.C.E.)

B	Babylonian Talmud
J	Jerusalem [Palestinian] Talmud
M	Mishnah
T	Tosefta
CM	*Commentary on the Mishnah*
MT	*Mishneh Torah*

Rabbinic Texts

The Mishnah has sixty tractates, divided into six orders. The traditional division has sixty-three tractates, with Bava Qamma, Bava Mesi'ah, and Bava Batra belonging to Tractate Neziqin and Makkot being a continuation of Sanhedrin. There are also minor tractates outside of the six orders. The Roman numerals indicate the volume of the Soncino translation of the Babylonian Talmud.

First Order: Zera'im Seeds

Ber Berakhot Blessings I
Pe'ah Corner of the Field II
Demai Doubtfully Tithed II
Kil Kil'ayim Mixtures [of Plants, Trees, and Animals] II
Shev Shevi'it Sabbatical Year II
Ter Terumot Heave Offerings II
Ma'as Ma'aserot Tithes II
Ma'asSh Ma'aser Sheni Second Tithe II
Hal Hallah Dough II
'Orl 'Orlah Tree's First Three Years II
Bik Bikkurim First Fruits II

Second Order: Mo'ed Appointed Time [Festival]

Shab Shabbat Sabbath III
'Eruv 'Eruvin Joining Domains IV
Pes Pesahim Paschal Lambs [Passover] V
Sheq Sheqalim Shekels [Dues for Temple]
Yoma The Day [of Atonement] VII
Suk Sukkah Booth [Festival of Tabernacles] VIII
Besah Egg [Preparing Food on Festivals] VI
RH Rosh Hashanah New Year VI
Ta'an Ta'anit Fast [Days] IX
Meg Megillah Scroll [of Esther] IX
MQ Mo'ed Qatan Minor Festivals VIII

Hag Hagigah Festival Offerings IX

Third Order: Nashim Women

Yev Yevamot Sisters-in-law [Levirate Marriage] X
Ket Ketubbot Marriage Deeds XI
Ned Nedarim Vows XII
Naz Nazir Nazirite XIII
Sot Sotah Suspected Adulteress XIII
Git Gittin Bills of Divorce XIV
Qid Qiddushin Betrothals XV

Fourth Order: Neziqin Damages

BQ Bava Qamma First Gate XVI
BM Bava Metzia Middle Gate XVII
BB Bava Batra Last Gate XVIII
San Sanhedrin [High Court of Law] XIX
Mak Makkot Lashes [Corporal Punishment] XX
Shev Shevu'ot Oaths XX
'Eduy 'Eduyyot Witnesses XXI
'AZ 'Avodah Zarah Idolatry XXI
Avot Ethics of the Fathers XXI
Hor Horayot Rulings XXI

Fifth Order: Qodashim Sacred Things

Zev Zevahim Animal Sacrifices XXII
Men Menahot Meal Offerings XXIII
Hul Hullin Unhallowed [Slaughter] XXIV
Bekh Bekhorot Firstlings XXV
'Arakh 'Arakhin Valuations [of Dedicated Objects] XXV
Tem Temurah Substitution [of Sacrifices] XXVI
Ker Keritot Excisions [for Intentional Sins] XXVI
Me'il Me'ilah Sacrilege XXVI
Tam Tamid Regular Daily Sacrifice XXVI
Mid Middot Measurements of the Temple XXVI
Kinnim Bird Nests [Sacrificial Birds] XXVI

Sixth Order: Tohorot Purity and Impurity

Kel Kelim Vessels [Ritual Impurity] XXVIII
Ohal Ohalot Tents [Ritual Impurity] XXVIII

Neg Nega'im Leprosy XXVIII
Parah Red Heifer XXVIII
Toh Tohorot Purification XXVIII
Miq Miqwa'ot Ritual Baths XXVIII
Nid Niddah Menstruating Woman XXVII
Makh Makhshirin Preparations [of Impure Foods Due to Liquids] XXVIII
Zav Zavim Those Suffering from a Discharge XXVIII
Tevul Tevul Yom Immersed During the Day XXVIII
Yad Yadayim Washing of the Hands XXVIII
'Uqsin Stems, Stalks [Ritual Impurity] XXVIII

Minor, or External, Tractates XXIX

ARN Avot of Rabbi Nathan
Sof Soferim Scribes
Sem Semahot Happy Occasions
Kal Kallah Bride
KalR Kallah Rabbati Long Tractate on Brides
DerR Derekh Eres Rabbah Long Tractate on Courtesy
DerZ Derekh Eres Zuta Short Tractate on Courtesy
Gerim Converts
Kutim Samaritans
'Avadim Slaves
Sefer Torah Torah scroll
Tef Tefillin Phylacteries
Sisit Fringes [of Tallit]
Mez Mezuzah Parchment Scroll on Doorposts

Halakhic Midrashim

MekRI Mekhilta de Rabbi Ishmael
MekRS Mekhilta de Rabbi Simon ben Yohay
SifraLev Sifra on Leviticus
SifreNum Sifre on Numbers
SifreDeut Sifre on Deuteronomy
MidTan Midrash Tannaim [Mekhilta] on Deuteronomy

Exegetical Midrashim

GenR Genesis Rabbah
LamR Lamentations Rabbah

Homiletic Midrashim

LevR Leviticus Rabbah
PRK Pesiqta de Rav Kahana
PesR Pesiqta Rabbati
Tan Tanhuma
TanB Tanhuma Buber
DeutR Deuteronomy Rabbah
ExR Exodus Rabbah
NumR Numbers Rabbah

Smaller Homiletic Midrashim

Aggadat Bereshit
Midrash Hashkem or We-Hizhir
Pesiqta Hadatta
Midrash wa-Yekhullu
Midrash Abkir

Midrashim on the Five Megillot (Scrolls)

LamR Lamentations Rabbah, ed. S. Buber, pp. 308–12
SongR Song of Songs [Canticles] Rabbah
Midrash Ruth
Midrash Qohelet [Ecclesiastes Rabbah]
Midrash Esther
Midrash Zuta on Song of Songs
Ecclesiastes Zuta
Aggadat Esther

Other Exegetical Midrashim

Midrash Jonah
Midrash Ps
Midrash Proverbs
Midrash Job

Other Haggadic Works

Megillat Ta'anit
Seder 'Olam [Rabbah]
Seder 'Olam Zuta
PRE Pirqe de Rabbi Eliezer
Josippon
Sefer ha-Yashar

Midrash wa-Yissa'u
Divre ha-Yamim shel Mosheh [The Life of Moses]
Midrash Petirat Aharon [Midrash of the Passing of Aaron]
Book of Eldad ha-Dani
Sefer Zerubbabel
Megillat Antiochos [Scroll of Antiochos or Book of the Hasmoneans]
Midrash Elleh Ezkerah [These I Will Remember, Ps 42:5]
Midrash 'Eser Galuttot [Midrash of the Ten Exiles]
Midrash wa-Yosha'
Midrash 'Aseret ha-Dibrot [Midrash of the Ten Commandments]
Midrash Esfah [Midrash on Numbers]
Midrash Al-Yithallel
Ma'aseh Books
Mishnat Rabbi Eliezer

Ethical Midrashim

DerER Derekh Eres Rabbah and Zutah
Tanna de-Be Elijah [Seder Elijah]
Midrash Ma'aseh Torah
Alphabet of Ben Sira
Midrash Temurah
Midrash Haserot wi-Yeterot

Esoteric Writings

Sefer Yesirah [Book of Creation]
Midrash Tadshe
Midrash Konen [on Creation]
The Greater and Lesser Hekhalot [Mystical Ascent to God's Throne]
Sefer Hekhalaot [3 Enoch or the Hebrew Book of Enoch]
Alphabet of Rabbi Aqiba
Sefer Raziel and Sefer ha-Razim [with a long version of Shi'ur Qomah]

Compilations

Yalqut Shim'oni
Yalqut ha-Makhiri
Yalqut Reubeni
Midrash ha-Gadol
Genesis Rabbati
Leqah Tov
Midrash Samuel

Genesis Zuta
Pitron Torah
Sefer ha-Liqqutim

Books of Mishneh Torah in Yale Judaica Series

Knowledge (I)
Love (II)
Seasons (III)
Women (IV)
Holiness (V)
Asseverations (VI)
Agriculture (VII)
Temple Service (VIII)
Offerings (IX)
Purity (X)
Torts (XI)
Acquisition (XII)
Civil Laws (XIII)
Judges (XIV)

Treatises of Mishneh Torah

The Mishneh Torah is divided into fourteen books; these are divided into treatises, then chapters that contain *halakhot* in the form of paragraphs.

Book of Knowledge

Foundations of the Law
Ethical Qualities
Torah Study
Idolatry
Repentance

Book of Love

Recitation of the Shema'
Prayer and the Priestly Blessing
Phylacteries Mezuzah and Torah scroll
Fringes
Blessings
Circumcision

Book of Seasons

Sabbath
Joining Domains
Resting on Tenth of Tishre (Day of Atonement)
Resting on Festivals
Leavened and Unleavened Bread
Rams Horn Booth and Palm Branch
Shekel Dues for Temple
Sanctification of the New Moon
Fast Days
Megillah [Purim] and Hanukkah

Book of Women

Marriage
Divorce
Levirate Marriage
Virgin Maiden
Wayward Woman

Book of Holiness

Forbidden Intercourse
Forbidden Foods
Slaughter

Book of Asseverations

Oaths
Vows
Nazirites
Valuation and Consecrations

Book of Agriculture

Diverse Kinds
Gifts to the Poor
Heave Offerings
Tithe
Second Tithe and Fourth Year's Fruit
First Fruits and Other Priestly Offerings
Sabbatical and Jubilee Years

Book of Temple Service

Temple
Temple Utensils and Servers
Entrance into Sanctuary
Things Forbidden for the Altar
Sacrificial Procedures
Daily and Additional Offerings
Offerings Rendered Unfit
Day of Atonement
Trespass

Book of Offerings

Passover Offering
Festal Offering
Firstlings
Offerings for Transgressions Committed Through Error
Those Whose Atonement Is Not Complete
Substituted Offerings

Book of Purity, or Cleanness

Corpse Impurity
The Red Heifer
Impurity of Leprosy
Those Who Render Couch and Seat Unclean
Other Fathers of Impurity
Impurity of Foodstuffs
Utensils
Immersion Pools

Book of Torts

Damage by Chattels
Theft
Robbery and Lost Property
Wounding and Damaging
Murderer and Preservation of Life

Book of Acquisition

Sales

Acquisition and Gifts
Neighbors
Agents and Partners
Slaves

Book of Civil Laws

Hiring
Borrowing and Depositing
Creditor and Debtor
Pleading
Inheritance

Book of Judges

Sanhedrin
Evidence
Rebels
Mourning
Kings and Their Wars

NOTES

For full bibliographical information, please visit: http://doubleday.com/maimonides.

INTRODUCTION

1. Bernard Lewis, *The Jews of Islam*, p. 8.

2. F. Braudel, *The Mediterranean and the Mediterranean World in the Age of Philip II*, trans. S. Reynolds, I, 278, 316.

3. Braudel, *The Mediterranean*, I, 276.

4. Most prominently in S. D. Goitein, "The Unity of the Mediterranean World in the 'Middle' Middle Ages," pp. 29–42, esp. pp. 29–35. See also S. D. Goitein, *A Mediterranean Society: The Jewish Communities in the Arab World as Portrayed in the Documents of the Cairo Geniza*, I, 42; henceforth *Med. Soc.*

5. Y. Avishur, *In Praise of Maimonides: Folktales in Judaeo-Arabic and Hebrew from the Near East and North Africa*, pp. 74, 86. The story first appeared in Gedaliah ibn Yahya (ca. 1515–1587), *Shalshelet ha-qabbalah*, p. 46a, and from there entered some mainstream biographies. It also shows up in a cycle of stories about Maimonides in Judeo-Arabic from Iraq.

6. Robin W. Winks, *The Historian as Detective: Essays on Evidence*. And see *The Detective as Historian: History and Art in Historical Crime Fiction,* ed. Lawrence A. Kreiser Jr. and Robin W. Winks.

7. Plutarch, "Life of Alexander the Great," ch. 1.

8. Leon Edel, *Writing Lives: Principia Biographia,* pp. 29, 161.

9. A. Ravitzky, "The Secrets of *The Guide of the Perplexed:* Between the Thirteenth and the Twentieth Centuries," *Studies in Maimonides,* ed. I. Twersky, pp. 159–207.

10. There is a painting of Saladin from this era that is considered to have been copied from his life. Access at members.eunet.at/kessler/105.jpg.

11. B. Ugolinus, *Thesaurus antiquitatum sacrarum* (Venice, 1744), I, ccclxxxiv. This portrait is the source for the popular likeness of Maimonides.

12. Ms. T-S 8 J 14.18, published by Paul Fenton, "A Meeting with Maimonides," pp. 1–4.

13. MT Ethical Qualities, v, 8–9.

14. Arabic-speaking authors invariably called him al-Ra'is (Head), sometimes adding that he was the Head over the Jews of Egypt.

15. The honorific byname (*kunya*) was Abu (father of) or Umm (mother of), usually with the name of the eldest son, as Abu 'Abdallah, or some quality of the bearer, such as Abu 'l-Fadl, "Possessor of Merit." If the name was biblical, the byname followed the biblical genealogy. For instance, as Jacob-Ya'qub was the son of Isaac-Ishaq, and the eldest son usually bore his grandfather's name, a man named Jacob-Ya'qub was given the honorific byname (*kunya*) Abu Ishaq. A man named Moses-Mosheh was given the byname Abu 'Imran ('Amram), as was Maimonides. Some scholars "correct" this to Ibn 'Imran.

16. Maimon ben Joseph, *Epistle of Consolation,* ed. and trans. L. M. Simmons, p. 15 (text)/86 (trans.).

17. This is the correct title, although *Moreh nevukhim* (without the article) is often

found. Both Arabic and Hebrew titles are in genitive construct; hence, *Guide* of *the Perplexed*, not *Guide* for *the Perplexed*.

18. Goitein's monumental *Mediterranean Society* is fundamentally based on Genizah documents.

19. See the colossal first volume published so far, *India Traders of the Middle Ages: Documents from the Cairo Geniza "India Book,"* ed. and trans. S. D. Goitein and Mordechai A. Friedman.

20. Augustine, *Contra Faustum,* 12.12, pp. 341–42; 16.21, p. 464; cited by Jeremy Cohen, *Living Letters of the Law*, p. 29.

21. Peter Alfonsi also assailed Islam, representing Muhammad as an impostor motivated by lust and political aspiration. He depicted the pre-Islamic rituals at Mecca as pagan and the Islamic pilgrimage to Mecca as corrupted by its origins. This was a view that Maimonides ostensibly rejected, asserting that Islam infused a pagan cult with monotheistic content. Alfonsi wrote an anthology of proverbs and fables, *Disciplina clericalis,* some from Arabic, that got into the *Gesta Romanorum* and Boccaccio; see *The 'Disciplina Clericalis' of Petrus Alfonsi,* ed. and trans. E. Hermes, with extensive discussion of the author and his times. At the end of his life, Alfonsi taught astronomy in England and France.

22. Samau'al al-Maghribi, *Ifḥām al-Yahūd (Silencing the Jews),* ed. and trans. M. Perlmann.

23. Abu 'l-Barakat Hibat Allah ibn Malka al-Baghdadi, called Awhad al-Zaman, born ca. 1077, died after 1164; see S. Pines, s.v. Abu 'l-Barakāt, *Encyclopaedia of Islam,* 2nd ed. (Leiden, 1954–2005), henceforth *EI*. Abu 'l-Barakāt converted to Islam in old age, according to reports, either out of "wounded pride" or fear. His pupil, Isaac son of Abraham Ibn Ezra, also converted to Islam, superficially it appears, and then rescinded. See Judah al-Harizi, *The Book of Taḥkemoni,* trans. D. S. Segal, ch. 3, pp. 45–46; Ms. T.-S. 13 J 18, f. 19; Goitein, "Rabbi Yehuda Hallevi in Spain in the Light of the Geniza Papers," 134–49, on 143, n. 10; *Med. Soc.,* II, 592, n. 19; *New Hebrew Poems from the Genizah,* ed. J. Schirmann, pp. 277–81; Isaac ben Abraham Ibn Ezra, *Poems,* ed. M. H. Schmelzer, Introduction, pp. 9–11.

24. The same attitude of skepticism is expressed in the expression *takafu' al-adilla* (which Josef van Ess takes to be equivalent *to isostheneia ton logon* of the ancient Skeptics); see his *Die Erkenntnislehre des 'Adudddin al-Ici,* pp. 223–25; M. Perlmann, "Ibn Hazm on the Equivalence of Proofs," pp. 279–90. Abu Muhammad Ibn Hazm (994–1064), living in Muslim Spain, cites among others two Jewish physicians who professed this doctrine; see also Kraemer, *Humanism in the Renaissance of Islam,* 2nd rev. ed., p. 190, n. 210.

25. Ross Brann, *Power in the Portrayal: Representation of Jews and Muslims in Eleventh-and Twelfth Century Spain,* ch. 2, "An Andalusi-Muslim Literary Typology of Jewish Heresy and Sedition," pp. 55–63.

26. For instance, Psalms 103:15–16 *(his days are as grass, as a flower of the field).*

27. See *The Guide of the Perplexed,* trans. S. Pines (Chicago, 1963), II, 11 (p. 276); and III, 31 (p. 524).

CHAPTER 1

1. Goethe, *The Collected Works, Selected Poems,* ed. C. Middleton, I, 132/133.

2. In the epilogue to his *Commentary on the Mishnah,* Toh, ed. and trans. Y. Qafih, p. 738. He wrote: "I am Moses son of Rabbi Maimon the Judge, son of Rabbi Joseph [II] the Sage, son of Rabbi Isaac the Judge, son of Rabbi Joseph [I] the Judge, son of Rabbi Obadiah [II] the Judge, son of Rabbi Solomon the Rav, son of Obadiah [I] the Judge (may the memory of the holy be a blessing)."

3. He actually wrote "in [14]79 of the Seleucid era [= 4928 A.M. = 1167/68 C.E.]." The Seleucid era, which began in 312/311 B.C.E., was used mainly on legal documents. Maimonides also gave his genealogy at the beginning of his *Epistle to Yemen,* but the text there is

abridged. See *Letters and Essays of Maimonides,* ed. and trans. I. Shailat [Heb.], p. 82: "From me, even I, Moses, son of Rabbi Maimon the Judge, son of Rabbi Joseph the Sage, son of Rabbi Isaac the Master, son of Rabbi Obadiah the Judge (may the memory of the righteous be a blessing)." For the syntax of "From me, even I," cf. Ezra 7:21. The style may be influenced by legal documents, for instance, Ms. T-S NS 309.12. Here three links have dropped out—Joseph I, Obadiah II, and Solomon. See also A. H. Freimann, "The Genealogy of Moses Maimonides' Family," pp. 9–32 on p. 10, n. 3. A Genizah document, listing prominent families in Cairo/Fustat, gives Maimonides' lineage down to his son Abraham. It corresponds to the list in the *Commentary on the Mishnah.* See also J. Mann, *The Jews in Egypt and in Palestine Under the Fāṭimid Caliphs,* II, 319 (Ms. T-S 8 K 22.6); Freimann, "Genealogy," pp. 11–12—"They are Israelites: Obadiah, Solomon, Obadiah II, Joseph I, Isaac, Joseph II, Maimon, David and Moses, Abraham." Se'adyah ben Danan gives a different lineage, changing the order, adding a generation, and varying the titles, in *Ma'amar 'al seder ha-dorot,* ed. C. del Valle and G. Stemberger, p. 70. See Freimann, "Genealogy," p. 12, n. 4.

4. See S. Z. Havlin, s.v. "Mosheh ben Maimon," *Hebrew Encyclopaedia,* xxiv, 536–42; idem, "Le-Toledot ha-Rambam," pp. 67–79, on p. 73: M. A. Friedman, "Notes by a Disciple in Maimonides Academy," pp. 523–83, on pp. 540–41, n. 84; idem, "New Sources for the Crusader Period," pp. 63–82, on p. 74, n. 33; idem, "Two Maimonidean Letters," *Me'ah She'arim: Studies in . . . Memory of Isadore Twersky,* ed. E. Fleischer et al., pp. 191–221, on pp. 202–3, n. 52. (All of the above are in Hebrew.) As scholars such as S. D. Goitein, J. Qafih, S. Z. Havlin, and M. A. Friedman have accepted the 1137/38 date, and the State of Israel inscribed it on the 100-shekel note bearing Maimonides' likeness, we should have no trouble accepting it.

5. In a note on his own birth date and the birth dates of his father and grandfather, David wrote in an addendum to Maimonides' *Commentary on [Bavli] Rosh ha-Shanah*: "Our Master Moses was born to his father, our Master Maimon, of blessed memory, on 14 Nisan [March 30], 1446 Seleucid Era, which David said is 4893 A.M. [rather 4895 = 1135 C.E.], in Cordova. And he retired from this world and gained the world to come in 1516 Seleucid Era [1204 C.E.] on Monday eve, 20 Teveth [December 13]."

6. David Yellin and Israel Abrahams, *Maimonides: His Life and Works,* 3rd rev. ed. (New York, 1972), pp. 7–8, said that Maimonides was born at one o'clock in the afternoon of March 30 (14 Nisan), 1135 C.E. The very hour of his birth was thus treasured in the loving memory of posterity. The exact hour was a later embellishment that did not appear in David ben Abraham's note. Nor did David say anything about lineage. Aaron ha-Kohen of Lunel, a contemporary of Maimonides (d. 1209/10), traced the Master's ancestry to Judah ha-Nasi in a letter to a colleague, and Solomon ben Simon Duran said that Maimonides' ancestors were the seed of David, King of Israel. The testimony of Simon Duran (1361–1444), of Majorca, is late and unfounded. Freimann says that the Judah ha-Nasi and King David traditions were influenced by the fact that Maimonides' descendants were Nagids in Egypt. The family of Judah ben Josiah ha-Nasi, a contemporary of Maimonides, traced its ancestry to King David, but this was expected of Nesi'im (princes of the House of David). See Maimonides, *Responsa,* ed. and trans. J. Blau, rev. ed., no. 373, p. 653; Freimann, "Genealogy," p. 10, n. 2. The Exilarchs in Iraq claimed Davidic descent.

7. Rabbi Maimon is the first of the dynasty, as far as we know, to have written books and responsa. See M. Steinschneider, *Die Arabische Literatur der Juden,* pp. 197–99; A. H. Freimann, "Responsa of R. Maimon the Dajjan," *Likkutei Tarbiz V: Studies on Maimonides,* Part One, ed. J. N. Epstein, p. 164.

8. Many had Arabic names ending with *-un,* such as Barhun, Zaydun, Hayyun, Khalfun, Fadlun. See also H. Z. Hirschberg, *A History of the Jews in North Africa,* 2nd rev. ed. (Leiden, 1974), I, 155; Goitein, *Med. Soc.,* I, 357–58.

9. It was not uncommon for Jews in this milieu to have bilingual names, conveniently a biblical name that also occurred in the Qur'an and sounded alike in both languages. A man named Abraham in Hebrew was Ibrahim in Arabic, Isaac was Ishaq, Moses was Musa,

David was Da'ud (or Dawud), Obadiah was 'Abdallah (or 'Ubaydallah), and Eli was 'Ali. The double names of Jews expressed their dual existence as citizens of two worlds, as did their Judeo-Arabic dialect.

10. The name of the river is from Arabic al-Wadi al-Kabir (the Great River).

11. *The History of the Mohammedan Dynasties in Spain*, trans. Pascual de Gayangos, I, 30; Robert Hillenbrand, "'The Ornament of the World': Medieval Córdoba as a Cultural Center," *The Legacy of Muslim Spain,* ed. S. K. Jayyusi, I, p. 118.

12. Janina M. Safran, *The Second Umayyad Caliphate*, p. 173.

13. It is often said that the Arabs transplanted the palm tree from Syria, yet many coins from Spain under the Carthaginians (third century B.C.E.) show a horse standing before a palm tree. Recemund's *Calendar*, or the *Calendar of Cordoba*, has the earliest record of crops introduced to Spain by Arabs: rice, sugar cane, aubergines, watermelons, and bananas. Rice was a specialty around Valencia, which had a sophisticated irrigation system. See Richard A. Fletcher, *The Quest for El Cid* (New York, 1990), p. 19.

14. *The History of the Mohammedan Dynasties in Spain,* trans. Pascual de Gayangos, I, 30–31.

15. Maimonides, *Responsa,* no. 310, p. 576.

16. Today's palace, the splendid Alcázar de los Reyes Cristianos—built by Alfonso XI in 1328—is not on the site of the original Muslim Alcázar, which was located where the Episcopal Palace now stands. Spanish *alcázar* is from Arabic *al-qasr,* meaning "castle" or "palace." The Arabic word is derived from Latin *castellum* ("fortress"), from *castra,* meaning "watchpost." Lat. *castellum* is diminutive of *castrum* (and gives us our "castle"). Many cities had an *alcázar*, the famous ones being in Seville, Segovia, and Toledo. The town Alcázar (de San Juan) in the plain of La Mancha, was the mise-en-scène for much of Cervantes' *Don Quixote.*

17. Constructed or reconstructed in 1314/15, it was dedicated after 1492 as a hermitage to Santa Quiteria, and then in 1588 it was given over to the brotherhood of the shoemakers guild, with the patronage of Saint Crispin and Saint Crispiniano. When it was being repared in 1884, a priest, Don Mariano Párraga, discovered the original plasterwork, and the synagogue was turned into a national monument the following year. See Jesús Peláez del Rosal, *The Synagogue,* trans. Patricia A. Sneesby, pp. 147–73.

18. See C. Brian Morris, *Son of Andalusia: The Lyrical Landscapes of Frederico García Lorca*, p. 384.

19. Maimonides gave rules of etiquette for right of way in congested lanes in MT Murder and Preservation of Life, xiii, 10–11. See BQ, ii, 10–11; J, BQ, iii, 5 (3d) and the discussion in S. Lieberman, *Tosefta ki-feshuṭah: A Comprehensive Commentary on the Tosefta*, Nez, 26–27. My experience in the narrow lanes of Fez is that the asses forge ahead, looking down, with no thought for pedestrians coming the other way.

20. The original mosque was built between 784 and 786 by 'Abd al-Rahman I on the site of the Visigoth Church of St. Vincent, which stood astride the ruins of a Roman Temple to Jupiter. After conquering Córdoba in 1236, King Ferdinand III of Castile made the mosque into a cathedral. This lasted for 300 years, but in the early sixteenth century, the cathedral clerics, with the support of Emperor Charles V, inserted a Gothic chapel in the center of mosque. Nevertheless, the Patio de los Naranjos, the minaret-like bell tower, and the name "La Mezquita" preserve the Islamic character of the edifice. Across the street today is the Hotel Maïmonide, which has a close-up view of the Mezquita.

21. Rodrigo Amador de los Ríos, *Inscripciones árabes de Córdoba* 2nd ed., pp. 183–84; Safran, The *Second Umayyad Caliphate*, p. 62.

22. J. C. Bürgel, "Ecstasy and Control in Andalusī Art," *The Legacy of Muslim Spain,* II, 626–38, p. 626.

23. See M. Streck, EI, s.v. "Ḳaysariyya."

24. Tanning was one of the despised professions. The tanner, dealing with animal hides, worked in a malodorous environment. Even in the talmudic period, tanning was a

despised profession. For the tanner (*bursi* < Grk *burseus*; *bursqi* < *bursiki* [tannery) in rabbinic sources, see T Qid (ed. Lieberman), ii, 4; and see B Pes 65a and Qid 82b; and see
Goitein, *Med. Soc.*, II, 265. The apostle Peter lodged for some time in Jaffa with a leather-
tanner named Simon (Acts 9:43; 10:6, 32).

25. We still have Córdoban leather (no longer from Córdoba), which is soft, fine, and
durable. The term "cordwainer," the medieval word for shoemaker or leather worker, from
French *cordonnier*, is derived from Córdoba, from which the best leather was brought to
England. Córdoban silk was called *qurtubi* from the name of the city. See Goitein, *Med.
Soc.*, IV, 169 and p. 402, n. 138, citing Serjeant, *Islamic Textiles*, p. 169 and *passim*. Muslim
jurists commended austerity and modesty in dress, and prohibited silk, as did *hadith*s ascribed to Muhammad. Only in Paradise will the righteous don garments of silk (Qur'an
22:23, 25:33, 76:12, 21). The prohibition did not deter the Syrian Umayyads and others from
wearing silk, and rulers bestowed honorary robes woven of silk and gold; see Y. K. Stillman, *Arab Dress*, pp. 22, 31, 33–35, 134–37.

26. MT Utensils, xxiv, 1.

27. For the cork oak in antiquity, see A. T. Fear, *Rome and Baetica: Urbanization in
Southern Spain C. 50 B.C.–A.D. 150*, p. 1. Even now, the cork oak grows mainly in the Mediterranean area. Cork is soft but durable, comfortable yet resilient, impacting shock and
protective, and therefore ideal for shoes, as Lady Rosina De Courcy, down on her luck but
practical, discovered in Anthony Trollope's *The Prime Minister*, p. 253. Weather never
frightened her because she had thick boots and cork soles. "'I think I owe my life to cork
soles,' said Lady Rosina enthusiastically" to the Duke of Omnium.

28. Juan Zozaya, "Material Culture in Medieval Spain," *Convivencia*, ed. Vivian B.
Mann et al., pp. 159–60.

29. The Mozarabs, in contrast to the *muwalladun*, who were Christian converts to Islam, remained Christians.

30. The words "Slav" and "slave" are related. The English word is from OFr *esclave*
from Med Lat *sclavus, sclava*, meaning both "Slav" and "slave."

31. Mikel de Epalza, "Mozarabs," in *The Legacy of Muslim Spain*, ed. Jayyusi, I, 149; D.
S. Ruggles, "Representation and Identity in Medieval Spain," in *Languages of Power in Islamic Spain*, ed. R. Brann, p. 78.

32. See David Wasserstein, "The Language Situation in al-Andalus," *Studies on the
Mûwaššah and the Kharja*, ed. Alan Jones and Richard Hitchcock, pp. 1–15.

33. Judeo-Arabic is a dialect of Middle Arabic, somewhere between Classical and
Modern Arabic. It was usually written in Hebrew script and contained an admixture of
Hebrew and Aramaic.

34. Abraham Ibn Daud, *The Book of Tradition (Sepher ha-Kabbalah)*, ed. and trans. G.
D. Cohen, pp. xxiii–xxiv.

35. Midrash, from *darash* ("study," "investigate"), refers to the homiletic exegesis of the
Bible as either Aggadic (legendary) Midrash or Halachic (legal) Midrash.

36. Ibn Daud, *The Book of Tradition*, p. 66; Salo W. Baron, *A Social and Religious History of the Jews*, 2nd ed., VI, 61. I take this to mean that Joseph ibn Abitur explained the
contents of the Talmud in broad strokes.

37. Employment of mercenaries was a formula for disaster in Muslim societies, as Ibn
Khaldun, the great fourteenth-century Tunisian historian (1332–1406), stressed throughout
his *Introduction to History* (*Muqaddimah*), trans. Franz Rosenthal. Machiavelli made the
same observation for the Italian city-states in *The Prince*, ch. 12, and *The Art of War*,
Book 1.

38. P. Chalmeta, EI, s.v. "al-Manṣūr bi'llāh." Although al-Mansur usurped power, he
was careful to keep the caliph as a figurehead and took the title "king" (*malik*). See David
Wasserstein, *The Caliphate in the West* (Oxford, 1993), pp. 17–27.

39. Sa'id al-Andalusi, *Science in the Medieval World*, trans. S. I. Salem and A. Kumar,
pp. 61–62. This is a translation of al-Andalusi's *Tabaqat al-umam*.

40. Wasserstein, *The Rise and Fall of the Party-Kings*, pp. 274–91; idem, *The Caliphate in the West*, p. 163.

41. See al-Maqqari, *The History of the Mohammedan Dynasties in Spain*, trans. Pascual de Gayangos, I, 34–36.

42. The Muslim eagerness to convert the Jews around this time, it seems, was due not only to the proximity of the year 500 A.H. (see below, p. 36), but to these Christian victories in their reconquest of Spain.

43. Haim Beinart, "The Jews in Castile," *Moreshet Sepharad: The Sephardi Legacy,* ed. H. Beinart, I, 21.

44. For the identification of Esau or Edom with Rome and accordingly Christianity, see J Ta'an, iv, 8, 68d; Gen R. LXV, 21; LXVII, 7; SifreDeut, XLI, ed. Finkelstein, p. 85. And see Louis Ginzberg, *The Legends of the Jews,* trans. H. Szold and P. Radin, V, 272, n. 19; G. D. Cohen, "Esau as Symbol in Early Medieval Thought," *Studies in the Varieties of Rabbinic Cultures*, pp. 243–69; and Moshe David Herr, EJ, s.v. "Esau."

45. The image of Judah ha-Levi, the "Sweet Singer of Zion," being stabbed through the heart by an Arab horseman before the gates of Jerusalem, which Heinrich Heine made famous in "Hebrew Melodies," is from a seventeenth-century historian. However, a report of his death in a letter written just three months after he arrived in the Holy Land, preserved in the Cairo Genizah, mentions the gates of Jerusalem and intimates that his death was unnatural. See S. D. Goitein, "Did Yehuda ha-Levi Arrive in the Holy Land?" pp. 245–50; and Moshe Gil and Ezra Fleischer, *Yehuda ha-Levi and His Circle*, pp. 254–56.

46. The name Almoravid is from Arabic al-Murabitun, "those dwelling in the frontier fortresses" (sing. *ribat*, cf. French *marabout*). Almohads is from al-Muwahhidun, "those who declare the unity [of Allah]."

47. See Y. K. Stillman, *Arab Dress*, pp. 17, 87–88, 94. Al-burnus has passed into Spanish as *albornoz*, and into English as "burnoose" and French as *burnous*.

48. The name Cid is from Arabic *sayyidi*, "my lord," vulgar Spanish Arabic *sidi*, rendered in Spanish as "mio Cid." *The Poem of the Cid* was titled *El Cantar de mio Cid*.

49. R. Le Tourneau, *The Almohad Movement in North Africa in the Twelfth and Thirteenth Centuries*; A. S. Halkin, "The History of Forced Conversion at the Time of the Almohads," *The Joshua Starr Memorial Volume*, pp. 101–10. David Corcos, "The Attitude of the Almohadic Rulers toward the Jews," pp. 137–160 (English summary, p. ii); reprinted in *Studies in the History of the Jews of Morocco*, pp. 319–42 (Hebrew section); Hirschberg, *A History of the Jews in North Africa*, I, 37, 123–27.

50. See J. F. P. Hopkins, EI, s.v. "Ibn Tūmart."

51. On Ibn Tūmart's religious thought, see I. Goldziher, *Le livre de Mohammed Ibn Toumert* (Algiers, 1903); R. Brunschvig, "Sur la doctrine du Mahdī Ibn Tūmart" *Ignace Goldziher Memorial Volume*, II, 1–13; idem, "Encore sur la doctrine du Mahdī," pp. 33–40; and D. Urvoy, "La pensée d'Ibn Tūmart," pp. 19–44.

52. Madeleine Fletcher, "Al-Andalus and North Africa in the Almohad Ideology," p. 240.

53. Ibid., p. 251.

54. Y. K. Stillman, *Arab Dress*, p. 95.

55. The Hijra was Muhammad's flight from Mecca to Medinah in 622, which became the first year of the Islamic calendar. Its first day is 1 Muharram, 1 A.H. (Anno Hegirae = Friday, July 16, 622 C.E. The famous theologian Abu Hamid al-Ghazali (d. 1111) was recognized as such a revivalist. He called his major work *Revival (Ihya') of the Religious Sciences*. See J. J. G. Jansen, EI, s.v. "Tadjdīd," citing A. J. Wensinck, *Concordance et indices de la tradition musulmane*, I, 364, for the tradition. Jansen notes that the self-renewal in modern times occurred when a new millennium of the Muslim calendar began on November 21/22, 1979, the beginning of 1400 A.H. A candidate for the title of Renewer was Rohallah Khomeini. The idea of renewal took hold of fundamentalist circles in their confrontation with the West.

56. See on the 500th year, M. A. Friedman, *Maimonides, the Yemenite Messiah and Apostasy*, pp. 15–17.

57. There is no record of such a promise. The Muslim leaders sought to strengthen Islam at this time by converting the Jews; see ibid., pp. 15–16.

58. Ibn Daud, *Book of Tradition*, p. 141, n. 459; and see Friedman, op. cit., p. 16, n. 20 for further sources.

59. See Friedman, op. cit., p. 17, n. 22, citing Abba Hillel Silver, *A History of Messianic Speculation in Israel*, pp. 68–69; Baron, *History*, V, 154, 200ff., 384, n. 65.

60. Abu Yusuf's suspicion of Jewish converts prefigured the Spanish Inquisition's doubts about the sincerity of "New Christians" in fourteenth- and fifteenth-century Spain. They were accused of "judaizing," although many had embraced Christianity in their hearts.

61. See Gad Freudenthal, "Les sciences dans les communautés juives médiévales de Provence," pp. 29–136 = "Science in the Medieval Jewish Culture of Southern France," pp. 23–58.

62. Comment on Ex 29:3; Norman Golb, *The Jews in Medieval Normandy: A Social and Intellectual History*, pp. 287–88.

63. Charles Homer Haskins, *The Renaissance of the Twelfth Century*; Robert L. Benson and Giles Constable (eds.), *Renaissance and Renewal in the Twelfth Century*; Robert N. Swanson, *The Twelfth Century Renaissance*; Anna Sapir Abulafia, *Christians and Jews in the Twelfth Century Renaissance*; and M.-D. Chenu, *Nature, Man, and Society in the Twelfth Century*, ed. and trans. J. Taylor and L. K. Little. The dominant motifs of the twelfth-century Renaissance in Europe were nature and reason, which infuse the thought of contemporary Spanish Jewish thinkers, such as Abraham Ibn Daud and Maimonides.

64. Brann, *Power in the Portrayal*.

65. Américo Castro, *The Spaniards: An Introduction to Their History*, trans. W. F. King and S. Margaretten; Thomas Glick, *Islamic and Christian Spain in the Early Middle Ages*, pp. 6–13; idem, *Convivencia*, "Introduction," pp. 1–2. The term *convivencia* had been used before Castro by Ramón Menéndez Pidal in his *Orígenes del español* in the sense of "coexistence of norms."

66. David Nirenberg, *Communities of Violence*, p. 9.

67. Ibid., pp. 38–40.

68. C. Sánchez-Albornoz, *Spain, A Historical Enigma*, translated by Colette Joly Dees and David Sven Reher.

69. Mark R. Cohen, *Under Crescent and Cross*, ch. 1.

70. Brann, *Power in the Portrayal*, p. 21.

71. Glick, *Convivencia*, "Introduction," pp. 4–5.

72. Glick, *Islamic and Christian Spain*, p. 135.

73. Ibid., p. 165.

74. *Guide*, II, 9 (pp. 268–69).

75. *Guide*, III, 48 (p. 598). The translator, S. Pines, says (n. 4) that Maimonides evidently meant the western Europeans in general.

76. The Arabs called the Europeans "Franks" (Ifranj), first those in Charlemagne's empire and then Europeans in general, exclusive of Spanish Christians. They generally called the Crusaders Ifranj, or else infidels, but never Crusaders. See Bernard Lewis, *The Muslim Discovery of Europe* (New York, 1982), p. 22. Index, pp. 342–43. Spanish and North African Arabs used Ifranj for Christians whom they knew. The more common name was Rum, which was equivalent to Ifranj. The notion that they were unhygienic was a prevalent stereotype. See Bernard Lewis and J. F. P. Hopkins, EI, s.v. "Ifrāndj."

77. Biographers have no definite information about Shakespeare between the time he made his way to London in the mid-1580s and the early 1590s. See Arthur Acheson, *Shakespeare's Lost Years in London 1586–1592* (London, 1920); and Stephen Greenblatt, *Will in the World* (New York, 2004), ch. 5.

CHAPTER 2

1. The belief in their antiquity and lineage was not far off the mark, as Jews emigrated to Hispania along with the Romans, their number increasing after the destruction of the Second Temple.

2. The Arabic expression '*indana* has no proper English equivalent; it means something like "by us" or "with us" or *chez nous*. See J. Blau, "'At Our Place in al-Andalus,' 'At Our Place in the Maghrib,'" in *Perspectives on Maimonides*, ed. Joel L. Kraemer, pp. 293–94.

3. See Isadore Twersky, *Introduction to the Code of Maimonides (Mishneh Torah)*, pp. 7–9.

4. Robert Brody, *The Geonim of Babylonia and the Shaping of Medieval Jewish Culture.*

5. The period of the Geonim was from the ninth to the eleventh century, after which the title was used as an honorific. The Gaon was "the Head of the Academy" (*rosh ha-yeshivah*), and the title is most likely from Rosh Yeshivat Ge'on Ya'aqov, "the Head of the Academy, which is the pride [*ge'on*] of Jacob." See Brody, *The Geonim of Babylonia*, p. 49.

6. E. Ashtor, *The Jews of Moslem Spain,* trans. A. Klein and J. M. Klein, II, 183; Joseph Rivlin, *Bills and Contracts from Lucena*, p. 28.

7. Cohen, Introduction to Ibn Daud, *The Book of Tradition*, pp. xviii–xix.

8. Abraham Ibn Daud related that Moses ben Enoch was one of four scholars taken captive by pirates. They brought him to Córdoba, where he was redeemed by the local people; *The Book of Tradition*, pp. 63–68. See Gerson D. Cohen, "The Story of the Four Captives," in *Studies in the Variety of Rabbinic Cultures,* pp. 157–208. The story is schematized and may not be a true description of events, but it faithfully represents the process of cultural transmission that took place.

9. Torah is from a word meaning "teach," and has the sense of "teaching." It applies in the first place to the Five Books of Moses (Genesis, Exodus, Leviticus, Numbers, Deuteronomy), and by extension to the whole of the Teaching, both the Written and the Oral Law (Talmud and Midrashim).

10. See in this volume below, p. 256.

11. See F. Gabrieli, EI, s.v. "Adab." The modern Hebrew word "polite" (*adiv*) is a neologism coined from this Arabic term.

12. Samuel's son's name was actually Jehoseph, a form that occurs once in the Hebrew Bible, in Psalm 81:6. (Bible translations do not indicate this.) According to tradition (see J Sot vii, 4, 21d), Jehoseph was the form written on the ephod of the priestly breastplate, where the twelve tribes appear in two columns, the additional *h* giving twenty-five letters on each side; see Maimonides, MT Temple Utensils and Servers, ix, 9. Some regarded the *h* as an abbreviation of the divine name; see Ibn Ezra on Psalm 81:6. Samuel's father's name was also Jehoseph.

13. See *Hebrew Ethical Wills*, ed. and trans. Israel Abrahams, I, 59. I have modified the translation.

14. *Selected Poems of Shmuel HaNagid*, trans. Peter Cole, p. 111.

15. James Dickie, "Granada: A Case Study of Arab Urbanism in Muslim Spain" in *The Legacy of Muslim Spain,* ed. Jayyusi, I, 88. This was the area where at the beginning of the twentieth century the famous composer Manuel de Falla resided, whose *Nights in the Gardens of Spain* reawaken the transcendent beauty of Andalusia. He was a friend of the immortal poet, Federico García Lorca, who lived in Granada and wrote exquisite verse about his homeland. I suggest the music and poetry as accompaniment to this chapter to sense the soul of Andalusia.

16. Ibn Daud, *The Book of Tradition*, ed. and trans. G. D. Cohen, p. 102 (translation slightly modified).

17. Jews with the name Samuel were often called Isma'il, which was, of course, a popular name in a Muslim environment. As Isma'il, his honorific name was Abu Ibrahim. Eli/'Ali was the most popular personal name at this time, as it served well in both societies. Jews did not use the name Muhammad and its variations such as Ahmad.

18. Ashtor, *The Jews of Moslem Spain,* II, 49–50.

19. Abu Marwan ibn Hayyan al-Qurtubi (987/88–1076) as cited by Lisan al-Din Ibn al-Khatib (1313–1375), *al-Ihata fi akhbar Gharnata* (*The Comprehensive History of Granada*), I, 446–48. See also *Rasa'il Ibn Hazm,* ed. I. 'Abbas, III, 10. And see Ross Brann, "Textualizing Ambivalence in Islamic Spain" in *Languages of Power,* ed. Brann, p. 114, where this is translated. I have retranslated the selection to bring out the meaning I find in some of its terms.

20. This was a *façon de parler.* Samuel belonged to an accursed people from the viewpoint of the author's religion.

21. The term *hilm,* a key concept in Arab-Islamic ethics, means "self-restraint," "forbearance," "patience." It is the restraint of someone powerful, such as Mu'awiya, first of the Umayyad caliphs of Syria (661–680), famous for this virtue. The person who possesses *hilm* is *halim,* and the noun/adjective is one of the ninety-nine beautiful names of Allah, so that we find the name 'Abd al-Halim (the Servant of the Forbearing One).

22. The term is *makr,* meaning "cunning, craftiness, slyness, wiliness, double-dealing, deception, trickery." This is not usually a praiseworthy quality and it sounds like a stereotypic label for a Jew. Yet as a courtier, one would have needed this quality.

23. Supplied by the editor.

24. He means Arabic and Hebrew and secular and traditional knowledge.

25. Abraham Gross, "Centers of Study and Yeshivot," *The Sephardi Legacy,* ed. Haim Beinart, I, 402.

26. A frequent blessing at the end of letters was: *Your sons will succeed your ancestors; you will appoint them princes throughout the land* (Ps 45:17).

27. Ashtor, *The Jews of Moslem Spain,* II, 98.

28. *Selected Poems of Shmuel HaNagid,* trans. Peter Cole, p. 56.

29. J. Schirmann, *The History of Hebrew Poetry in Muslim Spain,* ed. E. Fleischer, pp. 356–61.

30. Bernard Lewis, "An Ode Against the Jews," in *Islam in History,* new ed., pp. 167–74. See the text and translation in *Hispano-Arabic Poetry,* trans. James T. Monroe, pp. 206–12.

31. *Fara'id al-qulub* (*Duties of the Hearts*), v, 5; B. Safran, "Bahyah ibn Paquda's Attitude Toward the Courtier Class," *Studies in Medieval Jewish History and Literature,* ed. I. Twersky, pp. 155–58; Bernard Septimus, "Piety and Power in Thirteenth-Century Catalonia," ibid., pp. 197–230; and E. Gutwirth, "Hispano-Jewish Fortuna of Maimonidean Ideas on Wealth," Sobre la vida y obra de Maimonides, p. 298, n. 10.

32. Bahya Ibn Paquda lived at the end of the eleventh century in Andalusia, possibly in Saragossa; see Georges Vajda, EJ, s.v. "Bahya Ben Joseph Ibn Paquda.1" His *Duties of the Hearts* has been edited by A. S. Yahuda (1912) and Joseph Qafih (1972/73), and translated into English by M. Hyamson (1962) and Menahem Mansoor (1973). On his asceticism, see Vajda, *La théologie ascétique de Bahya Ibn Paquda*; A. Lazaroff, "Bahya's Asceticism Against Its Rabbinic and Islamic Background." And see Diana Lobel, *A Sufi-Jewish Dialogue: Philosophy and Mysticism in Bahya Ibn Paqūda's* Duties of the Heart.

33. Gerson D. Cohen traced Bahya's influence on Abraham Maimonides in "The Soteriology of Rabbi Abraham Maimuni." See also Safran, "Bahyah ibn Paquda's Attitude Toward the Courtier Class," p. 184, n. 4.

34. Naguib Mahfouz, the Egyptian novelist and Nobel Prize winner, in *Bayn al-Qasrayn,* called *Palace Walk* in translation, describes the father of the household, Ahmad 'Abd al-Jawad, after a night of carousing, getting up early in the morning to pray. "His boisterous nights were not able to make him forget his daytime duties." See *Palace Walk,* trans. William Maynard Hutchins with Olive E. Kenny, p. 15.

35. Eric Ormsby, "Ibn Hazm," in Menocal et al., *The Literature of al-Andalus,* p. 244. See Ibn Hazm's *The Ring of the Dove,* trans. A. J. Arberry, pp. 180–81.

36. Ross Brann, *The Compunctious Poet: Cultural Ambiguity and Hebrew Poetry in Muslim Spain.*

37. James Dickie, "The Hispano-Arab Garden: Notes towards a Typology," *The Legacy of Muslim Spain,* ed. S. K. Jayyusi, pp. 1020–21.

38. García Lorca, *Collected Poems,* introduction by Christopher Maurer, p. xl.

39. Maimonides, *Responsa,* no. 293, p. 548; *Letters,* ed. Y. Shailat, pp. 233, 684, n. 4. And see Ibn Daud, *The Book of Tradition,* pp. 97–98, and "Analysis and Interpretation," pp. 266–67, 294; Moses Ibn Ezra, *Book of Discussion and Commemoration,* ed. and trans. A. S. Halkin, pp. 54–56. Abraham Ibn Ezra, in his commentary on Obad 1:20, says that this was the Exile of Titus in 70 C.E., not the first exile in 587 B.C.E., as the exegete Moses Gikatilla thought. Ibn Daud also took it to be the Exile of 70 C.E. In this case, the Obadiah verse was a prophecy. Samuel ha-Nagid agreed with Gikatilla that Obadiah meant the exiles of 587 B.C.E.; see J. Schirmann and Fleischer, *History of Hebrew Poetry in Muslim Spain,* p. 17. See also N. Roth, "Maimonides as Spaniard: National Consciousness of a Medieval Jew," *Sobre la vida y obra de Maimonides,* p. 466; and M. A. Friedman, *Maimonides, the Yemenite Messiah and Apostasy,* pp. 50, 67–68.

40. The Aramaic Targum Jonathan identified Sefarad with Aspamia (from Latin Hispania), and this interpretation became widely accepted. The verse goes on to say, "They shall possess the towns of the Negeb," which was understood to mean Judea, the sense being that the exiles would return to a region that included Jerusalem and were hence from there. Sefarad in the verse was probably the city and province of Sardis in the Persian Empire (as of 545 B.C.E.), called Sparda in Old Persian, Saparda in Babylonian, and Sardeis in Greek; see Koehler, Baumgartner, *Hebrew and Aramaic Lexicon,* s.v. "Sefarad." In the same verse, the toponymic "Zarephath" occurs, which Jews later applied to France, though originally it was a town in Phoenicia (1 Kings 17:9).

41. Ibn Daud, *Book of Tradition,* ed. and trans. G. D. Cohen, "Analysis and Interpretation," pp. 276–77, 295. See also Brann, *The Compunctious Poet,* pp. 47–58; A. Sáenz-Badillos, "Philologians and Poets," in *Languages of Power,* ed. R. Brown, p. 74; Brann, *Power in the Portrayal,* p. 86; and see María Rosa Menocal, *Ornament of the World,* p. 79.

42. Consuelo López-Morillas, "Language," *The Literature of al-Andalus,* ed. María Rosa Menocal et al., pp. 43–45.

43. See Ibn Daud, op. cit., p. 270.

44. *Guide,* I, 71 (p. 175); II, 11 (p. 276); and III, 31 (p. 524).

45. For instance, the Shu'ubiyya movement rejected superiority of the Arabs, taking the form of an awakened national consciousness among subject populations. (See Qur'an 49:13 for *shu'ub,* nations.) The early Shu'ubis were Persians, but the name came to include others, such as the Egyptian Copts and the Berbers and Slavs in Andalusia. See I. Goldziher, "Die Su'ûbijja unter den Muhammedanern in Spanien"; H. A. R. Gibb, "The Social Significance of the Shu'ûbiyya"; R. P. Mottahedeh, "The Shu'ûbiyya Controversy and the Social History of Early Islamic Iran"; *Islam from the Prophet Muhammad to the Capture of Constantinople,* ed. and trans. B. Lewis, II, 201–6; J. M. Monroe, *The Shu'ûbiyya in al-Andalus*; H. T. Norris, "Shu'ûbiyya in Arabic Literature"; Jo Miller, "Islam, Arabism, and the Shu'ubiyya Literature of al-Andalus, c. 1060–1170," accessed at http://instruct1.cit.cornell.edu/courses/nes339/shu.html.

46. Neal Kozodoy, "Reading Medieval Hebrew Love Poetry," p. 115. Peter Cole's *The Dream of the Poem: Hebrew Poetry from Muslim and Christian Spain 950–1492* appeared (2007) too late for me to make use of it.

47. Ibid., pp. 117–18. Kozodoy appositely cites T. S. Eliot's "Tradition and the Individual Talent," stressing the notion of a living tradition residing in the poet's consciousness.

48. It is called *musivstil* (mosaic style); see David Yellin, *Theory of Spanish Poetry,* pp. 118ff. And see Dan Pagis, *Innovation and Tradition in Secular Poetry,* pp. 70ff.; Kozodoy, "Reading Medieval Hebrew Love Poetry," p. 118, n. 13.

49. See Kozodoy's analysis of the poem, pp. 121–26, and Scheindlin's commentary in *Wine, Women, and Death,* pp. 37–39.

50. In the *Book of Discussion and Commemoration,* ed. Halkin, pp. 134ff.

51. For a sense of the erotic language in the biblical text, see the translation by Ariel and Chana Bloch, *The Song of Songs: A New Translation*; and see Carey Ellen Walsh, *Exquisite Desire*. The commentaries by Marvin H. Pope (the Anchor Bible) and Tremper Longman III (the New International Commentary on the New Testament) are excellent on the language and love themes of Song of Songs, as is Michael V. Fox, *The Song of Songs and the Ancient Egyptian Love Songs*.

52. See Scheindlin, *The Gazelle*, pp. 37–38.

53. See Song 2:9, 17; 8:14; 4:5; 7:4.

54. Aharon Mirsky, "Hebrew Literary Creation," p. 171.

55. Jehoseph, son of Samuel ha-Nagid. said that his father's love poems were sacred, that the lover was the Congregation of Israel, and that whoever suspects him of the opposite will bear his sin. *Diwan Samuel*, ed. Sasson, p. 1; J. Schirmann, "The Ephebe in Medieval Hebrew Poetry," p. 98. There is no doubt, however, that they were on one level erotic poems.

56. See, for instance Qur'an 47:15, 55:72, 88:10–16.

57. Richard Ettinghausen, "Art and Architecture," pp. 284, 286.

58. The English "gazelle" is from Ar *ghazal* by way of OF *gazelle* < Sp *gacela*, *gacele*, *gacel* (OED).

59. See Jefim Schirmann, "The Ephebe in Medieval Hebrew Poetry." Norman Roth has treated the question of homoeroticism in Hebrew poetry in a series of stimulating studies—"Deal Gently with the Young Man: Love of Boys in Medieval Hebrew Poetry of Spain"; "My Beloved Is Like a Gazelle"; and "The Care and Feeding of Gazelles." Schirmann's view was that the homoerotic references did not necessarily reflect actual practice, whereas Roth put them in the context of the wider society, where homoeroticism in poetry was more than a literary motif.

60. Doris Behrens-Abouseif, *Beauty in Arabic Culture*, p. 59; Arie Schippers, *Spanish Hebrew Poetry and the Arabic Literary Tradition: Arabic Themes in Hebrew Andalusian Poetry*, pp. 120, 147, 152. The curly-haired youth, a prominent motif in this poetry, appears as an embodiment of the divine in Jewish mystical writings. See Song 5:11. ("His locks are curled and black as a raven"). In the Song of Glory, in the Sabbath Morning Service, God is compared to a young boy with curly hair, which can be traced to rabbinic mystical exegesis of Song of Songs; see S. Lieberman in Gershom G. Scholem, *Jewish Gnosticism Merkabah Mysticism, and the talmudic Tradition,* Appendix D, pp. 119–20.

61. Adding to the richly layered meaning is the fact that the homophone of Heb *sevi* also means "beauty," "glory," "magnificence" (2 Sam 1:19; Dan 11:16, 41).

62. Moses Ibn Ezra, *Diwan*, no. 54, trans. Arie Schippers, *Spanish Hebrew Poetry and the Arabic Literary Tradition*, p. 113 (substituting "his" for "its" in line 2a).

63. Al-Harizi, *Wanderings*, ed. Yahalom and Blau, p. 227. The son of Amram is Moses, the lawgiver. See Lev 18:22, which ends, "as one lies with a woman; it is an abhorrence."

64. *Responsa,* no. 269, pp. 515–16, from Aleppo. The complete version of the responsum is in no. 224. See Cf. MT Forbidden Foods, xi, 10. The responsum was apparently written before *The Mishneh Torah*, as Maimonides did not refer to the law code in the responsum. See A. H. Freimann's comment in Blau's edition of the responsa, p. 516, n. 8.

65. Maimonides used the word *nabdha*, which is date wine. In this responsum, he states that the Muslims (Ishmaelites) are not far from idolatry, as the people of Aleppo had claimed. See Goitein, *Med. Soc.*, V, 39–40. Later, in his responsum to Obadiah the Proselyte, he sought to establish that Islam was pure monotheism (see below, p. 312).

Chapter 3

1. MT Torah Study, i, 6.

2. T-S 20.138 verso; see Goitein, *Jewish Education in Muslim Countries*, p. 35; MT Torah Study, ii, 2.

3. This environment was similar to medieval France, where childhood did not exist

as we know it. Society viewed a youth of seven as a grown-up, and parents dressed children like young adults. See Philippe Ariès, *Centuries of Childhood*.

4. M. C. Lyons and D. E. P. Jackson, *Saladin: The Politics of the Holy War*, p. 3.

5. The Babylonian Talmud says (Meg 3a) that Onqelos translated the Pentateuch into Aramaic under the direction of Rabbi Eliezer ben Hyrcanus and Rabbi Joshua ben Hananyah. According to talmudic sources, he was also close to Rabban Gamliel of Yavneh. See Louis Isaac Rabinowitz, EJ, s.v. "Onkelos and Aquila."

6. Maimonides studied the entire Bible through once every year and made his own handwritten copy of the Torah; MT Torah scroll, viii, 4 and x, 10.

7. The term "Rabbanite" designates Jews who adhered to the Oral Law, embodied in the Talmud and Midrashim. They were opposed by the Karaites, who denied the Oral Law's validity and the authority of the Talmud. "Rabbinite" (with an *i*) refers to the rabbinic sages of the Talmud.

8. The law codes arranged talmudic discussions in a systematic organization of laws comprehensible to nonscholars. The *Sefer ha-halakhot* of Rabbi Isaac Alfasi (1013–1103) summarized the legal discussions of the Talmud and stated their legal conclusions, omitting nonlegal matters.

9. Joseph ben Judah Ibn 'Aqnin was the pupil of Maimonides whom we met in Fez (see above, p. 92). Judah ibn 'Abbas lived in Spain in the thirteenth century, wrote poetry and was the father of the apostate Samaw'al ben Judah al-Maghribi, author of *Silencing the Jews (Ifham al-Yahud)*.

10. *Halakhah* is "the sum total of rules and laws—derived from the Bible, from religious thought and teaching, from jurisprudence and custom—that govern all aspects of Jewish life." It is almost always said by scholars to be derived from *halakh*, "to go," but this is incorrect, and it should be rather traced to *halakh* in Ez 4:13 or to Aram *halkha*, having the sense of a (land) tax, thereby having the same meaning as Lat *regula*, which also signified a fixed land tax. The meaning of *halakhah* would be "fixed rule." See S. Lieberman, *Hellenism in Jewish Palestine*, p. 83; Shmuel Safrai, "Halakha," in *The Literature of the Sages*, ed. S. Safrai, First Part, pp. 121–209, on p. 121.

11. Ashkenazi Jews, or Ashkenazim, are Jews from Germany, France and the rest of Central Europe, many of whom emigrated to Eastern Europe.

12. MT Torah Study, ii, 5.

13. Goitein, *Med. Soc.*, III, 234–35.

14. B 'AZ 19b.

15. Grk *notarikon* and Lat *notaricum*, from *notarius*, "shorthand writer." In notarikon, either the words are shortened or one letter of each word is used. See M Shab, vii, 5; M. Berenbaum and F. Skolnik, *EJ*, 2nd ed., s.v. "Notarikon."

16. For the laws of prayer and festivals, see A. Marmorstein, "The Book *Laws of Prayer and Festivals* of Rabbi Maimon," pp. 182–84, and see I. M. Ta-Shma, EJ, s.v. "Maimon ben Joseph."

17. Ms. Vatican Neofiti 11, 128b–132b; see A. H. Freimann, "*Responsa* of Rabbi Maimon the Dajjan, the Father of Maimonides."

18. B San 105b.

19. The name Migash is apparently from Greek *megas*, meaning "great," which may point to a Byzantine origin of the family.

20. Born in Qal'at Bani Hammad in Algeria, Alfasi studied in Qayrawan, Tunisia, with Nissim ben Jacob Gaon and Rabbenu Hananel ben Hushiel. He settled in Fez (Ar Fas) and became the head of its academy. He was later called the RIF, an acronym for Rabbi Isaac of Fas.

21. Ibn Daud said that two men in his native country denounced Alfasi, forcing him to go into exile; *The Book of Tradition*, p. 84. See Hirschberg, *A History of the Jews in North Africa*, pp. 347–51. Often these denunciations were by enemies regarding tax issues and hidden treasures.

22. His responsa were later translated into Hebrew. See A. Grossman, "Legislation and Responsa Literature," *The Sephardi Heritage*, ed. H. Beinart, I, 192. Menachem Elon, *Jewish Law: History, Sources, Principles*, pp. 1476–7 and Appendix C.

23. The first edition of Alfasi's *Precepts* was Constantinople 1509. The book has been edited by N. Zaks. See S. Shefer, *Ha-Rif u-mishnato*; Menachem Elon, *Jewish Law: History, Sources, Principles*, I, 1168–70. The full title of Alfasi's code is *Sefer halakhot rabbati*; see S. Friedman's Introduction to *Sefer Halakhot Rabbati le-Rabbenu Yitzhak Alfasi*, pp. 52ff.

24. For the Babylonian Talmud, see H. L. Strack and G. Stemberger, *Introduction to the Talmud and Midrash*, pp. 208–44; Abraham Goldberg, "The Babylonian Talmud," *The Literature of the Sages,* ed. Safrai, pp. 323–45; and Neusner, *Judaism: The Classical Statement: The Evidence of the Bavli.* The word Gemara ("teaching") is used for the exposition of the Mishnah by Amoraim, and it therefore corresponds to Talmud; Strack and Stemberger, p. 183. On the Jerusalem Talmud, see Strack and Stemberger, pp. 182–207; Abraham Goldberg, "The Palestinian Talmud," *The Literature of the Sages,* pp. 303–22; and Neusner, *Judaism in Society: The Evidence of the Yerushalmi.*

25. The name "Abridged Talmud" for Alfasi's work occurs in Ibn Daud, *The Book of Tradition*, p. 84; and see Baron, *Social and Religious History*, VI, 368, n. 96; and Avraham Grossman, "Legislation and Responsa Literature," *The Sephardi Legacy*, ed. Haim Beinart, I, 192–93.

26. Elon, *Jewish Law*, III, 1139.

27. Ibid., I, 267–71; III, 1170.

28. Ibn Daud, *The Book of Tradition*, pp. 85–87; A. L. Grajevsky, *Rabbenu Yosef ha-Levi Ibn Migash;* I. M. Ta-Shma, EJ, 2nd ed., s.v. "Ibn Migash."

29. He was Abu 'l-Qasim Muhammad Ibn 'Abbad al-Mu'tamid (r. 1069–91) of the 'Abbadid dynasty of Seville. See David Wasserstein, *The Rise and Fall of the Party-Kings*, pp. 95, 123, 156–59, 289; R. P. Scheindlin, *Form and Structure in the Poetry of al-Mu'tamid Ibn 'Abbād*; E. Levi-Provençal and R. P. Scheindlin, EI, s.v. "al-Mu'tamid Ibn 'Abbād."

30. Alfasi's longevity was remarkable in those days, when disease was rampant and hard to cure. The physician Isaac Israeli of Qayrawan (ca. 855–ca. 955) lived to about one hundred, although he never married.

31. Ibn Daud added that "his exemplary traits were tangible proof of the fact that he himself was of the very seed of Moses, the most humble of all men"; see *Book of Tradition*, p. 273. As Exilarchs were deemed to belong to the seed of King David, Heads of Academies were deemed to belong to the seed of the lawgiver Moses.

32. *Commentary on the Mishnah*, ed. Y. Shailat, pp. 61–62 Hebrew/p. 357 Arabic. Others were equally flattering. Isaac ibn Albalia said that Ibn Migash "had been blessed with qualities that surpassed those of the outstanding men of the generation of Moses." On the literary productivity of Ibn Migash, see Israel M. Ta-Shma, *Studies in Medieval Rabbinic Literature, 2. Spain,* ch. 2.

33. Gil and Fleischer, *Yehuda ha-Levi and his Circle,* p. 59, n. 17.

34. Rabbi Joseph Migash, *Responsa*, no. 114. See Baron, *Social and Religious History*, VI, 115–16; Elon, *Jewish Law*, III, 1181–84; Goitein, *Med. Soc.*, II, 208 and 564, n. 7; and Ta-Shma, op. cit., pp. 41–46.

35. Relying upon previous responsa assumes the principle of adhering to decided cases, or *stare decisis* (Lat "to stand by that which is decided") in present legal parlance. When an issue has been decided, it becomes a binding precedent.

36. A dispute between Halfon ben Nethanal ha-Levi, the India trader and friend of Judah ha-Levi, and a scholar in Spain named Jacob, which is preserved in the Genizah, probably led to the query and response. Halfon had referred the scholar to a responsum of the Geonim, and his correspondent replied in a very discourteous letter that one could only decide legal questions by referring to the Talmud, and he would prove this by presenting the question to the Rav (meaning Ibn Migash) or to Isaac ben Judah Ibn Ghiyath. (The second name appears only partially.) Halfon had studied for a brief time with Ibn Migash.

See T-S 13 J 26.11, edited and translated into Hebrew in Goitein and Friedman, *India Traders,* iv, 44; and see Goitein, *Education,* pp. 167–69; and Gil and Fleischer, *Judah ha-Levi,* pp. 302–06. The correspondence took place in the winter of 1128/29. Goitein said that Jacob's letter to Halfon was the coarsest that he ever read in the Genizah.

37. Elon, *Jewish Law,* III, 1184.

38. Goitein, *Education,* pp. 153–54.

39. Abraham Gross, "Centers of Study and Yeshivot in Spain," *The Sephardi Legacy,* ed. Haim Beinart, I, 404.

40. U. Simon, "The Spanish School of Biblical Interpretation," ibid., p. 116.

41. Many works of Galen of Pergamon (131–201 C.E.) were translated from Greek into Arabic. See on the physician as philosopher P. Bachmann, *Galens Abhandlung darüber, dass der vorzügliche Arzt Philosoph sein muss.* In this influential book Galen was mainly interested in demonstrative proof (*apodeixis/burhān*) and in proper *diaresis (taqsīm)* into genera and species (see, e.g., p. 31). See also Jonathan Barnes, "Galen on Logic and Therapy."

42. Taqi al-Din Ibn Taymiyya (d. 1328), exemplifying this attitude, said that only science inherited from the Prophet Muhammad deserves to be called science, and the rest is either useless or not science at all; see *Majmu'at al-rasa'il al-kubra,* I, 238, cited by I. Goldziher, *Stellung der alten Islamischen Orthodoxie zu den Antiken Wissenschaften,* p. 6. Ibn Taymiyya is a source of inspiration for anti-Western jihadis nowadays.

43. See David King, *Astronomy in the Service of Islam.*

44. The expression *gezerat ha-kokhavim* (lit. "the edict of the stars") renders Ar *ahkam al-nujum,* lit. "decrees of the stars" or "judicial astrology," which studies celestial influence on human destinies. Astrology was called *ahkam al-nujum* to distinguish it from astronomy (*'ilm al-nujum*). *Ahkam,* however, does not mean "judgments," as it has been (mis)understood, giving rise to the widely accepted term, "judicial astrology." Rather *hukm* (sing.) is a type of reasoning involving inference of the unknown from the known, and *ahkam* are really astrological signs. Hebrew texts went with the sense of judgments, using the expressions *gezerat ha-kokhavim* (above) or *mishpete ha-kokhavim* (lit. "astral judgments").

45. See CM AZ, iii, 3; *Guide,* III, 29.

46. *Epistle on Astrology,* ed. Shailat, p. 482; trans. Ralph Lerner, p. 229. Maimonides wrote the epistle in Hebrew to the sages of Lunel on 11 Tishre 1506 S.E. (September 11, 1194). See below, ch. 21.

47. *Guide,* II, 25 (pp. 327–28).

48. Maimonides used the example of two asymptotic lines for illustrating something rational but unimaginable in *Guide,* I, 73 (p. 210). See Gad Freudenthal, "Maimonides' *Guide of the Perplexed* and the Transmission of the Mathematical Tract 'On Two Asymptotic Lines' in the Arabic, Latin, and Hebrew Traditions."

49. The first reference to these nine digits in the Arab world is said to be in the year 662 C.E. by the bishop Severus Sebokht, and the earliest study was by Ahmad ibn Ibrahim Uqlidisi (952 C.E.). The Hindus invented the decimal positional system before 600 C.E. In positional notation, the value of the number depends on its position. The value of the number 4 depends on whether it is in the column of the hundred, tens, or units. The Arabic word *sifr* was used for zero and is the source from which our word "cipher" is derived. It represents a vacant place in positional notation. The Babylonians used positional notation but not a decimal system and had no cipher, which Babylonian astronomers invented (from *ouden* = nothing). The Hindus adopted it from the Greeks. On number systems, see B. L. van der Waerden, *Science Awakening,* ch. 2.

50. With the Roman numeration, lacking zero, it was impossible to indicate the year zero. And hence we have a calendar jumping from 1 B.C.E. (−1) to 1 C.E. (+1). No one was born in the year zero. Yet people were born in 1000 and 2000 C.E. The theologian Franz Bibfelt wrote his dissertation on the problem of the year zero. See *The Unrelieved Paradox: Studies in the Theology of Franz Bibfelt,* ed. Martin E. Marty and Jerald C. Brauer.

51. The sexagesimal scale goes back to the ancient Sumerians and Babylonians. It has

the advantage over decimal notation in that 60 has eleven factors (1, 2, 3, 4, 5, 6, 10, 12, 15, 30, 60), while 10 has only four (1, 2, 5, 10). We divide hours into 60 minutes and minutes into 60 seconds, and divide the sky and circular planes into 360 degrees. The Babylonians divided the day into 24 hours, which is divisible by 6 and divides into 360 evenly. See D. E. Duncan, *Calendar*, p. 18. The sexagesimal system most likely influenced the six days of creation in Genesis, which (with the added Sabbath) gives us our seven-day week. Nowadays the binary system, using base 2, is ubiquitous because of its application to computers. In a decimal system, based on our ten fingers, digits ("fingers") are 0 through 9. In a binary system, digits are 0 and 1, based on electronic impulses (on or off), which is oddly called "digital."

52. Al-Khwarizmi's *Arithmetic* (ca. 825), preserved in twelfth-century Latin translations, noted a decimal system using zero, known in Europe as algorismus. See André Allard, "The Arabic Origins and Development of Latin Algorismus," and his "Arabic Mathematics in the Medieval West," p. 540. See A. I. Sabra, EI , s.v. "'Ilm al-Ḥisāb"; and M. Levey and M. Petruck, *Principles of Hindu Reckoning*.

53. *Commentary on Rosh ha-Shanah,* 22b (p. 18).

54. CM RH, ii, 9. Some scholars do not accept the authenticity of the commentary on *Rosh ha-Shanah*, partly because of this passage, on the assumption that Maimonides would not speak this way about himself.

55. Samuel Saqilli stated clearly that he copied the commentary in Acre from a Maimonides autograph. David II ha-Nagid, Maimonides' great-great-great-grandson, was in Acre at the time and obviously brought the manuscript there. Saqilli copied it, and his descendants disseminated it in Europe (where many copies of the commentary were circulated). See also *Hilkhot ha-Yerushalmi*, ed. Lieberman, Introduction, pp. 13–14; and Israel M. Ta-Shema, *Studies in Medieval Rabbinic Literature*, II, *Spain*, pp. 313–14. Ta-Shema explained how this autobiographical text appears at the end of Maimonides' *Commentary on the Mishnah*. The Great Sage was working on the commentary on the ship and had no other paper on which to write his description of the storm; hence he wrote it at the end of the commentary.

56. See Richard Walzer, *Greek into Arabic: Essays on Islamic Philosophy*; Franz Rosenthal, *The Classical Heritage in Islam*; Dimitri Gutas, *Greek Thought, Arabic Culture*. See also Kraemer, "The Intellectual Context of Medieval Jewish Thought," pp. 39–43.

57. *Guide*, I, 71 (p. 175). The priority of Moses to Plato was a motif of Jewish apologetic literature in the Hellenistic period (for instance, Philo). It was adopted by some of the Church Fathers and was widely held in Maimonides' time.

58. See Kraemer, "The Islamic Context of Medieval Jewish Philosophy," pp. 39–40.

CHAPTER 4

1. Umberto Eco, *The Name of the Rose*, p. 215.

2. Israel Efros edited two fragments of the Arabic original and the Hebrew translations of Moses Ibn Tibbon, Ahituv ben Isaac, and Joseph ben Joshua ben Vivas, and published an English translation of the work in *Maimonides' Treatise on Logic*. Mubahat Türker discovered two manuscripts of the treatise in Arabic, in Ankara and Istanbul, and published the text along with an introduction and Turkish translation; *Al-Makala fi Sina'at al-Mantiq de Musa ibn Maymun (Maïmonide)*. Efros subsequently published the entire Arabic text in Hebrew characters. Rémi Brague published the Arabic text with French translation in *Traité de logique*. On editions, see further Kraemer, "Maimonides on the Philosophic Sciences in his *Treatise on the Art of Logic*," p. 77, n. 1.

3. F. E. Peters, *Aristoteles Arabus*, pp. 17–30. See also Richard E. Rubenstein, *Aristotle's Children*, pp. 62 and 106–7.

4. This treatise is philosophic and as such is universal. Maimonides introduced the first chapter speaking of "we," meaning logicians. See also *Traité de logique*, ed. and trans. Rémi Brague, pp. 17–18.

5. The Hebrew translations of Ibn Tibbon and Ibn Vivas render *al-'ulum al-shar'iyya* by *ha-hakhamot ha-toriyyot,* suggesting Jewish legal sciences. Ahituv translates more correctly: *ha-hakhamot ha-datiyyot,* i.e., legal sciences in general.

6. The superscription to the work (in the editions by Efros) is *bismi 'llah al-rahman al-rahim* (in the name of God, the merciful, the compassionate), which appears at the head of the Surahs of the Qur'an (except Surah 9) and in daily prayers. It is referred to by the acronym *basmala.* Türker's edition has *bismi 'llah rabb al-'alamin,* an Arabic rendition of *In the name of the Lord, God of the world* (Gen 21:33), evidently a more accurate version of the original text. Maimonides began the three parts of the *Guide* as well as his halakhic works and his *Treatise on Resurrection* with this quotation from Genesis 21:33. For its meaning, see MT Idolatry, i, 3; *Guide,* II, 13 and 30; III, 29. His medical works, addressed to Muslim potentates, also begin with the *basmala.* According to H. Atay, in his edition of the *Guide* in Arabic letters, based upon Ms. Istanbul Jarullah 1279 (p. 7, n. 1), the manuscript reading of the superscription is *bismi 'llah al-rahman al-rahim.* It is most likely that a Muslim substituted the Islamic invocation for the biblical verse here and in the *Treatise on the Art of Logic.* On the superscriptions to Maimonides' works, see also S. Lieberman's Introduction to his edition of *Hilkhot ha-Yerushalmi,* p. 5, n. 7.

7. See Averroes, *The Decisive Treatise,* trans. George F. Hourani in *Averroes on the Harmony of Religion and Philosophy,* pp. 49 and 92, n. 59; *Decisive Treatise,* trans. Charles E. Butterworth, p. 8.

8. Averroes quotes an appropriate verse from the Qur'an: *Summon to the way of your Lord by wisdom and by good preaching, and debate with them in the most effective manner* (16:125). The *falasifa* (sg. *faylasuf* from Greek *philosophos*) were the Islamic Aristotelian philosophers (whose political philosophy was, however, Platonic).

9. Leo Strauss, "Maimonides' Statement on Political Science"; Lawrence V. Berman, "A Reexamination of Maimonides' Statement on Political Science."

10. Kraemer, "Maimonides on the Philosophic Sciences," p. 90.

11. Translating *umma* as "nation" is an anachronism if we think of the modern nation or nation-state, defined by government and territory. I mean by "nation" here a group of people who have a common ethnicity, culture, language or languages, and traditions, regardless of territory or government.

12. Aristotle, *Politics,* III, 14, 1285b33f.

13. See S. M. Stern, *Aristotle on the World State,* pp. 64–65. The text was ascribed to Aristotle in a letter to Alexander the Great and was available to medieval Jewish thinkers.

14. The Hebrew translations render the word *awamir* as *inyanim* (Ibn Tibbon) or *devarim* (Ahituv and Vivas), meaning "matters" or "things," as though the Arabic were *umur.* Both *awamir* and *umur* are plural formations of *amr,* the first having the sense of "commandments" and the second having the sense of "things."

15. See Kraemer, "Maimonides on the Philosophic Sciences," pp. 90–91, where the views of Harry A. Wolfson and Leo Strauss are criticized. Wolfson translated "the great nation" as "the great religion" and identified it with Judaism. Strauss identified the great nation with "any group constituted by a universalistic religion."

16. See L. Strauss, *What is Political Philosophy? and Other Studies,* p. 165; Brague, *Traité de logique,* p. 13. As Strauss says, these considerations are "necessarily somewhat playful. But they are not so playful to be incompatible with the seriousness of scholarship."

17. Maimonides wrote, "This number four is wondrous and should be an object of reflection," *Guide,* II, 10 (p. 272). See also *Guide,* I, 72 and III, 54, cited by Y. T. Langermann, "Maimonides and the Sciences," p. 172.

18. The expression "numerical signature" was suggested to me by Dr. Gad Freudenthal.

19. The Banu Hud reigned in the period of the party kings. D. M. Dunlop, EI, s.v. "Hūdids," calls him al-Mu'taman and says that he reigned until 1085. Bosworth, *The New Islamic Dynasties,* p. 19, gives the name as al-Mu'tamin and has him reigning in 474 A.H. = 1081/82. See also Wasserstein, *The Rise and Fall of the Party-Kings,* p. 94; Langermann, "Mathematical Writings," pp. 59–65; Samsò, "The Exact Sciences in al-Andalus," pp. 82,

133–36, 270, 331, 384; *Las Ciencias de los Antiguos en al-Andalus*, pp. 134–36; Charles Burnett, "The Translating Activity in Medieval Spain," p. 1041. A descendant of the Hudids taught *The Guide of the Perplexed* to a circle of Jews in Damascus at the end of the thirteenth century. This was the Sufi scholar Abu 'Ali al-Hasan Ibn Hud al-Judhami (d. 26 Sha'ban 699/ May 17, 1300), a nephew of al-Mu'tamin. His father was governor of the city of Murcia, but Abu 'Ali renounced the promise of *gloria mundi* for the patched garment of the ascetic. See Kraemer, "The Andalusian Mystic Ibn Hūd and the Conversion of the Jews."

20. Charles Burnett, "The Translating Activity in Medieval Spain," pp. 1041–42. The Banu Hud had to move to Rueda de Jalón after Saragossa fell to the Christians in 1118.

21. Abu Ja'far al-Khwarazmi was a mathematician, astronomer, and geographer, who lived circa 800–47 in Baghdad during the caliphate of al-Ma'mun, who stimulated recovery and translation of classical philosophy and science. He wrote a book on algebra, *al-Mukhtasar fi hisab al-jabr wa'l-muqabala*, which was translated by Robert of Chester and then by Gerard of Cremona. The European word "algebra" is from the word in his title *al-jabr*; see J. Vernet, EI, s.v. "al-Khwārazmī."

22. A. Djebbar and J. P. Hogendijk; see Samsó, "Exact Sciences," p. 954; Charles Burnett, "The Translating Activity in Medieval Spain," p. 1041.

23. Sonja Brentjes, EI, s.v. "Uķlīdis"; B. L. van der Waerden, *Science Awakening*, pp. 195–200.

24. Al-Nadim, *al-Fihrist*, trans. Bayard Dodge, p. 642; Ibn al-Qifti, *History of the Sages*, p. 108, Heath, *A Manual of Greek Mathematics*, p. 393; George Sarton, *Introduction to the History of Science*, I, 211.

25. Al-Nadim, *al-Fihrist*, p. 638; Heath, *Manual*, pp. 399–402; Sarton, *Introduction*, I, 253.

26. Al-Nadim, *al-Fihrist*, Index, p. 962; Ibn al-Qifti, *History of the Sages*, p. 66.

27. Al-Nadim, *al-Fihrist*, p. 630, 637–38, 646, 649; Heath, *Manual*, p. 352; Sarton, *Introduction*, I, 173.

28. Each of two integers is equal to the sum of the proper divisors of the other. The smallest pair are 220 and 284, as 220 has the proper divisors 1, 2, 4, 5, 10, 11, 20, 22, 44, 55, and 110, which have the sum of 284. The number 284 has the proper divisors 1, 2, 4, 71, and 142, which sum to 220. A perfect number is a natural number equal to the sum of its proper divisors, as 6 has the proper divisors 1, 2, and 3, which add up to 6. The numbers 28, 496, and 8,128 are also perfect numbers.

29. Al-Nadim, *al-Fihrist*, pp. 647–48; Ibn al-Qifti, *History of the Sages*, p. 115; Sarton, *Introduction*, I, 599; R. Rashed and R. Morelon, EI, s.v. "Thābit b. Qurra."

30. J. Vernet, EI, s.v. "Ibn al-Haytham." His problem, which appeared in Book V, was: Given a light source and a spherical mirror, at what point on the mirror will the light be reflected to the eye of an observer. It was solved elegantly by the Dutch mathematician Christiaan Huygens (1629–96).

31. Roshdi Rashed, "Geometrical Optics," p. 661.

32. Ibn al-Qifti, *History of the Sages*, pp. 317–19; followed by Bar Hebraeus, *Ta'rikh mukhtasar al-duwal*, p. 239.

33. The work is preserved in Ms. Manisa (Turkey), Genel 1706/6, folios 26b–33b. See F. Sezgin, *Geschichte des arabischen Schrifttums*, V, 141 and Y. T. Langermann, "The Mathematical Writings of Maimonides." Maimonides refers to Book II, theorem xiii of *The Conic Sections* in *The Guide of the Perplexed*, I, 73 (p. 210).

34. See also Roshdi Rashed, "al-Sijzî et Maïmonide: Commentaire mathématique et philosophique de la proposition 11–14 des Coniques d'Apollonius"; Gad Freudenthal, "Maimonides' *Guide of the Perplexed* and the Transmission of the Mathematical Tract 'On Two Asymptotic Lines' in the Arabic, Latin, and Hebrew Traditions," p. 114, n. 3. Rashed and Freudenthal raised doubts about its authorship by Maimonides, a skepticism they still hold, as Freudenthal informed me (personal communication). Freudenthal discussed Maimonides' example of two asymptotic lines (illustrating something rational but unimaginable) in *Guide*, I, 73, arguing that Maimonides' source was not Apollonius of Perga.

35. The literal meaning is *Treatise on Intercalation* (*'ibbur*), referring to intercalation (adding) of an extra month to the year to adjust a lunar calendar to the solar year.

36. See Neugebauer, "Astronomical Commentary," p. 147. Elsewhere, he notes that "the presentation of the material shows everywhere the great personality of the author and supreme mastery of a subject, worthy of our greatest admiration." See his "Astronomy of Maimonides," p. 324.

37. See 1 Chron 12:33 and the interpretation in GenR, lxxii.

38. MT Sanctification of the New Moon, xvii, 25 (with slight changes). Maimonides mentioned Greek books as still extant, and he quoted (ix, 1) a disagreement between Greek and Persian scholars. Aside from Ptolemy and classical sources, Maimonides relied mainly on Abu 'Abdallah al-Battani for information on mathematical astronomy. Neugebauer, "Astronomical commentary," p. 129. See also "The Astronomy of Maimonides," p. 324. Al-Battani (858–929) was a Muslim astronomer of Sabian ancestry.

39. Ed. A. Lichtenberg, *Qoves*, pp. 17a–20b; *Die aelteste atronomische Schrift*, trans. L. Dünner; *Lettre de Maïmonide sur le calendrier hébraïque*, ed. and trans. R. Weil and S. Gerstenkorn; and see E. Baneth, "Maimonides als Chonologe und Astronom." The treatise was written in Arabic, but all we have is a Hebrew version. Books on the calendar were titled *Ma'amar* or *Sefer ha-'ibbur* (*Treatise* or *Book of Intercalation*) or *Sod ha-'ibbur*, usually taken to mean *The Secret of Intercalation*. However, the original meaning of *sod* (a word that occurs in the Dead Sea Scrolls) was "council," the rabbinic court that established the calendar; see Sacha Stern, *Calendar and Community*, p. 190.

40. CM RH ii, 7 and Suk iv, 2. In his earlier work on the calendar, he stated explicitly that he was not giving the causes for phenomena, or scientific (proofs), but only premises and principles. See Aristotle, *Posterior Analytics*, I, 2, 71b 20–25. In CM 'Arakh ii, 2, he praised someone in Andalusia who had composed a fine composition on the calendar, probably alluding to Abraham bar Hiyya, whose *Sefer ha-'ibbur* he apparently used in Sanctification, ch. vi–x; see Obermann, Introduction, pp. xliv–xlv. Abraham Ibn Ezra as well wrote a *Book on the Calendar*, on seasonal cycles, new moons, and signs of the zodiac, which Maimonides would have known. Maimonides had no cause to mention his own early treatise on the calendar, especially as it was replaced by the mature treatment of the calendar in the *Mishneh Torah*.

41. The text of *Sanctification of the New Moon*, vi–x, was composed in 4926 A.M. (1166 C.E.). This is the earliest date Maimonides gave for its composition.

42. See *Sanctification of the New Moon*, trans. Solomon Gandz; and see Julius Obermann's Introduction to this volume, pp. xliv–xlv. For previous works, see Obermann, p. xlv, n. 35. And see Y. T. Langermann, "Maimonides and Astronomy: Some Further Reflections," pp. 8, 16. See in general Sacha Stern, *Calendar and Community*.

43. See also Obermann, "Introduction," pp. xxxi–xxxiii.

44. Consider 19 = 12 zodiacal signs + 7 planets (*Guide*, III, 29, pp. 519–20) and also the nineteen years of the Metonic cycle. That it took him twelve years to write was coincidental.

45. Obermann, "Introduction," p. xxx. He gave the year 1178 in four ways: 4938 A.M., 1489 S.E., 1109 years after the destruction of the Second Temple, and year seventeen of the 260th Metonic cycle.

46. *Ptolemy's Almagest*, trans. G. J. Toomer, p. 23.

47. *Responsa*, no. 134, pp. 251–55, on p. 252, where Maimonides explains that hours are seasonal as in the Talmud. And see *Commentary on the Mishnah*, Ber, i, 4.

48. Neugebauer, "Astronomical Commentary," p. 147, notes that the subdivision of the hour into 1,080 parts goes back to Old Babylonian times.

49. See David King, "Three Sundials from Islamic Andalusia," *Islamic Astronomical Instruments*, No. XV, p. 368, 389; J. Samsó, "Andalusian Astronomy: Characteristics and Influence," p. 6.

50. The sundial is in the Museo Arqueológico Provincial; see King, "Three Sundials," pp. 360–63, 367–68; B. R. Goldstein, EI, s.v. "Ibn al-Ṣaffār." Ibn al-Saffar also wrote a set of astronomical tables and a treatise on the use of the astrolabe.

51. These are dietary laws (*kashrut*).

52. Maimonides, *Commentary on the Mishnah*, ed. Shailat, p. 357 (Arabic) and p. 61 (Hebrew). See *Maimonides' Novellae on the Talmud (Hiddushe ha-Rambam la-Talmud: 'al she-tem 'esreh masekhtot)*, ed. Mordecai Judah Loeb Sachs. I. M. Ta-Shma, "Maimonides' Commentary to the Talmud."

53. *Hilkhot ha-Yerushalmi (The Precepts of the Jerusalem Talmud)*, ed. S. Lieberman.

54. I. Twersky, *Introduction to the Code of Maimonides*, p. 165. Twersky says "heretical rumblings," which implies people among the congregation of Israelites, whereas "heretics" (*minim*) here almost certainly refers to Christians or Jewish-Christians.

CHAPTER 5

1. The date is based on the fact that the superscription to Maimon ben Joseph's *Epistle of Consolation* says that he composed it in Fez in 1471 s.e. (1159/60 c.e.). Biographers say that the family came to Fez at the time, but this is not precise; the date is a *terminus ad quem*, the final temporal limit. They were there, but we do not know when they actually arrived.

2. Yellin and Abrahams, *Maimonides*, p. 26, stop short of saying that Ibn Shoshan was the reason for their coming to Fez, but accept the story that he was Maimonides' "companion and guide in his researches into Jewish lore." Heschel, *Maimonides*, p. 20, does not reject the story, and makes Ibn Shoshan a friend of the family, pp. 46–47. Zeitlin, *Maimonides*, p. 7, gives the Ibn Shoshan story total credence. A more recent biography, Ilil Arbel, *Maimonides*, p. 39, accepts the story and adds fanciful details: "and Rabbi Judah ibn Shoshan was indeed instrumental in aiding him, supplying books and introducing him to various scholars. They became close friends." H. Z. Hirschberg, *A History of the Jews in North Africa*, I, 136, accepts Ibn Danan's account (see next note) without demur. Salo W. Baron, *A Social and Religious History*, III, 291, n. 7 (from p. 290) correctly rejects the Ibn Shoshan account because it "gratuitously assumes that there were no scholars of equal standing in Cordoba," and it does not explain why Maimonides' entire family moved there. Baron suggested that supervision of *dhimmi*s was less strict in the Moroccan capital, which was out of reach of Crusaders. However, Fez was not the capital (Marrakesh was) and the reach of Crusaders did not influence events in Fez.

3. The story was told by Se'adyah ben Maimon Ibn Danan (late fifteenth century), *The Order of Generations (Seder ha-dorot)*, ed. C. del Valle and G. Stemberger, pp. 69–71 of text and pp. 136–40 of the translation; some of the elements are in A. Neubauer, "Une Pseudo-Biographie de Moïse Maïmonide," pp. 173–88. Se'adyah Ibn Danan lived four hundred years after the events. He was a learned judge in Granada and emigrated to Oran, Algeria, after the expulsion of Jews from Spain in 1492. The last part of his *Order of the Generations* is about Maimonides, whom he admired.

4. Joseph ben Judah Ibn 'Aqnin is often confused with Joseph ben Judah Ibn Simon, though they had different ancestral names ('Aqnin and Simon), careers, writings, locations, and bodies. There should be no debate about this. Ibn 'Aqnin appears to have remained in Morocco, whereas Ibn Simon, of Ceuta, came to Egypt, studied with Maimonides, and then emigrated to Aleppo. See the confusion in Yellin and Abrahams, *Maimonides*, p. 120–21; Heschel, *Maimonides*, pp. 166–74, who conflates the two men into one; Zeitlin, *Maimonides*, pp. 95ff., 126ff.; and Arbel, *Maimonides*, pp. 152–55. S. Munk already made a precise identification in "Notice sur Joseph ben-Iehouda," p. 20, as did D. H. Baneth, "Joseph Ibn Simon, the Important Pupil of Maimonides and Joseph Ibn 'Aqnin"; and idem, *Epistles*, Introduction, pp. 1–2. See also A. S. Halkin in his preface to Ibn 'Aqnin's *Commentary on Song of Songs*, p. 11; and Hirschberg, *History of the Jews in North Africa*, I, 356–59.

5. David Corcos, "The Attitude of the Almohadic Rulers Toward the Jews," pp. 157–59.

6. Ibrahim ibn Hamushk was the father-in-law of Ibn Mardanish, a Muslim of Span-

ish Christian ancestry, ruler of Murcia and Valencia, who fought the Almohads for control of central Andalusia—Jaen, Baeza, Cadix, Carmona, Córdoba, Seville, and Granada.

7. Braudel, *The Mediterranean*, I, 117: "The sea does not act as a barrier between the two great continental masses of Spain and North Africa; but rather as a river which unites more than it divides, making a single world of North and South, a 'bi-continent,' as Gilberto Freyre has called it."

8. See Paul Theroux, *The Pillars of Hercules*, pp. 1–4, an account of the Mediterranean. The enterprising Phoenicians had navigated beyond Gibraltar before 1100 B.C.E. and founded Cadiz on the western coast of the Iberian Peninsula. They named the rocks "the Pillars of Melkarth, Lord of the Underworld."

9. Some say not Mount Acha but rather Jabal Musa, to the west of Ceuta.

10. The name is said to be from Latin Septem Fratres after the seven peaks near the town. Nowadays, Ceuta and Melilla, on the coast to the east, are enclaves under Spanish control.

11. Goitein found that the fathers of around 85 percent of the thousands of persons who signed documents or letters in the Genizah were eulogized as dead. He estimated that only 15 percent of the population survived to the age of fifty. This surmise is based also on indirect evidence from what prevailed in ancient Greece, which he assumed was similar (*Med. Soc.*, V, 117–18).

12. Roger Le Tourneau, *Fez in the Age of the Marinides*, pp. 3–5.

13. Ibid., pp. 7–10.

14. H. Terrasse, *La Mosquée al-Qaraouiyin à Fès*.

15. The Marinids (or Merinids), Zanata Berbers from the northwest Sahara, defeated the Almohads and ruled in Morocco and the eastern Maghrib for a long period. See Bosworth, *The New Islamic Dynasties*, pp. 41–42; Maya Shatzmiller, EI, s.v. "Marīnids (Banū Marīn)"; Roger Le Tourneau, *Fez in the Age of the Marinides*.

16. Heschel, *Maimonides*, p. 15.

17. See V. J. Cornell, *The Way of Abū Madyan*; idem, *Realm of the Saint: Power and Authority in Moroccan Sufism*.

18. Kenneth Garden, "Al-Ghazali's Contested Revival: *Ihya' 'Ulum al-Din* and Its Critics in Khorasan and the Maghrib," Ph.D. thesis, University of Chicago, 2005.

19. See Nancy G. Siraisi, *Avicenna in Renaissance Italy;* idem, *Medieval and Early Renaissance Medicine*.

20. See Maimonides, *On Asthma*, ed. and trans. G. Bos, pp. xxv–xxvi.

21. But Tashufin ibn 'Ali, as we know, died by falling with his horse from a cliff overlooking the Mediterranean. Perhaps it was his father, 'Ali ibn Yusuf Ibn Tashufin (r. 1106–43), who was mistreated. The Great Theriac of Mithridates was a medical compound made of large amounts opium and many other ingredients, used as an antidote against snake venom and other bites as well as poisons. It was allegedly developed by King Mithridates V Eurgetes of Pontus (ca. 150–120 B.C.E.). Physicians in the Islamic world knew it from Galen's *Theriakē*. It was sometimes taken in small amounts as a preventive antidote. The opium was naturally addictive, and we can only wonder what effect this had on rulers and how much power it put into the hands of physicians.

22. Maimonides, *On Asthma*, ed. and trans. G. Bos, pp. 103–4.

23. The dirham was both a (silver) coin and a weight (= 3.25 grams); Goitein, *Med. Soc.*, I, 360. They gave the lad about 1.56 grams of the theriac.

24. Abu al-'Ala' Ibn Zuhr ibn 'Abd al-Malik of Córdoba was first of the famous Ibn Zuhr family of physicians (Manfred Ullmann, *Die Medizin im Islam*, p. 162). Sufyan is most likely Abu 'l-Hasan Sufyan al-Andalusi, who wrote a book on pharmaceuticals with the philosopher Ibn Bajja (Ibn Abi Usaybi'a, *Classes of Physicians*, pp. 516–17; Ullmann, op. cit., p. 276. See Maimonides, *On Asthma,* ed. and trans. G. Bos, p. 103, nn. 66 and 67). Abu Marwan 'Abd al-Malik ibn Abi 'l-Ala' Zuhr, or Ibn Zuhr (d. 1162) was the most famous of the

Ibn Zuhr family. He was known in Latin as Avenzoar. The physicians Averroes and Maimonides held him in great esteem. Abu Marwan was born in Seville but went to Morocco, where he administered to the Almoravid ruler 'Ali ibn Yusuf ibn Tashufin and to the Almohad ruler 'Abd al-Mu'min. His son, the physician Abu Bakr Muhammad ibn 'Abd al-Malik Ibn Zuhr al-Hafid, "the grandson" (d. 1199), was a friend of Maimonides. He was an outstanding poet, famous for his strophic poems (*muwashshahat*). See Ullmann, op. cit., pp. 162–63.

25. See Hirschberg, *History of the Jews in North Africa*, I, 351–52; Meyerhof, "L'oeuvre médicale de Maimonide," pp. 137–38. For ha-Levi's poem on the Jews of Seville and Ibn Qamniel, see *Diwan*, ed. H. Brody, I, 127–29, no. 88; Schirmann, *Hebrew Poetry in Spain and Provence*, I, pp. 447–49, no. 181. See also Judah ha-Levi, *Diwan*, I, pp. 176–77, no. 118.

26. On Abu Ayyub Solomon Ibn al-Mu'allim, see Schirmann, op. cit., pp. 541–43, Schirmann and Fleischer, *The History of Hebrew Poetry in Muslim Spain*, p. 433; Moshe Gil and Ezra Fleischer, *Yehudah ha-Levi and His Circle*, p. 70, n. 79 and p. 207, n. 131.

27. Ibn 'Aqnin, *Commentary on Song of Songs,* ed. and trans. A. S. Halkin, p. 490.

28. Song of Songs was admitted to the biblical canon as a mystical allegory, with the strong support of Rabbi Aqiba, who declared it the Holy of Holies (*M* Yad, iii, 5; T Yad, ii, 14). He was also quoted as saying that "whoever makes it a secular song has no share in the world hereafter" (T San xii, 10). Jewish exegetes, including Ibn 'Aqnin in his *Commentary on Song of Songs*, interpreted it allegorically as a mystical love song between God and the people of Israel or between the soul and God.

29. *On Asthma*, ed. and trans. G. Bos, pp. 76–78.

30. Ibid., pp. 99–100. It was not a laughing matter, but Maimonides' teacher appreciated his pupil's acumen and wit.

31. Ibid., Introduction, p. xxvi. Lieber suggests that "he appears to have studied medicine as a purely intellectual exercise, without any intention of pursuing a medical career." See "Maimonides the Medical Humanist," pp. 43–44. In fact, in Andalusia medicine was part of the scientific curriculum.

32. Meyerhof, *L'Explication des noms de drogues*, Introduction, p. xlvii; *On Asthma*, ed. and trans. Bos, Introduction, p. xxv.

33. *Aphorisms*, Book XXII, 35, trans. F. Rosner and S. Muntner, p. 118.

34. See A. S. Halkin, "The History of the Forced Conversion in the Days of the Almohads"; David Corcos, "The Attitude of the Almohadic Rulers Toward the Jews"; H. Z. Hirschberg, "The Almohad Persecutions and the India Trade"; idem, *A History of the Jews in North Africa*, I, 123–39; and M. Abumalham, "La conversión segun formularios notariales andalusíes: Valoración de la legalidad de la conversión de Maimónides."

35. Corcos, "The Attitude of the Almohadoc Rulers Toward the Jews."

36. See, for example, Jamil M. Abun-Nasr's *A History of the Maghrib in the Islamic Period*, pp. 87–103. He presents the Almohad movement as "one of religious reform," omitting the oppressive side of this reform (p. 87). See also Abdellatif Sabbane, *Le gouvernement et l'aministration de la dynastie Almohade* (XXe–XXXe siècles). Roger Le Tourneau, *The Almohad Movement in North Africa in the Twelfth and Thirteenth Century*, pp. 57–58, limits 'Abd al-Mu'min's severity against Jews and Christians to the conquest of Ifriqiya (roughly Tunisia nowadays), without a word about the Maghrib; and he notes (p. 77) that Almohad intolerance was at its greatest under Abu Yusuf Ya'qub, when suspected Jewish converts were forced to don ridiculous clothing for purposes of identification. H. Z. Hirschberg says, *A History of the Jews in North Africa,* I, 137, that Maimon's *Epistle of Consolation* and Maimonides' *Epistle on Forced Conversion* "do not point to outrages and bloody persecution" in Fez, citing as corroborating evidence Maimonides' testament to his son, Abraham, which is, however, inauthentic.

37. 'Abd al-Wahid al-Marrakushi, *al-Mu'jib fi talkhis akhbar al-Maghrib (The Wondrous Epitome of the History of the Maghrib)*, edited by R. Dozy as *The History of the Almohads*, p. 223; trans. E. Fagnan, *Histoire des Almohades*, pp. 264–65. See also Hirschberg,

History of the Jews in North Africa, I, 201–2; García-Arenal, "Jewish Converts to Islam," p. 238. The passage had been edited and translated by S. Munk in his 1842 article, "Notice sur Joseph ben Iehouda," pp. 40–42. Al-Marrakushi wrote this work in 621 A.H. = 1224/25. He is therefore almost a contemporary reporter of Almohad history, and he was present in Fez. In 1198/99, he met the physician Abu Bakr Ibn Zuhr. The elderly physician recited some of his poetry to young al-Marrakushi, a lad of fourteen. Al-Marrakushi also met a son of the philosopher Ibn Tufayl. On him, see Dozy's Preface to al-Marrakushi, *The History of the Almohads*, pp. v–xxi.

38. Joseph ben Judah Ibn 'Aqnin described disabilities imposed by the Almohads on the Jewish converts in a chapter of his *Tibb al-nufus* (*Medicine of the Souls*); see A. S. Halkin, "On the History of the Persecution in the Days of the Almohads," pp. 101, 106–10; Hirschberg, *History of the Jews in North Africa*, I, 202.

39. Immediately after this passage, al-Marrakushi said that in the days of Abu Yusuf, the philosopher Ibn Rushd suffered an inquisition (*mihna*, meaning "trial" or "ordeal") and books on philosophy were burned.

40. Israel Levin published an annotated text in his *Abraham Ibn Ezra Reader*, pp. 101–3. It had been published earlier by Israel Davidson, *Thesaurus of Mediaeval Hebrew Poetry*, I, 62–63. The poem was translated with accompanying text and comments by Leon J. Weinberger, *Twilight of a Golden Age*, pp. 96–100. See the translation in Ross Brann, *Power in the Portrayal*, pp. 121–22, his discussion on pp. 123–25, and his longer analysis in "Constructions of Exile in Hispano-Hebrew and Hispano-Arabic Elegies," where he compares Ibn Ezra's elegy with Abu 'l-Baqi al-Rundi's Arabic elegy on the fall of Seville to the Christians. The Arabic poem, Brann shows, stressed the temporary character of the Muslim withdrawal and the inevitable restoration of Spain to Islam, whereas Ibn Ezra linked the Almohad devastation with the Exile of the Jewish people from the Land of Israel. See also Mark R. Cohen, *Under Crescent and Cross*, pp. 182–84; and Gerald Nahon, "La elegia de Abraham ibn Ezra."

41. He ascribed the tragedy to the sins of Jews, thereby following an ancient theme found in rabbinic literature. The virtuous may suffer in this world to have their reward in the next world increased, but the generation of persecution is suffering punishment for its own sins.

42. The arrow is shot at Sarah, personifying the Israelite people. Ishmael was a bowman in Gen 21:20.

43. The verse, as the editor-translator G. D. Cohen notes, was cited by Ibn 'Aqnin in his description of the events; see A. S. Halkin, "On the History of the Persecution in the Days of the Almohads," p. 105, n. 41.

44. The year 4873 A.M. (=1112/13 C.E.) is incorrect for the beginning of Ibn Tumart's rule, which was rather 515 A.H./1121 C.E., when he was proclaimed as Mahdi.

45. The verse (Ps 83:5) is spoken by God's enemies who plot against his people. The enemies include the Edomites, the Ishmaelites, the Moabites, and the Hagrites, ten in all (Ps 83:6–9).

46. Silves in Portugal, near the Atlantic, seemed like the end of the world. Mahdiyya is in Tunisia. Hirschberg, *History of the Jews in North Africa*, I, 126, suggests that the reading should be Salé instead of Silves, as it had a Jewish community, whereas we do not hear of one at Silves.

47. Abraham Ibn Daud, *Book of Tradition,* pp. 87–88 (of the translation).

48. Ibid., pp. 96–97.

49. The document was first published by Y. M. Toledano, "Manuscript Documents." H. Z. Hirschberg published the text with his Hebrew translation in "The Almohad Persecutions and the India Trade" and gave an English translation in *History*, I, 127–29. See also Goitein, *Med. Soc.*, V, 59–61 (with partial translation); and *Med. Soc.*, VI, Cumulative Indices, p. 154; and M. García-Arenal, "Jewish Converts to Islam," pp. 236–37. The manuscript is now in the Sassoon Collection (*Ohel David*), no. 713, pp. 394–96. Goiten and Friedman,

India Traders, mention Sulayman ibn Abu Zikri often and suggest that he was an India merchant as was his father; see Index, p. 894.

50. Mirbat, meaning, "a place of anchorage," is a port on the coast in Dhofar Province about forty miles east of Salalah, nowadays in the Sultanate of Oman; C. E. Bosworth, EI, s.v. "Al-Mirbāṭ."

51. Sijilmasa, now in ruins, was 190 miles south of Fez, at the edge of the desert. The town thrived under the Almoravids, who linked the Sahara with the Mediterranean, using Sijilmasa as a staging area for Fez and Ifriqiya (modern Tunisia). In the eleventh and twelfth centuries, Sijilmasan merchants traded in Sudanese gold and African slaves; see M. Terrasse, EI, s.v. "Sidjilmāsa"; H. Terrasse, Notes sur les ruines de Sijilmasa. A Jewish community, with learned scholars, existed there from the tenth century or earlier. See Hirschberg, History of the Jews in North Africa, pp. 352–54.

52. The representative of the merchants was like a consul, who supervised warehouses and caravanserais and acted as a depositary and neutral arbiter for merchants. He was the legal representative for claims of foreign merchants, and hence many Muslim representatives were judges. He provided storage for merchandise; and if necessary he helped market it. The warehouse also served as a bourse. See Goitein, Med. Soc., VI, Cumulative Indices, p. 96, especially Med. Soc., I, 186–92. Jewish India trade was basically in the hands of Maghribi Jews. Letters from Abu Zikri's correspondence are preserved in Goitein and Friedman, India Traders; see Index, p. 861.

53. Hirschberg, "The Almohad Persecutions," p. 136; Goitein, Med. Soc., I, 192; IV, 189. Madmun ben Japheth was the husband of Abu Zikri's sister; see Med. Soc., V, 66–68 and VI, p. 64.

54. 'Abd al-Mu'min was actually from the village of Tagra in the north of present-day Oran. It was Abu Tumart who was from Sus. 'Abd al-Mu'min was called al-Kumi, of the Berber tribe of Kumya. Hirschberg's explanation in History, I, 127, that 'Abd al-Mu'min was from the Sus valley is misleading.

55. Tashufin ibn 'Ali (r 1142–1146) retreated to Oran, planning for an escape by sea to Andalusia, but he and his horse fell from a precipice on the coast and were found dead the next day by the Almohads, who sent the horse's head to 'Abd al-Mu'min; see E. Lévi-Provençal, Documents inédits d'histoire Almohade, pp. 159–60 (the version of al-Baydhaq) and p. 159, n. 5. 'Abd al-Wahid Marrakushi, History of the Almohads, ed. R. Dozy, p. 146; trans. E. Fagnan, p. 176, related that he went out armed, mounted on his gray mare, and fell into the sea. His enemies retrieved the body, crucified it, and then burned it. This detail is consistent with Solomon's account. Crucifixion is a Qur'anic punishment for making war against God and his messenger and striving after corruption in the earth (5:33), a vague crime that often applies to those who oppose the dynasty or those who are dissidents in an Islamic state. Most jurists say that the criminal must first be beheaded and not crucified alive, a ruling that the Almohads followed, although Malikis, Hanafis, and most Twelver Shi'is permit impalement of the living. See Kraemer, "Apostates, Rebels and Brigands," pp. 66–67.

56. The term afsha'a, a common word in Judeo-Arabic for "apostatize," is an Arabic verb derived from Hebrew pesha', meaning "transgression." See Goitein, Med. Soc., II, 300; V, 521, n. 59. Friedman, Maimonides, the Yemenite Messiah and Apostasy, p. 25, n. 49, observes that the term is not used for conversion to Christianity. See also Joshua Blau, A Dictionary of Mediaeval Judaeo-Arabic Texts, p. 504. Tilimsan is in today's Algeria near the Moroccan border on the main route leading from Oran and Sedi bel Abbes in Algeria to Oujda and Fez in Morocco.

57. The Jews had Islamic law on their side, as it prohibits forced conversion, though Shi'is in Iran and Yemen permitted it; Goitein, Med. Soc., V, p. 521, n. 60. We may wonder why the Almohads bothered negotiating, since they had all the divisions on their side. The reason is that the city surrendered and so deserved lenient conditions by Islamic laws of war. Furthermore, the Qur'an bids Muslims to call to the Lord's way with wisdom and good admonition and reason in the better way (16:125–26) before using force. The Almohads

engaged in religious debates with their foes from the time of the Mahdi Ibn Tumart. The negotiations were probably about money payments as well.

58. The text reads: *'ala yihud ha-shem*. The expression echos the Islamic *tawhid* (declaration of God's oneness) in the *shahada* and is used appropriately in the context of the Almohads, whose name (al-Muwahhidun) means those who unify (the name of Allah). See also Friedman, *Maimonides, the Yemenite Messiah and Apostasy*, p. 26, n. 50.

59. The judge Joseph ben 'Imran was a friend of Abraham Ibn Ezra and perhaps his benefactor when he visited the Maghrib; see Hirschberg, *History of the Jews in North Africa*, I, 128, n. 1, who says that he later returned to Judaism, but this is unclear; see pp. 352ff. See also N. Ben-Menahem, "Joseph ben 'Imran, Friend of Abraham Ibn Ezra."

60. The writer used the word *khawarij*, which was a religio-political sect (Kharijites) in North Africa and elsewhere, but he intended it in the sense of "rebels," which it occasionally means (from *kharaja 'ala*). See also Hirschberg, *History of the Jews in North Africa*, p. 521, n. 64. In al-Baydhaq's memoir (Levi-Provençal, *Documents inédits*, p. 162), an inhabitant of Fez called the Almohads *khawarij*. It was not uncommon for each side to view the other as insurgents against legitimate authority.

61. Meknes fell after Fez in 1150 following an obstinate fight against the Almohads; see al-Baydhaq's memoir in Levi-Provençal, *Documents inédits*, p. 165 and n. 2; C. Funck-Brentano, EI, s.v. "Miknas."

62. The next word is illegible. Goitein suggests the Arabic term for "Gibraltar." Friedman, *Maimonides, the Yemenite Messiah and Apostasy*, p. 25, deciphered it as "Tortosa."

63. Bijaya was actually conquered by the Almohads in 1152; Goitein, *Med. Soc.*, V, 521, n. 67. After defeating the Almoravids, they headed east toward Tunis in a campaign against incursions by troops of Roger II of Sicily. The proximity of Africa facilitated the Muslim conquest of Sicily in the ninth century, and in 1127 Muslim ships pillaged the Sicilian coast. Roger retaliated by sending expeditions to North Africa, gaining control over Gabes and then occupying al-Mahdiyya by 1141/42. See Donald Matthew, *The Norman Kingdom of Sicily*, pp. 57–58.

64. Goitein, *Med. Soc.*, V 59, says that the numbers, which are exaggerated, are consistent with what we know from Arabic sources, and signify that the male population was put to the sword and women sold into slavery.

65. Trans. Goitein in *Med. Soc.*, V, 60–61 and 107. I have altered the translation in several places.

66. Goitein, *Med. Soc.*, V, 61. Mallal is not his father, but a village in the region of Dar'a; Hirschberg, "The Almohad Persecutions," p. 151, note to line 19 and p. 352. This is, however, a very unusual patronymic.

67. Abu Zikri probably sent the Torah scroll as a donation for a synagogue. Now Ben Qadib has brought it back to Fustat.

68. The writer said that he was a *bazzaz* (cloth merchant) among the *qushashiyyin*; see Goitein, *Med. Soc.*, I, 438, n. 5. *Qushashi* is from the verb *qashsha*, meaning "to collect," "gather," "pick up from here and there." See Wehr, *Dictionary*, p. 894; Diem and Radenberg, *A Dictionary of the Arabic Materials*, p. 173; and Blau, *Dictionary,* p. 545.

69. E. Lévi-Provençal, *Documents inédits*, introduction, pp. ix–x; Troisième Partie, pp. 75–224; Hirschberg, *History of the Jews in North Africa*, I, 128.

70. Levi-Provençal, op. cit., pp. 181ff. and see p. 181, n. 1.

71. This sentence on the purge appears, according to Lévi-Provençal, in a marginal gloss on fol. 50 recto, p. 112 of the text (and see p. 185 of the translation). Cf. Le Tourneau, *The Almohad Movement*, p. 54.

72. Lévi-Provençal, op. cit., p. 184.

CHAPTER 6

1. The *shahada* says, "I attest that there is no god but God [Allah], and that Muhammad is the messenger of God." The first part is a simple declaration of faith in one God,

which a Jew could easily utter, but the second recognizes the prophetic status and message of Muhammad. Jews believe that the last prophet was Malachi.

2. See G. A. Wiegers, EI, s.v. "Moriscos"; L. P. Harvey, "Crypto-Islam in Sixteenth-Century Spain"; Harvey, "Moriscos," in *The Legacy of Muslim Spain*, ed. Jayyusi, I, 211–12. On Crypto-Muslims and Mudejars (Muslims) in sixteenth-century Spain, see Harvey, *Muslims in Spain 1500–1614*. The Mudejars receive much attention as well in his *Islamic Spain 1250 to 1500*.

3. This ruling creates problems for Muslims living in European countries as a minority, for they must either leave, get the host countries to acquiesce to all their religious requirements, or transform them into Islamic states.

4. L. P. Harvey, "The Mudejars," in *The Legacy of Muslim Spain*, ed. Jayyusi, I, 178–79.

5. Maimon's epistle was edited in Judeo-Arabic and translated into English by L. M. Simmons; it was translated into Hebrew by B. Klar and printed in English by Franz Kobler, *Letters of Jews Through the Ages*, I, 167–77. On the epistle, see M. Ben-Sasson, "The Prayer of the Forced Converts," especially pp. 155ff.; E. Schlossberg, "The Attitude to Islam and Its *Shemadot* of Rabbi Maimon the Judge"; H. Soloveitchik, "Ben ḥevel 'Arav le-ḥevel Edom," pp. 149–50.

6. *Epistle on Consolation*, ed. and trans. L. M. Simmons, pp. 5–6 (Heb)/71–72 (Eng.).

7. Cf. Qur'an 3:103.

8. The image of clinging to a rope by one's fingertips expresses the precariousness of their existence as Jews and the tolerance that Rabbi Maimon and later Moses ben Maimon had for "sinners." The picture of drowning is a poignant preshadowing of his son David's fate.

9. B Ber 29a.

10. Ed. and trans. Simmons, p. 15/86.

11. Saul Lieberman, "Persecution of the Israelite Religion," p. 363; idem, "Palestine in the Third and Fourth Centuries," pp. 113, 125.

12. The word *anusim* was used later for the Marranos of Spain and Portugal, also called *conversos* or New Christians.

13. See A. Grossman, "The Roots of Sanctification of the Name in Early Ashkenaz," p. 125.

14. G. Blidstein, "Maimonides and Me'iri on the Legitimation of Non-Judaic Religion"; Moshe Halbertal, *Between Torah and Wisdom: Rabbi Menachem ha-Meiri and the Maimonidean Halakhists in Provence*.

15. G. Vajda, "La polèmique anti-intellectuel de Joseph ben Shalom Ashkenazi," pp. 133–36; David Corcos, "The Attitude of the Almohadic Rulers Toward the Jews," p. 155, n. 77.

16. Al-Marrakushi, *al-Mu'jib fi talkhis akhbar al-Maghrib*, ed. Dozy, p. 224; trans. García-Arenal, "Jewish Converts to Islam," p. 238.

17. Shailat, "An Unknown Translation." This second translation is from Ms. Avraham Skandari of the *Responsa* = Ms. Bedahab of Freimann and Blau; see *Responsa*, ed. J. Blau, III, 27. It is now in the collection of M. Benayahu; see Benayahu, "Moses ibn Maimon's *Responsa*," *Sefer Zikaron le-Rav Nissim*, II, 201. And see Maimonides, *Letters*, ed. Shailat, pp. 28–29.

18. The *Iggeret ha-Shemad* was also called *Ma'amar Qiddush ha-Shem* (*Treatise on Sanctifying the [Divine] Name*). Abraham Geiger edited it in 1850 (*Iggereth ha-shemad leha-RaMbaM*). It has been edited more recently by J. Qafih, *Iggerot* (*Letters*) *by Moshe ben Maimon* (*Maimonides*), pp. 107–20, with an important Introduction. Y. Shailat based his edition, in *Iggerot ha-Rambam* (*Letters of Maimonides*), pp. 30–59, on Ms. Adler 2380 (translation A) and cited significant variants from other manuscripts and from the second Hebrew translation (B). An English translation by A. S. Halkin with a long discussion by D. Hartman is found in their *Crisis and Leadership: Epistles of Maimonides*, pp. 15–90. I have used my own translation, prepared for a volume of Maimonides' letters in the Yale Judaica Series. M. Friedländer doubted the epistle's authenticity in the Introduction to his translation of the *Guide*, pp. xxv–xxxvii, but few supported his view and no new knowledge has turned

up. Shailat's discovery of a second Hebrew translation proves that the epistle was written in Arabic. Expressions such as "madman" (*ha-meshugga'*) for the prophet of Islam are almost certainly by translators. Maimonides called Muhammad *al-shakhs* ("the individual" or "that person") in his *Epistle to Yemen*, which translators replaced with *ha-meshugga'*.

19. Judah ben mar Farhun fled at the beginning of the Almohad persecution in 1148 from Sijilmasa to Der'a in Morocco. See also Baneth, *Epistles*, p. 90, n. 11; Hirschberg, *History of the Jews in North Africa*, I, 353; and Goitein, *Med. Soc.*, V, 61, 522.

20. Maimonides, *Epistles*, ed. D. H. Baneth, p. 89.

21. Maimonides cited this verse in disapproval of long-windedness in CM Avot, i, 17; MT Ethical Qualities, ii, 4; and Impurity of Leprosy, xvi, 10.

22. He cited Deut 22:26, where the context pertains to an engaged girl who is forced by a man. The man is punished, *but you shall do nothing to the girl.* The verse is cited in B 'AZ 54a in connection with coercion to worship idolatry.

23. *Guide*, I, 50 (p. 111).

24. L. Gardet, EI, s.v. "Īmān"; Wensinck, *The Muslim Creed*.

25. See also M. Ben-Sasson, "The Prayer of Forced Converts," p. 15.

26. See MT Foundations of the Law, v, 3. The Name, used in the compounds "sanctification of the Name" and "desecration of the Name," is a substitute for "God."

27. See B Sot 36b on sanctifying the Name in public and private.

28. See Dan chs. 3 and 6.

29. B San 110b; MT Foundations of the Law, v, 4.

30. See B Ket 111a, where the rabbis admonish Israel not to ascend the wall, that is, not to rebel; and see similar counsel against making war in SongR, ii, 7; Mid Tan (Buber), addition to Parshat Devarim, iii, 3; Ibn Daud, *The Book of Tradition,* pp. 240–50; E. E. Urbach, *The Sages,* I, 679; II, 1002, n. 11.

31. See 1 Kings 12:20; M Avot v, 18, etc.

32. Many Islamic traditions depict the bliss a martyr (*shahid*) can expect: "All his sins will be forgiven; he will be protected from the torments of the grave; a crown of glory will be placed on his head; he will be married to seventy-two houris and his intercessioon will be accepted for up to seventy of his relations." See E. Kohlberg, EI, s.v. "Shahīd."

33. Trans. B: "in which it was fated that they be killed." The reference is to the Hadrianic persecutions in the wake of the Bar Kokhba revolt. Rabbi Meir was a third-generation Tanna (ca. 130–60). See *Letters*, ed. Shailat, pp. 37–41.

34. Rabbi Eliezer ben Hyrcanus was a second-generation Tanna (ca. 90–130 c.e.). See Y. D. Gilat, *Rabbi Eliezer ben Hyrcanus: A Scholar Outcast*; J. Neusner, *Eliezer ben Hyrcanus*.

35. Previously, in Foundations of the Law, v, 1, Maimonides said that under duress an Israelite should commit the transgression rather than be slain, citing Lev 18:5, *You shall keep my laws and my rules, by the pursuit of which man shall live: I am the Lord*. He added that if he allows himself to be slain rather than transgress, he is responsible for his own death. He alluded to this idea in the epistle: "his blood is on his own hands, and he endangers his own life." See I. Twersky, "Sanctifying the Name and Sanctifying Life," p. 168; E. Schlossberg, "Moses ben Maimon's Attitude to Islam," pp. 42ff.; D. Schwarz, "And He Shall Live by Them"; and M. Ben-Sasson, "The Prayer of Forced Converts," p. 163.

36. See B Pes 50a.

37. B Sot 36b. See also MT Foundations of the Law, v, 7 ("even if he takes your soul"). And see H. Soloveitchik, "Ben hevel 'Arav le-hevel Edom," p. 150.

38. See J Ned, iii, 9 (38b); B Qid 40a and San 107a and other sources cited in MT The Book of Knowledge, ed. Lieberman et al., p. 115, note to lines 23–24.

39. MT Foundations of the Law, v, 4.

40. See *Osar ha-Geonim* on B Qid 18a; Jacob Katz, "Though He Sinned, He Is Still an Israelite," pp. 262ff.

41. B San 44a.

42. For the difference between an oath (*shevu'ah*) and a vow (*neder*), see M Ned, ii, 2;

T Ned, i, 5; B Ned 2b; Lieberman, *Greek in Jewish Palestine*, p. 117. An oath invokes the divine name and obliges one to do something or to refrain or to confirm that something is true. A vow renders something forbidden to the person or renders one's property forbidden to someone else.

43. Maimonides gives similar advice to emigrate in the *Epistle to Yemen*, ed. Shailat, p. 92; trans. Kraemer, p. 111; and see MT Ethical Qualities, vi, 1; Torah Study v, 4. This is precisely the advice that Islamic law gives to Muslims living under non-Muslim sovereignty.

44. The idea of exile is stressed by al-Farabi in his discussion of the perfect state and the ignorant or depraved states. Al-Farabi posits the obligation to emigrate from "corrupt polities" in *Selected Aphorisms* (see Dunlop's Introduction to his edition and translation, p. 15; text, p. 164/trans., 72). The idea of *hijra*, or emigration, is a guiding principle for militant Islam nowadays and appears in the name of groups, such as al-Takfir wa 'l-Hijra (Declaring Heretical and Emigration). The exemplary hijra was, of course, that of Muhammad from Mecca to Medinah in 622 c.e.

45. MT Foundations of the Law, v, 4.

46. See *Letters*, ed. Shailat, p. 92, trans. J. L. Kraemer in R. Lerner, *Maimonides' Empire of Light*, p. 111.

47. "God knows the truth" and "God knows best," said by Muslim authors, are taken to be confessions of uncertaintly.

48. Lev 18:5; and see Deut 6:24f.; Ezek 18: 9, 20:11, 13, 21; 33:15. The meaning of the verse in Leviticus and its parallels is that "to follow the commandments is to choose life and blessing; not to follow them is to choose death and the curse" (Moshe Greenberg, *Commentary on Ezekiel 1–20*, p. 366). And see T Shab, xv, 17; B Yoma 85b, San 74a, 'AZ 27b and 54a, EcclR, i, 3; MT Foundations of the Law, v, 1 and 4; and Sabbath, ii, 3. See also I. Twersky, "Sanctification of the Name and Sanctification of Life," p. 168 and n. 3, where he observes that the formulation in the epistle is stronger and more uncompromising than in the *Mishneh Torah*, citing also *Letters*, ed. Shailat, p. 52.

49. T Shab xv, 17.

50. See MT Foundations of the Law, v, 7; Twersky, "Sanctification of the Name and Sanctification of Life," p. 167.

51. Maimonides did not quote these European scholars, and we have no evidence that he knew their writings. Rabbi Isaac ben Sheshet (d. Algiers 1408), who experienced the terrible persecutions of 1391 in Spain, decided in harmony with Maimonides' opinion that forced converts who could not escape, but followed the precepts of the Torah, even if only behind closed doors, are Israelites. Their wine is permissible; their ritual slaughter is trusted; their court testimony is accepted. See Rabbi Isaac ben Sheshet, *Responsa*, no. 4, and see also nos. 14 and 171.

52. Rabbenu Gershom Meor ha-Golah, *Responsa*, no. 4. A rescript is ascribed to Rabbenu Gershom prohibiting humiliation of repentants who had apostatized; Jacob Katz, "Though He Sinned, He Is Still an Israelite," p. 265 and n. 55; Avraham Grossman, "The Roots of Sanctification of the Name," p. 125, n. 52 and references there.

53. B San 44a; see Rashi, *Responsa*, nos. 168–71.

54. See also Rabbi Simon Duran, *Responsa*, II, no. 19; and see J. Katz, *Between Jews and Gentiles*, pp. 75ff.; and B. Netanyahu, *The Marranos of Spain*, pp. 8–9.

55. See Tosafot to B 'AZ 27b and 54a. The Tosafists were scholars, including Rashi's disciples and descendants (his grandsons, Samuel ben Meir, Jacob Tam, and Isaac ben Meir), who made additions (*tosafot*) to Rashi's commentaries on the Talmud; see E. E. Urbach, *Ba'ale ha-Tosafot (The Tosafists)*; and see J. Katz, "Sanctifiers of the Name," *Between Jews and Gentiles*, pp. 89ff. Maimonides refused to go beyond the law here; see I. Twersky, "Sanctifying the Name and Sanctifying Life," p. 168.

56. Josephus, *The Wars of the Jews*, trans. William Whiston, 7.8.1–7.9.2, pp. 914–22. The medieval *Book of Josippon* told the same story in a brief style; see *Book of Josippon*, ed. D. Flusser, I, 423–31.

57. See Benjamin Kedar, "The Masada Complex"; Bernard Lewis, *History—Remembered, Recovered, Invented*, pp. 3–41; Nachman Ben-Yehuda, *The Masada Myth: Collective Memory and Mythmaking in Israel*; Yael Zerubavel, *Recovered Roots: Collective Memory and the Making of Israeli National Tradition*, ch. 5. It was Yigael Yadin, excavator of Masada, who did the most in transforming its ruins into a myth of national revival, in *Masada: Herod's Fortress and the Zealots' Last Stand*.

58. See Judith Herman, *Trauma and Recovery*, pp. 39–42.

59. Robert Chazan, *European Jewry and the First Crusade*; *God, Humanity, and History: The Hebrew First Crusade Narratives*; Jeremy Cohen, *Sanctifying the Name of God*; Susan L. Einbinder, *Beautiful Death*. On Christian and Jewish martyrdom, see the innovative study by Daniel Boyarin, *Dying for God*.

CHAPTER 7

1. Ibn 'Aqnin, *Commentary on Song of Songs*, p. 398.

2. Obadiah was the ancestor of Maimonides, the progenitor of the family, called 'Abdallah or 'Ubaydallah in Arabic.

3. Ibn 'Aqnin, *Commentary on Song of Songs*, p. 430.

4. Jamal al-Din Ibn al-Qifti (b. 1172 in Qift, Upper Egypt, d. Aleppo 1248) studied in Cairo and then in 1187 went to Jerusalem, where his father was a deputy to al-Qadi al-Fadil. See R. Sellheim, "Review of *Inbāh ar-ruwāh 'an-nuhāh*"; A. Dietrich, EI, s.v. "Ibn al-Ḳifṭī." In 1201, he emigrated to Aleppo and gained the patronage of the Ayyubid ruler al-Zahir Ghazi. Ibn al-Qifti was in charge of the ministry of finance with the title al-Qadi al-Akram. After al-Zahir's demise, Ibn al-Qifti served his successor and then served as vizier to al-'Aziz from 1236 until 1248, when he died. His *History of the Sages* (*Ta'rikh al-hukama'*) was epitomized by his pupil Muhammad ibn 'Ali al-Khatibi al-Zawzani in 1249, soon after the author died. It has 414 biographies of physicians and scientists, including precious quotations from Greek authors not extant in their original language.

5. *History of the Sages*, p. 318; trans. Kraemer, "The Life of Moses ben Maimon," p. 424. The conclusion is based on the principle that there is no coercion in religion (*la ikraha fi 'l-din*) in Qur'an 2.256. Muslim legal sources support the view that conversion under duress is invalid. The Spanish Arabist Montserrat Abumalham cites Ibn al-'Attar (tenth century), an Andalusian Maliki from Maimonides' time, to the effect that forced conversion is unlawful: M. Abumalham, "La conversión segun formularious notariales andalusíes: Valoración de la legalidad de la conversión de Maimónides." See also Mark Cohen, *Under Crescent and Cross*, p. 176; M. García-Aranel, "Jewish Converts to Islam in the Muslim West," p. 235. Friedman, *Maimonides, the Yemenite Messiah and Apostasy*, p. 34, n. 67. D. S. Margoliouth claimed, however, that a Muslim who had been coerced to convert to another religion may plead force majeure, but not someone who converted to Islam; see "The Legend of the Apostasy of Maimonides," p. 539.

6. Yellin and Abrahams, *Maimonides*, p. 37, have "a Moslem poet and theologian, Abul-Arab Ibn Moisha," saving Maimonides from the fate of Ibn Shoshan, who was executed. That Ibn Mu'isha saved Maimonides is from a late distorted source, *Ta'rikh al-Islam* (*The History of Islam*) by the Damascene traditionist and historian Shams al-Din al-Dhahabi (1274–1348), which we shall consider anon. Subequent biographers repeat this information, and consequently an error of Yellin and Abrahams has been perpetuated for over a century.

7. S. Z. Havlin, "Mosheh ben Maimon," in *Hebrew Encyclopaedia*, vol. 24, pp. 536–42; R. Blachère, "Une source de l'histoire des sciences chez les Arabes." The greatest tribute to Ibn al-Qifti as a scholar was written by the famous biographer Yaqut ibn 'Abdullah al-Rumi al-Hamawi (1179–1229). He knew Ibn al-Qifti personally and wrote a long admiring entry on him in his biographical dictionary; see Yaqut, *Mu'jam al-udaba'*, vol. 15, no. 34, pp. 175–204.

8. See also Munk, "Notice sur Joseph ben Ioudah," p. 37. Two scholars, writing recently, support the theory that Maimonides lived outwardly as a Muslim in Fez; see J. Yahalom, "'Sayeth Tuviah ben Zidkiyah': The *Maqama* of Joseph ben Simon in Honour of Maimonides," p. 558; and M. A. Friedman, *Maimonides, the Yemenite Messiah and Apostasy*, pp. 28–29 and 35.

9. *History of the Sages*, p. 392.

10. See Kamal al-Din Ibn al-'Adim (b. Aleppo 1192, d. Cairo 1262), *Bughyat al-talab fi ta'rikh Halab (The Desirous Quest on the History of Aleppo)*, iv, 1828. On Ibn al-'Adim, see F. Rosenthal, *A History of Muslim Historiography*, Index; *Historians of the Middle East*, ed. B. Lewis and P. M. Holt, pp. 111–13; and B. Lewis, EI, s.v. "Ibn al-'Adīm." He was from a family of judges, his father being chief judge in Aleppo under the Zangids and Ayyubids. Ibn al-'Adim served the Ayyubids of Aleppo as secretary, judge, and vizier. He used copious sources and cited them carefully, giving the specific one for each report.

11. Ladhiqiyya (Latakia), named for Laodicea, the mother of Seleucus II of the Seleucid dynasty (third century B.C.E.), is the chief port of Syria. (After Alexander the Great's death on June 11, 323 B.C.E., his generals, called the Diadochi, ruled over his divided empire, the Seleucids being in charge in Syria.) The author of the narrative wants to stress that Abu 'l-'Arab was not heading for Aleppo.

12. Al-Zahir Ghazi (1173–1216), third son of Saladin, was first appointed by his father as regent in Aleppo in 1183 and eventually was made prince of the city in 1186, governing Aleppo and a wide territory surrounding it. In family power struggles, al-Zahir Ghazi tended to support his older brother al-Afdal. See S. Heidemann, EI, s.v. "al-Malik al-Ẓāhir Ghazī."

13. The name "Abu Musa" is, of course, wrong. He was Abu 'Imran Musa. Rum can also mean Europe, but Byzantium is more likely here. Ibn al-'Adim's informant, Taj al-Din Muhammad ibn Hashim, whom he cites again (x, 4688), was the main preacher in Aleppo and had contact with Abu 'l-'Arab ibn Mu'isha there.

14. That is, reverted to Judaism. Ibn Abi Usaybi'a, *Classes of Physicians*, p. 582. "It is said" usually implies qualified assent.

15. Rosenthal, *A History of Muslim Historiography*, pp. 129–30 and index; M. Bencheneb and J. de Somogyi, EI, s.v. "al-Dhahabī." He became blind toward the end of his life and was assisted by students. His *Ta'rikh al-Islam (History of Islam)* is a vast work, consisting of narrative history and brief biographies. It was abridged many times, six by al-Dhahabi himself.

16. Al-Dhahabi's text was cited by S. Munk, "Studien von Doctor Abraham Geiger, Rabbiner in Breslau" [Review of Geiger's edition of *Iggeret ha-Shemad*], p. 329, where he quoted the passage on "Ibn-Mo'îcha" (who became Ibn Moisha in Yellin and Abrahams and henceforth), and this was the basis of later references to the man. See Corcos, "The Attitude of the Almohadic Rulers Toward the Jews," pp. 144–52.

17. F. Rosenthal, EI, s.v. "Al-Ṣafadī." He was a government secretary in Cairo and Damascus, going back and forth, but also served in Aleppo. His enormous biographical encyclopedia of necrologies, *al-Wafi bi'l-wafayat*, is in the process of publication.

18. Margoliouth gives this longer account in "The Legend of the Apostasy of Maimonides."

19. The *tarawih* (sing. tarwiha) prayers on the nights of Ramadam included recitation of the Qur'an. See A. J. Wensinck, EI, s.v. "Tarāwīḥ." Ramadan commemorates the revelation of the Qur'an.

20. Muhyi 'l-Din Ibn al-Zaki Abu 'l-Ma'ali al-Qurashi, a Shafi'ite jurist (1155–1201), was a well-known judge, close to Saladin, who made him chief judge in Aleppo after he appointed his son al-Zahir Ghazi as ruler. See Baha' al-Din Ibn Shaddad, *al-Nawadir al-sultaniyya (The Rare and Excellent History)*, trans. D. S. Richards, p. 36; Lyons and Jackson, *Saladin*, p. 276; L. Pouzet, *Damas au VIIe/XIIIe siècle: Vie et structures réligieuses dans une métropole islamique*, pp. 44–45. Muhyi 'l-Din wrote an ode in praise of Saladin when the sultan conquered Aleppo (550 A.H. [1183–84]), in which he predicted Saladin's conquest of

Jerusalem. After Saladin did conquer Jerusalem, he chose Muhyi 'l-Din to be the first to give a sermon in the city (October 9, 1187). He was also the first to lead prayers after the death of Saladin. He had great prestige as a descendant of the third caliph 'Uthman ibn 'Affan.

21. Margoliouth points out chronological difficulties in "The Legend of the Apostasy of Maimonides," p. 540.

22. Friedman, *Maimonides, the Yemenite Messiah and Apostasy*, pp. 35–36. Similar Jewish accounts of Maimonides as a Muslim can be found in Yitzhak Avishur's *In Praise of Maimonides*; see his index, p. 377 and his introductory remarks on pp. 41–42. He believes that the Judeo-Arab narratives reflect the ones we find in Arabic sources.

23. E. Levi-Provençal and Ch. Pellat, EI, s.v. "al-Maḳḳarī." See *Nafh al-tib min ghusn al-Andalus* (*A Fragrant Scent from the Bough of Andalusia*), III, 326–27. The first part was translated into English by D. Pascual de Gayangos. This text was brought to my attention by Professor David Cook.

24. See Y. Avishur, *In Praise of Maimonides*, pp. 39–42. Jews knew the Muslim sources and reacted to them. It is mainly in stories about his attitude to Islam that we find allusions to his conversion.

25. Hirschberg, *History of the Jews in North Africa*, I, 139, says that "the majority left the Maghrib in response to Maimonides' advice and example," but does not summon evidence for this point. Obviously, many would have done so, however we do not know if they actually did or if they were a majority.

CHAPTER 8

1. Fernand Braudel, *The Mediterranean*, I, 237.

2. Olivia R. Constable, *Trade and Traders in Medieval Spain*, p. 28.

3. Braudel, op. cit., I, 103. Hugging the coast is called (from OF) cabotage. The Italians called it *cabotaggio* or *costeggiari*.

4. Goitein, *Med. Soc.*, I, 319.

5. Prawer, *The Jews in the Latin Kingdom of Jerusalem*, pp. 144–46, cites Christians, such as Bernard of Clairvaux.

6. Ed. Shailat, 224–25; trans. Kraemer, "The Life of Moses ben Maimon," pp. 421–22 (correct the erroneous October 12, 1166 in Kraemer's translation to 1165).

7. A copy of the text is preserved in Ms. Paris 336, f. 38b, and the same text from a different source appears in Elazar Aziqri, *Book of the Pious* (*Sefer haredim*), p. 66. It was published in *Jen Libanon; trois manuscrits inédits*, ed. J. Brill, p. 1. See also *Hiddushe ha-RaMBaM la-Talmud*, ed. Mordecai Judah Loeb Sachs, pp. 58–60. And see Joshua Prawer, *The Jews in the Latin Kingdom of Jerusalem*, pp. 141–42, for his translation.

8. His brother David had accompanied him, along with their father and Japheth, on the pilgrimages to Jerusalem and Hebron. Perhaps this refers to the safe arrival of David in Egypt, but we do not know.

9. This is based on *by the finger of God* in Ex 31:18 and Deut 9:10.

10. The expression *the man of God* is used for Moses in Deut 33:1, Josh 14:6, and Ps 90, and generally for men inspired or sent by God and having superhuman powers (e.g. Elijah in 1 Kings 17:24). It became a typical form of address used by people writing to and about Maimonides.

11. Olivia Remie Constable, *Housing the Stranger in the Mediterranean World: Lodging, Trade and Travel in Late Antiquity and the Middle Ages*, Index, s.v. "khān."

12. The quotations are from Ibn Jubayr, *Travels*, trans. Broadhurst, pp. 317–18, the year being 580 A.H./1184–85 C.E. Salih is mentioned in the Qur'an as a prophet sent to the people of Thamud, an ancient Arabian tribe (see, e.g., 7:73–79, 9:61–68; 26:141–59; 27:45–53).

13. Benjamin of Tudela, *Travels*, ed. Adler, pp. 19 and 31. Benjamin gave the number of Jews in each location, which is usually taken to mean Jewish households.

14. The source is Ps 47:5: *He chose our heritage for us, the pride of Jacob [ge'on ya'aqov] whom he loved. Selah*. The title Ga'on for Head of the Academy (Yeshivah) is an abbreviation of this expression; Gil, *In the Kingdom of Ishmael*, I, 122.

15. Al-Harizi, *The Book of Taḥkemoni*, trans. David S. Segal, p. 339.

16. Its names are 'Akko in Hebrew, 'Akka in Arabic, and Acre and St. Jean d'Acre for the Crusaders.

17. Palestine, Filastin (Ar), is classical Palestine (Grk Palaistinē, Lat Palaestina), the land of the Philistines. After the Jewish defeats by the Romans in 70 and 132–35 C.E., when Judaea was made captive by the victors, they called the country Syria Palaestina, later Palaestina, and expunged Judaea. In Byzantine times, there were three provinces of Palestine: Palaestina Prima (capital at Caesarea), Palaestina Secunda (capital at Scythopolis), and Palaestina Tertia (capital at Petra in what is Jordan today). In Maimonides' time, al-Sham served for Syria-Palestine, hence "Syro-Palestine." "The beautiful land" (ereṣ ha-sevī) is from Dan 11:16, 41.

18. Prawer, *The History of the Jews in the Latin Kingdom of Jerusalem*, p. 42.

19. Ms. JTS ENA 2727.28; trans. Goitein, *Med. Soc.*, I, 132; and see Prawer, op. cit., pp. 42–43, who notes that massacres of Muslims and Jews and annihilation of Jewish communities occurred in all the maritime cities of the area, except for Tyre and Ascalon.

20. Ibn Jubayr, *Travels*, trans. Broadhurst, Introduction, p. 17.

21. Al-Harawi (d. 1215) joined the court of al-Zahir Ghazi in Aleppo at the end of his life. He carried out diplomatic and intelligence missions and was familiar with government and warfare. See J. Sourdel-Thomine, "Le testament politique due Shaykh 'Alī al-Harawī"; and "Les conseils du šayḫ al-Harawī à un prince ayyūbide."

22. Usama Ibn Munqidh, *An Arab-Syrian Gentleman and Warrior in the Period of the Crusades: Memoirs of Usāmah ibn-Munqidh (Kitāb al i'tibār)*, trans. P. K. Hitti, p. 164. See Qur'an 112:1–4.

23. Usama Ibn Munqidh, *An Arab-Syrian Gentleman*, pp. 164–65.

24. Maimonides, *Responsa*, no. 350, pp. 627–28.

25. A sizeable immigration of French rabbis and their families swelled Acre's Jewish population. Prawer, *The History of the Jews in the Latin Kingdom of Jerusalem*, pp. 61–63. In 1210-11, around 300 rabbis from France and England emigrated to Acre, including Jonathan ben Jacob ha-Kohen of Lunel, with whom Maimonides had corresponded. Jonathan of Lunel was in the Land of Israel by 1210 in the first wave of French scholars from southern France; see E. Kanarfogel, "The 'Aliyah of 'Three Hundred Rabbis,'" p. 193. In about 1260 the French talmudist Rabbi Jehiel of Paris emigrated with his son and many disciples to Acre and founded a yeshivah, which became known as the Midrash ha-Gadol of Paris. The Kabbalist Abraham Abulafia resided there for a time, and Nahmanides (Rabbi Moses ben Nahman), who lived in Jerusalem, later moved to Acre and died there in 1270.

26. Prawer, *The History of the Jews in the Latin Kingdom of Jerusalem*, p. 143 and n. 40, pp. 54–55 and n. 33; *Letters*, ed. Shailat, pp. 191–92.

27. Maimonides, *Responsa*, nos. 119–49, pp. 205–86. See J. Mann, *The Jews in Egypt and in Palestine Under the Fāṭimid Caliphs*, II, 316.

28. In the twentieth century, the attitudes of Christians and Muslims to Jewish residence in Jerusalem were reversed, as the British Mandate for Palestine (1918–48) allowed it, whereas under Jordanian control (1948–67), for nineteen years, Jews were not permitted to visit Jerusalem.

29. On the conquest of Jerusalem and its effects, see Prawer, *The History of the Jews in the Latin Kingdom of Jerusalem*, pp. 46–49; August. C. Krey, *The First Crusade: The Accounts of Eyewitnesses and Participants*; J. S. C. Riley-Smith, *The First Crusade and the Idea of Crusading*; Thomas S. Asbridge, *The First Crusade: A New History*.

30. See J. Prawer, "The Latin Settlement of Jerusalem," pp. 490–503; idem, *Crusader Instititutions*, pp. 85–101.

31. Prawer, *The History of the Jews in the Latin Kingdom of Jerusalem*, p. 47, n. 4.

32. Cf. Ps 55:15. Modern translations take *ba-regesh* in the sense of "in a throng" or "together." Abraham Ibn Ezra (d. 1167), in his comment on the verse, understood it in this sense ("one group"); similarly Rashi: "with many people." In CM Avot, vi, 3, Maimonides explained *ba-regesh* first as "with many people" or "a gathering" and then cited the view that it means "in fear and trepidation." In MT Temple, vii, 5, he explained *ba-regesh* this way.

33. Usama Ibn Munqidh relates that when he visited Jerusalem he entered the al-Aqsa Mosque, occupied by Templars, and prayed in a small mosque, converted into a church, nearby. The Templars, who were his friends, he says, evacuated the small mosque for him to pray there; *An Arab-Syrian Gentleman and Warrior in the Period of the Crusades,* trans. P. K. Hitti, pp. 163–64.

34. J. Prawer discusses famous itineraries of Jewish visitors to Jerusalem at this time in *The History of the Jews in the Latin Kingdom of Jerusalem*, ch. 6. He remarks (on p. 143, n. 38) that "Maimonides states clearly that he entered the precinct of the Temple esplanade and also the Dome of the Rock." This is not the case however.

35. Prawer, op. cit., p. 131.

36. See MT Temple, vi, 14–16; vii, 7.

37. MT Fast Days, v, 16–17. B MQ 26a.

38. Prawer, op. cit., p. 139.

39. Ibid., pp. 40–41.

40. Benjamin of Tudela, *Travels*, p. 25.

41. Prawer, op. cit., p. 157. Nahmanides, *Criticisms on the Book of Commandments,* Positive, no. 4.

42. Prawer, op. cit., p. 158.

43. See also Twersky, "Maimonides and Eretz Yisrael," p. 262, n. 11.

44. MT Fast Days, v. 9; Twersky, ibid., pp. 288–89.

45. B Ket 110b. And see MT Kings and Their Wars, v, 12.

46. Deut 17:16; MT Kings and Their Wars, v, 7–8.

47. Twersky, "Maimonides and Eretz Yisrael," p. 257, n. 2.

CHAPTER 9

1. The Pharos lighthouse, a marvel of architecture and engineering, and one of the Seven Wonders of the World, guided ships to the harbor. Its cupola held a great concave mirror of polished metal that could project a beam visible from thirty-five miles away. In 1166, the Muslim traveler Abu Hajjaj al-Andalusi visited the lighthouse and depicted it as approximately 384 feet in elevation, the height of a forty-story building nowadays.

2. Goitein, *Med. Soc.*, I, 351.

3. Benjamin of Tudela, *Itinerary*, pp. 74–75; Ibn Jubayr, *Travels*, trans. R. Broadhurst, pp. 31–35.

4. P. Sanders, "The Fatimid State," p. 167–68.

5. Goitein, *Med. Soc.*, I, 32.

6. E. Ashtor, "The Number of Jews in Mediaeval Egypt," Part II, p. 12.

7. Sanders, loc. cit.

8. Goitein, *Med. Soc.*, II, 264; IV, p. 17–19. The quarter was called Mamsusa, Massasa, and Mussasa. Mamsusa appears to be the original form.

9. Wladyslaw B. Kubiak, *Al-Fustat: Its Foundation and Early Urban Development*, pp. 106–8.

10. N. A. Stillman, *The Jews of Arab Lands*, I, 48, n. 21, cites Goitein, *Med. Soc.*, II, 139–40, 438–39, and 469, Table 1. Ashtor gives a lower estimate of only 1,500 for Cairo/Fustat, which Stillman says holds for the period after 1201–2, when the community had been reduced by plague and famine. See Eliyahu Ashtor, "Prolegomena to the Medieval

History of Oriental Jewry," pp. 56–58. In "Some Features of the Jewish Communities in Medieval Egypt," pp. 63–64, Ashtor applies his estimate to the earlier period. See also "The Number of the Jews in Mediaeval Egypt," Part I, p. 10 and Part II, pp. 12–13.

11. I use the term "Iraqians" (called "Babylonians" in Jewish sources of this period) rather than "Iraqis," because Iraqis are nationals of present-day Iraq.

12. Goitein, "Bet ha-Kenesset." The material was incorporated into *Med. Soc.*, IV, 31–33. See also E. Ashtor, "Some Features of the Jewish Communities in Medieval Egypt," p. 62.

13. See M. A. Friedman, "A Controversy for the Sake of Heaven," p. 259.

14. Abraham mentions this in *Kifayat al-'abidin*, ed. Nissim Dana, p. 180. See also MT Torah Study, iv, 9, where it is said that the sanctity of the *bet midrash* transcends the sanctity of a synagogue.

15. For the synagogue, see P. Lambert, *Fortifications and the Synagogue: The Fortress of Babylon and the Ben Ezra Synagogue*; and for the Genizah, see also Goitein, *Med. Soc.*, I, 1–28; S. C. Reif, *A Jewish Archive from Old Cairo: The History of Cambridge University's Genizah Collection*.

16. Professor Norman Golb, of the University of Chicago's Oriental Institute, who has done important research on the Dead Sea Scrolls *and* the Cairo Genizah, says (private communication) that the Genizah is much more important than the Dead Sea Scrolls, and that there is no comparison between the two sources as far as the study of Jewish history is concerned.

17. Allan Whigham Prince, *The Ladies of Castlebrae: A Story of Nineteenth-Century Travel and Research*.

18. Agnes Lewis, *In the Shadow of Sinai (1895–1897)*, pp. 168–80. See also Margaret D. Gibson's *How the Codex Was Found*, based on her sister's diaries describing an expedition to St. Catherine's monastery at the foot of Mount Sinai, where they discovered a fourth-century Syriac version of the Gospels.

19. Schechter later became the first president of the Jewish Theological Seminary in New York. See Norman Bentwich, *Solomon Schechter: A Biography*.

20. The letter is preserved in the Genizah collection of the University of Cambridge Library.

21. The Church included Ecclesiasticus in the Greek Bible as a deuterocanonical book among the Wisdom Books (Proverbs, Job, etc.). Its original Hebrew, written in Jerusalem in 190 B.C.E., was known to St. Jerome and, of course, to the talmudic sages. Other surviving fragments of the Hebrew, aside from the ones in the Genizah, were found in a Qumran cave and at Masada. The book is also known in Greek as Wisdom of Jesus Ben Sirach (Ben Sira). See *The New Jerusalem Bible*, pp. 1076–78; *Jewish Writings of the Second Temple Period*, ed. Michael Stone, pp. 290–301.

22. Charles Taylor (1840–1908), Christian Hebraist, became Master of St. John's College, Cambridge, in 1881 and encouraged Solomon Schechter's interest in the Genizah. He edited *The Wisdom of Ben Sira* with Schechter in 1899.

23. Schechter published a report of his first findings in the *Times*, London, August 3, 1897, and in the *Sunday School Times*, Philadelphia, about the same date; reprinted in Schechter, *Studies in Judaism*, second series (1908). See also Norman Bentwich, *Solomon Schechter: A Biography*, pp. 126–35.

24. The 'Alids were descendants of 'Ali ibn Abi Talib, the cousin and son-in-law of Muhammad, who was the fourth caliph (r. 656–61). On Fatimid origins, see Michael Brett, *The Rise of the Fatimids: The World of the Mediterranean and the Middle East in the Tenth Century* C.E.; and *The Advent of the Fatimids: A Contemporary Shi'i Witness*, ed. and trans. by Wilfred Madelung and Paul E. Walker.

25. Jawhar had already conquered large parts of North Africa for the Fatimids. He rose from the lowly level of slave to the rank of state chancellor and general. The epithets attached to his name reveal both his humble origin and high station: al-Saqlabi (the Slav),

al-Siqilli (the Sicilian), or al-Rumi (the Greek), al-Katib (the State Chancellor), and al-Qa'id (the General); see H. Mones, EI, s.v. "Djawhar al-Ṣiḳillī."

26. When the Fatimids founded the city, the planet Mars, called al-Qahir (the Triumphant), whence the name Cairo, was in the ascendant.

27. Al-Azhar means "the shining," "the brilliant," "the splendid," related etymologically to Hebrew *Zohar* (the *Book of Splendor*), and may allude to Fatima, known as al-Zahra' (the Radiant). In the eighteenth century it gained the status of a university and has become the main Islamic place of higher learning in the world with branches in other Muslim countries.

28. J. Jomier, EI, s.v. "al-Azhar."

29. The Shi'a (Partisans) were supporters of 'Ali in the early controversies over succession to Muhammad. They claim that 'Ali, as a member of the prophet's family, was Muhammad's rightful heir rather than the actual successors—Abu Bakr, 'Umar, and 'Uthman—who allegedly usurped the rights of the family. The basic difference between the Sunnis and Shi'is pertains to the issue of succession and beliefs concerning the qualifications of the caliph. The Sunnis require that he be a descendant of Muhammad's tribe of Quraysh. The Shi'i believe that the imams (caliphs) must be descendants of Muhammad's own family, and that they are charismatic leaders who are infallible, divinely guided, and possess esoteric knowledge of the truth.

30. S. M. Stern, *Studies in Isma'ilism*, pp. 30ff.

31. Al Qa'im bi 'l-Haqq is the one who brings about justice. The title al-Qa'im also means "the one who arises." Qiyām is the appearance of the Mahdi. See Heinz Halm, *Shiism*, p. 38.

32. Heinz Halm, *The Fatimids and their Traditions of Learning*, pp. 71ff. D. Sourdel, EI, s.v. "Dār al-Ḥikma," says that it was administered by the chief missionary (*da'i al-du'at*), and was associated closely with teaching of Shi'i doctrine and also instruction in Isma'ili teachings. But cf. Paul Walker, "Fatimid Institutions of Learning," pp. 189ff., who says that it had no direct relationship with the Isma'ili mission. On the Fatimid Dar al-'Ilm, see Youssef Eche, *Les Bibliothèques arabes*, pp. 74–97; H. Halm, "Al-Azhar, Dar al-'Ilm, al-Rasad, Forschungs-und Lehranstalten der Fatimiden in Kairo," cited by Walker, p. 189, n. 48.

33. See also Walker, "Fatimid Institutions of Learning," p. 189, n. 49 for sources.

34. See M. C. Lyons and D. E. P. Jackson, *Saladin: The Politics of the Holy War*, p. 56.

35. Goitein, *Med. Soc.*, I, 71; II, 285–86.

36. Sanders, *Ritual, Politics, and the City*, p. 31.

37. See Alfred Ivry, "Islamic and Greek Influences on Maimonides' Philosophy"; "Neoplatonic Currents in Maimonides' Thought"; and "Ismāīlī Theology and Maimonides' Philosophy."

38. Frank Talmadge, "Apples of Gold: The Inner Meaning of Sacred Texts in Medieval Judaism."

39. Pines, "Translator's Introduction," p. xcvi. "Apophatic" is from Grk "to deny, to say no," which is what a negative theology does.

40. See *Guide* I, 59, and 60 (pp. 138–39) and Pines, "Shī'ite Terms and Conceptions in the *Kuzari*," pp. 296–97, citing al-Kirmani's *Rahat al-'aql*. On al-Kirmani, see D. De Smet, *La quiétude de l'intellect: Néoplatonisme et gnose ismaélienne dans l'oeuvre de Ḥamīd ad-Dīn al-Kirmānī (Xe/XIe s.)*; Paul E. Walker, *Ḥamīd al-Dīn al-Kirmānī: Ismaili Thought in the Age of al-Ḥākim*. See also S. M. Stern, *Studies in Early Ismā'īlism*, pp. 236–42.

41. See Halm, *The Fatimids and their Traditions of Learning*, p. 19, and Maimonides, *Commentary on the Mishnah*, Introduction to *Pereq Heleq*, ed. Shailat, Arab, p. 361; Heb, p. 131.

42. Pines calls them "Islamic internalists." See *Guide* II, 25 (p. 328).

43. Pines, "Shī'ite Terms and Conceptions in the *Kuzari*," Appendix VI, p. 294.

44. Al-Farabi, *Kitab al-milla*, p. 50; Alfarabi, *The Political Writings*, trans. C. E. Butterworth, *Book of Religion*, p. 99; Pines, op. cit., p. 297.

45. H. Daiber, "The Ismāīlī Background of Fārābī's Political Philosophy," p. 144, sug-

gests that al-Farabi's *Perfect State* was inspired by Isma'ili ideas and not the reverse. See also F. M. Najjar, "Fārābī's Political Philosophy and Shī'ism," pp. 57–72.

46. Majid Fakhry, *A History of Islamic Philosophy*, pp. 258–59; María Isabel Fierro Bello, *La heterodoxia en al-Andalus durante el periodo Omeya*.

47. See H. Grieve, *Studien zum jüdischen Neuplatonismus: Die Religionsphilosophie des Abraham Ibn Ezra*. And see *Neoplatonism and Jewish Thought*, ed. L. E. Goodman.

48. Ya'qub ibn Qillis is an outstanding example. See also S. M. Stern, "Fāṭimid Propaganda Among Jews," *Studies in Ismāʿīlism*, ch. 5, pp. 84ff.; *The Epistles of the Brethren of Sincerity*, IV, 105. These epistles express the views of a small, esoteric group of philosophers who had Isma'ili orientation without belonging to official Isma'ilism.

49. Bernard Lewis, "The Fatimids and the Route to India," pp. 52–53.

50. Goitein, *Letters of Medieval Jewish Traders*, p. 175.

51. Ibid., p. 186.

52. Goitein, *Med. Soc.*, I, 211.

53. See Ibn al-Qifti, *History of the Sages*, pp. 317–19.

54. Meyerhof, "L'oeuvre médicale de Maimonide," p. 138, placing the beginning of Maimonides' medical practice in 1167 as physician of al-'Adid.

55. Ibn al-Qifti, *History of the Sages*, p. 318.

56. See B. Lewis, "Maimonides, Lionheart, and Saladin," pp. 70–75; and "The Sultan, the King, and the Jewish Doctor," pp. 166–76.

57. Yellin and Abrahams, *Maimonides*, pp. 113–14.

58. Ibn al-Qifti, *History of the Sages*, p. 318, trans. Kraemer, "The Life of Moses ben Maimon," p. 423.

59. See below, ch. 22, n. 94.

60. CM Kelim, xvii, 16, ed. Qafih, p. 164. Mordechai Akiba Friedman called my attention to this passage.

61. See above, Introduction, p. 4. And see Maimonides, CM Nedarim, iii, 3.

62. K. N. Chaudhuri, *Trade and Civilisation*, p. 20.

63. At the beginning of his book *On Poisons and Their Antidotes*, Maimonides said that al-Qadi al-Fadil requested his help getting items that had to be imported for the antidotes known as the Great Theriac and the Electuary of Mithridates.

64. *Epistles*, ed. Baneth, p. 70, trans. Goitein, "Maimonides, Man of Action," p. 163.

65. Rabbi Asher ben Yehiel (b. ca. 1250 Germany, d. 1327 Toledo) applied this characterization to someone who had an occupation and devoted most, not all, of his time to study. On Maimonides' view of "his Torah is his profession," see Twersky, *Introduction to the Code of Maimonides*, pp. 5 and 81–83; E. Kanarfogel, *Jewish Education and Society in the High Middle Ages*, pp. 46 and 48.

66. CM Avot, iv, 7, ed. Qafih, p. 441–42. On this *mishnah* as reflecting the essence of Maimonides' social thought, see H. H. Ben-Sasson, *Reṣef u-temurah (Continuity and Variety)*, ed. J. R. Hacker, pp. 302, 312–15.

67. MT Torah Study, i, 9.

68. MT Gifts to the Poor, x, 18.

CHAPTER 10

1. Elon, *Jewish Law*, III, 1051–52. The word "Mishnah" is from the Hebrew root *sha-nah*, meaning to repeat, and therefore to learn and to teach, specifically to recite or teach the Oral Law (M Avot, iii, 8). The literature on the Mishnah is vast. A good starting point is Strack and Stemberger, *Introduction to the Talmud and Midrash*, pp. 119–66, with extensive bibliography. Another is Abraham Goldberg, "The Mishnah—A Study Book of Halakha," in *The Literature of the Sages*, Part One, ed. S. Safrai, pp. 211–81. See also D. W. Halivni, *Midrash, Mishnah and Gemara*; Jacob Neusner, *Judaism: The Evidence of the Mishnah*; and *Rabbinic Literature*, Part V (with bibliography on pp. 97–98); E. E. Urbach, EJ, s.v. "Mish-

nah." The Mishnah owes its existence to the real fear that, in the time of crisis following the destruction of the second commonwealth and the aborted revolt of Bar Kokhba, that the Oral Law would be forgotten if it were not written down. Its final editor was Rabbi Judah ha-Nasi. There are two useful English translations, one by Herbert Danby (1933) and a newer translation by a team of scholars under the editorship of Jacob Neusner (1988).

2. A Tanna is literally one who recites or repeats the law. It was applied to the teachers (Tannaim, Tannaites) active during the period of the Mishnah (until ca. 200 C.E.). The Tannaim are divided into five generations See Strack and Stemberger, *Introduction to the Talmud and Midrash*, pp. 72–91. Well-known Tannaim were Hillel and Shammai, Rabbi Johanan ben Zakkai, Rabbi Aqiba, and Rabbi Judah ha-Nasi.

3. Ibid., pp. 154–55.

4. Hence called "Ethics of the Fathers," a tractate to which Maimonides gave special attention.

5. Six probably alludes to the six orders of the Mishnah. Maimonides began his major works with poems.

6. B Ber 56a, San 37b.

7. Here he gave names of ancestors seven generations back. He wrote: "I began to compose this commentary when I was twenty-three years old, and I completed it in Egypt when I was thirty years old, in the year [14]79 s.e. [= 4928 A.M. = 1167/68 C.E.]." We do not know on which copy of the commentary he wrote this, whether on the fair copy (see below) or a prior draft copy; see Simon Hopkins, "The Textual Tradition of Maimonides' *Commentary on the Mishnah*," p. 113. Nor can we be sure that he meant thirty years old precisely, and not approximately. See also above, ch. 1, n. 3.

8. I have translated from CM *Tohorot,* ed. Qafih, pp. 737–38.

9. A facsimile edition of the fair copy was published by R. Edelmann in three volumes. See *Maimonidis Commentarius im Mischnam,* ed. S. D. Sassoon. A fair copy is a clean, finished copy after corrections are made to draft copies. The text of the commentary was edited and translated into Hebrew by Rabbi Joseph Qafih, *Mishnah 'im perush Rabbenu Mosheh ben Maimon: maqor we-targum.* The introductions to various parts of the Mishnah have been edited by Shailat, *Maimonides' Introductions to the Mishnah.*

10. This copy would normally be a final redaction and exemplar for all other copies. However, it was corrected throughout Maimonides' lifetime and even after his death. There were copies before this one that were used by Hebrew translators, who therefore preserve earlier readings that Maimonides removed from the fair copy. See Hopkins, "Textual Tradition," p. 113.

11. S. M. Stern, in *Maimonidis Commentarius im Mischnam*, "Ten Autographs by Maimonides," III, 186.

12. It is translated by Stern and Sassoon, Introduction, p. 15. However, I have retranslated it for greater terminological faithfulness.

13. Pocucke's teachers were the German Arabist, Matthias Pasor (Oxford) and William Bedwell, "the father of Arabic studies in England," vicar of Tottenham High Cross." See G. J. Toomer, *Eastern Wisedome and Learning,* pp. 116–66, 212–25, 271–78, 281–86. Pococke also planned to publish Maimonides' *Guide of the Perplexed.* He had several manuscripts and quoted from it in his publications. However, the plan did not come to fruition.

14. Sassoon, *Maimonidis Commentarius im Mischnam,* I, 31.

15. Maimonides' signature from this manuscript is often reproduced.

16. See Sassoon, Introduction, p. 49.

17. Maimonides' commentary is in six volumes, corresponding to the six orders of the Mishnah. The two exemplars at the Bodleian Library include three volumes (Huntington 117 has Vol. 1 and Pococke 295 has Vols. 4 and 5 together). S. M. Stern, "Autographs of Maimonides in the Bodleian Library," p. 182. The Sassoon collection at Letchworth had two more volumes, Ms. Sassoon 72 (vol. 2) and Ms. Sassoon 73 (vol. 3) that are now at the Jewish National and University Library.

18. See Sassoon, Introduction, pp. 34–35. Abraham told of a dream in which his father encouraged him to defend his books from attacks by critics. The son first protested that he had no time, whereupon his father urged him to defend his legacy before turning to his own writing; see Abraham's *Birkat Avraham* (*Blessing of Abraham*), ed. B. Goldberg, p. 3.

19. On discrepancies between the *Mishneh Torah* and *Commentary on the Mishnah*, see Elijah Mizrahi (fifteenth century), *Responsa* (Jerusalem, 5698), no. 5; S. Lieberman, *Hilkhot ha-Yerushalmi*, p. 6 and the extensive study by Marc B. Shapiro, "Principles of Interpretation in Maimonidean *halakhah*."

20. See for autographs of draft copies J. Blau and A. A. Scheiber, *An Autograph of Maimonides*; Simon Hopkins, *Maimonides's Commentary on Tractate* Sabbath.

21. Lieberman's Introduction to *Hilkhot ha-Yerushalmi*, p. 6; Sassoon, Introduction, pp. 32–33.

22. Maimonides, *Responsa*, no. 217, pp. 382–83. S. M. Stern translates the text verbatim on p. 184 and discusses it on pp. 184–85.

23. Abraham ben Maimon, *Responsa*, no. 81, p. 106.

24. Letter to Joseph, no. 6, ed. Baneth, *Epistles*, pp. 57–58.

25. Rabbenu Nissim ben Jacob Ibn Shahin (990–1062) was head of an academy in Qayrawan and in touch with Pumpedita in Iraq. *Megillat setarim* was written before 1051. See S. Abramson, *Rav Nissim Ga'on*; and Menahem Ben-Sasson, *The Emergence of the Local Jewish Community in the Muslim World: Qayrawan, 800–1057*, index, p. 577.

26. *The Book of Commandments* of Hefes ben Masliah was edited by B. Halper in 1915. See, for instance, *Responsa*, p. 383, no. 217, in which Maimonides refers to a first version of the *Commentary on the Mishnah*, where he followed the erroneous view of Rabbi Hefes in his *Book of Commandments*; and see n. 4 ad loc. See also *Responsa*, no. 217, p. 383, where he cites Rabbi Hefes as the source of an error and says that in about ten responsa he was misled by Geonim.

27. See Sassoon, Introduction, pp. 17-18, 41.

28. In editions of the Talmud it is called erroneously Introduction to Tractate Seeds (*Haqdamah le-Masekhet Zera'im*)—and this is how most writers refer to it—whereas it is actually an introduction to the entire Mishnah.

29. Seder Tohorot (Purities), the sixth order of the Mishnah, is a euphemism, as it concerns ritual defilements, plagues and leprosy, the red heifer, ritual baths, separation of a woman during her menstrual cycle, liquids that make food susceptible to ritual impurity, seminal emissions, etc. It is the longest order of the Mishnah. Maimonides' intense attention to minuscule details arouses admiration and wonder. His Introduction is a masterpiece of analytical organization and pedagogy, as he reduced exceedingly complicated details to general principles.

30. An unbroken line of tradition, called *tawatur*, was a principle of Islamic jurisprudence.

31. On *tafaqquh* as "study of the law," see Bloomberg, *Arabic Legal Terms*, p. 8.

32. This is the principle of *ijma'*, or consensus, in Islamic jurisprudence.

33. *Ijtihad* is an important concept in Islamic jurisprudence and refers to independent judgment and innovation in the law.

34. See M Eduy, i, 3.

35. The well-known Oven of Akhnai narrative (B BM 59a-b), in which Rabbi Eliezer ben Hyrcanus the Great proved a point of law by having miracles and a heavenly voice confirm his opinion against that of a majority of sages, is often taken to mean that the majority rules (see Ex 23:2). Its overall message, however, is that the sages should treat individuals having their own views with consideration and respect; see Jeffrey L. Rubenstein, *Talmudic Stories*, ch. 2. The account, as Rubenstein comments (p. 315, n. 2), has become part of Western culture.

36. *Commentary on the Mishnah*, Introduction, ed. Qafih, p. 4; ed. Shailat, Arabic, p. 328; Hebrew, p. 28.

37. B Sotah 13b; SifreDeut on 34:5; Mid Tan on Deut 34:5.

38. This kind of aside signals some esoteric level of meaning. Maimonides is probably alluding to Moses' mind becoming united with the Agent Intellect.

39. See Ginzberg, *Legends*, III, 109-114; 443-448; V, 417. The Apocryphal text, called *Testament of Moses*, was identified with a book called the *Assumption of Moses* in the Acts of the Council of Nicea and by A. M. Ceriani, who discovered it (1861), but *Testament of Moses* contains no narrative of Moses' ascent to heaven. The ascent may, however, have been mentioned in the second part of the apocalypse that is no longer extant; see J. Priest's introduction to the *Testament of Moses*, in *The Old Testament Pseudepigrapha: Apocalyptic Literature and Testaments*, ed. James H. Charlesworth, pp. 919–34.

40. The narrative is based on Surah 17 (*al-Isra'*) and the vision in which it culminated (Qur'an 53:1–18). See M. Asín Palacios, *La escatologia musulmana en la Divina Comedia* (abridged translation: *Islam and the Divine Comedy*); and Geo Widengren, *The Ascension of the Apostle and the Heavenly Book*; and James W. Morris, "The Spiritual Ascension: Ibn 'Arabī and the Mi'rāj."

41. Esoterically renders *nazar batin*. The expression "the pure good" occurs in the Arabic title, *Kalam fi mahd al-khayr* or *al-khayr al-mahd* (*Discourse on the Pure Good*), of a famous Neoplatonic work. It was translated into Latin and became known to the West as *Liber de causis* (*Book on Causes*). *Discourse on the Pure Good* is derived from *The Elements of Theology* by the Neoplatonist philosopher Proclus Diadochus (412–485).

42. B Qid 71a.

43. The verse and this interpretation appear in B Hag 13a, and they are cited in this sense also in CM Hag, ii, 1; MT Foundations of the Law, ii, 12.

44. The Isma'ilis taught their doctrines in sessions of wisdom (*majalis al-hikma*).

45. The image of a veil is used often by Maimonides as something that hides the truth, and we find it in al-Ghazali's writings, as well as in al-Suhrawardi and other mystics. It is already used in this sense in the Qur'an: *We have placed veils over their hearts, that they may not understand* (Qur'an 18:57).

46. See Louis Jacobs, *Principles of the Jewish Faith*; Menachem Kellner, *Dogma in Medieval Jewish Thought*; and Marc B. Shapiro, *The Limits of Orthodox Theology*. See the translation in Twersky, *A Maimonides Reader*, pp. 402–23. The text was edited with a German translation and notes by Dr. J. Holzer, *Mose Maimûni's Einleitung zu Chelek*.

47. See A. J. Wensinck, *The Muslim Creed*; W. M. Watt, EI, s.v. "'Aqīda."

48. The Mishnah is divided into orders, books, chapters, and sections, called *mishnayot*. I shall refer to each one as *mishnah* with a lowercase *m* to distinguish them from Mishnah, which is the name of the entire work.

49. On the Mishnah's interpreting biblical "all" as inclusive or absolute, see Alexander Samely, *Rabbinic Interpretation of Scripture in the Mishnah*, pp. 243–47.

50. The words "prescribed in the Torah" are omitted in some versions. The allusion may be to the Sadducees; see Sanders, *Paul and Palestinian Judaism*, pp. 149–52.

51. That is, noncanonical books.

52. The verse was used in amulets and elsewhere to ward off evil, thus a misuse of the divine name; see the amulet in J. Naveh and S. Shaked, *Amulets and Magic Bowls*, p. 99.

53. Urbach, *The Sages*, II, 652.

54. See David Flusser, *Judaism and the Origins of Christianity*, pp. 109–11, and especially p. 109, n. 23.

55. Flusser says that the first three Beatitudes depend on Isa 61:1–2. Isaiah begins: *The Spirit of the Lord God is upon me; because the Lord has anointed me to preach good tidings unto the meek.* The Christian community took the verse as a prophecy of the descent of the Holy Spirit upon Jesus when he was baptized.

56. See Urbach, *The Sages*, I, 29–31. The Israeli historian Yitzhaq Baer thought that the talmudic sages did have some familiarity with Greek thought; see his *Israel Among the Nations*.

57. M Avot, ii, 17.

58. See B San 99b–100a, where an Epicurean is said to be someone who disdains scholars, deriving the word by false etymology from *hefqerut*, Aramaic *afqiruta* (*afqaruta*), meaning "irreverence."

59. He cited Prov 2:19 and B San 38b.

60. MT Repentance, vii, 8.

61. B San 100b; and see J San, x, 1, 28a.

62. Alfasi and Maimonides evidently confused the ancient Ben Sira (Ecclesiasticus) with the medieval *Tales of Ben Sira*; see *The Tales of Ben Sira in the Middle Ages*, ed. Eli Yassif, p. 5.

63. See his *Silencing the Jews*, ed. and trans. M. Perlmann, pp. 72–74 (text).

64. See I. Goldziher, *Stellung der alten islamischen Orthodoxie zu den antiken Wissenschaften*, p. 6.

65. See E. P. Sanders, *Paul and Palestinian Judaism*, p. 151. He infers that the exclusions are based on the principle of "measure for measure." Those who deny the world hereafter do not merit a portion in it. If so, Sanders observes, the saying may be more homiletical than dogmatic.

66. Pines, "Translator's Introduction," p. cxix, suggests that raising people to this level of abstraction risks putting them on the royal road to philosophy. This may have been one of Maimonides' aims.

67. *Maimonides' Introductions to the Mishnah*, ed. Shailat, p. 187.

68. The hymn Yigdal, beginning, "May the living God be exalted," was written in fourteenth-century Rome; Ismar Elbogen, *Jewish Liturgy*, p. 77; Stefan Reif, *Judaism and Hebrew Prayer*, pp. 207, 211–13. Also, the principles in the form of articles of faith, each beginning with "I believe," became part of Jewish liturgy, chanted in the early morning service.

69. In ancient Greek philosophy and in modern taxonomy, individuals belong to a species that is a type within a class called a genus. Human beings, for example, belong to a species, distinguished by reason, that is within the genus animal. Individuals are also compound (not simple) and are infinitely divisible.

70. Here Maimonides added in the margin that the greatest principle of the Torah is that the world is created (*muhdath*) by God ex nihilo, and that he only had recourse to—he said, "hovered about"— the idea of eternity according to the philosophers (in the *Mishneh Torah*, Foundations of the Law, and in the *Guide*, II, 15–17, 25) so that the demonstration (*burhan*) of God's existence be absolute. On the marginal note, see Sassoon, Introduction, p. 33. The addition is in the facsimile of the fair copy, vol. II, p. 301, in the margin. It is semicursive, not as rounded as the text but less cursive than drafts of the *Guide*. This addition sounds like a clarification called for by the view, evidently already current, that Maimonides actually accepted the Aristotelian position that the universe was pre-eternal.

71. The Agent Intellect is a cosmic intellect that conveys divine messages to the human intellect. This is a philosophic description of prophecy derived from Muslim philosophers, such as al-Farabi and Ibn Sina.

72. The term *safwa* occurs in ha-Levi's *Kuzari* often in the sense of chosen and pure and is originally a Shi'i term; see Shlomo Pines, "Si'ite Terms and Conceptions in the *Kuzari*," pp. 167–72, 186, 195. The word used here is applied in Muslim texts (in the form *safwat Allah*) to Muhammad. Maimonides explained this principle at some length, stressing the differences between Moses and other prophets.

73. In Qur'an 4:164, God is described as speaking directly to Moses, whereas Muhammad receives the revelation through an intermediary, the angel Gabriel.

74. *Shi'ur qomah* is "the measurement of God's stature [body]." It is a corpus of texts speculating on these dimensions in a mystical mode. Maimonides deleted six Arabic words referring to the topic in the fair copy of the *Commentary on the Mishnah*, and we know the reading only from manuscripts prior to the fair copy. The expunged text is in the facsimile edition, *Maimonides Commentarius in Mischnam*, II, 302. See also Sassoon, Introduction, p. 33,

n. 4. On *Shi'ur qomah*, see Martin Samuel Cohen, *The Shi'ur Qomah: Texts and Recensions*. We shall return to *Shi'ur qomah* when we discuss Maimonides' responsa, below, ch. 17, p. 313.

75. Muslims called the Qur'an *kalam* (*Allah*), "God's speech."

76. This is a direct rejection of the Muslim claim that the Torah has been abrogated (*naskh*)—the term the Muslims used—and replaced by the Qur'an. He mentioned text and interpretation to include both the Muslims, who deny the validity of the text, and the Christians, who accept the text but deny its interpretation.

77. *Karet*, or excision, is death by means of Heaven (divine agency) for serious sins. Maimonides intended here being cut off from eternal life.

78. This principle is stated in only two Hebrew words. Maimonides adds that he has already explained it.

79. "Cutting the shoots" occurs in connection with the Tanna Elisha ben Abuya, who allegedly became a heretic after entering Pardes. See on the expression "cut the shoots," T (ed. Lieberman), Hag, ii, 3; B Hag 14b–15a; J Hag, ii, 1, 77b; Song R, i, 1. It was taken to mean either killing the students who were studying Torah or alienating them from study by means of heretical ideas. See also Alon Goshen-Gottstein, *The Sinner and the Amnesiac*, pp. 92–93. Maimonides described Elisha ben Abuya's transgression in *Guide*, I, 32 (pp. 68–69) as being an attempt to aspire to metaphysical things beyond our apprehension, citing the verse, *If you find honey, eat only your surfeit, lest you be filled with it and throw it up* (Prov 25:16). See also Sarah Stroumsa, "Elisha ben Abuyah and Muslim Heretics in Maimonides' Writings."

80. Simon Eppenstein, "Moses ben Maimon, ein Lebens und Charakterbild," pp. 6–7. Sarah Stroumsa addressed this topic in "Was Maimonides an Almohad Thinker?"

81. I. Goldziher, *Mohammed Ibn Toumert et la théologie de l'Islam*; "Die Bekenntnissformeln der Almohaden"; Robert Brunschvig, "Sur la doctrine du Mahdi Ibn Tūmart." Ibn Tumart's creed was translated into Latin by Mark of Toledo; see Marie-Thérèse d'Alverny, "Marc de Tolède, traducteur d'Ibn Tùmart."

82. See Shapiro, *The Limits of Orthodox Theology*, pp. 45–70. One of Maimonides' critics was the great Muslim theologian Ibn Taymiyya (d. 728 [1328]), who fought against the Crusaders and Mongols and is a source of inspiration for Islamic jihadist movements nowadays. Ibn Taymiyya criticized Maimonides for his denial of divine attributes. He pointed out that early Jewish authorities did not reject the attributes of God in the Torah; this was an innovation of philosophers such as Moses ben Maimon and Jewish Mu'tazilites such as the eleventh-century Karaite theologian Abu Ya'qub al-Basir. Jews were influenced by the Mu'tazilites, Ibn Taymiyya said, and therefore set down principles of Judaism. See his *Dar' ta'arud al-'aql wa-'l-naql* (*Preventing Conflict Between Reason and Tradition*), VII, 94.

83. A striking midrash in BR, viii, 10 (ed. Theodor-Albeck, pp. 63–64) states that when God created Adam, the ministering angels mistook Adam for God and wished to exclaim "holy" before him. See, in general, Yair Lorberbaum, *Image of God: Halacha and Aggada*.

84. See G. Scholem, *Jewish Gnosticism, Merkabah Mysticism and Talmudic Tradition*, especially ch. 6 and Appendix D by Saul Lieberman, "Mishnat Shir ha-Shirim."

85. *Guide of the Perplexed*, II, 26. And see Michael A. Fishbane, *The Garments of Torah*.

86. Maimonides, *Responsa*, no. 117, p. 200 (*Letters*, ed. Shailat, p. 574).

87. *Guide*, I, 36 (p. 85).

88. *Guide*, I, 35 (p. 80); III, 28 (p. 512).

89. See *Guide*, III, 36 (p. 539); and Arthur Hyman, "Maimonides' 'Thirteen Principles,'" p. 141.

90. Pirqe Avot is generally understood to mean "Chapters of the Fathers," meaning the main sages of the Mishnah. Avot, however, may mean "fundamental principles." It is unique in the Mishnah, as it does not concern law but ethics in the form of maxims, like Grk *gnōmē* and Lat *sententiae*. It cites authorities from the time of Simon the Just in 300 B.C.E. to Judah ha-Nasi in 200 C.E. See M. B. Lerner, "The Tractate Avot," *The Literature of the Sages*, Part One, ed. Safrai, ch. 5.

91. See also CM Introduction, ed. Qafih, Zera'im, pp. 29–31. Maimonides stressed that the tradition did not depend on individuals but on an unbroken line of groups of tradents.

92. Maimonides used Ar *ādāb* (pl. of *adab*) for the sayings in Avot. The word means "morals," "rules of conduct," and also "decorum" and "etiquette." It also has the sense of "aphorism," which fits here well. On *adab,* see also above, p. 45.

93. The "cure" is based on Galenic therapy by using extreme measures to swing back to the equilibrium.

94. *Zuhd* is the normal Arabic word for "abstemiousness" and "asceticism." He wanted judges to abstain from indulgence of desires, avarice, and ostentation.

95. Rabban Simon was the son of the previous teacher quoted in the chapter, Rabban Gamaliel.

96. The anecdote in almost identical language appears in Joseph Ibn 'Aqnin's *Hygiene of the Soul*, ed. and trans. A. S. Halkin, pp. 75–77. It is most likely copied from our text; see Halkin, p. 77, n. 15, with references. Ibn Gabirol included it in his *Choice of Pearls*, the chapter on silence. The wise man famous for silence was Secundus, whose sayings were translated into Arabic; see Ben Edwin Perry, *Secundus the Silent Philosopher*.

97. For the statement about Rav, see also MT Ethical Qualities, ii, 4. There, Maimonides wrote, "Of Rav, disciple of our sainted teacher [Rabbi Judah ha-Nasi] it was said that throughout his life he never indulged in idle conversation." Scholars have searched in vain for the talmudic basis of this anecdote. It is found in a Geonic source: *Osar ha-Geonim*, Shab, Teshuvot, par. 339. See MT Ethical Qualities, ii, 4, ed. Lieberman et al., p. 144, note ad loc. Add to their references *Teshuvot ha-*Geonim, Sha'are teshuvah, no. 178; *Sefer ha-orah*, part 1; *Sefer ha-eshkol*, ed. Albeck, ba'l qeri, 2a. This means not that Maimonides derived the statement from the Geonim but that he may have had the same source that they had. Nahmanides, in his comment on Lev 19:2, said that Rabbi Hiyya never indulged in idle conversation.

98. B Pes 3b.

99. See Joseph Schacht, *Introduction to Islamic Law*, pp. 121–22; Kraemer, "On Maimonides' Use of the Five Qualifications of Islamic Jurisprudence." Beyond the five there was *wara'* ("piety"), which Maimonides invoked as *middat hasidut* to forbid some acts that the law permitted.

100. *Avot* i, 16, p. 419.

101. Maimonides approved wine as beneficial to one's health when taken in moderation.

102. Using the qualification of recommended, Maimonides endorsed some Greek and Arab virtues. *Karam* is a quintessential Arab virtue with a wide range of meaning: generosity, honor, kindness, amicability, etc. See Introduction to *Avot*, ed. Qafih, p. 380; ed. and trans. Gorfinkle, p. 19/55, where Maimonides placed *karam* between pomp and meanness; see Aristotle, *Nicomachean Ethics*, II, 7, 1107b17–20. Maimonides generally favored exaggerating in the direction of humility; see *De'ot*, i, 5; ii, 3; and especially his comment on *Avot*, iv, 4, ed. Qafih, Neziqin, p. 438. On instilling courage as the goal of the forty years' wandering in the desert, see *Guide*, III, 32 (p. 528), and see Maimonides' *Book of Commandments,* neg. 58, pp. 55–56; and MT Kings and Their Wars, vii, 15 (beginning), where he mentioned the prohibition against cowardice in battle.

103. On strophic poetry, see James T. Monroe, *Hispano-Arabic Poetry*, pp. 28–33, 392; and for Hebrew versions, see S. M. Stern, *Les chansons mozarabes* and *Les vers finaux (kharjas) en espagnol dans les muwashshahs arabes et hébreux*. In MT Fasts, v, 14, Maimonides mentioned the rabbinic ordinance forbidding music and singing in commemoration of the destruction of the Temple. He included songs accompanying wine-drinking. See also below, p. 305.

104. It is not therefore poetry itself, or Arabic poetry, that Maimonides finds objectionable, rather its theme. If it arouses desire, it is reprehensible speech.

105. B San 101a.

106. Averroes, *Commentary on Plato's Republic*, trans. Lerner, p. 28.

107. There is, for instance, no mention of courage or honor in the Index to Daniel Boyarin's informative *Unheroic Conduct*. He did not discuss Andalusian, Maghribi, and Middle Eastern Jews, and our passage is not mentioned. We should also consider Samuel ha-Nagid, who commanded armies in the field (if we are to believe his poetry), and the Jewish long-distance traders, many of whom were rabbis but far from gentle, as is Boyarin's gentle rabbi who is said to be the male ideal in "Jewish society." There was, of course, no monolithic "Jewish society," rather Jewish *societies* in the plural. Writers unconsciously identify "Jewish society" with European Jewish society, although in the Middle Ages most Jews lived in the Middle East. Goitein discusses honor in *Med. Soc.*, V, 200–4, especially the term *'ird*, meaning "honor, name, reputation." (Nowadays Arabs use the word *'ird* for female honor and chastity.) See also Diem and Radenberg, *Dictionary*, p. 142.

CHAPTER 11

1. Saladin's full name and titles were al-Malik al-Nasir Abu 'l-Muzaffar Salah al-Dunya wa-'l-Din Yusuf ibn Ayyub. His title was Sultan, which had been used by the Sunni Saljuks, indicating control of a territory. The literature on Saladin is naturally vast, beginning with contemporaries' reports, such as Baha' al-Din Ibn Shaddad, whose *al-Nawadir al-sultaniyya* is available in a fine English translation by D. S. Richards as *The Rare and Excellent History of Saladin*. Of modern studies, there is Stanley Lane-Poole, *Saladin: All-Powerful Sultan and the Unifier of Islam*, first published in 1898. H. A. R. Gibb acquainted the reader with two of Saladin's biographers in *The Life of Saladin from the Works of 'Imad al-Din and Baha' al-Din*. Then there is Andrew S. Ehrenkreutz, whose *Saladin* is the first biography that was not encomiastic. This was followed by M. C. Lyons and D. E. P. Jackson, *Saladin: The Politics of the Holy War*, a comprehensive biography, using the correspondence of al-Qadi al-Fadil in addition to historians; and more recently Yaacov Lev, *Saladin in Egypt*. Ehrenkreutz wrote "Saladin's Egypt and Maimonides" for *Perspectives on Maimonides*, ed. J. L. Kraemer, and Michael Winter wrote "Saladin's Religious Personality, Policy, and Image" for the same volume.

2. Ayman F. Sayyid, *La capitale de l'Egypte jusqu'à l'époque fatimide*.

3. Ayyub is the Arabic name for biblical Iyyob, which is pronounced in English as Job. In Turkish it is the well-known name Eyup. Many of the names at this time were compounded with the word al-Din, which means "the Religion" or "the Faith." So Najm al-Din means "Star of the Faith," Salah al-Din means "Rectitude of the Faith," Asad al-Din means "Lion of the Faith," and Nur al-Din means "Light of the Faith." See Annemarie Schimmel, *Islamic Names*, pp. 61–63; and A. Dietrich, "Zu den mit *ad-din* zusammengesetzen islamischen Personennamen."

4. See N. Elisseeff, *Nūr ad-Dīn, un grand prince musulman de Syrie au temps des Croisades*, a three-volume study, and his article in EI, s.v. "Nūr al-Dīn Maḥmūd b. Zankī"; and C. E. Bosworth, *The New Islamic Dynasties*, pp. 190–91.

5. Lyons and Jackson, *Saladin*, p. 7. Ibn Shaddad was an official biographer, but even Saladin did not mention this expedition in his own narrative about his career. It is possible that he stayed behind in Syria.

6. Nur al-Din sent some of his own emirs along with Shirkuh, giving a total number of 2,000 cavalry. Saladin described "vast armies," and William of Tyre said that Shirkuh had 12,000 Turks, 9,000 fully armed, the rest archers; Lyons and Jackson, *Saladin*, p. 11.

7. W. B. Kubiak, "The Burning of Misr al-Fustat in 1168."

8. Neil D. MacKenzie, *Ayyubid Cairo: A Topographical Study*, p. 17.

9. Lyons and Jackson, *Saladin*, pp. 11–12.

10. In MT Ethical Qualities, iv, 16, Maimonides recommended a warm bath weekly, warning not to take it immediately after dinner. Most accounts ascribed Shirkuh's demise to a fatal bath, but there was one that said he had been poisoned; see H. Dajani-Shakeel, *Al-Qāḍī al-Fāḍil*, p. 116, citing Ibn Khallikan.

11. Sayyid, *La capitale de l'Egypte jusqu'à l'époque fatimide*, p. 566, citing the Egyptian writer on administration Shihab al-Din al-Qalqashandi (ca. 1355–1418), *Subh al-a'sha fi sina'at al-insha'*, X, 91–98, and other sources.

12. Many Armenians migrated to Egypt in the eleventh century, capitalizing on the penetration of Armenians into the vizierate, including the well-known Badr al-Jamali (r. 1074–1094), his son al-Afdal (r. 1094–1112), and the Christian Armenian amir Bahram, vizier to the caliph al-Hafiz (r. 1135–1137). Bahram brought Armenians to Egypt and commanded Armenian troops, but his Muslim troops refused to support him and he retired to a monastery in Ikhmin until the caliph invited him back to Cairo, where he resided in the caliphal palace.

13. P. Sanders, "Ritual, Politics, and the City," p. 97. The burning of the Mansuriyya Quarter and adjoining locales outside Bab Zuwayla brought great devastation; MacKenzie, *Ayyubid Cairo: A Topographical Study*, p. 179.

14. This was, of course, a Sunni gesture, as they accepted the Rashidun—Abu Bakr, 'Umar, 'Uthman, 'Ali—as legitimate, whereas the Shi'is believed that 'Ali was the rightful caliph after Muhammad's death and rejected the historical succession. The *khutba* is the sermon given at Friday midday prayers in a large congregational mosque, in which the name of the sovereign is mentioned. Changing that name means transferring allegiance to a new ruler.

15. See Ehrenkreutz, *Saladin*, pp. 93–95; Lyons and Jackson, *Saladin*, pp. 45–46; Sayyid, *La capitale de l'Egypte jusqu'à l'époque fatimide*, p. 566–67; M. Chamberlain, "The Crusader Era and the Ayyūbid Dynasty," p. 215.

16. Among the Shi'ites, 10 Muharram, the 'Ashura,' is a festival commemoring the death of Husayn, son of 'Ali, who was killed by Syrian Umayyad troops on that day in Karbala', Iraq.

17. Ehrenkreutz, *Saladin*, pp. 92–94, accepts that he was ill and adds that his physician suspended medication. Lyons and Jackson, *Saladin*, p. 45, accept that he was ill, but power politics also played a role in determining that Fatimid rule could not go on. See also Yaacov Lev, *Saladin in Egypt*, p. 83.

18. See B. Lewis, "Saladin and the Assassins."

19. He was Zayn al-Din 'Ali Abu 'l-Hasan al-Wa'iz (the Preacher), a Hanbali jurist from Damascus. See 'Abd al-Rahman Abu Shama, *Kitab al-Rawdatayn fi akhbar al-dawlatayn*, II, 282, 284; III, 214; and Isma'il Ibn Kathir, *al-Bidaya wa'l-nihaya*, XII, 244, 275. Another version names the emir Najm al-Din ibn Maṣāl, who aided Saladin at the siege of Alexandria and remained his close friend. See 'Imad al-Din al-Isfahani, *al-Barq al-Shami*, III, 127; Lyons and Jackson, *Saladin*, p. 67. The report that the Fatimid supporters approached Zayn al-Din is intriguing, as he was a Hanbali jurist and preacher. The Hanbalis are strict Sunnis. Yet in this period we occasionally find under the mask of a Sunni a believer in Shi'ism, even of the Isma'ili variety. The conspirators were presumably well informed about him.

20. Muhammad Mahir Hamadah, *al-Watha'iq al-siyasiyya wa 'l-idariyya*, pp. 208–12 (from Abu Shama, *Kitab al-rawdatayn*); Ehrenkreutz, *Saladin*, pp. 112–15; Lyons and Jackson, *Saladin*, p. 67; Dajani-Shakeel, "Egypt and the Egyptians: A Focal Point in the Policies and Literature of Al-Qāḍi al-Fāḍil," p. 31. Lev, *Saladin in Egypt*, pp. 86–94, doubts al-Qadi al-Fadil's account.

21. Lev, *Saladin in Egypt*, p. 93.

22. The Nizari Isma'ili movement began when the Fatimid caliph al-Mustansir died, in 487 (1094). There was a split over the succession, with a group led by the Persian Hasan-i Sabbah (d. 1124), supporting the eldest son, Nizar, as the Fatimid caliph, whereas the majority preferred his younger brother, al-Musta'ili.

23. Dante describes himself as being "like a friar who hears the sins of a perfidious assassin" (*io stava come 'l frate che confessa lo perfido assassin*); *The Divine Comedy: Inferno*, xix, 49–50.

24. M. G. S. Hodgson, *The Order of the Assassins*; B. Lewis, *The Assassins: A Radical Sect in Islam*; Farhad Daftary, *The Assassin Legends: Myths of the Isma'ilis*; M. Hodgson, EI, s.v. "Ḥasan-i Ṣabbāḥ"; Azim Nanji, EI, s.v. "Nizāriyya."

25. B. Lewis, "Saladin and the Assassins."

26. Ehrenkreutz, *Saladin*, pp. 148–49.

27. The Nizari fortresses were finally destroyed by the Mongols in 1256. The mission then moved to the Indian subcontinent, where the Nizaris were called Khojas. Their imam, Agha Khan, made his headquarters in Europe.

28. Baha' al-Din Ibn Shaddad, *The Rare and Excellent History of Saladin*, trans. D. S. Richards, p. 22.

29. Ehrenkreutz, *Saladin*, pp. 11, 187.

30. Nur al-Din died on May 15, 1174, following a fit of rage during a polo match. William of Tyre said of him that he was "the greatest persecutor of the Christian name and faith, but a just ruler, astute and far-sighted and, according to the traditions of his race, a religious man." See Lyons and Jackson, *Saladin*, p. 69.

31. Dajani-Shakeel, "Egypt and the Egyptians," p. 35, citing a manuscript of al-Fadil's correspondence. The word for prostitute is in the grammatical masculine gender, but it refers to a female.

32. On the Ayyubids, see especially Chamberlain, "The Crusader Era and the Ayyūbid Dynasty."

33. The Shafi'is and Malikis and two other Sunni schools of law—the Hanafi and Hanbali—are considered by Sunnis as legitimate interpretations of Islamic law, with all their differences in details, as distinct from the Shi'is, who are not. See Ira M. Lapidus, "Ayyubid Religious Policy and the Development of Schools of law in Cairo."

34. The favorite colors of Islam are black, white, and green. The 'Abbasids used black banners in their revolution against the Umayyads, believing that Muhammad used black banners in his military campaigns, and that it was a color of vengeance and revolt and had eschatological significance. It became the official color of the 'Abbasids when they were in power. The word for black (*aswad*) is related to the word (*sāda*) for reigning, mastering, and power; and black suggests night, darkness, and mystery. The Black Stone in the Ka'ba in Mecca has religious influence. The enemies of the 'Abbasids, the Umayyads, wore white. Shi'is used green and also white, a sign of mourning and purity. Yellow was assigned to Jews and Christians and was the color of their turbans and the badges on their garments.

35. The madrasa, a religious college, was established by the Baghdad caliphs to spread Sunni doctrine, in opposition to Shi'i-Isma'ili teachings. The first, al-Nizamiyya, in Baghdad, was founded by Nizam al-Mulk, the powerful vizier who was killed by an Assassin (Nizari Isma'ili), an act that shocked the Sunni world.

36. Winter, "Saladin's Religious Personality," p. 311, citing Ibn al-Athir, not a great lover of Saladin, in *al-Kamil fi 'l-ta'rikh*, XII, 63, and Gabrieli, *Arab Historians of the Crusades*, pp. 9, 110–11.

37. *The History of the Decline and Fall of the Roman Empire*, III, ch. lix, pp. 631–44. Gibbon used Baha' al-Din [Bohadin], *al-Nawadir al-sultaniyya*, translated into Latin by the Dutch orientalist Albert Schultens (1686–1750).

38. See Humphreys, *From Saladin to the Mongols*, p. 20.

39. His name was Abu 'Ali 'Abd al-Rahman. See A. H. Helbig, *Al-Qāḍī al-Fāḍil, der Wezīr Saladin's*; Dajani-Shakeel, *Al-Qāḍī al-Fāḍil 'Abd al-Raḥīm al-'Asqalānī*.

40. Al-Fadil wrote letters for Saladin, for his brother al-'Adil, and for himself. He portrayed Saladin favorably and was, according to the historian Yaacov Lev, Saladin's propagandist; *Saladin in Egypt*, pp. 25 et passim. He also wrote a diary titled *al-Mujaddidat* (*News*) that has survived in quotations by other authors, and he even penned a *diwan* of poetry.

41. There are various accounts of his background. According to some, the family migrated to Egypt after Ascalon fell to the Crusaders in 1153. Some say that the family origi-

nated in Beisan, in Palestine, or that the father was Qadi there; see Lev, *Saladin in Egypt*, pp. 14–15.

42. *Mahabba* can also mean "love." See Michael Chamberlain, "The Crusader Era and the Ayyūbid Dynasty," pp. 238–39; Paula Sanders, *Ritual, Politics, and the City*, p. 15. Many kinds of subordination exemplified *khidma*, as wives' service to husbands, the young to the old, and servants to their masters.

43. Al-Fadil is often called vizier, but it uncertain that he really bore this title. He may have performed the tasks of a vizier without having the name. Recall that his patron Saladin was a vizier (under the Fatimids) before becoming the Ayyubid sultan; see Lev, *Saladin in Egypt*, p. 22.

44. Lyons and Jackson, *Saladin*, p. 57.

45. Dajani-Shakeel, Al-Qāḍī al-Fāḍil 'Abd al-Raḥīm al-'Asqalānī, p. 25.

46. Lyons and Jackson, *Saladin*, pp. 56–57.

47. For al-Qadi al-Fadil's administrative roles, see A. H. Helbig, *Al-Qāḍī al-Fāḍil, der Wezīr Saladin's*, and H.-A. Hein, *Beiträge zur Ayyubidschen Diplomatik*; W. Björkmann, *Beiträge zur Geschichte der Staatskanzle*.

48. Dajani-Shakeel, in her book *Al-Qāḍī al-Fāḍil 'Abd al-Raḥīm al-'Asqalānī*, makes al-Qadi al-Fadil into a Palestinian nationalist, a heroic jihadist fighting to remove the Crusaders from holy soil, and she identifies the (Palestinian) Ascalonians in Egypt as the most devoted of the jihadists.

49. Ibid., p. 26, from al-Qadi al-Fadil's *diwan* of poetry, I, 91 (her translation).

50. Ibid., p. 36. Dajani-Shakeel relates (p. 38) that the medieval historian al-Maqrizi quoted many of al-Qadi al-Fadil's sayings on the merits of Egypt, and that in the nineteenth century Rifaʿa al-Tahtawi (1801–73) quoted them in his writings intended to shape a "national consciousness in modern Egypt."

51. MacKenzie, *Ayyubid Cairo: A Topographical Study*, pp. 35–36.

52. Lyons and Jackson, *Saladin*, p. 131. The Qadi warned al-Malik al-'Aziz 'Uthman, son of Saladin, who went with his father to Syria, not to eat fruit or imported meat in Damascus.

53. See MacKenzie, op. cit., pp. 67, 117; and Steven Harvey, "Maimonides in the Sultan's Palace," p. 74.

54. Al-Qadi al-Fadil brought scholars from all over the Islamic world to Egypt and extended patronage to them; Dajani-Shakeel, "Egypt and the Egyptians," p. 30; Lyons and Jackson, *Saladin*, pp. 275–76.

55. The Hebrew translation by Moses Ibn Ezra was edited by S. Muntner (1942). There exists an English translation of the Hebrew translation by F. Rosner (1984). See H. Friedenwald, *The Jews in Medicine*, I, 193–216, at 208–9.

56. Maimonides, like his Muslim friends, did not demonstrate here an understanding of the Crusaders' ideological motives.

57. Richard Gottheil, "An Answer to the *Dhimmis*," p. 397 (text), p. 430 (trans.). The Arabic title is *Radd 'ala ahl al-dhimma wa-man tabi'ahum* (Refutation of the *Dhimmis* and Their Followers). It was written between 1290 and 1293. Gottheil published it from a Columbia University manuscript. See also Leon Nemoy, "A Scurrilous Anecdote Concerning Maimonides." I have used their translations with some alterations.

58. Both Gottheil and Nemoy translate *fadil* here as "decent"; it usually means "virtuous" or "excellent."

59. The verb for "advise" (or "admonish") is related to *wasiyya*, a testamentary instruction to an heir. Nemoy suggested that Maimonides believed he was on his deathbed, but *wasiyya* does not necessarily require that.

60. Nemoy, "A Scurrilous Anecdote," p. 191, n. 16. He consulted with S. D. Goitein on this document.

61. Chamberlain, "The Crusader Era and the Ayyūbid Dynasty," pp. 217–31.

62. Ibid., p. 230.

63. The chief judge was 'Abd al-Malik ibn 'Isa Sadr al-Din Ibn Dirbas (Durbas) (d. 605 [1208-9]), an Ash'ari and Shafi'i of Kurdish background, who replaced a Shi'i judge on 23 Jumada II 566 = March 3, 1171. See Leiser, *Restoration*, p. 193 and 533, n. 17.

64. M. Chamberlain, "The Crusader Era and the Ayyūbid Dynasty," p. 215.

65. Named for its founder, Abu 'l-Hasan al-Ash'ari (873–935).

66. The change to Sunnism and Ash'ari *kalam* was expressed in calligraphy as well. The Fatimids used a cryptic, floriatic Kufic script for monumental inscriptions, expressing the duality of outer (*zahir*) and internal (*batin*) meanings of the Qur'an, while the Ayyubids used a more straightforward cursive, as in the al-Aqmar Mosque in Cairo (1125); see Madhuri Desai's review of Yasser Tabbaa, *The Transformation of Islamic Art During the Sunni Revival*, p. 563.

67. *Kitab hada'iq al-fusul* by Muhammad Hibat al-Makki, published as an appendix to *al-Iqtisad fi 'l-I'tiqad* of al-Ghazali.

68. *Guide*, I, chs. 71 and 73.

69. See Lev, *Saladin in Egypt*, pp. 188–89.

70. R. S. Humphreys, *From Saladin to the Mongols*, p. 27.

71. See H. Ziai,"The Source and Nature of Authority: A Study of al-Suhrawardi's Illuminationist Political Doctrine."

72. Ernest Renan, *Averroès et l'averroïsme*, p. 43. In 1192 the physician al-Rukn 'Abd al-Salam was accused of atheism, and his books were destroyed, a scene witnessed by Judah ben Joseph. See Munk, "Studien von Doctor Abraham Geiger, Rabbiner in Breslau" [Review of Geiger's edition of *Iggeret ha-Shemad*], p. 334, and "Notice sur Joseph ben Iehouda," pp. 8–19.

73. On the kuttab, see Björkmann, *Beiträge zur Geschichte der Staatskanzlei im islamischen Ägypten*, pp. 89–92.

74. D. H. Baneth, *Epistles*, no. 5, pp. 27–30.

75. He was al-Qadi al-Sa'id Hibatallah ibn Ja'far Ibn Sana' al-Mulk (ca. 550–608 A.H. [1155–1211 C.E.]). See Rikabi, *La poésie profane sous les Ayyûbids*, pp. 73–74 and M. 'Abdu'l-Haq's Introduction to Ibn Sana' al-Mulk's *Diwan*. The title of judge was honorary.

76. He did not, however, introduce the genre into Egypt as is sometimes maintained. The Alexandrinian Fatimid poet Zafir al-Haddad (d. 1134) had already written *muwashshahat*.

77. Comment on *Avot,* i, 16, ed. Qafih, p. 419.

78. *Classes of Physicians*, pp. 582–83; Kraemer, "The Life of Moses ben Maimon," p. 427 (trans. F. Rosenthal).

79. *Gems of Excerpts and Chaplets of Intellects*. See F. Rosenthal, "Maimonides and a Discussion of Muslim Speculative Theology," pp. 109–11.

80. Rosenthal identifies him as Abu 'l-Qasim 'Abd al-Rahman ibn 'Ali, d. 582 (1186/87).

81. See Pines, "Translator's Introduction," pp. lxxxiv, cxxiv–cxxxi; M. Schwarz, "Who Were Maimonides' Mutakallimūn?"

82. Goitein, "The Moses Maimonides–Ibn Sanā' al-Mulk Circle."

83. On the dinar, a gold coin (from Greek *denarion*, Lat *denarius*), see G. C. Miles, EI, s.v. "Dīnār." Goitein, *Med. Soc.*, I, 359, explains that two dinars were a monthly income adequate for a lower-middle-class family.

84. It is not definite, however, that Ibn al-Kallam was a full-fledged member of their circle.

85. See Kraemer, "Life of Moses ben Maimon," pp. 422–24.

86. 'Abd al-Latif's autobiography is excerpted at length by Ibn Abi Usaybi'a, *Classes of Physicians,* pp. 683–96. See also *Extrait de l'autobiographie d'A'bd* [sic] *el-Latif.*

87. 'Abd al-Latif wished to stress that Musa ibn Maymun came to him and not the reverse.

88. Maimonides wrote *The Guide of the Perplexed* in Judeo-Arabic in a Hebrew script. Writing it in Arabic entailed transcribing the Hebrew script into the Arabic alphabet.

89. This is the view of Leo Strauss in "The Literary Character of *The Guide of the Perplexed*" and elsewhere.

90. S. M. Stern, "A Collection of Treatises by 'Abd al-Laṭīf al-Baghdādī."

91. 'Imad al-Din described Saladin sitting with friends who were intellectuals; Lyons and Jackson, *Saladin*, p. 118.

92. See G. Makdisi, *The Rise of Humanism*, p. 87.

93. 'Abd al-Latif al-Baghdadi, *Kitab al-Ifada wa'l-i'tibar*, pp. 223–55, describing the events of 597 (1200/1). Al-Maqrizi (Wiet, *Traité*, 29ff.) mentions a severe famine and epidemic in 596 A.H. (1199/1200), caused by a decrease of the waters of the Nile. He adds that by April that year the bed of the Nile was dry. Al-Taghribirdi, *al-Nujum al-zahira*, VI, 173–74, records a decline of the Nile in 597 (1200/1), in the first year of the rule of al-Malik al-'Adil, noting that it was virtually unprecedented. Omar Prince Toussoun (Tusun), *Mémoire sur les anciennes branches du Nil*, II, 473, cites sources concerning a famine in 598 (1201/2), which went on from Shawwal 596 (began July 15, 1200) to Rajab 598 (began March 27, 1202).

94. See *Responsa,* no. 15, p. 22; and Eppenstein, *Moses ben Maimon*, p. 102, n. 3. Another reference to famine occurs in *Responsa*, no. 21. And in no. 118, in the colophon to a quire of queries by Se'adyah ben Berakhot, he mentions that he finished the edition in 1200 at Fustat, where great misery prevailed.

95. *Risala fi 'l-marad al-musamma diyabitis*, ed. Ghalioungui et al. And see *Der Diabetestraktat 'Abd al-Laṭīf al-Baghdādī's*, trans. Hans-Jürgen Thies. Maimonides refers to diabetes in his *Medical Aphorisms*, ed. Munter, Introduction, p. xii; text, pp. v, 13; vi, 9; viii, 69; xxiv, 39, 40. Galen stated that the disease is rare, and Maimonides never came across a case in the Maghrib, but saw several in Egypt, which he attributed to warm regions affecting the kidneys and possibly Nile water. See also Friedenwald, "Moses Maimonides," p. 205.

96. 'Abd al-Latif al-Baghdadi does not clarify whether Jews do not believe that Joseph ben Judah converted to Islam or whether he reverted outwardly to Judaism. Al-Baghdadi confirms Ibn al-Qifti's account of Joseph ben Judah's conversion to Islam in Morocco.

97. S. M. Stern, "A Collection of Treatises by 'Abd al-Latif," p. 54; Angelika Neuwirth, *'Abd al-Latif al-Bagdadi's Beartbeitung von Buch Lambda der Aristotelischen Metaphysik*. For his summary of Aristotle's *Metaphysics*, Book *Lambda*, Al-Baghdadi used also Alexander of Aphrodisias, *De providentia*; excerpts from the *Liber de Causis* and Proclus' *Institutio theologica*; and the *Theology of Aristotle* based on extracts from the *Enneads* of Plotinus. The Book *Lambda* text has a section (*fasl*) (16) that is a paraphrase of Alexander's *On the Principles of the* All (*Universe*), a work that influenced Maimonides. Neuwirth describes part one of the Book *Lambda* text as being strongly Aristotelian, and she mentions its use of the Aristotle commentators Alexander of Aphrodisias and Themistius. Part two is replete with Neoplatonic ideas and terminology. The one God is not the Aristotelian first mover but a personal God described as having *awliya'*, a word that means "saints" or "friends."

98. Al-Farabi's compendium of Plato's *Laws* was edited by F. Gabrieli, *Talkhīṣ Nawāmīs Aflāṭūn*.

99. See Al-Farabi, *Falsafat Arisṭāṭālīs*; M. Mahdi, *Al-Farabi's Philosophy of Plato and Aristotle*. For the harmony of Plato and Aristotle, see Al-Farabi, *Kitāb al-jāmi' bayn ra'yay al-hakīmayn*, *L'harmonie entre les opinions de Platon et d'Aristote*, ed. and trans. F. M. Najjar; *Deux traités philosophiques: l'harmonie entre les opinions des deux sages, le divin Platon et Aristotle*, trans. D. Mallet; *The Harmonization of the Two Opinions of the Two Sages: Plato the Divine and Aristotle*, trans. C. E. Butterworth, in Alfarabi, *The Political Writings*, pp. 125–67.

100. See *Guide*, III, 12; Pines, "Translator's Introduction," p. cxxxi. Maimonides said the same of Galen and Isaac Israeli. It was tantamount to saying that they were not Aristotelians. He implied, of course, that he was both physician and philosopher.

101. Ivry, "Neoplatonic Currents," p. 116, n. 3, refers to al-Baghdadi's possible influence on Maimonides; on p. 117, n. 5, he suggests his acquaintance with al-Baghdadi's work on the *Metaphysics*, which paraphrases the *Theology of Aristotle*.

102. Ibn Jubayr, *Travels*, trans. Broadhurst, pp. 43–44. Ahmed Issa Bey, *Histoire des Bimaristans-hôpitaux à l'époque islamique*, pp. 36–40. The word for hospital was *bimaristan*, from Persian. Nowadays, the Arabic word *mustashfa* is used in Arabic-speaking countries.

103. Goitein, *Med. Soc.*, I, p. 256, notes that in a petition to an Ayyubid sultan the physician Makarim ibn Ishaq asked for a lifetime appointment in the hospital of New Cairo with the usual salary of three dinars per month, giving us an idea of Abraham's situation.

104. M. Meyerhof, "Sultan Saladin's Physician on the Transmission of Greek Medicine to the Arabs," p. 169.

105. Ibn Abi Usaybi'a, *Classes of Physicians*, pp. 576–79; J. Vernet, EI, s.v. "Ibn Jamī'." On Ibn Jumay', see Meyerhof, "Sultan Saladin's Physician on the Transmission of Greek Medicine to the Arabs"; "Mediaeval Jewish Physicians," p. 450; "La serveillance des professions médicales et para-médicales chez les arabes," 119ff. and Appendice, p. 134; and see Paul Kraus, "*Min Minbar al-Sharq: Tabib Saladin*," and M. Ullmann, *Der Medizin im Islam*, pp. 164–65.

106. Abu Nasr 'Adnan 'Aynzarbi (d. 1153) served the Fatimid caliph al-Zafir (r. 1149–1154); Ullmann, op. cit., p. 161.

107. Ms. T-S NS 321.34, published by H. D. Isaacs, "An Encounter with Maimonides," pp. 42, 45, 47, which is a description by a man who visited him about an illness and asked to study medicine with him. Maimonides replied, "I shall speak on your behalf with al-Muwaffaq," meaning evidently Ibn Jumay'.

108. See P. Fenton, "The State of Arabic Medicine at the Time of Maimonides According to Ibn Jumay''s *Treatise on the Revival of the Art of Medicine*." The treatise has been edited and translated by H. Fähndrich.

109. Fenton, "The State of Arabic Medicine," p. 215.

110. The *qitara* or *qithara* is at the origin of the Spanish *guitarra*. Ibn Abi Usaybi'a, *Classes of Physicians*, pp. 581–82; Meyerhof, "Mediaeval Jewish Physicians," p. 446.

111. Al-Khabushani was a powerful figure. He was instrumental in the fall of the Fatimids, having given a legal opinion that the last Fatimid ruler al-'Adid may be deposed and executed as an offender against Islam; Lyons and Jackson, *Saladin*, p. 45; Ehrenkreutz, *Saladin*, p. 90. He advised Saladin to found a madrasa for Shafi'i jurists near al-Shafi'i's tomb; see Lev, *Saladin in Egypt*, p. 82.

112. The word for "obscure" is *mastur*, meaning also "chaste" and "blameless." Its basic meaning is "hidden," "covered." Its opposite is uncovering (*kashf*) the face; see M. R. Cohen, *Poverty and Charity in the Jewish Community of Medieval Egypt*, pp. 41–53.

113. Karaites were well represented among court physicians. Abu 'l-Bayan al-Sadid ibn al-Mudawwar (d. 1184 at the age of 83) administered to the last Fatimids and then to Saladin. Ibn Abi Usaybi'a, *Classes of Physicians*, pp. 579–80; Meyerhof, "Mediaeval Jewish Physicians," p. 445. He served in the Nasiri hospital. His teacher was Ibn Jumay'. Abu 'l-Fada'il Muhadhdhib ibn al-Nakid (d. 1188) was a physician, oculist, and popular teacher of medicine. His son Abu 'l-Faraj, also an oculist, converted to Islam, an act that may not have been rare in medical circles; Ibn Abi Usaybi'a, *Classes of Physicians*, p. 580; Meyerhof, "Mediaeval Jewish Physicians," p. 445.

114. Ibn Abi Usaybi'a, *Classes of Physicians*, pp. 651–59.

115. G. Makdisi, *The Rise of Humanism*, pp. 254ff.

116. *Classes of Physicians*, 582. Maimonides, *On Asthma*, ed. and trans. G. Bos, p. xxvii, n. 19.

117. Meyerhof, "Mediaeval Jewish Physicians in the Near East," p. 445, says that the Qadi was a lover and protector of Jewish physicians, and that by his influence about twelve came to high positions in the courts of Ayyubid rulers,

118. B. Lewis, "'Eber in Arabic Literature," pp. 171–78; idem, "Maimonides, Lionheart

and Saladin," pp. 70–75. Meyerhof, "Mediaeval Jewish Physicians," p. 447, states that Maimonides was physician to the last Fatimid caliph, al-'Adid, and that he also was recommended to the court of Saladin after 1171. See also above, ch. 9, n. 54.

119. E. Ashtor-Strauss, "Saladin and the Jews," pp. 311–12.

CHAPTER 12

1. Nesi'im were Jews descended from members of the family of David, much like the *ashraf* (sing. *sharif*), descendants of the family of Muhammad. The Exilarch, or Head of the Diaspora (Resh Galuta) in Babylonia, was a Nasi who achieved the leading position above other Nesi'im.

2. See Mann, *The Jews in Egypt and in Palestine*, I, 394; Goitein, *Med. Soc.*, II, 23; and Gil, *Documents*, I, 44.

3. The term *muqaddam* occurs often in our texts and in Arabic texts from the same milieu in the sense of one placed in front, thus a leader or official. A *muqaddam* was a judge and rabbi, occasionally layman, who was administrative and religious leader of local communities. The *muqaddam* of a town was like its mayor. See Goitein, *Med. Soc*, II, 68–75; VI, General Index, p. 78.; Ashtor, "Some Features of the Jewish Communities in Medieval Egypt," pp. 138–41; M. Cohen, *Jewish Self-Government*, pp. 202–4; Friedman, *Polygyny*, p. 315; and "Maimonides, Zuta and the Muqaddamin," passim.

4. The title of Nagid does not appear until ca. 1065 and does not come into continuous use until the thirteenth century; Goitein, "The Title and the Office of Nagid: A Reexamination," pp. 93–94; *Med. Soc.*, II, 23; Cohen, *Jewish Self-Government*, p. 28. In 1 Sam 9:16, etc., the word Nagid occurs in the sense of ruler appointed by God. It was the Jewish communal title for Ra'is al-Yahud, the title conferred by the government.

5. Goitein, *Med. Soc.*, II, 32.

6. Menahem Ben-Sasson, "Maimonidean Dynasty—Between Conservatism and Revolution."

7. Goitein, "The Title and the Office of Nagid: A Reexamination," p. 103; *Med. Soc.*, II, 31.

8. Friedman, "Maimonides, Zuta and the Muqaddamin," p. 3, n. 11, states that the consensus of the community usually came first.

9. Richard J. H. Gottheil, "An Eleventh-Century Document Concerning a Cairo Synagogue," p. 500; Goitein, "The Title and the Office of Nagid: A Reexamination," p. 98; idem, *Med. Soc.*, II, 27.

10. Benjamin of Tudela mentioned the number of Samaritans in towns he visited on his travels. In Ascalon, he found more Samaritans (300) than Rabbanites (200) and Karaites (40); see *Itinerary*, ed. Adler, p. 29; Mann, *The Jews in Egypt and in Palestine*, I, 170–71.

11. Bosworth, "Christian and Jewish Religious Dignitaries in Mamluk Egypt and Syria: Qalqashandi's Information on Their Hierarchy, Titulature, and Appointment (II)," p. 213.

12. M. Ben-Sasson, "Maimonidean Dynasty—Between Conservatism and Revolution."

13. Bosworth, loc. cit.

14. Shulamit Sela, "The Head of the Rabbanite, Karaite and Samaritan Jews," pp. 257–58.

15. Ibid., p. 260.

16. Bosworth, op. cit., pp. 212–14. See Qur'an, ix, 10.

17. Goitein, "The Title and Office of the Nagid: A Reexamination," p. 118; *Med. Soc.*, II, 38. The Nagid was not responsible for collection of the poll tax. However, he raised funds for those unable to pay.

18. Strauss-Ashtor, *History*, II, 244.

19. Goitein, "The Title and Office of the Nagid: A Reexamination," p. 118.

20. Ibid., p. 106.

21. Goitein, *Med. Soc.*, II, 168, explains that the Nagids were not supermen, citing the case of a Nagid who banned a man from the synagogue and then had to relent.

22. Strauss-Ashtor, *History*, II, 250–51, noting MT Sanhedrin, vi, 6–9; xxv, 8ff. The same author observes, pp. 255–56, that in the fifteenth century, a Nagid had a prison and imposed fines on Jews for going to gentile courts.

23. Richard J. H. Gottheil, "An Eleventh-Century Document Concerning a Cairo Synagogue," p. 501.

24. Khan, "Document of Appointment," in *Arabic Legal and Administrative Documents*, no. 121, pp. 460–66 (Ms. T-S Ar 38.93).

25. Ben-Sasson, "Maimonidean Dynasty—Between Conservatism and Revolution."

26. Goitein, *Med. Soc.*, II, 36–37.

27. Ibid., p. 168.

28. See Michael Cook's *Commanding Right and Forbidding Wrong in Islamic Thought*. The phrase is, of course, Qur'anic (see 3:104 and Cook, p. 13 for other references). Maimonides used the expression in the *Book of Commandments,* pos. 176, ed. Qafih, p. 148; trans. C. B. Chavel, pp. 187–88. For other Rabbanite and Karaite citations, see Cook, p. 572, n. 68.

29. TS Ar. 54.60, published by E. Ashtor, "Some Features of the Jewish Communities in Medieval Egypt," pp. 156–57; see Goitein, *Med. Soc.*, II, 528, n. 46; 535, n. 118. M. Ben-Sasson, "Maimonides in Egypt: The First Stage," pp. 18–19; Friedman, "Maimonides, Zuta and the Muqaddamin," pp. 476, 479–80. As Friedman observes, only the name Abu Sa'd occurs in the text. He and Goitein read his title as ha-Shevi'i, the Seventh, which was then changed to ha-Shishi, the Sixth. Ashtor's reading is al-Shami, the Syrian (or Syro-Palestinian). The Sixth (ha-Shishi) pertained to a rank in the *havurah* (fellowship) of the Academy, and it became a family name for his descendants. See Mann, *The Jews in Egypt and in Palestine*, I, 233–39; *Texts and Studies*, I, 255–62; Goitein, *Med. Soc.*, II, 32–33, 528 n. 46; M. Ben-Sasson, "Maimonides in Egypt," p. 18 and n. 27, citing also Goitein, *The Yemenites*, pp. 53–74.

30. *Mutawalli al-bab* is the title—also called *sahib al-bab*—second to the vizier. Ibn al-Sallar may well have been the chamberlain. He was governor of Alexandria and then vizier in 1149–53. But this happened before he was vizier, when al-Hafiz was the caliph. Ibn al-Sallar was a Sunni Egyptian who rose through the administration and the military. The name is written Salar and Sallar (arabicized), from Persian *sardar* and *salar* (army commander). See Leila S. al-Imad, *The Fatimid Vizierate*, p. 169; G. Wiet, EI, s.v. "al-'Adil b. al-Salar."

31. Goitein, *Med. Soc.*, II, 26.

32. Goitein, *Med. Soc.*, V, 426–28, citing Ms. T-S Misc. K 25.64; p. 628, n. 60; and also citing Mann, *The Jews in Egypt and in Palestine*, II, 292–94; *Texts and Studies*, I, 256–62. On Nethanel, see also Friedman, "Maimonides, Zuta and the Muqaddamin," pp. 482–84.

33. His protocol was "the Great Nasi, Head of the Exile of All Israel"; Mann, *The Jews in Egypt and in Palestine*, II, 209; S. Assaf, "Letters of Rabbi Samuel ben Eli and his Contemporaries," p. 67. In 1164, he was Exilarch in Fustat, two years after writing this letter, the date of which appears at the end (Assaf, p. 77).

34. A copy of the letter was brilliantly rejoined by S. Assaf from Genizah fragments found in three different libraries— Ms. 1131 of the Antonin Library in St. Petersbourg, Ms. T-S 8 J.2 of Cambridge University, and Ms. ENA 4011.74 of the Jewish Theological Seminary. The beginning is still lacking. See Assaf, "Letters of Rabbi Samuel ben Eli and His Contemporaries," pp. 66–71, 75–77, especially pp. 68–69. See also Mann, *The Jews in Egypt and in Palestine*, II, 467–69; *Texts and Studies*, I, 230–36; Goitein, *Med. Soc.*, II, 18; Friedman, "Maimonides, Zuta and the Muqaddamin," pp. 482–83. The copy, evidently made in Cairo-Fustat, was witnessed by Jacob ha-Kohen ben Joseph, who otherwise signed documents of Nethanel (Mann, *The Jews in Egypt and in Palestine*, I, 22, n. 1; II, 293, 366).

35. Assaf, "Letters of Rabbi Samuel ben Eli and His Contemporaries," p. 68. This took place in Baghdad, showing that the Exilarch's choice was ratified by the public.

36. Assaf, ibid., p. 73; Friedman, op. cit., p. 483, n. 15. They are said to be established before the God of their father forever and intended to help the sick and needy. It is easy to misread *huqqim* as "statutes," as this is the general meaning it has *in Hebrew,* but the Exilarch alluded to Arabic *haqq,* pl. *huquq,* which refers to payments.

37. Benjamin of Tudela, *Travels,* pp. 70–71.

38. Ibn Abi Usaybiʻa, *Classes of Physicians,* p. 580. The author used the title al-Raʾis. On Nethanel, see also Mann, *The Jews in Egypt and in Palestine,* II, 293; Goitein, "The Life of Maimonides," p. 31 and n. 5, citing TS 13 J 6, f. 27; *Med. Soc.,* II, 32, 244. The word for "government stipend" is *jāmakiyya.* It may also have the meaning of "salary given in dress," then "salary." See Goitein, *Med. Soc.,* II, 353; 604, n. 37 and 605, n. 12; Diem and Radenberg, *Dictionary,* p. 32; and H. Monés, EI, s.v. "Djāmakiyya."

39. TS 13 J 3.14; see Goitein, *Med. Soc.,* III 369, 409, 486.

40. TS 13 J 20.18 and 18 J 1.27; Goitein, *Med. Soc.,* III, 252, 482, n. 13.

41. Mann, *The Jews in Egypt and in Palestine,* II, 303; Goitein, "The Renewal of the Controversy over the Prayer for the Head of the Community at Abraham Maimuni's Time," p. 50. Moshe Gil vocalizes the word as *rashut;* thus *be-rashuteh* (under his authority), as in M. Avot, i, 10, where *rashut* means "authority," "leadership." *Reshut* is from *r-sh-h(w),* meaning "to permit, authorize, empower," and *rashut* is from *roʾsh,* meaning "head" or "authority." See Gil, *Documents,* I, 44; *In the Kingdom of Ishmael,* I, p. 90. Gil argues that *reshut* does not have the sense of "authority" or "jurisdiction." Jastrow, *Dictionary,* II, 1499, vocalizes the Hebrew form as *rashut* (power, authority, control) and Aramaic as *reshuta, reshu, rashuta,* with the same meaning. Sokolow, *Dictionary,* p. 530, gives *reshu* and *reshuta* for Jewish Palestinian Aramaic (control, permission). He rejects the distinction between *rashut* (< *roʾsh*) and *reshut,* because an Aramaic form of *reshut* should be *rishut,* which does not occur. In the language of our texts, *reshut* is used for "taking leave" and *rashut* refers to the Headship = *riyasa* in Arabic. The question is how to vocalize "under his jurisdiction." Is it *be-reshuteh* or *be-rashuteh?* The term *reshut* corresponds to *exousia* of the New Testament in the senses of permission, authority. It may also mean "power" and "sphere of dominion." See *A Greek-English Lexicon of the New Testament,* ed. W. Bauer, p. 278; *Theological Dictionary of the New Testament,* ed. G. Kittel and G. Friedrich, abridged by G. W. Bromiley, p. 238.

42. Ashtor, "Some Features of the Jewish Communities in Medieval Egypt," p. 143.

43. Friedman, "Rabbi Yeḥiel b. Elyakim's Responsum Permitting the *Reshut,*" p. 328.

44. The title Raʾis (from *raʾs,* "head"), or Rayyis, as it was often pronounced, might apply to a physician in charge of a hospital department, the chief physician in a place, or judges and ship captains. In fact, it denoted the chief or leader of any distinctive group, whether political, religious, or other. It is commonly used today in Arab counries for president, chairman, or prime minister (*raʾis al-wuzara'*). Rais/Raiz/Reiz came into English in the sixteenth century as a title for a ship captain. See also Mark Cohen, *Jewish Self-Government,* pp. 166–71.

45. Ibn al-Qifti, *History of the Sages,* p. 318; trans. Kraemer, "The Life of Moses ben Maimon," p. 423.

46. See Goitein, "The Life of Maimonides in Light of New Genizah Discoveries," pp. 29–42; "Moses Maimonides, Man of Action"; M. A. Cohen, "Maimonides' Egypt"; M. Ben-Sasson, "Maimonides in Egypt," pp. 11–13 and note 18. See the works of M. A. Friedman: "Moses ben Maimon in Legal Documents from the Geniza," "Was Maimonides 'Nagid' [=the Head of the Jews] in Egypt?" and "Maimonides, Zuta and the Muqaddamin."

47. Ibn al-Qifti, *History of the Sages,* p. 392, and Ibn Abi Usaybiʻa, *Classes of Physicians,* p. 582. Ibn al-Qifti says that Maimonides was Raʾis al-Yahud in his article on Joseph ben Judah, but that need not disturb us. Ibn Abi Usaybiʻa says that "he was Head over [the Jews] in Egypt" (*wa-kana raʾisan ʻalayhim fi 'l-diyar al-misriyya*), a statement that could not be clearer.

48. Cf. Goitein, "Moses Maimonides, Man of Action," pp. 165–66, who thinks that he became Ra'is again in 1195 or 1196.

49. That is, *reshuteh de-Adonenu Mosheh ha-Rav ha-Gadol be-Yisra'el*. Occasionally, the title did not include "in Israel." After it came the blessing "May his name be eternal" (Ps 72:17). The rest of the verse is "while the sun lasts, may his name endure."

50. See Mann, *The Jews in Egypt and in Palestine*, I, 234–37, II, 294; Goitein, "Moses ben Maimon, Man of Action," p. 160 and n. 23. An autograph of Maimonides from Ab-Elul (July–August) 1170 in TS Box 309, n. 12, according to which Maimonides received in the town of al-Mahalla nine dinars for release of captives, called him simply Rabbenu Mosheh ("our Master Moses"). See also Friedman, "New Sources for the Crusader Period," p. 72 and n. 30.

51. Mann, *The Jews in Egypt and in Palestine*, II, 294; Goitein, "The Life of Maimonides," p. 31 and n. 9. And see Friedman, "New Sources from the Geniza on the Crusader Period," p. 74 and n. 26.

52. Ms. T-S 13 J 3.15 dated Elul 1482 s.e./4931 a.m., which began August 4, 1171. See Reif, *Bibliography,* p. 153, and especially Goitein, *Med. Soc.*, I, 365. Friedman, "New Sources for the Crusader Period," p. 74.

53. The first ten days of Tishre 1483 s.e./4932 a.m. (=September 2–12, 1171). See Ms. T-S 10 J 26.4; Reif, *Bibliography*, p. 144, and especially Goitein, *Med. Soc.*, III, 276.

54. Dated Marheshvan 1483 s.e./4932 a.m. = October 1171; Ms. Vienna papyrus Erherzog Rainer H 20; Goitein, *Med. Soc.*, III, 367, n. 26; III, 453, n. 44. Acknowledgments of trousseaux were renewed after the burning of Fustat in 1168.

55. The date given is 1483 s.e.; Ms. T-S 12.572. See Reif, *Bibliography*, p. 240.

56. The first ten days of Adar I 1483 s.e. began January 29, 1172; Ms. T-S 10 J 26.13. See Reif, *Bibliography*, p. 144. The verso side has a list of accounts in the hand of the judge Samuel ben Se'adyah; Goitein, *Med. Soc.*, II, 485.

57. Ms. Or 1080 J 142 and also Misc. 25.53. See *Med. Soc.*, IV, 335ff.

58. S. D. Goitein published the text and an English translation of Ms. T-S J 2.78, which he titled "Maimonides' Installation as *Ra'īs al-Yahūd*," in "Moses Moses ben Maimon, Man of Action," pp. 161–62, 167. The document is in Hebrew except for a few words in the first two lines that are in Arabic. It is in the hand of the scribe Mevorakh ben Nathan.

59. Ms. T-S 12.822 was first edited and translated by Israel Friedlaender, "Ein Gratulationsbrief an Maimonides." See Reif, *Bibliography*, p. 246. This was an early Genizah publication. Friedlaender received the text from Solomon Schechter from a "special collection of Maimonidean Genizah texts in Cambridge." His readings are occasionally erroneous, and one needs to examine the original document closely.

60. Reading *[ado]nenu*. Only the bottom horizontal stroke of the penultimate *nun* is visible in the manuscript.

61. The appellation "our chariots and horsemen," used for Heads of the Jews, is based on 2 Kings 2:12 and 13:14, when Elijah went up in a whirlwind and Elisha cried, "Oh father, father! Israel's chariots and horsemen." This was understood to mean that Elijah was Elisha's master who taught him Torah. See B MQ 26a; Friedman, "Maimonides, Zuta and the Muqaddamin," p. 483.

62. See Lam 4:20: the breath of our life, the Lord's anointed.

63. *Alluf* was a sobriquet for great dignitaries in the Iraqian academy (*rashe yeshivot we-allufe torah*); see Mann, *The Jews in Egypt and in Palestine*, I, 114; Goitein, *Med. Soc.*, II, 22, 199.

64. The text has a reading that appears to be האש, meaning "fire," which is senseless here. I suggest that the writer first wrote הרב, and then corrected the resh to an *alif* and the bet to a *shin*, without correcting the *he'* to a *resh*. He intended to correct הרב (*ha-rav*) to ראש (*rosh*). For a different reading, see Friedlaender, "Ein Gratulationsbrief an Moses ben Maimon," p. 261, n. 2. The expression *rosh ha-roshim* ("Head of Heads," or "supreme Head") is the Hebrew equivalent of Arabic Ra'is al-Ru'asa', used by political leaders, for instance, the

vizier Abu 'l-Qasim, who became the Fatimid caliph al-Qa'im bi-Amri Allah (tenth century); see al-Taghribirdi, *al-Nujum al-Zahira*, V, 6, 10. It was used by the Copts as an honorific title of the patriarch; Cohen, *Jewish Self-Government*, p. 167.

65. To preserve the rhyme, the writer used a masculine plural (*nefashim*) of the word *nefesh*, which usually has a feminine plural (*nefashot*), having the meaning of "soul." *Nefashim* means "persons" in Ez 13:20 and is a *hapax legomenon* (occurring once in Scripture).

66. The more lengthy, clever, and effusive the description of the recipient, the more chance that a letter would be appreciated and taken seriously.

67. Maimonides alluded to such people in his letter to Japhet ben 'Ali. See below, p. 255.

68. Heb *haslaha* corresponds to Ar *sa'ada*, meaning "happiness" in the Aristotelian sense (Grk *eudaimonia*).

69. See also CM Avot i, 10 and *Guide*, III, 12 (pp. 445–46) on the danger of service to rulers.

70. This is from a letter that Maimonides wrote to Joseph ben Judah, consoling him for the death of a young girl; *Epistles*, ed. Baneth, pp. 93–94.

71. See Ms. Cambridge Or 1080 J 8. The 1173 date proposed here has been accepted by M. A. Friedman, "Maimonides, Zuta, and the Muqaddamin," p. 475, n. 11.

72. Mosseri VII-138.1 L-206. Misc. 28.2 invokes the authority of Sar Shalom ha-Levi Gaon in the last ten days of Adar, 14[...]4, which may be 1494/1183, began January 26, 1183, or (what is more likely) 1484, i.e., 1173.

73. See Goitein, "Life of Maimonides," 32–34; "Maimonides, the Man of Action," p. 165 and n. 42, where it is said that Sar Shalom reappears first in Nisan 1177, citing Bodl. Ms. Heb. b 13, f. 40 (Cat. 2834, no. 21); and then he appears with frequency until Iyyar 1196, for instance in TS 10 J 29, f. 4; TS 10 J 24, f. 7, written in his own hand; see *Med. Soc.*, II, 32–33 and 572, n. 49; V, 491; Ben-Sasson, "Maimonides in Egypt," p. 21, n. 34—"Maimonides served in this office between the first and second terms of Sar Shalom's rule, as well as after his second term." And see Friedman, "Maimonides, Zuta and the Muqaddamin," p. p. 476.

74. CM Bekhorot, iv, 4, ed. Sassoon, III, 632–33; ed. Qafih, Qodoshim, pp. 244–45. There are differences between the two texts, which I shall indicate when there is a change of meaning. He was mainly concerned at the beginning with the legal opinions of a jurisprudent (mufti), and this brought him to the issue of appointment of a chief justice and his jurisdiction. See Mann, *The Jews in Egypt and in Palestine*, II, 293-4; Twersky, *Introduction to the Code of Maimonides*, p. 82; Friedman, "Maimonides, Zuta and the Muqaddamin," p. 7. After the first words in his long commentary on Avot in the original manuscript there is the sign for an addition (after *wa-li-'ilmi aydan an*). Friedman thinks that Maimonides wrote additional words on a note that he pasted on the page, and the note was thereafter lost.

75. The fair text has *al-Sham wa'l-'Iraq*. The Hebrew translation in printed editions adds "the land of the West."

76. Nethanel was the Head of the Academy of the Diaspora and Sar Shalom was the Head of the Academy of the Pride of Jacob; Friedman, "Maimonides, Zuta and the Muqaddamin," p. 11.

77. The expression "embellishment [lit. "fattening"] of words" occurs in B BM 66a, for which Maimonides substituted "name" (in the singular). *Nu'ut* (sing. *na't*) means "titles" in Arabic historical texts.

78. A *bar be rav* is a pupil (B Berakhot 58a) and a *bar be rav de-had yoma* is a pupil of one day, that is, a tyro (B Hag 5b).

79. Rav in Hebrew, meaning "great," is used in the Talmud for master, in contrast to slave or pupil, and was given to the Babylonian (Iraqian) Amoraim. Related to rav was the title rabbi ("my master"), which was conferred upon Sages who had ordination by the Sanhedrin, limited in the talmudic period to the Land of Israel. The rav was someone whose legal opinions were authoritative, and who interpreted and taught the law and had a per-

sonal occupation. The title rabbi is applied in the Gospels to Jesus and John the Baptist, as well as to the Scribes, who are criticized for being avid for it.

80. Friedman, "Maimonides as Codifier," p. 226; "New Fragments," pp. 110–11.

81. *Responsa*, no. 191, p. 348. The local Jewish judge had testified before the Qadi that Jewish girls after marriage remained in the custody of their fathers; however, he was opposed by someone who was present in court. See below, pp. 301–02.

82. Goitein, *Med. Soc.*, II, 325–26, citing Tyan, *L'Organisation judiciaire*, pp. 219–30.

83. Muhammad Khalid Masud, Brinkley Messick, and David S. Powers, "Muftis, Fatwas, and Islamic Legal Interpretation," p. 3.

84. Goitein, "Political Conflict and the Use of Power," p. 174–75.

85. Goitein notes that Maimonides lived in Egypt for about forty years, yet no court record signed by him is found in the Genizah, whereas responsa are well represented; *Med. Soc.*, II, 326. When Maimonides is called Moses son of Maimon the judge, the title belongs, of course, to his father. See Friedman, "Two Maimonidean Letters," p. 202, n. 51.

86. See *Responsa*, no. 102, p. 172. See Goitein, *Med. Soc.*, II, 514, n. 26 on *muvhaq* as "presiding." And see Mann, *The Jews in Egypt and in Palestine*, II, 268.

87. On one document Maimonides signs *dayyan*, but not *ha-dayyan* because he was judge ad hoc for that specific legal procedure. See *Responsa*, no. 348, p. 625. This was a legal communal enactment concerning authorization of certain qualified rabbis to supervise marriage and divorce, signed by him and three colleagues. In *Responsa*, no. 309, p. 570, in the exchange of letters with Samuel ben Eli of Baghdad, he is called "our Master Moses the Presiding Judge" (*ha-dayyan ha-muvhaq*), but this was written by someone in Iraq. He is called the Great Rav in Israel (*ha-Rav ha-Gadol be-Yisra'el*) at least eighteen times in his responsa.

88. *Sayyiduna mufti al-milla*. A variant has *al-umma wa 'l-milla* (the nation and the religious community); see *Responsa*, no. 178, p. 326.

89. Goitein, *Med. Soc.*, II, 36ff.

90. For Maimonides' *moshav*, see *Responsa*, no. 6, p. 8; no. 15, p. 23; no. 106, p. 180; no. 260, p. 487; Index, p. 214—*moshav* (*bet din*). In references to enactments issued by him and his colleagues, people spoke of Maimonides and his court; see Friedman, *Polygyny*, p. 227. Goitein, "Documents on Abraham Maimonides and His Pietist Circle," pp. 186–87, cites Ms. T-S 10 J 13.8, an autograph of Abraham, with references to his *majlis*, which Goitein translates as *yeshivah*. He observes (in note 26) that *majlis* is usually translated as *moshav*, ("meeting place" or "meeting"), but here it is a place of study and prayer. Maimonides' *majlis*, in addition to convening as a court, was probably a place of study and prayer as well.

91. Hebrew *moshav* and *yeshivah*, as well as Arabic *majlis*, are derived from words meaning "to sit." See Goitein, *Med. Soc*, II, 196, 561, 566. On *yeshivah*, see Goitein, *Med. Soc.*, II, 5, 196. *Yeshivah*, Goitein suggests, may be a Hebrew equivalent of Greek *synhedrion* (Sanhedrin of the Talmud), which the New Testament understands in the sense of council. It means, literally, "place where people sit together." The scholars who interpreted the law, gave rulings, and decided questions that came before them. The *yeshivah* functioned as an academy, a parliament, and a supreme court. The *yeshivah* was sometimes called in Genizah documents "the Great Sanhedrin." The name *havurah*, literally "fellowship," or *havurat ha-sedeq*, "the righteous fellowship," included sages who could interpret and apply the law in actual life situations. Goitein notes (II, 196) that *havurat ha-sedeq* is reminiscent of the terminology of the Dead Sea Scrolls.

92. The elders acted as community leaders. Their number varied from three to seven to ten, etc. Maimonides said that there was no compulsory number; see Goitein, *Med. Soc.*, II, 58–61. And see Goitein, "Political Conflict and the Use of Power," p. 173. The nonrabbinical leaders, or elders, were the religiously learned merchants, bankers, physicians, etc. The business of the community was conducted by the elders. In order to be an elder, one did not need to be old. Think of the English word "senator" (< *senatus*), which means "elder" in Latin. Or think of Arabic *shaykh*, which means elder, but also chief, master, ruler, senator. *Majlis al-shuyukh* is council of elders, senate. Many Genizah documents refer to *ha-zaken*

ha-bakhur (the elder who is a young man). In *Responsa*, no. 271, p. 519, Maghribis asked about the seven notables of a city. Maimonides defined them as disciples of the wise, men of Torah and good deeds. See also MT Prayer and Priestly Blessing, xi, 17.

93. Israel Ta-Shema shows that Maimonides' entourage was divided into an inner circle, which had access to texts in Maimonides' house meant for the use of his close family and intimate disciples, and a wider circle. See his *Studies in Medieval Rabbinic Literature*, 2. *Spain*, pp. 311–12. M. A. Friedman has published notes of a pupil taken down in one of the Master's teaching sessions; see his "Notes by a Disciple in Maimonides' Academy Pertaining to Beliefs and Concepts and Halakha."

94. A. Freimann, Introduction, in *Responsa*, III, 41ff.

95. See *Responsa*, no. 191, pp. 347–48.

96. See *Responsa*, no. 409, p. 686.

97. Goitein, "Maimonides as Chief Justice," p. 191. This is clear from his signature in responsa—*we-khatav Moshe*, literally, "written by Moses." It is always possible, of course, that he conferred with others even when he signed by himself.

98. Cf. *Responsa*, pp. 152 and 172. It stands to reason that Maimonides did not object to these two senior members of his court answering on their own. Cf. ibid., no. 16, p. 24, which is headed: "This question was sent to Rabbi Isaac—certainly Isaac ben Sason—but was answered by Maimonides, as Rabbi Isaac was absent." See also the signature of Samuel ha-Levi in *Responsa*, nos. 11, 99, 102, 192, 232, 380, and 431; Isaac ben Sason in nos. 103 (as a *dayyan*), 173, 260 (with his motto, *yesha' yiqrav*), 408, 409; and both Isaac and Samuel in nos. 403, 408, 452.

99. M. A. Friedman, "Social Realities in Egypt and Maimonides' Rulings on Family Law," p. 226, observes that "it is not entirely clear why judges sometimes added their consenting opinions to Maimonides' responsa." See also Friedman, "New Fragments from the *Responsa* of Maimonides" pp. 110–11.

100. Num 11:12, Deut 1:16; B San 8a, MT Sanhedrin, xxv, 1–4.

101. Ibn al-Qifti gives information on his marriage and his wife's family; see *History of the Sages*, p. 318; trans. Kraemer, "The Life of Moses ben Maimon," p. 423.

102. Goitein, *Med. Soc.*, I, 48–49.

103. His full name was al-Shaykh al-Thiqa Abu 'l-Mahasin Mishael ben Isaiah ha-Levi. Government officials were sometimes given the sobriquet Thiqat al-Dawla, *thiqa* meaning "reliable." See also Mann, *The Jews in Egypt and in Palestine*, I, 226; II, 270, 319, 328, 563; Freimann, "The Genealogy of Moses Maimonides' Family," pp. 13–15; Gil, *Documents*, p. 261, n. 4; and Docs. 49, 75, 109 (called *ha-rofe'*, the Physician); Friedman, "Two Maimonidean Letters," p. 195.

104. Freimann, "Genealogy," pp. 13–14.

105. Ibn al-Qifti, *History of the Sages*, p. 318, trans. Kraemer, p. 423. It is called in Arabic a *mubadala* (exchange) marriage; see also Goitein, *Med. Soc.*, III, 32. Saladin and the son of the Fatimid vizier Shawar were rumored to be planning an exchange marriage to reinforce an alliance; see Lyons and Jackson, *Saladin*, p. 20.

106. Ibn al-Qifti, *History of the Sages*, p. 318; trans. Kraemer, p. 423. Abu 'l-Ma'ali is, strangely enough, mentioned among the Family of the Nagids of the House of Maimonides, where it is said that he died on 2 Tammuz 619 A.H./4982 A.M. (June 13, 1222); Brit Lib Or. 5549. See Mann, *The Jews in Egypt and in Palestine*, II, 328; Freimann, "Genealogy," p. 15.

107. Baneth, *Epistles*, p. 71.

108. Freimann, "Genealogy," p. 15.

109. M. A. Friedman, "Two Maimonidean Letters," pp. 194–211. The letter—JTS Marshall Case Ms. 8254.16 (ENA 2560)—and Hebrew translation are on pp. 209–11; facsimile opposite p. 199. The discussion here is indebted to this publication. Friedman thinks (p. 194, n. 13) that the handwriting resembles that of the judge Rabbi Mevorakh ben Na-

than ben Samuel the *haver*. However, he leaves the question open for further confirmation, and I am rather doubtful that the hand is of Mevorakh ben Nathan.

110. See *The Book of Commandments*, pos. 6; MT Ethical Qualities, vi, 2, where Maimonides advised that one should try to marry the daughter of a scholar; see B Pes 49a-b. Américo Castro, *The Spaniards*, p. 138, mentions the Spanish *hombres de bien* as strongly reminiscent of the *fijos d'algo* or *hijos de bien* (children of wealthy or noble origin), a Castilian expression translated from the Hebrew *ben tovim* (son of nobility and wealth). See also Gil, *Documents*, I, 44.

111. See Friedman, "Two Maimonidean Letters," p. 195, citing Freimann, "Genealogy," p. 10. Goitein observes that many of Mishael's ancestors had the epithet *hasid* (pious) attached to their names. Maimonides' son Abraham was later called *rosh kol ha-hasidim* (the Head of all the Pietists). Goitein believed that Abraham's pietism came from his mother's side, yet his paternal grandfather Maimon reflected the type of pietism we find in Bahya ibn Paqoda's *Duties of the Hearts*, and Moses ben Maimon had his own kind of mystical pietism.

112. See Friedman, "Two Maimonidean Letters," p. 196.

113. We need not assume that Maimonides married shortly before the birth of his son Abraham (1186), when he was about forty-eight years old. He was married long before this and may even have had daughters who are not mentioned in the sources; see Friedman, "Two Maimonidean Letters," p. 198.

114. Goitein states that in 1169, when Maimonides acted on behalf of the captives of Bilbays, he was already called *ha-rav ha-gadol*, "the Great Rav"; see "Moses Maimonides, Man of Action," p. 161. However, the circumstance and date are uncertain.

115. Rabbi Maimon was called "the Great Rav" when mentioned along with his son.

116. The epithet "ark of our covenant" was also applied to Abraham (see Friedman, "Two Maimonidean Letters," p. 211, n. 98). Friedman (p. 213) traces the description to Song R, i, 20 (on Song 1:3), where it applied to Rabbi Aqiba. Jonathan of Lunel called Moses ben Maimon "the tables of the covenant, the throne of glory, the place of our sanctuary"; Ms. Oxford Bodl. 11.33.

117. See Jer 51:5; lit. "not widowed." The same epithet for Abraham appears in his *Responsa*, no. 121, p. 206 (cited by Friedman, "Two Maimonidean Letters," p. 209, n. 85).

118. For *yehid ha-dor*, see Kraemer, "Six Letters," p. 86, n. 120. As Friedman observes, [*yehid*] *ha-zeman* reflects Arabic *awhad al-zaman* ("unique in his time") ("Two Maimonidean Letters," p. 210, n. 86).

119. Friedman, "Two Maimonidean Letters," pp. 198, 201.

120. Note that at this time Maimonides also ceased being Head of the Jews if my theory is correct.

CHAPTER 13

1. Ibn al-'Imad, *Shadharat al-dhahab*, II, 234, says that 'Abd al-Nabi was an Isma'ili (*batini*) and one of the Egyptian (Fatimid) propagandists (*du'at*). Al-Taghribirdi, *Nujum*, VI, 69, hints at this. The name 'Abd al-Nabi ibn al-Mahdi appears occasionally as Mahdi, without the definite article.

2. An eyewitness was the renowned historian-poet 'Umara al-Yamani (1121–74). See his *Ta'rikh al-Yaman*, ed. and trans. H. C. Kay as *Yaman, Its Early Mediaeval History*. And see G. R. Smith, *The Ayyubids and Early Rasulids*, pp. 56–62. On the Banu Mahdi, see G. R. Smith, EI, s.v. "Mahdids." Here too, the name appears occasionally as Mahdi without the definite article.

3. The chronology supports this. 'Umara al-Yamani refers to 'Abd al-Nabi in his narrative as al-Qa'im; H. Derenbourg, *'Oumâra du Yémen, sa vie et son œuvre*, I, 29. Al-Qa'im is short for *al-qa'im bi-amr Allah*, the one who executes God's command, or supports God's cause. Al-Qa'im also means the one who arises, and *qiyam* is the appearance of the Mahdi.

The Qa'im has been defined as "the Resurrector; he who rises up (to reestablish Truth)"; see Mohammad Ali Amir-Moezzi, *The Divine Guide in Early Shi'ism*, p. 104. Arab sources do not say that the Mahdids forced Jews to convert, but the edict was in the spirit of their restrictions. 'Abd al-Nabi was also called "the one who subdues the infidels and sinners."

4. Historical sources referring to him as a *khariji* intend the term in the sense of "rebel" (*kharaja 'ala*) not as leader of a Khariji sectarian movement. See, e.g., Ibn Khallikan, *Wafayat al-a'yan* (*Necrologies of Notables*), I, 306 and VII, 165. Yosef Tobi, "Conversion to Islam among Yemenite Jews under Zaidi Rule," p. 106, argues that 'Abd al-Nabi belonged to the Khariji sect, and his policy of imposing Islam on the Jews should be viewed against this background.

5. Smith, *The Ayyūbids and Early Rasūlids*, II, 32–33, 41–46. According to one account, 'Umara al-Yamani, court poet of Turan Shah, encouraged his patron to invade Yemen; see Abu Shama, *al-Rawdatayn (The Two Meadows)*, II, 271, quoting 'Imad al-Din, *al-Barq al-Shami*. Ibn Shaddad, cited there, reports that Saladin took the initiative in dispatching his brother.

6. See, e.g., al-Taghribirdi, *Nujum*, vi, 23, 69; Ibn al-Athir, *Kamil*, X, 52–53. 'Umara al-Yamani helped by describing the country for Turan Shah. See also Smith, *The Ayyūbids and Early Rasūlids*, pp. 31–49; Chamberlain, "The Crusader Era and the Ayyūbid Dynasty," p. 217.

7. Maimonides mentioned Balaam's prophecy regarding the advent of King David and the Messiah in MT Kings and Their Wars, xi, 1 and he discussed Balaam's role as prophet in *Guide*, II, 41, 42, 45 and III, 22. For a thorough discussion, see Friedman, *Maimonides, the Yemenite Messiah and Apostasy*, pp. 50–63.

8. Hartman, *Crisis and Leadership*, pp. 202–10, doubts that Maimonides believed in the tradition.

9. See Gerson D. Cohen's description of messianism in *Book of Tradition,* p. 288; and in his "Messianic Postures of Ashkenazim and Sephardim." pp. 273–74, 280–85, and 292–93. Messianic aspirations were at a peak in eleventh- and twelfth-century Andalus. Solomon Ibn Gabirol, Abraham Ibn Ezra, Judah ha-Levi, Abraham bar Hiyya, Judah ben Barzillai, Moses Ibn Ezra, Abraham Ibn Daud, and Moses Maimonides regarded messianism as a central pillar of their religious thought.

10. The Qur'an says that Jews and Christians claim that they are sons of God and his loved ones (Qur'an 5:18) and also claim that only they will enter paradise (2:111).

11. *It was not because you were more numerous than any other people that the Lord set his heart on you and chose you—for you were the fewest of all peoples* (Deut 7:7).

12. See also *Guide*, II, 39; III, 26, 39, 49.

13. Amalek: Ex 17:8–13; Sisera: Judg. 4–5; Sennacherib: 2 Kings 18:13–19:37; Nebuchadnezzar: 2 Kings 24 and 25. The Roman emperors Titus and Hadrian show up in Aggadic sources.

14. The new faction is Islam.

15. The name is followed by an imprecation, "may his bones be ground to dust." It appears in rabbinic sources after the names of Hadrian, Nebuchadnezzar, etc., sometimes in Aramaic as *shehiq temaya*. It is difficult to know whether the author added the imprecation or whether it was added by scribes, which is more likely.

16. B Yev 45a–46a, 70a; Qid 68b, 70a, 71b, 75b; MT Forbidden Intercourse, xv, 3; *Enc. Tal.*, viii, s.v. "*goy*," col. 291 and n. 71.

17. Cf. B Sab 104b, for instance, makes Jesus the son of Pandera (or Pandira, etc.), the paramour of his mother; and see T Hul, ii, 24; J AZ, ii, 2, p. 40d; and Lam R, v, 16. B San 67a says explicitly that Jesus was born out of wedlock. See R. T. Herford, *Christianity in the Talmud and Midrash*, pp. 35ff. The story of Joseph Pandera occurs also in the *Toledot Yeshu*, a medieval compilation of Jewish texts on Jesus; ed. S. Krauss, *Das Leben Jesu nach jüdischen Quellen*. And see *Jesus Through Jewish Eyes*, ed. A. Shan'an, pp. 63–68. All versions portray

Mary favorably, from a good family, and married to a nobleman, descended from King David; J. Dan, EJ, "Toledot Yeshu."

18. T San, x, 11; B San 43a, 67a (in uncensored versions). The accusation was sorcery, deceiving and leading astray (into apostasy); see also Herford, *Christianity in the Talmud and Midrash*, pp. 78ff.

19. See MT Kings and Their Wars, xi, 4 (uncensored) in *The Book of Judges*, trans. A. M. Hershman, p. xxiii. Rashi on the Daniel verse cites Se'adyah Gaon as saying that Daniel was referring to the nation of Esau and his sect (Christianity).

20. See below, n. 28. If Maimonides is referring to Paul, the words "a long time after Jesus" are imprecise.

21. Here we find Maimonides acknowledging that the Jews were responsible for the death of Jesus as punishment for the transgressions cited in n. 18 above.

22. See MT Kings and Their Wars, xi, 4 (uncensored), where Maimonides says that both Jesus and Muhammad paved the way for the Messiah to prepare the world to worship God. See below, chapter 18.

23. "Innovation" (*bid'a*) has a negative connotation in an Islamic context and means also "heresy."

24. Cf. Ha-Levi, *Kuzari*, II, 32; III, 9.

25. *Guide*, II, 19; III, 19, 32.

26. For secondary literature, see Gehman, "Maimonides and Islam"; Hourani, "Maimonides and Islam"; Novak, "The Treatment of Islam and Muslims in the legal writings of Maimonides"; Posen, "Die Einstellung des Maimonides zum Islam und zum Christentum"; Schlossberg, "Maimonides's Attitude to Islam."

27. The synoptic Gospels represent Jesus rather as not opposing any teaching of the Written or Oral Law and as carrying out the commandments.

28. Maimonides was influenced by Islamic sources in holding that the main doctrines of Christianity were introduced by Paul. See P. S. van Koningsveld, "The Islamic Image of Paul and the Gospel of Barnabas." See also S. Pines, "The Jewish Christians," who claims that this view of Paul, found in some Islamic texts, goes back to early Jewish-Christian sources.

29. On the rational and moral virtues, see Maimonides, Eight Chapters, chs. 2 and 7; see Gorfinkle, trans., pp. 49 and 80. See also CM Avot, I, 17; II, 5; iv, 21; v, 7, 14; *Treatise on the Art of Logic*, ch. 14. *Guide*, III, 54. The division is Aristotelian (*aretai ēthikai* and *dianoētikai*); see *Nicomachean Ethics*, I, 2; II, 1; *Eudemian Ethics*, II, 1.

30. The key expressions derived from al-Farabi are *al-jam' al-ilahi fadil, al-milla al-fadila*. The adjective *fadil* has the senses of "virtuous," "excellent," "preeminent." Al-Farabi's ideal of the virtuous city or religious community is traceable to Platonic antecedents.

31. See also ha-Levi, *Kuzari*, iv, 23. The commentator Jacob ben Hayyim perceived the similarity between the views of ha-Levi and Maimonides; see *Qol Judah* on *Kuzari*, iv, 22, 23; Halkin, *Epistle to Yemen*, Introduction, p. xiv, n. 91.

32. See al-Farabi's *Kitab al-huruf* (*Book of Letters*), p. 154; Berman, "al-Farabi, Disciple of Maimonides," p. 162. In the same work, p. 131, al-Farabi explains the priority of philosophy to religion (cf. *The Attainment of Happiness*, trans. Mahdi, p. 45, par. 55 end). The passage is treated by Berman, op. cit., pp. 156–58.

33. MT Kings and Their Wars, xi, 4 (in uncensored texts). Cf. Halkin, *Epistle to Yemen*, Introduction, p. xiv. See also ha-Levi, *Kuzari*, iv, 23, for a similar idea; and Friedman, *Maimonides, the Yemenite Messiah and Apostasy*, p. 80.

34. He used the word *dhalla*; see Lane, *Lexicon*, p. 973: "to render submissive." The word *dhalil* is "low, base, vile," also "easy to rule." Judah ha-Levi also used it ("the lowly religion") in the rhyming Arabic title of the *Kuzari*. See also P. F. Kennedy, *The Wine Song*, p. 237, n. 127. Maimonides signed a letter to Samuel Ibn Tibbon (1199), "May your peace, my friend, son and pupil, increase and may salvation be at hand for a poor and miserable people" (*'ani wa-dal*); *Letters*, ed. Shailat, p. 554.

35. See also Qur'an 5:60. Speaking of the People of the Book (Jews and Christians), we

find: *Those whom Allah cursed and was angry with, and made some into apes and swine, and those who worshiped error [idols] are worse in rank, and more astray from the right path.* See also 1:7 (Surat al-Fatiha), where God is said to be angry with one group (the Jews) and the other (the Christians) are said to go astray. For Jews as apes, see also 2:65 and 7:166.

36. Cohen, *Under Crescent and Cross*, pp. 198–99.

37. See also Blau, *Dictionary*, pp. 717–18, where vexatious and provocative harm are noted.

38. See Urbach, *The Sages*, I, 679; II, 1002, n. 11; and Ibn Daud, *The Book of Tradition,* pp. 240–50 ("The Prices of Miscalculation and Indiscretion").

39. See Tar Jon ad loc.; Halkin, *Epistle to Yemen*, p. 96, n. 142; and *Languages of Power*, ed. Ross Brann, p. 120 and n. 35.

40. A verse before this, 120:5, says, *Woe is me . . . that I must live among the tents of Kedar.* Kedar was a descendant of Abraham by Hagar, mother of Ishmael, and epynomous ancestor of Arab tribes in northern Arabia (Gen 25:12–13; 1 Chron 1:29).

41. The verse is a refrain in Song of Songs (2:7, 3:5, 5:8, 8:4). The lovesick girl adjures her friends in the name of animals—a substitute for God's name in an oath—not to arouse love until the ripe time.

Chapter 14

1. Goitein, *Med. Soc.*, I, 290, 295–96, 305–7; and see H. Kindermann, *"Schiff" im Arabischen: Untersuchung über Vorkommen und Bedeutung der Termini*, pp. 16–17, 26, 35, 64, 81–82, 95–97.

2. Goitein, *Med. Soc.*, I, 298. See also Maimonides, *Responsa*, no. 405, p. 682, for a query concerning two men entrusted to carry a parcel with them on the Nile. Fearing theft, they placed it near the captain, but when he tossed the ship's rope overboard the parcel went flying into the river and could not be found. Maimonides did not hold the two men responsible for the loss.

3. Goitein, *Med. Soc.*, I, 299.

4. The name is from Coptic *phion* ("the sea," for Lake Qarun), with its chief city, Madinat al-Fayyum, near the ruins of ancient Crododopolis-Arsinoë. See P. M. Holt, EI, s.v. "Al-Fayyūm."

5. See Golb, "The Topography of the Jews of Medieval Egypt," Part 1, p. 268. Se'adyah Gaon translates names of the garrison cities Pithom and Raamses in Ex 1:11 as Fayyum and 'Ayn al-Shams, using contemporary names.

6. The Fayyum's link with the Joseph legend probably goes back to an ancient Jewish settlement there in the third century B.C.E.

7. From Coptic Shmin, Greek Khemmis; Byzantine Panopolis; see G. Wiet, EI, s.v. "Akhmīm"; Goitein, *Med. Soc.*, I, 298.

8. Ibn Jubayr, *Travels*, trans. Broadhurst, pp. 53ff., depicts customs officials in Akhmim performing vigorous body searches on merchants to find money hidden in their clothing.

9. See Goitein, *Med. Soc.*, I, 298, where he says that it was "an unpleasant surprise." Akhmim, however, was just that kind of place.

10. Our friend Ibn Jubayr appears to be ingeniously intimating Hermetic-Gnostic motifs.

11. See Asclepius, III, 24b, in *Hermetica*, ed. and trans. Walter Scott, pp. 340–41; and *Hermetica* trans. B. P. Copenhaver, p. 81; and G. Fowden, *The Egyptian Hermes*, pp. 13, 39.

12. The discovery of the Nag Hammadi library (in 1945) is one of the great manuscript finds in modern times, along with the Dead Sea Scrolls and the Cairo Genizah. See J. Robinson (ed.), *The Nag Hammadi Library in English*. The best-known writings are *The Jung Codex*, *The Gospel of Truth*, and *The Gospel of Thomas*. See also B. Layton, *The Gnostic Scriptures*; and E. H. Pagels, *The Gnostic Gospels*.

13. Ibn Jubayr arrived at Qus on Thursday 24 Muharram 579 A.H. (= May 19, 1183), having been on the Nile for eighteen days. See *Travels*, trans. Broadhurst, p. 57. As Qus is about three hundred miles from Fustat, he traveled about sixteen miles a day. See also the same itinerary, of the trader Joseph Lebdi, in Goitein and Friedman, *India Traders,* pp. 187–92. Customs dues were high, six dinars at one point, aside from tips (and bribes).

14. Goitein, *Med. Soc.*, I, 298, and n. 28, citing Ms. Or 1080 J 26.

15. Benjamin of Tudela found three hundred Jews in Qus shortly before 1168; see *Itinerary*, trans. M. N. Adler, pp. 69, 74. This appears to be the total population, not just males or taxpayers; see Goitein, *Med. Soc.*, II, 45, 258; III, 278; IV,'44, 350. And cf. E. Ashtor, "The Number of Jews in Mediaeval Egypt," p. 14; Golb, "The Topography of Jews in Medieval Egypt," Part 2, pp. 136–37.

16. Ms. T-S NS 321.1; Goitein, *Med. Soc.*, I, 298 at n. 27; V, 31–32.

17. Ibn Jubayr, *Travels*, trans. Broadhurst, pp. 57–58. See J.-Cl. Garcin, *Un centre musulman de la Haute-Egypte médiévale: Qūṣ*; Paula A. Sanders, "The Fatimid State," pp. 168–69; J.-Cl. Garcin, EI, s.v. "Qūṣ."

18. A *rafiq* was de rigueur for such journeys. See Goitein, *Med. Soc.*, I, 347–48, citing the Arabic proverb, "The companion [*rafiq*] is more important than the route taken [*tariq*]."

19. See also Goitein, *Med. Soc.*, I, 276ff., on desert travel.

20. After 'Aydhab's destruction (in 1428), Suwakin (ca. two hundred miles south) and later Port Sudan, thirty-six miles to the north, took its place as main Sudanese ports on the Red Sea. See M. Jules Couyat, "Les routes d'Aidhab"; G. W. Murray, "Aidhab"; A. Paul, "Aidhab: A Medieval Red Sea Port"; and J.-Cl. Garcin, "Jean-Léon l'Africain et 'Aydhab."

21. See Paul, "Aydhab," p. 62.

22. Ibn Jubayr, *Travels*, trans. Broadhurst, pp. 63–66. Ibn Jubayr reviled the Beja tribesmen and their exploitation of pilgrims. The only cure for them, he said, was the sword. He advised pilgrims to take a circuitous route by way of Baghdad, Acre, Alexandria, Sicily, even a Rumi (Christian) ship to Ceuta in Morocco (which is what he had done). Ibn Jubayr stayed in 'Aydhab for twenty-three days, suffering a meager diet and poor health before taking a *jalba* boat to Jedda.

23. Ibn Jubayr, *Travels*, trans. Broadhurst, p. 67. *'Ifrit* acquires the sense of a cunning and powerful chthonian power.

24. Goitein and Friedman, "Ben Yīju," p. 283, from *India Book*, III, 39; see Goitein and Friedman, *India Traders,* pp. 719, n. 21 and p. 720. Al-Wahrani, *Manamat*, p. 19, gives a definite wordplay on *'aydhab/'adhab*. Ibn Jubayr also used the pun; see *Travels*, trans. Broadhurst, p. 48.

25. Goitein, *Med. Soc.*, I, 42.

26. Therefore given the shelf mark of Or 1081 J 1. The Or 1080 and 1081 series are manuscripts that were acquired for the Cambridge University Library before Schechter's material arrived. The writing is a clear Spanish semicursive. See also Reif, *Jewish Archive*, pp. 172–73.

27. See Goitein, *Letters*, pp. 209–12. The narrative here is based on my own translation of the letter, but Goitein's decipherment was crucial.

28. We gather that indigo, used as a dye, was not then in demand in Cairo. On the product in general, see J. Balfour-Paul, *Indigo in the Arab World.*

29. The *NJPS* translation renders the word "discourse" (*siyaḥ*) as "ranting," because the young man in the verse, a messenger of the prophet Elisha, is described there as mad. David means: "You know his character."

30. See Goitein, *Med. Soc.*, I, 161, on female brokers. The sexual mores of the time in both the Islamic environment and in Jewish society required that wives stay at home. They were restrained from entering public space and from having any contact with men other than their husbands. However, we find in Genizah documents that women were more mobile and more independent than legal norms prescribed. It is hard to estimate the num-

ber of female businesswomen, but they existed, especially among unmarried women, including widows.

31. The house of a Sitt Ghazal, obviously a wealthy woman, is mentioned often in records dating from 1181–83. It was situated near the Gate of the Well of the Synagogue of the Palestinians (the Ben Ezra Synagogue); see Goitein, *Med. Soc.*, II, 431. Sitt, meaning "mistress" or "female ruler," is the colloquial form of *sayyidat*, originally an honorary title that became part of a personal name, as here; *Med. Soc.*, III, 316.

32. Bu is short for Abu, common for men from North Africa (and still gives us names such as Boumediene). The Dahlak islands are a group of some one hundred and twenty-five small islands adjacent to the west coast of the Red Sea. Dahlak was then the main southern port of the western border of the Red Sea about five hundred miles south of 'Aydhab and three hundred and fifty miles north of Aden.

33. A *jalba* (pl. *jilab*) is a large barge used on the Red Sea and the Gulf of Aden. The word is from Port-Span *gelba/gelva*, with another form, *gallevat*, giving Eng "jolly-boat." See H. Kindermann, *"Schiff" im Arabischen*, pp. 19–20. See also G. R. Tibbetts, *Arab Navigation*, pp. 47, 264; C. E. Bosworth, EI, s.v. "Safîna."

34. David refers to M Ber, ix. 3. We learn from here that in these circumstances Moses would offer prayers of entreaty or supplication. In his legal compendium (MT Prayer, i, 2; Blessings, i, 3), he classified prayer as praise, supplication, and thanksgiving, and in *The Guide of the Perplexed*, I, 59 and III, 51, he distinctly favored prayers of praise and thanksgiving over entreaty. See Ehud Benor, *Worship of the Heart*, pp. 96–98 and 114–15.

35. To say that a letter is written in haste was a literary topos to excuse brevity and stylistic shortcomings, but in this case it also happened to be true.

36. The Muslim calendar is lunar (ca. 354 days), independent of the solar year (ca. 365 days) and the seasons, so that a lunar year retreats about eleven days every solar year, with the months rotating throughout the year and Ramadan falling at a different time each year.

37. In 4929 A.M. (1168/69 C.E.) 22 Iyyar was on 21 Sha'ban 564 A.H. (= May 20, 1169); in 4930 A.M. (1169/70 C.E.) it was on 20 Sha'ban 565 A.H. (= May 9, 1170); in 4931 (1170/71) it was on 21 Sha'ban 566 (April 29, 1171). From 1172 and for the next three decades the Muslim month of Ramadan preceded the Jewish month of Iyyar. See also Goitein, *Letters*, p. 208.

38. M. A. Friedman, "Notes by a Disciple," pp. 540–41, n. 84. Shailat, *Letters*, pp. 72–73, 198, claims that David returned from that trip and died during a second voyage to India in 1176–77.

39. See, all by Goitein, "From the Mediterranean to India: Documents on the Trade to India, South Arabia and East Africa from the Eleventh and Twelfth Centuries"; "Letters and Documents on the India Trade in Medieval Times"; *Letters of Medieval Jewish Traders*; and *Mediterranean Society*.

40. See L. Casson, *Ships and Seamanship in the Ancient World*, pp. 9–10; Hourani, *Arab Seafaring*, pp. 87–98, and additional notes by John Carswell, pp. 151–52; C. E. Bosworth, EI, s.v. "Safîna." C. Meyer, *Glass from Quseir al-Qadim*, pp. 111–12, thinks that sewn vessels were used for the most part but not always. Vergil describes Aeneas crossing the Styx in a sewn skiff (*cumba sutilis*), *Aeneid*, VI, 413, and St. Jerome compares chastity to a fragile sewn boat (*fragilem et sutilemm ratem*) (*Epistles*, 128), cited by Casson, p. 9, n. 25. Carswell, in Hourani, *Arab Seafaring*, p. 151, notes that the Pharaonic "Cheops Ship" was a sewn vessel.

41. Ibn Jubayr, *Travels*, trans. Broadhurst, p. 65.

42. Hourani, *Arab Seafaring*, p. 90; Chaudhuri, *Trade and Civilisation in the Indian Ocean*, pp. 148–50.

43. See Goitein and Friedman, *India Traders*, Introductory Remarks to ch. 3, pp. 157–64.

44. See W. Daum, "From Aden to India and Cairo: Jewish World Trade in the Eleventh and Twelfth Centuries"; R. B. Serjeant, "Early Islamic and Mediaeval Trade and Commerce in the Yemen"; and R. E. Margariti, *Aden and the Indian Ocean Trade*.

45. Chaudhuri, *Trade and Civilisation in the Indian Ocean*, p. 107.

46. *Letters*, ed. Shailat, pp. 228–30. Only one of the extant manuscripts gives the date of the letter, which Shailat reads as Shevat 1496 s.e. (= January–February 1185), the same as the reading given by A. Freimann, *Alummah*, Additions and Corrections, p. 157, which is corroborated by M. A. Friedman. As Maimonides wrote that he received the evil tidings eight years previously, this would have been in 1177.

47. The epithet *he-hakham ha-mevin* appears as a requirement for studying mystical works in the Talmud; see T Hag (ed. Lieberman), ii, 1 and B Hag 11b, etc.

48. Cf. Deut 31:17 and Ps 71:20.

49. The accusations may have pertained to Maimonides' conversion to Islam in Fez and his reverting to Judaism in Egypt, something that came up again later in his life when Abu 'l-'Arab Ibn Mu'isha came to Egypt.

50. Cf. 2 Sam 19:8.

51. Maimonides used verses from Scripture to describe his symptoms, taking three of the afflictions from the curses of the Mosaic covenant upon those who do not obey (Deut 28:15–68). In MT Acquisition and Gifts, viii, 2, he used the expression "prostrate in bed" (*nofel 'al ha-mittah*) in the sense of "dangerously ill" (*shekhiv mera'*). Severe inflammation (*shehin ra'*) (Deut 28:35 and Job 2:7) can also mean "grievous boils" (NRSV); Alter has "evil burning rash," but *ra'* does not mean "evil" here, and *shehin* may have been worse than a rash. Syriac *shuhana* means "ulcer," "boil." In Job *shehin* is a skin disease. See Koehler, Baumgartner, and Richardson, *Lexicon*, s.v. *shehin*. The sixth plague visited on the Egyptians (Ex 9:8–11) as punishment was *shehin*, meaning "boils" or "blisters." *Shehin* was the punishment of a student of Rabbi [Judah ha-Nasi], who endeavored to explain the Account of the Chariot; J Hag, ii, 1 (77a); Preuss, *Biblical and talmudic Medicine*, p. 343. According to M Nega'im, ix, 1, *shehin* is a general term for different kinds of skin lesions. Fever (*daleqet*) (Deut 28:22) is from a root meaning "burn." In J Ter, viii, 3 (45c), *daleqet* is most likely a fever; see Preuss, p. 160. A fever was not regarded as a symptom, rather as an illness. *Timhon levav* is rendered in *NJPS* as "dismay." NRSV has "confusion of the mind" and NJB has "distraction of the mind." Alter, being literal, has "confounding of the heart," but the heart was the seat of the mind.

52. Cf. Ex 2:22, 18:3, where the biblical Moses says, "I have been a stranger in a foreign land," meaning Egypt. A foreign land, as opposed to eternal life, also suggests life in this world, where one's soul is estranged from its proper home.

53. Cf. Hos 11:8.

54. The biblical Jacob says this upon learning that Joseph had been torn by a savage beast.

55. The term is *harsha'ah*, which occurs often in the Talmud; see, e.g., B Shev 31a. And see MT Ethical Qualities, v, 13, where Moses ben Maimon disapproves of scholars acting as sureties or trusties or accepting power of attorney. He discusses the function in MT Agents and Partners, iii.

56. Cf. 2 Samuel 23:5.

57. Cf. Jon 4:9.

58. See, for instance, B Ber 10b, 63b on being hospitable to scholars.

59. See Isa 3:3; lit. "expert enchanter."

60. See Goitein, *Med. Soc.,* V, 236.

61. See Ibid., V, 249.

62. *Guide*, I, 54 (p. 123); II, 28 (p. 336); III, 12 (p. 448); and I, 5 (p. 29). See Pines, "Translator's Introduction," p. lxi, n. 8.

63. S. Freud, *Mourning and Melancholia (Trauer und Melancholie)*. There is no need to accept Freud's topography of the mind to appreciate this work. For contemporary use of the model, see Julia Kristeva's *Black Sun: Depression and Melancholia*, and Jonathan Lear's *Love and Its Place in Nature*, pp. 158ff.

64. We find David's widow listed as a recipient of public charity. See Ms. T-S K 15.30; Goitein, *Med. Soc.*, II, 448. She collected "a quarter and an eighth of a *wayba* [of grain]," the equivalent of a gallon and a half gallon (Goitein, *Med. Soc.*, II, 445).

65. Goitein, *Med. Soc.*, V, 116, makes this observation in connection with Maimonides' response to David's drowning. He first thought that the severity was due to Moses' sensitivity, but later concluded that he was "a child of his time and society." It was likely both.

66. L. Febvre, *A New Kind of History and Other Essays*, pp. 8–9; Kraemer, *Humanism in the Renaissance of Islam*, pp. 21–22.

67. See A. J. Heschel, *Maimonides*, p. 138; Yellin and Abrahams, *Maimonides*, p. 48 ("abandoned commerce in favor of medicine"); S. Zeitlin, *Maimonides*, p. 53; E. Lieber, "Maimonides the Medical Humanist," p. 45, citing F. Rosner, "Moses Maimonides the Physician," p. 4.

CHAPTER 15

1. Yahya son of Zachariah (Zikri) is the Arabic name of John (Yahya < Johanan) the Baptist; see Qur'an (five times), Surahs 3:39, 6:85, 19:7, 12, 21:90. What is the meaning of Zuta's taking the sobriquet Sar Shalom, a name given to Jesus? I wonder whether Zuta's claim to be the precursor of the Messiah, or the Messiah himself, was related to these names of his. *The Scroll of Zuta the Wicked* (see below) says that Maimonides removed an image from the synagogue and purified it after overcoming Zuta. Was this image related to Christianity?

2. The Book of Esther is read in synagogues on Purim from a scroll called *Megillat Esther* (*The Scroll of Esther*).

3. Cf. Ben-Sasson's somewhat different reconstruction, "Maimonides in Egypt," pp. 6–19.

4. Mann, *The Jews in Egypt and in Palestine*, I, 235.

5. Neubauer, "Egyptian Fragments," p. 542, says that Maimonides *crushed* Zuta, but this sounds extreme. At this point, a section of the *Scroll* may be missing, where the outcome of Maimonides' intervention is related; see D. Kaufmann, "The Egyptian Sutta-Megilla," p. 172.

6. Friedman, "Maimonides, Zuta and the Muqaddamin," p. 7, stresses Maimonides' role in the bans, singling out in particular his activity in the ban of al-Mahalla (see below, ch. 16, pp. 290–91).

7. See S. M. Stern, "The Succession to the Fatimid Imam al-Āmir," p. 211, on Fatimid pretenders under the Ayyubids.

8. Dirgham, who became vizier, was then chief chamberlain.

9. Neubauer, "Egyptian Fragments," p. 542

10. On the judges Elazar ha-Kohen and Ephraim and their controversy, see the discussion in Miriam Frenkel, *The Jewish Community of Alexandria*, I, 148–57.

11. Frenkel, *Jewish Community*, Appendix, no. 30, pp. 99–102/103–9, ms. T-S 16.272. Goitein, *Med. Soc.*, II, 62 and 535, n. 118, dates the letter to around 1180. Its writer refers to Ephraim in the first person.

12. The word for rabble is Ar *safāsuf*, from Heb *asafsuf*. The *ansar* in the early days of Islam were the Medinan "Helpers" of Muhammad, who joined the Muhajirun, "the Emigrants," who made the hijra with him from Mecca to Medinah. In another letter, we find Alexandrian cobblers rebelling against authority; Goitein, *Med. Soc.*, II, 62–63.

13. Abu 'l-Tahir Ibn 'Awf (d. 1184/85) was a famous jurist in Alexandria, called the Shaykh of Alexandria. He was one of the scholars who taught Saladin and later instructed his son al-Afdal. In 1138, the vizier Ridwan ibn al-Walakhshi (r. 1136–38) established a madrasa in Alexandria for teaching the Maliki school of jurisprudence, and appointed Ibn 'Awf as its director. He owned a large house in Alexandria in which a group of jurists convened. When Shirkuh wrote to Alexandria in 562 (1166/67), calling for help against the Crusaders and Shawar, they joined him, sending weapons with a nephew of Ibn 'Awf. Al-

exandria was a center of Sunni resistance during the Fatimid period, dominated by the Maliki school. See Ayman al-Sayyid, *al-Dawla al-Fatimiyya*, p. 387, and Frenkel, *The Jewish Community of Alexandria*, Appendix, p. 108, note to recto, line 30.

14. Frenkel, op. cit., Appendix, p. 108, note to recto, line 30, says that he is apparently the Alexandrian jurist Abu 'l-Qasim ibn Mahluf al-Maghribi (d. 1181). An Abu 'l-Qasim al-Nisaburi, a *hadith* scholar who taught Saladin, is mentioned by Ibraham ibn Muhammad Ibn Duqmaq (d. 1407), *Intisar li-wasitat 'iqd al-amsar*, p. 17, n. 5 and by Ahmad ibn 'Ali al-Maqrizi (1364-1442), *al-Suluk li-ma'rifat duwal al-muluk*, I, 140.

15. Haggai Ben-Shammai, "Eschatological Messages," showed that both *gaon* and *iqtidar* have the meaning of "pride," "arrogance," "pretense," and "ascribing power to one-self" in Arabic translations of Scripture by Se'adyah Gaon and others. There is a reference to Zuta below (verso, line 21), said to be called al-Muqtadir, which may have been a title that his followers bestowed upon him having a messianic significance. As he also claimed to be head of an academy, he was called Gaon. Whereas the Zuta Scroll said that he claimed to be a precursor of the Messiah, here we find that Zuta claimed to be the Messiah himself. See also Friedman, "Maimonides, Zuta and the Muqaddamin," p. 512.

16. Immolation was a punishment in Islamic law used against apostates after they were decapitated by the sword; see J. L. Kraemer, "Apostates, Rebels and Brigands," pp. 44–45. The alleged apostasy of Zuta and his followers was accompanied by rebellion against the state, for which the punishment was impaling; see ibid., pp. 67–68.

17. Verso, line 14. This is my reading on the basis of the document and an excellent photograph. Frenkel follows Goitein's typed transcription of the document (usually done by an advanced graduate student). However, his handwritten copy, done in the Cambridge library on August 17, 1976, reads correctly (in my view), "R' Menasheh."

18. For the jurist Ibn Za'farani, see al-Maqrizi, *Itti'az al-hunafa' bi-akhbar al-a'immah al-Fatimiyyin al-khulafa'*, III, 163.

19. For his correspondence with Maimonides, see below, ch. 16, pp. 280–83.

20. *Letters*, ed. Shailat, pp. 434, 436–54.

21. Menahem Ben-Sasson, "Maimonides in Egypt," has argued for this interpretation, citing (p. 23, notes 37 and 38) earlier scholars who identified Zuta with Sar Shalom, such as Samuel A. Poznanski, David Kaufmann, and Simon Eppenstein. Jacob Mann found it absurd that Zuta could be the Gaon Sar Shalom, who was widely accepted by Jewish communities according to his correspondence; see *The Jews in Egypt and in Palestine*, I, 234–45; *Texts and Studies*, I, 416–17. See also Goitein, *Med. Soc.*, II, 32–33; "Moses Maimonides, Man of Action," p. 166, cited by Ben-Sasson. Friedman supports Ben-Sasson in "Maimonides, Zuta and the Muqaddamin," pp. 490–91.

22. Abraham ben Moses Maimonides, *Kifayat al-'abidin* (*The Sufficiency of Worshipers*), ed. Nissim Dana, p. 180; M. Ben-Sasson, "Maimonides in Egypt," p. 13; Friedman, "Maimonides, Zuta and the Muqaddamin," p. 2.

23. The title *sar ha-sarim* for "chief of chiefs" occurs in Dan 8:25.

24. See *Qoves*, ed. Lichtenberg, II, 36d.

25. S. Sela, "Queries on Astrology Sent from Southern France to Maimonides," p. 96.

CHAPTER 16

1. Erwin Graef, "Religiöse und rechtliche Vorstellung über Kriegsgefangenen in Islam und Christentum." The Arabic terms used for redemption, *fida'* (related to Heb *pidyon*) and *iftikak*, are used in Jewish documents of the period.

2. *Travels*, trans. Broadhurst, pp. 322–23. See Cl. Cahen, "Ibn Jubayr et les Maghrébins de Syrie."

3. J. Brodman, "Ransoming Captives in Crusader Spain: The Order of Merced on the Christian-Islamic Frontier"; idem, *Ransoming Captives in Crusader Spain*; and see Y.

Friedman, "Women in Captivity and Their Ransom During the Crusader Period," and her "The Ransom of Captives in the Latin Kingdom of Jerusalem." Friedman cites C. Osiek, "The Ransom of Captives: Evolution of a Tradition" (on p. 179, n. 7).

4. Mann, *The Jews in Egypt and in Palestine*, I, 87–94; Goitein, *Med. Soc.*, II, 137; Bareket, *The Jewish Leadership in Fustat*, p. 71.

5. A. Munk, "A New Responsum of Moses ben Maimon," pp. 329–31, reprinted in Blau, *Responsa*, IV, 41.

6. MT Gifts to the Poor, viii, 10.

7. See B BB 8b. In saying that there is no commandment more meritorious, the Talmud cites Jer 15:2. It is told of Rabbi Phinehas ben Jair that he went to ransom captives, and because he was fulfilling this duty, a river parted to enable him to cross (B Hul 7a; J Dem 1, 3).

8. Notice that he cited seven biblical verses.

9. See Goitein, *Palestinian Jewry*, pp. 312ff.; *Letters*, ed. Shailat, pp. 60ff.; Friedman, "New Sources from the Genizah on the Crusader Period." The receipt dated July 24 to August 3, 1170 is preserved in T-S NS Box 309.12v; see Goitein, op. cit., pp. 316–18; idem, "Moses Maimonides, Man of Action," p. 160. The verso was reedited in *Letters*, ed. Shailat, pp. 70–71.

10. Ms. T-S NS 309.12 is dated Elul 1481 s.e. (began August 14, 1170). Ms. ENA 2896 has a date that is, however, unclear. Another ransoming incident in 4940 a.m. (1179/80) is mentioned in *Responsa*, no. 452, pp. 733–34.

11. ENA 2896 and T-S 16.9. However, if Ms. ENA 2896 is from a later period, then the occasion may not have been the fall of Bilbays. Fund-raising campaigns sometimes lasted for years, so Bilbays cannot be excluded even by a later date.

12. Mevorakh's documents are attested for the years 1150–81. He was responsible for writing more than a hundred Genizah documents; see Goitein, "Moses Maimonides, Man of Action," p. 156; *Med. Soc.*, II, 514, sect. 22. He wrote T-S J 2.78, a document on Maimonides' appointment as Head of the Jews, and also a letter of congratulations on his wedding.

13. Ms. T-S 16.9, edited by Goitein in *Palestinian Jewry*, pp. 314–16; see also Goitein, "Moses Maimonides, Man of Action," pp. 158–59, for a partial English translation. It was reedited in *Letters*, ed. Shailat, pp. 66–68. The document is large, measuring 31 by 22 cm. Its beginning and end are lacking. It is in the writing of Mevorakh ben Nathan. Between the lines of the circular there is a poem written once the circular was disposable.

14. The word is *misrayim*. Arabic *misr* was usually Fustat, but here *misrayim* is probably both Cairo and Fustat; Goitein, *Palestinian Jewry*, p. 315, n. 12. The Hebrew is in rhymed prose. Goitein (n. 14) connects the bad times with the burning and pillaging of Fustat.

15. Poor people, in petitions for communal aid, often described themselves as *munqati'un*, meaning without family, relatives, or friends—"cut off" and without support.

16. Either the signatures of the captors or the released captives—the text is unclear— who would promise to repay what they could. The captives had to contribute according to their means, and Maimonides wanted to assure that they acknowledged this; see Goitein, *Palestinian Jewry*, p. 315, n. 16; idem, "Moses Maimonides, Man of Action," p. 158, n. 14. Shailat thinks that the judges Hiyya and Ephraim are meant, who should acknowledge how much was paid.

17. Here he is simply called Aaron. Aaron ha-Levi ben Jacob ha-Melammed is presumably the same who appears as a *parnas* (welfare official) in other appeals, such as Mss T-S NS 309.12 and ENA 2896. He later signed a document of manumission in Cairo (T-S NS J 484).

18. Ms. ENA 2896. See R. Margulies, "Zwei autographische Urkunden von Moses und Abraham Maimuni," pp. 8–13, an edition and translation (German) with a facsimile. This document was loaned to Margulies by Solomon Schechter.

19. *Palestinian Jewry*, pp. 312–13. Goitein also used the facsimile published by Norman Bentwich in his biography of Solomon Schechter (*Solomon Schechter: A Biography*, opposite

p. 143). He published a translation into English in "Moses Maimonides, Man of Action," pp. 156–57. See also the brief excerpt by Mann, *The Jews in Egypt and in Palestine*, II, 316–17.

20. See M. A. Friedman, "New Sources from the Genizah on the Crusader Period," p. 75. Friedman discusses the dating (pp. 72–75) and offers improved readings and an excellent facsimile reproduction (p. 73). See also *Letters*, ed. Shailat, p. 64 text/p. 65 translation, with poor-quality facsimile on p. 63. There is a fine facsimile in Sassoon, *Moses b. Maimon Commentarius in Mischnam*, I, XXII. One must not rely on facsimiles for readings. In this instance, the space after the date is smudged and what is a particle of ink looks like a dark spot.

21. Margulies read Tammuz תפד = 1484 s.e. = 1173 c.e. Bentwich took the date to be 1172 c.e. Goitein has Tammuz פד or [1]480, which began June 27, 1169. There is a presumption in favor of Margulies' dating of 1484 s.e. (1173 c.e.), as he saw the document in ca. 1900, and a final ד may have been more obvious then. Friedman also read 1484 s.e. = 1173, and this is what I discerned. Those who do not see the remnant of a third letter have not worked from the manuscript, but from unreliable reproductions.

22. See Friedman, "New Sources," p. 75, n. 39, for corrections of Goitein's edition. Some words seen by Goitein are no longer visible. The reading of this line is tentative in places.

23. A *firnas* (Ar) or *parnas* (Heb) by the name of Rabbi Halfon appears in a similar capacity in T-S NS 309.12.

24. Ar *taghtanimu*. The word has the basic sense of "take war booty," "capture."

25. Goitein, *Med. Soc.*, V, 366–72. See above in chapter 4.

26. *Responsa*, no. 449, pp. 729–32; IV, 26; see Goitein, *Med. Soc.*, V, 366–67, with a translation of this passage that is actually a loose paraphrase.

27. Maimonides cites B Gittin 61a, where it is said: "Our Rabbis have taught: 'We support the poor of the gentiles [*goyim*] along with the poor of [the people of] Israel, and visit the sick of the gentiles along with the sick of [the people of] Israel, and bury the poor of the gentiles along with the dead of Israel, in the interests of peace.'" His decision was moderate and tolerant, yet his citation of this talmudic passage pertaining to gentiles reveals his attitude toward the Karaites.

28. Goitein, *Med. Soc.*, V, 22–23. Often someone would dedicate property as a pious foundation (*qodesh* or *heqdesh*), usually for synagogues or the poor, to avoid inheritance taxes by making it communal property and having one's relatives administer it. It was administered by a supervisor appointed by the court, who had to be religious, trustworthy, and experienced in negotiating transactions. See MT Gifts to the Poor, ix, 1; *Responsa*, no. 54, pp. 89–90. The Islamic *waqf* is similar in that a person performs a pious act by declaring property unalienable and appoints public recipients of its yields, intended as charity for the poor, for the jihad, and for travelers.

29. See Kraemer, "A Jewish Cult of the Saints in Fāṭimid Egypt."

30. Al-Maqrizi, *al-Khitat*, II, 465 (Gottheil, "An Eleventh-Century Document," p. 503). See also Yaqut, *al-Mushtaraḳ*, p. 182.

31. Yosef Sambari, *Sefer Divrei Yosef*, ed. Shimon Shtober, pp. 158–59.

32. T-S 20.117r. See Reif, *Bibliography*, p. 267.

33. The physical segregation did not prevent men from meeting women in the synagogue courtyard. In a touching letter (Ms. T-S 8 J 17.3rv) from a certain Bu 'l-Faraj to Umm Joseph, he says that he was in distress from the day that she met him in the synagogue and cannot stop thinking about her. The letter was written to the famous judge Rabbi Elijah ben Zechariah, who would presumably read the letter to her. Goitein refers to another aspect of the letter in *Med. Soc.*, II, 144.

34. See MT Resting on Festivals, vi, 19–21. And cf. MT Palm Branch, viii, 12–15, on celebrating the festival of Tabernacles. The court should appoint officers on festival days to patrol and inspect parks, orchards, and riverbanks, to ensure that men and women do not

gather there to eat and drink together and be led into immorality, nor to rejoice freely inside their houses, overindulging in wine, and be led into immorality there either.

35. The document was written by Mevorakh ben Nathan, Maimonides' confidant and secretary. It is Ms. T-S 10 J 32.12, partly edited by S. D. Goitein, "New Documents," pp. 711, and 718–19 (Appendix II) (on p. 711 folio 12 is omitted from the classmark, and *tusamma* is read mistakenly for *tasmah*; see corrections and notes in Goitein, *Tarbiz,* 24 (1955), p. 468; and see Goitein, *Med. Soc.,* II, 485, App. C, sec. 36; V, 22–23, and 510, n. 64. See also N. Golb, "The Topography of the Jews of Medieval Egypt," *JNES* 24, p. 255; *JNES* 33, p. 125; Strauss-Ashtor, *History of the Jews,* I, 245–46; II, 385. See Reif, *Bibliography,* p. 146.

36. Goitein, *Med. Soc.,* V, 22–23.

37. Arabic Box 54.66, May 1235. On Hananel, see Goitein, *Letters,* p. 57, and "Chief Justice Hananel ben Samuel." See Reif, *Bibliography,* p. 197; and P. B. Fenton, "A Re-Discovered Description of Maimonides by a Contemporary."

38. Gil, *Pious Foundations,* pars. 55–57.

39. T-S 8 J 15.17. The letter was published by Goitein, in "A Letter to Moses b. Maimon Concerning Pious Foundations," and then by Gil, *Documents,* no. 94, pp. 363–66. The document was written in ca. 1171. See also Goitein, *Med. Soc.,* II, 421.

40. T-S NS J 193; and see on Meir ben Hillel, Frenkel, *The Jewish Community of Alexandria,* I, 139–47.

41. See Goitein, "A New Autograph by Maimonides and a Letter to Him from His Sister Miriam"; Gil, *Documents,* pp. 321–22; *Letters,* ed. Shailat, pp. 242–45 (with facsimile).

42. Goitein, 188, n. 14, takes *watiq* to be an abbreviation for *talmid watiq,* noting that it is not the Arabic word *wathiq* ("trustworthy"). See also Friedman, "New Fragments from the Genizah of Moses ben Maimon's *Responsa,*" p. 452, n. 35. Goitein mentions that a man named Watiq received a salary from the community of Fustat of 16 dirhams per month in Elul, Tishre, and Marḥeshvan, 1181 (Ms. Oxford, Heb. f 56, f. 43 [2821, 16]), and 10 dirhams per month for Nisan in 1182 (T-S 8 J 11, f. 7).

43. T-S 10 J 4, f. 11v. See Assaf, *Meqorot,* pp. 158–59; Gil, *Documents,* no. 75, pp. 319–21.

44. See Kraemer, "A Jewish Cult of the Saints."

45. Gil, *Documents,* 322, n. 2, takes the gentilic to be from al-Sharah (in what is nowadays Jordan). The man was obviously a Muslim.

46. Described by Goitein in "A Jewish Addict to Sufism," pp. 291–304.

47. Ms. D[avid]K[aufmann] XXI (A41), ed. and trans. M. Gil, *Documents,* no. 77, p. 323–24. See also Gil, Introduction, 104 (par. 136). And see Goitein, *Med. Soc.,* II, Appendix A, 41 (pp. 419–20). Gil estimates the date of the letter at around 1185, since repairs of the caravanserai of the pious foundation are noted in another document dated in 1183/84. See Bodl. Ms. Heb. f 56.59–61, published by Gil, *Documents,* no. 89, 350ff.

48. The word for caravanserai is *funduq,* a hostel for sojourners and resort for the indigent, from Grk *pandocheion* (Goitein, *Med. Soc.,* IV, 29–30). Olivia Remie Constable's *Housing the Strangers in the Mediterranean World* treats the institutions of *funduq, pandocheion,* and *fondaco.* The first references to *pandocheion* are from the Athenian area in the fifth century B.C.E. It continued as Arabic *funduq* and Italian *fondaco* throughout the Mediterranean area for two millennia. The institutions served "not only as hostelries, but also as commercial depots, warehouses, emporia, tax-stations, offices, taverns, prisons and brothels." Today, *funduq* is used for "hotel" in Arabic and *fondaco* is "warehouse" in Italian; see Constable, Introduction, p. 2. In Mishnaic Hebrew the form is *pundaq* (Aramaic *pundeqa*).

49. The poll tax was onerous, and failure to deliver led to arrest. By saying there is no harm, Moses ben Maimon and his academy may have wished to deflect criticism that direct payment was being made to a scholar. See Gil, *Documents,* Introduction, p. 104 (par. 136). Gil cites Goitein *Med. Soc.,* II, App. A, sec. 41, to the effect that the document was unsigned, and suggests the existence of differences of opinion among the members of the *majlis,* including perhaps even an objection by Maimonides himself. However, if the document is a draft, the absence of signatures may not be significant.

50. See Frenkel, *The Jewish Community of Alexandria*, I, 157–64. His written documents are preserved for the years 1195 to 1212.

51. Maimonides states that Jewish courts invoked the death penalty in eleventh- and twelfth-century Spain; see CM Hul, i.

52. In Andalusia and the Maghrib the Islamic Maliki school of law prevailed, which emphasized the force of customary law (*'adah*).

53. See Frenkel, *The Jewish Community of Alexandria*, I, 165–71. Anatoli's written documents are preserved for the years 1199 to 1229.

54. Elon, *Jewish Law*, II, 681–82.

55. The scriptural basis for the authority of rabbinic councils is Deut 17: 11 or 32: 7; see B Shab 23a; MT Rebels, i, 1–2. See E.A. Urbach, *The Halakha, Its Sources and Development*, pp. 11–25 ; Goitein, *Med. Soc.*, II, 65–66.

56. On the edict of Rabbenu Gershom, see Elon, *Jewish Law*, II, 783–86; and see Avraham Grossman, *Pious and Rebellious*, pp. 70–78. The enactment came to be called "the ban [*herem*] of Rabbenu Gershom." A second enactment imposed a ban on a husband who divorced his wife against her will.

57. Elon, *Jewish Law*, II, pp. 682–83. p. 683, n. 16; see pp. 715–27 in regard to majority and minority in communal enactments, and pp. 762–63 as to the rule that no legislation should be enacted unless the majority of the public can conform to it. See also Y. Baer, "The Foundations and the Origins of the Organization of the Jewish Community in the Middle Ages," p. 7, n. 18.

58. Elon, *Jewish Law*, II, 715; Alfasi, *Responsa*, no. 13.

59. Elon, ibid., II, p. 755, 758–59.

60. Friedman, "Maimonides as Codifier," p. 228.

61. Friedman, "Maimonides, Zuta and the Muqaddamin," stresses the importance of enactments for Maimonides' leadership and for his struggle against Zuta.

62. See M. A. Friedman, "R. Yeḥiel b. Elyakim's Responsum," where the issue of *re-shut* and this responsum are discussed.

63. SifreDeut, xcvi; B Yev 13b, 14a; MT Idolatry, xii, 14.

64. *Responsa*, no. 242, pp. 434–44, on p. 444.; *Letters*, ed. Shailat, pp. 175–85.

65. Avraham Grossman, *Pious and Rebellious*, pp. 109–10.

66. The name of the father is a blank space in Ms. S. Even early scribes could not read it. In *Responsa*, no. 2, p. 2, an Abraham the *haver* is mentioned but without additional information.

67. *Responsa*, no. 234, pp. 426–28; Friedman, "Maimonides as Codifier," p. 230.

68. *Responsa*, no. 348, p. 624–25. Sambari, *Sefer divre Yosef*, ed. Shtober, p. 219; Abraham ben Moses, *Responsa*, 106, pp. 183, 189. See Eppenstein, *Moses ben Maimon*, p. 56; Friedman, *Polygyny*, p. 227. Friedman, "Maimonides as Codifier," p. 231–32, esp. n. 33. On the date, see S. D. Goitein, "A New Autograph by Maimonides and a Letter to Him from His Sister Miriam," p. 184, n. 2. And see *Med. Soc.*, II, 74.

69. Friedman: "Maimonides as Codifier," p. 231–32, 234; see Abraham Maimonides, *Responsa*, no. 106, pp. 182–83, 189.

70. *Responsa*, no. 347, p. 624. Friedman, "Maimonides as Codifier," p. 233. See Sambari, *Sefer divre Yosef*, ed. Shtober, p. 220, who says that the rabbis who signed the previous enactment also signed this, which makes sense, as an enactment was by consensus. The text we have omits their names.

71. See MT Forbidden Intercourse, xxi, 29. A man should not marry a woman in one city and another woman in another city.

72. Marriage xiv, 2; See *Responsa* of the Geonim, *Sha'are sedeq*, iii, 1, 3; and Alfasi, *Responsa*, no. 120, on the ancient Spanish custom concerning this.

73. B Yev 37b, Yoma 18b.

74. See Friedman, "Maimonides as Codifer," p. 234.

75. A marriage could only end and the woman become free by a bill of divorce or reli-

able evidence that the husband had died. If he abandoned her or was absent, and she could not prove that he died, she could not remarry. The reason Jewish law stipulated that the woman could not remarry was to avoid a situation in which she took another husband and then the first came back, as in Natalie Davis, *The Return of Martin Guerre*.

76. Goitein, *Med. Soc.*, III, 190, 466, n. 143.

77. For gentile courts, see *Responsa*, no. 408, pp. 685–86; and Sambari, *Sefer divre Yosef*, ed. Shtober, p. 220.

78. MT Marriage, xiv, 3.

79. B Yev 65a.

80. Friedman, "Maimonides as Codifier," p. 234.

81. *Responsa*, no. 373, pp. 650–55.

82. *Responsa*, no. 270, p. 516. From Genizah, T-S 16.135. Published by S. Assaf, "A Question and Answers by Maimonides," in *Melilah*, 3–4 (1950), pp. 224–29 with a translation by E. Strauss (-Ashtor) and corrections by D. H. Baneth. See additional text in *Responsa*, vol. IV, 8–10. The beginning of the enactment was discovered by Goitein, in T-S 13 J 25.16.

83. See Goitein and Friedman, *India Traders*, Introduction to section 1, ch. 2 on Abraham Ben Yiju and his family, pp. 52–89; Goitein, *Med. Soc.*, III, 43; IV, 382, 429; V, 562; *Responsa*, pp. 516–18, 624, 655; Friedman, *Polygyny*, 26 and n. 77; Friedman and Goitein, "Ben Yijū," pp. 285ff; and Kraemer, "Women Speak for Themselves," p. 197.

84. Text: *be-lev shalem* (Isa 38:3, etc.) *we-da'ata shelemata*, a tautological repetition of the Hebrew in Aramaic. The idiom in pure Aramaic is found twice in Hayya Gaon, *Book of Legal Documents (Sefer shetarot)*, Appendix 4.

85. See Deut 29:11; MT Oaths, ii, 4.

86. Actually written Rayyis.

87. MT Evidence, x, 1. And see Oaths, i, 1–2, and many other places.

88. On the judge Manasseh ben Joseph, see Goitein, *Med. Soc.*, Index, p. 67. Manasseh acted as judge from as early as 1164 and "retired" in 1219; Goitein, *Med. Soc.*, II, 514, no. 27. Samuel ben Se'adyah and Manasseh ben Joseph signed by their first names in a case of inheritance in 1182 (Goitein, *Med. Soc.*, III, 278, and 489 n. 8), and they signed a betrothal document in September 1184; see Goitein, *Med. Soc.*, III, 92 and n. 82 on p. 445.

89. M. Ben-Sasson, "Maimonides in Egypt," p. 14, with references to Goitein and others who identified Abu Zikri of the al-Mahalla controversy with Zuta.

90. See Ms. Bodl. Heb. b. 13 (2834, 22), ff. 13–14; Mann, *The Jews in Egypt and in Palestine*, I, 222, n. 2; Fleischer, *Eretz-Israel Prayer and Prayer Rituals as Portrayed in the Geniza Documents*.

91. MT Prayer and the Priestly Blessing, xiii, 1-2.

92. Mann, *Texts and Studies*, I, 416ff.; Goitein, *Med. Soc.*, II, 52ff.

CHAPTER 17

1. See S. B. Freehof, *A Treasury of Responsa*, for examples of this genre; and see Elon, *Jewish Law*, IV, Subject Index, pp. 2207–8.

2. K. Pennington, "Spirit of Legal History."

3. The queriers collected answers in bundles, and students copied and published them. See *Qobes Teshuvot ha-Rambam we-Iggerotaw*, ed. A. Lichtenberg, II, 16a.

4. On this and the following, see Elon, *Jewish Law*, III, 1460–61.

5. *Responsa*, no. 14, pp. 20–21. The query was about 275 words long, asking whether the sabbatical year, when debts were canceled, also cancels a debt based on the marriage contract, to which Maimonides responded, "It cancels" in one word and then signed "Moses" for "Moses signed." He had obviously lost his patience. See also Elon, *Jewish Law*, III, 1477, n. 80. To a question of sixty-seven words on the liability of a ritual slaughterer (*shohet*) for damages when he caused an animal to be unfit for eating, he replied in two words ("He

is liable to pay"); see *Responsa*, no. 435, p. 714. He replied to a long query of the judge Phineas ben Meshullam about a decision of the Alexandrian judge, which he sent for Maimonides' perusal, in seven words—"His decision was correct and requires no discussion"; *Responsa*, no. 412, pp. 689-90.

6. M. A. Friedman, "Responsa of Abraham Maimuni," p. 267.

7. *Responsa,* Introduction, III, 17–18.

8. T-S 20.133; ed. Kraemer, "Four Geniza Letters Concerning Maimonides," pp. 394–98. Almost half of the document is torn vertically, making deciphering very tricky.

9. See Goitein, *Med. Soc.*, I, 40, 42, 211, 325; II, 221.

10. See Goitein, *Med. Soc.*, I, 475, n. 2. Goitein notes that we have no responsa addressed to Maimonides from northern France or England. A distant country would normally be Morocco, called *al-Maghrib al-aqsa* = furthest, or most distant West. But in correspondence with the rabbis of southern France, the term "distant country" referred to France and Provence.

11. *Responsa*, no. 3, pp. 3–4.

12. MT Divorce, xi, 18; M Yev, iv, 10; B Yev 41b. Whatever woman was divorced or widowed should not be married or betrothed without waiting ninety days so as to ascertain if she is pregnant. Similarly, in Muslim law there was a period of time, called `idda*, during which a woman who is divorced or widowed or whose marriage was annulled must wait before she may remarry. A divorcee and a woman whose marriage was annulled must wait three months (or menstrual cycles); a widow must wait for four months and ten days. See Qur'an 2:228 and 234 and 65:4.

13. See MT Evidence, x, 1 and ff.

14. See MT Divorce, I, 17, where it is said that if the witnesses, or even one of the two, are ineligible, the bill of divorce is invalid because it is inherently fraudulent.

15. A person about to commit a grave sin must be forewarned to distinguish between the unwitting and presumptuous transgressor, and he must acknowledge the warning before he can be held responsible for his transgression; see B San 8b, 40a-b; MT Sanhedrin, xii, 1–3.

16. See Deut 24:4, where the reason given is that if she marries another man she has been defiled, and returning to her first husband would be abhorrent to the Lord. See also B Yeb 52b; J Yeb xiv, 14 (2a); Maimonides, *Book of Commandments*, fifth principle; neg. 356; MT Divorce, xi, 12; Forbidden Intercourse, xviii, 7.

17. Schacht, *Introduction to Islamic Law*, p. 164. An evasion, *tahlil* ("making lawful"), existed, whereby a man would marry the divorced wife and immediately suspend the marriage following consummation, which was often feigned.

18. *Responsa*, no. 15, p. 22.

19. The deaths of father and son may have been from a disease, such that both died around the same time.

20. The word *qilla* means "scarcity," but like English "dearth" it may also mean famine. The famine is most likely the one that took place in 598 A.H. (1201/1202).

21. The inquirers feared that a Muslim court may be appealed to if the matter is not handled properly by the Jewish court. Goitein, *Med. Soc.*, III, 265, calls attention to a case in which a woman was denounced for divorcing her husband before a Muslim judge. From the time of Roman sovereignty over Judea, Jews sought to preserve judicial autonomy and refrained from appealing to gentile courts, called `arkha'ot* (Grk *archeia*) *shel goyim*.

22. Necessity (*darura*) is a concept in Islamic law, in which it means taking into consideration the force of circumstances. In this case, the authors of the query went over the heads of two courts of law and appealed to Maimonides and his council because (1) the lower courts contradicted one another and (2) the case had bearing on the welfare of the entire community. The first court had decided that the creditors may take the debt from the land, on the assumption that the woman was divorced and the self-ransom was valid; and the second court had ruled that the woman may not remarry, as she had lost two husbands,

implying that she was still married to husband number two when he died, thus suggesting that the self-ransom was invalid.

23. *Maslaha* (or *al-maslaha al-'amma*) is a technical term in Islamic jurisprudence referring to the general welfare of society, which is often taken into consideration in judicial rulings and in juristic works. Jewish law has a similar principle, *mipne tikkun ha-'olam* ("a precaution for the general good") (M. Git, iv, 2–5; Tos. Git, iv (iii); and the concept of *mipne darkhe shalom* ("in the interests of peace"); see M. Git, v, 8–9; T Git, v (iii), 4–5.

24. That is, to her third husband. See MT Forbidden Intercourse, xxi, 31, where it is stated that if a woman married two husbands successively and both died, she is considered a "killer wife" (*qatlanit*) and ought not marry a third; but if she nevertheless does so, she need not be divorced. See Friedman, *Polygyny*, p. 343. And see Joseph Caro's (*Kesef Mishneh*) long comment on the place.

25. See Wael B. Hallaq, *A History of Islamic Legal Theories*, pp. 117, 123–24, 144–47, and esp. 160–61; idem, "'*Iftā*' and *Ijtihād* in Sunnī Legal Theory."

26. B Yev 64b. Amoraim ascribed the deaths to the woman's bad luck or her sexuality, which would endanger future husbands. See the discussion in Grossman, *Pious and Rebellious*, pp. 262–72, on "the murderous wife."

27. Responsum no. 218, pp. 384–88. He did not, to be sure, know about hemophilia as a hereditary disorder, but experience showed that a problem with blood coagulation existed in the family.

28. The note on the place (p. 387, n. 12) by A. Freimann points out that in the *Responsa* of Joseph ibn Migash, no. 103, the marriage of a "killer wife" is forbidden, and Freimann raises the question whether the responsum is authentically by him. The responsum stresses that prohibiting a third marriage is the law, that the sages declared it forbidden. Its tone suggests that some rabbis were permitting such marriages, letting the groom decide for himself.

29. Grossman, *Pious and Rebellious*, pp. 267–68.

30. For the Islamic provisions, see Yvon Linant de Bellefonds, *Traité de droit musulman comparé*, II, 423–47; Asaf A.A. Fyzee, *Outlines of Muhammadam Law*, pp. 155ff.; *Law in the Middle East*, ed. Majid Khadduri and Herbert J. Liebesny, pp. 135, 156, 162. See also 'Ali al-Khafif, *Les dissolutions du mariage*. And for Jewish law, see especially Goitein, *Med. Soc.*, III, 267; and Friedman, "The Ransom-Divorce."

31. *Responsa*, no. 191, pp. 347–48. Legal maturity began at the age of twelve years and one day for females and thirteen years and one day for males; see MT Marriage, ii, 1–2, 10–12; B Nid 46a, 47a, 65a; Yev 80a-b, 97a.

32. J. Schacht, *Introduction to Islamic Law*, pp. 160–63.

33. Goitein, *Med. Soc.*, I, 136–37.

34. *Responsa,* no. 211, p. 373; See Goitein, *Med. Soc.*, I, 136–37.

35. NRSV has: *It is time for the Lord to act, for your law has been broken.*" NJB: "*It is time to take action, Yahweh* (on the basis of one manuscript and Jerome's translation). The legal maxim meant that it was time for a reform of the law. See M Ber, ix, 5; B Ber 54a, 63a and parallels. See *Responsa*, no. 256, p. 475, and Abraham Maimonides, *Kifayat al-'abidin*, p. 195; *Guide*, Introduction, p. 16, where he cited this adage along with, *Let all your acts be for the sake of Heaven* (M Avot, ii, 12). Pines translates: "It is time to do something for the Lord," and so on. See also below, ch. 19, p. 375 and n. 95.

36. *Responsa*, no. 110, pp. 189–91. The word *hadhayan* has the basic meaning of "delirium," "hallucination"; hence "drivel," "jabber." See S. Stroumsa, "'Ravings': Maimonides' Concept of Pseudo-Science."

37. The word *sukham* means "black matter," "soot," "charcoal," hence "smut" and by extension "nonsense," see E. W. Lane, *An Arabic-English Lexicon*, IV, 1326.

38. The elder obviously did not say that the words of God were nonsense, but rather the sermon based upon them.

39. MT Ethical Qualities, vi, 8; Repentance, iii, 14.

40. See MT Torah Study, vi, 1; vii, 1. But in the *Mishneh Torah* Maimonides did not mention giving the benefit of the doubt and overlooking slips and lapses. He said that an elderly sage who has transgressed should be flogged privately in his own home (to avoid shame), and that a court should never place a ban upon a scholar.

41. See Frenkel, *The Jewish Community of Alexandria*, p. 151 and doc. 28, where Rabbi Elazar disturbed a sermon of Rabbi Ephraim during their dispute.

42. *Responsa*, no. 165, p. 314. See Goitein, *Med. Soc.*, II, 168, noting Maimonides' criticism of the lax synagogue decorum, with reference also to Abraham; see *Responsa*, II, 314–17, 467–68, 475; Abraham ben Maimon, *Highways of Perfection*, I, 45.

43. See Goitein's description in *Med. Soc.*, II, 222–23.

44. See MT Torah scroll, x, 4, where Maimonides mentioned silver and golden pomegranates as decorations on Torah scrolls. A Torah scroll is covered with a mantle over which is an adorned breastplate on a chain, like the breastplate of the high priest in the Jerusalem Temple. The scroll is rolled around wooden staffs topped by a crown or pomegranates. The pomegranate fruit, with its lush red seeds, is an ancient symbol of fertility that decorated the garments of the high priest (Ex 28:33–34, 39:24) and the capitals of two columns of the Temple (1 Kings 7:42). See I. Elbogen, *Jewish Liturgy: A Comprehensive History*, trans. R. P. Scheindlin, p. 360.

45. M Avot, iv, 6. See MT Ethical Qualities, v, 3 on drunkenness as desecration of God's Name (*hillul ha-shem*).

46. *Responsa*, no. 224, p. 398, Shailat, p. 425ff. See Farmer, *Maimonides on Listening to Music*, 11–14 (text), 15–17 (translation). The beginning of the query and response are quoted at the beginning of responsum no. 269, pp. 515–16.

47. See on this Henry G. Farmer, EI, s.v. "Mizmār."

48. J. During, EI, s.v. "Samā'."

49. Farmer, "Maimonides on Listening to Music," p. 5.

50. Ibid., pp. 8–9.

51. *Responsa*, no. 204, p. 360, See Goitein, *Med. Soc.*, I, 365; II, 296.

52. MT Sabbath, vi, 17; B AZ 22a. A number of Geonic responsa had adopted this position.

53. Goitein, *Letters of Medieval Jewish Traders*, p. 9.

54. M. A. Friedman, "Rabbi Moses ben Maimon in Legal Documents from the Genizah," pp. 177–88. See Nahum Rakover, *Agency and Authorization in Hebrew Law*.

55. *Responsa*, p. 520, no. 272. This is an autograph from the Genizah that had been in the Library of the Jewish Community of Cairo. It was edited and translated by B. Halper, "An Autograph Responsum of Maimonides." Mr. Jack Mosseri sent it to Solomon Schechter, then President of the Jewish Theological Seminary, who handed it over to Halper for publication. There is a photograph in Halper, Fig. 1, opposite p. 225, and in *Corpus Codicum Hebraicorum*, I, LV.

56. See B Shev 31a.

57. See MT Ethical Qualities, v, 13, where the conduct of a scholar is described. Among other things, he does not act as a surety or trustee or accept power of attorney. See also MT Agents and Partners, iii, 5.

58. *Avot*, i, 8 and CM ad loc. And see MT *Sanhedrin*, xxi, 11. This was true of pious men in Islamic societies as well because of pressures on judges toward favoring one side over another.

59. *Responsa*, no. 274, p. 522. This is a Maimonides autograph. Its beginning is T-S.10. K8.3 and it continues with T-S.8.K.13.8. The latter was published by Friedländer in *MGWJ*, 52, 621-25 with a photograph of the response. Baneth translated it into Hebrew, correcting Friedländer, in *Responsa*, ed. A. Freimann, no. 385, p. 352. A photograph of T-S.8.K.13.8 is in Corpus Codicum Hebraicorum, I, 1, p. LIV.

60. See MT Ethical Qualities, vii, 2.

61. *Responsa*, no. 276, p. 524. It is an autograph from the Genizah, Ms. Brit. Mus. Mar-

goliouth 567b. See photograph there, Vol. 2, Plate b. And see the photo in *Corpus Codicum Hebraicorum*, p. LIII. It was first published by Margoliouth, *JQR*, vol. 11, p. 539. A photograph of the fragment in the British Library is on a postcard that was sold there. M. A. Friedman, "New Fragments of Maimonides' *Responsa*," pp. 117–20, published two prior versions.

62. See Isaiah 2:18, 10:10.

63. Cf. Isaiah 42:21.

64. This was added as an afterthought once the query was finished. The verse is from Ps 84:7. On dots that appear above the words in the manuscript, see Friedman, "Polygamy: Documents and *Responsa* from the Genizah," p. 189, n. 101.

65. MT Oaths, vi, 1. See Friedman, "New Fragments of Maimonides' *Responsa*," p. 120, n. 6.

66. The responsa were published by Blau, II, no. 293, pp. 548–50; no. 436, pp. 714–16; no. 448, pp. 725–28. See also the comment on the correspondence by Freimann, p. XLVI (Blau, III, 44–45).

67. In Ms. Oxford 2670/2 and the first edition of responsa (Constantinople 1517).

68. On the Christian Obadiah, who converted to Judaism, see the series of studies by Norman Golb: "Obadiah the Proselyte: Scribe of a Unique Hebrew Manuscript with Lombardic Neumes"; "Concerning Obadiah the Proselyte and His Musical Work"; "The Music of Obadiah the Proselyte and His Conversion"; "Megillat Obadiah Hager"; and "The Autograph Memoirs of Obadiah the Proselyte."

69. Haggai Ben-Shammai, "Eschatological Messages in Se'adyah's Translations," p. 214, n. 65.

70. The text has Merqulis, as in rabbinic literature. Mercurius is the Roman god (Grk Hermes), whose worship by casting stones is mentioned in M San vii, 6. See also B San 64a; M 'AZ, iv, 1; T 'AZ , vi, 13–15; B 'AZ 50a; Hul 133a; TY 'AZ, iv, 4 (43d), xvii, 20 (28d). And see Maimonides, CM to San vii, 6 (p. 185); MT Idolatry, iii, 5. See also on Mercurius, S. Lieberman, "Palestine in the 3rd and 4th Centuries," Appendix, in *Texts and Studies*, p. 165. Maimonides' overly detailed discussion of the idolatrous practices at the pre-Islamic Ka'ba leads Prof. Alyssa Gray to suggest that he was not completely forthright in his view that Islam was pure monotheism.

71. Heb. *yihud*; cf. Arabic *tawhid*, which has the same meaning, as we have seen.

72. The word is *dofi*, which B. Septimus, "Petrus Alfonsi and the Cult at Mecca," renders as "doubt," citing "Maimonides' own usage." But beyond the texts he cites there are others where *dofi* means "defect" or "reproach." See MT Oaths, xii, 12; Creditor and Debtor, xxii, 2; Evidence, i, 4.

73. Maimonides has in mind Qur'an 9:30, where it is said that the Jews call 'Uzayr (Ezra?) the son of Allah; see H. Lazarus-Yafeh, *Intertwined Worlds*, pp. 50–74.

74. See Septimus, "Petrus Alfonsi and the Cult at Mecca," p. 522, n. 23, for an explanation of the juxtaposition of these verses.

75. Maimonides stresses that Judaism is the real Abrahamic faith, in contradistinction to the claims made in the Qur'an that Islam was brought into being when Abraham bound his son Isaac.

76. Gershom Scholem, EJ, s.v. "Shi'ur Komah"; A. Altmann, "Moses Narboni's 'Epistle on Shi'ur Qomā'"; M. S. Cohen, *The Shi'ur Qomah: Liturgy and Theurgy in Pre-Kabbalistic Jewish Mysticism*; idem, *The Shi'ur Qomah: Texts and Recensions*; David Blumenthal, "A Philosophical-Mystical Interpretation of a Shi'ur Qomah Text"; and "Maimonides' Intellectualist Mysticism and the Superiority of the Prophecy of Moses."

77. According to S. Abramson, in Blau, *Responsa, Addenda et Corrigenda*, p. 124, the responsum is preserved also in Ms. Berlin 102, fol. 162b, where the title suggests that the people of the Maghrib asked Maimonides this question (see also colophon on p. 204). Maimonides' reply began with "The response of Moses son of Maimon (of blessed memory) to the men of the Maghrib."

78. He used the term *darshanin al-Rum*. The word Rum, like Edom, refers either to Rome, to the Byzantine Empire, or to Christian Europe in general. Here he probably meant Europe. (See also Qafih's translation in CM Neziqin, p. 213, n. 42.) In the copious literature on *Shi'ur qomah*, scholars say that Maimonides ascribed *Shi'ur qomah* to the Romans, Greeks, or Byzantines, taking the word Rum in its narrow sense.

79. See Z. Ankori, *Karaites of Byzantium*, 256, n. 19; 393, n. 102. Ankori notes (n. 102) that Karaites actually waged war against rabbinic midrashim of *Shi'ur qomah,* yet they themselves were accused of the same.

80. *Responsa*, no. 117, p. 200; *Letters*, ed. Shailat, pp. 574–75. Abramson in his addenda to Blau, in III, 124, adds D. Sasson, *Corpus Codicum Hebraicorum*, I, 1, p. 33, n. 4 (Heb, p. 18, n. 16).

81. G. Scholem, *Jewish Gnosticism*, pp. 36–55 et passim; I. Gruenwald, *From Apocalypticism to Gnosticism*, pp. 213–17; M. Cohen, *The Shi'ur Qomah* (texts); idem, *Liturgy*, 32–33, cites our responsum and compares it with the version in the *Mishnah Commentary*. Saul Lieberman writes in Scholem, *Jewish Gnosticism*, p. 124, that in his youth Maimonides believed in the sacredness of *Shi'ur qomah*, following *Yesod mora'* by Abraham ibn Ezra, ch. 12.

82. See CM Introduction to San, x (Pereq Heleq), ed. Qafih, p. 213 and n. 42; and Introductions to *The Commentary on the Mishnah* and to Pereq Heleq, ed. Shailat, p. 371 (Ar)/p. 143 (Heb), and n. 27.

83. Maimonides mentioned in the *Guide*, Introduction, p. 9, a Book of Prophecy and a Book of Correspondence on talmudic homiletics, but he changed his mind and wrote the *Guide* instead, incorporating parts of these discarded works.

84. *Responsa*, nos. 119–50, pp. 205–86.

85. *Responsa,* no. 150, p. 285.

86. B *Shab* 75a.

87. The rest is: "of him Scripture says, but who do not regard the deeds of the Lord, neither have they seen the work of his hands" (Isa 5:12).

88. The source of this *baraita* is unknown. In MT Foundations of the Law, ii, 2, Maimonides wrote, "As the Sages have said in the matter of love, that from it you come to recognize him who spoke and the world came into being"; see the note ad loc. in the edition of Lieberman et al. See also MT Foundations of the Law, iv, 12, trans. Lerner, p. 152. It is possible that in our responsum Maimonides substituted God's works for his words. See *Book of Commandments*, Pos, no. 3, and *Guide*, III, 28. The source is not in SifreDeut, we-ethanan, 33 (Friedman, 74a) or SifreDeut 'eqev 49 (85a), for in his *Book of Commandments*, Maimonides cited Sifre on Deut 6:5. See also ARN, 37, in Version A, p. 55b [Kister]. See *Book of Commandments,* pos. 3; *Guide*, III, 28; Professor Saul Lieberman informed me that he did not know the rabbinic source for the *baraita* cited in the name of Rabbi Meir. It is cited in the name of Rabbi Meir in Midrash Tannaim on Deut 6:6, but with the theme "these words." Maimonides replaced "God's words" with "God's works."

CHAPTER 18

1. See the English translation by Charles B. Chavel, *The Commandments*. Joseph Qafih published the Arabic original with translation and commentary.

2. See Chaval, *The Commandments*, Foreword, p. xi.

3. Ibid., p. xv.

4. Twersky, *Introduction to the Code of Maimonides*, pp. 25–26.

5. *Book of Commandments*, Introduction.

6. Twersky, *Introduction to the Code of Maimonides*, p. 330; *Languages of Power*, ed. Ross Brown, pp. 72–72.

7. See Moshe Greenberg, "Bible Interpretation as Exhibited in the First Book of Maimonides' Code," p. 421; Twersky, *Introduction,* p. 145

8. Hyam Soleveitchik, in a lecture at New York University, March 21, 2004, drew

attention to the poetic aspect of MT Sabbath, and by implication the entire *Mishneh Torah*, by which he meant, inter alia, multiplicity of meanings and interpretations. See his *"Mishneh Torah: Polemic and Art."*

9. See M. Carruthers, *The Book of Memory*, pp. 7–8.

10. MT Introduction, trans. R. Lerner, p. 140.

11. See Birger Gerhardssohn, *Memory and Manuscript*; Jacob Neusner, *The Memorized Torah: The Mnemonic System of the Mishnah*; Michael D. Swartz, *Scholastic Magic: Ritual and Revelation in Early Jewish Mysticism*, Part I, chapter 2; Goitein, *Med. Soc.*, II, 174–75. And see Mary Carruthers, *The Book of Memory: A Study of Memory in Medieval Culture*; and Francis A. Yates, *The Art of Memory*.

12. P. Hadot, *Philosophy as a Way of Life*.

13. He related the episode to the Alexandrian Judge Phineas ben Meshullam; see *Letters*, ed. Shailat, pp. 444–45.

14. For a detailed treatment of Maimonides' motives and goals in writing the *Mishneh Torah*, see Twersky, *Introduction to the Code of Maimonides*, pp. 61–81. And see Maimonides' explanation in MT Introduction, trans. Lerner, pp. 139–40. Maimonides' reference to the disappearance of the wisdom of the wise is an allusion to Isaiah 29:4, which is cited verbatim in *Guide*, II, 11 (p. 276), where loss of wisdom and reversion to ignorance are mentioned. For a thorough account of Maimonides' gloomy view of contemporary cultural and intellectual decline, see Twersky, *Introduction to the Code of Maimonides*, pp. 62–64, 476. He saw his enterprise as an act of recovery and revival.

15. The Oral Law is the necessary authoritative interpretation of the Written Law, the text of the Torah given to Moses at Sinai, which is obscure and in need of interpretation, and therefore the Oral Law is coeval with it. While the Oral Law depends upon the Written Law as its interpretation, the Written Law would be a dead letter without the Oral Law. On the Oral Law, see S. Safrai, *The Literature of the Sages,* ed. Safrai, ch. 2; and see A. Goldberg, ch. 4, "The Mishnah," After the destruction of the Second Temple in 70 C.E., the sages feared that the oral tradition would be lost, making compiling of the Mishnah a necessity.

16. *Letters*, ed. Shailat, pp. 558–59.

17. Ms. B: the words of Rav Ashe. See *Letters*, ed. Shailat, p. 114 and n. 15. Maimonides mentions Ravina and Rav Ashe in the Introduction to the *Mishneh Torah* as the final Sages of the Gemara, and Rav Ashe as the compiler of the Babylonian Talmud; see also CM Introduction, Ar, pp. 356–57/Heb pp. 60–61.

18. *Responsa*, IV, 33; *Letters*, ed. Shailat, p. 558.

19. *Binah we-hokhmah*. The two usually appear reversed as *hokhmah we-binah*, as in the liturgy (MT Book of Love, trans. M. Kellner, Appendix, p. 175). In *Book of Commandments*, second principle, Maimonides takes *binah we-hokhmah* to refer specifically to astronomy, as he does in his *Epistle on Astronomy*. See also ch. 21, n. 32.

20. Cf. Jer. 49:7, *Has counsel vanished from the prudent?*

21. According to the expression in B Shab 83b; Git 57b. See MT Torah Study, iii, 12. Joseph ben Judah was then in Aleppo.

22. T San (Zuckermandel), xi, 6; xiv, 1; Neg vi, 1; B Sot 44a; San 51b, etc.

23. This is rare testimony about the spiritual condition of Jews who settled in India. Accordingly, many had become distracted by business and other concerns.

24. The term *'illegim* means "stammerers," and is the semantic equivalent of Arabic *'ajam*, used for non-Arabs in general and Persians in particular. See CM Ned, i, 2; Nazir, i, 1. Arabic *'ilj*, pl. *'uluj*, which is etymologically equivalent to Hebrew *'illeg*, pl. *'illegim*, means indigenous population, non-Arabs, etc. In his letter to Samuel Ibn Tibbon (see below, p. 439), Maimonides says that Samuel resides among the *'illegim*, those who do not speak Arabic.

25. Ms. B adds *we-'osin*, that is, they carry out the law literally.

26. Letter to Joseph ben Judah, ed. Baneth, pp. 50–54; trans. Kraemer, "The Life of Moses ben Maimon," p. 425.

27. See *Guide*, I, 34 (p. 75).

28. The expressions "the time to come" and "when envy and ambition disappear" are messianic; see Kraemer, "Maimonides' Messianic Posture," p. 113.

29. See I. Twersky, "*The Mishneh Torah* of Maimonides," p. 217; and Idem, *Introduction to the Code of Maimonides,* p. 207.

30. MT Kings and Their Wars, xi, 1.

31. MT Introduction, trans. Lerner, p. 140.

32. This text was published by A. S. Halkin and was included in the 1985 edition of Baneth's *Epistles,* iv, pp. 423–24, and probably belongs to letter no. 6. See also *Letters,* ed. Qafih, pp. 135–36. And see Elon, *Jewish Law,* III, 1222-23, but he calls the man Joseph Ibn 'Aqnin.

33. MT Introduction, trans. Lerner, p. 140.

34. See Elon, op. cit, III, 1216–21.

35. *Letters,* ed. Shailat, p. 439. See also Twersky, *Introduction to the Code of Maimonides,* p. 32; Elon, op. cit, III, 1145–46.

36. See Elon, op. cit, III, 1223–25. Abraham ben David, called RaBaD, wrote law codes and commentaries on Mishnah, Talmud, and Midrash. He wrote critical glosses (*hassagot*) on Alfasi's *Precepts* and Maimonides' *Mishneh Torah.* His *hassagot* on the *Mishneh Torah* were published along with the text beginning with the Constantinople edition of 1509. Abraham ben David was the father of the famous early Kabbalist, Isaac the Blind. See I. Twersky, *Rabad of Posquières, a Twelfth-Century Talmudist.*

37. The Muslim theologian Abu Hamid al-Ghazali began his great juridical/theological *Ihya' 'ulum al-din* (*Revivication of the Religious Sciences*) with the Book of Knowledge; see Franz Rosenthal, *Knowledge Triumphant,* p. 96, observing that Maimonides' Book of Knowledge, at the beginning of the *Mishneh Torah,* "owes its title, its being, and its place to the attitude of Muslim civilization toward 'knowledge.'" Al-Ghazali's Book of Knowledge is available in a translation by Nabih Amin Faris.

38. MT Foundations of the Law, ii, 1–5.

39. *Guide,* III, 28 (pp. 512–13).

40. MT Foundations of the Law, i, 1. Note Maimonides' use of the verb "to know," and compare al-Farabi's reference to the things all the people of the perfect state ought to know in common; *Perfect State,* ch. 17, pp. 277–79. The affinity between the two conceptions becomes even more obvious when the ideas corresponding to Foundations of the Law, I, 1–6 in *Guide* I, 69–71 and II, 1 are compared with the opening of al-Farabi's work. I have shown in "Alfarabi's Opinions of the Virtuous City and Maimonides' Foundations of the Law" that the exposition of these foundations follows structurally and thematically the fundamental beliefs, or opinions, posited by al-Farabi for the virtuous city.

41. See *Book of Commandments,* pos. 3, where Maimonides stressed testaments and commandments along with God's actions in the world as the object of contemplation that leads to love of God.

42. The Hebrew word *sham* is an Arabism, from Ar *thamma,* meaning "there is . . ." As only the consonants are given in the text, it is often misread and even vowellized in some texts and discussions as *shem,* meaning "name."

43. The first four words in Hebrew (= "The fundamental principle and the pillar of the sciences") contain the acrostic *y-h-w-h* (*Yesod Ha-yesodot We-'amud Ha-hokhmot*), which is the Tetragrammaton (*yahweh*). "The fundamental principle and the pillar of the sciences," a philosophic locution, is by this means identified with the God of creation and revelation. Likewise, Maimonides' poem at the beginning of the *Guide* has twenty-six words, the *gematria,* or numerical equivalent, of the Tetragrammaton.

44. This is the outer sphere of the universe according to Ptolemaic astronomy.

45. *Guide,* I, 71 (pp. 181–82).

46. *Guide,* II, 1 (p. 246).

47. The equation is essential, for the God whose existence is demonstrated by the philosophical method is the first mover and not the God of creation and revelation in the Torah. Cf. Strauss, "Introductory Essay," pp. 1ii-1iii.

48. *Kuzari*, I, 11, ed. D. H. Baneth and H. Ben-Shammai, pp. 9–10; Pines, "Shī'ite Terms and Conceptions in the *Kuzari*," pp. 209-10, 255; Strauss, "The Law of Reason in the *Kuzari*," p. 113.

49. "The Memorial," Blaise Pascal, *Pensées and Other Writings*, trans. Honor Levi, p. 178, and note on p. 244–45. Pascal recorded a revelatory experience.

50. MT 'Avodah Zarah, iii, 3.

51. See, for instance, *Bereshith Rabbah*, xxxix.1; ed. Theodor-Albeck, I, 365.

52. See also *Guide* I, 13 (p. 282), II, 39 (p. 379) and III, 29 (p. 517).

53. MT Repentance, iii, 6–8. See Arthur Hyman, "Maimonides' 'Thirteen Principles'," pp. 131–33.

54. The word *qa'ida* means "base," "basis," "foundation," and is often used by Maimonides and others for a basic teaching of religion as in *qawa'id al-din*, basic principles of religion. (It is in use nowadays as the name of the militant jihadist group under the leadership of Osama bin Laden.)

55. *Guide*, II, 13 (p. 282).

56. MT Foundations of the Law, ii, 2, trans. Lerner, p. 144.

57. Heb *ribbon ha-'olamim,* which occurs very often in both Talmuds and in Midrashim, is presumably the source of Ar *rabb al-'alamin* in Qur'an 1:2.

58. Elsewhere, he cited Rabbi Meir instead of the sages. And see Foundations of the Law, iv, 12, trans. Lerner, p. 152.

59. *Guide*, III, 28 (pp. 512–13).

60. MT Foundations of the Law, ii, 9–10. *Guide*, I, 60 (p. 146).

61. MT Foundations of the Law, i, 9–10.

62. *Guide* I, 68 (p. 163). For the dictum on the self-thought of the divine mind, see Aristotle, *Metaphysics*, Book Lambda, 7, 1072b19–20; 9, 1075a3–5. It was adopted by Muslim philosophers; see al-Farabi, *Risala Fi 'l-'aql (De intellectu)*, ed. M. Bouyges, pp. 35–36; *al-Madina al-fadila (The Perfect State)*, ed. and trans. R. Walzer, pp. 70–73. See also Maimonides, CM Avot, iii, 20 (ed. Qafih, p. 436).

63. *Guide*, I, 68 (pp. 163, 165, 166). Yahya ibn 'Adi, Ibn Zur'a and other Christian Arab philosophers interpreted the dictum about intellect in a Christological, Trinitarian manner. The Jacobite Yahya ibn 'Adi, for instance, compared the hypostasis of Father with the intellect, the Son with the intelligizer, and the Spirit with the intelligized. See Kraemer, *Humanism in the Renaissance of Islam*, p. 118.

64. "Translator's Introduction," pp. xcvii–xcviii; idem, "Limitations of Knowledge," pp. 93–94; and see M. Schwarz, *Guide of the Perplexed*, p. 173.

65. Wehr, *Dictionary*, p. 299. cf. *Guide* II, 40 (p. 381).

66. For instance, J. Ber, ix, 2 and B Ber 58a.

67. I have used the text of S. Lieberman et al., *Sefer Hamada (Book of Knowledge)*, and the translations of M. Hyamson, *The Book of Knowledge,* and R. Weiss and C. E. Butterworth, *The Ethical Writings of Maimonides*.

68. Jerome Kagan, *Galen's Prophecy: Temperament in Human Nature; The Nature of the Child*.

69. Lat *temperamentum* = "mixture" (Grk *krasis*). The Arabic word for temperament, *mizaj*, which underlies Heb *mezeg*, also means "mixture." "Humor" is from L. *humorem*, or *umorem*, meaning "bodily fluid" or "moisture."

70. Kagan, *Galen's Prophecy*, p. 8.

71. CM Avot, v, 19; MT Ethical Qualities, i, 1; and *Guide*, II, 40.

72. MT Ethical Qualities, i, 2; iv, 20. See Aristotle, *Ethics*, II, 1, 1103a15–b25.

73. CM Avot, ii, 1; MT Ethical Qualities, ii, 4, cf. Al-Ghazali, *Ihya'*, III, 53.

74. MT Ethical Qualities, ii, 1, trans. Weiss and Butterworth, pp. 30–31. Maimonides then quoted Isa 5:20 and Prov 2:13.

75. H. A. Davidson, "Maimonides' *Shemonah Peraqim* and al-Farabi's *Fusul al-Madani*," p. 39, *Eight Chapters*, III, p. 6.15.26 = *Aphorisms*, ed. and trans. D. M. Dunlop, par. 37/

ed. F. Najjar, p. 56 (41). Maimonides interpolates examples of unfit foods and omits *Aphorisms*, p. 57.3–5 on the virtues. The text in MT Ethical Qualities is virtually identical to that of *Eight Chapters,* omitting a few examples of unfit foods.

76. See al-Farabi, *al-Siyasa al-madaniyya* (*The Political Regime*), ed. F. M. Najjar; trans. idem in *Medieval Political Philosophy: A Sourcebook,* ed. R. Lerner and M. Mahdi, pp. 38–39. Maimonides evidently had these passages in mind in MT Ethical Qualities, ii, 1 and *Eight Chapters* III.

77. See also al-Ghazali, in *Riyadat al*-Nafs, *Ihya'*, III, 61: "The physicians [of the soul] are the wise [*al-'ulama'*]," an idea that Maimonides expressed in the same language.

78. Aristotle, *Topics,* I, 1, 100b21; I, 10, 104a8–12.

79. MT Ethical Qualities, ii, 2. Galen recommended this technique, as did Plato and others; see Galen's *De placitis Hippocratis et Platonis*. Galen said that Asklepios used this method to produce catharsis of the soul; Galen, *De sanitate tuenda*, Book 1, chap. 8 (VI:1–452, ed. Kuhn, p. 41).

80. *Kitab al-milla* (*Book of Religion*), ed. M. Mahdi, p. 57; trans. C. E. Butterworth in *Alfarabi, The Political Writings,* pp. 104–05. Al-Ghazali mentioned the same technique in Riyadat al-Nafs, *Ihya'*, III, 61; trans. T. J. Winter, *Al-Ghazālī on Disciplining the Soul,* pp. 43–44.

81. MT Ethical Qualities, i, 5. See M Avot, v, 7, 10–14; *Guide*, III, 53–54.

82. Ibn Hazm was aware of his own character defects, in particular his tendency toward anger and pride. In a confessional passage in his ethical treatise, *Kitab al-akhlaq wa'l-siyar,* ed. and trans. N. Tomiche as *Epître morale,* he pondered his own deficiencies and specified his obsessive need to be always right as most blameworthy. See Eric Ormsby, "Ibn Hazm," in the *Literature of al-Andalus*, ed. Maria-Rosa Menocal, p. 240, citing paras. 96–114. The main objective of his ethics was to overcome anxiety, which emerges as an aim in Maimonides' ethics and in *The Guide of the Perplexed.*

83. Consider *Who is a hero? He who conquers his inclination*; *see* M Avot, iv, 1, citing Prov 15:16, and see Prov 16:32.

84. MT Ethical Qualities, ii, 3; CM Avot, iv, 4; B Sot 4b.

85. M Avot, iv, 4.

86. MT Ethical Qualities, ii, 3.

87. In the *Eight Chapters*, ch. 4, where Maimonides similarly disapproved of the behavior of ascetics, he did not mention Christian monks; trans. Weiss and Butterworth, pp. 69–71.

88. See Eight Chapters, iv; MT Ethical Qualities, iii, 1.

89. Eliezer Diamond, *Holy Men and Hunger Artists*, treats sexuality, eating, and drinking.

90. See also CM Avot, v, 13.

91. The translation reflects Maimonides' understanding of the verse, based on rabbinic exegesis. See Sifre Numbers, Naso', xxx; B Ta'an 11a. *NJPS* has: *[The priest shall] make expiation on his behalf for the guilt that he incurred through the corpse.* The Nazirite needs expiation because a person died near him, thereby defiling his consecrated hair.

92. Midrash Ecclesiastes Rabbah commented, saying that "whoever is compassionate when he should be ruthless is eventually ruthless when he should be compassionate." King Saul had pity on Agag, king of the Philistines, yet eventually gave orders to Doeg the Edomite to kill the priests of Nob, who protected David, and he put to the sword men, women, children, infants, oxen, asses, and sheep (1 Sam 22:17–19).

93. Or "obscenity." The word is *tiflut* (see M Sot, iii, 4; B Sot 20a and 21b; J Sot, iii, 18 [3d]), from *tafel,* meaning "insipid," "dull," "without salt" (see Job 6:6), hence "nonsense." In rabbinic Hebrew, it also has the sense of "obscenity" or "wantonness"; see Jastrow, *Dictionary*, p. 1687. Here *tiflut* may have both senses.

94. SifreDeut, xlvi (ed. Finkelstein, p. 104); Maimonides, *Book of Commandments,* pos 11; T. Ilan, "A Window into the Public Realm: Jewish Women in the Second Temple Period," p. 48.

95. Petahiah of Regensburg, *Sibbub*, ed. Grünhut, pp. 9ff.; Baron, *Social and Religious History*, V, 323, n. 89.

96. This was true in the period of the talmudic sages also. A woman was permitted to write her own bill of divorce; see M Git, ii, 5. However, Torah scrolls, tefillin, and mezuzot written by women are invalid; B Men 42b. See Ilan, "A Window," p. 50–51.

97. B Qid 29b; MT Torah Study, i, 1.

98. MT Torah Study i, 13. The principle is that someone who is commanded and performs is superior to someone who is not commanded and performs; see B BQ 38a, 87a and 'AZ 3a, Eight Chapters, ch. 6, trans. Weiss and Butterworth, pp. 78–80.

99. Even in the Talmud the words of Rabbi Eliezer are softened. The Mishnah quotes him as saying "taught her *tiflut*," whereas the Gemara has him saying, "*as if he had* taught her *tiflut*," which is the version Maimonides cited, modifying Rabbi Eliezer's statement even further by substituting *divre havay* (nonsense) for *tiflut*, which, as we saw, can mean "obscenity" or "wantonness." (He used *divre havay* also for the anthropomorphic representations of God by the common people, who were misled by their imagination.)

100. Elijah J. Schochet and Solomon Spiro, *Saul Lieberman: The Man and His Work*, pp. 13 and 107, n. 293.

101. MT Prayer and Priestly Blessing, iv,16; B Ber 31a, San 22a, and J Ber, v, 1.

102. MT Prayer and Priestly Blessing, xi.

103. It was specifically forbidden by the Pact of 'Umar for churches and synagogues to be higher than mosques.

104. MT Prayer and Priestly Blessing, xi, 4.

105. *Enjoy life with the wife whom you love* (Eccl 9:9).

106. B Yev 62b; Gen R, xvii, 2. See *Book of Women*, trans. Isaac Klein, Introduction, pp. xxi–xxii; David M. Feldman, *Birth Control in Jewish Law*, pp. 33–34. See also *Book of Commandments*, pos. 213.

107. MT Ethical Qualities, v, 11.

108. The context in Deut 20 is exempting certain men from battle—those who recently built a house, planted a vineyard, or paid the bride-price for a wife. This is the actual order, not as Maimonides quoted it. See M Sot, viii, 2; Tos Sot, vii, 18; B Sot 43a-b. It is unlikely that Maimonides misquoted. Perhaps he reversed the order of income and housing because it makes better sense to have income come first. In MT Kings and Their Wars, vii, 3, he quoted the order precisely. Moshe Greenberg observed that "Maimonides' manipulation of the order of items in the first series in an interesting display of hermeneutical liberty; see "Bible Interpretation as Exhibited in the First Book of Maimonides' Code," p. 430.

109. The general imprecation is in the previous verse (Deut 28:29): "you shall not prosper in your ventures." The reverse order in 28:30, with vineyard last, implies that the correct order is vineyard, house, wife, which is the way Maimonides presented Deut 20:5–7.

110. In CM Avot, v, 21, which lists eight ages of human life, with marriage coming at the age of eighteen, Maimonides commented that one gets married at eighteen and pursues a worldly occupation at twenty. Jaques in Shakespeare's *As You Like It*, II, 2, 138–65, observes that the acts of a man are in seven ages; see David Bevington, *Shakespeare: The Seven Ages of Human Experience*, 2nd ed., pp. 3–6. The psychologist Eric Erikson, in *Childhood and Society*, postulated eight stages of human psychosocial development as our *mishnah* does.

111. MT Torah Study, i, 5.

112. MT *Marriage*, xv, 2–3. This is the first commandment in the Torah (Gen 1: 28). The end of the verse speaks of conquest; hence the tradition inferred that women were not the intended subject. See M Yev, vi, 6 and B Yev 65b, where it is said that the obligation applies to the man and not the woman.

113. B Qid 29b.

114. Simon ben 'Azzai, called Ben 'Azzai, was a second-century Tanna, one of the four who entered Paradise (*pardes*) and engaged in theosophic speculation, from which only Rabbi Aqiba emerged unharmed. See Gershom Scholem, *Jewish Gnosticism*, pp. 14–19;

Strack and Stemberger, *Introduction to the Talmud and Midrash*, p. 82. Ben 'Azzai remained unmarried because his heart yearned for Torah; see B Yev 63b.

115. Goitein, *Med. Soc.*, III, 69–70. See for details on marriage, pp. 47–159. For the rabbinic definitions, see Satlow, *Jewish Marriage in Antiquity*, pp. 73–89.

116. *Book of Women*, trans. I. Klein, Introduction, p. xxv.

117. The poet John Milton admired the contractual (not sacramental) nature of marriage in the Hebrew Bible and the Talmud, which he heard about from his friend John Seldon, who had read Maimonides' code of law.

118. Jacob Dienstag, "Christian Translators of Maimonides' *Mishneh Torah* into Latin"; Aaron L. Katchen, *Christian Hebraists and Dutch Rabbis: Seventeenth-Century Apologetics and the Study of Maimonides'* Mishneh Torah.

119. Jason P. Rosenblatt, *Renaissance England's Chief Rabbi: John Selden*. See also Fania Oz-Salzburger, "The Jewish Roots of Western Freedom."

120. Matthew Biberman, "Milton, Marriage, and a Woman's Right to Divorce."

121. MT Ethical Qualities, iv, 19. In the rest of the paragraph he warned against sexual dissipation as debilitating, citing Solomon, *Give not your strength unto women* (Prov 31:3), the words of the mother of Lemuel, king of Massa.

122. A *mokh* was a tuft of wool or cotton. Used before or during intercourse, it was like a tampon; if afterward it was a postcoital absorbent; Feldman, *Birth Control in Jewish Law*, p. 170.

123. Ibid., p. 169–70, cites (in n. 1) T Nid, ii, 6; B Yev 12b; Ket 39a; Nid 45a; Ned 35b. See also Michael L. Satlow, *Tasting the Dish*, p. 232.

124. Feldman, op. cit., p. 208.

125. Ibid., p. 304.

126. MT Marriage, xiii, 1–10.

127. MT Marriage, xiii, 11.

128. MT Marriage, xiii, 11. Rabbinic law permits a husband to prevent his wife by force from going out to the marketplace; see GenR, viii, 12, ed. Theodor-Albeck, p. 66.

129. Goitein, *Med. Soc.*, III, 153, suggests that the remark alludes to Muhammad's Farewell Sermon. Upon returning from the Farewell Pilgrimage on 18 Dhu 'l-Hijja 10 (March 16, 632), at Ghadir Khumm, Muhammad is quoted as having said, "Your wives are like prisoners of war; they have no free disposition over themselves." See also Qur'an 33:33, where Muhammad's wives are instructed to stay in their houses.

130. MT Marriage, xiii, 11; B Yev 77a. Grossman, *Pious and Rebellious*, pp. 105–6, observes that there is no talmudic basis for the limitation on women to go out once or twice a month, and that Maimonides was under the influence of Muslim society. Grossman says that Solomon ben Abraham Ibn Parhon, a twelfth-century Spanish lexicographer, wrote that in the Land of Israel, Iraq, and Spain women covered their faces with a veil, leaving a hole opposite one eye to see, whereas in Christian countries women went out with uncovered faces. Grossman cites his *Mahberet he-'arukh*, p. 57b and M. A. Friedman, "The Ethics of Medieval Jewish Marriage," which has a detailed discussion of the seclusion of women.

131. Marriage, xxiv, 12.

132. See Friedman, *Polygyny*, pp. 55ff.

133. See M. Elon, *Jewish Law*, II, 784–86.

134. Marriage xiv, 3; B Yev 65a, Niddah 17a; Grossman, *Pious and Rebellious*, pp. 78–82.

135. When J. Blau's Hebrew translation has the word *haser* ("residence"), translators into English take it to mean "courtyard," but the word *haser* renders Arabic *dar*, which means "residence." This was an edifice of rooms or apartments built around an inside courtyard.

136. *You may marry such women as seem good to you, two, three, or four; but if you fear you will not be equitable, then marry only one, or your slaves; so it is more likely you will not be partial* (Qur'an 4:3).

137. Marriage, xiv, 4; B Yev 44a.

138. David Novak, "Jewish Perspectives on Sex and Family," pp. 278–79. See MT Marriage, i, 4; *Guide*, III, 49 (p. 603). A concubine (from Latin meaning "lying together") or handmaid cohabits with a man outside of marriage, and in Hebrew and Muslim law she is a secondary, inferior wife, as Hagar was to Abraham and Bilhah to Jacob. The word "polycoity" is probably better than "concubinage." See Naomi Steinberg, *Kinship and Marriage in Genesis*, p. 15 and ch. 2. Whereas a Muslim man is permitted up to four (concurrent) wives, he may have as many concubines as he can handle.

139. On concubinage in the Talmud, see Michael L. Satlow, *Jewish Marriage in Antiquity*, pp. 192–95.

140. MT Marriage, xv, 17; B Sot 3a; BamR, ix, 2.

141. MT Marriage, xv, 17–18.

142. MT Marriage, xv, 19–20.

143. See Grossman, *Pious and Rebellious*, ch. 10.

144. See Goitein, *Med. Soc.*, III, 184–89.

145. This is cited by Grossman, "Violence Against Women," pp. 187–88. The ruling is assigned to Rav Yehuday Gaon (eighth century), but Grossman rejects this ascription.

146. M Ket, v, 5.

147. MT Marriage, xxi, 10.

148. Book of Women, trans. Isaac Klein, Introduction, p. xxxv–vi. Klein gives examples of European rabbis who strongly opposed wife beating.

149. Marriage, xxi, 10. See also Grossman, *Pious and Rebellious*, p. 221. A man who injures his wife, however, is obliged to pay her; see MT Wounding and Damaging, iv, 16.

150. See Goitein, *Med. Soc.*, III, 185.

151. An exception may be Spain, where wife beating among Jews was rampant; see M. Assis, "Sexual Behaviour," p. 34. Assis considers this as part of a general violent tendency in Hispano-Jewish society; see also Assis, "Crime and Violence."

152. Boyarin, *Unheroic Conduct*, 163–64. (The source should be cited as Ishut [Marriage], the first treatise in the Book Nashim [Women].) He cites Avraham Grossman, "Violence," p. 193, on the possibility that a court is doing the flogging, without taking a position on the issue.

153. See Rabbi Joseph Qafih's commentary on Marriage, xxi, 10, p. 436; Grossman, *Pious and Rebellious*, p. 220. Davidson, *Moses Maimonides,* p. 230, writes: "And in a singularly distasteful ruling, Maimonides decides that a husband can force a recalcitrant wife 'even with a whip' to perform the household chores that rabbinic law has laid down as her wifely obligations." The author prefers Abraham ben David's ruling as being what one hopes Jewish judges facing the situation would do, which is to withhold nourishment from (allegedly) recalcitrant wives, that is, starve them into compliance! Surely Maimonides' ruling, properly understood, which places judgment and punishment in the hands of a court, is superior from a humane viewpoint. The danger in Davidson's misreading is that it gives latitude to observant Jews, who follow Maimonides' decisions, to indulge in wife-beating by right, and it condones a method of coercion (withholding food) that is cruel and unusual punishment.

154. MT Marriage xv, 7.

155. MT Gifts to the Poor, vii, 10.

156. MT Sanhedrin xviii, 5.

157. M Git, ix, 10.

158. MT Divorce, i, 2.

159. MT Gifts to the Poor, vii, 2.

160. MT Gifts to the Poor, vii, 7; B Git 59b, 61a; BB 9a; Pe'ah, viii, 5.

161. MT Gifts to the Poor, x, 1–6; B BB 9a, Yev 79a, Shab 139a. I have omitted the biblical citations.

162. MT Gifts to the Poor, x, 7–14. I have omitted verses and references to precedents cited in the Talmud. See also Julie Salamon's *Rambam's Ladder*.

163. M Sheq, v, 6; B BB 10b. One should make sure that the person in charge is trustworthy, as was Hananyah ben Teradion; a second generation Tanna B AZ 17b.

164. MT Gifts to the Poor, x, 16; B Ket 50a.

165. MT Marriage, xii, 14.

166. MT Rebels, vi, 3 under honoring one's parents.

167. See MT Gifts to the Poor, iv, 13; SifreDeut, xv, 17; B BM 17a.

168. See Feldman, *Birth Control in Jewish Law,* pp. 271–75; Fred Rosner, *Medicine in the Mishneh Torah of Maimonides*; and Daniel Schiff, *Abortion in Judaism.* The Catholic view, from St. Augustine on, has been that the soul enters the body at conception, making the embryo a full human being and hence inviolable.

169. M Ohal, vii, 6; T Yev, ix; B San 72b; J Shab, xiv, 4; San, viii, end; Feldman, *Birth Control in Jewish Law,* p. 275; Daniel Schiff, *Abortion in Judaism,* p. 36.

170. See B San 72b; J San, viii, 9; Feldman, *Birth Control in Jewish Law,* p. 276.

171. MT Murder and Preservation of Life, i, 9.

172. This continues the discussion in the previous *halakha,* where Maimonides cited, *Your eye shall have no pity* (Deut 25:11) with reference to saving the pursued from the pursuer even at the cost of the pursuer's hand or life; see Schiff, *Abortion in Judaism,* p. 59. The *rodef* is a pursuer, assailant, or aggressor, on the verge of committing rape or murder. Others may use whatever means necessary to prevent the crime, even killing the pursuer.

173. The phrase "as one pursuing" (*ke-rodef*) raises a question of interpretation. Does it mean "like a pursuer" or "as a[n actual] pursuer?" See Schiff, *Abortion in Judaism,* pp. 82–83.

174. Lit., "the nature of the world." This corresponds to the rabbinic reference to an act of God. Maimonides considered the moment of birth to be when the infant comes to the end of the vaginal canal and most of its forehead has appeared (MT Forbidden Intercourse, x, 6), but some rabbinic texts say when most of the baby has emerged, or the head, or most of the baby and the head; see Schiff, *Abortion in Judaism,* p. 36, n. 37.

175. He also added the method of drugs; see B Nid 30b. On the innovation of Maimonides' position, making the fetus a pursuer, see also Schiff, *Abortion in Judaism,* p. 60.

176. See Feldman, *Birth Control in Jewish Law,* pp. 273, 277.

177. See B San 72b; Schiff, *Abortion in Judaism,* pp. 49ff., 60.

178. See J. Preuss, *Biblical and talmudic Medicine,* p. 420; Schiff, *Abortion in Judaism,* pp. 61–63.

179. D. B. Sinclair, "Legal Basis for the Prohibition on Abortion," p. 121 (cited by Schiff, p. 61, n. 9). Rabbi Shneur Zalman of Lublin (d. 1902), however, pointed out that in MT Wounding and Damaging, viii, 15, Maimonides gave the example of one passenger on a ship throwing overboard the baggage of another on a sinking ship, as the baggage is "like a pursuer." See Schiff, *Abortion in Judaism,* pp. 103–4.

180. I benefited greatly from a discussion with my niece Alyssa Gray about the apparent illogicality of Maimonides' position, and she suggested this solution.

181. B San 57b; see MT Kings and Their Wars, ix, 4; x, 11; Schiff, *Abortion in Judaism,* pp. 52 and 62.

182. B San 59a.

183. Feldman, *Birth Control in Jewish Law,* p. 281.

184. M BQ, v, 3; B BQ 49a.

185. MT Kings and Their Wars, ix, 4; see B San 57b. Maimonides mentions other cases, including euthanasia, in which a Noahide is put to death, and asserts that in none of them is an Israelite put to death; see also Murder and the Preservation of Life, i, 13; ii, 2, 6, 8; B Nid 44a.

186. In the state of Israel, abortion laws are restrictive, permitting abortion only for the sake of a woman's physical or mental health. A woman must appear before a committee, including a physician (in obstetrics and gynecology), another physician (a family doctor,

psychiatrist, internist, or gynecologist) and a social worker, with at least one woman present on each committee; *Jerusalem Report*, February 12, 2001, http://www.jewishvirtuallibrary. org. For further information about Jewish views on abortion nowadays, see Daniel Eisenberg, "Abortion in Jewish Law," *Society Today: Science and Medical*, May 30, 2004; http:// www.aish.com/societyWork/sciencenature.

187. MT Mourning, iv, 5; M Sem, i, 1–6; B MQ 16b, Shab 151b. See Fred Rosner, "Euthanasia"; Byron Sherwin, "A View of Euthanasia."

188. These things are done after someone dies. The jaws are tied so that the mouth will not be open. However, when a person is dying, this may hasten his or her death and it is not done.

189. Rubbing and washing are done after the person dies. These things were mentioned in M Sem, i, 3 and Sem, Baraitot min Evel Rabbati, iii, 1. Rosner observes that Maimonides has added rubbing and washing to his talmudic source; "Euthanasia," p. 357. The sand and salt were intended to keep him alive.

190. The idea of a flickering flame is mentioned in M Semahot, i, 4 (in the name of Rabbi Meir) and in B Shab 151b. When someone touches a flickering candle, even to keep it burning, it is often extinguished. Maimonides adds the possibility of being in a swoon.

191. I. Jakobovits, *Jewish Medical Ethics*, pp. 123–25; "The Dying and Their Treatment in Jewish Law"; see Rosner, "Euthanasia," p. 362, n. 52.

192. For further discussion on recent halackhic decisions, see Jakobovits and Rosner in previous note, and see K. J. Kaplan and M. B. Schwartz, *Jewish Approaches to Suicide, Martyrdom, and Euthanasia*.

193. T San, ix, 11; B Ket 37b, B Pes 75a and parallels.

194. *Book of Commandments* pos. 9; MT Kings and Their Wars, viii, 11; MT Sabbath, xx, 14; MT Idolatry, x, 6; MT Circumcision; i, 6; MT Forbidden Intercourse, xiv, 7. See B San 56b–57a and Hul 92a, J 'AZ, ii, 1; GenR, xvi, 6 (Lieberman, *Greek in Jewish Palestine*, p. 81, n. 104). The Noahides are the descendants of Noah, hence the entire human race. See Aaron Lichtenstein, *Seven Laws of Noah*; David Novak, *The Image of the Non-Jew in Judaism: An Historical and Constructive Study of the Noahide Laws*; Schwarzschild, "Do Noachites Have to Believe in Revelation?"; Faur, "The Basis for the Authority of the Divine Commandments According to Maimonides." These laws may be considered valid by natural right in the sense that they set forth the minimal conditions for political life.

195. MT Kings and Their Wars, ix, 4; see B San 57b. The reasoning of the rabbis appears to be that the Noahides are bound by the pre-Mosaic legislation in Gen 9:5–6. The Talmud (B San 57b) cites verse 6 (as a prohibition of abortion).

196. MT Kings and Their Wars, viii, 11. As accepted on the basis of a reasoned conclusion alone, they are not absolute obligations, since reason may justify breaching them for pragmatic reasons, whereas divine commands have an absolute claim. (I heard this explanation from Professor Saul Lieberman.)

197. For the evidence, see *talmudic Encyclopedia*, vi, 290; J. Katz, *Shelosha mishpatim apologetiyyim be-gilgulehem*, pp. 270–90, esp. pp. 270–77; J. Faur, "The Basis for the Authority of the Divine Commandments According to Maimonides," p. 47, n. 45; Twersky, *Introduction to the Code of Maimonides*, p. 455, n. 239. The printed editions, from the first edition of Rome 5240 A.M. (1480/81 C.E.), have *we-lo'*. Once this (incorrect) reading got into the first edition, it was copied by subsequent printed editions. M. Fox prefers this reading ("nor is he one of their wise men"). See "Maimonides and Aquinas on Natural Law," pp. xii–xv; *Interpreting Maimonides*, pp. 124–51, esp. 132–33. He holds that Maimonides strongly rejected all claims of natural law predicated upon right reason (p. 130), hence he did not agree that gentiles who recognize the seven Noahide laws by reason are sages (p. 132).

198. On this passage and later discussions, see L. Strauss, *Spinoza's Critique of Religion*, pp. 23–25; S. S. Schwarzschild, "Do Noachites Have to Believe in Revelation?" And see Novak, *The Image of the Non-Jew*. The exclusion of wise gentiles from the world hereafter contradicts Maimonides' view that immortality is a state accessible to gentiles.

199. L. Strauss, "Natural Law," p. 140. And see his *Natural Right and History*, p. 158, on the Averroist view of Marsilius of Padua, which understands natural right as following from necessary and universal convention.

200. MT King and Their Wars xi, 3–4. On resurrection at the time of the messianic advent, see, e.g., Se'adyah Gaon, *Book of Doctrines and Beliefs,* trans. Rosenblatt, pp. 264, 309; Hayya Gaon, in Rabbi Abraham ben `Azriel, `Arugat ha-Bosem, I, 249, 261. As is well known, Maimonides' omission of resurrection in the eschatological drama disturbed a number of critics, who took this as a sign that he rejected belief in it, prompting his reply in the *Treatise on Resurrection.*

201. MT Kings and Their Wars, xi, 4. The passage is translated by Hershman in the Introduction to his translation of the *Book of Judges*, pp. xxiii–xxiv. It occurs in the first edition (Rome 1480/81) and was also preserved by Moses ben Nahman (Nahmanides); see Lea Naomi Goldfeld, "The Laws of Kings, Wars and the King Messiah According to Maimonides' *Mishneh Torah*," p. 244.

202. MT Repentance, ix, 1. Maimonides, like Spinoza after him, regarded the rewards promised in the Torah to be of this world. Yet Maimonides viewed them as a means for attaining the ultimate reward, whereas Spinoza thought that the material rewards of the Bible were their final end; see Spinoza, *Tractatus Theologico-Politicus*, III, 48; V, 69–70.

203. MT Repentance, ix, 2.

204. B 'AZ 54b.

205. B Ber 34b in the name of Samuel. In MT Kings and Their Wars, xii, 1, Maimonides said that prophecies envisioning a change in nature are hyperbolic. He said the same in his Introduction to San, x (Pereq Heleq) and *Epistle on Resurrection*, trans. Hillel G. Fradkin, p. 167.

206. Introduction to San, x (Pereq Heleq), ed. Qafih, p. 207. Maimonides referred to the sages' saying, *The Land of Israel is destined to produce cakes and wool robes.* See B Shab 30b and Ket 111b. Whereas in the *Mishneh Torah,* he spoke in general of abundant goods and delicacies, in the *Commentary on the Mishnah* he had used more concrete and picturesque language. Maimonides' emphasis on the persistence of class distinctions between rich and poor contrasted with the revolutionary programs of many messianic movements.

207. *Treatise on Resurrection*, trans. Fradkin, p. 167.

208. See *Historia animalium*, IX, 1, 608b30f.

209. *Guide*, III, 11 (pp. 440–41).

210. *Guide*, III, 33 (p. 532).

211. See S. M. Stern, *Aristotle on the World State*, pp. 7–8.

212. MT Kings and Their Wars, xii, 5.

213. Ibid., xii, 4; Repentance, ix, 8.

214. Cf. *For the earth shall be filled with awe for the glory of the Lord as waters cover the sea* (Hab 2:14).

CHAPTER 19

1. *Guide*, Epistle Dedicatory, p. 4. See, e.g., *Theology of Aristotle*, IV, 41–42, ed. P. Henry and H.-R. Schwyzer, *Plotini Opera*, II, p. 381, on writing for the few.

2. *Guide*, Epistle Dedicatory, p. 3.

3. R. Drory, "The *Maqama*," in *The Literature of al-Andalus,* ed. M. R. Menocal et al., ch. 8; C. Brockelmann (Ch. Pellat), EI, s.v. "Maqāma." It is translated as "assembly," "session," "séance." The word *maqama* is from *qama*, meaning "to rise," "to stand," and hence "to stay in a place," "abode where one stays." See R. Blachère, "Etude semantique sur le nom *maqāma*."

4. A. Mirsky, "Hebrew Literary Creation," *The Sephardi Legacy*, ed. Haim Beinart, I, 179.

5. Maimonides used "perfect" in the sense of acccomplished or consummate in knowledge and virtue, not totally without blemish.

6. *Maqasid al-mutakallimin* may allude to the title of al-Ghazali's work *Maqasid al-falasifa*; see Baneth, *Epistles*, p. 8, on line 15, and see *Guide*, I, chs. 71–76.

7. The rest of the verse is *and recorded genuinely truthful sayings*. Where Maimonides quotes this verse, as in CM Introduction to San, x (Pereq Heleq), third group, and *Epistle on Astrology*, trans. Lerner, p. 178, it relates to the discovery of the truth. He alludes to Joseph's desire to pursue metaphysical matters.

8. Pines trans. "strange notion," but *gharib* also means "wondrous" and the like, which is its meaning here; see also Avraham Nuriel, *Concealed and Revealed in Medieval Jewish Philosophy*, pp. 158–64.

9. See *Epistles*, ed. Baneth, Introduction, p. 2. The *Guide* was undertaken before Maimonides had a son, that is, before 1186.

10. Maimonides used the expression occasionally despite his rejection of predestination. See CM Eight Chapters, chs. 2 and 8 on determinism and free will. In MT Repentance, vi, 3 and 5, God's determination is equated with divine wisdom or with the way of the world; and see *Guide*, III, 17.

11. Baneth distinguishes between completion of the *Guide* and completion of its publication; see *Epistles*, Introduction to epistle no. 6, p. 37, n. 1.

12. Baneth, *Epistles*, pp. 67–68.

13. The Eastern quire had five sheets folded in half (bifolia), into ten leaves written on both sides (recto and verso folios), giving twenty pages of writing. The word for "quire" is *quntres* < Grk *chartēs* (papyrus). Heb *qartes*, "paper," "document" (and nowadays "ticket") is from the same Greek word. Cf. Ar *qirtas* (paper). The English word "quire" denotes four sheets of paper doubled into eight leaves in medieval manuscripts, ultimately from Lat *quatern,* a set of four (OED). As Maimonides sent Joseph six quires, there were some 120 pages of writing. He said that he got them from someone, hence they were not in his handwriting. His own manuscripts of the *Guide*, such as T-S 10 K a4, had about twenty-five lines per page and about nine words per line, or about 225 words per page.

14. Baneth (p. 37, n. 1) suggests that this refers to Part I, chapter 71 or 71–72, but I believe that Maimonides sent more. The *sadr* is presumably the Introduction at the beginning of Part I.

15. Ms. S has "the pious judge Abu 'l-Mahasin." In his letter to Rabbi Phineas, judge of Alexandria, he twice mentioned "the pious judge," who may be Isaac ben Sason, Maimonides' close colleague. A better candidate is the judge Hananel, who did do copying and was also called "the pious judge." Abu 'l-Mahasin is the teknonym (*kunya*) of Maimonides' father-in-law, Mishael al-Shaykh al-Thiqa, but this may not be the same person. Maimonides said "none other" because it was unusual for men of this stature to function as copyists.

16. Maimonides was afraid that some Jews would show the book to Muslims. 'Abd al-Latif al-Baghdadi reported that Maimonides "wrote a book for the Jews and called it *Kitab al-dalala*, and cursed whoever would write it in a non-Hebrew script"; cited in Ibn Abi Usaybi'a, *Classes of Physicians*, p. 687. See above, p. 209.

17. Maimonides alluded to Jews who would report him to the Muslim authorities. For the concept "the wicked among Israel" (*rish'e yisra'el*), see T San (Zuckermandel), xiii, 2; B Sot 48b, 110b; MT Sabbath, l, 15; Evidence, xi, 10.

18. *Epistles*, ed. Baneth, Epistle to Joseph, no. 8, pp. 93–94.

19. Cf. Isa 9:5.

20. Cf. Ruth 4:15. See Baneth, *Epistles*, pp. 9–16. Joseph became Maimonides' pupil before his son, Abraham, was born (1186).

21. Baneth, *Epistles*, p. 10, n. 1, sees here a positive attitude to Muslim Sufis, found also in the writings of his son, Abraham, who described the Sufis as following in the ways of the prophets of Israel. See *High Ways of Perfection (Kifayat al-'abidin)*, ed. and trans. S. Rosenblatt, pp. 48–53. Rosenblatt covers only Part 2, section 4, Part 2, Chapters XI–XXIII, a frac-

tion of the entire work. See also David Blumenthal, "Maimonides' Intellectualist Mysticism and the Superiority of the Prophecy of Moses."

22. The title "Introduction" is given by Pines in square brackets; see p. 5. Pines calls it (p. 10) "Introduction to the First Part," yet it seems to have been an Introduction to the *Guide* as a whole.

23. See *Guide*, I, 14 (p. 40).

24. *Guide*, I, Introduction (p. 5).

25. See Miriam Galston's discussion of multilevel writing in *The Political Philosophy of al-Farabi*, passim (Index, p. 238).

26. *Guide*, III, 51 (p. 619).

27. See Sarah Stroumsa's edition of Joseph ben Judah, *Silencing Epistle Concerning the Resurrection of the Dead*, Introduction, p. xi, with a somewhat less sanguine assessment.

28. On Joseph, see S. Munk, "Notice sur Joseph ben Iehouda"; D. H. Baneth, "Joseph Ibn Simon, the Important Pupil of Maimonides and Joseph Ibn 'Aqnin" and "Some Philological Remarks Concerning Yosef ben Yehuda ben Shimon's Metaphysical Treatise."

29. Ibn al-Qifti, *History of the Sages*, pp. 392–34.

30. His *ḳunya* (teknomyn) Abu 'l-Hajjaj was conventional for men named Joseph. As a Muslim, he was Abu 'l-Hajjaj Yusuf ibn Yahya.

31. It was for a short time. Maimonides mentioned in *Guide*, II, 24 (p. 322) that apart from astronomy there was insufficient time to begin another theoretical study with him.

32. Joseph may have taken a land route to India. His being a commerçant as well as a scholar and physician is a phenomenon that should no longer surprise us. Joseph's teacher, Moses ben Maimon, had contact with him in matters concerning the India trade.

33. He ministered to al-Malik al-Zahir Ghazi, son of Saladin, who was ruler of Aleppo and its territories.

34. Ibn Abi Usaybi'a, *Classes of Physicians*, p. 696.

35. This is the only report known to me saying that Joseph studied *medicine* with Maimonides.

36. Faris al-Maymun al-Qasri (d. Ramadan 616 = November-December 1219) was an army commander and had a reputation for bravery. Yaqut, *Mu'jam al-buldan*, IV, 354, takes the name al-Qasri from the two Fatimid palaces (*qasrani*) in Cairo. He was with 'Izz al-Din Jurayk when he raided Yavneh in January and February 1192, and commanded a raiding party that ambushed the Franks outside the city. He died in Aleppo. See Abu Shama, *al-Rawdatayn fi akhbar al-dawlatayn*, IV, 298; Ibn Abi Usaybi'a, *Classes of Physicians*, p. 696; Yusuf Ibn Taghribirdi, *al-Nujum al-zahira*, VI, 137; Ibn al-Athir, al-*Kamil fi'-ta'rikh*, X, 213; Lyons and Jackson, *Saladin*, p. 346. S. Munk thought that Joseph ben Judah may have met Ibn al-Qifti in al-Qasri's residence; "Notice sur Joseph ben-Iehouda," p. 11, n. 1.

37. Joseph Sadan, "Rabbi Judah al-Harizi as a Cultural Intersection"; and Aharon Mirsky, *EJ*, s.v. "Alharizi."

38. See Yahalom and Blau, *The Wanderings of Judah Alharizi*, p. 210 and n. 232. On his translation of the *Guide*, see Moritz Steinschneider, *Die Hebraeischen Übersetzungen des Mittelalters*, pp. 428–32, and Yair Shifman, "On Different Ways of Translating *The Guide of the Perplexed* and Their Philosophical Meanings," and Shiffman's "The Differences Between the Translations of Maimonides' *Guide of the Perplexed* by Falaquera, Ibn Tibbon, and al-Harizi, and the Textual and Philosophical Implications."

39. His translation was based on a secondary Arabic version made from Samuel Ibn Tibbon's Hebrew translation. See D. H. Baneth, "Rabbi Judah al-Harizi and the Three Translations"; Yahalom and Blau, *The Wanderings of Judah Alharizi*, p. 191.

40. Chapter on Poems, ed. Yahalom and Blau, vi, 73 [12], p. 201.

41. Yahalom and Blau, *The Wanderings of Judah Alharizi*, p. xv. See the Chapter on Poets, version 5, ed. Yahalom and Blau, p. 179; and S. M. Stern, "An Unpublished *Maqama* by Al-Harizi," p. 208.

42. Pleiades has seven stars and is known to be a guide at night.

43. Baneth, *Epistles*, p. 23. The marriage was consummated in the bridal chamber, where the bride remained probably for the week of festivities. It was then, after Joseph had known her, that she was unfaithful.

44. Ibn 'Ubaydallah is the name of Maimonides' family after his eponymous ancestor. This, as far as I know, is the first time Ibn Rushd (Averroes) is associated with the *Guide*.

45. *Kesil* also may be taken as alluding to Maskil of Joseph's *maqama*. The imagery of the *maqama* is the background to the figures used here. Maskil wished to marry Yemimah, who was under the protection of the Nasi Moses ben Maimon.

46. Cf. Esther 4:16.

47. Cf. Lev 19:19 and Deut 22:9. The two kinds to witness are Maimonides and Ibn Rushd.

48. Combining Lam 4:5 and Exod 17:12, in which the stem *'-m-n* is used in two different senses, and alluding to a third, faithfulness, thus a triple paronomasia. "Steady in the heavenly sphere" alludes to Pleiades.

49. Gen. 38:15. Tamar had covered her face, and so her father-in-law, Judah, took her for a cult prostitute. By rabbinic times, covering of the face was a sign of modesty and the biblical text became puzzling. Various explanations were given, one being that she kept her face covered out of modesty in her father-in-law's home, and therefore he did not recognize her on the road. See B Meg 10b; Sot 10b; BerR lxxxv, 15–16. Maimonides meant that his "daughter" was modest, but Joseph took her for a prostitute. He also alluded to the veiled, esoteric nature of the *Guide*.

50. Munk, "Notice sur Joseph b. Jehuda," p. 59. Munk was first in the modern period to edit Joseph's allegorical letter.

51. Baneth considered (*Epistles,* p. 26) Maimonides' allegorical letter to Joseph one of the best creations in all of Jewish literature.

52. *Guide*, Introduction, pp. 5–6.

53. *Guide*, Introduction with Respect to This Treatise, pp. 16–17.

54. Leo Strauss quoted this remarkable sentence twice in "How To Begin To Study *The Guide of the Perplexed*," p. xiii and lvi, at the beginning and the end of his essay, changing the word order, but not inadvertently, as some have thought.

55. The poem is based on Isa 35: 8: *And a highway shall appear there, / which shall be called the Sacred Way. / No one unclean shall pass over it.* Ms. T-S J 2.39 23.5 × 16, a fragment of the Dedicatory Epistle to *The Guide*, has three lines written in his own hand, beginning *de'i holekh* ("My knowledge goes forth").

56. See MT Repentance viii, 4, where "the Sacred Way" is a metaphor for an eternal life of bliss.

57. Gematria (< Grk *geōmetria*) is assigning numerical value to letters of the alphabet, giving a word a numerical value.

58. The poem has nineteen words (12 + 7) and is in the meter *ha-shalem/al-kamil* ("the perfect").

59. See *Guide,* III, 54 (end) (p. 638). Before the poem Maimonides cited Isa 35:5 and 9:1, whose theme is light.

60. On *dalala*, see Gil Anidjar, *"Our Place in al-Andalus,"* ch. 1. The word and its root (*dalla*) are used in the *Guide* to mean "indicate, signify, and also infer" (from a proof text or other evidence). See also José Faur, *Homo Mysticus*, p. 50 on *dalala* as a signpost. He associates this with perplexity and the task of the *Guide*'s author to communicate "by insinuation rather than by imparting authoritative, objective knowledge." See also Faur, *Homo Mysticus*, pp. 52, 168, and 208.

61. The Arabic title, *Dalalat al-ha'irin,* means *hora'at ha-nevukhim, Guiding the Perplexed*. The translation *Moreh ha-nevukhim*, which Maimonides himself used, is not quite accurate. As for the original, Arabic title, Avner Giladi, "A Short Note on the Possible Origin of the

Title *Moreh ha-Nevukhim*," suggested that Maimonides may have found it in al-Ghazali's *Ihya' 'ulum al-din,* citing II, 10 and IV, 2, where one finds: *dalil al-mutahayyirin.* However, a phrase closer to Maimonides' title is preserved in Ahmad b. Muhammad al-Maqqari's *Nafh al-tib min ghusn al-Andalus al-ratib,* V, 324 and VI, 325, namely, *dalil al-ha'irin.*

62. The Arabic translators Eustathius, Mattā b. Yūnus, and Naẓīf b. Yumn al-Rūmī used *taḥayyur* and *ḥayra* for *aporia* in Aristotle's *Metaphysics* (e.g. 1045a7, 1075a5, 993a4); see S. M. Afnan, *Philosophical Terminology in Arabic and Persian,* p. 84. I do not agree with some that by starting with perplexity Maimonides alluded to Aristotle's statement that philosophy begins in *wonder (thaumazein)*; see *Metaph.,* I, 2, 982b12.

63. For Socrates, according to Plato's *Meno* 79e5–80c6, inquiry began with his placing himself and others in a state of perplexity *(aporein)*; see Jacob Klein, *A Commentary on Plato's Meno,* p. 88.

64. *Guide,* Introduction, pp. 5–6 (emphasis added).

65. See Michel Foucault, *The Care of the Self, Vol. 3 of The History of Sexuality,* especially Part II: "The Cultivation of the Self."

66. *Philosophy as a Way of Life,* ed. Arnold Davidson, trans. Michael Chase, Introduction, pp. 19–20.

67. *Du musst dein Leben ändern*; *Archaischer Torso Apollos, Neue Gedichte/New Poems,* trans. Stephen Cohn, p. 142/143.

68. As a letter, we expect it to be called a *risala.* In the text, Maimonides called it a *maqala* (treatise). The Arabic terms, however, are often interchangeable; see A. Arazi and H. Ben-Shammai, EI, s.v. "Risāla."

69. See *Guide,* Introduction, p. 6.

70. The Account of the Beginning pertains to the Creation narrative and the Account of the Chariot to Ezekiel's vision of the divine chariot, or divine throne (Ezek 1:1–3:15). See L. Strauss, "The Literary Character of *The Guide for the Perplexed,*" p. 54.

71. M Hag, ii, 1.

72. See Gershom Scholem, EJ, s.v. "Kabbalah."

73. B Suk 28a, BB 134a, MT Foundations of the Law, iv, 13.

74. *Third Enoch or the Hebrew Book of Enoch,* ed. H. Odeberg; Ithamar Gruenwald, *Apocalyptic and Merkavah Mysticism*; David J. Halperin, *The Merkabah in Rabbinic Literature*; idem, *The Faces of the Chariot: Early Jewish Responses to Ezekiel's Vision*; Peter Schaefer, *Synopse zur Hekhalot-Literatur*; idem, *Geniza Fragmente zur Hekhalot-Literatur*; James R. Davila, "The Dead Sea Scrolls and Merkavah Mysticism"; idem, *Descenders to the Chariot: The People Behind the Hekhalot Literature*; Vita Daphna Arbel, *Beholders of Divine Secrets: Mysticism and Myth in Hekhalot and Merkavah Literature.* See also R. Goctschcl (ed.), *Prière, Mystique et Judaisme*; M. Bar-Ilan, *Thc Mysteries of Jewish Prayer and Hekhalot*; and M. D. Swartz, *Mystical Prayer in Ancient Judaism: An Analysis of Ma'aseh Merkavah.*

75. See especially Rahel Elior, *The Three Temples.*

76. See, e.g., Moshe Idel, *Maïmonide et la mystique juive.*

77. *Tosefta ki-fshuṭah,* ed. Lieberman, Hag, ii, 1–3, p. 1287–88. B Hag 11b, 13a; MT Foundations of the Law, ii, 11–12; iv, 11, 13, *Guide,* I, 33 (p. 72); III, 5 (p. 425).

78. We find the method of dispersion *(tabdid)* in alchemical writings, which were esoteric and used this method of concealment along with alphanumeric symbolism *(gematria)*; see *Guide,* Introduction, pp. 6–7; Paul Kraus, *Jābir Ibn Ḥayyān: Contribution à l'histoire des idées scientifiques dans l'Islam,* pp. 32, 42–43, 49, and 336; Rémi Brague, "Paul Kraus: Person und Werk (1904–1944)," p. 5, mentions *tabdid* with regard to Maimonides. Kraus, *Contribution,* p. 49, quotes Jabir as saying that the wisdom of Plato is dispersed throughout his writings, and that a great effort is needed to disengage it. On Jabir ibn Hayyan, see also P. Lory, *Dix traités d'alchimie,* and the bibliography cited.

The magical tome called *Picatrix* (*Ghayat al-hakim, The Aim of the Sage*), on the talismanic art, magic, and astrology, is a very disorderly book, with an erratic sequence of chapters and much irrelevant material. Subjects that should be together are asunder, sequences are broken. See Martin Plessner, Introduction, pp. lix–lxxv. The mode of presentation is intentional. The same is true of the famous encyclopedia of the Brethren of Sincerity (*Ikhwan al-Safa'*).

79. Leo Strauss recommended this way of reading Plato's works. See, for instance, his *City and Man*, p. 60, where he says that there is nothing by chance, arbitrary, or haphazard in Plato's dialogues, and they must be read with exceeding care.

80. *Guide*, Introduction, pp. 7–8. The image of lightning recalls early Arabic odes, in which lightning is depicted as piercing dark clouds over distant mountains. Pines, "The Limitations of Human Knowledge," pp. 89–90, says that Maimonides received the lightning image from Ibn Sina's *al-Isharat wa'l-tanbihat* (see Ibn Sina, *Isharat*, ed. J. Forget, 202–3). See also Pines, Translator's Introduction, pp. lxviii, cv. Al-Ghazali adopted Avicennan ideas in the Metaphysics of the *Intentions of the Philosophers*, on vision, prophecy, and miracles. In the vision of the unknown, the soul must liberate itself from the body and remove the veil of the senses; then it rises to the supernal world, where things appear to it in a moment, brief as a lightning flash. This is the first level of prophecy. The image of lightning was used later by Ibn Bajja; see *al-Ittisal*, pp. 114–15. Ibn Tufayl, *Hayy ibn Yaqzan*, p. 6 (text), p. 96 (trans.), mentions "delightful glimpses of the truth, strokes of lightning as it were, which no sooner flash than they disappear," adding, "Now, if he persists in his disciplinary practice, these ecstatic glimpses multiply." See also *Guide*, III, 51, (p. 625). Maimonides teaches that the dark night is illumined for the prophet by lightning flashes from on high, but for the philosopher only by the "small light" reflected by pure gleaming bodies; see L. Strauss, *Philosophy and Law*, trans. E. Adler, pp. 108–10, 140, n. 16. Strauss followed a comment of Shem tov Ibn Falaquera on *Guide*, III, 51, where he cited Abu Bakr (Ibn Bajja) as saying that the symbol of lightning flashes in the dark parallels the Platonic image of the cave and the sun in the *Republic*; see Ibn Falaquera, *Moreh ha-Moreh*, ed. Y. Shiffman, p. 318. For Maimonides, only the prophets live outside the cave and see the sun itself, whereas the philosophers see merely an image of it.

81. Pines translates (*Guide*, p. 8): "all the sages possessing knowledge of God the Lord." But I think that *kull hakim ilahi rabbani* should be translated "every sage who is a metaphysician." See also Munk, *Le Guide des égarés*, I, 12, n. 1. Friedländer, *Guide*, p. 10, translates, "great theological scholars." Fox, *Interpreting Maimonides*, p. 267, takes Friedlander to task for translating *ilahi* as "theologian," but Friedländer was innocent.

82. See also al-Farabi, *Kitab al-jam' bayn ra'yā 'l-ḥakīmayn*, pp. 84–85; trans. Mallet, pp. 64–65; and Kraemer, "The Islamic Context," p. 50. See the biography of Aristotle by al-Mubashshir b. Fatik, *Mukhtar al-hikam*, p. 184; trans. I. Düring, *Aristotle in the Biographical Tradition*, p. 201 (and see his comment, p. 433). Avicenna mentioned the same correspondence in *Fi ithbat al-nubuwwa*, in *Tis' rasa'il fi 'l-hikma wa-'l-tabi'iyyāt*, p. 85; trans. M. E. Marmura, *Medieval Political Philosophy: A Sourcebook*, ed. Lerner and Mahdi, p. 116. And see Galen, *Compendium Timaei Platonis*, ed. Paul Kraus and Richard Walzer, p. 3, on Aristotle's terse, obscure style. On the terse, compressed, precise style of Aristotle's acroamatic works as opposed to the popular style of his dialogues, see the testimonies in *The Works of Aristotle*, trans. David Ross, XII, *Select Fragments*, p. 5. Greek *akroamatikos* means "*designed for hearing only*, the *esoteric* doctrines of philosophers, delivered orally"; Liddell-Scott, *Greek-English Lexicon*, p. 56. The *Guide*, we have seen, was a written substitute for oral dialogue.

83. On preference for oral instruction in Plato, see, e.g., *Phaedrus* 276A–277A; Seventh Letter, 344e. See also al-Farabi's introduction to his *Compendium of Plato's Laws*, ed. Fr. Gabrieli, pp. 3–4.

84. *Guide*, Introduction, pp. 10–12.

85. See also Ibn Rushd, *The Decisive Treatise*, trans. Butterworth, p. 11. And see F. Talmage, "Apples of Gold," p. 314.

86. *Guide*, Introduction, pp. 11–12.

87. Y. Yovel, *Spinoza and Other Heretics*, I, 143, says that Maimonides was Spinoza's

mentor in rhetorical matters and addressing the multitude. Primary in philosophical rhetoric is the use of "metaphoric-systematic equivalence."

88. *Guide,* III, 32 (p. 525). Cf. Spinoza's *deus sive natura* in Ethics, II, 206–7, 213, ed. E. Curley, pp. 114, 118–19 (Penguin Classics) and *The Collected Works,* I, pp. 544 and 548. Spinoza intends by nature an active force, *natura naturans.* Whenever Maimonides says, "I mean to say," the reader needs to be alert. Pines remarks, "Translator's Introduction," p. xcvi, n. 66, that Spinoza's expression "may have been, at least in part, suggested by this passage of *The Guide.*" See also Moshe Idel, *"Deus sive Natura"*; and Carlos Fraenkel, "Maimonides' God and Spinoza's *Deus sive Natura.*"

89. Ethics, Prop. 29–31, ed. Curley, p. 434. Spinoza's distinction between *natura naturans* and *natura naturata* (nature as experienced by us) (see H. A. Wolfson, *The Philosophy of Spinoza,* I, 216, 252–55, 371) is found in medieval Arabic texts as *al-ṭabīʿa al-ṭābiʿa* and *al-ṭabīʿa al-maṭbūʿa*; see my *Philosophy in the Renaissance of Islam,* p. 177.

90. *Theological-Political Treatise,* vi, 8–9; trans. Jonathan Israel, pp. 86–87.

91. See Faur, *Homo Mysticus,* pp. 49–50.

92. Kraemer, "Islamic Milieu," p. 61.

93. To remind the reader, Judeo-Arabic, the language of the *Guide,* was generally written in Hebrew characters. See above in this chapter, n. 16.

94. *Guide,* Introduction with Respect to This Treatise, p. 16.

95. Ps 119:126; M Ber ix, 5; B Ber 54a, 63a, Yoma 69a and parallels. See also *Responsa,* no. 211, p. 375; no. 256, p. 475. This was understood to mean, "When it is time to act for the Lord, you may abrogate the Torah," the sense being that you may infringe a precept to conserve the entire Torah.

96. M Avot, ii, 12 (Pines, p. 16, n. 62, has Aboth, ii, 17).

97. Jacob I. Dienstag, "Biblical Exegesis of Maimonides in Jewish Scholarship."

98. See Twersky, *Introduction to the Code of Maimonides,* p. 144–54, on Maimonides' philological-lexicographical material in the *Mishneh Torah.* Strauss, "How to Read," p. xxv, observes that in *Guide,* I, 1–49, thirty chapters are lexicographic, whereas in the rest of the treatise at most two are such, namely, I, 66 and I, 70.

99. See Aristotle, *Categories* , I, 1a, 1–12; *Topics,* I, 15, 106a, 9; Harry A. Wolfson, "The Amphibolous Terms in Aristotle, Arabic Philosophy and Maimonides."

100. *Guide,* I, 27 (p. 57). On Onqelos, see Rafael B. Posen, *The Consistency of Targum Onqelos' Translation.*

101. Maimonides cited Onqelos in *Book of Commandments,* pos. 36 and neg. 128; MT Forbidden Intercourse, xii, 13 and Mourning, v, 19. In Marriage, viii, 4 he referred to being able to read Onqelos; see B Qid 49a. Maimonides used Onqelos to support his non-literal interpretation of Scripture, as in *Guide* I, 2. See Possen, *The Consistency of Targum Onqelos' Translation,* p. 75, n. 1.

102. Onqelos was a convert to Judaism, and Maimonides stressed this by using the epithet, *ha-ger,* meaning "the Proselyte."

103. *Guide,* II, 33 (p. 366). Eliezer ben Hyrqanos and Joshua ben Hananyah were second-generation Tannaim (40–80 c.e.); see Strack and Stemberger, *Introduction to the Talmud and Midrash,* pp. 77–78.

104. For Word (*memra*), see Onqelos on Gen 21:20, 23; 28:15; 39:2. For Indwelling (*shekhinta*), see Ex 15:17, 20:21, 25:8. For Glory (*yeqara*), see Gen 28:13, Ex 3:1, 24:13. The terms are in Aramaic, the language of his translation, and they all signify God's presence.

105. See *Guide,* I, 21 (pp. 48–49), where Maimonides approved of Onqelos' translation. And see *Guide,* I, 54 (p. 124). In *Guide,* Part I, Maimonides used the Qur'anic term *sakina* in at least four chapters (chapters 10, 21, 22, 25), surely not to avoid the rabbinic term *shekhinah,* for he also uses that (for instance, chapters 21, 23, 25, 27, 28, 76). See Qur'an 9:40; 48:4, 18, 26. See also n. 122 below.

106. See Ex 25:8, 29:45–46, Num. 35:34; 1 Kings 6:13, etc.; Kaufmann Kohler and Ludwig Blau, *JE,* s.v. "Shekhinah."

107. Zech 8:3, Ps 135:21, 1 Chron 23:25.

108. Deut 33:16.

109. Exod 24:16–17. On *doxa* in the New Testament as "brightness, splendor, radiance," expanding in meaning to "glory, majesty, and sublimity," see William F. Arndt and F. Wilbur Gingrich, *A Greek-English Lexicon of the New Testament*, p. 203. In the Apocrypha and the New Testament, the word "radiance" (Grk *doxa*) refers to a divine presence, like Aramaic *yeqara*, as in Lk 2:9—"the glory of the Lord [*doxa kuriou*] shone around them." Jn 1:14 has both *logos* (= *memra*) and *doxa* (= *yeqara*). In Rev 21:3, there is a reference to "the tabernacle [*skēnē*] of God." *Skēnē* is a perfectly good Greek word, and the translation makes sense, but the context requires something like "presence," and one wonders whether *skēnē* may be deformed from *shekhinah*.

110. Maimonides identified the permanence of God's Indwelling, or his created light, with the permanence of his providence; see *Guide*, I, 25 (p. 55); 28 (p. 60). The created light is identical in medieval Jewish thought with the term *kavod* (glory) as an emanated divine light. See Harry A. Wolfson, *Crescas' Critique of Aristotle*, pp. 460–61. Maimonides appears to have identified Word-Indwelling-Glory with the Agent Intellect.

111. See Se'adyah Gaon, *Book of Beliefs and Opinions*, ii, trans. S. Rosenblatt, chs. 8 and 10. See also Se'adyah's *Commentary on Daniel*, ed. J. Qafih, pp. 134–36; Ha-Levi, *Kuzari*, ii, 4, 7, 8; iv, 3, 14. For "revealed light" and "created light" in prophecy, see the Hebrew translation of the *Guide* by Michael Schwarz, I, p. 38 n. 6; and *Guide*, I, 10, 19, 25, 26, 27, 28, 64, 76; II, 10, 18, 19, 25, 27, 76; III, 7.

112. *Guide* I, 1. See also MT Foundations of the Law, iv, 1.

113. *NJPS* translates Elohim as "divine beings." Following Onqelos, Maimonides took Elohim in the sense of rulers, the meaning it has in Ex 22:8, according to some interpreters. See T Shev, iii, 8 (Zuckermandel); B San 3b, J San, i, 18. See also the philosophic allegory in *Guide*, II, 30; Warren Z. Harvey, "Maimonides and Spinoza on the Knowledge of Good and Evil"; and S. Pines, "Truth and Falsehood Versus Good and Evil."

114. The Arabic text has *rajul 'ulumi*, an awkward expression. It is used to render *ho mathematikos* (mathematician) in the Arabic translation of Aristotle's *De anima* (403b15) by Ishaq ibn Hunayn. See S. M. Afnan, *A Philosophical Lexicon in Persian and Arabic*, p. 200; *Aristotelis De Anima,* ed. 'A. Badawi, p. 7, line 15. Or perhaps Maimonides meant a man of the sciences, that is, a scientist.

115. The words *hasan* and *qabih* render *to kalon* (morally noble) and *to aischron* (morally base); see, for instance, Aristotle, *Rhetorica* 1366a24, in the old Arabic translation, *al-Khitaba*, ed. 'A. Badawi, p. 38, line 9. See also al-Farabi, *Talkhis Nawamis Aflatun* (*Compendium Legum Platonis*), ed. and trans. Fr. Gabriel, ii, 1, p. 12, line 11 (*jamil* and *qabih*; cf. Laws 654a); cf. also iii, 2, p. 17, line 17. M. Fox, *Interpreting Maimonides*, p. 136, rejected Pines' translation, "fine and bad," opting for "beautiful and ugly" instead. However, the context relates to moral, not aesthetic, judgment, and Fox did not justify his translation on the basis of the Arabic text. His translation buttresses his view that Maimonides thinks of moral behavior as relating to the beautiful and the ugly, which pertain to subjective taste or social convention (p. 133). Cf. also S. Schwarzschild, "Do Noachites Have to Believe in Revelation?" p. 43, who also considers this terminology aesthetic. In Greek and Arabic, however, these terms have an ethical connotation.

116. See also *Treatise on the Art of Logic*, ed. and trans. Efros, ch. 8, p. 17/47. The self-evident propositions are: perceptions, first intelligibles, conventions, and traditions. In his *Epistle on Astrology*, Maimonides lists three sources of knowledge, omitting conventions; see *Letters*, ed. Shailat, p. 479; trans. R. Lerner, p. 179.

117. Spinoza, *Ethics*, ed. and trans. E. Curley, IV, 68, p. 584.

118. *Guide*, I, 2 (p. 25).

119. Spinoza, *Ethics*, II, 44, p. 480.

120. Theologico-Political Treatise, ed. J. Israel, v, 19, p. 79.

121. *Shekhinah* appears in *Guide*, I, 10, 21, 22, 23, 25, 27, 28, 76; II, 42, 45; III, 41, 45, 52; *Eight Chapters,* iv, vii; Commentary on Avot, iv, 4. *Book of Commandments,* pos. 6, 31, 96, 109, 209; neg. 68, 74, 252. The word occurs at least thirty-six times in the *Mishneh Torah:* in the Book of Knowledge—Foundations of the Law, vii, 5; Ethical Qualities, vi, 2, 4; Torah Study, v, 1, 8; Repentance, vii, 6, 7; viii, 2. See also Strauss, "How To Begin To Study *The Guide of the Perplexed*," pp. xxxi–xii.

122. Maimonides used Ar *sakina* instead of Heb *Shekhinah* four times—in *Guide*, I, 10 (p. 36); I, 21 (p. 48); I, 22 (p. 52); and I, 25 (p. 55). It is used with *hulul,* a term in mysticism that also occurs in Christian (for Incarnation) and Shi'i (the divine element in the Imam) texts. It is translated here as "descent" or "coming down." The context is prophecy, though in *Guide*, I, 25, it is the created light in a place or the permanence of providence. He used Heb *Shekhinah* in Part I, chapters 21, 23, 25, 27, 28, and 76 (x 2). The question is why he used both Arabic and Hebrew for the same concept.

Muslim scholars have taken *sakina* in the Qur'an and *hadith* as meaning "tranquility," from the Arabic root *sakana,* but it is almost certainly derived from Hebrew *shekhinah.* See, for instance, Qur'an 2:248. M. A. S. Abdel Haleem and M. Fakhry, to cite recent translations, take it as "tranquility," following traditional commentaries, but it makes little sense in the context. A. J. Arberry, being more cautious, used "shechina." R. Paret understands it to be the dwelling or presence of God, corresponding to Heb *shekhinah.* In another verse, "He sent down the Shechina upon them, and rewarded them with a nigh victory" (48:18, Arberry), *sakina* almost certainly means "presence" and not "tranquility."

T. Fahd, EI, s.v. "Sakīna," defines the root *s-k-n* as meaning "to go down, rest, be quiescent, inhabit." Fahd derives Ar *sakina* from Heb *Shekhinah,* noting that native Arab scholars do not. Once you accept that the Qur'an is the literal word of Allah, you cannot very easily derive any of its vocabulary from foreign sources. See Arthur Jeffrey, *The Foreign Vocabulary of the Qur'an.*

123. Yehuda Ratzaby, *A Dictionary of Judaeo-Arabic in R. Se'adyah's* Tafsir, p. 129.

124. *Guide*, I, 21 (p. 49)

125. Strauss, "How To Begin To Study *The Guide of the Perplexed*," p. xxxii. He suggests that while Shekhinah is bound to Israel, providence is bound to intellect. Yet Shekhinah is linked to prophecy, which is not exclusively a possession of the people of Israel.

126. The created light is identical in medieval Jewish thought with the term *kavod* (glory) as an emanated Divine Light. See Wolfson, *Crescas' Critique of Aristotle*, pp. 460–61. God's Glory takes on three meanings in the *Guide* (as Wolfson explains): (1) a divine emanation, called "the created light" (as in Ex 24:16); (2) the divine essence; (3) the human glorification or conception of God. The expression sometimes means the created light which God causes to show in a certain place (*Guide*, I, 64).

127. *Guide*, I, 25 (p. 55).

128. *Guide*, I, 23 (pp. 52–53).

129. *Guide*, I, 44 (p. 95).

130. *Guide*, I, 24 (p. 54).

131. On divine anger, see *Guide*, I, 24, 36; II, 23, 29; III, 28, 30; III, 48.

132. *Guide*, I, 36 (p. 84).

133. *Guide*, I, 62 (p. 152) and I, 63 (p. 154). For a profound explanation of *ehyeh asher ehyeh,* see James Kugel's *How to Read the Bible,* p. 211.

134. See Gen 2:4 and 4:26 for first instances of the tetragrammaton. It was pronounced *adonay* in the Massoretic text from the first century c.e. onward; see s.v. in Koehler, Baumgartner, Walter, *The Hebrew and Aramaic Lexicon of the Old Testament,* CD-ROM edition. A conflate of the consonants *y-h-w-h* of *yahweh* and the vowels *a-o-a* of *adonay* gave rise to *yahowah,* becoming Jehovah, a mispronunciation mixing what was written with what was read, first attested in 1381 and in general use from ca. 1500. The etymology of *y-h-w-h* is unknown. The *Lexicon* notes: (1) to blow, fall; (2) to be; to call into existence; (3) to be pas-

sionate, act passionately; (4) to speak; (5) to call ecstatically. In Hellenistic gnostic and Greek and magical papyri the name became *Yao*.

135. See *JSB* on the verse. A classic case of desacrilization is Shakespeare's use of God's self-designation of Ex 3:14 as a thunderous self-reference in Sonnet 121.9, "I am that I am." In the previous line the word "will" occurs; see Helen Vendler, *The Art of Shakespeare's Sonnets*, p. 513. Iago pronounces its negation by saying, "I am not what I am," in *Othello* I, 1, 65.

136. *Guide*, I, 57 (pp. 132-33), along with Avicenna.

137. This is what Maimonides means in MT Foundations of the Law, i, 1.

138. *Guide*, I, 58 (p. 135).

139. cf. *Guide*, II, 1, no. 3; I, 57 (p. 132).

140. *Guide*, I, 58–59 (pp. 134–43). Avicenna had espoused the doctrine of negative attributes, meaning that essential attributes ascribed to God (existing, one, wise, powerful) do not have a positive sense but must be understood as denying their opposite.

141. Maimonides understood the word *dumiyah* to mean silence. Modern versions take it in the sense of "befitting" (*Praise befits you in Zion, O God*). See also *Guide*, I, 51 (p. 112), where, introducing negation of attributes, he cites Ps 4:5: *Commune with your heart upon your bed, and be silent*. See also I, 59 (p. 140) and II, 5 (p. 260). Rashi on Psalm 65:2 takes it in the sense of silence. See also Ps 22:3 and 39:3. Ibn Ezra gave both meanings but favored silence. See also B 'Eruv 19a and Meg 18a; Bahya ibn Paquda, *Duties of the Hearts*, I, 10. On Ps 4:5. Samuel Terrien intimates a cultivation of mystic silence, trust in the Lord, tranquility, security, and quietude; *The Psalms,* p. 98.

142. Pines, "Limitations of Knowledge."

143. Topics, I, 11, 104b1–105a9.

144. See al-Farabi, *Kitab al-jadal*, ed. R. al-'Ajam, in *al-Mantiq 'inda al-Farabi*, III, 80–2; and Georges Vajda, "À propos d'une citation non identifiée d'al-Farabi dans le '*Guide des egarés*,'" pp. 43–50.

145. Ibn Tufayl was silent about the difference between the God of creation and Aristotle's first mover.

146. Barry S. Kogan, *Averroës and the Metaphysics of Causation,* pp. 209–22.

147. See Kraemer, "The *Jihād* of the *Falāsifa*," for the concept of rhetorical accommodation.

148. *Guide*, II, 26, pp. 330–32. See also II, 30, p. 349, where the passage is cited very briefly.

149. The *Chapters of Rabbi Eliezer* is dated to the eighth century C.E., that is, the Muslim period, and is falsely ascribed to the famous second-century Tanna Eliezer ben Hyrcanus, also called Eliezer the Great. Chapters of Rabbi Eliezer is a midrashic account of the biblical narrative, from the Creation story through the Book of Esther. As occasionally happens, Maimonides did not quote the text precisely. He omitted words and phrases, some perhaps because his source was faulty, but also, as is likely, to condense the passage to its essence. *Guide,* II, 26 occurs somewhere around the middle of the *Guide*.

150. GenR, III, 4. For references to earlier midrashim, to Philo, and to the Zohar, see L. Ginzberg, *Legends of the Jews*, V, 8. And see Urbach, *The Sages*, I, 209. For the development of this idea in the Kabbalah, see I. Tishby, *The Wisdom of the Zohar*, II, 552f.; A. Altmann, "A Note on the Rabbinic Doctrine of Creation."

151. Here the text has "upon the water and the water froze and became earth," which Maimonides omitted.

152. Pines translates the adjective *gharib* as "strangest," but the word often has the sense of "wondrous" and "extraordinary." In any case, it should not be taken to suggest that Maimonides rejected Eliezer the Great's statement. See also above, n. 8.

153. The Platonic idea of a Demiurge, or Craftsman, bringing the visible world from disorder to order (*Timaeus* 30A)—a *formatio mundi*—was appealing to Islamic philosophers. The Arabic version of Galen's *Compendium of the Timaeus* uses the language of creation, with Plato's Demiurge becoming "Allah" and *al-khaliq* (the Creator). The Platonic

model of the Demiurge as efficient cause was joined with Neoplatonic emanation, giving rise to a theory of eternal creation. This idea conformed with Qur'anic verses depicting Allah as the Creator who does not cease to create (al-khallaq) (10:4, 34; 30:11, 36:81, etc.). See Kraemer, "The Islamic Context," pp. 48–49. Marc B. Shapiro has shown in a fine conspectus that the major medieval Jewish philosophers, including Maimonides, held a Platonic view of creation; see *The Limits of Orthodox Theology,* pp. 71–77. Shapiro mentions Abraham Ibn Ezra, Judah ha-Levi, Samuel Ibn Tibbon, Gersonides, Shem Tov Falaquera, Abraham Abulafia, Hisday Crescas, and Joseph Ibn Kaspi. They adopt Averroes' formula of God's eternally transforming the world from non-being into being. Ultimately, it is the ontological dependence of the world on God that matters rather than a *creatio ex nihilo* myth. Leo Strauss urges us to compare Guide, III, 17 with III, 23 and II, 13 with II, 32, where repetitions introduce new viewpoints, and the second comparison implies a Platonic view of creation; "The Literary Character of the *Guide for the Perplexed,*" p. 63. See also his *Philosophy and Law,* pp. 74–75. And see Norbert M. Samuelson, *Judaism and the Doctrine of Creation*; Kenneth Seeskin, *Maimonides on the Origin of the World,* each with a section on Plato's *Timaeus*; and T. M. Rudavsky, *Time Matters: Time, Creation, and Cosmology in Medieval Jewish Philosophy,* especially pp. 5, 10–12, 18.

154. As was his wont, Maimonides had philosophic interpretations for most of Rabbi Eliezer's myth, but not for "the light of [God's] garment." He said that he had no figurative interpretation (*ta'wil*) and worried that it would confuse someone such as Joseph ben Judah, a learned man who cleaved to the law. Nevertheless, he identified this light with celestial matter.

155. Maimonides then cited a statement of Rabbi Eliezer in Genesis Rabbah that the creation of all that is in the heavens derives from the heavens, and the creation of all that is on earth derives from the earth; see GenR, xii, ed. Theodor-Albeck, pp. 109–10 (correct Pines, p. 332, n. 10, which has GenR, x); B Yoma 54b. See also QohR, iii, in the name of Rabbi Hiyya bar Joseph. The heavens were a fifth essence, quintessance, or ether, which Aristotle depicted as an unchangeable, perfect substance. They were translucent, and each sphere rotated in a perfect circular motion without friction.

156. For instance, GenR, iii, 4, ed. Theodor-Albeck, pp. 19–20, quoted by Altmann, "A Note on the Rabbinic Doctrine of Creation," pp. 129–30.

157. See J. Levenson, *Creation and the Persistence of Evil,* p. 5.

158. Ibid., p. 59.

159. Gershom Scholem, *Major Trends in Jewish Mysticism,* pp. 170, 173.

160. *Guide,* II, 6 (pp. 262–63). The word for "host" is *pamalya,* which is from Lat *familia* (p. 263, n. 16). Pines observes that the source for the quotation is unknown. See Schwarz's Hebrew translation, I, 279; and Lenn E. Goodman, "Maimonidean Naturalism," p. 161, on the Platonic aspect, citing also Idel on its importance for Kabbalah.

161. Pines translates, "from him." Cf. Timaeus 28Aff. on the eternal model imitated by the demiurge

162. *Guide,* II, 6, p. 263; B San 38b; J San, i; Mid ha-Gad, Bereshit, 55.

163. *Letter on Astrology,* trans. Lerner, pp. 181–82.

164. *Guide,* II, 30 (p. 349) cites GenR, iii, 7, ed. Theodor-Albeck, p. 23. See also EcclesR, iii, 11; MidPs, xxxiv.

165. "And there was evening and morning" implies that they had been present before the events of Creation, for God did not command that there be. Maimonides understood Rabbi Judah's view as agreeing with the Aristotelian concept that time always existed.

166. The text says *we-hinneh,* "and, behold, it was very good" (KJV), indicating that God now realizes that this one is very good. *Hinneh,* which is cognate to Arabic *inna,* need not always be translated. It does not, of course, mean "behold" or "look." It is asseverative or emphatic and draws attention to something. Robert Alter's excellent translation of the Pentateuch translates *we-hinneh* as "look" in many places where it functions exactly as *inna.*

167. The possibility exists that he had a different text. Yet if no such readings show up anywhere else, chances are that he quoted freely.

168. See his discussion of *Guide*, II, 26, above.

169. Kraemer, "Islamic Context," pp. 48–49.

170. In the *Wisdom of Solomon*, 11:18, we find creation depicted as shaping the world out of unformed matter as in *Timaeus* 50D.

171. Foundations of the Law vii, 1. For the most thorough treatments of prophecy in general and in Maimonides in particular, see Howard Kreisel, *Prophecy: The History of an Idea in Jewish Philosophy*.

172. CM Introd, ed. Shailat, p. 331 (Ar) p. 31 ; *Guide*, II, 32 (pp. 361–62). For courageous, see Avot iv, 1; ShP, vii, trans. Weiss and Butterworth, p. 81. On sound body, see MT Ethical Qualities, iv, 1.

173. B Shab 92a ("The Shekhinah rests only upon someone wise, courageous, wealthy, and tall"); cf. Ned 38a. Maimonides cited B Shab 92a in some of the passages in the previous note. He omitted tall as a criterion. (Was he tall?) The Talmud may have seen height as a leadership quality, as in the case of King Saul.

174. Al-Farabi, *Perfect State*, ed. and trans. Walzer, pp. 247–49 and pp. 439, 444–50 (commentary).

175. See *Guide*, II, 32, 38, III, 45 and 51. In Maimonides' statement of the sixth of his thirteen principles in the *Commentary on the Mishnah*, his language is philosophical: "Then this intellect conjoins with the Agent Intellect, and an exalted emanation overflows upon [the prophets] from it."

176. See al-Farabi's *Perfect State*, ed. and trans. Walzer, ch. 17, pp. 279–81. On his theory of prophecy, and especially the role of the faculty of imagination, see R. Walzer, "Al-Farabi's Theory of Prophecy and Divination," *Greek into Arabic*, pp. 206–19. *Rumuz* often renders *parabolai* or *mythoi* in translation literature. On Aristotle's use of *ibdalat* and Plato's employment of this technique in the *Timaeus* (upon which Alfarabi comments disapprovingly); see *Utterances Employed in Logic* (*Kitab al-alfaz al-musta'mala fi 'l-mantiq*), pp. 90–91. In this context Alfarabi also comments on the terms *rumuz* and *alghaz*, observing that there is no need to investigate (i.e., in a book on philosophical expressions) statements, the philosophy of which resembles lies (or "fables"), lit. "adornments," "embellishments" (*zakharif*). He adds, however, that while such lies may be repugnant in the various kinds of philosophical disciplines, they are perhaps indispensable in rhetoric and in the statements employed in political affairs.

177. The literature on providence in Maimonides is vast. These are some of the studies: Z. Diesendruck, "Samuel and Moses Ibn Tibbon on Maimonides' Theory of Providence"; Leo Strauss, "Der Ort der Vorsehungslehre nach der Ansicht Maimunis"; Leonard Kravitz, "The Revealed and the Concealed—Providence, Prophecy, Miracle and Creation in *The Guide*"; Alvin J. Reines, "Maimonides' Concepts of Providence and Theodicy"; Charles Touati, "Les deux theories de Maïmonide sur la Providence"; Charles M. Raffel, *Maimonides' Theory of Providence*; David Burrell, "Maimonides, Aquinas and Gersonides on Providence and Evil"; Alfred L. Ivry, "Providence, Divine Omniscience and Possiblility: The Case for Maimonides"; and Gad Freudenthal, "Maimonides' Stance on Astrology in Context: Cosmology, Physics, Medicine, and Providence."

178. *Guide*, II, 13 (p. 285); II, 32 (p. 360); III, 17 (p. 464).

179. *Guide*, III, 12.

180. This is an allusion to Aristotle's *On Generation and Corruption* (*Coming-into-Being and Passing Away*).

181. *De usu partium humani corporis*, III, 10, ed. Kuhn, p. 238; Guide, III, 12, p. 444, n. 13).

182. The examples are telling. David ben Maimon went on a sea voyage and Moses served kings. Yet Maimonides would presumably not say that either was seeking luxuries. The addressee, Joseph ben Judah, also served a king and went on a voyage to India.

183. Pines translated *fayd* as "overflow." Other translations of this Neoplatonic concept are "emanation," "efflux," and "influence."

184. *Guide*, III, 17 (471–72).

185. This is how Gersonides later understood the matter of intellect as our link to providence.

186. *Guide*, III, 18 (p. 474).

187. *Guide*, III, 18 (p. 476).

188. *Nicomachean Ethics*, x, vii, 8, 1177b14.

189. Shem Tov ben Joseph ben Shem Tov is the last known descendant (fifteenth century) of the Shem Tov family. He wrote a commentary in the *Guide* and pursued Aristotelian studies in an Averroistic mode. See Pines, Translator's Introduction, lxvi–lxvii.

190. *Guide*, III, 17 (p. 465).

191. *Guide*, III, 17 (pp. 466–67).

192. *Guide*, II, 12 (p. 280).

193. *Guide*, III, 52 (p. 629); Pines, "Translator's Introduction," p. cxv.

194. *Guide*, III, 16 (pp. 461–62).

195. *Guide*, III, 51 (pp. 624–25) (Pines translates *nazar* as "speculation," but "insight" catches the meaning better.)

196. Cf. *Guide*, I, 23 (p. 53), where Maimonides speaks of God's returning to his place (Hosea 5:15) as the removal of the Shekhinah, following which is a privation of providence among us. This is also called God's hiding his face (Deut. 31:17): "For a privation of providence leaves one abandoned and a target to all that may happen and come about, so that his ill and weal come about according to chance. How terrible is this threat!" And in the following chapter (I, 24, p. 54), Maimonides identifies removal of providence with "hiding of the face" and with "returning" or "turning away" and "anger."

197. See *Guide*, I, 49 (p. 108); and III, 18.

198. By Don Oldenburg, *Washington Post*, Saturday, January 8, 2005, page C01, http://www.washingtonpost.com.

199. *Guide*, III, 23 (p. 496). God's knowledge, purpose, and providence are unlike ours. Knowing this we bear our misfortunes lightly and do not doubt his knowledge and providence, but rather increase our love.

200. *Guide*, III, 24 (p. 497).

201. B Shab 88b, Yoma 23a, Git 36b; MT Ethical Qualities, ii, 3.

202. Compare *Guide*, III, 17 (p. 469) with pp. 471–74. On p. 471, Maimonides said, "As for my own belief with regard to this fundamental principle, I mean divine providence." His own belief, as distinct from traditional belief, is based on the intention of "the book of God and of the books of our prophets." See also *Guide*, III, 20 (p. 481) ("What I myself say . . .").

203. Guide, III, 17 (p. 470). He then quoted the Torah of Moses our Master and the talmudic sages, who said, *There is no death without sin, and no suffering without transgression* (B Sab 55a). See also III, 24 (p. 498), where he said that this is a principle of the law and the opinion of the talmudic sages.

204. *Guide*, III, 14 (p. 457). Maimonides presented a similar view in MT Foundations of the Law, ii, 2.

205. See MT Foundations of the Law, iv, 12.

206. Diels and Kranz, *Die Fragmente der Vorsokratiker*, 80b1.

207. Job 38–41; *Guide*, III, 23 (pp. 496–97).

208. Lenn E. Goodman, "Maimonides' Responses to Saadiah Gaon's Theodicy," p. 289.

209. *Guide*, III, 10 (pp. 439–42).

210. See Gersonides, *The Wars of the Lord*, trans. Seymour Feldman, II, 149–50.

211. On preservation of the species as a good, see *Guide*, III, 10 (p. 440); III, 12 (p. 443).

212. See Gen 1:31 and *Guide*, III, 13 (p. 453). GenR, ix, 5, ed. Theodor-Albeck, p. 70. See

for Maimonides' interpretation, Sarah Klein-Braslavi, *Maimonides' Interpretation of the Story of Creation*, ch. 4.

213. "Perhaps when the chapters of *The Guide of the Perplexed* which treat this matter reach you, this principle will become sufficiently clear to you, with God's help." They are *Guide*, III, 10–12.

214. *Guide*, III, 10 (p. 440), citing GenR, li, 3, ed. Theodor-Albeck, p. 535. The saying is in the name of Rabbi Hanina ben Pazzi.

215. See Strauss, "How To Begin To Study *The Guide of the Perplexed*," p. xiii.

216. *Guide*, III, 46–47. This is the eleventh class of commandments according to the enumeration in the *Guide*, which was included in the *Mishneh Torah* in two books, the Book of Temple Service (VIII) and the Book of Offerings (IX). On reasons for the commandments, see Josef Stern, *Problems and Parables of Law*.

217. *Guide*, III, 46 (p. 585). Elsewhere, he described the Sabians as believing in spirits that can be made to descend among men. They also made talismans; *Guide*, I, 63 (p. 153). *Jinn* is an Arabic word for "demon," occurring frequently in the Qur'an (2:32, 18:48, 55:14, 72:1, etc.). "Men and *jinn*" occurs in the sense of all beings. In pre-Islamic Arabia, the *jinn* were desert nymphs or satyrs. Islam scholars accepted them completely and even discussed their legal status. Philosophers (e.g., al-Farabi, Ibn Sina), however, tended to doubt their existence. See D. B. MacDonald and H. Massé, EI, s.v. "Djinn." English "genie" (Fr *génie*) was used to translate *jinn* in the *Thousand and One Nights* because of the similarity in sound and meaning. "Genie" is from Lat *genius* (Eng "genius") in the sense of one's attendant god or spirit that accompanies a person from birth. It is curious and coincidental that Arabic *jinn* may also be derived from Lat *genius*. (The Arabic word *majnun,* "crazy," means possessed by a *jinn*.)

218. Maimonides identified the *jinn* of the Sabians with the goat-demons forbidden in Leviticus. The *se'irim* may have been like satyrs, half goat and half human.

219. In describing the cult of the Sabians in *Guide*, III, 29 (p. 521), he mentioned their setting up of monumental stones, which may be intended to evoke the black stone in the Ka'ba at Mecca.

220. See Pines, "Translator's Introduction," pp. lxxii–iv.

221. G.W.F. Hegel, *Lectures on the Philosophy of World History*, trans. H. B. Nisbet, pp. xxv, xxviii, 89.

222. Arabic *kamal* is usually translated as "perfection," which is, however, misleading, as it implies flawlessness. It means rather "fulfillment," when a human being realizes what it is to be human, becoming what he or she is.

223. E. Goldman, "The Special Worship of Those Who Perceive the Truths"; David Blumenthal, "Maimonides' Intellectualist Mysticism"; idem, "Maimonides: Prayer, Worship and Mysticism"; Andrew L. Gluck, "The King in His Palace: Ibn Gabirol and Maimonides"; Steven Harvey, "Maimonides in the Sultan's Palace"; David Shatz, "Worship, Corporeality and Human Perfection: A Reading of *The Guide of the Perplexed* III.51–54."

224. Sudan in the text refers to the people in the "lands of the blacks" (*bilad al-sudan*), the territories south of the Sahara from the Atlantic to the Nile. Galen and Arab geographers classified them as being at a low level of civilization; see Bernard Lewis, *Race and Slavery in the Middle East*, pp. 50–53. By including the Turks, Maimonides showed that this category was not racial. He used the Greek theory of climes, a clime (Gr *klima*, Ar *iqlim*) being a zone of the earth marked by longitude and latitude. The accepted number was seven zones, outside of which were the countries to the far north and to the south of the Equator. The favored climes for culture and intellectual development were the moderate climes, especially the fourth, which signified moderation. People of Iraq and Spain were proud to be favored by their position in the most moderate clime, promising good character, harmonious balance, and intelligence. See A. Miquel, EI, s.v. "Iklim."

225. He has in mind heretics.

226. On each of the levels, Maimonides first described the individual's position with

respect to the palace and later identified the level of knowledge, except for the seventh level where only the position is given.

227. T Hag, ii, 6; J Hag, ii, 1 (p. 77a); B Hag 15a; Lieberman, *Tosefta Kifshuṭah*, Hag, pp. 1292–94; Lieberman, "How Much Greek in Jewish Palestine," pp. 137–39; and E. E. Urbach, *The Sages*, pp. 189–90. Simon ben Zoma (usually just Ben Zoma) was a second-generation Tanna, one of the four who entered Pardes; see Strack and Stemberger, *Introduction*, p. 82. The correct reading, according to Lieberman, *Tosefta Kifshuṭah*, Hag, p. 1294, is "Ben Zoma is already outside," followed by the statement that a few days later Ben Zoma died." The narrative surrounding "Ben Zoma is still outside" is arcane. Accordingly, he was lost in thought when Rabbi Joshua greeted him thrice, and he did not answer. Rabbi Joshua asked him what was the matter, and Ben Zoma explained that he was contemplating the Account of the Beginning and referred to the upper and lower waters and the verse "And the spirit of God was hovering" (Gen 1:2), "like a bird flying with fluttering wings, its wings all but touching [the nest]." Rabbi Joshua said to his disciples, "Ben Zoma has gone." Then Ben Zoma replied, "*Lo' me'ayin*," which means "Not from nothing" or "Not whence."

S. Lieberman explains that Ben Zoma was contemplating questions that Gnostics raised. He found the correct reading of the GenR text in a Genizah palimpsest, reproduced in *Palestinian Syriac Texts* by Lewis and Gibson (namely, the Scottish sisters of Genizah fame, Agnes Smith Lewis and Margaret Gibson): *lo' me'ayin Rabbi*, meaning "nothing from nothing, Rabbi," which Lieberman interpreted as, "I am nothing who comes from nothing." The Gnostics would ask, "From where do you come, and whither are you going?"

I think that the reply "nothing from nothing," pertained rather to the Account of the Beginning, which Ben 'Azzai said he was contemplating. In fact, Lieberman mentioned (p. 139, n. 24) the Epicurean phrase *ouden ginetai ek tou mÿ ontos,* "Nothing comes into being from nonbeing." Ben 'Azzai was asserting that creation was not from nothing, a view that he alludes to in other pronouncements as well.

228. This was said of Moses.

229. *Guide* III, 51 (p. 621).

230. MekhS, xxii, 25; SifreDeut, xii; MidTan, xi, 13; B Ta'an 2a; J Ber, iv, 1 (7a); and see MT Prayer and the Priestly Blessing, i, 1. Service of the heart, or prayer, replaced service in the form of sacrifices in the holy sanctuary.

231. *Guide*, III, 51 (p. 621). See Guide, II, 12 and 37.

232. B Shab 149a. The statement slightly changes scriptural "Do not turn to idols" (Lev 19:4). The Talmud understood it to mean not to look at idols and images, a sense that Maimonides gave it in *Book of Commandments,* neg. 10 and in MT Idolatry, ii, 2.

233. Pines translates "bed." The word is *sarir*, which is like Persian *takht*, having the meaning of "seat" or "throne," and then "a raised seat or bench," or "a sofa" (like a *chaise longue*). See J. Sadan, *Le mobilier au proche orient mediéval*, pp. 32–51; Ghada al-Hijjawi al-Qaddumi, *Kitab al-hadaya wa'l-tuhaf* (*Book of Gifts and Rarities*), p. 436.

234. *Guide*, III, 51 (p. 623). See also III, 8 (p. 433). And see Ibn Sina *On Prayer*; Pines, Translator's Introduction, p. cii. Spinoza taught the intellectual love of God (*amor dei intellectualis*) (*Ethics*, V, prop. 33).

235. Aristotle mentioned the pleasure humans have in sensation and thought; see *Nicomachean Ethics*, x, 4, 1174b20–21; *Metaph*, i, 1, 980a21–22; Wolfson, *Spinoza*, II, 302. Plotinus associated joy with ecstatic experiences. And see Descartes, *Principia philosophiae*, iv, 190: *gaudium intellectuale*.

236. Traditional Jewish exegesis on Song of Songs usually saw the woman as the congregation of Israel and the beloved as God, as Judah ha-Levi did in Kuzari, ii, 24. Maimonides' pupil Joseph Ibn 'Aqnin in his commentary on the verse also gave it an individualistic and philosophic interpretation. Reason speaks to the Agent Intellect and says, "I am sleeping while I am attached to a physical body in this world, while my heart is awake and ready for my beloved." See his *Commentary on Song of Songs*, ed. Halkin, p. 262.

237. Pines translated: "This rank is not a rank that, with a view to the attainment of

which, someone like myself may aspire for guidance." In his note (p. 624, n. 32), he explains that the Arabic can have two meanings, giving the one accepted above as the second possibility.

238. *Guide*, III, 51 (p. 627).

239. The Hebrew word *hashaq* is etymologically related to Arabic *'ashiqa*, both meaning "to love passionately," the noun forms being *hesheq* and *'ishq*. See Gen 34:8 and Deut 21:11. Ps 91:14, cited here, is the only place in Scripture where it is used with respect to loving God. See Georges Vajda, *L'Amour de Dieu dans la theologie juive du Moyen Age*, p. 135, n. 4. On Maimonides' possible sources, see S. Harvey, "The Meaning of Terms Designating Love in Judaeo-Arabic Thought and Some Remarks on the Judaeo-Arabic Interpretation of Maimonides." Blumenthal, "Maimonides: Prayer, Worship, and Mysticism," notes that Maimonides mentions passionate love (*'ishq*) seven times in the chapter.

240. MT Foundations of the Law ii, 2; iv,12; Repentance v, 3.

241. *Guide* III, 51 (p. 627).

242. The Sages taught (B BB 17a) that the saying of Scripture, *And Moses the servant of the Lord died there in the land of Moab by the mouth of the Lord* (Deut 34:5) indicates that his death was by a kiss. The same expression is used of Aaron (Num 33:38). Miriam also died by a kiss, but the phrase *by the mouth of the Lord* was not appropriate, as she was a female. See on the motif Michael A. Fishbane, *The Kiss of God: Spiritual and Mystical Death in Judaism*, and for Maimonides, see pp. 24–30, 39–41, and 46.

243. *Guide*, III, 52-54. He drew from Aristotle's *Ethics* and Ibn Bajja's *Letter of Farewell*. See Berman, *Ibn Bajjah and Maimonides*, pp. xix (English summary) and p. 139; Altmann, "Maimonides' 'Four Perfections,'" and "On Maimonides' View of the Aim of Human Existence." See also Isaac Heinemann, *Die Lehre von der Zweckbestimmung des Menschen im griechisch-römischen Altertum und im jüdischen Mittelalter*, pp. 61–74. H. Blumberg, "Alfarabi, Ibn Bajja, and Maimonides on the Conduct of the Solitary: Sources and Influences"; Menachem Kellner, *Maimonides on Human Perfection*; idem, "Politics and Perfection: Gersonides vs. Maimonides"; Lawrence Kaplan, "'I Sleep but My Heart Awaketh': Maimonides on Human Perfection"; Menachem Kellner, *Maimonides on Human Perfection*; Joel L. Kraemer, "Ibn Bajja y Maimònides: sobre la perfecciòn humana"; Ralph Lerner, "Maimonides' Governance of the Solitary"; idem, "Maimonides' Vorbilder menschlicher Vollkommenheit"; David Shatz, "Worship, Corporeality and Human Perfection: A Reading of *The Guide of the Perplexed* III.51–54"; Ruth Ben-Meir, "On the Perfection and Purpose of Man—Gersonides and His Predecessors."

244. *Guide*, III, 54 (p. 635).

245. Here and elsewhere Maimonides used the language of pious exhortation, as al-Ghazali did in his *Revivication of Religious Sciences*.

246. S. Pines, in "The Limitations of Human Knowledge," argued that Maimonides was skeptical regarding knowledge of metaphysical things and denied the possibility of conjunction with the Agent Intellect and knowledge of spiritual forms.

247. Cf. also Aristotle's observation that while it is worthwhile to attain the end merely for one man, it is finer and more godlike to attain it for a nation or for city-states (*Ethics*, I, 2, 1094b7–10).

CHAPTER 20

1. See Caroline Walker Bynum, *The Resurrection of the Body in Western Christianity, 200–1336*; Neil Gillman, *The Death of Death: Resurrection and Immortality in Jewish Thought*; and Alan F. Segal, *Life After Death: A History of the Afterlife in the Religions of the West*. And see R. Lerner, *Maimonides' Empire of Light*, ch. 4.

2. The Book of Daniel is said to have been written in the period of Antiochus IV Epiphanes (175–63 B.C.E.).

3. H. A. Wolfson, *Philo*, Index s.v. "Soul, Resurrection."

4. See Segal, *Life After Death*, p. 376; Gillman, *The Death of Death*, pp. 117 and 122.

5. M San, x, 1.

6. Jn 5:28–29; 6:39–40; 11:23–26; Lk 14:14. Against the Sadducees, see Matt 22:23–33; Mk 12:18–27; Lk 20:27–40. See Bynum, *The Resurrection of the Body*, pp. 18 and Segal, *Life After Death*, pp. 555–58.

7. Acts 17:16–21, 32.

8. In Ps 88, sermo ii, n. 5, cited in the *Catholic Encyclopedia*, s.v. "General Resurrection."

9. *Yawm al-din* in the Qur'an = *yom ha-din* of the Jewish tradition.

10. Toshihiko Izutsu, *Ethico-Religious Concepts in the Qur'ān*, p. 125. See also Qur'an 75:1–6.

11. See al-Ghazali's *Incoherence of the Philosophers* (*Tahafut al-falasifa*), trans. Michael E. Marmura, Twentieth Discussion, pp. 212–29.

12. See Aristotle, *De anima*, 430a23; cf. *De gen. an.* 736b27.

13. *Metaph.*, XII, 9, 1074b 34. See above, pp. 330–31.

14. See *Mantiq al- mashrqiyyin*, p. 3; *Tis' rasa'il*, pp. 114–16.

15. *In al-Risala al-adhwiyya fi amr al-ma'ad*, ed. Sulayman Dunya, p. 53.

16. Ibid.

17. The *Book of the Decisive Treatise* (*Fasl al-maqal*), trans. Charles E. Butterworth, p. 10.

18. Averroes' *Tahafut al-Tahafut* (*The Incoherence of the Incoherence*), trans. S. van den Bergh, I, 359.

19. On Gaon Samuel ben Eli, Head of the Great Yeshivah in Baghdad, see Maimonides, *Letters*, ed. Shailat, pp. 273–422; S. Assaf, "A Collection of Epistles by Samuel ben Eli and His Contemporaries"; M. Gil, *In the Kingdom of Ishmael*, I, pars. 262–66, pp. 448ff.; Y.T. Langermann, *Yemenite Midrash: Philosophical Commentaries on the Torah*, pp. 297–302; idem, "The Letter of Rabbi Shmuel ben Eli on Resurrection."

20. Benjamin of Tudela said that the Gaon's genealogy went back to Moses. *Travels,* trans. Adler, p. 60. This was a typical counter to the Exilarchs' claim that their genealogy was traceable to King David.

21. *Epistles*, ed. Baneth, no. 6, pp. 54–64.

22. *Epistles*, ed. Baneth, no. 7, pp. 85–90. The letter to Joseph was first published by S. Munk, "Notice sur Joseph ben Iehouda," pp. 67–71. See also *Letters*, ed. Shailat, p. 419.

23. See also *Guide*, III, 51 (p. 622), where the verse is cited and interpreted.

24. The title Rosh ha-Seder, or Head of the Row, originally went to the head of one of the seven rows of members in the academy, where they sat in fixed places in order of rank. At this time, it was used for the Head of the Academy, which Joseph was in Aleppo. See Goitein, *Med. Soc.*, II, 198–99.

25. B BM 32b. Maimonides changed the text by inserting that the enemy has priority. The talmudic text says that it is a commandment, or good deed (*mitzvah*), to help the enemy load.

26. See *Letters*, ed. Shailat, pp. 402–18. Only part of the original Arabic has been preserved. The responsa sections of the letter in their Hebrew version were published in *Responsa*, II, no. 313, pp. 580–82 and no. 320, p. 588.

27. See *Epistles*, ed. Baneth, pp. 85–88.; *Letters*, ed. Shailat, pp. 395, 402.

28. See also CM Avot, i, 16. On Moses ben Maimon's attitude to language, see also Twersky, *Introduction*, pp. 324, 354.

29. The word Ar *iftiyat* (< *fata*) means "betrayal," "treason," "offense." The Hebrew translation of the letter takes it in sense of "slander." The same term is used in the *Treatise on Resurrection* in a similar context, where Moses ben Maimon claimed that certain views were unfairly ascribed to him.

30. For "cunning knave" (*rasha' 'arum*), see M Sot, iii, 4; B Ket 95b; Sot 21b; J Sot, iii, 4 (18c); CM Avot, v, 14.

31. See also below, p. 420.

32. See Mann, *Texts and Studies*, I, 230ff. and above, p. 221, on the Exilarch's letter to Nethanel; and see also Robert Brody, *The Geonim of Babylonia*, p. 41.

33. *Epistles*, ed. Baneth, p. 62. The issue of the divorce is unclear. Ms. Neofiti has Heb *ha-ta'ut* (the error), presupposing an original Arabic *al-ghalat* (Baneth). This may have been corrupted into *al-get/ha-get* ("the divorce").

34. See *Epistles*, ed. Baneth, p. 64. Of course, this may not have been the house Maimonides lived in from the beginning of his stay in Fustat.

35. He was Judge Samuel ben Se'adyah ha-Levi of Fustat, an associate of Maimonides and member of his rabbinical court. His dated documents run from 1165 to 1203; see Goitein, *Med. Soc.*, Indices, s.v. "Samuel ben Sa'adya." See *Responsa*, ed. Blau, Index, p. 220, and Mss. T-S J 2.78 and 12.428.

36. For *dikka*, see Sadan, *Mobilier*, 56, 123 and Index, 171 (*siège, banc*, "buffet"). According to Sadan, the *dikka* (and *dukkān*) is a seat, counter, or platform, in a garden or in a house, fixed or mobile, generally made of wood.

37. For various interpretations of Maimonides' position, see, for instance, H. Blumberg, "The Problem of Immortality in Avicenna, Maimonides and St. Thomas Aquinas"; J. Finkel, "Maimonides' *Treatise on Ressurection*: A Comparative Study"; R. S. Kirchner, "Maimonides Fiction of resurrection," R. Lerner, *Maimonides' Empire of Light*, pp. 42–55; A. S. Halkin and D. Hartman, *Crisis and Leadership*, pp. 246–63. J. L. Teicher doubted the authenticity of the treatise in his "Maimonides' *Treatise on Resurrection*, a Thirteenth-Century Forgery"; I. Sonne convincingly replied in "A Scrutiny of the Charges of Forgery Against Maimonides' *Letter on Resurrection*." Naomi Vogelman-Goldfeld followed her teacher Teicher in her *Moses Maimonides' Treatise on Resurrection*. All doubts have been set aside by Y. T. Langermann's "The Letter of Rabbi Shmuel ben Eli on Resurrection" and Sarah Stroumsa's *On the Beginnings of the Maimonidean Controversy in the East: Yosef ibn Shim'on's Silencing Epistle Concerning the Resurrection of the Dead*. Joseph's *Epistle* was a defense of Maimonides' position, written prior to Maimonides' own treatise.

38. Ibn Shaddad, *The Rare and Excellent History of Saladin*, trans. D. S. Richards, p. 20. Ibn Shaddad served Saladin from 1188 to 1193 and then became advisor to al-Zahir Ghazi, a role that al-Suhrawardi had filled prior to 1191.

39. The treatise was edited and translated by Joshua Finkel, and translated by Hillel G. Fradkin in Lerner, *Maimonides' Empire of Light*, pp. 154–77. See also the translation by Fred Rosner with an essay on the resurrection debate by Daniel Jeremy Silver and a bibliography of editions, translations and studies by Jacob I. Dienstag. I have used my own translation here.

40. The expression *thalith thalatha* is from Qur'an 5:73, a verse that brands the Christians unbelievers. Maimonides seems to have derived his knowledge of Christianity from Islamic sources.

41. *Ta'ala 'amma* . . . is a Qur'anic locution; see, e.g., 6:100, 17:42. For the Christian belief in the Trinity, see *Guide*, I, 50 (p. 111). Maimonides, as we see here, considered Christians to be polytheists; see also MT Idolatry, ix, 4.

42. Reading *al-bulh* (pl.) as suggested by Baneth, "Maimonides' Treatise," p. 37, and accepted by Qafih and Shailat. Finkel preferred the reading: *al-milla* ("our religious community").

43. See above, p. 181.

44. *Guide*, I, 71.

45. See B San 90b; CM Int San, x (Pereq Heleq), fifth group.

46. Maimonides' position on individual immortality is unclear. He cited Ibn Bajja's view that eternal souls are not multiple but one, united with the Agent Intellect. See *Guide*, I, 74, p. 221 seventh way; Pines, "Translator's Introduction," p. civ; Pines, "Maimonides," *DSB*, p. 30.

47. MT Repentance, viii, 3.

48. At a later time, Spinoza argued (in *Theological-Political Treatise*, ch. 5) that the

ceremonial law only promised temporal physical happiness and the security of the Hebrew kingdom, and that it was only valid while that kingdom lasted.

49. MT Repentance, iii, 5–14, stressing that they are twenty four, afraid that a transcriber would omit one, and then someone might say, "He did not mention it." He did the same in his *Treatise on the Art of Logic*, where he enumerated logical terms. As you may recall, I remarked in the discussion of the logic treatise that he used enumeration as a mnemonic device.

50. MT Repentance, viii, 3.

51. MT Repentance, viii, 2. See B Ber 17a. And see ARN, A, ch. 1, s.v. *ḳesad nivra'*. In CM Int San, x (Pereq Heleq), ed. Shailat, p. 366 (Ar)/p. 136 (Heb trans) and in MT Repentance, viii, 2, he wrote "intercourse," *tashmish* (*ha-mittah*). The Soncino and Vilna editions of the Talmud have "procreation" (*periyah u-reviyah*), as does Ms. Oxford opp. Add., fol. 23. Both Ms. Florence 7–9 I II and Paris 671 omit the phrase altogether. Unfortunately, the Genizah remnants of B Berakhot do not have folio 17a. Se'adyah Gaon, in his *Beliefs and Opinions*, ix, 4, has "neither intercourse nor procreation" (*we-lo' tashmish we-lo' holadah*). Nahmanides on Ex 16:6 omits "reproduction," as does Rabbenu Bahya on Deut 30:15. But in *Torat ha-Adam*, no. 124, Nahmanides has *tashmish*. And see *Zohar*, II, Mishpatim, 116a (*tashmish ha-mitta*). The three functions of eating, drinking and intercourse (Ar *nikah*) are conjoined often in the *Guide,* e.g., II, 36; III, 8 (especially), 12, 33.

52. See A.J. Wensinck and Ch. Pellat, EI, s.v. "Ḥūr." Philosophers and Sufis tried to interpret these references in a more spiritual sense. In *hadith* their age is given as thirty-three, the age of Jesus. Jesus will have a hundred houris to keep him company. Women will meet their husbands again in Paradise and remarry. The assumption is that they would consider this a reward.

53. B Ber 17a; MT Repentance, viii, 2.

54. Ibn Rushd said the same thing in his *Kashf al-adilla*. Close to the same language is found in Ibn Rushd, *al-Kashf 'an manakij al-adilla*, p. 139.

55. On angels as separate intellects, see, e.g., MT Foundations of the Law, ii, 5–8; *Guide*, I, 49, 70, 72, 74, II, 2, 4,6 (*nota bene*), 10, 12, 14, 18, 42; III, 45.

56. Joseph ben Judah, *Silencing Epistle*, ed. Stroumsa, Introduction, p. vii.

57. The Christian scholar Bar Hebraeus wrote about the influence of this interpretation on Jewish communities. See P. Fenton, "A Yemenite Polemical Work Against Maimonides: The Imam al-Shaukani and his Book Concerning the Hereafter," And see Joseph ben Judah, *Silencing Epistle*, ed. Stroumsa, Introduction, p. vii.

58. Abraham ben David of Posquières, the author of animadversions on the *Mishneh Torah*, wrote in his comment on Repentance, viii, 2, "The words of this man [Maimonides] seem to me very near to him who says there is no resurrection of the body but only of the soul. By my life, this is not the view of the sages!"

59. The term *raj'a* for "resurrection" is taken from Islamic terminology. Maimonides' response to the Yemenites is not known to be extant. Shailat (*Letters*, p. 349, line 1, note) mentions a text in a Yemenite commentary on the Torah written three hundred years after this treatise that appears to refer to Maimonides' reply.

60. Ed. Shailat, p. 367 (Ar text)/p. 138 (Heb trans.).

61. The expressions *al-mashhura al-ma'luma* and *al-mujma' 'alayha* convey emphatically that the belief is based on tradition and consensus, *ijma'*. As a foundation of Islamic law, *ijma'* is the unanimous consensus of the *umma*, or more specifically of the religious authorities, *ulema*, on a legal regulation.

62. See B San 92b, where the discussion is whether the dead brought back to life in the vision of dry bones (Ezekiel 37:1–14) was real or a parable; and see Moses ben Maimon, CM Introduction to San, x (Pereq Heleq), third group; MT Foundations of the Law, vii, 3; *Guide*, II, 46.

63. The word *ikhtilaf*, used here, is a technical term in Islamic jurisprudence for difference of opinion among juridical schools and authorities.

64. Moses ben Maimon, CM Sot, iii, 5; San, x, 3; Shev, i, 4; see also *Book of Commandments*, neg. 133.

65. CM Introduction to San, x (Pereq Heleq), ed. Shailat p. 368 (Ar)/138–39 (Heb).

66. For the expression, see, e.g., Qur'an 28:63.

67. The root principle is God. The expression here is *kefirah ba-'iqqar*. See MT Foundations of the Law, i, 6 (*kofer ba-'iqqar*) and Ethical Qualities, vii, 3.

68. See MT Kings and Their Wars, xii, 1, where this is said to be a parable. In *Guide*, III, 11, the parabolic sense is implied. Se'adyah Gaon, *Beliefs and Opinions*, trans. Rosenblatt, VIII, 8, pp. 318–19, disputes the view that it is a parable. See also Finkel, *Treatise on Resurrection*, p. 96, n. 26, citing Abraham Ibn Ezra and David Qimhi.

69. MT Kings and Their Wars, xii, 1(where the language is different); cf. Repentance, ix, 2. *Guide*, II, 29; and see III, 11.

70. In the Introduction to Part III of the *Guide* (p. 416), on his discussion of the Account of the Chariot, Maimonides says that he followed "insight [*hads;* Pines; "conjecture"] and supposition," for "no divine inspiration [*wahy* Pines, "revelation")" came to him to instruct him about the intention of the subject, nor did he receive what he believed from a teacher. He then recognized the possibility that his interpretation may be wrong. Finally, "rightly guided reflection and divine aid" moved him to the the position he held.

71. See MT Kings and Their Wars, xii, 1–2.

72. *Guide*, Introduction, p. 6; and see II, 29 (p. 338).

73. M Avot, v, 5 (and Maimonides' comment ad loc.); ARN, B, ch. 39 (s.v. *'asharah nissim*); B Yoma 21a.

74. See CM Eight Chapters, viii, trans. Weiss and Butterworth, p. 87; CM Avot, v, 5; *Guide*, I, 73, seventh premise; II, 19, 25.

75. The text has *holekh* instead of *noheg* ("follows"); see MT Repentance, ix, 2. Ibn Tibbon's translation preserves *noheg*. See B AZ 54b; San 42a; CM Eight Chapters, ch. 8; Melakhim, xii, 1; *Guide*, II, 29

76. Cf. the expression "We do not mention miracles" in T Yev (Lieberman), xiv, 6; B Ber 60a; Yev 121b, etc.; and see Rashi on B Hul 43a, s.v. en mazkirin. And consider the sayings "We do not bring proof from the charob" or "We do not bring proof from the fools" and the like in B Baba Mesi'a 59b and Nid 30b. Maimonides' quotation conflates the two. See also CM Yevamot, xvi, 4, where the text is as here.

77. See in this chapter, n. 37.

78. *Guide*, III, 28 (p. 512).

79. See *Guide*, I, 33 (pp. 70–72), on the need to educate the young and undeveloped according to their capacity, gradually, and by accepting tradition. See also Strauss, "How To Begin To Study *The Guide of the Perplexed*," p. xxxvi.

80. See al-Farabi, *Kitab al-Jadal*, ed. R. al-'Ajam, pp. 29–38 and p. 60. Carlos Fraenkel, *From Maimonides to Samuel ibn Tibbon*, p. 284, compares necessary beliefs to necessary lies in Ibn Rushd, where the Muslim philosopher was using Plato.

81. Dialectical and rhetorical statements are used in religious discourse, whereas the sciences use demonstrative (proven) propositions.

82. See also Ibn Sina, *Kitab al-Shifa', al-Mantiq, al-Jadal*, ed. I. Madkour, 11–14.

CHAPTER 21

1. Saul Lieberman, "How Much Greek in Jewish Palestine?" p. 135. Prof. Lieberman said this by way of introducing Gershom Scholem's second lecture on Merkavah Mysticism and Jewish Gnosticism, but the actual statement, which I heard, was more pithy—"Nonsense is nonsense, but the history of nonsense is scholarship."

2. *Letters*, ed. Shailat, pp. 475–76.

3. Jonathan emigrated to the Land of Israel in 1210 with about 310 French and English rabbis and died soon thereafter. See Israel Moses Ta-Shma, EJ, s.v "Jonathan ben David

ha-Kohen of Lunel." Lunel in Provence was located close to the Mediterranean, west of the Rhone, between Arles and Montpellier.

4. A. Marx, "The Correspondence Between the Rabbis of southern France and Maimonides about Astrology," p. 333. On Maimonides' astrology, see G. Freudenthal, "Maimonides' Stance on Astrology in Contest; H. Kreisel, "Maimonides' Approach to Astrology"; Y. T. Langermann, "Maimonides' Repudiation of Astrology"; R. Lerner, "Maimonides' Letter on Astrology"; D. Schwartz, *Astral Magic in Medieval Jewish Thought*.

5. Cf. Deut 34:10.

6. The harbinger of the Messiah sometimes comes to see himself as the fulfillment. See also Friedman, *Maimonides, the Yemenite Messiah and Apostasy*, p. 131. The Lunel sages had written about a harbinger, and perhaps that influenced Maimonides' formulation in his reply.

7. This resembles the Shiʻi doctrine of *ghayba*, the belief that the dead Imam is in occultation and will return as the Mahdi.

8. See below, p. 435 and Friedman, *Maimonides, the Yemenite Messiah and Apostasy*, p. 45.

9. Alexander Marx, "Correspondence," pp. 343–49. See S. Sela, "Queries on Astrology Sent from Southern France to Maimonides."

10. This is a clever combination of Gen 38:19 with Esth 5:1 (see Rashi ad loc.) and Ezek 16:10.

11. These are throne names of the royal child. *JSB* explains that Semitic names were often based on sentences describing a god. Christian tradition ascribes the titles to Christ, something the authors, living in a Christian environment, may have known. They omitted "Counselor" and "God."

12. Isa 9:5 (beginning).

13. Isa 11:5. The chapter describes a descendant of David who will reign in Jerusalem and ends on a messianic note.

14. Cf. EsthR (Vilna ed.), ii, 4.

15. Literally: "made handles for it." See B ʻEruv 21b, Yev 21a, SongR (Vilna), i, 8; Rashi on Eccl 12:9.

16. Cf. Isa 23:13.

17. Cf. Ps 48:14. *Passegu* is translated by RSV as "go through." But cf. Rashi ad loc. and on Num 21:20 ("raise").

18. Deut 3:25. The "good hill country" was identified in many Midrashim with Jerusalem, and "the Lebanon" with the holy sanctuary because its cedar wood came from Lebanon (1 Kings 5:22–24). A popular midrash, however, related Lebanon to the sanctuary because it whitens the sins of Israel, where "whitens" (*malbin*) is from a root whose consonants are the same as those for "Lebanon." See SifreDeut, xxviii; B Yoma 39b; ARN, version B, xxv, etc.

19. Cf. Isa 28:12.

20. Samuel Ibn Tibbon calls Maimonides' concilium a *havurah* ("fellowship"). See above, ch. 12, n. 9.

21. B Shab 156a, Ned 32a.

22. Harkavy, *Teshuvot ha-Geonim,* no. 390, p. 207, with minor changes; Marx, "Correspondence," p. 343, n. 5.

23. *Ribbon ha-ʼolamim*, ("Lord of the Worlds") which occurs often in rabbinic literature; see, e.g., AdRN, B, ch. 25, s.v. "*Kevan she-raʼah*," B Ber 17a, 19a, etc. And cf. Arabic *rabb al-ʻalamin*, a precise counterpart, in the opening surah (al-Fatiha) of the Qurʼan.

24. M Ber, ix, 3; MT Blessings, x, 22.

25. Cf. Micah 5:4, where the same words have a different meaning.

26. See Josh 2:12.

27. One manuscript has *moshav zeqenim* ("council of elders"). See Num 24:21 (*etan moshavekah*), and 1 Kings 8:2 (*yerah ha-etanim*). According to the Midrash, the *etanim* are the

ancestors Abraham, Isaac, Jacob; see J Rosh Ha-Shanah, i, 2, p. 56d. The word *yerah* = "moon," "month" was given to Lunel; Provence was called Yerah ha-Etanim, "the Moon of the Ethanim," from 1 Kings 8:2, where it means "month of the Ethanim." The Ethanim in Midrash are the Patriarchs, but here it refers to the sages of Provence. See *Responsa* of Rabbi Solomon ben Adret, I, no. 418 (Rabbis of France); *Responsa* of the sages of Provence, I, no. 9.

28. See Micah 6:2.

29. Gad Freudenthal, "Les sciences dans les communautés juives médiévales de Provence: leur appropriation, leur rôle."

30. First edition has "in the city of Marseilles" (Shailat, p. 478).

31. *Responsa,* IV, 33; *Letters,* ed. Shailat, p. 558.

32. Text: *Binah we-hokhmah.* The two usually appear in the order "wisdom and discernment" (*hokhmah we-binah*), as in the liturgy (see MT Book of Love, trans. M. Kellner, p. 175). The phrase is from Isa 11:2. It appears in Deut 4:6 as "your [plural for "the people of Israel"] wisdom and discernment" (*hokhmatkhem u-binatkhem*), which is taken in B Shab 75a to be astronomy. He cites this in *Book of Commandments,* second principle, where *binah we-hokhmah* refer to astronomy, as we have it here. See above, ch. 18, n. 19.

33. The reference is to the duty of a brother of a deceased man to take his widow as his wife, or else to undergo a ceremony of refusal; see Deut. 25:5–10. Maimonides suggests that the Torah is a widow and the men of Lunel the brother of the deceased.

34. Trans. Alter, who notes the nuance, "to lead the forces in battle." See also Num 27:17. Moses says this to all Israel at the beginning of the epilogue of Deut (31-34).

35. This is from a part of Isaiah (chs. 40–66) containing Songs of the Suffering Servant, or Servant of the Lord, identified in Jewish exegesis with the people of Israel or the Messiah. A text in the Talmud (B Sot 14a) notes the view that it depicts Moses. Others, including Se'adyah Gaon, took it as referring to Jeremiah. Christians believe that it prefigures the coming of Jesus, who is viewed as the Suffering Servant (Acts 8:26–40).

36. Cf. Zeph. 3:20.

37. See MT Idolatry, especially i–ii, x–xi.

38. See I. Twersky, *Rabad of Posquières*, p. 125; *Letters,* ed. Shailat, p. 302; al-Harizi, *Wanderings,* ed. Yahalom and Blau, no. 492, p. 224.

39. cf. Se'adyah Gaon, *Beliefs and Opinions*, trans. Rosenblatt, p. 16. See also *Treatise on Logic,* ch. 8; *Guide,* I, 50.

40. See *Epistle to Yemen*, trans. Kraemer, p. 122.

41. Josephus stated that miscalculating celestial portents and other omens was one cause for the revolt against the Romans and its four-year duration (Josephus, *Wars*, vi, 5, 3). Maimonides knew what warfare was, as he witnessed the military preparations by Saladin and the Ayyubids in their struggle against the Crusaders.

42. For the expression "root of idolatry" (*'iqqar 'avodah zarah*), see Mid Lev R (Margoliouth), xxxiii, 6; MT Idolatry, i, 1.

43. See also MT Idolatry, i, 1 (where the word *kesilut* ("foolishness") is used; cf. *kesil* = Orion); Repentance, v, 4.; and See CM 'AZ, iv, 7; and especially MT Idolatry, xi, 16.

44. This would hold true for Aristotle, for example. Otherwise, Maimonides' observation is wrong, as Arabic and Hebrew versions of the astrological works of Ptolemy, the *Tetrabiblos* and *Centiloquium*, were extant, unless Maimonides meant that those who accepted astrology were not really sages. This would not be true either. Eudoxus of Cnidus (408–355 B.C.E.), a founding father of Greek astronomy, also knew the principles of universal and meteorological astrology. Hipparchus (fl. 146–127 B.C.E.) investigated the correspondence of planetary signs with ethnic groups and geography and between the human body and planets.

45. "Chasdeans and Chaldeans" is a doublet. The biblical form for Chaldeans, *Kasdim*, is derived from the eponymous ancestor Kesed (see Gen 22:22; and see Ezekiel 23:14 and II Chronicles 36:17). In the book of Daniel the Babylonian astrologers are called Kasdim

(Chaldeans), and in Aramaic Kasda'ei (2:2, 4, 5, 10; 4:14; 5:7, 11). Greek texts have *Chaldaioi*. Rabbinic literature has Heb *Kaldiyyim* and Aram *Kalda'e*; B Pes 113b, Shab 119a, 156b, Yev 21b, where they are regarded as astrologers. The phonetic variation from *s* to *l* appears in Akkadian of the second millennium B.C.E. onward. On these people and magic, see *Guide*, III, 37 (where the Sabians are added).

46. Cf. MT Idolatry, xi, 16.

47. *Guide*, III, 17. And see above, p. 392.

48. For "chance occurrence," Maimonides used an Aramaic expression (*aqra'i be-'alma hu'*) familiar from the Talmud; see, e.g., B Yoma 23a, San 25b.

49. CM Introduction to San, x (Pereq Heleq), Tenth Principle; Ber, ix, 7; *Guide*, III, 17, fifth opinion.

50. B Shab 55a; Lev R (Vilna ed.), xxxii; Qoh R, v, 4; Mid Zuta Qoh, v, 4.

51. MT Repentance, v, 2; cf. also Ethical Qualities, i, 2–3.

52. The hemistichs of the Isaiah verse are inverted here, probably because he quoted from memory.

53. According to the view of some rabbinic sages. See *Guide*, III, 17 (p. 470), where Maimonides cites the rabbinic view "There is no death without sin, and no sufferings without transgression" (B Shab 55a). In the same chapter (p. 468) he cites the (Mu'tazilite) view (but with some disapproval) that suffering and death are for a greater good.

54. Surely Maimonides knew that great scientists, such as al-Kindi and al-Biruni, wrote on astrology. Consider especially al-Biruni's synopsis of astrology, including also astronomy, arithmetic, and geometry, in *The Book of Instruction in the Elements of the Art of Astrology* (*al-Tafhim li-awa'il sina'at al-tanjim*). It is true, however, that Spanish astronomers known to Maimonides were less inclined to engage in astrology; for instance, Abu Ishaq al-Zarqali (d. ca. 1087), called Azarquiel; Jabir ibn Aflah al-Ishbili (Geber), who flourished in the first half of the twelfth century; and Abu Ishaq al-Bitruji, known as Alpetragius in Latin, who flourished in Seville ca. 1190. There were Jewish astrologers, such as Abraham bar Hiyya and Abraham Ibn Ezra, both serious astronomers as well.

55. But some manuscripts give the year as 11 Tishre 1507 S.E. (= 4956 S.E.) (September 17, 1195).

56. Z. Diesendruck, "Samuel and Moses Ibn Tibbon on Maimonides' Theory of Providence"; Georges Vajda, "An Analysis of the *Ma'amar Yiqqawu ha-Mayim* by Samuel Ibn Tibbon"; Giuseppe Sermoneta, "Shmuel Ibn Tibbon's Criticism of the Maimonidean Theory of Intellect"; Aviezer Ravitsky, "Samuel ibn Tibbon and the Esoteric Character of *The Guide of the Perplexed*"; Steven Harvey, "Did Maimonides' Letter to Samuel ibn Tibbon Determine Which Philosophers Would Be Studied by Later Jewish Thinkers?" *Otot ha-shamayim: Samuel Ibn Tibbon's Hebrew Version of Aristotle's* Meteorology, ed. and trans. Resianne Fontaine; Y. Tzvi Langermann, "A New Source Concerning Samuel ibn Tibbon's Translation of *The Guide of the Perplexed* and His Comments on It"; Yair Schifman, "The Differences Between the Translations of the Maimonides' *Guide of the Perplexed* by Falaquera, Ibn Tibbon, and al-Harizi, and the Textual and Philosophical Implications"; C. Fraenkel, *From Maimonides to Samuel ibn Tibbon: The Transformation of the* Dalalat al-Ha'irin *into the* Moreh ha-Nevukhim; James T. Robinson, *Samuel Ibn Tibbon's Commentary on Ecclesiastes*; Robert Eisen, "Samuel ibn Tibbon on the Book of Job."

57. See Steinschneider, *Die Hebraeischen Übersetzungen*, pp. 4, 215.

58. Gad Freudenthal, "Les Sciences dans les communautés juives médiévales de Provence: leur appropriation, leur rôle."

59. The Hebrew with facing English pages were published by Israel Abrahams in *Hebrew Ethical Wills*, pp. 51–92. Wills were also popular in Arabic literature, called *wasiyya*, etymologically related to Heb *sawa'ah* (with metathesis). They were often ascribed to great figures such as 'Ali ibn Abi Talib. Maimonides left an ethical will for Abraham. The problem is that it is almost certainly inauthentic.

60. The details emerge from the correspondence between Maimonides and the sages of Lunel and from Samuel Ibn Tibbon's Introduction (Apologia) to his translation, published by Yehudah Even Shmuel in his edition of Ibn Tibbon's translation, 117–22. (The editor's name is not *Ibn* Shmuel, a mistake often made, even on the English title page of the Mossad Harav Kook New Revised Edition.)

61. Maimonides first sent in ca. 4957 = 1196/97 the first two parts of *The Guide* in Arabic, which were given to Samuel to translate into Hebrew.

62. I have had occasion to refer to a new Hebrew translation by Michael Schwarz, which is excellent and has copious notes. Previously Joseph Qafih had published a translation, based on the Munk-Joel edition and several Yemenite manuscripts, to accompany his Arabic edition of the *Guide*.

63. Baneth, "Maimonides as His Own Translator," p. 101. See also Schwarz's translation, p. 745.

64. *Milhamot ha-Shem* (*Wars of the Lord*), ed. R. Margaliyot, p. 53.

65. Baneth, "Maimonides as His Own Translator."

66. Leo Strauss and Shlomo Pines differed over method in translating the *Guide* into English. Strauss made specific suggestions to Pines in their correspondence in the late 1950s and also wanted him to translate literally and consistently. Pines wanted to make the text as translucid as possible and add notes. Strauss wanted to preserve some opaqueness and to refrain from explanatory remarks.

67. *Letters,* ed. Shailat, pp. 550–51; trans. Kraemer, "The Life of Moses ben Maimon," p. 428. The letter is signed 8 Tishre 4960 = September 30, 1199. It is not certain that all parts of the letter were written at the same time.

68. See also Maimonides' letter to Joseph ben Judah, ed. Baneth, no. 6, p. 52, where he said that the *Mishneh Torah* had reached "the ends of the inhabited earth" (Ar *'imran* = Grk *oikoumenÿ*); and see above, p. 317.

69. The document is preserved in TS AS 149.41. See Friedman, "Two Maimonidean Letters," pp. 191–94.

70. The letter puts to rest much speculation on Maimonides' motives for discouraging Samuel's visit. Jacob Levinger suggested that Maimonides was trying "to hint to Ibn Tibbon that he should not expect to hear more revelations of Maimonides' views of esoteric problems, such as providence, even in private conversation." See A. Ravitzky, "Samuel Ibn Tibbon and the Esoteric Character of *The Guide of the Perplexed*," pp. 87–123, especially n. 132; and idem, "R. Shmuel Ibn Tibbon and the Secret of *The Guide of the Perplexed*," p. 45, n. 135. See also Schwarz, *The Guide of the Perplexed*, p. 744. Ravitzky stressed that Maimonides' lack of welcome had repercussions on the nature of the relationship between the Master and his translator in the years 1199–1204. He concluded ("Samuel Ibn Tibbon and the Esoteric Character," pp. 122–23) that "we have no answer to these questions" and "the ultimate question of the intention and aims of the Master himself is thereby not solved."

71. Maimonides addressed Samuel as "the sage" in his letter to him and in a letter to the Lunel sages, ed. Shailat, p. 530, 531, 558.

72. See Rashi on B San 106b. The expression occurs in Maimonides' (ascribed) Letter to Hisday ha-Levi (*Letters*, ed. Shailat, pp. 673–84).

73. Abu Bakr Muhammad ibn Zakariyya'al-Razi, known to the Europeans as Rhazes (ca. 854–925 or 935) was a philosopher, physician, and alchemist, one of the important "freethinkers" in Islamic civilization. See the articles on him by Lenn E. Goodman, in the *Encyclopedia of Islam* and in *History of Islamic Philosophy*, ed. Seyyed Hossein Nasr and Oliver Leaman. And see Sarah Stroumsa, *Freethinkers of Medieval Islam*, ch. 3.

74. See A. Altmann and S.M. Stern, *Isaac Israeli: A Neoplatonic Philosopher of the Early Tenth Century*.

75. The biblical quotation is usually understood in a negative sense, but Maimonides does not mean it that way. Joseph ibn Saddiq was also from Córdoba, therefore Maimonides could easily have known him, except that Maimonides and his family left Córdoba when he

was ten, so it is hard to conceive of him knowing the man and his discourse. The best explanation, if we stick to a 1137/38 birthdate for Maimonides, is to say that he knew him after 1148.

76. The book is also known as *al-Siyasa al-madaniyya, The Political Regime*. See the translation of selections by Fauzi M. Najjar, in *Medieval Political Philosophy: A Sourcebook*, ed. R. Lerner and M. Mahdi, pp. 31–57.

CHAPTER 22

1. The Supreme Judge (*qadi al-qudat*) was 'Abd al-Malik ibn 'Isa Sadr al-Din ibn Dirbas (Durbas) (d. 605[1208/9]), an Ash'ari and Shafi'i of Kurdish background, who replaced a Shi'i judge on 23 Jumada II, 566 = March 3, 1171. See Leiser, *Restoration*, p. 193 and 533, n. 17. He served until 18 Rab'i I, 590 = March 13, 1194, when he was replaced by Zayn al-Din 'Ali ibn Yusuf al-Dimashqi. See al-Maqrizi, *Suluk*, I, 1, 46, 121. Al-Wahrani said of Sadr al-Din that in addition to intelligence and sound judgment he had the merit of "keeping himself from bribery and banquets." See Lyons and Jackson, *Saladin*, pp. 44, 119, 152; al-Wahrani, *Manamat*, pp. 16, 52, 54, 95, 189–90. A document from the Cairo Genizah (Ar. Box 40.126), cited by Goitein, *Med. Soc.*, I, 188 and translated in *Letters of Mediaeval Jewish Traders*, pp. 270–71, refers to a notary of a warehouse (*dar al-wikala*) named Sadr al-Din, which Goitein takes as a title. I suggest that "the excellent Qadi Sadr al-Din" is most likely Sadr al-Din ibn Dirbas.

2. Baneth, the editor, notes that physicians did not receive payment from dignitaries but were rewarded with gifts.

3. But in Maimonides' letter to Samuel Ibn Tibbon (above, p. 440), written about eight years later, he spoke of giving medical attention to the common along with the noble.

4. See above, p. 209.

5. See above, pp. 88–91.

6. Ibn al-Qifti, *History of the Sages,* p. 317.

7. See *Sharh asma' al-'uqqar (L'explication des noms de drogues)*, ed. and trans. M. Meyerhof, Introduction, pp. viii–ix. And see his "Medieval Jewish Physicians in the Near East," p. 448.

8. Taqi al-Din ruled in Hamat from 1178 to 1191. He died on October 10, 1191. See Lyons and Jackson, *Saladin,* pp. 37, 44, 68, 91, etc.

9. For the Arabic text, see H. Kroner, *Eine medicinische Maimonides-Handschrift aus Granada*. Kroner also edited the Hebrew translation of Zerahia ben Shealtiel Gracian (thirteenth century) in *Ein Beitrag zur Geschichte der Medizin des xii. Jahrhuderts*. Two works on sexual intercourse are ascribed to Maimonides, one longer with nineteen chapters and a shorter work of ten. F. Rosner accepts S. Muntner's argument that the long version is not by Maimonides. Both are translated in M. Gorlin, Maimonides' "On Sexual Intercourse." For the short version, see F. Rosner, *Maimonides' Medical Writings (Treatise on Poisons, Hemorrhoids, Cohabitation)*, pp. 155ff., and *Sex Ethics in the Writings of Moses Maimonides*, pp. 17–40. Rosner translates into English Zerahia ben Shealtiel's Hebrew translation. Maimonides' attitude to sex was discussed by W. Zev Harvey, "Sex and Health in Maimonides" and M. Idel, "*Sitre* 'Arayot in Maimonides' Thought."

10. CM Avot, i, 5; *Guide,* III, 8 (pp. 434–35); 12 (p. 445); 33 (p. 533); 49 (pp. 606–9).

11. Lyons and Jackson, *Saladin*, p. 372.

12. Porter to Macduff in Shakespeare, *Macbeth*, II, iii, 33.

13. Myrrh, which we associate with frankincense, goes back to Ak *murru*, Heb *mor*, Ar *murr*, and Grk *murra*. It is a gum resin aromatic; see Song i, 3. Amber (Ar and Heb *'anbar*) is a resin oil. The Latin name of nutmeg (*Myristica fragrans*) defines it well, both words meaning fragrant.

14. Goitein, *Med. Soc.*, II, 240–41.

15. D. H. Baneth, "A Doctor's Library in Egypt in the Days of Maimonides."

16. S. D. Goitein, *Jewish Education in Muslim Countries*, p. 76.

17. S. D. Goitein, "The Medical Profession in the Light of the Cairo Geniza Documents," p. 177; *Med. Soc.*, II, 240–41; Franz Rosenthal, "The Physician in Medieval Muslim Society," p. 477 and n. 4.

18. J. O. Leibowitz, "Maimonides on Medical Practice," p. 313. It is an old truth in medical practice, already expressed in Hippocrates' first aphorism, that the physician must "also make the patient, the attendants, and the externals cooperate" (translation by Francis Adams).

19. Samuel Kottek, "Maimonides: Rabbi, Philosopher and Physician," p. 338–39.

20. Maimonides, *Art of Cure: Extracts from Galen*, ed. and trans. Uriel S. Barzel, p. 108, cited in *On Asthma*, ed. and trans. G. Bos, p. 123.

21. Franz Rosenthal, "'Life Is Short, the Art Is Long': Arabic Commentaries on the First Hippocratic Aphorism." The Latin expression *ars longa vita brevis*, "art is long, life is brief," was used by Roman writers and orators, including Horace and Lucius Annaeus Seneca (4 B.C.E.–65 C.E.), who used it in *De brevitate vitae*, but it was generally attributed to Hippocrates, speaking of medical practice: "Life is short, the art long, opportunity fleeting, experiment treacherous, judgment difficult." Maimonides cited the saying in *Aphorisms of Hippocrates*, p. 8 and *Aphorisms of Moses*, p. 11.

22. Elinor Lieber, "Maimonides, the Medical Humanist," p. 53.

23. See also Gerrit Bos, "Ibn al-Jazzār on Medicine for the Poor and Destitute," p. 365.

24. Goitein, *Med. Soc.*, II, 252.

25. See F. Rosenthal, "The Physician in Medieval Muslim Society," pp. 487–88; Michael W. Dols, *Medieval Islamic Medicine: Ibn Ridwan's Treatise on the Prevention of Bodily Ills in Egypt*, p. 37; Emilie Savage-Smith, "Medicine," p. 933.

26. Meyerhof, Introduction; J. O. Leibowitz, "Maimonides on Medical Practice," pp. 309–17; Lieber, "Maimonides the Medical Humanist," p. 46. See Sherwin B. Nuland's *Maimonides,* pp. 154–85, on "Maimonides, Physician."

27. For the Arabic Galen tradition, see R. Walzer, EI, s.v. "Djālīnūs."

28. See above, pp. 331–32.

29. Thomas Glick, "Science," in *Convivencia*, ed. Vivian B. Mann, Thomas F. Glick, and Jerrilynn D. Dodds, p. 83.

30. See Maimonides, *On Asthma*, pp. 95–96.

31. Ibid., p. 96.

32. Kottek "Maimonides: Rabbi, Philosopher and Physician," p. 338; Lieber "Maimonides the Medical Humanist," p. 46. This comes across in a discussion that took place in 1050 C.E. between a Muslim physician in Cairo, who had learned medicine theoretically, and his Christian opponent in Bagdad, who had studied with a man of experience; Joseph Schacht and M. Meyerhof, *The Medico-philosophical Controversy Between Ibn Butlan of Baghdad and Ibn Ridwan of Cairo.*

33. Maimonides' *Commentary on the Aphorisms of Hippocrates*, trans. Fred Rosner, pp. 14-23. Sarah Stroumsa, "Al-Fārābī and Maimonides on Medicine as a Science." Stroumsa mentions (pp. 244–47) Moses di Rieti (d. 1388) and his *Small Temple* (*Miqdash me'at*), a poem modeled on Dante's *Divine Comedy*, in which di Rieti used Maimonides' classification. He also wrote a commentary on Maimonides' *Chapters of Moses* (*Fusul Musa*).

34. *Epistles*, ed. Baneth, pp. 69–70; *On Asthma* ed. and trans. Bos, Introduction, p. xxix.

35. As nature heals, so it may prevent healing. Now matter how skilled the physician is, he is like a seaman thwarted by the waves.

36. On this passage, see Y. Gellman, "Maimonides and the Cure-all Book," p. 192.

37. J. O. Leibowitz, "Maimonides on Medical Practice," p. 310.

38. Ibid. and citing parallel in *Regimen of Health*, trans. A. Bar-Sela, H. E. Hebbel, and E. Faris, pp. 20–21. "In similar conditions nature is self-sufficient and it is not necessary to support her by medication."

39. Leibowitz observes that Maimonides' principles of medical practice remind one of Sir William Osler, as Dr. Macht once noted in an address to the Medical History Club in 1935; D. Macht, "Moses Maimonides, Physician and Scientist."

40. Maimonides, *On Asthma*, ed. and trans. G. Bos, pp. 82–83.

41. In the nineteenth century, Jacob Bigelow of Boston revived the doctrine. "It was he who made the first effective protest in America against ill-chosen drugs and large doses, and against excessive blood-letting. He embodied in his *Discourse on Self-limited Diseases* the idea that many disorders if left to the natural recuperative powers of the patient would disappear more rapidly than from excessive medical treatment.

"Of this lecture Dr. Oliver Wendell Holmes (*Proceedings of the American Academy of Arts and Sciences,* 1879, p. 16) said that it exerted more influence upon medical practice in America than any work that had ever been published in this country." Coined by the great Bostonian in spiritual kinship was the sage of Fostat, the term "self-limited disease" became a common expression. Maimonides brought a biological principle near to the practice of medicine; Leibowitz, "Maimonides on Medical Practice," pp. 311–12.

42. *On Asthma*, p. 94.

43. Ibid.

44. Ibid. For both quotations and the paraphrase, see Hippocrates, *Epidemics,* 6.5.1 (trans. Jones, 255): "The body's nature is the physician in disease. Nature finds the way for herself, not from thought. . . . Well trained, readily and without instruction, nature does what is needed."

45. Ibid., p. 94, n. 30. The idea of nature being endowed with virtues such as industriousness, skill, wisdom, and justice is a prominent theme in Galen's works; see Galen, *On the Usefulness of the Parts,* trans. May, 1:10-11. For further references, see p. 137.

46. *On Asthma*, p. 46 and n. 31, where Bos cites Galen's *On the Usefulness of the Parts,* trans. May, I, 251–52 and *On the Natural Faculties,* ii, 9, trans. Brock, pp. 214–15. Bos observes (p. 131) that "divine providence" is "nothing other than his adaptation of the Galenic concept of 'Nature.'"

47. There is a vast amount of medical lore in the Talmud; see especially Julius Preuss, *Biblical and talmudic Medicine*. Maimonides did not regard talmudic medicine as obligatory, and only cited it when it conformed with Greek, Roman, and Arabic medicine. His son Abraham wrote in his *Treatise on the Homilies of the Sages*, in *Wars of the Lord*, p. 84 (cited in *Mishneh Torah*, ed. Lieberman, p. 150 to line 1), surely echoing his father, that we are not obligated by the greatness of the talmudic sages in interpreting the Torah to accept their views in medicine, physics, and astronomy. Cf. *Guide,* III, 14 (pp. 458–59) on the Sages and astronomy. Rav Sherira Gaon in a responsum took the same position on the sages and medicine; *Osar ha-Geonim*, Gittin, *Responsa,* par 376 (cited by Lieberman et al.).

48. *On the Causes of Symptoms*. ed. and trans. J. O. Leibowitz and S. Marcus, pp. 151–53. See Lieber, "Maimonides the Medical Humanist," pp. 55–57.

49. See MT Ethical Qualities, iv, 1. See *Regimen of Health,* trans. Bar-Sela et al., trans. Bar-Sela et al., p. 6, and Lieber, "Maimonides the Medical Humanist," p. 44.

50. See also *Guide,* II, 37 on magic.

51. MT Idolatry, xi, 11; B San 101a.

52. Cf. MT Idolatry 11.12, on the Torah being medicine for the soul.

53. *Regimen of Health,* p. 19.

54. B BB 58b.

55. *Medieval Islamic Medicine,* trans. Michael W. Dols, chap. 12, 43b.

56. *Aphorisms of Moses,* nos. 26 and 28.

57. Galen, *De sanitate tuenda,* Book 5, ch. 5, ed. Kuhn); Rosner-Muntner, *Aphorisms of Moses,* II, nos. 46 and 62; Leibowitz-Marcus, *On the Causes of Symptoms,* 151-52.

58. Lieber, "Maimonides the Medical Humanist," p. 40.

59. Meyerhof in the Introduction to *L'explication des noms de drogues,* pp. xxiii, lxv-lxvi.

60. Ibid., pp. xxiii, lxv–lxvi. Al-Idrisi served in the court of Roger II of Sicily and wrote a famous geographical work, the *Book of Roger*, and a treatise on simple drugs with synonyms for each. On Abu 'l-Muna al-Kohen al-'Attar, see also A. Dietrich, EI, s.v. "al-Kohen al-'Aṭṭār"; Goitein, *Med. Soc.*, II, 265, and 582, n. 24. He wrote in 1259/60 for his own use and for his son a book on medicaments based on the literature and his own experience: *The Store Guide on Medicaments for the Human Species* (*Minhaj al-dukkan fi 'adwiyat naw' al-insan*). It was written for pharmacists rather than physicians and gained popularity.

61. Ibn al-Baytar was born in Malaga, ca. 1190, and died in 1248 in Damascus. He first studied medicine and collected herbs in Seville before traveling in North Africa, Asia Minor, and Syria, finally settling in Egypt, where the Ayyubid sultan al-Malik al Kamil (r. 1218–38) made him chief herbalist in Cairo. Maimonides' son, Abraham, served the same sultan and presumably knew Ibn al-Baytar. Perhaps this helps explain how he came to edit Maimonides' book. In Damascus he taught Ibn Abi Usaybi'a. See Ullmann, *Die Medizin in Islam*, 1978, pp. 280–83; J. Vernet, in *DSB*, I, 538; and idem, EI, s.v. "Ibn al-Bayṭar."

62. *On Asthma*, p. 89 and n. 22—Hippocrates, *Epidemics*, 1.2.11 (trans. Jones, 165): "As to diseases, make a habit of two things—to help, or at least to do no harm." C. Sandulescu, "Primum non nocere: Philological Commentaries on a Medical Aphorism."

63. Leibowitz, "Maimonides on Medical Practice," p. 312. The book *On Asthma* was written for an anonymous, high-ranking patient and contains general advice on health.

64. *On Asthma*, p. 85. Here Maimonides advised, in the name of Abu Bakr al-Razi, that one can dispense with a physician more than one needs him.

65. Ibid.

66. Ibid., pp. 87–88.

67. Ibid., pp. 89–90.

68. Maimonides gave an exact quotation from Galen, *In Hippocratis Epidemiarum*, 1.2.53, ed. Wenkebach and Pfaff, p. 76 lines 3–16; ibid., p. 90, n. 23. The Galen text is reproduced by Bos on pp. 136–37.

69. Ibid., pp. 93–94 and commentary by Bos, p. 137; *Regimen of Health*, trans. Bar-Sela et al., p. 21, where Maimonides refers to Aristotle's *De sensu et sensatu*. The quotation is not found in the Aristotle text as we have it.

70. Barbara Floyd, University Archivist, University of Toledo, http://www.cl.utoledo. edu/canaday/quackery/quack2.html.

71. Maimonides, *On Asthma*, p. 95.

72. Ibid., p. 95 and n. 33. Hebrew translations render *fudala'* as *hasidim: Mss.* B and A read "the pious."

73. Ibid., pp. 110–11. Maimonides had used this text in the *Guide*, I, 31 (pp. 66–67); see Pines, "Translator's Introduction," pp. lxvii–lxviii; and Leibowitz, "Maimonides on Medical Practice," p. 317. The fourth cause of dissension, added by Maimonides, is crucial, as it applies to a traditional religious society.

74. Maimonides, *On Asthma*, p. 109.

75. Ibid., Introduction, p. xlvii and text, p. 96.

76. Ibid., Introduction, p. xlvii, and text p. 98.

77. Ibid., Introduction, p. xlvii and text, p. 102.

78. Leibowitz, "Maimonides on Medical Practice," pp. 313–14.

79. Maimonides, *On Asthma*, pp. 95–96.

80. Maimonides, *Regimen of Health*, p. 25.

81. Maimonides, *On Asthma*, pp. 24–25. Bos cites Maimonides' statement in *Regimen of Health*, p. 16, that Hippocrates summed up the entire regimen of health in two points, that a person should not eat to surfeit and should not neglect exercise; see *On Asthma*, p. 127.

82. Maimonides, *Regimen of Health*, p. 17; *On Asthma*, p. 26 and comment by Bos, p. 128.

83. Maimonides, *Regimen of Health*, p. 17; *On Asthma*, p. 27.

84. *Regimen of Health*, p. 25.

85. Eight Chapters, I; MT Ethical Qualities, ii, 1; Weiss and Butterworth, p. 31.

86. Eight Chapters, I, trans. Weiss, p. 61.

87. *Regimen of Health,* pp. 25–27.

88. The text reads *al-mawa'iz wa-'l-adab,* which the English translations render: "admonitions and disciplines." However, in the *daf' al-hamm* (banishing of grief) literature, which influenced Maimonides, these terms are used in the sense given here; see, e.g., Samir, "Bar Hebraeus, le 'Daf' al-Hamm' et les 'Contes Amusants,'" p. 144.

89. Galen mentions death induced by anger or by excessive pleasure (*De locis affectis*, v, 2; Kuhn, VIII, 301–2; Daremberg, II: 627); see Leibowitz and Marcus, p. 15.

90. P. Hadot, *Philosophy as a Way of Life,* p. 83.

91. *On the Causes of Symptoms*, ed. and trans. J. O. Leibowitz and S. Marcus, Introduction, p. 15. The editors note that oxtongue steeped in wine is prescribed by a number of ancient medical practitioners, among them Dioscorides, *De materia medica* (IV, 126 [128]). See *On the Causes of Symptoms*, fol. 133v.

92. See *On the Causes of Symptoms*, p. 51, note to line 8. They had experiments performed showing that the plant has a tranquilizing effect in animals.

93. *Regimen of Health,* pp. 23–24.

94. See *On the Causes of Symptoms*, p. 107, notes to lines 3–4. See above, p. 516, n. 59.

95. *Regimen of Health,* p. 26; Weiss and Butterworth, *On the Management of Health,* pp. 108–9.

96. Eight Chapters in *Ethical Writings of Moses*, trans. Weiss and Butterworth, p. 75 (and see Introduction, p. 14).

97. In MT Repentance, viii, 6, beautiful forms (*surot na'ot*) are beautiful women (the ones Muslims envision in paradise), so here beautiful forms are probably comely women (and young men). See also Friedman, *Maimonides, the Yemenite Messiah and Apostasy*, p. 141, n. 233.

98. Eight Chapters in *Ethical Writings of Moses*, trans. Weiss and Butterworth, p. 75 (and see Introduction, p. 14).

99. See R. Klibansky et al., *Saturn and Melancholy*, 15ff.

100. I. Kant, "Analytic of the Sublime," *Critique of Judgment,* trans. J. H. Bernard, p. 117. See Klibansky, p. 122.

101. Twersky, *Introduction to the Code of Maimonides*, p. 67.

102. Maimonides regarded despondency and subjugation to the will of others as a great barrier to intellectual activity, viewing melancholy as a deterrent to creativity on an individual and communal level. He believed that prophecy does not come to someone in a state of despondency, and that the Jewish people during their long period of exile and sorrow were deprived of creativity and genius.

103. *Guide*, II, 11 (p. 276).

104. Maimonides combined B Ber 57b and San 38a, which speak of any man and not just a scholar, and do not mention a bed prepared, with Shab 25b, which mentions "a bed prepared and a wife adorned for scholars."

105. Eight Chapters, trans. Weiss and Butterworth, p. 77.

106. S. W. Jackson, *Melancholia and Depression*, pp. 73–74.

107. Ibid., p. 59.

108. Al-Kindi, *Fi daf' al-hamm*, ed. Ritter and Walzer, *Studi su Al Kindi II,* p. 11. The editors cite consolation literature of Stoic thinkers, such as Cicero, Plutarch, and Seneca.

109. *Essays on Philosophical Counselling*, ed. Ran Lahav and Maria da Venza Tillmans, p. 260.

110. Maimonides, *On Asthma,* pp. 81–82.

Epilogue

1. The letter is preserved in T-S 16.290, and was first published by D. H. Baneth, "From the Correspondence of Maimonides," pp. 50–56. See also Goitein, "The Life of Maimonides in the Light of New Genizah Discoveries," p. 35, and his *Med. Soc.*, II, 252; Sassoon, *Maimonidis Commentarius*, I, plate lvii. It was edited and translated by Kraemer, "Two Letters," pp. 92–98.

2. See M. A. Friedman, "Notes by a Disciple in Maimonides' Academy," p. 526. The Master riposted Samuel Ibn Tibbon's desire to visit him by saying the same thing. He would only be able to see him in a study hall, not a seminar or a tutorial.

3. See Sassoon, Introduction, p. 33. Corrections in the text of his *Commentary on the Mishnah* go from rounded to cursive to trembling. The signature in Plate XXIV, which appears often in reproductions, is wavering.

4. Al-Harizi, *Wanderings*, ed. Yahalom and Blau, p. 211, poem no. 57, lines 253–55.

INDEX